Skill Acquisition in Sport

Success in sport depends upon the athlete's ability to develop and perfect a specific set of perceptual, cognitive and motor skills. Now in a fully revised and updated new edition, *Skill Acquisition in Sport* examines how we learn such skills and, in particular, considers the crucial role of practice and instruction in the skill acquisition process.

Containing 13 completely new chapters, and engaging with the significant advances in neurophysiological techniques that have profoundly shaped our understanding of motor control and development, the book provides a comprehensive review of current research and theory on skill acquisition. Leading international experts explore key topics such as:

- attentional focus;
- augmented feedback;
- observational practice and learning;
- implicit motor learning;
- mental imagery training;
- physical guidance;
- motivation and motor learning;
- neurophysiology;
- development of skill;
- joint action.

Throughout, the book addresses the implications of current research for instruction and practice in sport, making explicit connections between core science and sporting performance. No other book covers this fundamental topic in such breadth or depth, making this book important reading for any student, scholar or practitioner working in sport science, cognitive science, kinesiology, clinical and rehabilitation sciences, neurophysiology, psychology, ergonomics or robotics.

Nicola J. Hodges is Associate Professor in the School of Kinesiology, at the University of British Columbia, Canada, where she studies motor skill learning and correlates of expert performance. She has contributed to the understanding of processes involved in learning from observation and instruction and practice behaviours for elite performance.

A. Mark Williams is Professor of Motor Behaviour in the Research Institute for Sport and Exercise Sciences at Liverpool John Moores University, UK. He has published widely in areas related to expertise, skill acquisition and motor control and learning.

Skill Acquisition in Sport

Research, theory and practice

Second edition

**Edited by Nicola J. Hodges
and A. Mark Williams**

LONDON AND NEW YORK

First edition published 2004

This edition first published 2012
by Routledge
2 Park Square, Milton Park, Abingdon, Oxon OX14 4RN

Simultaneously published in the USA and Canada
by Routledge
711 Third Avenue, New York, NY 10017

Routledge is an imprint of the Taylor & Francis Group, an informa business

British Library Cataloguing in Publication Data
A catalogue record for this book is available from the British Library

Library of Congress Cataloging-in-Publication Data
Skill acquisition in sport: research, theory and practice/edited by Nicola J.
Hodges and Mark A. Williams.
p. cm.
Includes bibliographical references and index.
1. Sports sciences—Research. 2. Perceptual–motor learning—Research. 3.
Motor ability—Research. I. Hodges, Nicola J., 1970– II. Williams, A. M. (A.
Mark), 1965–
GV558.S57 2012
796.07—dc23
2011051494

ISBN: 978-0-415-60784-1 (hbk)
ISBN: 978-0-415-60786-5 (pbk)
ISBN: 978-0-203-13371-2 (ebk)

Typeset in Goudy
by Prepress Projects Ltd, Perth, UK.

Printed and bound in Great Britain by
CPI Group (UK) Ltd, Croydon, CR0 4YY

Contents

Figures

Tables

Contributors

Bruce Abernethy, PhD

Faculty of Health Sciences
The University of Queensland
Brisbane
Australia

Neil B. Albert, PhD

Spencer Foundation
Chicago
Illinois
USA

David Anderson, PhD

Department of Kinesiology
San Francisco State University
California
USA

Duarte Araújo, PhD

Faculty of Human Kinetics
Technical University of Lisbon
Portugal

Sian L. Beilock, PhD

Department of Psychology
The University of Chicago
Illinois
USA

Michael Borich, PhD

Department of Physical Therapy
Faculty of Medicine
University of British Columbia
Vancouver
Canada

Lara Boyd, PhD

Department of Physical Therapy
Faculty of Medicine
University of British Columbia
Vancouver
Canada
and Brain Research Centre
University of British Columbia
Vancouver
Canada

Gavin Breslin, PhD

Sport and Exercise Science Research Institute
University of Ulster
Newtownabbey
Northern Ireland

Chris Button, PhD

School of Physical Education
University of Otago
New Zealand

Paul Campagnaro, MSc

Motor Skills Lab
School of Kinesiology
University of British Columbia
Vancouver
Canada

Mark Campbell, PhD

Department of Physical Education and Sport Sciences
University of Limerick
Ireland

Joe Causer, PhD

Discipline of Exercise and Sport Science
The University of Sydney
Australia

Jia Yi Chow, PhD

National Institute of Education
Nanyang Technological University
Singapore

Jean Côté, PhD

School of Kinesiology and Health Studies
Queen's University
Kingston
Ontario
Canada

Keith Davids, PhD

School of Human Movement Studies
Queensland University of Technology
Brisbane
Australia

Terry Eskenazi, MSc

Donders Institute for Brain, Cognition, and Behaviour
Radboud University Nijmegen
Netherlands

Damian Farrow, PhD

School of Sport & Exercise Science
Institute of Sport, Exercise and Active Living
Victoria University
Melbourne
Australia
and The Australian Institute of Sport
Canberra
Australia

Paul Ford, PhD

Research Institute for Sport and Exercise Sciences
Liverpool John Moores University
UK

Adam Gorman, PhD candidate

AIS Movement Science – Skill Acquisition, Australian Institute of Sport
School of Human Movement Studies
The University of Queensland
St Lucia
Australia

Nicola J. Hodges, PhD

Motor Skills Laboratory
School of Kinesiology
University of British Columbia
Vancouver
Canada

Paul Holmes, PhD

Institute for Performance Research
Manchester Metropolitan University
UK

Robert Hristovski, PhD

Sts. Cyril and Methodius University
Skopje
Macedonia

Christopher M. Janelle, PhD

Department of Applied Physiology and Kinesiology
University of Florida
Gainesville
USA

Carly Kontra, MA

Department of Psychology
The University of Chicago
Illinois
USA

Timothy D. Lee, PhD

Department of Kinesiology
McMaster University
Hamilton
Ontario
Canada

Rebecca Lewthwaite, PhD

Rancho Los Amigos National Rehabilitation Center
Downey
California
USA

Oliver Logan

English Institute of Sport
Lilleshall National Sports Centre
Shropshire
UK

Keith Lohse, MA

Motor Skills Laboratory
School of Kinesiology
University of British Columbia
Vancouver
Canada

Tadhg MacIntyre, PhD

School of Sports Studies
University of Ulster
Northern Ireland

Richard Magill, PhD

Steinhardt School of Culture, Education, and Human Development
New York University
USA

David Mann, PhD

Institute of Human Performance
The University of Hong Kong
China

Rich Masters, PhD

Institute of Human Performance
The University of Hong Kong
China

Aidan Moran, PhD

School of Psychology
University College Dublin
Ireland

Jennifer Murphy-Mills, MSc

School of Kinesiology and Health Studies
Queen's University
Kingston
Ontario
Canada

Stafford Murray

English Institute of Sport
Manchester
UK

Nicole Ong, MSc

Motor Skills Lab
School of Kinesiology
University of British Columbia
Vancouver
Canada

Pedro Passos

Faculty of Human Kinetics
Technical University of Lisbon
Portugal

Jamie Poolton, PhD

Institute of Human Performance
The University of Hong Kong
China

Luc Proteau, PhD

Département de Kinésiologie
Université de Montréal
Quebec
Canada

Richard A. Schmidt, PhD

Professor Emeritus
Department of Psychology
UCLA
Los Angeles
California
USA
and Human Performance Research
Marina del Rey
California
USA

Natalie Sebanz, PhD

Donders Institute for Brain, Cognition, and Behaviour
Radboud University
Nijmegen
Netherlands
and Department of Cognitive Science
Central European University
Budapest
Hungary

Charles H. Shea, PhD

Department of Health and Kinesiology
Texas A&M University
College Station
USA

Regis Thouvarecq, PhD

Sciences du Sport et Education Physique
Université de Rouen
France

Maxime Trempe, PhD

Département de Kinésiologie
Université de Montréal
Quebec
Canada

Robrecht Van Der Wel, PhD

Department of Psychology
Rutgers University
New Brunswick
New Jersey
USA

Joan N. Vickers, PhD

Faculty of Kinesiology
University of Calgary
Alberta
Canada

Katie Wadden, MSc

Department of Physical Therapy
Faculty of Medicine
University of British Columbia
Vancouver
Canada

A. Mark Williams, PhD

Research Institute for Sport and Exercise Sciences
Liverpool John Moores University
UK

David L. Wright, PhD

Department of Health and Kinesiology
Texas A&M University
College Station
USA

Gabriele Wulf, PhD

Department of Kinesiology
University of Nevada
Las Vegas
USA

Preface

N. J. Hodges and A. M. Williams

The field of skill acquisition is in an exciting period owing to the broad interest in learning processes and their applications across a variety of disciplines and professions (e.g. rehabilitation/medicine, computer science, psychology, engineering and sport). Moreover, there have been significant technical developments in the field that have facilitated understanding of the mechanisms underpinning learning (e.g. brain imaging and stimulation devices, physiological measurement tools and robotic interfaces). These advances in technology have enabled scientists to ask more refined questions influencing theory, research and applied practice in equal measure. We are therefore very pleased and excited to showcase the second edition of this book, which attempts to highlight the dynamic and vibrant nature of the field and the novelty of approaches and ideas that have evolved since the previous edition.

The new edition of the book is revamped with 21 new chapters focusing on traditional topics (e.g. feedback, practice scheduling and perceptual–cognitive skill) as well as new ones that have gained prominence over recent years (e.g. joint action and coordination, imagery and observation, and developmental readiness for motor learning). We have a list of contributors from all around the globe including Australia, Canada, France, Hong Kong, Ireland, Macedonia, the Netherlands, New Zealand, Northern Ireland, Portugal, Singapore, the UK and the USA. A novel section includes two chapters that focus on applied issues in order to illustrate the increasing translational impact of this field of study, particularly with high-level athletes. In these last chapters, insights from the Asia-Pacific and from the UK illustrate the challenges and opportunities presented when attempting to translate research into practice and how work undertaken in the field can inform research and theoretical development.

The book is broadly divided into five parts, namely 'Presenting information', 'Optimizing practice conditions', 'Issues in motor learning', 'Skilled performance' and 'Research, theory and practice: challenges and solutions'. In the opening section on 'Presenting information', there are four chapters that address issues related to the effective presentation of instructions, feedback and demonstrations. *Magill and Anderson* provide a review of the role of augmented feedback in motor learning. The chapter contains a number of practical illustrations of how technical advances in sport have allowed feedback to be used in relatively novel and innovative ways. In the second chapter, *Ong and Hodges* show how mixed schedules of demonstrations and physical practice can potentially aid skill learning by promoting the acquisition of different types of knowledge. They suggest ways in which the usefulness of demonstrations can be optimized, particularly in regard to when and how frequently they should be presented. In the third chapter, *Lohse, Wulf and Lewthwaite* illustrate the pervasive effects of attentional focus on motor skill learning, with particular reference to the measurement of efficiency. An externally directed focus of attention affects learning outcomes as well as how these are achieved. In the final chapter in this section, *Masters and Poolton* revisit the topic of implicit motor learning and show how this field of research has progressed over the last decade. They show how methods of presenting information (e.g. through analogies or at a subliminal level of awareness) can impact long-term retention, particularly under conditions that simulate competitive situations and pressures. They offer some interesting speculations about the evolutionary mechanisms underpinning the effectiveness of more implicit learning techniques.

In the second part, we present five chapters that have implications for how practice should be structured and organized to bring about effective motor skill learning. In the first chapter, *Lee* reminds us how important it is to structure practice appropriately to enhance learning, rather than to gain fast yet temporary performance benefits. He provides a concise review of the contextual interference literature, with a focus on contemporary research. In the second chapter, *Moran, Campbell, Holmes and MacIntyre* review the potential of covert methods of practice, including imagery and action observation, to enhance learning. They discuss how these practice methods (both cognitive and neurophysiological) can help refine and enhance motor skill learning. An ecological, constraints-based view of learning is considered in the third chapter by *Davids, Araújo, Hristovski, Passos and Chow*. These authors offer thought-provoking ideas concerning instruction pedagogy that places emphasis on the individuality of the learner and the practice environment. We return to more traditional, information processing-based methods of studying and inferring learning in the fourth chapter, by *Shea and Wright*. These authors provide an overview of contemporary research and theory relating to sequence learning and what this means for how movements are remembered and may be generalized to new contexts. In the final chapter of this part, *Hodges and Campagnaro* evaluate the benefits and costs associated with providing physical guidance during motor skill learning. They consider how advances in rehabilitation and robotics have implications for effective physical guidance techniques in sport.

A total of five chapters are presented in the third section. These chapters relate to broader issues in motor skill learning, including the role of motivation, sleep and rest, and the underlying neurophysiology of motor learning. *Lewthwaite and Wulf* remind us of the often-neglected role of affect and emotion in teaching, and highlight the effectiveness of various practice methods, including feedback and instruction, providing interesting examples of how practice can be enhanced by subtle manipulations to the beliefs and motivations of the learner. In the next chapter, *Trempe and Proteau* review a burgeoning area of interest pertaining to the learning that takes place between practice sessions. They provide a stimulating evaluation of current evidence relating to the value of rest (and sleep) for motor learning. This chapter is followed by an equally fascinating discussion on developmental markers of readiness for motor skill acquisition by *Anderson, Magill and Thouvarecq*. Although primarily giving a historical review of critical and sensitive periods of development, these authors make a compelling case for the need for researchers and practitioners to consider when sport-related practice should start to be of most benefit to the learner. Next, *Eskenazi, van der Wel and Sebanz* present an informative discussion of research relating to shared or joint actions, which has implications for coordinative behaviours required in opponent or team sports and games. They focus on the types of processes engaged when individuals share in tasks or goals and what this means for performance and learning. In the final chapter in this part, *Wadden, Borich and Boyd* review the neurophysiology of motor learning. These authors provide a comprehensive and current review of research in this area and attempt to illustrate how understanding of the neurophysiology of learning and skilled performance can help us develop better environments to promote performance enhancement.

The acquisition of expertise is the primary focus in the fourth section of the book. We present five chapters related to skill learning in elite, high-performance athletes. *Côté, Murphy-Mills and Abernethy* present the developmental model of sport participation, which details two potential pathways to success in sport. They review support for their model and then go beyond this to present seven clear and testable postulates about the relative benefits of early versus late specialization in sport. In the next chapter, *Abernethy, Farrow, Gorman and Mann* consider how skilled athletes can be differentiated from their less-skilled counterparts in terms of perceptual-cognitive skills related to attention and anticipation. In the following chapter, *Causer, Janelle, Vickers and Williams* evaluate how effectively this knowledge has filtered down to aid training of athletes. They focus on methods employed to train 'quiet eye' as well as 'game intelligence' skills such as anticipation and decision-making. The final two chapters in this part provide a somewhat different focus from the first three in that skilled performers are studied to help understand how actions and sensory–motor experiences influence perception and cognitions and the memory and transfer of skills across contexts. *Kontra, Albert and Beilock* show us how movement experiences and skilled performance in sports such as ice hockey can impact on the way we look at the world and make sense of situations. They argue that movement in general can impact on classroom learning. *Breslin, Schmidt and Lee* then provide examples of what they term 'especial skills'. These skills seem to be caused by high amounts of practice under specific conditions and are evidenced by significantly superior performance in one context (such as the free-throw line in basketball), in comparison with other distances and what would be predicted based on generalization theories of learning.

We conclude our book with two chapters that engage discussion about the difficulties and successes in moving from and between research, theory and practice. *Williams, Ford, Causer, Logan and Murray* continue this discussion by drawing upon their recent experiences working with elite athletes in the English Institute of Sport. *Button and Farrow* provide a Southern Hemisphere perspective, based on their roles as academic researchers and applied sport scientists in New Zealand and Australia respectively. In both chapters, attempts are made to engage the reader in understanding how the various topics addressed in this book have led to interventions with elite athletes, and hence these last two chapters serve an additional summative role for the book as a whole.

Our broad aims in compiling these chapters and bringing together world leaders in this field are to (a) continue to stimulate research interest; (b) provide a one-stop source for students of motor learning in undergraduate and graduate classes; and (c) provide a resource for practitioners looking to employ an evidence-based framework to guide their coaching practice. We acknowledge that the book will probably be more accessible to academics and students of movement science disciplines (e.g. Sport and Exercise Science, Kinesiology, Human Kinetics, Physical Therapy) than people without this background, but our hope is that the material presented will motivate these individuals to disseminate the knowledge presented across a range of different learning and performance environments.

Acknowledgements

This book is of course possible only because of the amazing bunch of researchers who have agreed to contribute their time, thoughts and work. Thank you so much for sharing your research and ideas with us.

Nicola Hodges

I would like to acknowledge the major government funding sources in Canada (SSHRC, CIHR and NSERC) that have enabled me to spend the time on this book project, to conduct the research that informs our understanding of motor skill acquisition, and most importantly to support the students who have formed a critical part of my research programme over the past decade. I would especially like to thank the graduate and undergraduate students who assisted with informal reviews of the chapters: Paul Campagnaro, Tom Coppola, Chris Edwards, David Hendry, Bev Larssen, Shannon Lim, Dana Maslovat, Des Mulligan, Nicole Ong and Katie Wadden. Especial thanks to Bev for last-minute help with manuscript preparation.

Love and thanks to Stuart for his support of my work and for Elara and Mera, and to my family and friends here in Canada and in England, especially Mum and Dad.

Mark Williams

I would like to thank my wife, Sara, and three sons, Thomas, Matthew and Alex. Without their unquestioning support, this book would not have been possible.

Part I
Presenting information

1 The roles and uses of augmented feedback in motor skill acquisition

Richard A. Magill and David I. Anderson

When a golfer hits a ball two types of feedback are available. Feedback is available from various sensory systems as a natural part of performing the skill, such as proprioceptive and tactile feedback from the sensory receptors in the muscles, joints, vestibular apparatus, and skin, visual feedback from the eyes, and auditory feedback from the middle and inner ears. All of these physiological systems provide performance-based feedback that informs the golfer about the success of hitting the ball. The utility of these sensory feedback sources depends on the specific characteristics of the golf shot situation. The second type of feedback, which may or may not be available to the golfer, comes from information that is not inherent to the task, such as from a coach, teacher, trainer, or training device. This latter type of feedback adds to the natural sensory feedback and can be provided in a variety of ways, such as in auditory, visual, proprioceptive, or tactile form.

Researchers who study the acquisition of motor skills and practitioners who teach or coach sports skills can profit considerably from knowing about these two types of feedback. For the researcher, an understanding of these types of feedback provides insights into the learning process, which is at the heart of our comprehension of skill acquisition. For the practitioner, knowledge about these types of feedback can provide the foundation for developing instruction and practice strategies that will facilitate the learning, or enhance the performance, of skills.

In this chapter, we focus on the second of the two types of feedback. We begin with a consideration of the terminology associated with this type of feedback, which has been a long-standing unresolved issue within the research and practitioner communities. We then consider the functions of this type of feedback in sports skills learning and performance. Next, we discuss various ways in which this feedback has been used to enhance performance and learning of sports skills and then propose some theoretically derived principles and guidelines for its optimal use. Finally, we conclude with our views of some specific directions for future research to enhance our understanding of the function and use of this type of feedback in sports.

Clarification of terminology

A persistent issue within the motor learning, motor control, sport psychology, and sport pedagogy literatures is a lack of consistency in designating terms that identify the two types of feedback described earlier. A primary concern has been the terms that should identify each type of feedback and the criteria for determining specific characteristics of each category. Although an elaboration of this terminology concern goes beyond the scope of this chapter, it is discussed elsewhere (e.g., Magill, 2010; Schmidt & Lee, 2011).

In this chapter, we use the term *task-intrinsic feedback* to specify the type of feedback referred to earlier as sensory feedback. An important advantage of the term task-intrinsic feedback is its acknowledgement of the skill-specific nature of sensory feedback sources associated with performing sport skills. The second type of feedback described earlier will be referred to in this chapter as *augmented feedback* (others have used terms such as *external* and *extrinsic feedback*). The word *augmented* refers to *adding to or enhancing* something. For example, when a coach tells a volleyball player that his or her hands were improperly spaced when hitting a set, the coach enhances the task-intrinsic feedback available to the athlete while performing the set. Some researchers have argued for the need to subdivide augmented feedback into two separate types, namely knowledge of results (KR) and knowledge of performance (KP). Although arguments have been made for this distinction (e.g., Magill, 2010), we will not use these terms, because of their inconsistent use and the fact that many researchers consider the distinction arbitrary, but designate the type of augmented feedback according to its specific characteristics and content.

Functions of augmented feedback

When augmented feedback is given to an athlete it can function in at least three ways. One is to facilitate the learning of a new skill by providing performance-based information that allows the athlete to determine what he or she should continue to do and what not continue to do. Another function is to enhance the performance of well-learned skills by providing information that allows the athlete to determine how to improve performance in specific contexts and situations. Third, augmented feedback functions as motivation to continue to practice a skill or to continue to participate. These three functions demonstrate that augmented feedback can serve multiple roles in any learning or performance situation.

Forms and uses of augmented feedback

Augmented feedback can be presented in many forms that range from verbal to sophisticated displays of information on a computer. In this section, we discuss various ways that people have implemented augmented feedback in sports practice (i.e., training) or competitive situations.

Verbal augmented feedback

When a coach tells an athlete what he or she did right or wrong during the performance of a skill, the coach provides verbal augmented feedback. Although there are several issues of concern when verbally providing augmented feedback, we focus on two in this discussion: the amount of information that should be provided and the content of the information.

The amount of verbal augmented feedback

Because sports skills typically involve the sequential movement of many body parts, the performer will potentially make many movement-related errors. As a result, there is a tendency for coaches to give too much movement-related information when they provide verbal feedback. Researchers in the areas of human attention and memory have established that people can process or remember only a limited amount of information at any one time. Because augmented feedback requires information to be remembered and used, it follows that the amount of information provided should be limited to amounts the athlete can use effectively. Although often interpreted as referring to giving too much information, the "limited" characteristic should also be seen as giving the "minimum" amount of information the performer needs or can use to achieve the function that the augmented feedback is serving when it is provided.

The basis for determining the upper limits of the amount of information to give as augmented feedback comes from short-term memory, or working memory, research. Classic research by Miller (1956), among others, shows that people have difficulty processing and remembering more than five to nine verbal items. Because it is difficult to determine what constitutes an item in the terms employed by Miller when we apply his conclusions to verbal augmented feedback statements, we propose a general rule. The rule is to provide information about one specific error observed in the performance of the activity. This rule seems especially critical for beginners, who have difficulty determining which errors they are making and have almost no basis for determining how to correct these errors (e.g., Fitts & Posner, 1967; Gentile, 2000). It is important to note here that, although this general rule has theoretical support, it lacks direct empirical support. Indirect empirical support can be demonstrated from dual-task interference research in which performance of a single motor activity is superior to performance of the same activity performed simultaneously with a cognitively demanding activity. For example, an increasing amount of evidence has shown that driving a vehicle is negatively affected when the driver simultaneously engages in a conversation on a mobile phone (e.g., Drews, Pasupathi, & Strayer, 2008).

The content of verbal augmented feedback

Determining the content of verbal feedback is closely related to determining the amount of feedback to give athletes (see reviews by Hodges & Franks, 2008; Wulf & Shea, 2004). That is, what should the coach actually say to the athlete? At least three points should be considered to answer this question. One is that *the verbal statement must be meaningful to the athlete*. The athlete must be able to use the information to correct an error in a way that will improve his or her performance. The importance of information meaningfulness has been supported by research reported several decades ago in which attention and memory were investigated in relation to motor skill acquisition. For example, Shea (1977) demonstrated that, for remembering an arm position in space, a clock-face verbal label (such as 2 o'clock) resulted in better remembering than a meaningless three-letter syllable. Winther and Thomas (1981) similarly demonstrated a positive benefit of the clock-face label for 7-year-old children who were asked to remember specific limb positions in space.

Another essential consideration in the decision to limit the amount of verbal augmented feedback to one specific error in performance is determining which error should be singled out. It would be a rare occurrence if the athlete made only one movement error. If the coach is to specify only one error for the athlete to correct, then on what basis does the coach determine that error? Magill (2010) proposed a two-step process based on research findings concerning the needs of learners during the early stage of learning skills (e.g., Hodges & Franks, 2008). First, the coach prioritizes the list of errors in terms of how important each is to correct to improve performance. The importance should be established on the basis of how critical the part of the skill in which the error occurred is to successfully performing the activity (Arend & Higgins, 1976). Second, the error that is highest on this priority list should be the one that is the basis for the verbal feedback statement.

A good example of research evidence supporting this two-step process is provided in an experiment by Weeks and Kordus (1998) (replicated recently by Wulf, Chiviacowsky, Schiller, & Ávila, 2010), in which 12-year-old boys, who were beginners in soccer, practiced throw-ins. The players were attempting to accurately throw in a ball a specified distance. To provide verbal augmented feedback, the researchers constructed a priority list of eight "form cues," such as "the feet, hips, knees, and shoulders should be aimed at the target." If a player's throw-in demonstrated an error in this part of the activity, it was the basis for the verbal feedback statement the player received (see Table 1.1 for examples of the form cues and the number of times they were presented). A similar approach was reported by

Table 1.1 The aspects of form that were provided as knowledge of performance (KP) most frequently in the Weeks and Kordus (1998) study on soccer throw-ins

Form cue	Group	
	100% KP	*33% KP*
The feet, hips, knees, and shoulders should be aimed at the target, feet shoulder-width apart	59	18
The arms should go over the head during the throw and finish by being aimed at the target	103	34
There should be no spin on the ball during flight	182	52
The ball should be released just in front of the head	78	29

Source: adapted from Weeks and Kordus (1998).

Note
The numbers indicate the raw frequencies with which each statement was given to the 100% and 33% KP groups.

Magill and Schoenfelder-Zohdi (1996) for teaching beginners a rhythmic gymnastics rope skill, and by Rucci and Tomporowski (2010) for improving performance on a weight-training skill. In each of these studies, this two-step process for giving feedback was effective in facilitating learning.

A third verbal feedback content consideration concerns the degree to which the statement indicates how to correct an identified error. Currently, two approaches are proposed to address this concern in the research literature. One is that, for the beginner, the error should be identified along with movement-specific information about how it should be corrected. The second approach states that the error should be identified, but the correction information should be less specific so that the learner is encouraged to search actively for ways to correct the error. Unfortunately, few attempts have been made to compare the effectiveness of these two approaches, although see Tzetzis, Votsis, and Kourtessis (2008) for a recent exception. The second approach would likely be more applicable to skilled performers.

Non-verbal forms of augmented feedback

Researchers have reported the use of many different forms of augmented feedback that are not verbally presented to a learner. As technology has improved and become more accessible to coaches and trainers, there has been an increase in use of augmented feedback involving computer-based technology. It is difficult to specify cogently which parameters of non-verbal augmented feedback are likely to have the greatest influence on learning because the effectiveness of any parameter will be a function of what parameters of the task need to be modified (e.g., spatial parameters, temporal parameters, coordination, movement scaling) as well as characteristics of the task and learner. Consequently, in this section, we discuss some examples of the various types of technology-based augmented feedback in sport settings. This discussion is not intended to be exhaustive of the various types of non-verbal forms of augmented feedback, nor of the sport settings in which they are used. The intent is to provide examples that establish the variety of types and uses of non-verbal forms of augmented feedback.

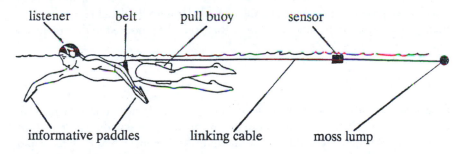

Figure 1.1 The experimental set-up used by Chollet et al. (1992) to provide augmented feedback on whole-body fluctuations in speed and hand propulsive force to competitive swimmers. Image provided courtesy of D. Chollet.

Gymnastics

Researchers in France (Baudry, Leroy, Thouvarecq, & Chollet, 2006) attached a custom-built goniometer to the upper spine and back of the knee of gymnasts to provide concurrent auditory feedback on body segment alignment during the circle movement on a pommel horse. A buzzer sounded when the gymnast's trunk–leg flexion was greater than 20°. Training involved performing circles on the pommel horse with the instruction to "keep the body as straight as possible." Assessment of body segmental alignment showed that the gymnasts who trained with the device for 300 circles improved during training and maintained their acquired performance level 2 weeks later when tested without the device. By comparison, a control group that experienced the same amount of training without the augmented feedback device showed no improvement during training.

Swimming

A speed sensor attached to the waist and hand paddles equipped with pressure sensors (see Figure 1.1) was used with skilled swimmers (14–18 years) to relay auditory information (variations in pitch) on whole-body fluctuations in speed and hand propulsive force (Chollet, Madani, & Micallef, 1992). The swimmers practiced the front crawl stroke during 3 days of training. All the swimmers benefited from the biofeedback training when assessed during training and 15 days later without the devices, when compared with a control group of swimmers who trained without the biofeedback devices.

Rowing

Smith and colleagues (e.g., Smith & Loschner, 2002) have undertaken a systematic search for biomechanical variables that correlate with boat speed and can be presented to rowers as augmented feedback. In a notable study, Spinks and Smith (1994) provided elite rowers with a computer-generated profile of the relation between the position of the handle (corresponding to oar angle) and the force on the handle (corresponding to the torque on the oar) during each stroke on a maximum ergometer test. The rowers were also provided with a template of an idealized force–angle profile. The concurrent augmented visual feedback led to a significant increase in the maximum amount of work that could be produced in the ergometer test.

Netball

Researchers at the Australian Institute of Sport (Helmer, Farrow, Lucas, Higgerson, & Blanchonette, 2010) devised a wearable nylon lycra sleeve with two embedded strain sensors to provide auditory information (drum beats) when the elbow and wrist approximated a particular range of motion during a modified netball throwing/shooting skill (i.e., throwing accuracy task). The drumbeats highlighted the desired tempo for shooting the ball accurately. The augmented feedback training group received the augmented feedback throughout four practice sessions (200 shots total), whereas a control group wore the sleeve, but received no auditory augmented feedback. The auditory feedback was used with different degrees of success by the 16-year-old participants. However, two notable features of the results were that the device encouraged more movement exploration during practice and it often led to poorer performance early in practice before enhancing performance later.

Running

Visual and auditory augmented feedback was used in a study by Eriksson, Halvorsen, and Gullstrand (2011) to modify the running mechanics of nationally ranked male and female Swedish athletes. Visual augmented feedback was displayed on a television monitor in front of each runner on a treadmill. Three vertical bars indicated the vertical displacement of each step, step length, and mechanical power/energy consumption. Bar heights indicated moment-to-moment values during running, and marks on each bar indicated target values for each variable. Prerecorded verbal instructions on how to correct technique errors depicted on the visual display were presented through a wireless headset as auditory feedback. The volume of the recording was proportional to the amount of error and the amount of correction required, and when no instructions were heard the running mechanics of interest were at target levels. In nearly all cases the athletes were able to modify the parameters of their running technique on which they were provided with augmented feedback.

Rifle shooting

In two studies from Finland, augmented feedback was provided in different ways to aid rifle stability while shooting. In one study (Mononen, Viitasalo, Konttinen, & Era, 2003) learners were provided with visual augmented feedback relating to the kinematics of the rifle barrel. The kinematic display was presented after each trial along with shot accuracy data. During the 4 weeks of training (480 shots at target) a group of military conscripts (non-elite shooters) who experienced the augmented kinematic feedback had higher shooting accuracy scores and lower shooting score variability than a group not trained with the kinematic feedback. This difference held for 2 days post training, but not on a test given 10 days post training. However, the differences held for 2 and 10 days when concurrent auditory feedback (variations in pitch) was used to provide information about rifle stability during training (Konttinen, Mononen, Viitasalo, & Mets, 2004).

Weight training

Two studies involving weight training provide examples of how non-verbal and verbal forms of augmented feedback can be combined to benefit sports skill learning and performance. In a study by Winchester, Porter, and McBride (2009) video and verbal information combined improved performance on the power snatch by trained university athletes. The athletes saw on a computer monitor a video of the bar paths of each of their power snatches in a previous set (i.e., summary feedback) and received verbal feedback about how to adjust their technique to produce the ring a training period of 3 days/week over 4 weeks, the athletes vement than a no-augmented feedback control group on the path (displacement) and kinetics (peak power and peak force) during their lifts. Rucci and Tomporowski (2010) showed similar benefits when combining video and verbal augmented feedback for improving weight training performance.

Golf

In a study that demonstrates some additional limitations to the use of video as augmented feedback, Bertram, Marteniuk, and Guadagnoli (2007) trained novice and skilled golfers to improve their swing characteristics. The benefits of video feedback were limited to the skilled players and actually impeded the improvement of the novice golfers. Unlike the studies just discussed involving video feedback and weight training (Rucci & Tomporowski, 2010; Winchester, Porter, & McBride, 2009), no verbal augmented feedback was added to the video feedback training, which suggests that the novices may have needed the combination of video and verbal augmented feedback to improve.

Shooting skills in ice hockey

An often overlooked type of augmented feedback is self-modeling, which refers to observing one's self performing a skill. The intent is to engage the person in comparing his or her recent performance, which was at a lower than desired level, with his or her own performance of the skill when it was performed at a desired level. In a study by Feltz, Short, and Singleton (2008) university ice hockey players viewed videotapes of previous performances of their shooting skills in which they exhibited correct elements of performance that resulted in positive outcomes. Following a 5-week intervention in which one group of players viewed self-modeling videotapes while a control group of players did not, shooting accuracy tests showed the beneficial effects of observing the self-modeling videotapes. The self-modeling experience positively influenced the players' shooting skill self-efficacy in addition to their shooting accuracy.

In summary, augmented feedback can be provided in a variety of forms to enhance performance and learning; however, convenience dictates that coaches commonly use verbal feedback about the errors that are most critical to successful performance. Coaches need a thorough understanding of the skills they are teaching so that the critical elements of each skill can be prioritized for potential use as augmented feedback. To be effective, the feedback must be meaningful to the learner (e.g., limb positions can be referenced to a familiar frame of reference such as a clock face) and the amount provided after each practice attempt should be minimized (e.g., limit to one error) so as to not overburden the learner's information processing capabilities. A number of non-verbal methods of providing augmented feedback have been shown to facilitate sport skill learning. Although it is difficult to specify the most effective ways to present non-verbal augmented feedback because of the range of parameters that could potentially be modified for a given skill, we recommend that practitioners adhere to the principles of meaningfulness and minimization of information when designing systems to present this type of feedback. We will take up these issues again in the following sections of the chapter.

Theory-based guidelines for providing augmented feedback

The scheduling of augmented feedback has been studied more extensively than any other variable that influences performance and learning, and important principles have been discovered about how to provide augmented feedback so that it facilitates rather than hinders learning. These principles have been based on the *guidance hypothesis* and the various ideas that have contributed to the development of that hypothesis.

The guidance hypothesis

The guidance hypothesis was proposed by Salmoni, Schmidt, and Walter (1984) following a comprehensive review of the KR literature. The hypothesis states that augmented feedback plays a major role in scaffolding the learning process by helping the learner discover how to accomplish the goal of the task. However, like any scaffold or crutch, the learner can become dependent on augmented feedback if it diverts attention away from discovering how to accomplish the goal of the task in the absence of augmented feedback. If scheduled inappropriately, augmented feedback can become an essential part of the task or it can prevent the learner from processing critical sources of task-intrinsic feedback or engaging in important aspects of action planning that are essential to task success.

Several aspects of scheduling are likely to lead to dependence on augmented feedback. An increased dependence occurs if augmented feedback is provided too quickly after a practice attempt (Swinnen, Schmidt, Nicholson, & Shapiro, 1990), if it is provided concurrently during performance (Vander Linden, Cauraugh, & Greene, 1993), or if it is provided too frequently during practice or in a manner that is too easy to use (Winstein & Schmidt, 1990). The likelihood that a learner develops a dependence on augmented feedback can be reduced by delaying its provision over trials (Anderson, Magill, & Sekiya, 1994), delaying it over trials and providing it in summary form (Lavery, 1962) or as an average (Young & Schmidt, 1992), or making the provision of augmented feedback contingent on the magnitude of errors made by the learner (Sherwood, 1988). Allowing learners to self-select the trials on which they receive augmented feedback (Patterson & Carter, 2010) or estimate their errors before receiving feedback (Hogan & Yanowitz, 1978) has also proved to be effective in minimizing dependency.

The relation between task-intrinsic feedback and augmented feedback makes a major contribution to whether a learner will become dependent on augmented feedback. Annett and Kay (1957) noted that learners will have a preference for using augmented feedback whenever it is provided because augmented feedback is typically presented in terms of fairly well-known, and therefore meaningful, scales (cm, inches, seconds), whereas no scale may initially exist for comparing task-intrinsic feedback to the goal of the task. Annett (1961) suggested that errors on a retention test without augmented feedback would be highest when the augmented feedback provided during practice was maximally informative and the intrinsic feedback was minimally informative. Building on this idea, subsequent research-ers suggested that dependence on augmented feedback would likely occur when augmented feedback was considerably easier to detect and interpret than intrinsic feedback (Armstrong, 1970; Lintern, 1980). This latter premise has been validated in recent research (Anderson, Magill, & Sekiya, 2001; Blandin, Toussaint, & Shea, 2008; Maslovat, Brunke, Chua, & Franks, 2009). For example, Anderson et al. (2001) showed that learners became dependent on augmented feedback when task-intrinsic feedback was made less familiar by adding elastic resistance to an aiming movement, even when augmented feedback was made more difficult to use and should have discouraged dependency.

Augmented feedback is most effective when it facilitates the learner's discovery of the critical sources of task-intrinsic feedback that are essential for controlling performance in the absence of augmented feedback. Making augmented feedback difficult to use is one way to encourage exploration of the critical sources of task-intrinsic feedback that are essential for success. In a study by Anderson, Magill, Sekiya, and Ryan (2005), when KR about the accuracy of an aiming movement was delayed by two trials, participants reported using more sources of intrinsic feedback during practice and changing the sources attended to across practice than when it was provided directly after each trial (see Figure 1.2). Importantly, delaying KR over trials facilitated retention.

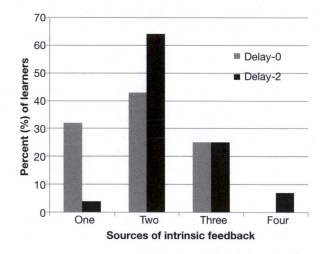

Figure 1.2 Percentage of learners who reported using one, two, three, or four sources of intrinsic feedback (hand location, movement distance, movement time, spring tension) in the Anderson et al. (2005) study. Delay-0 refers to KR given directly after each trial and Delay-2 refers to KR given after a delay of two trials. Adapted from Anderson et al. (2005).

How robust is the guidance hypothesis?

Attempts have been made to qualify the guidance hypothesis by highlighting how task and learner characteristics interact with augmented feedback to influence performance and learning (Guadagnoli & Lee, 2004; Wulf & Shea, 2004). Guadagnoli and Lee (2004) discussed the importance of the learner's skill level and the complexity of the task as determinants of the most appropriate way to schedule augmented feedback. As skill level increases and task complexity decreases, augmented feedback can be made more difficult to use to decrease the likelihood the learner will develop a dependency on this important source of information. However, when skill level is low and task complexity is high, the learner will likely need the guidance provided by augmented feedback to find appropriate ways to improve performance. Wulf and Shea (2004) have taken a different approach to qualifying the guidance hypothesis, arguing that recent findings on the effects of augmented feedback on complex skill learning challenge the fundamental tenets of the hypothesis.

In an experiment on augmented feedback and complex task learning (Wulf, Shea & Matschiner, 1998), concurrent augmented feedback provided throughout practice of a ski-type movement on a simulator resulted in superior retention performance compared with faded feedback (50% feedback) even though feedback was no longer available in retention. In this study, participants learned to make large-amplitude, lateral back-and-forth movements with concurrent augmented feedback provided on an oscilloscope about the time at which they shifted weight from one foot to another to push themselves further along the simulator trackway. The onset of force relative to the position of the feet on the trackway is correlated with movement amplitude.

As Wulf and Shea (2004) point out, the performance of the 100% group seems to run counter to the predictions of the guidance hypothesis, particularly as the augmented feedback was provided concurrently and on 100% of trials; two characteristics of augmented feedback scheduling likely leading to dependency. However, the finding can be explained by the guidance hypothesis if the relation between the salience of task-intrinsic and augmented feedback is taken into account. The augmented feedback was likely difficult to interpret early in learning, whereas the learners could easily discern the amplitude of the platform movements through task-intrinsic feedback. As the learners became more proficient at using the augmented feedback, they could continuously calibrate their adjustments to the timing of force onset with the amplitude of their movements. When the augmented feedback was removed, they still had task-intrinsic feedback about the amplitude of platform movement to gauge the success of their adjustment strategies. So, consistent with earlier ideas that have contributed to the guidance hypothesis (e.g., Annett, 1961), dependence on augmented feedback did not occur because of the highly salient nature of task-intrinsic feedback. However, we predict that dependence would develop on a complex task with less salient task-intrinsic feedback. Such dependencies have been noted for bimanual coordination tasks in which intrinsic feedback about the relative temporal–spatial position of the arms is difficult to gauge without augmented feedback (e.g., Maslovat et al., 2009).

Interactions between augmented feedback and attentional focus also provide a challenge to the guidance hypothesis according to Wulf and Shea (2004). The Wulf et al. (2010) replication of the Weeks and Kordus (1998) soccer throw-in study provides an excellent example of this interaction. Weeks and Kordus (1998) originally showed that 33% augmented feedback on the critical form elements of the throw-in led to better performance on a retention test than 100% augmented feedback. Wulf et al. (2010) replicated the original groups and added two new groups that received 33% or 100% augmented feedback on the critical form elements, but with statements that induced an external focus of attention. For example, the internal focus instruction "the back should be arched at the beginning of the throw" was changed to "produce a 'C' at the beginning of the throw." The pertinent finding was that the 100% external focus feedback group had significantly higher form scores on immediate and delayed transfer tests without augmented feedback than the other groups, though there were no group differences in practice, retention, or transfer for throwing accuracy.

The above findings seem inconsistent with predictions of the guidance hypothesis, although they can be reconciled with the guidance hypothesis if the relation between task-intrinsic and augmented feedback is considered. Wulf and colleagues essentially provided learners with the scale that Annett and Kay (1957) said was lacking for most sources of intrinsic feedback early in learning. The form statements were reworded so that they provided familiar, more *meaningful* labels for the critical sources of task-intrinsic feedback the learners needed to process to be successful on the task. The learners were then able to use those sources of information more effectively to improve performance.

In summary, the guidance hypothesis appears robust. Practitioners should not predict the same pattern of performance changes in practice, retention, and transfer when the same scheduling manipulations are used for simple and complex tasks. Performance with augmented feedback and after it has been withdrawn will reflect the interactions among the schedule of augmented feedback and the characteristics of task-intrinsic feedback and augmented feedback. The likelihood of dependence on augmented feedback can be reduced by making task-intrinsic feedback more meaningful or easier to use or by making augmented feedback more difficult to use.

Future directions

Despite the considerable attention that has been given to augmented feedback in motor skill learning, there is much work still to be done to identify how to utilize it effectively. In this final section, we provide some suggestions for future research directions.

On which aspect of performance to provide augmented feedback

It is ironic that much more attention has been given to how to schedule augmented feedback than on which aspect of performance to provide feedback. We have been guilty of "putting the cart before the horse." Although many creative and ingenious ways have been developed for providing augmented feedback, the content of augmented feedback has been based largely on intuition rather than on scientific principles. In tasks whose goal is to produce a particular movement pattern, such as in diving, gymnastics, and figure skating, the coach's job is simplified because the feedback strategy of prioritizing errors in performance, described earlier in the chapter, can be implemented quite simply. However, the practitioner's job is more difficult when the goal of the task does not specify the movement pattern needed to achieve the goal.

Consider an experiment by Wallace and Hagler (1979), regarded as one of the best examples of the effectiveness of KP for improving motor skill learning. Students who were not experienced basketball players practiced one-handed free-throw shooting with the non-dominant hand with either augmented feedback about the movement form or verbal encouragement. Despite similarities between the two groups early in practice, the group receiving augmented feedback about movement form scored considerably more points than the verbal encouragement group during the later stages of practice and when augmented feedback was removed. Clearly, the augmented feedback facilitated performance and learning. However, did learners receive augmented feedback on the aspects of their movement form that were needed to maximize or optimize performance? A discriminant analysis of the biomechanical factors contributing to successful free-throw shooting performance by Hudson (1985) suggests not. Hudson found that very few of the kinematic measures she examined (including release angle and velocity), that is the type of variables used as augmented feedback by Wallace and Hagler (1979), correlated with successful performance. The variable that provided the best predictor of successful shooting was the stability of the whole-body center of gravity (COG) at the point of release.

Of course, providing a player with information about his or her COG stability would be very difficult for a basketball coach. However, the key point is that few systematic attempts have been made to identify the parameters that are most closely associated with success on a task and to utilize those parameters as feedback for improving performance. Smith and colleagues have attempted such an analysis for rowing (e.g., Smith & Loschner, 2002) and a similar analysis of visual search strategies in soccer has been used to train anticipatory skills in goalkeepers (e.g., Savelsbergh, van Gastel, & van Kampen, 2010), though we are not aware of attempts to do so in other sports. We recommend that coaches and researchers take a more systematic approach to determining the parameters that are most predictive of success on tasks and studying the effects on performance and learning of presenting those parameters as augmented feedback. There is much to be learned and gained in this area.

How to provide augmented feedback and where to direct attention

The content of augmented feedback is closely related to the question of how to provide augmented feedback and where to direct attention. This notion is well illustrated by the way in which augmented feedback has been used to facilitate the learning of laboratory-based, bimanual coordination tasks. These tasks require participants to learn to coordinate two limbs or joints in a specific pattern, usually an oscillating pattern that has the motion of one limb cycle temporally shifted relative to the motion of the other limb's cycle. It is quite clear in this type of task that augmented feedback can be useful if it highlights the relative motions between the two limbs. A question is whether this may best be accomplished by highlighting the critical positions of each limb in its cycle with a light or a tone. These methods have certainly been used successfully; however, the best method is to transform the augmented feedback so that the relative motions of each limb are represented by a single point on a computer screen and the required coordination pattern is described by a familiar shape, such as a circle, that the point must trace. This type of augmented feedback makes a difficult task quite simple and researchers have established that learners can use it (and variations) with little practice to perform a wide range of coordinated movement patterns that are normally very difficult to control (e.g., Mechsner, Kerzel, Knoblich, & Prinz, 2001; Wilson, Snapp-Childs, Coats, & Bingham, 2010).

One reason that augmented feedback transformed into a perceptually simple and salient event is so effective might be that it encourages an external focus of attention. Prinz and colleagues (e.g., Mechsner et al., 2001; Prinz, 1997) have argued that an external focus of attention is beneficial to performance and learning because actions and movements are planned and represented in terms of their perceptual consequences. This idea is highly similar to Fowler and Turvey's (1978) notion that actors are generally more concerned with controlling events than controlling movements. In addition, focusing on the movement effect can encourage more automatic control processes (Wulf & Prinz, 2001). As noted earlier, Wulf and colleagues have already suggested that direction of attention can play an important role in determining the effectiveness of augmented feedback. Although we have questioned whether the findings reported by Wulf et al. (2010) were a function of an external focus of attention or transformation of the ease with which task-intrinsic feedback could be interpreted and processed, it is noteworthy that providing feedback on movement effects can facilitate changes in movement form in addition to changes in movement outcome.

The importance of providing feedback about movement consequences on movement execution in skilled soccer players was recently shown by Ford, Hodges, and Williams (2007). The players kicked soccer balls to a target while being prevented from seeing the trajectory of the ball or the final outcome. They were shown accurate or erroneous (75 cm lower than actual) ball trajectories on videotape and provided with accurate information about the ball's landing position relative to the target. The important finding was that players receiving erroneous videotape feedback modified their movement patterns to kick the ball higher in the retention test without augmented feedback, leading to target overshooting. Consequently, the players' movement patterns were intimately coupled to the event (ball trajectory and landing position) they were attempting to control.

Consistent with the recommendations made by Wulf and colleagues, it is our view that coupling manipulations of augmented feedback with manipulations of direction of attention could provide useful insights into the process by which augmented feedback influences learning and, consequently, present new ways in which augmented feedback can be provided to facilitate learning. An additional benefit of this research endeavor is that it would help tie together two of the issues just discussed in this and the preceding section. In the discussion of the need to investigate the aspects of performance on which to provide augmented feedback, we noted that Hudson (1985) found that the stability of the whole-body COG at the point of release was the best predictor of successful shooting. When considered in terms of attention focus, augmented feedback specifically directed toward this aspect of performance would direct the performer's attention focus internally. However, it is possible to predict that directing the performer's attention externally could result in an improvement in COG stability. Research is needed, however, to determine the specific movement outcome variable that would result in this type of learning and performance benefit. Clearly, considerable scope for research exists in this area.

Augmented feedback effects over extended periods of practice

Finally, an area that needs clarification is the effects of augmented feedback over extended periods of practice. Volume of practice interacts with a number of variables that influence motor skill learning (Anderson et al., 2005). Practice is particularly relevant in the context of augmented feedback because the sources of task-intrinsic feedback used by learners are known to change as skill is acquired (Anderson et al., 2005; Fuchs, 1962). Thus, the most helpful type of augmented feedback is likely to vary as a function of the individual's stage of learning or level of skill or age. Few attempts have been made to discern how the content of augmented feedback might need to change as the learner progresses through different phases of learning, yet tailoring augmented feedback to the learner's skill level is likely essential to ensuring continued skill development.

Blandin et al. (2008) have highlighted again the important parallels between the guidance hypothesis and the specificity of practice effect. The latter refers to the fact that performance becomes increasingly tied to the sources of information available to support performance as practice increases. In essence, the more a source of information is utilized the more essential it becomes. Consequently, dependence on augmented feedback is likely to increase as a function of the amount of practice a learner has had in utilizing this feedback. This notion has particularly important implications for those interested in learning that occurs over the long periods of time typically deemed necessary to acquire expertise in a task.

Conclusions

Augmented feedback can play a number of roles in motor skill learning, ranging from enhancing to degrading skill acquisition. Researchers and practitioners have devised clever ways to provide augmented feedback in the context of sport skill learning and performance. However, a more principled approach is needed to determine the most appropriate content of augmented feedback. At present, the most viable way for the coach or teacher to determine content is to use intuition and experience to rank those aspects of performance deemed critical for success and provide augmented feedback on the aspect that is ranked highest on the list and needs correction. Augmented feedback can be provided in a number of ways to minimize the likelihood of dependency, including reducing its frequency, delaying it over trials, delaying it over trials and providing it in summary or average form, providing augmented feedback only after a threshold of error has been exceeded, or allowing learners to self-select the schedule on which augmented feedback is provided. Ultimately, dependence on augmented feedback is a function of the characteristics of task-intrinsic feedback, the content of augmented feedback, and how it is provided to the learner. Further insights into the role of augmented feedback and the ways in which it can be used to enhance performance and learning can be gleaned by focusing on what aspects of a task to provide feedback on, how to present it, and how it interacts with the learner's focus of attention and stage of learning.

References

Anderson, D. I., Magill, R. A., & Sekiya, H. (1994). A reconsideration of the trials–delay of knowledge of results paradigm in motor skill learning. *Research Quarterly for Exercise and Sport, 65,* 286–290.

Anderson, D. I., Magill, R. A., & Sekiya, H. (2001). Motor learning as a function of KR schedule and characteristics of task-intrinsic feedback. *Journal of Motor Behavior, 33,* 59–66.

Anderson, D. I., Magill, R. A., Sekiya, H., & Ryan, G. (2005). Support for an explanation of the guidance effect in motor skill learning. *Journal of Motor Behavior, 37,* 231–238.

Annett, J. (1961). *The role of knowledge of results in learning: A survey.* Technical Report No. 342-3, U. S. Naval Training Device Center, Port Washington, LI, New York.

Annett, J., & Kay, H. (1957). Knowledge of results and "skilled performance." *Occupational Psychology, 31,* 69–79.

Arend, S. & Higgins, J. R. (1976). A strategy for the classification, subjective analysis, and observation of human movement. *Journal of Human Movement Studies, 2,* 36–52.

Armstrong, T. R. (1970). *Feedback and perceptual–motor skill learning: A review of information feedback and manual guidance training techniques.* Technical Report No. 25, Human Performance Center, University of Michigan, Ann Arbor.

Baudry, L., Leroy, D., Thouvarecq, R., & Chollet, D. (2006). Auditory concurrent feedback benefits on the circle performed in gymnastics. *Journal of Sports Sciences, 24,* 149–156.

Bertram, C. P., Marteniuk, R. G., & Guadagnoli, M. A. (2007). On the use and misuse of video analysis. *International Journal of Sports Science & Coaching, 2,* 37–46.

Blandin, Y., Toussaint, L., & Shea, C. H. (2008). Specificity of practice: Interaction between concurrent sensory information and terminal feedback. *Journal of Experimental Psychology: Learning, Memory, and Cognition, 34,* 994–1000.

Chollet, D., Madani, M., & Micallef, J. P. (1992). Effects of two types of biomechanical bio-feedback on crawl performance. In MacLaren, D., Reilly, T., & Lees, A. (Eds.), *Biomechanics and medicine in swimming: Swimming science VI* (pp. 57–62). London: E & FN Spon.

Drews, F. A., Pasupathi, M., & Strayer, D. L. (2008). Passenger and cell phone conversations in simulated driving. *Journal of Experimental Psychology: Applied, 14,* 392–400.

Eriksson, M., Halvorsen, K. A., & Gullstrand, L. (2011). Immediate effect of visual and auditory feedback to control the running mechanics of well-trained athletes. *Journal of Sports Sciences, 29,* 253–262.

Feltz, D. L., Short, S. E., & Singleton, D. A. (2008). The effect of self-modeling on shooting performance and self-efficacy with intercollegiate hockey players. In Simmons, M. P., & Foster, L. A. (Eds.), *Sport and exercise psychology research advances* (pp. 9–18). Hauppauge, NY: Nova Biomedical Books.

Fitts, P. M., & Posner, M. I. (1967). *Human performance*. Belmont, CA: Brooks/Cole.

Ford, P., Hodges, N. J., & Williams, A. M. (2007). Examining action effects in the execution of a skilled soccer kick by using erroneous feedback. *Journal of Motor Behavior, 39,* 481–490.

Fowler, C. A., & Turvey, M. T. (1978). Skill acquisition: An event approach with special reference to searching for the optimum of a function of several variables. In Stelmach, G. E. (Ed.), *Information processing in motor control and learning* (pp. 1–40). New York: Academic Press.

Fuchs, A. H. (1962). The progression–regression hypothesis in perceptual–motor skill learning. *Journal of Experimental Psychology, 63,* 177–182.

Gentile, A. M. (2000). Skill acquisition: Action, movement, and neuromotor processes. In Carr, J. H., & Shepherd, R. B. (Eds.), *Movement science: Foundations for physical therapy* (2nd edn., pp. 111–187). Rockville, MD: Aspen.

Guadagnoli, M. A., & Lee, T. D. (2004). Challenge point: A framework for conceptualizing the effects of various practice conditions in motor learning. *Journal of Motor Behavior, 36,* 212–224.

Helmer, R. J. N., Farrow, D., Lucas, S. R., Higgerson, G. J., & Blanchonette, I. (2010). Can interactive textiles influence a novice's throwing technique? *Procedia Engineering, 2,* 2985–2990.

Hodges, N. J., & Franks, I. M. (2008). The provision of information. In Hughes, M., & Franks, I. M. (Eds.), *Essentials of performance analysis: An introduction* (pp. 21–39). London: Routledge.

Hogan, J. C., & Yanowitz, B. A. (1978). The role of verbal estimates of movement error in ballistic skill acquisition. *Journal of Motor Behavior, 10,* 133–138.

Hudson, J. L. (1985). Prediction of basketball skill using biomechanical variables. *Research Quarterly for Exercise and Sport, 56,* 115–121.

Konttinen, N., Mononen, K., Viitasalo, J., & Mets, T. (2004). The effects of augmented auditory feedback on psychomotor skill learning in precision shooting. *Journal of Sport & Exercise Psychology, 26,* 306–316.

Lavery, J. J. (1962). Retention of simple motor skills as a function of type of knowledge of results. *Canadian Journal of Psychology, 16,* 300–311.

Lintern, G. (1980). Transfer of landing skill after training with supplementary visual cues. *Human Factors, 22,* 81–88.

Magill, R. A. (2010). *Motor learning and control: Concepts and applications* (9th edn.). New York: McGraw-Hill.

Magill, R. A., & Schoenfelder-Zohdi, B. (1996). A visual model and knowledge of performance as sources of information for learning a rhythmic gymnastics skill. *International Journal of Sport Psychology, 27,* 7–22.

Maslovat, D., Brunke, K. M., Chua, R., & Franks, I. M. (2009). Feedback effects on learning a novel bimanual coordination pattern: Support for the guidance hypothesis. *Journal of Motor Behavior, 41,* 45–54.

Mechsner, F., Kerzel, D., Knoblich, G., & Prinz, W. (2001). Perceptual basis of bimanual coordination. *Nature, 414,* 69–73.

Miller, G. A. (1956). The magical number seven plus or minus two: Some limits on our capacity for processing information. *Psychological Review, 63,* 81–97.

Mononen, K., Viitasalo, J. T., Konttinen, N., & Era, P. (2003). The effects of augmented kinematic feedback on motor skill learning in rifle shooting. *Journal of Sports Sciences, 21,* 867–876.

Patterson, J. T., & Carter, M. (2010). Learner regulated knowledge of results during the acquisition of multiple timing goals. *Human Movement Science, 29,* 214–227.

Prinz, W. (1997). Perception and action planning. *European Journal of Cognitive Psychology, 9,* 129–154.

Rucci, J. A., & Tomporowski, P. D. (2010). Three types of kinematic feedback and the execution of the hang power clean. *Journal of Strength and Conditioning Research, 24,* 771–778.

Salmoni, A. W., Schmidt, R. A., & Walter, C. B. (1984). Knowledge of results and motor learning: A review and critical reappraisal. *Psychological Bulletin, 95,* 355–386.

Savelsbergh, G. J. P., van Gastel, P. J., & van Kampen, P. M. (2010). Anticipation of penalty kicking direction can be improved by directing attention through perceptual learning. *International Journal of Sport Psychology, 41,* 24–41.

Schmidt, R. A., & Lee, T. D. (2011). *Motor learning and control: A behavioral emphasis* (5th edn.). Champaign, IL: Human Kinetics.

Shea, J. B. (1977). Effects of labeling on motor short-term memory, *Journal of Experimental Psychology: Human Learning and Memory, 3,* 92–99.

Sherwood, D. E. (1988). Effect of bandwidth knowledge of results on movement consistency. *Perceptual and Motor Skills, 66,* 535–542.

Smith, R. M., & Loschner, C. (2002). Biomechanics feedback for rowing. *Journal of Sports Sciences, 20,* 783–791.

Spinks, W. L., & Smith, R. M. (1994). The effects of kinetic information feedback on maximal rowing performance. *Journal of Human Movement Studies, 27,* 17–35.

Tzetzis, G., Votsis, E., & Kourtessis, T. (2008). The effect of different corrective feedback methods on the outcome and self confidence of young athletes. *Journal of Sports Science and Medicine, 7,* 371–378.

Swinnen, S. P., Schmidt, R. A., Nicholson, D. E., & Shapiro, D. C. (1990). Information feedback for skill acquisition: Instantaneous knowledge of results degrades learning. *Journal of Experimental Psychology: Learning, Memory, and Cognition, 16,* 706–716.

Vander Linden, D. W., Cauraugh, J. H., & Greene, T. A. (1993). The effect of frequency of kinetic feedback on learning an isometric force production task in nondisabled subjects. *Physical Therapy, 73,* 79–87.

Wallace, S. A., & Hagler, R. W. (1979). Knowledge of performance and the learning of a closed motor skill. *Research Quarterly, 50,* 265–271.

Weeks, D. L., & Kordus, R. N. (1998). Relative frequency of knowledge of performance and motor skill learning. *Research Quarterly for Exercise and Sport, 69,* 224–230.

Wilson, A. D., Snapp-Childs, W., Coats, R., & Bingham, G. P. (2010). Learning a coordinated rhythmic movement with task-appropriate coordination feedback. *Experimental Brain Research, 205,* 513–520.

Winchester, J. B., Porter, J. M., & McBride, J. M. (2009). Changes in bar path kinematics and kinetics through use of summary feedback in power snatch training. *Journal of Strength and Conditioning Research, 23,* 444–454.

Winstein, C. J., & Schmidt, R. A. (1990). Reduced frequency of knowledge of results enhances motor skill learning. *Journal of Experimental Psychology: Learning, Memory, and Cognition, 16,* 677–691.

Winther, K. T., & Thomas, J. R. (1981). Developmental differences in children's labeling of movement. *Journal of Motor Behavior, 13*, 77–90.

Wulf, G., Chiviacowsky, S., Schiller, E., & Ávila, L. T. G. (2010). Frequent external-focus feedback enhances motor learning. *Frontiers in Psychology, 1*, 1–7. doi: 10.3389/fpsyg.2010.00190

Wulf, G., & Prinz, W. (2001). Directing attention to movement effects enhances learning: A review. *Psychonomic Bulletin & Review, 8*, 648–660.

Wulf, G., & Shea, C. H. (2004). Understanding the role of augmented feedback: The good, the bad and the ugly. In Williams, A. M., & Hodges, N. (Eds.), *Skill acquisition in sport: Research, theory and practice* (pp. 121–144). London: Routledge.

Wulf, G., Shea, C. H., & Matschiner, S. (1998). Frequent feedback enhances complex motor skill learning. *Journal of Motor Behavior, 30*, 180–192.

Young, D. E., & Schmidt, R. A. (1992). Augmented feedback for enhanced skill acquisition. In Stelmach, G. E., & Requin, J. (Eds.), *Tutorials in motor behavior II* (pp. 677–693). Amsterdam: Elsevier.

2 Mixing it up a little

How to schedule observational practice

Nicole T. Ong and Nicola J. Hodges

Much has been written on the potential effectiveness of observational practice and learning and on the content of effective demonstrations (see Hodges, Williams, Hayes & Breslin, 2007; Maslovat, Hayes, Horn & Hodges, 2010; McCullagh, Law & Ste-Marie, in press). In this chapter we review research that has addressed two specific questions: when and how should demonstrations be provided?

Coaches often use demonstrations to relay a strategy and/or show what motor skill is to be performed or how. Demonstrations can occur at any time: before physical practice, during or after physical practice, as and when instructors deem necessary (external control), or when learners are given the autonomy to request a demonstration (self-control). In some contexts, the term *observational practice* refers to the viewing of demonstrations before any physical practice, whereas demonstrations that take place after physical practice or are interspersed with physical practice are commonly referred to as *observational learning*. In the former case, researchers are able to make conclusions about the unconfounded effects of watching on physical performance, retention and transfer (see Vogt & Thomaschke, 2007). In the latter case, observational learning allows researchers to study the potential beneficial effects of observation and physical practice combined. This combined method is more typical in sports. In this chapter we will use the term *observational practice* to refer to a period of practice when a model is viewed before, during or after a period of physical practice, such that, unlike previous definitions, we include within this term literature on both observational practice and observational learning.

Mixed schedules of observation and physical practice

There are a limited number of studies in which researchers have directly manipulated the interspersing of demonstrations with physical practice. Although it has been typical for demonstrations to be provided before as well as during physical practice (i.e. observe, attempt, observe, . . .), this type of mixed practice has typically been compared with no-observation and instruction-only control groups and less so with physical practice or pure observation groups. Despite the generally positive conclusions associated with these former comparison groups (Ashford, Bennett & Davids, 2006), a lack of comparison with pure observation and physical practice prevents conclusions about the relative effectiveness of this combined method.

Physical practice is usually found to be more effective than pure observational practice for outcome success on immediate and delayed tests of retention (e.g. Blandin, Proteau & Alain, 1994; Buchanan, Ryu, Zihlman & Wright, 2008; Maslovat, Hodges, Krigolson & Handy, 2010). However, this finding is modified by the task and by whether learning is assessed in a short, no-feedback retention test or through a reacquisition phase. In the latter case, the later addition of physical practice and feedback can negate any potential detriments associated with observation only and potentially lead to benefits (e.g. Blandin, Lhuisset & Proteau, 1999; Boutin, Fries, Panzer, Shea & Blandin, 2010; Vogt, 1996). With respect to task dependencies, differences in favour of physical practice seem to be more likely for tasks that could be considered complex, requiring the interaction of different effectors (such as those that might be involved in juggling, swimming, gymnastics), in comparison with tasks that place more emphasis on the sequencing of task components (arguably a more cognitive–perceptual–motor skill, such as the choreography of dance moves). For these latter types of skills, there has been evidence that pure observational practice can be as effective as or more effective than physical practice in retention tests (e.g. Badets, Blandin & Shea, 2006; Black, Wright, Magnuson & Brueckner, 2005).

There is more ambiguity in the research literature in regard to the relative effectiveness of combined or mixed schedules of observational and physical practice (in which overall amount of practice time has been controlled) in comparison with pure physical practice. Whereas some researchers have not shown differences in retention between mixed practice schedules and pure physical practice, when additional feedback and instructions have been available during practice (e.g. Magill & Schoenfelder-Zohdi, 1996) a number of studies show benefits of mixed compared with pure physical practice schedules.

Using a video-game task, a group that received alternating physical and observational practice performed with less error in a transfer task than a pure physical practice group (Shea, Wright, Wulf & Whitacre, 2000). However, the groups did not differ in retention. Often transfer effects are seen as evidence of a more abstract, visual–spatial or cognitive type of learning, which might involve the learning of a rule or strategy that can be applied in novel contexts (e.g. Hikosaka, Nakamura, Sakai & Nakahara, 2002). The finding of Shea and colleagues appears to strengthen the hypothesis that observation and potentially mixed practice schedules promote a more flexible type of learning than physical practice.

Positive support for a mixed schedule of observational and physical practice was also shown by Vinter and Chartrel (2010) when comparing children who were learning cursive writing for the first time. Visual–motor training (i.e. both physical practice and observation of letters being reproduced dynamically onto a screen) resulted in both faster and more fluent movements during earlier sessions of physical practice than visual or motor training only (physical practice with static display of letters). Findings support the proposition that interspersing observation with physical practice allows the learner to acquire the skill more proficiently than either process alone, as a result of either the interaction or the summation of the two processes. Not only can the learner see what to do and potentially acquire strategies to aid performance, but these strategies can be integrated into physical practice to promote more effective movement execution. Similar conclusions have been made by Deakin and Proteau (2000), who, using a puzzle task with relatively low motor demands, found no significant differences between a pure physical practice and mixed practice groups in retention. The pure observation group did not perform as accurately as the physical practice and mixed groups in the first block of retention, but with a few physical practice trials the groups did not differ. These data show that observation can be as effective as physical practice if interspersed with physical practice in order that these benefits be realized.

In our laboratory, we have begun to look at how observers learn to adapt to consistent changes in their environment, perhaps analogous to learning to kick or run in a muddy field, move in water or play video games with novel visual–motor mappings between the sensory information and the input device, such as a joystick or mouse (Larssen, Ong & Hodges, in press; Ong & Hodges, 2010; Ong, Larssen & Hodges, 2012). In one study, a mixed practice group (75% observational practice, 25% physical practice) was compared with a physical practice and pure observation group. The task involved aiming in an environment where the visual feedback was rotated clockwise by 30° (see Figure 2.1). This mixed group was able to aim more accurately to targets during practice than the physical practice group (see Figure 2.2; Ong et al., 2012). In immediate retention, both groups were equally accurate and did not differ in accuracy from the pure observation group.

Although observers learn from watching, (see Figure 2.2; Larssen et al., in press; Ong & Hodges, 2010; see also Mattar & Gribble, 2005), we have not seen

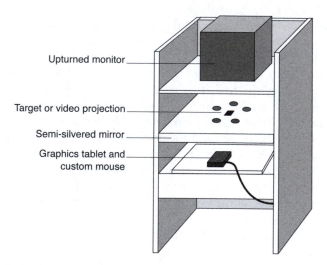

Upturned monitor

Target or video projection

Semi-silvered mirror

Graphics tablet and custom mouse

Figure 2.1 Diagram of mirror-box set-up to study visual–motor adaptation. Images of targets or of a video are projected onto a semi-silvered mirror from an upturned monitor. Participants watch or perform reaching movements on a graphics tablet using a specialized mouse.

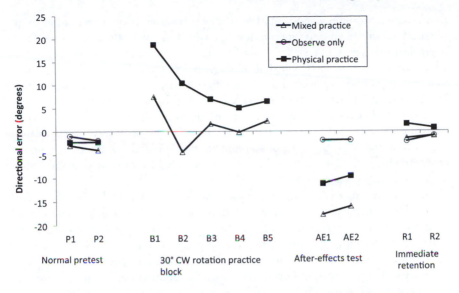

Figure 2.2 Mean directional constant error (degrees) for three groups of participants (Observe, Physical practice or Mixed practice, 25% = physical practice) aiming in normal and rotated environments, across five blocks (B) of practice (trials = 200) in the clockwise (CW) rotated environment (data shown for trials in which vision of the hand was occluded), in a normal environment post test to test for after-effects and again in the CW environment (immediate retention). Data adapted from Ong, Larssen and Hodges (2012).

after-effects (i.e. consistent bias in aiming after adapting to the rotated environment), following a period of observational practice. Therefore, there has been no evidence that motor planning processes have (implicitly) changed, related to the updating of an internal model (see Ong & Hodges, 2010 for a more detailed discussion). However, the mixed practice group in this experiment (Ong et al., 2012) surprisingly showed more pronounced after-effects than the pure physical practice group, despite the fact that the majority of their practice was observational (Figure 2.2).

It seems that this schedule of mixed practice fortified the adaptation experience – involving explicit, strategically driven learning processes, which best described the manner of learning for the observational practice participants, as well as implicit, motorically driven learning processes, which best described learning for physical practice individuals. These latter processes are presumed to be acquired on a slower time scale than the former strategic processes (see Gentile, 1998; Huang & Shadmehr, 2009; Smith, Ghazizadeh, & Shadmehr, 2006), but they are meant to be more robust and less prone to forgetting (see also Willingham, 1998). Therefore, combining observational and physical practice potentially serves to garner benefits from both these processes.

In a subsequent study, we found that observers showed better recall of a previously physically practised rotation if they subsequently observed rather than physically practised an opposite rotation (Larssen, Ong & Hodges, in press). That is physical practice of one skill, followed by observation of another, was better for later execution of the first skill than physical practice throughout. We suggested that these benefits were realized through a more strategic type of learning afforded by observational practice (as additionally evidenced by slower reaction times and more explicit knowledge), which did not interfere with the more implicit (motor) adaptation encouraged through physical practice. Therefore, observation does not appear to result in the updating of an implicit, internal model of the sensorimotor environment, such that multiple skills can potentially be more easily retained and performed back to back.

In summary, mixed practice methods have been shown to be beneficial for aiding skill learning and promoting retention and transfer of a skill. Some of the costs associated with either method in isolation (i.e. pure physical or observational practice) are potentially offset by this type of practice. Whereas physical practice might lead to more robust learning, yet less flexible transfer, observational practice generally shows the reversed pattern of results. Combining both forms of practice appears to negate some of the forgetting associated with observational practice as well as aiding transfer, which seems to be a positive feature associated with observation. Further research is required to test these hypotheses more generally.

Dyad learning as mixed practice

Another form of mixed practice which has received attention is dyad learning, whereby one individual watches as the other practices (e.g. Shea, Wulf & Whitacre, 1999; Shebilske, Regian, Arthur & Jordan, 1992; also McCullagh, Law & Ste-Marie, in press). In dyad practice, physical practice and observational practice are usually alternated between two participants. The learner gets to observe and practise and potentially be motivated by practising alongside a peer (McNevin, Wulf & Carlson, 2000). Shebilske and colleagues had dyads of participants physically control half of a complex video task while observing and reacting to their partners' actions. Each dyad participant alternated between control of the mouse and control of the joystick so that they received only half of the physical practice that participants in an individual group received. The performance of the dyads in retention was no different from the individual practice group, suggesting that participants learnt through observation and/or through the combination of observing and interacting with their partner, allowing them to develop shared representations of the task (Sebanz, Knoblich & Prinz, 2003). Without comparisons with a pure observation group it is not possible to isolate the main cause of this effect. Irrespective, learners were able to halve their physical practice time through this combined, peer-based method of learning, which can have important ramifications for learning under conditions where physical practice time is potentially compromised by costs, safety concerns or injury/impairments.

In subsequent work by Shea et al. (1999; Shea, Wright, Wulf & Whitacre, 2000) similar effects were shown in a two-person response video-game task and a balance task. In the latter, observational practice was alternated with physical practice, eliminating the shared task component of the previous work. Again, dyad learners required only half the amount of physical practice to achieve a similar level of retention to participants who physically practised alone. An alternating, mixed schedule improved training efficiency by increasing the number of learners trained for absolute practice time and/or reduced the absolute amount of physical practice necessary to acquire a certain level of proficiency. These benefits were not seen if a full period of observation followed or preceded physical practice, suggesting that benefits were derived from interspersing action observation with action execution.

These benefits appear to be related to the level of engagement engendered from alternating watching and doing and the processing activities that take place following an action. When additional opportunities to refine an attempted movement are afforded following either physical practice or observation, the processes involved in error detection and correction are potentially elaborated or enhanced (Shea et al., 1999). We suggest that the benefits of interspersing physical and observational practice could be related to the concurrent development of the motor skill, enabling more skilled perception and 'better' or more meaningful information to be gleaned from watching. In studies of brain neurophysiology, perceptual processes are more likely to involve cortical, motor-related areas if the observer has had action experience (e.g. Calvo-Merino, Glaser, Grèzes, Passingham & Haggard, 2005; Cross, Hamilton & Grafton, 2006).

Therefore, mixed schedules of practice, whereby physical practice is alternated in a dyad situation with a partner, or alone through demonstrations, can potentially afford a number of benefits to the learner over and above that experienced through either physical or observational practice alone. These benefits may be mediated by more cognitive or strategic processes, enabling better detection of errors (Blandin, Lhuisset & Proteau, 1999; Hodges, Chua & Franks, 2003) and greater engagement and attention (Bandura, 1986), and/or by the promotion of more motorically driven, implicit processes. In the former case, learners may be able to avoid self-initiated errors after seeing those in others, or they might observe strategies to help correct potential errors after watching. Given that dyadic, alternating practice should allow both learners to develop at similar rates, the information gleaned from watching should be matched to the stage of learning and proficiency of the pair. With respect to the latter case, there is some evidence that the motor system can be engaged during motor learning, at least at a cortical level (Frey & Gerry, 2006), and that motor experience facilitates this level of activation.

Optimizing observation and physical practice ratios

Generally more demonstrations are better than fewer (e.g. Carroll & Bandura, 1990; Weeks & Choi, 1992). However, there is a paucity of data with respect to the optimal ratio of demonstrations relative to physical practice (for exceptions see Laguna, 2000; Sidaway & Hand, 1993). In the study by Laguna (2000), participants were required to execute position-specific arm actions, under specific timing requirements. Five types of practice ratios were studied: 100% physical practice,

100% observational practice and three types of mixed observation and physical practice (25%, 50% or 75% physical practice). Regardless of the ratio, the mixed groups performed with lower spatial and timing errors than both the 100% physical practice and the 100% observation groups (see Figure 2.3).

In terms of the three types of mixed practice, more physical than observational practice was better for spatial/position accuracy, whereas there was a trend for the reverse with respect to temporal accuracy (i.e. more demonstrations were better). These results somewhat concur with the extant literature. For example, when learning how to coordinate joints in a specialized wrist–elbow coordination task, Buchanan, Ryu, Zihlman and Wright (2008) found that relative timing between these joints improved with observation (see also Breslin, Hodges, Williams, Curran & Kremer, 2005, 2006). They did not find improvements in the overall accuracy of the movement, nor in the overall speed following only observational practice in comparison with control conditions. Buchanan and colleagues argued that the relative timing reflected acquisition of more general features of the movement, and hence that observational practice generally enhances the acquisition of movement form or global task features rather than the appropriate scaling of an action to specific environmental demands (see Scully & Newell, 1985). Importantly, however, Buchanan and colleagues did not provide physical practice. In the studies by Breslin and colleagues, an observational learning paradigm was used in a cricket bowling task, whereby demonstrations and practice attempts were interspersed. In this case, demonstrations (of various types) aided both the correct relative timing of the motions of the bowling arm as well as the overall movement time in comparison with control conditions (see also Hayes, Hodges, Scott, Horn & Williams, 2006).

As mentioned at the beginning of the chapter, demonstrations seem to be limited in their effectiveness for the acquisition of complex tasks such as learning

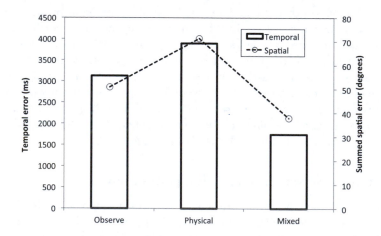

Figure 2.3 Data from the delayed retention test (average of blocks 5–8) for the 100% model and physical practice groups and the average of the three mixed practice groups for both spatial error (degrees) and temporal error (ms), adapted from tables in Laguna (2000).

between-limb relative motion information, even when combined with physical practice attempts (Breslin et al., 2006; Hodges & Franks, 2000; Magill & Schoenfelder-Zohdi, 1996; Maslovat, Hodges et al., 2010). Therefore, although observation and physical practice might differentially impact learning of specific task components, their role is not without ambiguity and their relative effectiveness will be related to the type of skill.

It has also been suggested that, in the early stage of practising a difficult task, most of a learner's cognitive resources are channelled into the execution of the task itself (what to do), leaving little capacity for other processing activities. In such instances, interspersing observational practice might allow the learner to process strategies and/or attend to elements of the task that might not have been possible with only physical practice until learners become more skilled (Wulf & Shea, 2002). Given this, mixed practice schedules are expected to aid the processing of information about what to do as well as how to do it, which might be especially important early in practice and for practice of difficult skills. In the next section, we expand on this question regarding when in practice demonstrations are most beneficial.

When to provide demonstrations

According to Bandura (1986), a performer first acquires a cognitive representation of a movement pattern or skill through selective attention to a demonstration, followed by the ability to code what they see in some symbolic form. In one study, viewing more demonstrations (eight vs two) resulted in a more accurate cognitive representation of a relatively complex arm movement sequence, as assessed through recognition tests (Carroll & Bandura, 1990). This cognitive representation is believed to be a type of 'perceptual blueprint' that guides the later execution of actions. A more accurate cognitive representation was positively correlated to accuracy of later movement execution (Carroll & Bandura, 1985, 1987, 1990). Hence, early observation of a skill can be beneficial for motor learning, promoting the acquisition of an appropriate cognitive representation. Although this perspective is relatively well supported, there are skills for which acquiring such a 'blueprint' may be particularly difficult or not helpful, such as those which require the interaction of limbs into novel patterns of coordination (such as juggling and potentially some gymnastics or swimming skills).

In previous work from one of us, demonstrations early in the skill acquisition process did not aid acquisition for novel bimanual coordination skills when feedback was available to guide learning (e.g. Hodges & Franks, 2000, 2002; Maslovat, Hodges et al., 2010). We did, however, see benefits from demonstrations in terms of perceptual–cognitive improvements (Hodges, Chua & Franks, 2003; Maslovat, Hodges et al., 2010). It appears that, at least for these types of complex coordinative skills, improvements in perceptual abilities do not necessarily translate into improved action abilities. The understanding that comes from physical experience is arguably different from that garnered through observation such that action experience and ability aid perceptual understanding in a different way from the reverse (i.e. observational experience aiding later action). What is likely to be undisputed, however, is that, early in learning, cognitive-based processes play a primary role in guiding learning with respect to picking up strategies and rules for effective performance (e.g. Gentile, 1998; Willingham 1998, 2001), although, as explained earlier, this strategic type of learning may be more prone to being forgotten.

The timing of when demonstrations were provided was manipulated by Weeks and Anderson (2000). Two mixed practice groups received the same number of demonstrations, but one group received demonstrations before and during early practice and another only during practice. The former 'before + during' group showed more accurate movement form in both immediate and delayed retention tests (see Figure 2.4). A third group, which received demonstrations only before practice, also performed more accurately in retention than the group that saw demonstrations only during practice. The authors proposed a few explanations for the less accurate form shown by the mixed 'during' group.

Provision of demonstrations throughout acquisition might have resulted in a dependency, negating the need for learners to form their own reference or perceptual blueprint, so that retention performance without demonstrations was impoverished. Also, if demonstrations were used as augmented feedback for physical practice trials too far into practice, error detection and correction mechanisms may have been suppressed. However, the difference found between the two mixed groups may be not (or not only) a result of 'late' demonstrations, but rather a benefit of the early provision. Weeks and Choi (1992) reported similar benefits for multiple demonstrations (up to five) over a single pre-practice demonstration. As it is not possible to isolate the difference in retention form accuracy to either one of the two potential causes, research is necessary to determine if additional pre-practice demonstrations lead to superior form retention or if demonstrations late into practice are detrimental for learning. We suggest one other explanation that requires testing. It could be that the learners who received demonstrations before or early in practice

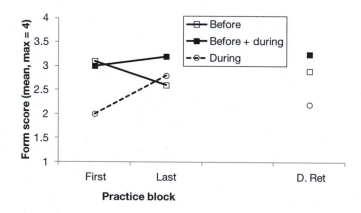

Figure 2.4 Average form accuracy data from the first and last blocks of practice and a 48-hour delayed retention test (D. Ret) of a volleyball serve for three groups that received all demonstrations 'Before' practice, a combined schedule of 'Before + During' or just 'During' practice. Data adapted from graphs of Weeks and Anderson (2000).

attained a more stable movement (plateaued) earlier than the group that had to wait to receive demonstrations during practice. Therefore these earlier groups had more 'correct' physical practice (at least with respect to their form accuracy) and hence might have acquired a 'stronger' representation of the volleyball serve.

Some researchers have compared the impact of providing a demonstration immediately *before* a physical practice trial ('proactive demonstration') versus a demonstration immediately *following* a physical practice trial ('retroactive demonstration'). Richardson and Lee (1999) compared the learning of gestures of the American manual alphabet following either proactive demonstrations or retroactive demonstration protocols, such that in the latter case the learner had to guess or remember what the letter looked like before attempting, rather than being directed by a proactive demonstration. The authors proposed that proactive demonstrations would be more likely to serve as prescriptive instructions to learners, whereas retroactive demonstrations would serve as post-execution feedback, providing comparative information.

Proactive demonstrations resulted in acquisition performance that was more accurate than retroactive demonstrations, yet a drop in accuracy was found for the proactive group in retention, whereas some improvement in accuracy was found for the retroactive group (although the groups were not statistically different in terms of retention). The authors concluded that retroactive demonstrations promoted retrieval practice that involved more cognitive effort than that required to generate a gesture after watching a demonstration. This retrieval practice appears to lead to a greater permanence and stronger retention than the typical proactive method (for related research related to the timing of demonstrations and instructions see Ong, Bowcock & Hodges, 2010; Patterson & Lee, 2005). However, the benefits associated with retroactive demonstrations, or visual cueing of a desired action after a physical practice attempt, disappears when learners are given control over when they wish to practise (Patterson & Lee, 2010), suggesting that reducing the frequency of proactive demonstrations, in a manner that is performance dependent, alleviates potential guiding effects.

At first glance, these advantages associated with retroactive demonstrations might seem contrary to what we have suggested above about providing demonstrations early in practice, given that it would potentially hinder cognitive effort. Although some pre-practice information or demonstration is potentially helpful early in acquisition to help understand the goal requirements and potentially form a perceptual blueprint (if the task is so amenable to such a representation), thereafter demonstrations may be most effective if provided sparingly and following a practice attempt, rather than preceding it. To our knowledge, the frequency of demonstrations has not been explicitly manipulated in order to determine whether it is better to give demonstrations after a series of trials (in a summary format) or in a faded schedule (when they are gradually reduced). However, when people have choice over the frequency of demonstrations, requests are typically limited to fewer than 10% of trials in a more faded schedule (e.g. Wrisberg & Pein, 2002). With respect to post-practice feedback, summary or faded methods of practice have been more effective in promoting retention when the feedback is no longer available, in comparison with providing feedback on every trial. Arguably, too much guidance prevents the learner from applying the requisite cognitive effort and sensory processing necessary for effective learning (see Hodges & Franks, 2008; Winstein & Schmidt, 1990; Wulf & Shea, 2004).

One other finding, related to the issue of when to provide demonstrations, pertains to literature in which learning and expert or correct models have been compared. Although research findings are somewhat mixed with respect to their relative effectiveness (e.g. Brown, Wilson, Obhi & Gribble, 2010; George, Feltz & Chase, 1992; Gould & Weiss, 1981), in the former case the learner does not get to see a correct model until later in learning, whereas in the latter case a correct model is seen throughout. Although this has not been explicitly discussed before, we posit that some of the potential benefits of learning models is that the learner is more engaged (retroactively) in figuring out what to do than in the case of expert models (although of course the error information provided through learning versus correct models might be equally or more beneficial). There is some evidence that mixed models, that is a combination of both novice and expert models, are beneficial for transfer of simple timing skills in comparison with either type of model (Anfard & Proteau, 2011).

Self-controlled observational learning

There have been a number of studies showing that giving learners control (or self-regulation) over aspects of their practice is beneficial for motor skill acquisition (e.g. Chiviacowsky & Wulf, 2002, 2005). Several mechanisms have been proposed for the superiority of learners' self-control over aspects of their own practice. It is believed to (1) increase active involvement and motivation in learners, resulting in 'deeper' information processing; (2) give learners the option of receiving information or feedback when they need it; and (3) enable learners to extract more, or more relevant, information on important components of the skill (Chiviacowsky & Wulf, 2005).

A self-controlled practice schedule has been studied with respect to how individuals choose to use/request demonstrations. Wrisberg and Pein (2002) studied three groups of novices learning the badminton long serve. Participants were assessed on their retention accuracy and movement form after a self-controlled schedule of demonstrations during physical practice, 100% demonstrations (no physical practice) or 100% physical practice (no demonstration). Surprisingly, the groups were not different in outcome accuracy during retention. However, the 100% demonstration and self-control participants significantly improved in movement form compared with the no-demonstration group. This finding fits with earlier research showing that demonstrations are important for acquiring an accurate 'blueprint' of the desired movement goal. However, there was no yoked schedule group (i.e. matched to the self-group) in this study; the addition of one would allow conclusions about whether it was the frequency or schedule of demonstrations or self-control that aided movement form.

Wulf, Raupach and Pfeiffer (2005) extended this research by comparing delayed retention performance of the basketball jump shot between a self-control group and a yoked group. No difference was found between the groups in terms of outcome accuracy, but a significant advantage was found in terms of movement form for the self-control group, suggesting that it is the timing that is important (i.e. performance-dependent information) rather than the frequency or schedule. The self-control group requested a demonstration on only 6% of practice trials. In Wrisberg and Pein's study, demonstrations were also relatively infrequent (~ 10%), suggesting that the perceived benefits from demonstrations are limited.

In our own work, we have shown that the frequency of augmented information requests (i.e. expert demonstrations, instructions or video feedback) during the practice of three different types of Frisbee disc-throwing skills was low. As shown in Figure 2.5, novice participants requested this information on only 9% of practice trials, which increased to 20% for a group who were judged to be experts in another motor domain (i.e. music). As discussed before, providing demonstrations through-out practice is expected to lead to overdependence on such instruction, therefore potentially impairing the development of error detection and correction capabilities in learners (Weeks & Anderson, 2000). Whether learners have some insight into the potentially guiding role of this information, that demonstrations have only a perceived limited usefulness, or they value physical practice over instruction is not clear. We do have some evidence that observers believe they are learning and improv-ing after watching demonstrations (in a two-ball juggling task), but that this seems to plateau quite early in practice (after about 10–20 observation trials) and the percep-tions are not well correlated with actual performance (Coppola & Hodges, 2011).

As with other studies, we found that the novice group in the disc-throwing study tended to request augmented information (AI) on more accurate trials (see Figure 2.6), (providing a reinforcing role, Chiviacowsky & Wulf, 2002; Hodges, Edwards, Luttin & Bowcock, 2011). The music experts, however, who had significant

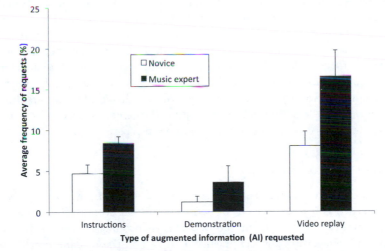

Figure 2.5 Frequency of augmented information requests during a self-regulated practice ses-sion across two groups of novices in a Frisbee disc-throwing task (one group was skilled in music). Based on data from Hodges et al. (2011).

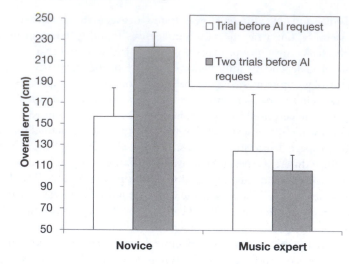

Figure 2.6 Average error on the trial preceding the request for augmented information (AI) in comparison with their error two trials before this request for the novices and music experts (see Hodges et al., 2011 for details of study).

experience practising and learning in another domain, requested information on more errorful trials, thereby using the demonstrations and other sources of information to try to improve performance. Our music experts also showed higher form scores than the novice group, suggesting that the higher frequency of information and/or performance-dependent timing of information, aided later performance.

There is limited knowledge about the type of information that is used by experts when viewing demonstrations of well-learned skills. Hars and Calmels (2007) examined the type of information that elite gymnasts perceived when they observed their own performance. The gymnasts reported more attention to specific movement characteristics (such as epochs of movement or parts of the body), rather than kinematic (relative motion and timing) information. It may be that when performers have had sufficient physical practice, observations function more as augmented feedback to fine-tune the performers' actions (i.e. more of a scaling role). Our data from the disc-throwing experiment seem to confirm this feedback-serving hypothesis in as much as demonstrations were requested when errors were relatively high although the experts in this study were not domain experts.

Summary and conclusions

Empirical evidence generally supports a mixed schedule of physical and observational practice as it leads to levels of performance that do not differ from actual physical practice in retention and transfer. This is encouraging news as this mixed method of interspersing physical practice with demonstrations anecdotally seems to be common practice in coaching arenas. There is also evidence that a mixed practice schedule might be beneficial in terms of flexibility and generalizability to new versions of a practised task. What is perhaps surprising is that there appears to be room to cut back on the amount of physical practice when demonstrations are available, that is demonstrations can compensate for physical practice, which could be beneficial for sports that have potentially high physical and mental costs (e.g. diving, gymnastics, wrestling) as well as economic costs (e.g. ski-jumping).

We suspect that mixed practice has some motivational benefits that have not been examined to date. Interspersing physical practice with demonstrations, particularly if these are of different models, would arguably make learning more interesting. Further, replacing physical practice with observation has obvious benefits in terms of reducing the risk of factors associated with injury and fatigue from physical practice. In terms of unexplored questions, it is clear that we know very little about the role of demonstrations later in the skill acquisition process and particularly how demonstrations are used by more skilled athletes. We suspect that skilled performers would request such information more infrequently than less skilled performers, because they have less to learn, but it might be the case that the action experience of the skilled performer allows them to extract more meaningful information from a demonstration (of their self or others).

There is also only a limited knowledge as to the optimal ratio of demonstration to physical practice. Although there is evidence that as little as 25% physical practice can match or potentially exceed benefits from 100% physical practice (Ong et al., 2012), with the exception of Laguna (2000), there have not been direct comparisons of ratios within studies in terms of their effects on perceptions of performance and potential motivational factors, performance, learning and transfer.

One other potential area of research, to which we have given only scant attention in this review, is the neurophysiology of observational practice with respect to effective practice scheduling. Although there is significant evidence that observational practice can promote neurophysiological changes in cortical and subcortical areas of the brain (e.g. Frey & Gerry, 2006; Stefan, Classen, Celnik & Cohen, 2008) and potentially modulate observational learning (Brown, Wilson & Gribble, 2009), there have not been attempts to look at the modulation of motor-related cortical pathways as a function of when in practice observation trials are received. For example, although we know that observing movement error in others recruits similar brain regions to those activated when observing self-produced error (Malfait et al., 2010) and that early and late in practice motor-related areas of the brain can be activated (Vogt et al., 2007), we do not know whether interspersed observation and physical practice modulates this pattern of activation nor how perceptions of errors in others changes with learning when practice is interspersed with demonstrations. We do know, from transcranial magnetic stimulation studies, that motor-evoked potentials are increased when movement observation is combined with physical practice (e.g. Celnik et al., 2006).

Finally, although we have discussed the potentially mediating role of task factors (such as requirements of different components of the task and task difficulty) and how these might interact with observation scheduling, there is more room for study. It seems as though mixed practice schedules are most beneficial for tasks that are relatively complex, with subtle execution requirements (in comparison with either physical or observational practice in isolation). To our knowledge, only in one study has task difficulty been manipulated with respect to the scheduling of demonstrations. In this study, task difficulty (high or low concept difficulty) did not moderate the effectiveness of retrieval practice (proactive versus retroactive demonstration of a to-be-performed letter action, Patterson & Lee, 2005).

Therefore, in general, mixed schedules of observation and physical practice, with some pre-practice demonstrations and alternating models during practice, seem to have considerable applied learning value. The frequency of demonstrations during practice should be controlled by the learner and, if not, then the optimal amount of demonstrations seems to be around 10–20% of practice trials. The instructor should also pay attention to when demonstrations are provided. Although in general a greater frequency of demonstrations early in practice is more beneficial than later, the practitioner also needs to be cognizant of the potential retention disadvantages associated with providing demonstrations before a practice attempt, rather than after.

References

Ashford, D., Bennett, S. J., & Davids, K. (2006). Observational modeling effects for movement dynamics and movement outcome measures across differing task constraints: A meta-analysis. *Journal of Motor Behavior, 38*, 185–205.

Badets, A., Blandin, Y., & Shea, C. H. (2006). Intention in motor learning through observation. *Quarterly Journal of Experimental Psychology, 59*, 377–386.

Bandura, A. (1986). *Social foundations of thought and action: A social cognitive theory.* Englewood Cliffs, NJ: Prentice Hall.

Black, C. B., Wright, D. L., Magnuson, C. E., & Brueckner, S. (2005). Learning to detect error in movement timing using physical and observational practice. *Research Quarterly for Exercise & Sport, 76*, 28–41.

Blandin, Y., Lhuisset, L., & Proteau, L. (1999). Cognitive processes underlying observational learning and motor skills. *Quarterly Journal of Experimental Psychology, 52*, 957–979.

Blandin, Y., Proteau, L., & Alain, C. (1994). On the cognitive processes underlying contextual interference and observational learning. *Journal of Motor Behavior, 26*, 18–26.

Boutin, A., Fries, U., Panzer, S., Shea, C. H., & Blandin, Y. (2010). Role of action observation and action in sequence learning and coding. *Acta Psychologica, 135*, 240–251.

Breslin, G., Hodges, N. J., Williams, A. M., Curran, W., & Kremer, J. (2005). Modelling relative motion to facilitate intra-limb coordination. *Human Movement Science, 24*, 446–463.

Breslin, G., Hodges, N. J., Williams, A. M., Curran, W., & Kremer, J. (2006). A comparison of intra- and inter-limb relative motion information in modelling a novel motor skill. *Human Movement Science, 25*, 753–766.

Brown, L. E., Wilson, E. T., & Gribble, P. L. (2009). Repetitive transcranial magnetic stimulation to the primary motor cortex interferes with motor learning by observing. *Journal of Cognitive Neuroscience, 21*, 1013–1022.

Brown, L. E., Wilson, E. T., Obhi, S. S., & Gribble, P. L. (2010). Effect of trial order and error magnitude on motor learning by observing. *Journal of Neurophysiology, 104*, 1409–1416.

Buchanan, J. J., Ryu Y. U., Zihlman, K., & Wright, D. L. (2008). Observational practice of relative but not absolute motion features in a single-limb multi-joint coordination task. *Experimental Brain Research, 191*, 157–169.

Calvo-Merino, B., Glaser, D. E., Grèzes, J., Passingham, R. E., & Haggard, P. (2005). Action observation and acquired motor skills: An fMRI study with expert dancers. *Cerebral Cortex, 15,* 143–1249.

Carroll, W. R., & Bandura, A. (1985). Role of timing of visual monitoring and motor rehearsal in observational learning of action patterns. *Journal of Motor Behavior, 17,* 69–85.

Carroll, W. R., & Bandura, A. (1987). Translating cognition into action: The role of visual guidance in observational learning. *Journal of Motor Behavior, 19,* 385–398.

Carroll, W. R., & Bandura, A. (1990). Representational guidance of action production in observational learning: A causal analysis. *Journal of Motor Behavior, 22,* 85–97.

Celnik, P., Stefan, K., Hummel, F., Duque, J., Classen, J., & Cohen, L. G. (2006). Encoding a motor memory in the older adult by action observation. *NeuroImage, 29,* 677–684.

Chiviacowsky, S., & Wulf, G. (2002). Self-controlled feedback: Does it enhance learning because performers get feedback when they need it? *Research Quarterly for Exercise & Sport, 73,* 408–415.

Chiviacowsky, S., & Wulf, G. (2005). Self-controlled feedback is effective if it is based on the learner's performance. *Research Quarterly for Exercise & Sport, 76,* 42–48.

Coppola, T. M., & Hodges, N. J. (2011). Insights into procedural ability following observational practice of a 2-ball juggling action. *Journal of Sport & Exercise Psychology, 33,* S66.

Cross, E. S., Hamilton, A. F. d.C., & Grafton, S. T. (2006). Building a motor simulation de novo: Observation of dance by dancers. *NeuroImage, 31,* 1257–1267.

Deakin, J. M., & Proteau, L. (2000). The role of scheduling in learning through observation. *Journal of Motor Behavior, 32,* 268–276.

Frey, S. H., & Gerry, V. E. (2006). Modulation of neural activity during observational learning of actions and their sequential orders. *Journal of Neuroscience, 26,* 194–201.

Gentile, A. M. (1998). Implicit and explicit processes during acquisition of functional skills. *Scandinavian Journal of Occupational Therapy, 5,* 7–16.

George, T. R., Feltz, D. L., & Chase, M. A. (1992). Effects of model similarity on self-efficacy and muscular endurance: A second look. *Journal of Sport & Exercise Psychology, 14,* 237–248.

Gould, D., & Weiss, M. (1981). The effect of model similarity and model talk on self efficacy and muscular endurance. *Journal of Sport Psychology, 3,* 17–29.

Hars, M., & Calmels, C. (2007). Observation of elite gymnastic performance: Processes and perceived functions of observation. *Psychology of Sport & Exercise, 8,* 337–354.

Hayes, S. J., Hodges, N. J., Scott, M. A., Horn, R. R., & Williams, A. M. (2006). Scaling a motor skill through observation and practice. *Journal of Motor Behavior, 38,* 357–366.

Hikosaka, O., Nakamura, K., Sakai, K., & Nakahara, H. (2002). Central mechanisms of motor skill learning. *Current Opinion in Neurobiology, 12,* 217–222.

Hodges, N. J., Chua, R., & Franks, I. M. (2003). The role of video in facilitating perception and action of a novel coordination movement. *Journal of Motor Behavior, 35,* 247–260.

Hodges, N. J., Edwards, C., Luttin, S., & Bowcock, A. (2011). Learning from the experts: Gaining insights into best practice during the acquisition of three novel motor skills. *Research Quarterly for Exercise & Sport, 82,* 178–188.

Hodges, N. J., & Franks, I. M. (2000). Focus of attention and coordination bias: Implications for learning a novel bimanual task. *Human Movement Science, 19,* 843–867.

Hodges, N. J., & Franks, I. M. (2002). Modelling coaching practice: The role of instruction and demonstration. *Journal of Sport Sciences, 20,* 793–811.

Hodges, N. J., & Franks, I. M. (2008). The provision of information. In Hughes, M., & Franks, I. M. (Eds), *Essentials of performance analysis* (pp. 21–39). London: Routledge.

Hodges, N. J., Williams, A. M., Hayes, S. J., & Breslin, G. (2007). What is modeled during observational learning? *Journal of Sports Sciences, 25,* 531–545.

Huang, V. S., & Shadmehr, R. (2009) Persistence of motor memories reflects statistics of the learning event. *Journal of Neurophysiology, 102*, 931–940.

Laguna, P. L. (2000). The effect of model observation versus physical practice during motor skill acquisition and performance. *Journal of Human Movement Studies, 39*, 171–191.

Larssen, B., Ong, N. T., & Hodges, N. J. (in press). Watch and learn: Seeing is better than doing when acquiring consecutive motor tasks. *PLoS One.*

Magill, R. A., & Shoenfelder-Zhodi, B. (1996). A visual model and knowledge of performance as sources of information for learning a rhythmic gymnastics skill. *International Journal of Sport Psychology, 27*, 7–22.

Malfait, N., Valvear, K., Culham, J., Anton, J., Brown, L., & Gribble, P. (2010). fMRI activation during observation of others' reach errors. *Journal of Cognitive Neuroscience, 22*, 1493–1503.

Maslovat, D., Hayes, S. J., Horn, R., & Hodges, N. J. (2010). Motor learning through observation. In Elliott, D., & Khan, M. A. (Eds), *Vision and goal-directed action: Neurobehavioural perspectives* (pp. 315–339). Champaign, IL: Human Kinetics.

Maslovat, D., Hodges, N. J., Krigolson, O. & Handy, T. (2010). Observational practice benefits are limited to perceptual improvements in the acquisition of a novel coordination skill. *Experimental Brain Research, 204*, 119–130.

Mattar, A. A. G., & Gribble, P. L. (2005). Motor learning by observing. *Neuron, 46*, 153–160.

McCullagh, P., Law, B., & Ste-Marie, D. (in press). Modeling and performance. In Murphy, S. (Ed.), *The Oxford Handbook of Sport & Performance Psychology.* New York, NY: Oxford University Press.

McNevin, N. H., Wulf, G., & Carlson, C. (2000). Effects of attentional focus, self-control, and dyad training on motor learning: Implications for physical rehabilitation. *Physical Therapy, 80*, 373–385.

Ong, N. T., Bowcock, A., & Hodges, N. (2010). Manipulations to the timing and type of instructions to examine motor skill performance under pressure. *Frontiers in Movement Science & Sport Psychology, 1*, 1–13.

Ong, N. T., & Hodges, N. J. (2010). Absence of after-effects for observers after watching a visuomotor adaptation. *Experimental Brain Research, 205*, 325–334.

Ong, N., Larssen, B., & Hodges, N. (2012). In the absence of physical practice, observation and imagery do not result in the updating of internal models for aiming. *Experimental Brain Research, 218*, 9–19.

Patterson, J. T., & Lee, T. D. (2005). Learning a new human–computer alphabet: The role of similarity and practice. *Acta Psychologica, 120*, 267–287.

Patterson, J. T., & Lee, T. D. (2010). Self-regulated frequency of augmented information in skill learning. *Canadian Journal of Experimental Psychology, 64*, 33–40.

Richardson, J. R., & Lee, T. D. (1999). The effects of proactive and retroactive demonstrations on learning signed letters. *Acta Psychologica, 101*, 79–90.

Rohbanfard, H., & Proteau, L. (2011). Learning through observation: a combination of expert and novice models favors learning. *Experimental Brain Research, 215*, 183–197.

Scully, D. M., & Newell, K. M. (1985). The acquisition of motor skills: Toward a visual perception perspective. *Journal of Human Movement Studies, 12*, 169–187.

Sebanz, N., Knoblich, G., & Prinz, W. (2003). Representing others' actions: just like one's own? *Cognition, 88*, B11–B21.

Shea, C. H., Wright, D. L., Wulf, G., & Whitacre, C. (2000). Physical and observational practice afford unique learning opportunities. *Journal of Motor Behavior, 32*, 27–36.

Shea, C. H., Wulf, G., & Whitacre, C. (1999). Enhancing training efficiency and effectiveness through the use of dyad training. *Journal of Motor Behavior, 31*, 119–125.

Shebilske, W. L., Regian, J. W., Arthur, W., & Jordan, J. A. (1992). A dyadic protocol for training complex skills. *Human Factors, 34*, 369–374.

Sidaway, B., & Hand, M. J. (1993). Frequency of modeling effects on the acquisition and retention of a motor skill. *Research Quarterly for Exercise & Sport, 64*, 122–125.

Smith, M. A., Ghazizadeh, A., & Shadmehr, R. (2006). Interacting adaptive processes with different timescales underlie short-term motor learning. *PLoS Biology, 4*, e179.

Stefan, K., Classen, J., Celnik, P., & Cohen, L. G. (2008). Concurrent action observation modulates practice-induced motor memory formation. *European Journal of Neuroscience, 27*, 730–738.

Vinter, A., & Chartrel, E. (2010). Effects of different types of learning on handwriting movements in young children. *Learning and Instruction, 20*, 476–486.

Vogt, S. (1996). The concept of event generation in movement imitation: Neural and behavioural aspects. *Corpus, Psyche et Societas, 3*, 119–132.

Vogt, S., Buccino, G., Wohlschläger, A. M., Canessa, N., Shah, N., Zilles, K., et al. (2007). Prefrontal involvement in imitation learning of hand actions: Effects of practice and expertise. *Neuroimage, 37*, 1371–1383.

Vogt, S., & Thomaschke, R. (2007). From visuo-motor interactions to imitation learning: Behavioural and brain imaging studies. *Journal of Sports Sciences, 25*, 3–23.

Weeks, D. L., & Anderson, L. P. (2000). The interaction of observational learning with overt practice: Effects on motor skill learning. *Acta Psychologica, 104*, 259–271.

Weeks, D. L., & Choi, J. (1992). Modelling the perceptual component of a coincident-timing skill: The influence of frequency of demonstration. *Journal of Human Movement Studies, 23*, 201–213.

Willingham, D. B. (1998). A neuropsychological theory of motor skill learning. *Psychological Review, 105*, 558–584.

Willingham, D. B. (2001). Becoming aware of motor skill. *Trends in Cognitive Science, 5*, 181–182.

Winstein, C. J., & Schmidt, R. A. (1990). Reduced frequency of knowledge of results enhances motor skill learning. *Journal of Experimental Psychology: Learning, Memory, and Cognition, 16*, 677–691.

Wrisberg, C. A., & Pein, R. L. (2002). Note on learners' control of the frequency of model presentation during skill acquisition. *Perceptual & Motor Skills, 94*, 792–794.

Wulf, G., Raupach, M., & Pfeiffer, F. (2005). Self-controlled observational practice enhances learning. *Research Quarterly for Exercise & Sport, 76*, 107–111.

Wulf, G., & Shea, C. H. (2002). Principles derived from the study of simple motor skills do not generalize to complex skill learning. *Psychonomic Bulletin & Review, 9*, 185–211.

Wulf, G., & Shea, C. H. (2004). Understanding the role of augmented feedback: The good, the bad, and the ugly. In Williams, A. M., & Hodges, N. J. (Eds), *Skill Acquisition in Sport: Research, Theory and Practice* (pp. 121–144). London: Routledge.

3 Attentional focus affects movement efficiency

Keith R. Lohse, Gabriele Wulf, and Rebecca Lewthwaite

Introduction

Without doubt, motor behavior is subject to a variety of social–cognitive–affective influences (Lewthwaite & Wulf, 2010a). For instance, the instructions or feedback given to learners not only provide them with "cold" information about the task, what to do, or how to correct errors, but also influence the learner's emotional state directly impacting on the performance, learning, and control of movements (e.g., Lewthwaite & Wulf, 2010b). This effect is exemplified by how small differences in the wording of instructions or feedback influence performance and learning (e.g., Hutchinson, Sherman, Martinovic, & Tenenbaum, 2008; Jourden, Bandura, & Banfield, 1991; Wulf & Lewthwaite, 2009). One line of research in which differential effects on motor skill learning as a function of instructions have been found consistently is research on attentional focus (see Wulf, 2007a, 2007b). Specifically, if attention is directed to the performer's body movements (i.e., inducing an internal focus of attention), motor learning is generally hampered compared with attention directed at the movement effect (i.e., inducing an external focus).

Most researchers examining attentional focus effects have assessed movement *effectiveness*, using outcome measures such as accuracy in hitting a target (e.g., Bell & Hardy, 2009; Marchant, Clough, & Crawshaw, 2007) or producing a certain amount of force (e.g., Freedman, Maas, Caligiuri, Wulf, & Robin, 2007; Lohse, 2011; Lohse, Sherwood, & Healy, 2011), the minimization of deviations from a balanced position (Chiviacowsky, Wulf, & Wally, 2010; Wulf, McNevin, & Shea, 2001), postural sway (Laufer, Rotem-Lehrer, Ronen, Khayutin, & Rozenberg, 2007; Wulf, Mercer, McNevin, & Guadagnoli, 2004), or movement speed (Fasoli, Trombly, Tickle-Degnen, & Verfaelllie, 2002; Porter, Nolan, Ostrowski, & Wulf, 2010; Totsika & Wulf, 2003). In the first study that demonstrated the effectiveness of instructions inducing an external relative to an internal focus of attention (Wulf, Höß, & Prinz, 1998), the learning of dynamic balance tasks was enhanced when participants' attention was directed to the movements of the platform on which they were standing (specifically, wheels on a ski simulator platform or markers on a stabilometer platform; Wulf et al., 1998, Experiments 1 and 2 respectively) as compared with the movements of their feet. Group differences were seen on delayed retention tests without focus instructions or reminders, suggesting that they reflected differential effects on learning. Since then, numerous researchers have replicated the benefits of instructions or feedback inducing an external focus.

Several studies have demonstrated learning advantages of an external focus for sport skills, such as hitting a golf ball (e.g., Bell & Hardy, 2009; Wulf, Lauterbach, & Toole, 1999; Wulf & Su, 2007), basketball free-throw shooting (Al-Abood, Bennett, Hernandez, Ashford, & Davids, 2002; Zachry, Wulf, Mercer, & Bezodis 2005), dart throwing (Marchant et al., 2007), and volleyball serves and soccer kicks (Wulf, McConnel, Gärtner, & Schwarz, 2002). Overall, the benefits of an external compared with an internal focus have been shown not only for a variety of skills, but also for levels of expertise and age groups, as well as healthy individuals and those with motor impairments. Many of these findings related to movement effectiveness have been reviewed elsewhere (see Wulf, 2007a, 2007b).

In this chapter, we review mostly newer studies that have been concerned with movement *efficiency* as a function of attentional focus. The efficiency of movement production is a central characteristic of skill (Guthrie, 1952). As individuals become more skilled, their movements not only become more accurate and consistent, but are also performed more efficiently (Sparrow & Newell, 1998). A movement pattern is considered more efficient or economical if the same movement outcome is achieved with less energy expended. Although distinctions between the terms *efficient* and *economic* have been made (e.g., Sparrow & Newell, 1998), here we will use them interchangeably.

An important prediction is that movements should be more efficient when the performer uses an external as opposed to an internal focus. In the following sections, we first briefly discuss explanation(s) for the effects of attentional focus, and then review attentional focus studies in which researchers have examined what can be interpreted as measures of movement efficiency, such as electromyographic (EMG) activity and oxygen consumption. We conclude by reviewing how the focus of attention might enhance learning and performance by improving movement efficiency, and make recommendations for athletes, coaches and therapists who can manipulate the focus of attention in applied settings to optimize performance.

How does attentional focus affect performance and learning?

The differential effects of internal versus external foci have been explained within the constrained action hypothesis (Wulf, McNevin, & Shea, 2001), according to which an internal focus on the body induces a conscious type of control. As a consequence, individuals tend to constrain their motor system by interfering with automatic control mechanisms that have the capacity to control movements effectively and efficiently. In contrast, focusing on the movement effect promotes a more automatic mode of control. That is, it allows for the utilization of unconscious, fast and reflexive control processes, with the result that the desired outcome is achieved almost as a by-product. Several converging lines of research support this notion. These include demonstrations of reduced attentional capacity demands with an external focus of attention (Wulf, McNevin, & Shea, 2001), high-frequency movement adjustments (e.g., McNevin, Shea, & Wulf, 2003; Wulf, Shea, & Park,

2001), and reduced pre-movement times, representing more efficient motor planning (Lohse, 2012).

A number of alternative explanations for the attentional focus effects have been suggested, ranging from visual advantages (e.g., Maurer & Zentgraf, 2007; Russell, 2007) to a greater functional relevance (e.g., Hommel, 2007; Künzell, 2007; Wrisberg, 2007; Ziessler, 2007) or reduced information-processing demands of an external relative to an internal focus (Poolton, Maxwell, Masters, & van der Kamp, 2007). However, none of these explanations can account for the entirety of the findings documented in the literature (see Wulf, 2007a, 2007b). For example, visual information is often controlled or prevented between attention focus conditions. In this way, identical visual information is available in both internal and external focus conditions, and any performance or learning differences between conditions are attributable to attention and not visual information (e.g., McNevin & Wulf, 2002; Wulf et al., 1998; Wulf, McNevin, & Shea, 2001).

Also, the idea that an external focus is more functionally relevant or goal directed cannot explain some key findings, such as differential balance performance when the focus is on the feet as opposed to boards (Totsika & Wulf, 2003), rectangles (Landers, Wulf, Wallmann, & Guadagnoli, 2005), or wheels (Wulf et al., 1998) under one's feet. From a functional relevance perspective, it is also not clear, for example, why increasing the distance of the external focus from the body, such as the distance of markers from the feet on balance tasks (e.g., McNevin et al., 2003), would enhance the effectiveness of the external focus (for further arguments against alternative views, see Wulf, 2007c).

More recently, Wulf and Lewthwaite (2010) have expanded the constrained action notion by suggesting how a one- or two-word difference in instructions might create a chain of events resulting in differential control of movement. The internal focus of attention may act as a self-invoking trigger in that references to one's body parts or bodily movement, such as those involved in the internal focus conditions, may facilitate access to the self-construct and related self-evaluative and self-regulatory processing. Conditions that invoke the *self* (e.g., internal focus instructions) may result in "micro-choking" episodes. The self-construct appears to be highly accessible, implicitly or explicitly, in many circumstances, including all movement contexts and laboratory experimental settings, influencing thoughts, actions, and behavior (see Bargh & Morsella, 2008; Chartrand & Bargh, 2002; Leary, 2004; Stapel & Blanton, 2004). Self-focused attention (Carver & Scheier, 1978) or self-related processing may produce something akin to a series of ongoing "micro-choking" episodes with attempts to right thoughts and bring emotions under control. The resulting attempts to harness thoughts and emotions may explain the effects of attentional focus on the efficiency of movement production, which we review next.

Attentional focus and movement efficiency

A series of recent studies have yielded findings strongly suggesting that changes in motor control as a function of attentional focus underlie differences in outcome. These studies also provide indirect evidence (maximum force production, movement speed, endurance) or direct evidence (EMG activity, oxygen consumption) that the focus of attention affects movement efficiency – generally demonstrating that training with an external focus enhances not only effectiveness, but also efficiency, allowing for better or equal production of outcomes with less physiological and mental effort.

Maximum force production

Many tasks require the production of maximum forces. These tasks include those in which one's own body (e.g., high jump, long jump, pole vault, basketball dunk) or an object has to be propelled (e.g., discus, hammer, football), as well as static force production tasks sometimes used for diagnostic purposes (e.g., dynamometry). Maximum force production requires and may be tantamount to an optimal activation of agonist and antagonist muscles, as well as optimal muscle fiber recruitment within a muscle or motor unit. Unnecessary co-contractions, imperfect timing, and/or direction of forces would result in less-than-maximal force output. Studies demonstrating that maximum force production varies under external versus internal focus conditions strongly suggest differences in muscular coordination, or movement efficiency (for a review, see Marchant, 2011).

In a series of experiments, maximum vertical jump height has been found to be increased with an external relative to an internal or uninstructed attentional focus (Wulf & Dufek, 2009; Wulf, Dufek, Lozano, & Pettigrew, 2010; Wulf, Zachry, Granados, & Dufek, 2007). A within-participant design was used in those studies, in which all participants performed the task under different focus conditions in a counterbalanced order. Thus, any differences in jump height could be attributed to differences in the coordination of the forces between and/or within muscles. The measurement device (Vertec) used to record jump height consisted of plastic rungs at different heights that the participant reached for during the jumps. Participants were instructed to concentrate on the tips of their fingers in the internal focus condition and on the rungs in the external focus condition, and no focus instructions were given in the control condition. The results of Wulf, Zachry, et al. (2007, Experiment 1) showed that participants jumped significantly higher in the external focus condition than in either the internal focus or the control conditions, with the last two resulting in similar jump heights. Furthermore, the vertical displacement of the center of mass (COM) was greatest when participants were instructed to adopt an external focus. A subsequent study demonstrated that, in addition to increased jump height and COM displacement, impulses as well as joint moments about the ankle, knee, and hip joints were significantly greater in the external focus condition (Wulf & Dufek, 2009) (see Figures 3.1 and 3.2). Thus, increased jump height with an external focus was achieved through greater force production.

Long-jump performance has also been found to be enhanced with an external relative to an internal focus (Porter, Ostrowski, Nolan, & Wu, 2010). A between-participant design was used in that study, and participants in the internal focus group ($n = 60$) were instructed to focus on extending their knees as rapidly as possible, whereas external focus group participants ($n = 60$) were asked to focus on

Figure 3.1 Jump-and-reach task used in the study by Wulf and Dufek (2009).

jumping as far past the start line as possible. The average jumping distance was 10 cm greater with an external (187 cm) than with an internal focus (177 cm). These findings nicely illustrate the generalizability of the external focus advantages for tasks requiring the production of maximum forces.

Beneficial effects of an external focus on maximum force production have also been shown by Marchant, Greig, and Scott (2009). Using an isokinetic dynamometer, these researchers asked experienced exercisers to produce maximum voluntary contractions of the elbow flexors, with the goal of producing maximal force over the full movement range, under internal (i.e., focus on arm muscles) or external focus conditions (i.e., focus on the crank hand-bar). They found that participants produced significantly greater peak joint torque when they focused externally than when they are focused internally.

Clearly, the "maximum" force an individual can produce is not fixed. It is well known that certain situations, such as those in which someone's life is in danger, enable individuals to produce greater forces than under normal circumstances. Also, "psyching-up" has been found to increase force production (Tod, Iredale, McGuigan, Strange, & Gill, 2005). However, it is interesting that even a simple change in a person's attentional focus can result in an increase in force production.

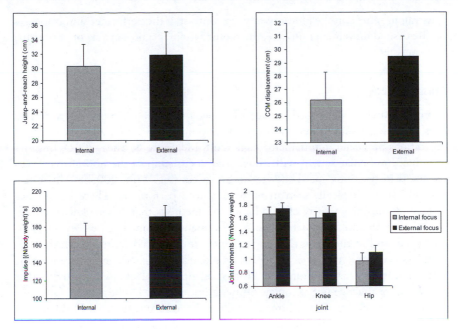

Figure 3.2 Jump-and-reach height, change in center-of-mass (COM) vertical displacement, impulse, and ankle, knee, and hip joint moments of the right extremity as a function of internal versus external focus in the study by Wulf and Dufek (2009).

Given that the performance benefit of an external focus has been found not only with respect to an internal focus but also when compared with control conditions, these findings suggest that external focus instructions enhance maximum force production above and beyond what a person would "normally" achieve.

Aside from a more efficient and effective recruitment of motor units (see below), a "freeing" of the body's degrees of freedom as a result of an external focus may contribute to the increased force output. There is converging evidence to suggest that an internal focus has a constraining effect on the motor system – by linking semi-independent body segments – with a detrimental effect on efficient movement production. In Wulf and Dufek's (2009) study using the jump-and-reach task, for example, joint moments around various joints (i.e., ankle, knee, hip) were correlated with each other when an internal focus on the finger was adopted, presumably resulting in a "freezing" of degrees of freedom (Vereijken, van Emmerik, Whiting, & Newell, 1992), but not with an external focus on the rungs. Also, there were more negative correlations between joint moments and outcome-related variables, such as jump height, with an internal focus but not with an external focus. For soccer kicks, Ford, Hodges, Huys, and Williams (2009) also found higher correlations across the displacements of various joints when the players' focus was on their body movements (internal) than with a focus on the ball trajectory (external). These results suggest that attempts to "force" an effective outcome by trying to control one's body movements are generally not very successful, because they tend to have a constraining effect on the motor system. In contrast, if the performer simply focuses on the desired movement outcome, the motor system is quite capable of optimizing that outcome.

Muscular activity

Several researchers have used surface EMG as a measure of muscle recruitment, thus providing a more direct measure of movement efficiency. Along with demonstrations of greater automaticity (e.g., Wulf, McNevin, & Shea, 2001), findings of reduced muscular activity with an external focus support the notion that external focus instructions speed the learning process (see Wulf, 2007b). This effect parallels what is typically seen in more advanced performers. There is evidence from studies using a variety of paradigms and methods that, when skill execution becomes automatized through practice, movement outcome (e.g., weight lifted) is enhanced, and at the same time movements are produced more efficiently (e.g., with less neuromuscular activity). For example, using magnetic resonance imaging (MRI) researchers have demonstrated increased efficiency in muscle recruitment as a function of practice (e.g., Conley, Stone, Nimmons, & Dudley, 1997; Green & Wilson, 2000; Ploutz, Tesch, Biro, & Dudley, 1994). Thus, reduced EMG activity with external focus relative to internal focus (or no) instructions provides further evidence that the learning process is facilitated by an external focus.

In a first study, Vance, Wulf, Töllner, McNevin, and Mercer (2004) recorded EMG activity of the agonist (biceps brachii) and antagonist (triceps brachii) muscles in the biceps curl under different attentional focus conditions. Reduced integrated EMG (iEMG) activity was found when participants adopted an external focus of attention than when they adopted an internal focus. Interestingly, this was the case for both the biceps and triceps muscles. In a follow-up study, Marchant, Greig, and Scott (2008) used an isokinetic dynamometer, allowing them more effective control of both movement time and range. These authors also added a control condition to assess EMG activity in external and internal focus conditions relative to one without focus instructions. Marchant et al. (2008) replicated the finding of Vance et al. (2004) in that externally focused instructions were again associated with lower EMG activity than internal focus instructions. In the control condition, similar levels of EMG activity were seen as in the internal focus condition. This latter finding suggests that, even in experienced performers, adopting an external focus can further promote movement efficiency (resembling findings of increased movement accuracy in skilled performers with external focus instructions; Wulf & Su, 2007).

Measures of EMG have also been applied to study how attentional focus affects the neuromuscular system while shooting free-throws with a basketball (Zachry, Wulf, Mercer, & Bezodis, 2005). In this experiment, participants were instructed to focus on either the motion of their wrist (internal focus) or the basketball hoop (external focus). Free-throw accuracy was greater in the external focus condition, and there was reduced EMG activity in the biceps and triceps brachii during the shooting motion when participants adopted an external focus of attention. Thus, congruent with the results of Vance et al. (2004), in the Zachry et al. (2005) study EMG activity was affected in muscle groups that participants were not specifically instructed to focus on. This finding suggests that the effects of the performer's attentional focus "spread" to other muscle groups – increasing inefficiency with an internal focus.

Lohse, Sherwood, and Healy (2010) used a dart-throwing task to examine accuracy and EMG activity as a function of attentional focus. In their study, participants were instructed to focus on either the flight of the dart (external) or the movement of their arm (internal), and participants were reminded at the beginning of each block of trials that, when they made errors (i.e., failed to hit the bulls-eye), they should correct their errors by changing the motion of their arm or the flight of the dart, respectively. An external focus of attention not only improved throwing accuracy but also resulted in reduced EMG activity in the triceps muscle of the throwing arm, thus confirming previous findings (e.g., Zachry et al., 2005).

In addition to measuring EMG activity, a few researchers have used an integrated fast Fourier transform of the raw EMG data to analyze the power spectral density of the recorded EMG. The spectral density represents how power is distributed across different frequencies in the EMG waveform, and represents physiological changes in motor unit recruitment that underlie changes in surface EMG. For instance, Vance et al. (2004) calculated the mean power frequency (MNF) of voluntary contractions in the biceps curl. In early repetitions, an external focus of attention led to smaller MNF than an internal focus of attention, suggesting that externally focusing attention improves movement economy at the level of muscle fiber recruitment. A smaller MNF suggests that fewer muscle fibers are being recruited, because muscle fibers are recruited incrementally (Olsen, Carpenter, & Henneman, 1968).

Increases in power spectral density (both MNF and median power frequency, MDF) are indicative of increased motor unit recruitment because recruitment of larger motor units with faster conduction velocities shifts the MDF/MNF upward (Arendt-Nielsen, Mills, & Forster, 1989; Farina, Fosci, & Merletti, 2002; Lindstrom, Magnusson, & Peterson, 1970; Solomonow et al., 1990). The power spectrum, however, seems to be insensitive to increased discharge rates and therefore is diagnostic only of increased motor unit recruitment (Lago & Jones, 1977; Van Boxtel & Schomaker, 1984) and only during isometric contractions (Farina, 2006; Farina, Merletti, & Enoka, 2004) when previous research on the focus of attention used dynamic contractions (e.g., a biceps curl, shooting a basketball, or throwing a dart).

Because previous research on attentional effects in muscle recruitment has studied dynamic contractions, instead of isometric contractions, there are some inconsistencies in findings about the effects of attention on MNF/MDF (compare Lohse et al., 2010, and Vance et al., 2004). Lohse et al. (2011) addressed this discrepancy by using an isometric force production task in which the length of the muscle does not change. Participants pressed against a force platform with their dominant foot, trying to produce a target force that was 30% of their maximum force while surface EMG measurements were taken from the soleus (agonist) and tibialis anterior (antagonist). Participants were given verbal feedback about their accuracy after each 4-s trial. There was no difference in the accuracy of forces produced in early trials but, over the course of training, mentally focusing on the force platform (external focus) led to more accurate force production than focusing on one's own muscles that were actually producing the force (i.e., focusing on the agonist muscle, or internal focus).

An external focus also led to reduced surface EMG amplitude (as a percentage of EMG activity during a maximum voluntary contraction, %MVC) and reduced MDF in the antagonist muscle. Thus, when participants adopted an external focus of attention, they reduced the amount of co-contraction between the agonist and antagonist muscles, resulting in a more efficient pattern of motor unit recruitment both within and between muscles (reduced MDF and reduced co-contraction, respectively). Figure 3.3 shows hypothetical efficient and inefficient patterns of muscle activation for completing this plantar flexion task. Figure 3.4 shows representative raw data from three participants showing significantly less efficient neuromuscular coordination while focusing internally (i.e., intermuscular coordination is impaired through greater co-contraction of the soleus and anterior tibialis; intramuscular coordination is also impaired, shown by increased MDF indicating unnecessary motor unit recruitment within the muscles).

In the experiment by Lohse, Sherwood, and Healy (2011), there was evidence for more effective performance within a single experimental session (i.e., greater improvement in accuracy as function of external focus), but what about long-term learning? In a follow-up experiment, Lohse (2012) trained participants to produce either 25% or 50% of their MVC in an identical plantar flexion task. Participants trained under either external (focusing on the force platform) or internal focus conditions (focusing on the agonist muscle). Although both groups had equal accuracy in early trials, by the end of training (60 trials), the external focus group

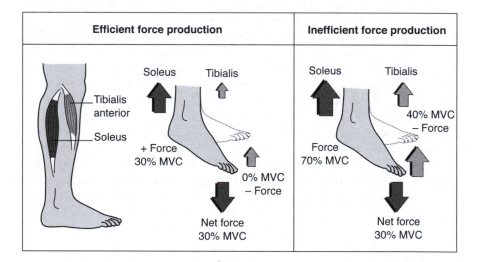

Figure 3.3 In the isometric plantar flexion task (Lohse et al., 2011), the soleus is the agonist muscle and the tibialis anterior is the antagonist. The left side of the figure depicts efficient force production, with little co-activation of the antagonist muscle. The right side depicts inefficient force production, with increased co-activation of the antagonist muscle but the same amount of total force being produced.

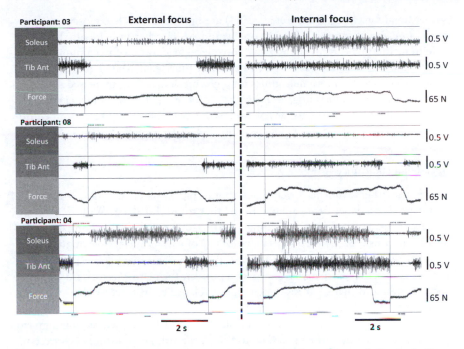

Figure 3.4 Example raw data from three participants (who showed strong behavioral effects of shifting the focus of attention), showing trials from the external focus phase (on the left) and the internal focus phase (on the right). Surface electromyography (sEMG) activity in the soleus, sEMG activity in the tibialis anterior, and force are shown as a function of phase and time (adapted from Lohse et al., 2011).

was significantly more accurate than the internal focus group. One week later, both groups returned to the laboratory for retention and transfer testing. Not only did the external focus participants remain significantly more accurate on the retention test, they significantly outperformed the internal focus group on the transfer test, suggesting that an external focus of attention improved participants' ability to re-parameterize the movement to remain accurate at new percentages of their MVC.

Finally, the production of *greater* maximal forces with an external focus (e.g., Marchant et al., 2009; Wulf & Dufek, 2009; Wulf, Dufek, Lozano, & Pettigrew, 2010) has been shown to be accompanied by *reduced* muscular activity. In the study by Marchant et al. (2009), a focus on the crank bar while performing biceps curls resulted not only in increased peak joint torque, but in less EMG activity than with an internal focus on the arm muscles. In line with those findings, Wulf and colleagues (2010) found that jump height was greater and, at the same time, EMG activity was lower in various leg muscles with an external focus than with an internal focus. Overall, the findings demonstrating greater force production with reduced muscular activity with an external focus clearly point to a greater efficiency in movement production in comparison with an internal focus.

Based on findings indicating that maximal (e.g., Marchant et al., 2008) and submaximal forces (e.g., Lohse et al., 2011) are produced with less muscular energy when an external focus is adopted, one would predict that individuals should be able to maintain a certain submaximal force level (e.g., 80% of maximum) longer, or increase the force level for a given period of time (e.g., 10 s). Thus, one might expect to see shorter movement times for a given distance (i.e., increased speed) in bicycling, and the like, or more repetitions in lifting the same ction, we review studies in which movement speed and endur- attentional focus conditions have been examined.

Speed and endurance

A few researchers who have examined attentional focus effects have used movement speed as a dependent variable. In the first study (Totsika & Wulf, 2003), two groups of participants practiced riding a pedalo: an apparatus that consists of two small platforms (one for each foot) between sets of wheels and moves by alternately pushing the upper platform forward and downward, similar to the pedals on a bicycle. Instructing participants to focus on pushing the platforms forward (external focus) resulted in increased movement speed relative to instructing them to focus on pushing their feet forward (internal focus). This finding was observed not only during the practice phase but also on transfer tests, which included requirements to perform the task under time pressure, to ride backward, or to count backward (i.e., with attention being directed elsewhere). Thus, participants who had received external focus instructions during practice not only learned a more efficient method of controlling the pedalo, but were able to transfer this newly learned skill to novel situations (i.e., riding backward) and situations with increased pressure to perform (i.e., time pressure).

A similar finding was observed by Porter, Nolan, Ostrowski, and Wulf (2010), who found that external focus instructions reduced the time taken to complete a whole-body agility task. In this task, participants completed an agility "L" run (which consists of a weaving run around three cones set 5 m apart) under external focus, internal focus, or control conditions. Participants had to run through the course as quickly as possible and with maximum effort. External focus instructions, which directed their attention toward accelerating between the cones and pushing off the ground in the turns, significantly decreased running time relative to both internal focus instructions, in which participants were asked to focus on moving their legs as fast as possible and planting their foot firmly in the turns, and a control condition.

An external focus of attention has also been found to increase movement speed in swimming. Recent reports suggest that giving swimmers external focus instructions related to the arm stroke in crawl swimming (e.g., "pushing the water back") was more effective than internal focus instructions that directed attention towards the swimmer's arms (e.g., "pulling your hands back"). This effect was demonstrated in both intermediate swimmers (Freudenheim, Wulf, Madureira, Pasetto, & Corrêa, 2010) and experts (Stoate & Wulf, 2011). These findings have obvious practical implications. For instance, in elite junior swimmers, an external focus of attention increased swim speed (i.e., reduced swim time) by an average of 0.18 s in a 25-yard (~23 m) crawl. In the 2008 Olympics, the difference between first place and second place in the men's 50-m crawl was only 0.15 s, and in the women's 50-m crawl 0.11 s. Thus, a swimmer's focus of attention could potentially determine his or her place on the medal stand.

It is also interesting to note that both of these studies used control conditions in which swimmers were not given specific instructions on how to focus their attention and were simply encouraged to swim as fast as possible. Intermediate swimmers performed similarly in the internal focus and control conditions (Freudenheim et al., 2010), whereas in experts the control and external focus conditions resulted in similar swim times (Stoate & Wulf, 2011). These results suggest that, whereas an instructed external focus enhanced movement automaticity and efficiency in less skilled participants, movements were already so highly automatized in experts that an external focus provided no additional advantage, or that experts had already discovered the value of an external focus and adopted one on demand or habitually (e.g., Gray, 2004). Self-report data from the Stoate and Wulf study indicated that experts' "normal" focus (i.e., in the control condition) differed among participants, however. Whereas some swimmers reported more of an internal focus in the control condition (e.g., hip rotation, spinning arms, high elbow), others reported focusing on the overall outcome (e.g., speed, tempo, going fast, swimming hard) or "nothing." Interestingly, those who adopted an internal focus in the control condition had slower swim times (13.55 s) than those who did not (13.02 s). These group differences in the control condition are consistent with the notion that an internal focus disrupts automaticity and results in poorer performance Thus, when movements are controlled automatically at a high level of skill, external focus instructions *may* only help to reinforce a learned focus of attention, but feedback inducing an internal focus should clearly be avoided.

Finally, Marchant, Greig, Bullough, and Hitchen (2011) demonstrated the influence of attentional focus on muscular endurance in trained individuals performing exercise routines. The authors measured the number of repetitions to failure during various exercises with weights corresponding to 75% of each participant's repetition maximum. The exercises included bench press tests on a Smith machine (allowing for vertical movement only), free bench press, and a free squat lift. External focus instructions directed participants' attention to the movement of the bar being lifted and the force exerted against it, whereas internal focus instructions referred to movements of the limbs involved in the exercise (i.e., arms, legs). With an external focus, participants produced a significantly greater number of repetitions than with an internal focus in all three exercises. In addition, the number of repetitions exceeded those performed under control conditions (except for the restricted bench press on the Smith machine). Intriguingly, the effect size of the attentional focus manipulation increased as the movements became more complex; the effect size was smallest for the Smith machine bench press, in which the dimensions of movements are constrained, and greatest for the free squat, which is the most complex movement pattern, with the free bench press in between the two. The increasing magnitude of effect sizes suggests that the benefit of an external focus might increase as movement complexity increases (see also Wulf, Töllner, & Shea,

2007). Overall, these findings demonstrate that the attentional focus adopted or induced through instruction has a significant influence on muscular endurance.

Oxygen consumption

An interesting example of how changing the focus of attention can improve movement efficiency comes from a study by Schücker, Hageman, Strauss, and Völker (2009). These authors had skilled runners focus their attention internally on a movement-relevant aspect of the task (running form), internally on a movement-irrelevant aspect of the task (breathing), or externally on a video display that simulated running outdoors, while running on a treadmill. For three 10-min periods each, runners concentrated on the running movement (internal focus), on their breathing (internal focus), or on the virtual surroundings (external focus) in a counterbalanced order. Consistent with previous research showing improved movement efficiency, Schücker and colleagues found improved metabolic efficiency with an external focus of attention, in that an external focus resulted in reduced oxygen consumption during the running task compared with either of the internal foci.

Implications for practice

As research on the focus of attention continues to demonstrate, even subtle differences in the wording of instructions or feedback that a participant is given can have profound effects on behavior and the underlying physiology. Thus, instructors, coaches, therapists, and performers themselves need to be aware of how these differences affect performance and should develop effective strategies to keep the performer's attention focused externally on the intended effects of their movements. Internally focusing on one's own movements constrains the motor system and leads to movements that are not only less accurate but also less efficient at the neuromuscular level. Numerous studies have shown that not only will an external focus of attention create a more efficient movement with the same outcome (e.g., same weight being lifted, same distance being run), but also that it can lead to more efficient movement with a significantly enhanced outcome (e.g., improved accuracy in dart throwing, increased jump height in the vertical jump, increased force production).

Although the attentional focus effect is well established in the motor behavior literature, the translation of this research into practice has been relatively slow. For example, in a recent analysis of feedback statements used by physiotherapists in their treatment of patients with stroke, Durham, Van Vliet, Badger, and Sackley (2009) found that 95.5% of feedback statements were related to the patient's body movements. Similarly, in interviews of track and field athletes competing at the outdoor national championships, 84.6% reported that their coaches gave instructions related to body and limb movements (Porter, Wu, & Partridge, 2010). As a consequence, the majority of athletes (69.2%) indicated that they focused internally when competing. Interestingly, as Porter et al. (2010) noted, the coaching literature for track and field coaches as well the curriculum for USA Track and Field coaches lacks content on motor learning and control. Thus, there is clearly potential to improve performance in various fields through the education of practitioners.

It is also important to remember that there is no "one-size-fits-all" approach to directing attention. Although an external focus of attention is generally beneficial to learning and performance across a wide variety of tasks and populations (see Wulf, 2007b, for a review), there may be differences, for instance, in the optimal external focus of attention between experts and novices. An external focus of attention is generally beneficial for both experts and novices (e.g., Wulf & Su, 2007); however, there is some evidence that novices benefit from a more proximal external focus (Wulf, McNevin, Fuchs, Ritter, & Toole, 2000) and the experts benefit from a more distal focus (Bell & Hardy, 2009). That is experts can focus on controlling events farther down the kinetic chain than novices, who lack the necessary ability to control physically or temporally distant events. Consider, for example, a novice pool player who might focus only as far out as the cue meeting the cue-ball. In contrast, an expert might be focused past the cue, the cue-ball, the target ball, and the target pocket, to something as distal as the placement of the cue-ball for the next shot. Similarly, a novice tennis player may not have a procedural concept of how to hit an ace, so focusing on hitting one would be meaningless from a motor control standpoint, and the novice would benefit from a more proximal external focus (e.g., focusing on the angle of the racket at ball contact). A world-class player, on the other hand, can focus not only on hitting an ace on his or her serve, but probably on a very specific flight path for the ball to set up the shot he or she wants if the serve is returned (Ford, Hodges, Huys, & Williams, 2006). The optimal focus of attention is presumably more distal for the expert because experts have much more detailed action concepts than novices (Schack, 2004; Schack & Mechsner, 2006), which makes it meaningful for experts to direct their focus farther down the chain of kinetic events in the action. Future studies may help identify optimal attentional foci for different tasks and skill levels.

Moreover, it would be interesting to further elucidate how attentional focus affects movement efficiency at a more central level. How does brain activity change when a certain task is performed under different focus conditions? Moreover, what effect does practice with different attentional foci have on brain activity in the long term, as evidenced, for example, by the amount of brain activation (Wu, Kansaku, & Hallett, 2004), effective connectivity of the brain motor networks (Wu, Chan, & Hallett, 2008), or changes in gray matter volume (Taubert et al., 2010)?

References

Al-Abood, S. A., Bennett, S. J., Hernandez, F. M., Ashford, D., & Davids, K. (2002). Effects of verbal instructions and image size on visual search strategies in basketball free throw shooting. *Journal of Sports Sciences, 20*, 271–278.

Arendt-Nielsen, L., Mills, K. R., & Forster, A. (1989). Changes in muscle fiber conduction velocity, mean power frequency, and mean EMG voltage during prolonged submaximal contractions. *Muscle & Nerve, 12*, 493–497.

Bargh, J. A., & Morsella, E. (2008). The unconscious mind. *Perspectives on Psychological Science, 3*, 73–79.

Bell, J. J., & Hardy, J. (2009). Effects of attentional focus on skilled performance in golf. *Journal of Applied Sport Psychology, 21*, 163–177.

Carver, C. S., & Scheier, M. F. (1978). Self-focusing effects of dispositional self-consciousness, mirror presence, and audience presence. *Journal of Personality and Social Psychology, 36*, 324–332.

Chartrand, T. L., & Bargh, J. A. (2002). Nonconscious motivations: Their activation, operation, and consequences. In Tesser, A., Stapel, D. A., & Wood, J. V. (Eds.), *Self and motivation: Emerging psychological perspectives* (pp. 13–41). Washington, DC: American Psychological Association.

Chiviacowsky, S., Wulf, G., & Wally, R. (2010). An external focus of attention enhances balance learning in older adults. *Gait & Posture, 32*, 572–575.

Conley, M. S., Stone, M. H., Nimmons, M., & Dudley, G. A. (1997). Resistance training and human cervical muscle recruitment plasticity. *Journal of Applied Physiology, 83*, 2105–2111.

Durham, K., Van Vliet, P. M., Badger, F., & Sackley, C. (2009). Use of information feedback and attentional focus of feedback in treating the person with a hemiplegic arm. *Physiotherapy Research International, 14*, 77–90.

Farina, D. (2006). The interpretation of the surface electromyogram in dynamic contractions. *Exercise and Sport Sciences Reviews, 35*, 121–127.

Farina, D., Fosci, M., & Merletti, R. (2002). Motor unit recruitment strategies investigated by surface EMG variables. *Journal of Applied Physiology, 92*, 235–247

Farina, D., Merletti, R., & Enoka, R. M. (2004). The extraction of neural strategies from the surface EMG. *Journal of Applied Physiology, 96*, 1486–1495.

Fasoli, S. E., Trombly, C. A., Tickle-Degnen, L., & Verfaellie, M. H. (2002). Effect of instructions on functional reach in persons with and without cerebrovascular accident. *American Journal of Occupational Therapy, 56*, 380–390.

Ford, P., Hodges, N. J., Huys, R., & Williams, A. M. (2006). The role of external action-effects in the execution of a soccer kick: A comparison across skill-level. *Motor Control, 10*, 386–404.

Ford, P., Hodges, N. J., Huys, R., & Williams, A. M. (2009). Evidence for end-point trajectory planning during a kicking action. *Motor Control, 13*, 1–24.

Freedman, S. E., Maas, E., Caligiuri, M. P., Wulf, G., & Robin, D. A. (2007). Internal vs. external: Oral-motor performance as a function of attentional focus. *Journal of Speech, Language, and Hearing Science, 50*, 131–136.

Freudenheim, A. M., Wulf, G., Madureira, F., Pasetto, S. C., & Corrêa, U. C. (2010). An external focus of attention results in greater swimming speed. *International Journal of Sports Science & Coaching, 5*, 533–542.

Gray, R. (2004). Attending to the execution of a complex sensorimotor skill: Expertise differences, choking, and slumps. *Journal of Experimental Psychology: Applied, 10*, 42–54.

Green, R. A. R., & Wilson, D. J. (2000). A pilot study using magnetic resonance imaging to determine the pattern of muscle group recruitment by rowers with different levels of experience. *Skeletal Radiology, 29*, 196–203.

Guthrie, E. R. 1952). *The psychology of learning.* New York: Harper & Row.

Hommel, B. (2007). Goals, attentions, and the dynamics of skill acquisition: Commentary on Wulf. *E-Journal Bewegung und Training (E-Journal Movement and Training), 1*, 4–14. Retrieved May 13, 2011, from http://www.sportwissenschaft.de/fileadmin/pdf/BuT/hossner_wulf.pdf.

Hutchinson, J. C., Sherman, T., Martinovic, N., & Tenenbaum, G. (2008). The effect of manipulated self-efficacy on perceived and sustained effort. *Journal of Applied Sport Psychology, 20*, 457–472.

Jourden, F. J., Bandura, A., & Banfield, J. T. (1991). The impact of conceptions of ability on self-regulatory factors and motor skill acquisition. *Journal of Sport & Exercise Psychology, 8*, 213–226.

Künzell, S. (2007). Optimal attentional focus in practical sport settings: Always external or task specific. *E-Journal Bewegung und Training (E-Journal Movement and Training), 1*, 27–28. Retrieved May 13, 2011, from http://www.sportwissenschaft.de/fileadmin/pdf/BuT/hossner_wulf.pdf.

Lago, P., & Jones, N. B. (1977). Effect of motor unit firing time statistics on EMG spectra. *Medical and Biological Engineering and Computing, 15*, 648–655.

Landers, M., Wulf, G., Wallmann, H., & Guadagnoli, M. (2005). An external focus of attention attenuates balance impairment in patients with Parkinson's disease who have a fall history. *Physiotherapy, 91*, 152–158.

Laufer, Y., Rotem-Lehrer, N., Ronen, Z., Khayutin, G., & Rozenberg, I. (2007). Effect of attention focus on acquisition and retention of postural control following ankle sprain. *Archives of Physical Medicine and Rehabilitation, 88*, 105–108.

Leary, M. R. (2004). *The curse of the self: Self-awareness, egotism, and the quality of human life.* New York: Oxford University Press.

Lewthwaite, R., & Wulf, G. (2010a). Grand challenge for movement science and sport psychology: Embracing the social-cognitive-affective-motor nature of motor behavior. *Frontiers in Psychology.* doi: 10.3389/fpsyg.2010.00042.

Lewthwaite, R., & Wulf, G. (2010b). Social-comparative feedback affects motor skill learning. *Quarterly Journal of Experimental Psychology, 63*, 738–749.

Lindstrom, L. R., Magnusson, R., & Peterson, I. (1970). Muscular fatigue and action potential conduction velocity changes studied with frequency analysis of EMG signals. *Electromyography, 4*, 341–353.

Lohse, K. R. (2012). The influence of attention on learning and performance: Pre-movement time and accuracy in an isometric force production task. *Human Movement Science, 31*, 12–25.

Lohse, K. R., Sherwood, D. E., & Healy, A. F. (2010). How changing the focus of attention affects performance, kinematics, and electromyography in dart throwing. *Human Movement Science, 29*, 542–555.

Lohse, K. R., Sherwood, D. E., & Healy, A. F. (2011). Neuromuscular effects of shifting the focus of attention in a simple force production task. *Journal of Motor Behavior, 43*, 173–184.

Marchant, D. C. (2011). Attentional focusing instructions and force production. *Frontiers in Psychology.* doi: 10.3389/fpsyg.2010.00210.

Marchant, D. C., Clough, P. J., & Crawshaw, M. (2007). The effects of attentional focusing strategies on novice dart throwing performance and their task experiences. *International Journal of Sport and Exercise Psychology, 5*, 291–303.

Marchant, D. C., Greig, M., Bullough J., & Hitchen, D. (2011). Instructions to adopt an external focus enhance muscular endurance. *Research Quarterly for Exercise and Sport, 82*, 466–473.

Marchant, D. C., Greig, M., & Scott, C. (2008). Attentional focusing strategies influence bicep EMG during isokinetic biceps curls. *Athletic Insight.* Retrieved July 26, 2010, from http://www.athleticinsight.com/Vol10Iss2/MuscularActivity.htm.

Marchant, D. C., Greig, M., & Scott, C. (2009). Attentional focusing instructions influence force production and muscular activity during isokinetic elbow flexions. *Journal of Strength and Conditioning Research, 23*, 2358–2366.

Maurer, H., & Zentgraf, K. (2007). On the how and why of the external focus learning advantage. *E-Journal Bewegung und Training (E-Journal Movement and Training), 1*, 31–32. Retrieved May 13, 2011, from http://www.sportwissenschaft.de/fileadmin/pdf/BuT/hossner_wulf.pdf.

McNevin, N. H., & Wulf, G. (2002). Attentional focus on supra-postural tasks affects postural control. *Human Movement Science, 21,* 187–202.

McNevin, N. H., Shea, C. H., & Wulf, G. (2003). Increasing the distance of an external focus of attention enhances learning. *Psychological Research, 67,* 22–29.

Olsen, C. B., Carpenter, D. O., & Henneman, E. (1968). Orderly recruitment of muscle action potentials. *Archives of Neurology, 19,* 591–597.

Ploutz, L. L., Tesch, P. A., Biro, R. L., & Dudley, G. A. (1994). Effect of resistance training on muscle use during exercise. *Journal of Applied Physiology, 76,* 1675–1681.

Poolton, J. M., Maxwell, J. P., Masters, R. S.W., & van der Kamp, J. (2007). Moving with an external focus: Automatic or simply less demanding. *E-Journal Bewegung und Training (E-Journal Movement and Training), 1,* 43–44. Retrieved May 13, 2011, from http://www.sportwissenschaft.de/fileadmin/pdf/BuT/hossner_wulf.pdf.

Porter, J. M., Nolan, R. P., Ostrowski, E. J., & Wulf, G. (2010). Directing attention externally enhances agility performance: A qualitative and quantitative analysis of the efficacy of using verbal instructions to focus attention. *Frontiers in Psychology.* doi: 10.3389/fpsyg.2010.00216.

Porter, J. M., Ostrowski, E. J., Nolan, R. P., & Wu, W. F. W. (2010). Standing long-jump performance is enhanced when using an external focus of attention. *Journal of Strength & Conditioning Research, 24,* 1746–1750.

Porter, J. M., Wu, W. F. W., & Partridge, J. A. (2010). Focus of attention and verbal instructions: Strategies of elite track and field coaches and athletes. *Sport Science Review, 19,* 199–211.

Russell, D. M. (2007). Attentional focus of the invariant control variables. *E-Journal Bewegung und Training (E-Journal Movement and Training), 1,* 47–48. Retrieved May 13, 2011, from http://www.sportwissenschaft.de/fileadmin/pdf/BuT/hossner_wulf.pdf.

Schack, T. (2004). The cognitive architecture of movement. *International Journal of Sport & Exercise Psychology, 2,* 403–438.

Schack, T., & Mechsner, F. (2006). Representation of motor skills in human long-term memory. *Neuroscience Letters, 391,* 77–81.

Schücker, L., Hageman, N., Strauss, B., & Völker, K. (2009). The effect of attentional focus on running economy. *Journal of Sport Sciences, 12,* 1242–1248.

Solomonow, M., Baten, C., Smith, J., Baratta, R., Hermens, H., D'Ambrosia, R., & Shoji, H. (1990). Electromyogram power spectra frequencies associated with motor unit recruitment strategies. *Journal of Applied Physiology, 68,* 1177–1185.

Sparrow, A. W., & Newell, K. M. (1998). Metabolic energy expenditure and the regulation of movement economy. *Psychonomic Bulletin & Review, 5,* 173–196.

Stapel, D. A., & Blanton, H. (2004). From seeing to being: Subliminal social comparisons affect implicit and explicit self-evaluations. *Journal of Personality and Social Psychology, 87,* 468–481.

Stoate, I., & Wulf, G. (2011). Does the attentional focus adopted by swimmers affect their performance? *International Journal of Sport Science & Coaching, 6,* 99–108.

Taubert, T., Draganski, B., Anwander, A., Müller, K., Horstmann, A., Villringer, A., & Ragert, P. (2010). Dynamic properties of human brain structure: Learning-related changes in cortical areas and associated fiber connections. *Journal of Neuroscience, 30,* 11670–11677.

Tod, D. A., Iredale, K. F., McGuigan, M. R., Strange, D. E. O., & Gill, N. (2005). "Psyching-up" enhances force production during the bench press exercise. *Journal of Strength and Conditioning Research, 19,* 599–603.

Totsika, V., & Wulf, G. (2003). The influence of external and internal foci of attention on transfer to novel situations and skills. *Research Quarterly Exercise and Sport, 74,* 220–225.

Van Boxtel, A., & Schomaker, L. R. B. (1984). Influence of motor unit firing statistics on the median frequency of the EMG power spectrum. *European Journal of Applied Physiology, 52,* 207–213.

Vance, J., Wulf, G., Töllner, T., McNevin, N. H., & Mercer, J. (2004). EMG activity as a function of the performers' focus of attention. *Journal of Motor Behavior, 36,* 450–459.

Vereijken, B., van Emmerik, R. E. A., Whiting, H. T. A., & Newell, K. M. (1992). Free(z)ing degrees of freedom in skill acquisition. *Journal of Motor Behavior, 24,* 133–142.

Wrisberg, C. A. (2007). An applied sport psychological perspective on the relative merits of an external and internal focus of attention. *E-Journal Bewegung und Training (E-Journal Movement and Training), 1,* 51–52. Retrieved May 13, 2011, from http://www.sportwissenschaft.de/fileadmin/pdf/BuT/hossner_wulf.pdf.

Wu, T., Chan, P., & Hallett, M. (2008). Modifications of the interactions in the motor networks when a movement becomes automatic. *Journal of Physiology, 586,* 4295–4304.

Wu, T., Kansaku, K., & Hallett, M. (2004). How self-initiated memorized movements become automatic: A functional MRI study. *Journal of Neurophysiology, 91,* 1690–1698.

Wulf, G. (2007a). Attentional focus and motor learning: A review of 10 years of research (Target article). *E-Journal Bewegung und Training (E-Journal Movement and Training), 1,* 4–14. Retrieved May 13, 2011, from http://www.sportwissenschaft.de/fileadmin/pdf/BuT/hossner_wulf.pdf.

Wulf, G. (2007b). *Attention and motor skill learning.* Champaign, IL: Human Kinetics.

Wulf, G. (2007c). Methods, findings, explanations, and future directions: Response to commentaries on "Attentional focus and motor learning." *E-Journal Bewegung und Training (E-Journal Movement and Training), 1,* 57–64. Retrieved May 13, 2011, from http://www.sportwissenschaft.de/fileadmin/pdf/BuT/hossner_wulf.pdf.

Wulf, G., & Dufek, J. S. (2009). Increased jump height with an external focus due to enhanced lower extremity joint kinetics. *Journal of Motor Behavior, 41,* 410–409.

Wulf, G., Dufek, J. S., Lozano, L., & Pettigrew, C. (2010). Increased jump height and reduced EMG activity with an external focus of attention. *Human Movement Science, 29,* 440–448.

Wulf, G., Höß, M., & Prinz, W. (1998). Instructions for motor learning: Differential effects of internal versus external focus of attention. *Journal of Motor Behavior, 30,* 169–179.

Wulf, G., Lauterbach, B., & Toole, T. (1999). Learning advantages of an external focus in golf. *Research Quarterly for Exercise and Sport, 70,* 120–126.

Wulf, G., & Lewthwaite, R. (2009). Conceptions of ability affect motor learning. *Journal of Motor Behavior, 41,* 461–467.

Wulf, G., & Lewthwaite, R. (2010). Effortless motor learning? An external focus of attention enhances movement effectiveness and efficiency. In Bruya, B. (Ed.), *Effortless attention: A new perspective in the cognitive science of attention and action.* Cambridge, MA: MIT Press.

Wulf, G., McConnel, N., Gärtner, M., & Schwarz, A. (2002). Enhancing the learning of sport skills through external-focus feedback. *Journal of Motor Behavior, 34,* 171–182.

Wulf, G., McNevin, N. H., Fuchs, T., Ritter, F., & Toole, T. (2000). Attentional focus in complex motor skill learning. *Research Quarterly for Exercise and Sport, 71,* 229–239.

Wulf, G., McNevin, N. H., & Shea, C. H. (2001). The automaticity of complex motor skill learning as a function of attentional focus. *Quarterly Journal of Experimental Psychology 54A,* 1143–1154.

Wulf, G., Mercer, J., McNevin, N. H., & Guadagnoli, M. A. (2004). Reciprocal influences of attentional focus on postural and supra-postural task performance. *Journal of Motor Behavior, 36,* 189–199.

Wulf, G., Shea, C. H., & Park, J. H. (2001). Attention and motor learning: Preferences for and advantages of an external focus. *Research Quarterly for Exercise and Sport, 72,* 335–344.

Wulf, G., & Su, J. (2007). External focus of attention enhances golf shot accuracy in beginners and experts. *Research Quarterly for Exercise and Sport, 78*, 384–389.

Wulf, G., Töllner, T., & Shea, C. H. (2007). Attentional focus effects as a function of task difficulty. *Research Quarterly for Exercise and Sport, 78*, 257–264.

Wulf, G., Zachry, T., Granados, C., & Dufek, J. S. (2007). Increases in jump-and-reach height through an external focus of attention. *International Journal of Sport Science and Coaching, 2*, 275–282.

Zachry, T., Wulf, G., Mercer, J., & Bezodis, N. (2005). Increased movement accuracy and reduced EMG activity as a result of adopting an external focus of attention. *Brain Research Bulletin, 67*, 304–309.

Ziessler, M. (2007). Effect codes are important for learning and control of movement patterns. *E-Journal Bewegung und Training (E-Journal Movement and Training), 1*, 55–56. Retrieved May 13, 2011, from http://www.sportwissenschaft.de/fileadmin/pdf/BuT/hossner_wulf.pdf.

4 Advances in implicit motor learning

Richard S. W. Masters and Jamie M. Poolton

Advances in implicit motor learning

Much of the way in which humans respond and adapt to the environment occurs implicitly, without conscious awareness and often without intention (e.g., Frensch, 1998; Reber, 1967). Conscious processes are constrained by limits to the information-processing capacity of the brain (e.g., Baars, 1998; Kahneman, 1973), so it is not surprising that implicit (unconscious) processes underlie our interaction with the environment. Nor is it surprising that evolution has selected advantages of implicit (unconscious) learning, given that learning is a biological imperative, which provided our ancestors with a significant survival advan_____ _____ ____.

What is implicit learning?

To operationalize implicit learning is challenging and much debated (see Frensch & Rünger, 2003). It is generally agreed that implicit learning is the antithesis of explicit learning, during which purposeful hypothesis testing exposes rules and knowledge thought to govern effective behavior. In the 1960s, Arthur Reber used artificial grammar learning to examine how people learned compound rules governing complex tasks. Participants were not informed of the rules, but when later asked to determine whether unfamiliar exemplars followed the same rules they were surprisingly accurate, despite negligible conscious knowledge of the rules (see Pothos, 2007). Reber (1989) considered implicit learning to be the accrual of knowledge that "in some raw fashion, is always ahead of the capability of its processor to explicate" (p. 229).

Implicit learning has also been investigated using the serial reaction time task (SRTT), in which people are asked to react as quickly as possible by pressing a key to match positions indicated on a monitor. The order of positions on the monitor is repeated over numerous trials in a sequence that can involve many key presses. Although most participants are unaware of a repeating sequence, their responses become so fast that they anticipate the next position, suggesting that they have learned the sequence implicitly (e.g., Jiménez & Mendez, 1999; Nissen & Bullemer, 1987). One of the strengths of the SRTT is that informing participants of the repeating sequence establishes a test of explicit, rather than implicit, learning (Curran & Keele, 1993; Willingham, Nissen, & Bullemer, 1989), with learners accruing knowledge of the sequence consciously. A dissociation between performance and conscious knowledge has also been demonstrated in learning sequences of events or detecting covariations between stimuli (e.g., Lewicki, Hill, & Bizot, 1988; Willingham et al., 1989), in interactive computer-simulation tasks (e.g., Berry & Broadbent, 1984; Broadbent, Fitzgerald, & Broadbent, 1986) and in studies that shape behavior without verbal rule-governed contingencies (e.g., Hefferline, Keenan, & Harford, 1959; Svartdal, 1995).

The rise of implicit *motor* learning

It is now 20 years since Masters (1992) first showed the advantages of acquiring ontogenetic skills implicitly, without orchestration by explicit (conscious) processes. Ontogenetic skills extend fundamental movement skills for specialized purposes in a specific environment (e.g., the Fosbury flop). Prior to 1992, fundamental movements (e.g., key-presses) rather than ontogenetic skills had been used in implicit learning studies to gain insight into the acquisition of abstract, unconscious knowledge. Researchers had shown little interest in the consequences of *implicit motor learning* for performance of the movements per se (e.g., Green & Flowers, 1991, 2003; Pew, 1974).

Masters (1992) alleged that ontogenetic skills are often acquired explicitly, with too great a contribution from consciousness. He argued that they can be acquired implicitly, with negligible conscious involvement. Implicit motor learning was expected to minimize the accrual of explicit knowledge about the movements or prevent conscious access to the knowledge, in either case, reducing the opportunity for conscious thought processes to destabilize performance through effortful, conscious processing of the movements (a phenomenon described as "reinvestment"; see Masters & Maxwell, 2008).

To cause implicit motor learning, Masters (1992) asked participants to learn a golf putting skill while concurrently carrying out a highly demanding letter generation task (see Baddeley & Hitch, 1974), which exploited enough processing capacity to inhibit conscious awareness of performing each putt. Participants reported very little knowledge of how they putted (unlike participants who were taught explicitly or left to learn by discovery). Self-report is not a convincing gauge of the awareness of task-relevant knowledge, given that it may not expose all of the relevant knowledge or access the *actual* knowledge that results in learning (e.g., Shanks & St John, 1994). Nevertheless, when asked to describe what they knew of their golf putting skill, many of the implicit learners reported merely that they putted by feel or intuition, a characteristic typically reported of implicit learning (e.g., Berry & Dienes, 1993).

Additionally, when those who learned implicitly were asked to perform in conditions designed to imitate real-life psychological pressures, they displayed no disruption of their putting, unlike the explicit learners and the discovery learners. These findings have been replicated repeatedly (e.g., Hardy, Mullen, & Jones, 1996) and, as recently as 2007, Mullen, Hardy, and Oldham (2007) posted evidence "firmly supporting the advantages of implicit over explicit practice in high anxiety conditions" (p. 155). However, the dual-task approach possesses an Achilles heel; inevitably, it slows the rate of learning compared with explicit or even discovery learning (see Figure 4.1).

MacMahon and Masters (2002) sought to resolve the problem by evoking a popular multi-component model of working memory, first proposed by Baddeley and Hitch (1974; see Baddeley, 2007). Typically, learners conceive and test hypotheses about movement solutions in a strategic trial-and-error fashion (e.g., Klayman & Ha, 1987; Ohlsson, 1996) made possible by the information storage and manipulation capabilities of working memory (e.g., Berry & Broadbent, 1984). MacMahon and Masters argued that concurrent letter generation caused implicit motor learning by preventing the use of working memory for hypothesis testing, but was so demanding that little attention could be directed to the motor task for learning. They tested if it was possible to disrupt hypothesis testing, but not motor learning, with dual-tasks that interfered not with control of attention but with temporary storage of verbal information before it could be used for hypothesis testing. The tasks (repetition of a simple word, unattended speech) were designed to disrupt subvocal rehearsal within the phonological loop, a slave system of working memory that holds verbal information until it can be used. In two studies, rate of motor learning was not slowed by either task, but nor was hypothesis testing disrupted.

Clearly, to fully disrupt hypothesis testing, dual-tasks must increase attention demands so much that motor learning slows (e.g., Maxwell, Masters, & Eves, 2000). Regardless, learners seldom report no task-relevant knowledge, so it is important to acknowledge that there are few if any forms of learning that are purely explicit or purely implicit (e.g., Seger, 1994; Sun, Merrill, & Peterson, 2001; Willingham, 1998). With these constraints in mind, methods have been devised to promote implicit motor learning without enforced control of attention, allowing the contribution of implicit processes to motor learning to be redressed more passively.

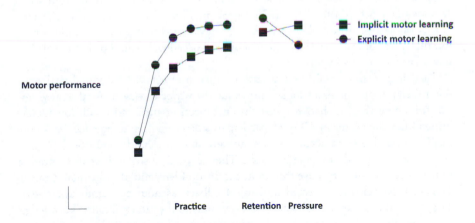

Figure 4.1 A stylized representation of the influence of implicit motor learning by means of dual-task techniques and explicit motor learning by means of instructions or discovery on the performance of ontogenetic movement skills during and after practice or under performance pressure.

Hampering hypothesis testing

Visual, auditory, proprioceptive, and tactile feedback is available to appraise movements, although often *visual* feedback supersedes all else when movement outcomes are appraised (Kelso, 1982). Masters (2000) argued that novices would be unlikely to test hypotheses if visual feedback was not available, so working memory would be by-passed during learning and accrual of task-relevant knowledge would be minimal. In a golf putting task, however, participants simply switched to testing hypotheses about the proprioceptive and tactile feedback that *was* available, whenever visual feedback about movement outcomes was absent (Maxwell, Masters, & Eves, 2003). Additionally, putting performance was later disrupted in a dual-task test, suggesting that working memory was not by-passed during learning. To prevent testing of hypotheses about proprioceptive and tactile feedback, Maxwell et al. (2003) asked participants to perform a visual search task immediately after striking each putt. Hypothesis testing was reduced and performance was not subsequently disrupted in a dual-task test, suggesting that working memory was by-passed during the learning process and that implicit motor learning occurred. The drawback was that the absence of outcome feedback restricted improvements in accuracy.

Marginally perceptible outcome feedback

Masters, Maxwell, and Eves (2009) proposed a solution, in the knowledge that two thresholds of awareness exist. One is objective; a person claims to be unaware of a stimulus and discriminates it at no better than chance (guessing). The other is subjective; a person claims to be unaware of a stimulus yet discriminates it better than chance (e.g., Cheesman & Merikle, 1984). As ability to detect a stimulus decreases, observers become less confident of their observations and eventually claim to be unaware of the stimulus. Nevertheless, observers display forced identification accuracy above chance. Masters et al. (2009) presented knowledge of results to learners at this "subjective" threshold of awareness. They argued that learning would occur, but that a lack of conscious awareness of outcome feedback would prohibit working memory from testing hypotheses.

Participants struck 500 putts toward an unseen target without visual feedback. After each putt, participants looked into a tachistoscope to view a visual representation of where the ball had stopped. In an objective threshold condition (determined individually, mean 7.33 ms), participants detected no outcome feedback and displayed no change in accuracy. In a supraliminal threshold condition (100 ms), participants detected outcome feedback. They learned to strike the ball accurately to the target. In the subjective threshold condition (determined individually, mean 11.71 ms), participants detected outcome feedback without conscious awareness. They learned to strike the ball almost as accurately to the target. Explicit knowledge of the putting task was low in each condition, possibly because the lag between putting and viewing feedback in the tachistoscope disrupted hypothesis testing.

Farrow and Abernethy (2002) reduced the salience of the stimulus–response mapping in a different way to examine whether perceptual cues could be acquired implicitly to improve anticipation of serve direction in tennis. In an explicit condition, players were instructed to search for cues available in occluded footage of expert tennis serves. In an implicit condition, players were asked to predict the speed of the serves, in order to deflect attention away from conscious processing of anticipation-related information (e.g., see also Poulter, Jackson, Wann, & Berry, 2005; Vinter & Perruchet, 1999). Participants in the implicit condition reported little explicit knowledge of cues, but their ability to predict serve direction improved significantly compared with the explicit learners (although the effect dissipated in delayed testing).

There is no *mistaking* implicit motor learning!

Working memory is deployed during learning to actively identify and correct performance mistakes (Baddeley & Wilson, 1994), but Prather (1971) observed that learning is passive when mistakes are negligible (i.e., errorless conditions). Maxwell, Masters, Kerr, and Weedon (2001) therefore proposed that hypothesis testing can be avoided by constraining the number of errors. This was achieved by initiating practice from distances so close to the target that participants seldom missed. Errors were promoted by initiating practice from distances so far from the target that novices missed often. After each block of trials, participants moved to an incrementally easier (errorful protocol) or more difficult (errorless protocol) distance. Few errorless learning protocols prohibit errors unequivocally, but it is conventional to use the term *errorless* to differentiate them from *errorful* interventions, which do not prohibit errors (e.g., Clare et al., 2000). Fewer errors occurred over the full range of distances in the errorless protocol. Performance was more accurate in a delayed retention test and, unlike the errorful protocol (or a control), performance was unaffected by a concurrent tone-counting task, suggesting that working memory was not significantly involved in the putting task. Surprisingly, errorless participants did not report less task-relevant knowledge than errorful participants.

Explicit hypothesis testing escalated in the errorless protocol when putting distances reached a critical increment at which errors became prominent (generally 100 cm). Despite this, performance appeared to be supported by implicit processes, so in a second experiment Maxwell et al. (2001) asked novice participants to putt from incrementally increasing distances that evoked a low frequency of errors (25 cm, 50 cm, 75 cm) or incrementally decreasing distances that evoked a high frequency of errors (175 cm, 150 cm, 125 cm). Performance by the errorless learners (low frequency) was superior to performance by the errorful learners (high frequency) in a transfer test at an intermediate distance (100 cm), and consistent with the first experiment they were unaffected by a concurrent tone-counting task, suggesting that working memory was not deployed to support putting performance. Moreover, errorless learners displayed less evidence of hypothesis testing, as ratified by video analysis of the number of visible adjustments to technique (indicative of hypothesis testing). By constraining the *early learning* environment to limit errors (i.e., 150 trials only), it seems that implicit motor processes can be evoked ahead of conscious, effortful processes that are predicted by stages of learning models (e.g., Fitts & Posner, 1967; Shiffrin & Schneider, 1977). Even if the environmental constraints allow accrual of task-relevant knowledge later in learning, advantages associated with implicit motor processes may remain. Supporting this claim, Lam, Maxwell, and Masters (2010) showed that probe reaction times did not slow as putting distance increased in an errorless protocol (and errors increased), implying that the attention requirements of the movement did not change. These findings are consistent with bottom-up models of learning, in which implicit supporting knowledge is learned first and explicit knowledge accumulates afterwards (e.g., Sun, Slusarz, & Terry, 2005).

Poolton, Masters, and Maxwell (2005) examined this further by introducing movement instructions at the outset of errorless learning (top-down) or after an initial brief period of implicit, errorless learning (bottom-up). The top-down approach promoted unstable performance when participants were required to complete a concurrent tone-counting task, whereas the bottom-up approach promoted stable performance despite the belated introduction of explicit knowledge (cf. Ong, Bowcock, & Hodges, 2010).

Stable, comfortable movement solutions are usually adopted at the outset of learning (Zanone, Monno, Temprado, & Laurent, 2001), but ontogenetic skills may oblige choreographed movement solutions for best practice (e.g., the Fosbury flop). A top-down approach is often adopted to initially modify movements consciously with instructions, but the result can be neither stable nor comfortable. Incremental errorless learning may permit gradated modifications of movements with minimal disturbance of their stability, comfort or attention requirements.

In recent years, the clinical utility of implicit motor learning has been examined using errorless learning in rehabilitation (e.g., Orrell, Eves, & Masters, 2006), child development (Capio, Poolton, Sit, Holstrom, & Masters, 2011), the elderly (Chauvel et al., 2012), and surgery (e.g., Masters, Lo, Maxwell, & Patil, 2008). In movement-disordered populations, pressures to move effectively often cause people to rely too heavily on conscious processes, presumably to manage the movements or to preserve their integrity (e.g., Fasotti & Kovacs, 1995; Masters, Pall, MacMahon, & Eves, 2007; Stapleton, Ashburn, & Stack, 2001; Wong, Masters, Maxwell, & Abernethy, 2008). Masters, MacMahon, and Pall (2004) asked people with Parkinson's disease to learn to strike a target accurately in either unconstrained (explicit) or error-constrained (implicit) conditions. No performance differences were evident in delayed retention tests. However, the implicit learning condition culminated in less task-relevant knowledge and no disruption of hitting accuracy while counting backwards. Physiotherapists often protest that patients can modify their movements when explicitly requested to during therapy, yet upon leaving the clinic they revert to pre-therapy movement patterns. Conscious control of new movements is highly effortful and difficult to maintain so it is not surprising that challenges of moving in the real world undermine their use. Orrell et al. (2006) asked stroke patients to keep a platform horizontal in conditions in which it rotated unstably (errorful protocol) or in which it initially was stable but gradually became less stable (errorless protocol). In a transfer test requiring concurrent digit recall while balancing, stroke patients who learned using the errorless protocol displayed improved balance performance relative to balance only, and the stroke patients who learned using the errorful protocol displayed disrupted balance performance. Presumably, the errorless protocol reorganized balance control at an implicit level, leaving working memory free to carry out the digit recall task.

Probing objective evidence of implicit processes

Lam, Masters, and Maxwell (2010; see also Lam, Maxwell, & Masters, 2010) showed that simple verbal RTs to random auditory probes were slower during both preparation and execution of putts that followed unsuccessful trials rather than successful trials. They argued that this corresponds to explicit construction of a motor hypothesis to correct the error (preparation phase) followed by conscious online implementation of the motor solution required to test the hypothesis (execution phase). Similarly, Koehn, Dickinson, and Goodman (2008; see also Rabbitt, 1967) showed that probe reaction times (RTs) were slower when errors occurred on the preceding trial. Work by Gray (2004) and Wong, Masters, Maxwell, and Abernethy (2009) substantiates this claim. Baseball batters in a slump (i.e., high error) and elderly fallers (i.e., serious error) were very accurate (compared with batters on a streak or elderly non-fallers) at recalling the position of their limbs at the exact moment that a random tone sounded, when batting or walking respectively. Hyperawareness of limb position suggests that prior errors increased the propensity for conscious monitoring and control of the movements, as predicted by the Theory of Reinvestment (Masters, 1992; Masters & Maxwell, 2008).

Further evidence that implicit motor learning reduces conscious involvement in movement has been shown using electroencephalography (EEG) to measure co-activation or coherence between different regions of the brain. Low coherence indicates that regions function autonomously, whereas high coherence indicates mutual reliance (e.g., Nunez, 1995). Low coherence between the T3 and Fz regions, particularly in the alpha2 bandwidth, is common in highly practiced performers (e.g., Deeny, Hillman, Janelle, & Hatfield, 2003; Hatfield, Haufler, Hung, & Spalding, 2004). The left temporal region (T3) is associated with explicit, verbal processes (e.g., Haufler, Spalding, Santa Maria, & Hatfield, 2000; Springer & Deutsch, 1998) and the frontal midline region of the brain (Fz) is associated with movement planning (Kaufer & Lewis, 1999). These findings confirm that explicit verbal involvement in movement reduces with automaticity, but it is work by Zhu, Poolton, Wilson, Maxwell, and Masters (2011a) that confirms that implicit motor learning allows skills to be acquired without conscious verbal involvement. Implicit (errorless) learners demonstrated less alpha2 T3–Fz coherence when putting than explicit (errorful) learners. Moreover, they displayed no change in coherence under performance pressure, whereas coherence increased significantly in explicit learners, implying that conscious verbal involvement in the movements was heightened by the desire to perform well. These findings were substantiated by Zhu, Poolton, Wilson, Maxwell, and Masters (2011b) using a surgical laparoscopy skill.

Analogical inferences for implicit motor learning

A different method to invoke implicit processes during motor learning uses analogy learning (e.g., Gentner, 1983; Shustack & Anderson, 1979) to guide learners to stable motor solutions with limited accrual of explicit knowledge (Masters, 2000). Analogies allow individuals to make inferences about concepts with little awareness of the rules that underlie the concepts (Donnelly & McDaniel, 1993). If a person knows how a pump works, it becomes relatively easy to infer how the heart works.

Liao and Masters (2001) examined whether Pythagoras's theorem could be used as an analogy to teach beginners the concept of an overspin table tennis forehand shot. Learners were instructed to swing the bat up the hypotenuse of an imagined right-angled triangle each time that they struck a forehand shot. Unlike literally instructed participants, analogy learners accrued little conscious knowledge of how they executed shots, and performed without disruption in attention-demanding or pressured conditions. Liao and Masters (2001) concluded that analogies can be used as *biomechanical metaphors* to promote implicit motor learning by describing the higher-order relationships underlying a motor task without presenting individual rules. Recent work supports this claim, showing that an analogy had "an immediate effect on deployment of the attention of novices during movement" (Koedijker et al., 2011, p. 7, Experiment 2). Novice Chinese table tennis players were presented with explicit instructions (five rules) or a culturally modified analogy (Poolton, Masters, & Maxwell, 2007a; Figure 4.2) and immediately performed counterbalanced blocks of trials under different demands. In both groups, performance was disrupted by speeded hitting or skill-focused conditions; however, only participants using the analogy instruction were impervious to dual-task conditions (word monitoring), suggesting that presenting underlying knowledge of the task as

Figure 4.2 Poolton et al. (2007a) found that, despite displaying a clear understanding of the Euclidean geometry underlying the concept of a right-angled triangle analogy (i.e., Pythagoras's theorem), Chinese learners often failed to apply the concept to their movements when endeavoring to hit an overspin table tennis shot. Poolton et al. therefore developed and validated a culturally relevant analogy that communicated the same principles, but in a different guise ("move the bat as if it is traveling up the side of a mountain").

higher-order relationships, rather than explicit rules, liberated working memory to monitor words.

Many studies have demonstrated that novices instructed by analogy learn in ways that are characteristic of implicit motor learning. They display minimal accrual of, or access to, task-relevant knowledge and resilient (or improved) performance in the face of pressure or multi-tasking (e.g., Law, Masters, Bray, Bardswell, & Eves, 2003; Masters, Poolton, Maxwell, & Raab, 2008; Poolton, Masters, & Maxwell, 2006; Tse, Masters, Whitehill, & Ma, 2012). Lam, Maxwell, and Masters (2009b) demonstrated unimpaired dual-task performance of a seated basketball shooting task after analogy learning, but not explicit learning, confirming that analogy learning by-passes involvement of working memory in performance. The analogy learners were instructed to "shoot as if you are trying to put cookies into a cookie jar on a high shelf," whereas the explicit learners were instructed with eight literal rules designed to elicit the same movement solution. Analogy learners reported minimal task-relevant knowledge, and the movements did not differ kinematically across groups.

Lam, Maxwell, and Masters (2009a) demonstrated unimpaired performance by analogy learners but not explicit learners on the same basketball task under pressure, but found that vocal probe RTs were slower for both groups during movement preparation. Although unsurprising for the explicit learners (see Holroyd, Yeung, Coles, & Cohen, 2005), this finding was at odds with the view that working memory is spare for other processing in skills learned by analogy; shorter probe RTs should have occurred. If the attention demands were similar for the two types of learning, why then was performance of explicit learners impaired? The explicit learners reported much more task-relevant knowledge than the analogy learners, so it is likely that processing this knowledge in working memory disrupted their performance under pressure. Koedijker, Oudejans, and Beek (2007) came to the same conclusion when they found that instructions to learn a table tennis forehand by analogy, or by attending to movement execution or the ball at all times, resulted in uniformly low accrual of task-relevant knowledge, compared with explicit instructions, yet only the explicit learners displayed disrupted performance under pressure.

The potential advantages of implicit motor learning that purportedly are associated with using analogy instructions have not always been agreed. Koedijker, Oudejans, and Beek (2008) replicated Liao and Masters (2001), but required participants to learn table tennis forehands by explicit instructions or by analogy for many more trials (10,000). Differences in performance were not evident early or late in learning when participants were tested in low- or high-pressure trials or under dual-task conditions. Koedijker et al. (2008) concluded that it is unnecessary to minimize accrual of task-relevant knowledge when acquiring ontogenetic skills. It is possible, however, that the fast-paced practice design employed in the study (50 trials per minute) afforded little opportunity for participants to consciously process task-relevant information. Consequently, implicit motor learning may have occurred in the explicit condition, explaining the lack of differences. Partly corroborating this argument, the explicit learners reported less task-relevant knowledge at the end of learning than the beginning, suggesting that it was discarded, forgotten, or consolidated in implicit memory (e.g., Schacter, 1987). Speeded learning warrants future consideration as an implicit motor learning technique.

An evolving explanation for implicit motor learning

What, then, explains the apparent advantages of implicit motor learning? Why does the performance of people who learn implicitly sometimes even improve in response to prejudicial challenges, such as pressure or attention loading? Hardy et al. (1996) suggested that continuous production of a secondary response during practice causes participants to become desensitized to "self-generated verbal distractions" that typically occur when state anxiety increases (see Eysenck, 1979). No clear evidence has emerged to support or refute this explanation (e.g., Mullen & Hardy, 2000; see also Mullen, Hardy, & Tattersall, 2005), but the evidence demonstrates that advantages of implicit motor learning surface even when paradigms are used that do not entail continuous production of a secondary response during practice.

A parsimonious explanation is that "almost everything we do, we do better unconsciously than consciously" (Baars, 1998, p. 73), so unconscious, implicit processes are far more efficient at controlling ontogenetic skills than conscious, explicit processes. Consequently, performance improves whenever unconscious motor control occurs, or disruptive residual conscious processes dissipate (Jackson, Ashford, & Norsworthy, 2006).

Alternatively, implicit processes are embedded in neuroanatomical brain structures that phylogenetically are older and more sophisticated than explicit processes (e.g., Reber, 1992). Reber argued that non-verbal implicit processes preceded explicit verbal processes and that extended selective pressures modified them to be more stable and resilient than their recently evolved cousins. In particular, implicit processes are resilient in many contexts in which explicit processes are fragile, including psychiatric disorders (Abrams & Reber, 1988), brain damage (e.g., Cohen & Squire, 1980; Nissen & Bullemer, 1987), cognitive loads (e.g., Frensch, Wenke, & Rünger, 1999; Hayes & Broadbent, 1988), and time constraints (e.g., Allen & Reber, 1980; Orrell, Eves, Masters, & MacMahon, 2007).

Given that "the modern mind is a mosaic structure of cognitive vestiges from earlier stages of human emergence" (Donald, 1991, p. 3), it is likely that phylogenetically old processes remain intact and can be invoked by implicit motor learning. Corroborating this claim, Poolton, Masters, and Maxwell (2007b) and Masters, Poolton, and Maxwell (2008) showed that implicit motor learning confers resilience in the face of physiological fatigue. Failure to perform skills effectively despite fatigue (e.g., missile throwing) would have been catastrophic for our ancestors. Participants in both studies learned a novel throwing task implicitly or explicitly through errorless or errorful learning. Poolton et al. (2007b) asked the learners to perform the throwing task accurately under conditions of severe anaerobic fatigue, whereas Masters, Poolton, and Maxwell (2008) asked the learners to perform the throwing task accurately under conditions of severe aerobic fatigue. In both studies, participants who learned implicitly, and presumably were reliant on sophisticated unconscious vestigial processes, displayed stable performance, whereas participants who learned explicitly did not.

Conclusions

The chapter opened by summarizing the extensive literature that has been published on implicit learning of cognitive skills and presenting the case for implicit learning of ontogenetic *movement* skills that are not universally acquired and require specialized coordination of many degrees of freedom to achieve specific motor objectives. Early work in implicit motor learning was discussed and we provided a rationale for why implicit motor learning techniques that persuade learners to avoid testing hypotheses are preferred to demanding dual-task methods that thwart working memory involvement. Techniques were described (i.e., errorless, analogy, minimal, and marginal feedback) that generally cause learners to engage in less hypothesis testing about their movements than explicit learners and to be unable to report more than a small amount of explicit knowledge about the movement solution. Electroencephalography (Zhu et al., 2011a, 2011b) provides objective evidence that implicit learners utilize minimal verbal involvement in their movements, as implied by reduced co-activation of specific motor and verbal areas during performance. Participants consistently display unimpaired motor performance when asked to engage in concurrent tasks that require the services of working memory or when they perform in conditions designed to increase their performance anxiety. In fact, improved performance is not uncommon.

The model that we have applied has largely been based on a bottom-up approach (see Sun et al., 2001) in that we seek to engage implicit, procedural learning processes at the outset of skill acquisition (explicit, declarative knowledge may later accrue harmlessly, as Poolton et al., 2005, showed). Our findings imply that implicit motor learners do not need to progress through an initial cognitive stage of learning as suggested by top-down stages of learning models (e.g., Fitts & Posner, 1967). We have proposed an evolutionary explanation for the advantages associated with implicit motor learning, which is based upon Reber's (1992) proposition that unconscious, implicit processes are biologically more stable than explicit conscious processes. We even used the evolutionary argument to make clear predictions about the effect of implicit motor learning on motor performance under taxing physical fatigue conditions and presented data that supported our predictions.

An important question remains. How exactly do these implicit motor learning techniques have their effect? Is an apparent lack of or lack of access to explicit task knowledge causal of the effects and advantages of implicit motor learning or merely a by-product? Do the techniques result in motor performance that entirely by-passes the executive functions of working memory, or, by removing the working memory load created by explicit knowledge, does implicit motor learning simply make it easier for the central executive to run performance? Alternatively, do the techniques train the central executive so that it is better able to cope with demands such as a concurrent secondary task, by shifting or inhibiting attention (see Miyake et al., 2000)? Perhaps implicit motor learning techniques help performers know what information to discard, guiding them to rely on simple heuristic performance cues (Gigerenzer, 2007). It is likely that the data that we have reported can be interpreted to support any of these possibilities, but for now, to paraphrase Reber (1989), our understanding "in some raw fashion, is . . . ahead of [our] capability [to] explicate" (p. 229).

Acknowledgment

Dr. Jon Maxwell (a.k.a. Jonny Max) contributed in many ways to this chapter, despite passing away on Sunday 25 January 2009. We were privileged to work with him.

References

Abrams, M., & Reber, A. S. (1988). Implicit learning: Robustness in the face of psychiatric disorders. *Journal of Psycholinguistic Research, 17,* 425–439.

Allen, R., & Reber, A. S. (1980). Very long term memory for tacit knowledge. *Cognition, 8,* 175–185.

Baars, B. J. (1998). *A cognitive theory of consciousness.* New York: Cambridge University Press.

Baddeley, A. (2007). *Working memory, thought, and action.* Oxford: Oxford University Press.

Baddeley, A. D., & Hitch, G. (1974). Working memory. In Bower, G. A. (Ed.), *Recent Advances in Learning and Motivation, Vol. 8.* New York: Academic Press.

Baddeley, A. D., & Wilson, B. A. (1994). When implicit learning fails: Amnesia and the problem of error elimination. *Neuropsychologia, 32,* 53–68.

Berry, D. C., & Broadbent, D. E. (1984). On the relationship between task performance and associated verbalisable knowledge. *Quarterly Journal of Experimental Psychology, 36A,* 209–231.

Berry, D. C., & Dienes, Z. (1993). *Implicit learning: Theoretical and empirical issues.* Hove, UK: Lawrence Erlbaum Associates.

Broadbent, D. E., Fitzgerald, P., & Broadbent, M. H. P. (1986). Implicit and explicit knowledge in the control of complex systems. *British Journal of Psychology, 77,* 33–50.

Capio, C. M., Poolton, J. M., Sit, C. H. P., Holstrom, M., & Masters, R. S. W. (2011). Reducing errors benefits the field-based learning of a fundamental movement skill in children. *Scandinavian Journal of Medicine and Science in Sports.* doi: 10.1111/j.1600-0838.2011.01368.x.

Chauvel, G., Maquestiaux, F., Hartley, A., Joubert, S., Diderjean, A., & Masters, R. S. W. (2012). Age effects shrink when motor learning is predominantly supported by nondeclarative, automatic memory processes: Evidence from golf putting. *Quarterly Journal of Experimental Psychology, 65,* 25–38.

Cheesman, J., & Merikle, P. M. (1984). Priming with and without awareness. *Perception and Psychophysics, 36,* 387–395.

Clare, L., Wilson, B. A., Carter, G., Breen, K., Gosses, A., & Hodges, J. R. (2000). Intervening with everyday memory problems in dementia of Alzheimer type: An errorless learning condition approach. *Journal of Clinical and Experimental Neuropsychology, 22,* 132–146.

Claxton, G. (1997). *Hare brain, tortoise mind.* London: Fourth Estate.

Cohen, N. J., & Squire, L. R. (1980). Preserved learning and retention of pattern analyzing skill in amnesia: Dissociation of knowing how and knowing that. *Science, 210,* 207–209.

Curran, T., & Keele, S. W. (1993). Attentional and nonattentional forms of sequence learning. *Journal of Experimental Psychology: Learning, Memory, and Cognition, 19,* 189–202.

Deeny, S. P., Hillman, C. H., Janelle, C. M., & Hatfield, B. D. (2003). Cortico-cortical communication and superior performance in skilled marksmen: An EEG coherence analysis. *Journal of Sport and Exercise Psychology, 25,* 188–204.

Donald, M. (1991). *Origins of the modern mind: Three stages in the evolution of culture and cognition.* Cambridge, MA: Harvard University Press.

Donnelly, C. M., & McDaniel, M. A. (1993). Use of analogies in learning scientific concepts. *Journal of Experimental Psychology: Learning, Memory, and Cognition, 19,* 975–987.

Eysenck, M. W. (1979). Anxiety, learning and memory: A reconceptualization. *Journal of Research in Personality, 13*, 363–385.

Farrow, D., & Abernethy, B. (2002). Can anticipatory skills be learned through implicit video-based perceptual training? *Journal of Sports Sciences, 20*, 471–485.

Fasotti, L., & Kovacs, F. (1995). Slow information processing and the use of compensatory mechanisms. In Chamberlain, M. A., Neumann, V., & Tennant, A. (Eds.), *Traumatic brain injury rehabilitation service, treatments and outcomes* (pp. 141–152). London: Chapman & Hall.

Fitts, P. M., & Posner, M. I. (1967). *Human performance.* Belmont, CA: Brooks/Cole.

Frensch, P. A. (1998). One concept, multiple meanings: On how to define the concept of implicit learning. In Stadler, M. A., & Frensch, P. A. (Eds.), *Handbook of implicit learning* (pp. 47–104). Thousand Oaks, CA: Sage.

Frensch, P. A., & Rünger, D. (2003) Implicit learning. *Current Directions in Psychological Science, 12*, 13–18.

Frensch, P. A., Wenke, D., & Rünger, D. (1999). A secondary tone-counting task suppresses performance in the Serial Reaction Task. *Journal of Experimental Psychology: Learning, Memory, and Cognition, 25*, 260–274.

Gentner, D. (1983). Structure-mapping: A theoretical framework. *Cognitive Science, 7*, 155–170.

Gigerenzer, G. (2007). *Gut feelings: The intelligence of the unconscious.* New York: Viking.

Gray, R. (2004). Attending to the execution of a complex sensorimotor skill: Expertise differences, choking, and slumps. *Journal of Experimental Psychology: Applied, 10*, 42–54.

Green, T. D., & Flowers, J. H. (1991). Implicit versus explicit learning processes in a probabilistic, continuous fine-motor catching task. *Journal of Motor Behavior, 23*, 293–300.

Green, T. D., & Flowers, J. H. (2003) Comparison of implicit and explicit learning processes in a probabilistic task. *Perceptual & Motor Skills, 97*, 299–314.

Hardy, L., Mullen, R., & Jones, G. (1996). Knowledge of conscious control of motor actions under stress. *British Journal of Psychology, 87*, 621–636.

Hatfield, B. D., Haufler, A. J., Hung, T. M., & Spalding, T. W. (2004). Electroencephalographic studies of skilled psychomotor performance. *Journal of Clinical Neurophysiology, 21*, 144–156.

Haufler, A. J., Spalding, T. W., Santa Maria, D. L., & Hatfield, B. D. (2000). Neuro-cognitive activity during a self-paced visuospatial task: Comparative EEG profiles in marksmen and novice shooters. *Biological Psychology, 53*, 131–160.

Hayes, N. A., & Broadbent, D. E. (1988). Two modes of learning for interactive tasks. *Cognition, 28*, 249–276.

Hefferline, R. F., Keenan, B., & Harford, R. A. (1959). Escape and avoidance conditioning in human subjects without their observation of the response. *Science, 130*, 1338–1339.

Holroyd, C. B., Yeung, N., Coles, M. G. H., & Cohen, J. D. (2005). A mechanism for error detection in speeded response time tasks. *Journal of Experimental Psychology: General, 19*, 163–191.

Jackson, R. C., Ashford, K. J., & Norsworthy, G. (2006). Attentional focus, dispositional reinvestment, and skilled motor performance under pressure. *Journal of Sport & Exercise Psychology, 28*, 49–68.

Jiménez, L., & Mendez, C. (1999). Which attention is needed for implicit sequence learning? *Journal of Experimental Psychology: Learning, Memory, & Cognition, 25*, 236–259.

Kahneman, D. (1973). *Attention and effort.* Englewood Cliffs, NJ: Prentice-Hall.

Kaufer, D. I., & Lewis, D. A. (1999). Frontal lobe anatomy and cortical connectivity. In Miller, B. L., & Cummings, J. L. (Eds.), *The human frontal lobes: Functions and disorders* (pp. 27–44). New York: Guilford Press.

Kelso, J. A. S. (1982). *Human motor behavior: An introduction.* Hillsdale, NJ: Lawrence Erlbaum.

Klayman, J., & Ha, Y. W. (1987). Hypothesis testing in rule discovery: Strategy, structure and content. *Journal of Experimental Psychology: Learning, Memory, and Cognition, 15,* 596–604.

Koedijker, J. M., Oudejans, R. R.D., & Beek, P. J. (2007). Explicit rules and direction of attention in learning and performing the table tennis forehand. *International Journal of Sport Psychology, 38,* 227–244.

Koedijker, J. M., Oudejans, R. R.D., & Beek, P. J. (2008). Rule formation and table tennis performance following explicit and analogy learning over 10,000 repetitions. *International Journal of Sport Psychology, 39,* 237–256.

Koedijker, J. M., Poolton, J. M., Maxwell, J. P., Oudejans, R. R. D., Beek, P. J., & Masters, R. S. W. (2011). Attention and time constraints in perceptual–motor performance: Instruction, analogy and skill level. *Consciousness & Cognition, 20,* 245–256.

Koehn, J. D., Dickinson, J., & Goodman, D. (2008). Cognitive demands of error processing. *Psychological Reports, 102,* 532–538.

Lam, W. K., Masters, R. S. W., & Maxwell, J. P. (2010). Cognitive demands of error processing associated with preparation and execution of complex movement. *Consciousness & Cognition, 19,* 1058–1061.

Lam, W. K., Maxwell, J. P., & Masters, R. S. W. (2009a). Analogy learning and the performance of motor skills under pressure. *Journal of Sport & Exercise Psychology, 31,* 337–357.

Lam, W. K., Maxwell, J. P., & Masters, R. S. W. (2009b). Analogy versus explicit learning of a modified basketball shooting task: Performance and kinematic outcomes. *Journal of Sports Sciences, 27,* 179–191.

Lam, W. K., Maxwell, J. P., & Masters, R. S. W. (2010). Probing the allocation of attention in implicit (motor) learning. *Journal of Sport Sciences, 28,* 1543–1554.

Law, J., Masters, R. S. W., Bray, S., Bardswell, I., & Eves, F. (2003). Motor performance as a function of audience affability and metaknowledge. *Journal of Sport & Exercise Psychology, 25,* 484–500.

Lewicki, P., Hill, T., & Bizot, E. (1988). Acquisition of procedural knowledge about a pattern of stimuli that cannot be articulated. *Cognitive Psychology, 20,* 24–37.

Liao, C.-M., & Masters, R. S. W. (2001). Analogy learning: A means to implicit motor learning. *Journal of Sport Sciences, 19,* 307–319.

MacMahon, K. M. A., & Masters, R. S. W. (2002). The effects of a secondary task on implicit motor skill performance. *International Journal of Sport Psychology, 33,* 307–324.

Masters, R. S. W. (1992). Knowledge, knerves and know-how: The role of explicit versus implicit knowledge in the breakdown of a complex motor skill under pressure. *British Journal of Psychology, 83,* 343–358.

Masters, R. S. W. (2000). Theoretical aspects of implicit learning in sports. *International Journal of Sport Psychology, 31,* 530–541.

Masters, R. S. W., Lo, C. Y., Maxwell, J. P., & Patil, N. G. (2008). Implicit motor learning in surgery: Implications for multi-tasking. *Surgery, 143,* 140–145.

Masters, R. S. W., MacMahon, K. M. A., & Pall, H. S. (2004). Implicit motor learning in Parkinson's disease. *Rehabilitation Psychology, 49,* 79–82.

Masters, R. S. W., & Maxwell, J. (2008). The Theory of Reinvestment. *International Review of Sport & Exercise Psychology, 1,* 160–183.

Masters, R. S. W., Maxwell, J. P., & Eves, F. F. (2009). Marginally perceptible outcome feedback, motor learning and implicit processes. *Consciousness & Cognition, 18,* 639–645.

Masters, R. S. W., Pall, H. S., MacMahon, K. M. A., & Eves, F. F. (2007). Duration of Parkinson disease is associated with an increased propensity for "reinvestment." *Neurorehabilitation & Neural Repair, 21,* 123–126.

Masters, R. S. W., Poolton, J. M., & Maxwell, J. P. (2008). Stable implicit motor processes despite aerobic locomotor fatigue. *Consciousness & Cognition, 17*, 335–338.

Masters, R. S. W., Poolton, J. M., Maxwell, J. P., & Raab, M. (2008). Implicit motor learning and complex decision making in time constrained environments. *Journal of Motor Behavior, 40*, 71–79.

Maxwell, J. P., Masters, R. S. W., & Eves, F. F. (2000). From novice to knowhow: A longitudinal study of implicit motor learning. *Journal of Sport Sciences, 18*, 111–120.

Maxwell, J. P., Masters, R. S. W., & Eves, F. F. (2003). The role of working memory in motor learning and performance. *Consciousness & Cognition, 12*, 376–402.

Maxwell, J. P., Masters, R. S. W., Kerr, E., & Weedon, E. (2001). The implicit benefit of learning without errors. *Quarterly Journal of Experimental Psychology, 54A*, 1049–1058.

Miyake, A., Friedman, N. P., Emerson, M. J., Witzki, A. H., Howerter, A., & Wager, T. D. (2000). The unity and diversity of executive functions and their contributions to complex "frontal lobe" tasks: A latent variable analysis. *Cognitive Psychology, 41*, 49–100.

Mullen, R., & Hardy, L. (2000). State anxiety and motor performance: Testing the conscious processing hypothesis. *Journal of Sport Sciences, 18*, 785–799.

Mullen, R., Hardy, L., & Oldham, A. (2007). Implicit and explicit control of motor actions: Revisiting some early evidence. *British Journal of Psychology, 98*, 141–156.

Mullen, R., Hardy, L., & Tattersall, A. (2005). The effects of anxiety on motor performance: A test of the conscious processing hypothesis. *Journal of Sport & Exercise Psychology, 27*, 212–225.

Nissen, M. J., & Bullemer, P. (1987). Attentional requirements of learning: Evidence from performance measures. *Cognitive Psychology, 19*, 1–32.

Nunez, P. L. (1995). *Neocortical dynamics and human EEG rhythms.* New York: Oxford University Press.

Ohlsson, S. (1996). Learning from performance errors. *Psychological Review, 103*, 241–262.

Ong, N. T., Bowcock, A., & Hodges, N. J. (2010). Manipulations to the timing and type of instructions to examine motor skill performance under pressure. *Frontiers in Movement Science & Sport Psychology, 1.* doi: 10.3389/fpsyg.2010.00196.

Orrell, A. J., Eves, F. F., & Masters, R. S. W. (2006). Motor learning of a dynamic balancing task after stroke: Implicit implications for stroke rehabilitation. *Physical Therapy, 86*, 369–380.

Orrell, A. J., Eves, F. F., Masters, R. S. W., & MacMahon, K. M. A. (2007). Implicit sequence learning processes after unilateral stroke. *Neuropsychological Rehabilitation, 17*, 335–354.

Pew, R. W. (1974). Human perceptuo-motor performance. In Kantowitz, B. H. (Ed.), *Human information processing: Tutorials in performance and cognition.* New York: Erlbaum.

Poolton, J., Masters, R. S. W., & Maxwell, J. P. (2005). The relationship between initial errorless learning conditions and subsequent performance. *Human Movement Sciences, 24*, 362–378.

Poolton, J. M., Masters, R. S. W., & Maxwell, J. (2006). The influence of analogy learning on decision-making in table tennis: Evidence from behavioural data. *Psychology of Sport & Exercise, 7*, 677–688.

Poolton, J. M., Masters, R. S. W., & Maxwell, J. P. (2007a). Development of a culturally appropriate analogy for implicit motor learning in a Chinese population. *Sport Psychologist, 21*, 375–382.

Poolton, J. M., Masters, R. S. W., & Maxwell, J. P. (2007b). Passing thoughts on the evolutionary stability of implicit motor behaviour: Performance retention under physiological fatigue. *Consciousness & Cognition, 16*, 456–468.

Poulter, D. R., Jackson, R. C., Wann, J. P., & Berry, D. C. (2005). Perceptual anticipation and awareness: Learning to predict soccer penalty kick direction. *Human Movement Science, 24*, 345–361.

Pothos, M. E. (2007). Theories of artificial grammar learning. *Psychological Bulletin, 133*, 227–244.

Prather, D. C. (1971). Trial-and-error versus errorless learning: Training, transfer and stress. *American Journal of Psychology, 84*, 377–386.

Rabbitt, P. M. (1967). Time to detect errors as a function of factors affecting choice-response time. *Acta Psychologia, 27*, 131–142.

Reber, A. S. (1967). Implicit learning of artificial grammars. *Journal of Verbal Learning & Verbal Behavior, 6*, 855–863.

Reber, A. S. (1989). Implicit learning and tacit knowledge. *Journal of Experimental Psychology: General, 118*, 219–235.

Reber, A. S. (1992). The cognitive unconscious: An evolutionary perspective. *Consciousness & Cognition, 1*, 93–113.

Schacter, D. L. (1987). Implicit memory: History and current status. *Journal of Experimental Psychology: Learning, Memory, & Cognition, 13*, 501–518.

Schustack, M. W., & Anderson, J. R. (1979) Effects of analogy to prior knowledge on memory for new information. *Journal of Verbal Learning and Verbal Behavior, 18*, 565–583.

Seger, C. A. (1994). Implicit learning. *Psychological Bulletin, 115*, 163–196.

Shanks, D. R., & St. John, M. F. (1994). Characteristics of dissociable human learning systems. *Behavioral & Brain Sciences, 17*, 367–447.

Shiffrin, R. M., & Schneider, W. (1977). Controlled and automatic human information processing II: Perceptual learning, automatic attending, and a general theory. *Psychological Review, 84*, 127–190.

Springer, S. P., & Deutsch, G. (1998). *Left brain right brain.* New York: Freeman/Worth.

Stapleton, T., Asburn, A., & Stack, E. (2001). A pilot study of attention deficits, balance control and falls in the subacute stage following stroke. *Clinical Rehabilitation, 15*, 437–444.

Sun, R., Merrill, E., & Peterson, T. (2001). From implicit skills to explicit knowledge: A bottom-up model of skill learning. *Cognitive Science, 25*, 203–244.

Sun, R., Slusarz, P., & Terry, C. (2005). The interaction of the explicit and the implicit in skill learning: A dual-process approach. *Psychological Review, 112*, 159–192.

Svartdal, F. (1995). When feedback contingencies and rules compete: Testing a boundary condition for verbal control of instrumental performance. *Learning & Motivation, 26*, 221–238.

Tse, A. C. Y., Masters, R. S. W., Whitehill, T., & Ma, E. P. M. (2012). The use of analogy in speech motor learning. *International Journal of Speech Learning & Pathology, 14*, 84–90.

Vinter, A., & Perruchet, P. (1999). Isolating unconscious influences: The neutral parameter procedure. *Quarterly Journal of Experimental Psychology, 52A*, 857–875.

Willingham, D. B. (1998). A neuropsychological theory of motor skill learning. *Psychological Review, 105*, 558–84.

Willingham, D. B., Nissen, M. J., & Bullemer, P. (1989). On the development of procedural knowledge. *Journal of Experimental Psychology: Learning, Memory, & Cognition, 15*, 1047–1060.

Wong, T., Masters, R. S. W., Maxwell, J. P., & Abernethy, B. A. (2008). Reinvestment and falls in community-dwelling older adults. *Neurorehabilitation & Neural Repair, 22*, 410–414.

Wong, W. L., Masters, R. S. W., Maxwell, J. P., & Abernethy, B. (2009). The role of reinvestment in walking and falling in community-dwelling older adults. *Journal of the American Geriatrics Society, 57*, 920–922.

Zanone, P. G., Monno, A., Temprado, J. J., & Laurent, M. (2001). Shared dynamics of attentional cost and pattern stability in the control of bimanual coordination. *Human Movement Science, 20,* 765–789.

Zhu, F. F., Poolton, J. M., Wilson, M. R., Maxwell, J. P., & Masters, R. S. W. (2011a). Implicit motor learning promotes low verbal-analytical involvement in motor performance: Neural co-activation as a yardstick of movement specific reinvestment. *Biological Psychology, 87,* 66–73.

Zhu, F. F., Poolton, J. M., Wilson, M. R., Maxwell, J. P., & Masters, R. S. W. (2011b). Implicit motor learning promotes neural efficiency during laparoscopy. *Surgical Endoscopy and Other Interventional Techniques, 25,* 2950–2955.

Part II

Optimizing practice conditions

5 Contextual interference

Generalizability and limitations

Timothy D. Lee

Interest in practice schedules has motivated motor learning research for many years. Distribution of practice was an early example, in which longer rest intervals, inserted between periods of practice, produced better retention than short rest intervals. The distribution of practice effect had implications for theory (e.g., Ammons, 1947; Hull, 1943) and practical applications for training efficiency and effectiveness in industry (e.g., Baddeley & Longman, 1978) and sport (e.g., Dail & Christina, 2004), and remained a driving force in motor learning research for several decades. The distribution of practice effect had a particularly large influence on the learning of continuous motor skills, such as tracking, but the effect was smaller when rest periods were applied to discrete skills (Lee & Genovese, 1988).

Researchers interested in the learning of discrete motor skills frequently turn their attention to the contextual interference (CI) effect. Similar to distribution of practice, CI concerns how practice is structured during the training environment, but in contrast to distribution of practice, in which only one task was typically practiced, CI concerns how the organization of practice for multiple skills influences performance and learning. The implications of CI research for motor learning theory and applications to training are many and are discussed in this chapter.

What is the CI effect?

Perhaps the best way to understand the CI effect is to describe how it is studied, and there is no better point to begin than with Shea and Morgan (1979). Their study was straightforward: two groups of participants responded to colored light stimuli with one of three patterns of arm movements. The goal was to respond to a stimulus by picking up a tennis ball from the apparatus base, knocking over three of the six small barriers located on the base, and then replacing the ball. Three light colors were used as stimuli, each associated with a specific movement pattern (defined by the order of barriers). The task goal was to respond to the light quickly and accurately (i.e., correct sequence of barrier contacts), with reaction time, movement time, and response errors as the dependent variables. Participants in the experiment practiced each of the three tasks for 18 trials, for a total of 54 trials. Half of the participants in each group returned for retention tests after one of two delay periods: one subgroup after a brief delay (10 min), the other after a much longer delay (10 days).

The primary experimental manipulation was the practice schedule by which participants completed their trials during the learning period. One group, the *blocked-practice order group*, completed all 18 trials for any one pattern before another block of trials on a different pattern was undertaken. The other group, the *random practice-order group*, completed only one, or at most two, trials of any pattern before practice on another pattern was undertaken. The order of practice for the random group was unsystematic, except that no more than two trials of any one pattern was completed in succession and that three trials of each pattern were completed after every set of nine trials.

The results of the Shea and Morgan (1979) study for response time are illustrated in Figure 5.1. During the practice period (left side of Figure 5.1), the blocked group attained a large performance advantage compared with the random group within the first block of nine trials, and this performance advantage was maintained throughout the entire practice period. The response times demonstrated by the blocked and random groups reflected large differences, perhaps due to (a) enhanced performance for the blocked group caused by repeatedly performing the same task, (b) a decrement for the random group caused by the frequent task switching, or (c) some combination of these two influences. However, the differences between the blocked and random groups exhibited during the practice period could not be described as being due to differences in *learning*; inferences about learning could only be made by examining the impact of these practice schedules in tests of retention (for a more complete discussion of the distinction between performance and learning, see Schmidt & Lee, 2011). Shea and Morgan conducted two retention tests that allowed a more appropriate examination of any differences that may have occurred because of learning. The practice groups performed these retention test trials using both random and blocked test orders.

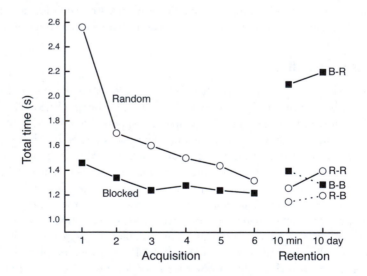

Figure 5.1 Results of the Shea and Morgan (1979) study.

The results of the retention tests are presented in the right side of Figure 5.1. These retention test scores can be considered from two different perspectives. First, from a perspective that considers each group's retention performance *relative to the end of the practice period*, the blocked group's performance diminished slightly when tested in blocked-ordered retention trials (designated with the "B-B" label in Figure 5.1), but dropped off dramatically in randomly ordered retention trials (B-R). In contrast, the random group maintained their level of performance when tested in randomly ordered trials (R-R), and improved their level of performance in the blocked-ordered retention trials (R-B). However, a more direct comparison of the effects of these practice schedules is from a perspective of their *relative impact on retention*. For blocked-ordered retention trials, previous practice in the random practice schedule (R-B) provided a small but important advantage compared with having practiced in the blocked schedule (B-B). For the randomly ordered retention trials, having previously practiced in the random schedule (R-R) provided a rather large advantage relative to the blocked schedule group (B-R).

Shea and Morgan (1979) found that blocked practice facilitated *performance during* acquisition trials, but that the random group facilitated *learning as a result* of these practice trials. This pattern of results has become synonymous with what is now called the CI effect (after Battig, 1979) and greatly puzzled researchers who had been conducting motor learning research. After all, how could a variable that had such a large impact on acquisition performance have an equally large, *but opposite*, effect on learning? Such an effect was considered counterintuitive, if not bizarre, on the basis of theoretical and practical accounts of motor learning at the time.

On the generality of the CI effect

Hundreds of studies have been performed by researchers since the time that Shea and Morgan (1979) published their findings, and reviews of this work abound (Barreiros, Figueiredo, & Godinho, 2007; Brady, 1998, 2004; Lee & Simon, 2004; Magill & Hall, 1990; Merbah & Meulemans, 2011). Many of these reviews provide excellent insights into the limitations of the CI effect. The intention in this chapter is to present some key findings in the literature that illustrate the generalizability of the CI effect and to identify, specifically, some factors to which CI is *not limited*. Shea and Morgan (1979) used a laboratory task that was learned in a very short practice period and demonstrated differences among young adults in a speeded movement task. A survey of the literature conducted since Shea and Morgan's experiment was published reveals that the impact of their findings has extended well beyond these modest beginnings. The goal is to impress upon the reader that these effects apply *not just to* (1) laboratory tasks practiced in a single session, (2) task outcomes, (3) young adults, (4) *motor* learning, and (5) learners who are expecting the effect. The intention is to summarize evidence for an effect that is both wide-ranging and cross-disciplinary – one that touches upon a fundamental feature of human learning.

1. CI is not limited just to laboratory tasks, practiced in a single session

A hallmark of an important effect in a field of study is its generalizability beyond the laboratory, and research by Goode and Magill (1986) represented an early extension of CI research outside the laboratory. The study compared novices who practiced three types of badminton serves (long, short, and drive serves) for nine sessions, over a 3-week period, before performing retention and transfer tests. Goode and Magill used methods for the blocked practice group that were slightly different from the Shea and Morgan procedures: practice of one type of serve was conducted in a blocked order *within* a session, but *repeated* once each week, resulting in three sessions of blocked practice on each serve, separated by blocked practice sessions on the other serves. In the Shea and Morgan study there was no return to a task once a practice block had been completed. Thus, Goode and Magill used a less "extreme" form of blocked practice than had Shea and Morgan – "extreme" in the sense of a continuum, where at one end a task is practiced repeatedly for a series of trials and then never practiced again (which is typical of many training regimes, sport skill classes, and university courses in which a limited amount of time is available for instruction). Nevertheless, this less extreme form of blocked practice resulted in acquisition performance that was superior to random practice during the acquisition sessions, but inferior to random practice in a retention test. Moreover, a transfer test, in which serves were made from the left service side (all practice sessions were performed from the right service court), produced much better performance by the random group than the blocked group. Thus, among the many significant contributions of this study was the demonstration of a CI effect in a recreational task, over multiple practice sessions, using valid measures of learning, and despite the fact that they used a less extreme form of blocked practice.

Another frequently cited study of random and blocked practice reported findings in which a sport skill (baseball batting) involved participants who were already highly experienced in the task. Hall, Domingues, and Cavazos (1994) recruited members of a collegiate baseball team and gave them "extra" batting practice twice a week over a period of 6 weeks. Each player received 15 pitches of three different types (fastballs, curveballs, and change-ups), ordered in blocked or random schedules during each batting practice session. A group of controls did not engage in the extra practice sessions. The findings of the Hall et al. (1994) study are presented in Figure 5.2.

Several points should be noted when reviewing the data presented in Figure 5.2. First, blocked practice was conducted in an even *less* "extreme" manner than in Goode and Magill. Blocked practice on each of the pitch types was conducted within *each* of the practice sessions, and still performance during the two recorded practice sessions was better than performance by participants in the random group. Thus, perhaps it should not be surprising that retention performance (in both blocked and randomly ordered trials), was significantly better by the blocked group than by the control group, which had received no extra batting practice during the 6-week period. Nevertheless, this blocked-practice group performed both retention tests more poorly than members of the random group, replicating the essential findings of Shea and Morgan (and Goode & Magill, 1986). Another important

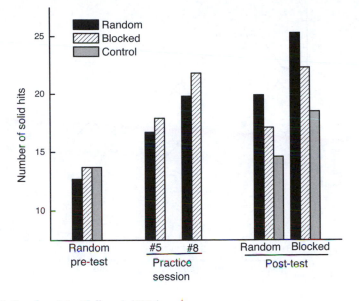

Figure 5.2 Results of the Hall et al. (1994) study.

finding to remember is that these results were produced with members of a collegiate baseball team, who, presumably, had less "room" for improvement than the novices used in the Shea–Morgan and Goode–Magill studies.

2. CI is not limited just to task outcomes

The CI effect in Shea and Morgan (1979) was an observed reduction in response time and errors. For Goode and Magill (1986) the outcome measured was the final location of the badminton serves; for Hall et al. (1994) it was the number of baseballs contacted with a solid hit. A question that remains unanswered from these studies is whether CI represents more than just an effect on observable task outcomes. Does CI have a direct influence on changes in movement control? A study by Tsutsui, Lee, and Hodges (1998) suggests so.

Studies of bimanual coordination reveal that rhythmic movements of the upper limbs tend to fall naturally into one of two coordination timing patterns – in-phase (or 0° relative-phase timing) and anti-phase (180° relative-phase timing) – but that other timing patterns can be acquired with practice (for review, see Kelso, 1995; Swinnen & Wenderoth, 2004). In Tsutsui et al. (1998, Experiment 2), participants learned to perform bimanual timing patterns of 45°, 90°, and 135° relative phase. Participants in the blocked group practiced 45 trials of one pattern on the first day, 45 trials of another pattern on a second day, and 45 trials of the remaining pattern on the third day (an "extreme" type of blocked practice, as in Shea & Morgan). Participants in the random group performed 15 trials of each pattern on each of the three practice days. As revealed in Figure 5.3, the first block of 15 trials on each day of practice was performed with similar overall relative timing error by the random

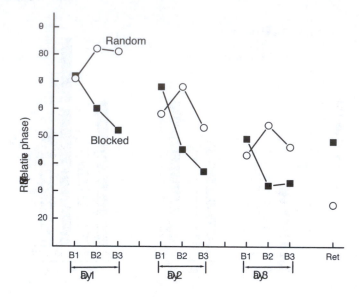

Figure 5.3 Results of the Tsutsui et al. (1998) study.

and blocked groups (remember that the blocked group was practicing a previously unlearned pattern at the start of each day of practice). However, trials 16–45 (blocks 2 and 3) were performed better by the blocked group on each practice day, consistent with the typical CI effect in acquisition. A retention test, performed 1 week later, demonstrated that random practice resulted in a significant and permanent coordination learning advantage, relative to the blocked group. That is a relatively permanent improvement in the capability to perform coordination patterns that were previously not part of the learner's repertoire had been facilitated by random practice.

Neuroscientific evidence also suggests that blocked and random practice have different manifestations in terms of brain activity. In a study by Cross, Schmitt, and Grafton (2007), groups of blocked-ordered and random-ordered participants practiced a finger-sequencing task and found typical CI effects during acquisition trials and in retention. In addition, Cross et al. examined pre-movement study times: the amount of time that an individual voluntarily chose to prepare for the upcoming trial. Replicating previous studies (Immink & Wright, 1998; Lee, Magill, & Weeks, 1985), participants who engaged in random practice self-selected longer study times prior to movement execution than did individuals during blocked practice. However, as a key additional feature during these study times, Cross et al. (2007) examined the blood flow activity in selected regions of the brain using fMRI (functional magnetic resonance imaging) techniques. These fMRI data were collected during the early and later stages of acquisition performance and revealed considerable differences in the regions of the brain that are known to be involved in movement preparation. Levels of fMRI activity are believed to be strongly associated with mental processing, leading Cross et al. to suspect that random practice activated greater movement preparation processes during practice than in blocked practice, especially late in learning. These behavioral and neurophysiological findings were subsequently replicated and extended by Wymbs and Grafton (2009) using a within-participant design.

One of the brain regions identified by Cross et al. (2007) and Wymbs and Grafton (2009) was the M1 (primary motor cortex) region, ipsilateral to the limb involved in learning. In a follow-up experiment, Cohen, Cross, Wymbs, and Grafton (2009) paired TMS (transcranial magnetic stimulation) to the ipsilateral M1 with the presentation of the movement stimuli with the intention of disrupting movement preparatory processing during random practice. Compared with practiced movement sequence controls (i.e., without paired TMS pulses), the patterns learned under simultaneously paired TMS were performed more poorly on a retention test conducted 1 day later, suggesting that the TMS had disrupted the learning of preparatory processes during practice. A potential limitation of the Cohen et al. (2009) study was the absence of blocked control groups that did or did not receive the TMS during practice trials. Lin, Fisher, Winstein, Wu, and Gordon (2008) and Lin, Winstein, Fisher, and Wu (2010) included these important control conditions and extended the Cohen et al. findings. Lin et al. (2008, 2010) found that the random-practice advantage in retention was eliminated when TMS was applied to the M1 region, contralateral to the arm practiced, immediately *after* trial feedback was presented. However, the typical CI effect was observed in learners who received either no TMS or a sham TMS procedure (in which an auditory click was accompanied by a slight pressure on the scalp, instead of the TMS). Thus, despite differences between the studies reviewed above in terms of where the TMS was applied (ipsilateral or contralateral to the moving arm) and when it was delivered (during movement preparation or after feedback was delivered), application of TMS to the M1 appeared to disrupt the retention of movement patterns practiced in a random order. The evidence from these fMRI and TMS studies suggests that CI has an effect not only on the behavioral expression of motor learning, but also on specific neural activities that underlie this expression, and implicate specific planning and/or reflective processes as the locus of the CI effect. More will be presented about these theoretical issues later in the chapter.

3. CI is not limited just to young adults

Two studies, one with children and the other with older adults, demonstrate that CI is not limited just to the learning of motor skills by healthy, young university students. In three experiments reported by Ste-Marie, Clark, Findlay, and Latimer (2004), children between the ages of 5 and 8 years practiced handwriting various characters according to blocked or random schedules. In one study, for example, young children practiced the individual letters "h," "a," and "y" and were required to perform a transfer test in which the word "hay" was written. The group who had practiced these individual letters in a random order performed "hay" much faster than the blocked group, yet without a sacrifice in writing quality.

Towards the other end of the age continuum, Lin, Wu, Udompholkul, and

Knowlton (2010) examined CI effects in younger adults (mean age 30 years) and older adults (mean age 65 years). Random and blocked subgroups of both ages performed three 4-element (stimulus–response) reaction-time sequences over two consecutive days of practice and a retention test 3 days later. Although the younger adults performed faster overall than the older adults, typical CI effects were found for both: blocked practice resulted in faster response times than random practice during acquisition, but the random subgroups performed faster in retention than the blocked subgroups. A similar, beneficial effect on retention for learning ATM (automatic teller machine) procedures following random practice was found in younger and older adults by Jamieson and Rogers (2000). The above studies suggest that CI effects are not limited to young adults serving as participants in a motor learning experiment. Furthermore, the Jamieson and Rogers study suggests that the CI effect may apply to other types of learning, which is examined next.

4. CI is not limited just to motor learning

An interesting, and more recent, trend in the literature has been the study of CI in research areas not specifically related to motor learning (see also Schmidt & Bjork, 1992). For instance, participants in Kornell and Bjork's (2008) study learned to identify 12 painters by studying six samples of their works of art. Participants studied half of the artists' samples in a blocked order and the others were studied in an interleaved order (a more "structured" type of random practice). Following this study period, the participants were presented with 48 previously unseen samples of the artists' work in a random order, and their task was to select the correct identity of the artist from a multiple choice list (followed by corrective feedback). The results of these transfer trials are presented in Figure 5.4, with the results of the first image from each artist presented in "test block 1," and so forth. The results revealed a large advantage for having previously studied the artists' samples in an interleaved order. Moreover, this advantage persisted throughout the 48 transfer trials, despite the corrective, augmented feedback that was provided after each test. Similar findings were found in a follow-up experiment that included older adults (mean age 77 years) as participants (Kornell, Castel, Eich, & Bjork, 2010).

Other examples of the beneficial impact of random practice in non-motor learning tasks have now been reported. Carlson and Yaure (1990) found that individuals learning Boolean logic rules by switching between problems that used a different function were faster in problem-solving transfer trials than participants who repeatedly practiced using the same function. Rohrer and Taylor (2007; Taylor & Rohrer, 2007) found improved transfer accuracy following random practice of problems in mathematics compared with blocked practice. Helsdingen, van Gog, and van Merriënboer (2011a, 2011b) found random advantages following practice on complex, problem-solving judgment tasks. These findings extend the range of tasks, perceptual, motor, and cognitive, for which random practice advantages have been demonstrated.

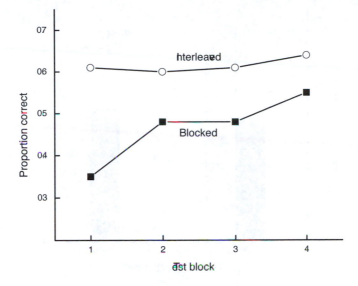

Figure 5.4 Results of the Kornell and Bjork (2008) study.

5. CI is not limited to learners who expect the effect

A methodological issue that could undermine all of the findings listed above would be validated if participants who practiced in random and blocked schedules *expected* to perform in retention tests at a certain level, and then did so. Such a methodological artifact, a type of expectancy bias effect, might suggest that individuals learned to the degree that simply matched their preconceived expectations. For example, if participants in a random practice group expected to learn better than those in a blocked group, and did so, then perhaps the findings are at least partially confounded by this expectancy bias. Simon and Bjork (2001), however, not only refuted this suggestion, but found that learners performed in retention tests at a level that was in stark contrast to their expectations.

In Simon and Bjork's (2001) study, random and blocked practice schedule participants underwent typical experimental protocols, and replicated the classic CI findings in acquisition and retention performance. During the acquisition phase learners were asked to predict, in terms of performance error, how accurate they expected their retention performance to be 1 day later. Also, when these learners did return a day later, they were asked once again to predict their performance on the retention test. Not surprisingly, the participants' predictions about their future retention performance, made during the acquisition trials, corresponded closely with their actual performance in these acquisition trials. One day later, learners in the blocked group still maintained that they would perform well in the retention test, and their predicted judgments of retention error were much less (i.e., at a performance level that was better) than the learners in the random group. However, as illustrated in Figure 5.5, members of the blocked group were clearly overconfident

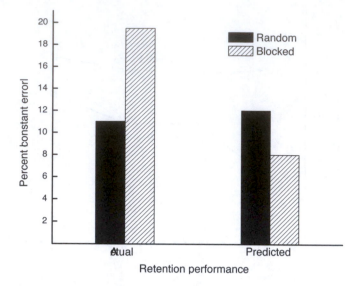

Figure 5.5 Results of the Simon and Bjork (2001) study.

in their ability to perform the retention test, and members of the random group were, perhaps, surprised by their retention performance.

A similar and dramatic level of misattribution about learning was present in the Kornell and Bjork (2008) experiments discussed earlier. Kornell and Bjork asked participants to identify artists from paintings presented during blocked and interleaved samples of the artists' work (their participants saw six artists in a blocked order and the other six artists in an interleaved order). After the four test blocks had been completed, Kornell and Bjork told the participants about the experimental manipulations (blocking vs. interleaving the study paintings) and asked which method they perceived to be more effective. Although interleaved practice resulted in test trial performance that was far superior to blocked practice, Kornell and Bjork found that 78% of their participants (94 out of 120 individuals) believed that they had learned more in the blocked trials than during interleaved practice (a similar result was also found in Kornell et al., 2010).

These findings suggest that CI is *not* a manifestation of expected outcomes, but in fact occurs *despite* the actual outcomes of the test trials. The vast majority of participants remained convinced that blocked study would be better than interleaved study, even though the reverse was actually true. The conclusions of Kornell and Bjork suggest that learners typically believe the "illusion that a sense of ease or fluency accompanies effective learning, whereas a sense of difficulty signifies ineffective learning . . . [in many] types of learning, spacing appears to be sometimes, if not always, a desirable difficulty" (Kornell & Bjork, 2008, p. 591).

To sum up, the impact of the Shea and Morgan (1979) experiment provided a modest start to what has become an area of intensive research in motor learning.

During this time, the effects of blocked and random practice have been extended to different population groups, tested in a variety of skills, demonstrating changes not only in in task outcomes but also in the learners' central nervous system, and despite the fact that the learners themselves were probably highly skeptical of the results of these studies.

What *are* the limits to the CI effect?

The evidence presented above might appear to suggest that the CI effect is an enormously robust effect with magic-bullet implications for learning. This is not so. Numerous researchers have failed to find beneficial effects of random practice when compared with blocked practice, particularly in studies involving the acquisition of sport-specific skills (e.g., see Brady, 1998). Some studies found a random practice advantage in retention or transfer in the absence of a detrimental effect in acquisition, leading them to question whether or not there is such a thing as a "typical CI effect." The order of retention and transfer trials seems to have a moderating effect on the size of random/blocked differences in some studies, but not always. Moreover, the CI effect appears to be larger when examined in discrete skills than in continuous skills, but this is not always the case either (e.g., as in the Tsutsui et al., 1998 study discussed earlier). Issues of statistical power may account for some of these discrepancies, but it is doubtful that this explanation extends very far.

There are two general conclusions however, that appear to have few exceptions:

1 When *acquisition performance* differences exist between individuals who practice according to blocked and random schedules, the advantage almost always favors the blocked practice group. Only rarely does random practice exceed blocked practice in acquisition performance outcomes (e.g., accuracy, speed, quality, and so on).
2 When *learning* differences exist between individuals who practice according to blocked and random schedules, the advantage almost always favors the random practice group in tests of retention and transfer.

So, what are these "almost always" exceptions? Some investigations have suggested that a blocked schedule is superior to random when the amount of practice is very limited. For example, in Shea, Kohl, and Indermill's (1990) findings, retention following blocked practice was better than after random practice when each task to be learned was performed for only 10 trials each. The reverse (i.e., the typical CI effect) was found, however, when retention was assessed following 80 trials of practice on each task. These findings, along with others, suggest that blocked practice may be more beneficial than random practice when the demands on learning are made particularly difficult as a function of the amount of practice, the nature of the task, and/or the capabilities of the learner. These (and other) exceptions and detailed findings are reviewed more thoroughly in Wulf and Shea (2002) and Guadagnoli and Lee (2004).

Theoretical implications of CI

A number of hypotheses for the CI effect have been suggested since the original publication of Shea and Morgan's results, each one emphasizing the cognitive operations of the learner as an integral part of the learning process. Two ideas in particular, seem to have maintained their presence in the literature.

One view, sometimes called the *elaboration and distinctiveness* hypothesis (Shea & Morgan, 1979; Shea & Zimny, 1983), suggests that the CI effect is caused by the contrast that occurs when multiple tasks are practiced together. In blocked practice, tasks are practiced virtually in isolation, and therefore there is little opportunity to gain knowledge from the comparison and contrastive nature of practicing sets of task combinations in succession, as in the case of random practice. The retention difference is due to the differences in elaborative and distinctive processing that are promoted in random practice, and/or degraded by blocked practice, and the result that these processes contribute to the durability of the memories.

The other view, sometimes called the *forgetting and reconstruction* hypothesis (Lee & Magill, 1983, 1985), suggests that the CI effect is due to the planning processes that are influenced by the spacing of practice (Cuddy & Jacoby, 1982). In blocked practice, short-term forgetting due to memory decay and/or interference is minimal, which limits the amount of new planning that is required in repeated practice. Short-term forgetting is abundant during random practice, requiring that learners undertake more extensive planning operations. The retention effect is due to the differences in the amount of planning that is promoted in random practice and/or diminished by blocked practice; greater planning processes enhance learning (see also the TMS and fMRI evidence reviewed above).

Although the two views differ in the details of their hypotheses about learning mechanisms, they share commonalities too. For example, cognitive operations provide the basis for both views, and in particular the role of memory processes, both short- and long-term, are the foundation for the learning differences that distinguish between random and blocked practice schedules.

Future directions for CI research

Experiments examining CI using neuroscience methods (e.g., fMRI and TMS) have begun (see 'On the generality of the CI effect' above) and hold the potential to provide new evidence that will confirm or refute existing theoretical positions, or provide new theories for the reasons why learning is different under random and blocked practice schedules. At the same time, new behavioral paradigms are being developed to explore CI. Some researchers have suggested that practice schedules that are specifically tailored to the individual needs of the learner can be as effective as, or more so than, random practice. Several different methods have been used to tailor these practice schedules, and include (1) self-selected practice methods, in which the learner is provided with the opportunity to define the order in which tasks are practiced (Hodges, Edwards, Luttin, & Bowcock, 2011; Keetch & Lee, 2007); (2) reference-based contingencies, in which the decision to repeat the same task or switch to a new task is based on a performance algorithm (Simon, Lee, &

Cullen, 2008); and (3) adapted practice schedules, which are specifically tailored to provide more or less practice as needed, and which change the difficulty of the task based on the learner's progress (Choi, Qi, Gordon, & Schweighofer, 2008). The study of CI as an expanded study of effects influencing the acquisition of motor, perceptual and cognitive tasks is likely to continue to grow. In more than 30 years of study since Shea and Morgan (1979) first reported their findings, CI continues to remain a "hot topic" in the literature, with no signs of cooling down in the near future.

References

Ammons, R. B. (1947). Acquisition of motor skill: I. Quantitative analysis and theoretical formulation. *Psychological Review, 54*, 263–281.

Baddeley, A. D., & Longman, D. J. A. (1978). The influence of length and frequency of training session on the rate of learning to type. *Ergonomics, 21*, 627–635.

Barreiros, J., Figueiredo, T., & Godinho, M. (2007). The contextual interference effect in applied settings. *European Physical Education Review, 13*, 195–208.

Battig, W. F. (1979). The flexibility of human memory. In Cermak, L. S., & Craik, F. I. M. (Eds.), *Levels of processing in human memory* (pp. 23–44). Hillsdale, NJ: Erlbaum.

Brady, F. (1998). A theoretical and empirical review of the contextual interference effect and the learning of motor skills. *Quest, 50*, 266–293.

Brady, F. (2004). Contextual interference: A meta-analytic study. *Perceptual and Motor Skills, 99*, 116–126.

Carlson, R. A., & Yaure, R. G. (1990). Practice schedules and the use of component skills in problem solving. *Journal of Experimental Psychology: Learning, Memory, and Cognition, 16*, 484–496.

Choi, Y., Qi, F., Gordon, J., & Schweighofer, N. (2008). Performance-based adaptive schedules enhance motor learning. *Journal of Motor Behavior, 40*, 273–280.

Cohen, N. R., Cross, E. S., Wymbs, N. F., & Grafton, S. T. (2009). Transient disruption of M1 during response planning impairs subsequent offline consolidation. *Experimental Brain Research, 196*, 303–309.

Cross, E. S., Schmitt, P. J., & Grafton, S. T. (2007). Neural substrates of contextual interference during motor learning support a model of active preparation. *Journal of Cognitive Neuroscience, 19*, 1854–1871.

Cuddy, L. J., & Jacoby, L. L. (1982). When forgetting helps memory: An analysis of repetition effects. *Journal of Verbal Learning and Verbal Behavior, 21*, 451–467.

Dail, T. K., & Christina, R. W. (2004). Distribution of practice and metacognition in learning and retention of a discrete motor task. *Research Quarterly for Exercise and Sport, 75*, 148–155.

Goode, S., & Magill, R. A. (1986). Contextual interference effects in learning three badminton serves. *Research Quarterly for Exercise and Sport, 57*, 308–314.

Guadagnoli, M. A., & Lee, T. D. (2004). Challenge point: A framework for conceptualizing the effects of various practice conditions in motor learning. *Journal of Motor Behavior, 36*, 212–224.

Hall, K. G., Domingues, D. A., & Cavazos, R. (1994). Contextual interference effects with skilled baseball players. *Perceptual and Motor Skills, 78*, 835–841.

Helsdingen, A. S., van Gog, T., & van Merriënboer, J. J. G. (2011a). The effects of practice schedule and critical thinking prompts on learning and transfer of a complex judgment task. *Journal of Educational Psychology, 103*, 383–398.

Helsdingen, A. S., van Gog, T., & van Merriënboer, J. J. G. (2011b). The effects of practice schedule on learning a complex judgment task. *Learning and Instruction, 21*, 126–136.

Hodges, N. J., Edwards, C., Luttin, S., & Bowcock, A. (2011). Learning from the experts: Gaining insights into best practice during the acquisition of three novel motor skills. *Research Quarterly for Exercise and Sport, 82*, 178–187.

Hull, C. L. (1943). *Principles of behavior.* New York: Appleton-Century-Crofts.

Immink, M. A., & Wright, D. L. (1998). Contextual interference: A response planning account. *Quarterly Journal of Experimental Psychology, 51A*, 735–754.

Jamieson, B. A., & Rogers, W. A. (2000). Age-related effects of blocked and random practice schedules on learning a new technology. *Journal of Gerontology: Psychological Sciences, 55B*, P343–P353.

Keetch, K. M., & Lee, T. D. (2007). The effect of self-regulated and experimenter-imposed practice schedules on motor learning for tasks of varying difficulty. *Research Quarterly for Exercise and Sport, 78*, 476–486.

Kelso, J. A. S. (1995). *Dynamic patterns: The self-organization of brain and behavior.* Cambridge, MA: MIT Press.

Kornell, N., & Bjork, R. A. (2008). Learning concepts and categories: Is spacing the "enemy of induction"? *Psychological Science, 19*, 585–592.

Kornell, N., Castel, A. D., Eich, T. S., & Bjork, R. A. (2010). Spacing as the friend of both memory and induction in young and older adults. *Psychology and Aging, 25*, 498–502.

Lee, T. D., & Genovese, E. D. (1988). Distribution of practice in motor skill acquisition: Learning and performance effects reconsidered. *Research Quarterly for Exercise and Sport, 59*, 277–287.

Lee, T. D., & Magill, R. A. (1983). The locus of contextual interference in motor-skill acquisition. *Journal of Experimental Psychology: Learning, Memory, and Cognition, 9*, 730–746.

Lee, T. D., & Magill, R. A. (1985). Can forgetting facilitate skill acquisition? In Goodman, D., Wilberg, R. B., & Franks, I. M. (Eds.), *Differing perspectives in motor learning, memory, and control* (pp. 3–22). Amsterdam: Elsevier.

Lee, T. D., Magill, R. A., & Weeks, D. J. (1985). Influence of practice schedule on testing schema theory predictions in adults. *Journal of Motor Behavior, 17*, 283–299.

Lee, T. D., & Simon, D. (2004). Contextual interference. In Williams, A. M., & Hodges, N. J. (Eds.), *Skill acquisition in sport: Research, theory and practice* (pp. 29–44). London: Routledge.

Lin, C. H., Fisher, B. E., Winstein, C. J., Wu, A. D., & Gordon, J. (2008). Contextual interference effect: elaborative processing or forgetting–reconstruction? A post hoc analysis of transcranial magnetic stimulation–induced effects on motor learning. *Journal of Motor Behavior, 40*, 578–586.

Lin, C. H., Winstein, C. J., Fisher, B. E., & Wu, A. D. (2010). Neural correlates of the contextual interference effect in motor learning: A transcranial magnetic stimulation investigation. *Journal of Motor Behavior, 42*, 223–232.

Lin, C. H., Wu, A. D., Udompholkul, P., & Knowlton, B. J. (2010). Contextual interference effects in sequence learning for young and older adults. *Psychology and Aging, 25*, 929–939.

Magill, R. A., & Hall, K. G. (1990). A review of the contextual interference effect in motor skill acquisition. *Human Movement Science, 9*, 241–289.

Merbah, S., & Meulemans, T. (2011). Learning a motor skill: Effects of blocked versus random practice. A review. *Psychologica Belgica, 51*, 15–48.

Rohrer, D., & Taylor, K. (2007). The shuffling of mathematics practice problems boosts learning. *Instructional Science, 35*, 481–498.

Schmidt, R. A., & Bjork, R. A. (1992). New conceptualizations of practice: Common principles in three paradigms suggest new concepts for training. *Psychological Science, 3*, 207–217.

Schmidt, R. A., & Lee, T. D. (2011). *Motor control and learning: A behavioral emphasis* (5th edn.). Champaign, IL: Human Kinetics.

Shea, C. H., Kohl, R., & Indermill, C. (1990). Contextual interference: Contributions of practice. *Acta Psychologica, 73*, 145–157.

Shea, J. B., & Morgan, R. L. (1979). CI effects on the acquisition, retention, and transfer of a motor skill. *Journal of Experimental Psychology: Human Learning and Memory, 5*, 179–187.

Shea, J. B., & Zimny, S. T. (1983). Context effects in memory and learning movement information. In Magill, R. A. (Ed.), *Memory and control of action* (pp. 345–366). Amsterdam: Elsevier.

Simon, D. A., & Bjork, R. A. (2001). Metacognition in motor learning. *Journal of Experimental Psychology: Learning, Memory, and Cognition, 27*, 907–912.

Simon, D. A., Lee, T. D., & Cullen, J. D. (2008). Win–shift, lose–stay: Contingent switching and contextual interference in motor learning. *Perceptual and Motor Skills, 107*, 407–418.

Ste-Marie, D. M., Clark, S. E., Findlay, L. C., & Latimer, A. E. (2004). High levels of contextual interference enhance handwriting skill acquisition. *Journal of Motor Behavior, 36*, 115–126.

Swinnen, S. P., & Wenderoth, N. (2004). Two hands, one brain: Cognitive neuroscience of bimanual skill *Trends in Cognitive Sciences, 8*, 18–25.

Taylor, K., & Rohrer, D. (2010). The effects of interleaved practice. *Applied Cognitive Psychology, 24*, 837–848.

Tsutsui, S., Lee, T. D., & Hodges, N. J. (1998). Contextual interference in learning new patterns of bimanual coordination. *Journal of Motor Behavior, 30*, 151–157.

Wulf, G., & Shea, C. H. (2002). Principles derived from the study of simple skills do not generalize to complex skill learning. *Psychonomic Bulletin & Review, 9*, 185–211.

Wymbs, N. F., & Grafton, S. T. (2009). Neural substrates of practice structure that support future off-line learning. *Journal of Neurophysiology, 102*, 2462–2476.

6 Mental imagery, action observation, and skill learning

Aidan Moran, Mark Campbell, Paul Holmes, and Tadhg MacIntyre

Introduction

One of the most remarkable capacities of the mind is its ability to simulate sensations, actions and other types of experience. As Crisp, Birtel, and Meleady (2011) proclaimed recently, "the ability to envisage a world different from that which we know is one of the defining characteristics of human experience" (p. 261). To illustrate a mundane application of this process, if you close your eyes, you should be able to "see" yourself throwing a bright yellow tennis ball up in the air (a visual mental image) and then "feel" yourself bouncing it (a kinaesthetic or "feeling-oriented" mental image). For over a century, researchers have investigated the construct of *mental imagery* or the cognitive simulation process by which we can represent perceptual information in our minds in the absence of appropriate sensory input (Munzert, Lorey, & Zentgraf, 2009). More recently, another mental simulation process that has attracted attention from cognitive neuroscientists and sport psychologists is "motor imagery" (sometimes called "movement imagery"; Holmes, Cumming, & Edwards, 2010) or the mental rehearsal of actions without any overt motor output (see review by Moran, Guillot, MacIntyre, & Collet, in press). Research on motor imagery is important in psychology because it provides an empirical window on consciousness and movement planning, rectifies a relative neglect of non-visual types of mental imagery, and has practical implications for skill learning and skilled performance in special populations (e.g., elite athletes).

Perhaps not surprisingly, mental simulation processes such as motor imagery are crucial to success in sport. This claim is supported by anecdotal, descriptive, and experimental evidence. At the anecdotal level, for example, consider the remarkable imagery skills of Michael Phelps, the 14-times Olympic gold medal winner in swimming (see Figure 6.1).

Explaining his psychological preparation for swimming competitions, he revealed that "I can visualize how I want the perfect race to go. I can see the start, the strokes, the walls, the turns, the finish, the strategy, all of it" (Phelps, 2008a, p. 8). Furthermore, he highlighted his reliance on kinaesthetic imagery when he said that

> swimmers like to say that they can "feel" the water . . . I didn't have to fight the water. Instead, I could feel how I moved in it. How to be balanced. What might make me go faster or slower. (Phelps, 2008b, p. 10)

Figure 6.1 Michael Phelps, the 14-times Olympic gold medal winner in swimming. Courtesy of Inpho Photography.

At the descriptive level, Taylor, Gould, and Rolo (2008) showed that imagery use was one of the strongest predictors of athletic success in a sample of US Olympians. Finally, at the experimental level, Caliari (2008) found that table tennis players who participated in a mental imagery intervention program to rehearse a stroke symbolically (the forehand drive) improved significantly relative to those in a control group. Clearly, mental imagery training can facilitate the learning and performance of sport skills (Weinberg, 2008). Not surprisingly, the value of using mental imagery to rehearse actions and movements has been acknowledged in other fields of skilled performance. For example, in medicine, motor imagery training can enhance surgical performance (Arora et al., 2010, 2011) and is helpful in facilitating upper-limb recovery after stroke (e.g., Braun, Beurskens, Borm, Schack, & Wade, 2006; Nilsen, Gillen, & Gordon, 2010).

In the present chapter, we explore the role of mental imagery (and the related cognitive process of observation; see Holmes & Calmels, 2008, 2011) in skill learning and skilled performance in sport. We begin by explaining the nature, characteristics (including neural substrates), and measurement of mental imagery. Next, we shall summarize the effects of "mental practice" (a systematic form of covert rehearsal in which people imagine themselves performing an action without engaging in the actual physical movements involved) on skill learning and skilled performance in sport. We then consider the neuroscience of "action observation":

the fact that when we watch someone performing an action that lies within our motor repertoire, our brains simulate performance of that action and sketch recent research findings on the relationship between imagery, action observation, and skill learning. Finally, we outline some potentially fruitful new directions for research on mental imagery, observation and skill learning in sport.

Mental imagery: nature, characteristics, and measurement

According to researchers, mental imagery has at least three key characteristics: it is multi-sensory, can be classified into different types, and shares certain neural substrates and cognitive mechanisms with other mental processes. As Hardy, Jones, and Gould (1996) proposed, mental imagery is "a symbolic sensory experience that may occur in any sensory mode" (p. 28). Therefore, we have the capacity to imagine "seeing," "hearing," "tasting," "smelling," and "feeling" simulated actions and experiences. As imagery is multi-sensory in nature, different *types* of mental imagery have been identified. However, imagery researchers in sport psychology and cognitive neuroscience differ considerably in their postulated typologies of imagery. For example, some sport psychology researchers have developed typologies based on intended functions of imagery. Martin, Moritz, and Hall (1999) distinguished between "motivation general – mastery" (e.g., imagining staying focused after making an error in a competition), "motivation general – arousal" (e.g., imagining the stress and/or excitement associated with competition), "motivation specific" (e.g., imagining achieving a personal best or winning a medal), "cognitive general" (e.g., imagining a game plan for a competitive event), and "cognitive specific" (e.g., mentally practicing a skill) imagery. By contrast with this functional approach, cognitive neuroscientists have adopted a mechanistic typology: distinguishing between the visual, spatial and motor imagery processes that are postulated to underlie the imagery experience. In this regard, Kozhevnikov, Kosslyn, and Shepard (2005) have postulated two distinct cognitive systems that encode and process visual information in different ways. Object-based imagery represents the shape and color information of objects, whereas spatial imagery represents location information. More recently, "motor imagery" processes or the "covert simulation of movement" (Holmes, 2007, p. 1) have begun to attract research attention in neuroscience.

Historically, motor imagery processes have been measured using standardized psychometric tests (e.g., the Vividness of Movement Imagery Questionnaire, VMIQ; Isaac, Marks, & Russell, 1986), qualitative procedures (Moran & MacIntyre, 1998), psychophysiological techniques (e.g., Guillot, Collet, et al., 2009) and chronometric tools (i.e., those in which the time-course of information-processing activities is used to draw inferences about cognitive mechanisms; see review by Guillot & Collet, 2005). In an effort to combine these measures, Collet, Guillot, Lebon, MacIntyre, and Moran (2011) proposed a formula by which a novel "motor imagery index" (MII) can be calculated using a combination of six specific component scores. These scores include self-estimations of imagery quality, psychometric assessment of imagery vividness, three psychophysiological indices (derived from electrodermal and cardiac recordings), and estimation of the difference between actual and imagined duration of movement execution. According to Collet et al. (2011), the MII is especially helpful to imagery researchers in sport psychology. It is flexible and relatively easy to calculate because most of its components (specifically, the qualitative, psychometric, and chronometric ones) do not require any specialist measurement equipment.

The second notable feature of mental imagery is that, although it is unobservable, it can be measured indirectly through individual variations in such dimensions as "vividness" (i.e., apparent realism, clarity, or richness) and "controllability" (i.e., the ease with which a given mental image can be manipulated by the person who generates it); (Moran, 1993). Over the past century, these two dimensions of imagery have been targeted by psychologists in their attempt to measure individual differences in people's use of, and ability in, imagery (see Morris, Spittle, & Watt, 2005). For example, the vividness of an image can be assessed using self-report scales in which people are asked to comment on certain experiential aspects of their mental representation. In this regard, Roberts, Callow, Hardy, Markland, and Bringer (2008) developed the VMIQ-2. This test consists of 12 items and assesses the ability to form mental images of various motor tasks (e.g., running, kicking a stone) and then to rate the resultant images on a Likert-type scale from 1 ("perfectly clear and vivid") to 5 ("no image at all"). The VMIQ-2 displays impressive factorial validity and acceptable concurrent and discriminate validity. The controllability dimension of a mental image can be measured objectively by requesting people to complete tasks which are known to require imagery abilities. For example, in the "Group Mental Rotations Test" (GMRT; Vandenberg & Kuse, 1978), people are required to make judgments about whether or not the spatial orientation of certain three-dimensional target figures matches (i.e., is congruent with) or does not match (i.e., is incompatible with) various alternative shapes. MacIntyre, Moran, and Jennings (2002) reported moderate positive correlations between scores on this latter test and finish position among a sample of canoe-slalom world cup competitors.

The third important aspect of mental imagery concerns its neurological substrates. Specifically, researchers have shown that motor imagery shares some neural pathways and mechanisms with like-modality perception (Farah, 1984; Kosslyn, 1994) and with the preparation and production of movements (Decety & Ingvar, 1990; Jeannerod, 1994, 2001). In short, there are close parallels between perceiving, imagining, and motor control (planning and executing actions). Recognition of these parallels led to the "functional equivalence" hypothesis (e.g., Finke, 1979; Jeannerod, 1994; see review by Moran et al., in press) or the proposition that cognitive simulation processes (e.g., imagery) share, to some degree, certain representations, neural structures, and mechanisms with like-modality perception and with motor preparation and execution processes. For example, neuroimaging studies show that mentally simulated and executed actions rely on similar neural representations and activate many common brain areas such as the primary motor cortex, supplementary motor area, premotor areas, and cerebellum (de Lange, Roelofs, & Toni, 2008; Munzert et al., 2009). Similarly, a meta-analysis by Grèzes and Decety (2001) revealed that motor imagery, movement execution, and action observation activate overlapping foci in the supplementary motor area, dorsal pre-motor cortex, supramarginal gyrus, and superior parietal lobe. As Macuga and Frey (2012) have recently pointed out, however, there has been no satisfactory direct test of the functional equivalence hypothesis because of the failure to study motor imagery, movement execution and action observation processes within a single paradigm.

Mental practice

As explained earlier, the term *mental practice* (MP; also known as *symbolic rehearsal* or *covert rehearsal*) refers to the systematic use of mental imagery to rehearse an action in one's imagination without engaging in the actual physical movements involved. For over a century, the effects of MP on skilled performance have been investigated by researchers in psychology. To illustrate, James (1890) claimed rather counterintuitively that, by anticipating experiences imaginatively, people actually learn to skate in the summer and to swim in the winter. The typical experimental paradigm used to study MP effects involves a comparison of the pre- and post-intervention performance of four groups of participants: those who have engaged only in physical practice of the skill in question (the physical practice group, PP); those who have mentally practiced (the mental practice group, MP); those who have alternated between physical and mental practice (PP/MP); and, finally, participants in a non-practice control condition. After a pre-treatment baseline test has been conducted on a designated skill, participants are randomly assigned to one of these conditions (PP, MP, PP/MP, or control). Normally, the cognitive rehearsal that occurs in the MP treatment condition is guided by a mental imagery script that describes the motor actions to be executed in clear and vivid detail (see Morris et al., 2005). After this MP intervention has been applied, the participants' performance on the target skill is re-tested. If the performance of the MP group is significantly superior to that of the control group, then a positive effect of mental practice is deemed to have occurred.

Empirical findings on mental practice

Scientists interested in imagery have established a number of conclusions about the efficacy of mental practice (see reviews by Driskell, Copper, & Moran, 1994; Schuster et al., 2011). These conclusions may be summarized as in Table 6.1.

First, MP can improve the learning and performance of a variety of motor skills. These skills include self-paced activities such as golf putting (Bell, Skinner, & Fisher, 2009; Ramsey, Cumming, & Edwards, 2008) and the high-jump (Olsson, Jonsson, & Nyberg, 2008) as well as skills involving an opponent and anticipation, such as the service return in tennis (Robin et al., 2007). Mental practice interventions have also been applied successfully to enhance performance in music (Johnson, 2011), dance (Bolles & Chatfield, 2009), and medical surgery (Arora et al., 2011). Second, there is evidence (see Driskell et al., 1994) that MP, when combined and alternated with physical practice, tends to produce superior skill learning to that resulting from either mental or physical practice conducted

Table 6.1 Empirical findings on mental practice (MP): selected studies

Empirical finding	Illustrative authors (year)	Skill/task in question	Conclusion
1	Bell, Skinner, & Fisher (2009)	Golf putting	MP improves skill learning and skilled performance
	Ramsey, Cumming, & Edwards (2008)	Golf putting	
	Robin et al. (2007)	Service return in tennis	
2	Malouin, Richards, Durand, & Doyon (2009)	Rising and sitting movements after stroke	MP combined and alternated with physical practice (PP) produces better outcomes than PP alone
3	Smith, Collins, & Holmes (2003)	Strength performance on a finger strength task	MP can improve performance on tasks involving physical strength
	Reiser, Büsch, & Munzert (2011)	Strength performance in bench pressing, leg pressing, triceps extension, calf raising	
4	Arvinen-Barrow, Weigand, Thomas, Hemmings, & Walley (2007)	Use of specific types of mental imagery	Expert athletes tend to use mental imagery for skill rehearsal more frequently than do relative novices
5	Goss, Hall, Buckolz, & Fishburne (1986)	Acquisition of various movement patterns	Imagery ability mediates the relationship between MP and performance

alone. In stroke rehabilitation, MP combined with physical practice yields better outcomes in movement recovery than does physical practice alone (Malouin, Richards, Duran, & Doyon, 2009; Page, Levine, & Leonard, 2007). In attempting to explain the mechanisms underlying such MP effects in rehabilitation settings, Welfringer, Leifert-Fiebach, Babinsky, and Brandt (2011) postulated that motor imagery training facilitates activation of pre-motor circuits in the damaged hemisphere with consequent stimulation of associated sensory cells. Third, although Feltz and Landers (1983) concluded that MP is more effective for the improvement of cognitive rather than motor components of sport skills, there is research evidence that MP can increase physical strength performance (Smith, Collins, & Holmes, 2003; Reiser et al., 2011). Fourth, the expertise level of the performer appears to moderate the effects of MP on performance. For example, Driskell et al. (1994) concluded that expert athletes tend to benefit more from MP than do novices, regardless of the type of skill being practiced (either cognitive or physical). Also, Arvinen-Barrow, Weigand, Thomas, Hemmings, and Walley (2007) found that elite athletes tend to use mental imagery more frequently for skill rehearsal than do novice counterparts. However, these last authors cautioned that there has been considerable inconsistency among imagery researchers in the way in which the skill level of participants has been dichotomized (i.e., elite versus novice). Finally, there is some evidence (e.g., Goss, Hall, Buckolz, & Fishburne, 1986) that imagery ability (or a person's capacity for forming "vivid, controllable images and retaining them for sufficient time to effect the desired imagery rehearsal"; Morris, 1997, p. 37) mediates the relationship between MP and motor skill performance. To summarize, numerous researchers have indicated that MP can enhance skill learning and skilled performance in athletes. As Munroe-Chandler and Morris (2011) have noted, however, relatively little research has been conducted on the efficacy of imagery in improving strategic aspects (e.g., developing game-plans) of sporting performance. Nevertheless, the distinction between skill and strategy is not completely clear-cut. For example, MacIntyre and Moran (2007b) argued that the attempt to decouple skills from strategies is often difficult because of the continuous nature of executed movements in sport.

Validation of mental practice research

Although there is an abundance of research on the efficacy of MP, there is at least one unresolved question – a validation issue – that afflicts this field. Specifically, how do we know that people who *claim* to be using imagery when engaged in MP are actually doing so? In other words, how can we validate people's subjective reports about their imagery experiences? One way of addressing this issue is to use custom-designed manipulation checks or verification procedures that attempt to assess the ease and accuracy with which participants adhered to the imagery instructions/script (see Cumming & Ramsey, 2009). An alternative solution to this validation problem comes from research on the *mental travel* chronometry paradigm (Guillot & Collet, 2005). According to the functional equivalence hypothesis, imagined and executed actions rely on similar motor representations and activate some common brain areas (e.g., the pre-motor and primary motor cortices). Consequently, there should be a close correspondence between the time required to perform simulated actions *mentally* and that required for *actual* performance. This hypothesis has been corroborated empirically (Guillot & Collet, 2005; Guillot, Louis, & Collet, 2010). Moran and MacIntyre (1998) validated the veracity of canoe-slalomists' imagery reports by comparing the congruence between the imagined time and the real time required by these athletes to navigate their courses in competition. More recently, a review by Guillot, Hoyek, Louis, and Collet (2012) concluded that elite athletes are typically more accurate than novices in estimating the imagined duration of executed actions.

Theories of mental practice

In general, four main theories have been postulated to explain MP effects; the neuromuscular model (e.g., Jacobson, 1932), the cognitive or symbolic approach (e.g.,

Denis, 1985), the bio-informational theory (e.g., Lang, 1979) and, most recently, the PETTLEP approach (Holmes & Collins, 2001). According to the neuromuscular model, MP effects are mediated by faint activity in the peripheral musculature (Moran, 2012). Advocates of this theory postulate that there is a strong positive relationship between the muscular activity elicited by imagining a given skill and that detected during actual execution. Unfortunately, there is mixed empirical support for this hypothesis. For example, whereas Guillot et al. (2007) discovered electromyographic activity during motor imagery, Gentili, Papaxanthis, and Pozzo (2006) failed to do so. Next, according to the cognitive approach, MP facilitates the coding and rehearsal of key elements of the skilled task. In contrast with neuromuscular accounts of MP, cognitive (or symbolic learning) models attach little importance to what happens in the peripheral musculature of the performer. They focus on the possibility that mental rehearsal strengthens the brain's central representation or cognitive "blueprint" of the skill being imagined (Roosink & Zijdewind, 2010). Although this approach has a plausible theoretical rationale, it is challenged by evidence that MP can improve people's performance of strength tasks, which, by definition, contain few cognitive components. Another problem for symbolic theorists is that they find it difficult to explain how MP can enhance the performance of expert athletes, who, presumably, already possess well-established blueprints or motor schemata for the movements being imagined. Bio-informational theory has at its core the interaction of three different factors: the environment in which a given movement is performed ("stimulus" information such as "feeling" the soft ground as one imagines teeing up a ball in golf), what is felt by the performer while the movement occurs ("response" information such as feeling a slow, smooth practice swing on the imaginary tee-box), and the perceived importance of this skill to the performer ("meaning" information such as feeling slightly anxious because other people are watching as one prepares to drive the ball). Of these factors, the response information is especially significant because it reflects how a person would *actually* react in the real-life situation being imagined. Therefore, bio-informational theorists postulate that imagery scripts that are heavily laden with response propositions should elicit greater MP effects than those without such information. The bio-informational approach has been influential in highlighting the value of "individualizing" imagery scripts so that they take account of the personal meaning that people attribute to the skills or movements that they wish to rehearse. Finally, the most recent theoretical approach to MP is known by the acronym PETTLEP (Holmes & Collins, 2001). In this model, P refers to the athlete's Physical response to the sporting situation imagined, E is the Environment in which the imagery is performed, T is the imagined Task, T refers to Timing (i.e., the pace at which the imagery is performed), L is a Learning or memory component of imagery, E refers to the Emotions elicited by the imagery, and P designates the type of visual imagery Perspective used by the practitioner (i.e., whether he or she imagines the movement from a "first-person" perspective, imagining/seeing oneself performing a given action, or from a "third-person" perspective, imagining/seeing either oneself or someone else performing the action). The PETTLEP model proposes that, when used to enhance performance, imagery interventions should replicate not only athletes' sporting situation but also the emotions that they experience when performing their skills. Although the predictions of the PETTLEP model have not been tested extensively to date, available empirical results are generally supportive. Smith, Wright, Allsopp, and Westhead (2007) compared the use of PETTLEP imagery training with traditional MP techniques and with physical practice in developing gymnasts' jump skills. The PETTLEP ———— proved its proficiency in these skills, whereas the traditional ———— ot.

Motor imagery, action observation, and skill

So far, we have provided evidence to support the effectiveness of motor imagery as an intervention technique for improving skill acquisition. Because few researchers have adequately addressed the validation problem (i.e., the issue of how we know for sure that people who *claim* to be using imagery when engaged in MP are actually doing so), some psychologists (e.g., Holmes & Calmels, 2008, 2011; Holmes et al., 2010) have turned to action observation as either a possible replacement for, or an adjunct to, mental imagery. Many of the factors that have been examined as moderators of the relationship between imagery and skilled performance have become popular in observation research. For example, intervening variables such as visual perspective, movement agency (self or other), viewing angle (allocentric or egocentric position relative to the action), task type (e.g., form-based versus perceptually driven; see Holmes & Calmels, 2011), and timing issues (e.g., real time, slow motion, or speeded) have been studied by action observation investigators. Holmes and Calmels (2011) postulated that observation, when delivered through video-based media, can offer solutions to many of the challenges encountered when delivering imagery interventions, such as increased control over image content.

Let us now summarize some emerging findings about the efficacy of observation interventions in sport settings and how best to integrate them with imagery approaches. To begin, mental skills training through the practice of action observation, just as we have described for motor imagery, can improve sporting performance (e.g., Ram, Riggs, Skaling, Landers, & McCullagh, 2007; Ramsey, Cumming, & Edwards, 2008). A clue to the likely mechanisms underlying these effects comes from the discovery that action observation and motor imagery processes share certain neural representations (see Conson, Sarà, Pistoia, & Trojano, 2009; Holmes et al., 2010). For example, these two processes tend to elicit activation in the primary and premotor cortex, supplementary motor area, cerebellum, and basal ganglia. Many of the cortical circuits that are activated when people execute actions are activated when people observe someone else executing these actions. A degree of interpersonal motor resonance between observer and executer (activation of the two motor systems), or intrapersonal resonance between visual and motor areas, during skill learning has been postulated. Such resonance may provide support for the idea that these shared motor regions are important for action recognition, goal recognition, and action anticipation through the simulation of the observed (or imagined) action (see Uithol, van Rooij, Bekkering, & Haselager, 2011). In this sense, the "shared" motor resonance translates the observed action into a general understanding of the action; the more familiar the observed action, the greater the motor resonance that can be seen in functional magnetic resonance imaging (fMRI) and transcranial magnetic stimulation (TMS) studies. As we have explained earlier, this abstract idea of linking several cognitive processes (e.g., motor imagery, action observation, and motor control) has been termed "functional equivalence" in the literature (e.g., the PETTLEP model; Holmes & Collins, 2001). Proponents of the PETTLEP approach have suggested that imagery and action observation can be optimized by including practice-related characteristics such as holding task-specific equipment or adopting task-relevant positions to perform the imagery or observation.

Recently, researchers using TMS have demonstrated that observing another person's actions can modulate the excitability of this shared corticospinal system (see Loporto, McAllister, Williams, Hardwick, & Holmes, 2011). This effect may reflect increased pre-motor activity, seen as increases in motor-evoked potential (MEP) amplitude. This increase in activity may occur because observation not only influences activity in corticocortical connections from pre- to primary motor cortex but also contributes to skill learning. This network has been proposed to form part of the *human action observation network*: a network of pre-motor and parietal areas similar to the *mirror neuron system* – a brain region that is postulated to underlie people's ability to infer the goals and intentions of others by observing and imitating their actions – found in primates (Di Pellegrino, Fadiga, Fogassi, Gallese, & Rizzolatti, 1992). Transcranial magnetic stimulation is an effective, non-invasive method of stimulating the brain and peripheral nervous system and provides researchers with a useful approach to examine the central mechanisms underlying movement imagery and action observation. For example, MEP amplitude during action observation and motor imagery of finger–thumb opposition was compared with imagery ability as measured using the VMIQ-2 (Williams, Pearce, Loporto, Morris, & Holmes, 2012). Significant increases in MEP amplitude were recorded during the experimental conditions with a significant correlation between imagery MEP change and imagery ability, leading the authors to propose that corticospinal activation during imagery seems to be strongly related to imagery ability. This last finding suggests that individual differences in imagery ability (e.g., vividness) need to be controlled for if neurological mechanisms are to be elicited in support of skill learning.

In addition to the TMS evidence for a neural mechanism to support action observation as part of the skill acquisition process, electroencephalography (EEG) enables suitable measurement of changes in cortical activity that may be associated with motor skill learning and performance. In this regard, recent research provides further support for the utility of the action observation network. In two detailed studies of action execution and observation, comparisons between simple and complex movement conditions displayed a number of significantly similar synchronization patterns across the two conditions (Calmels, Hars, Holmes, Jarry, & Stam, 2008; Calmels et al., 2006). Although they did not yield an identical match of EEG cortical indicators between observation and execution conditions, the preceding studies provide support for a postulated central action–execution matching system that might be important for skill acquisition.

Researchers have shown that, before voluntary movement production, there is an increase in electrical activity in motor areas of the brain known as the movement-related cortical potential (MRCP) (see Figure 6.2).

A component of the MRCP, the *Bereitschaftspotential* (BP, or "readiness potential"), is a negative slope that occurs just before movement onset (see Shibasaki & Hallett, 2006). The BP is followed by a steeper gradient negativity; the negative slope. The final component is the motor potential, which is concomitant with movement onset. The amplitude and onset times of these components vary depending on the physical and psychological characteristics of the forthcoming movement (Birbaumer, Elbert, Canavan, & Rockstroh, 1990). The MRCP seems, therefore, to reflect the cortical activity involved in planning and preparing to perform voluntary movements (Shibasaki & Hallett, 2006). Also, there are recorded differences in the MRCP amplitude and onset times between expert and novice performers (e.g., Wright, Holmes, Di Russo, Loporto, & Smith, 2011); expert performers show smaller-amplitude and later-onset MRCP profiles than novices. The experienced performers are able to plan and perform the task with a reduced cortical activity compared with novices. The phenomenon is termed *neural efficiency*, and the differences are attributed to long-term training by the expert group. This profile has been shown in expert and novice pistol shooters (Fattapposta et al., 1996), and kendo martial art performers (Hatta, Nishihira, Higashiura, Kim, & Kaneda, 2009). Wright et al. (2011) have also reported, in a group of novice guitarists, that the MRCP profile can be trained to reach that of an experienced group in as little

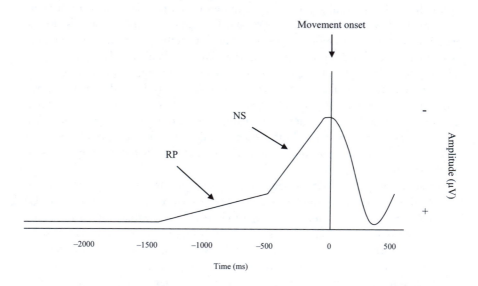

Figure 6.2 A schematic representation of the movement-related cortical potential (MRCP). Time 0 ms on the horizontal axis indicates the point of movement onset. The pre-movement components, termed the readiness potential (RP) and the negative slope (NS), are thought to reflect the cortical activity involved in planning and preparing to perform voluntary movement.

as 5 weeks. Studies are ongoing in our own laboratories to investigate whether or not observation and imagery are able to contribute to modifications of the MRCP profile. What is not yet known, however, is if the reduced MRCP activity is commensurate with altered activity elsewhere (e.g., in the basal ganglia and cerebellum). In future, research that attempts to combine EEG with fMRI may be able to address this unresolved issue.

New directions for research on imagery and action observation

At least five new directions may be identified for future research on imagery and action observation processes. First, little is known as yet about athletes' "meta-imagery" processes: their beliefs about the nature and regulation of their own imagery skills (see MacIntyre & Moran, 2010; Moran, 2002). This scientific neglect of what athletes know about their own imagery processes is surprising in view of the abundance of anecdotal insights into imagery that are available from sports performers. More generally, however, there is evidence that people's intuitive theories about their own mental imagery processes are often inaccurate. Denis and Carfantan (1985) discovered that a majority of participants (undergraduate students) in their study regarded as implausible the MP effect (see earlier in this chapter): the idea that systematic use of mental imagery could enhance the performance of motor skills. Unfortunately, although some researchers (e.g., MacIntyre & Moran, 2007a, 2007b; Munroe, Giaccobi, Hall, & Weinberg, 2000) have asked sport performers to indicate why, where, how, and when they use mental imagery, there has been little progress in developing either a psychometric test or a coherent theory of meta-imagery processes in athletes. Clearly, these unresolved issues require research attention. In a related vein, it is interesting to note that Pearson, Rademaker, and Tong (2011) have recently investigated people's metacognitive insights into their own visual imagery processes.

Second, research is needed to investigate the use of chronometric methods (mentioned briefly earlier) to validate athletes' reports of their imagery experiences. If imagined and executed actions rely on similar motor representations and activate certain common brain areas (e.g., the parietal and prefrontal cortices, the pre-motor and primary motor cortices), the temporal organization of imagined and actual actions should be similar, leading to a close correspondence between the time required to *mentally* perform a given action and that required for its *actual* execution.

Third, although imagery researchers in sport psychology (e.g., Morris et al., 2005) have typically advocated that athletes should use all of their sensory modalities in their simulation of action, the efficacy of this multi-modal approach has not yet been evaluated comprehensively. In order to address this unresolved issue, future research could use diary studies with elite athletes to determine the extent to which multi-modal images are generated.

Fourth, research is required on the relationship between action observation, motor imagery, and action execution. In this regard, a potentially promising line of inquiry concerns the study of eye movements. Such movements not only provide objective tools for studying online cognitive processing in imagery and action observation but could also be used to draw inferences about the shared neural network system that underlies these activities. McCormick, Causer, and Holmes (under review) used the classic "reach and grasp" task design (Fadiga, Fogassi, Pavesi, & Rizzolatti, 1995) to demonstrate similarities in visual fixation times and number of visual fixations across motor imagery and observation conditions. These authors also investigated visual perspective with the "reach–grasp–place" being shown in the first- and third-person perspectives. Some differences in the dependent variables between perspectives were evident in both observation and imagery conditions, providing further support for a shared neural representation between observation and imagery processes. Another potential use of eye-movement data in imagery research is to elucidate the extent to which eye–hand coordination during *imagined* movements is similar to that which occurs during *actual* (i.e., physically executed) movements. Heremans et al. (2011) investigated the role of eye movements during motor imagery training. They found that, although eye movements elicited during imagery did not affect the temporal parameters of trained hand movements (reaching task), they did help to achieve maximal gains in movement accuracy and efficiency. These findings were most pronounced in conditions with high accuracy demands. Additional research is required to establish the implications of these findings for motor imagery training.

Finally, an exciting and potentially fruitful new direction concerns the development of methodologies for the investigation of the unique neural mechanisms underlying motor imagery, motor execution, and action observation. Macuga and Frey (2012) devised an fMRI paradigm in which these three processes were examined using a task involving people's performance on a repetitive bimanual finger-tapping test. There was only partial support for the hypothesis that imagery and action observation processes activate the same neural representations subserving execution of the same action. Clearly, such results challenge researchers in this field to differentiate between distinctive and overlapping neural mechanisms underlying motor imagery, motor execution, and action observation processes.

In conclusion, this chapter investigated the nature and implications of the relationship between mental imagery, action observation, and skill learning and skilled performance. We began with a brief introduction to the nature, neural substrates, and measurement of mental imagery. After that, we summarized research findings on the effects of mental practice on skilled performance and suggested some ways in which the veracity of people's reports on their imagery processes could be validated objectively. Then, following clarification of the neuroscience of observation, we outlined some key research findings on the relationship between observation, imagery, and skill learning. The final section of the chapter sketched some new directions for future research on imagery and action observation processes.

References

Arora, S., Aggarwal, R., Sevdalis, N., Moran, A., Sirimanna, P., Kneebone, R., & Darzi, A. (2010). Development and validation of mental practice as a training strategy for laparoscopic surgery. *Surgical Endoscopy*, 24, 179–187.

Arora, S., Aggarwal, R., Sirimanna, P., Moran, A., Grantcharov, T., Kneebone, R., Sevdalis, N., & Darzi, A. (2011). Mental practice enhances surgical technical skills: A randomized controlled study. *Annals of Surgery, 253,* 265–270.

Arvinen-Barrow, M., Weigand, D. A., Thomas, S., Hemmings, B., & Walley, M. (2007). Elite and novice athletes' imagery use in open and closed sports. *Journal of Applied Sport Psychology, 19,* 95–104.

Bell, R. J., Skinner, C. H., & Fisher, L. A. (2009). Decreasing putting yips in accomplished golfers via solution focused guided-imagery: a single subject research design. *Journal of Applied Sport Psychology, 21,* 1–14.

Birbaumer, N., Elbert, T., Canavan, A. G., & Rockstroh, B. (1990). Slow potentials of the cerebral cortex and behavior. *Physiological Reviews, 70,* 1–41.

Bolles, G., & Chatfield, S. J. (2009). The intersection of imagery ability, imagery use, and learning style. *Journal of Dance Education, 9,* 6–16.

Braun, S. M., Beurskens, A. J., Borm, P. J., Schack, T., & Wade, D. T. (2006). The effects of mental practice in stroke rehabilitation: A systematic review. *Archives of Physical Medicine and Rehabilitation, 87,* 842–852.

Caliari, P. (2008). Enhancing forehand acquisition in table tennis: The role of mental practice. *Journal of Applied Sport Psychology, 20,* 88–96.

Calmels, C., Hars, M., Holmes, P. S., Jarry, G., & Stam, C. J. (2008). Non-linear EEG synchronization during observation and execution of simple and complex sequential finger movements. *Experimental Brain Research, 190,* 389–400.

Calmels, C., Holmes, P., Jarry, G., Lévèque, J.-M., Hars, M., & Stam, C. J. (2006). Local cortical activity prior to, and during, observation and execution of sequential finger movements. *Brain Topography, 19,* 77–88.

Collet, C., Guillot, A., Lebon, F., MacIntyre, T., & Moran, A. (2011). Measuring motor imagery using psychometric, behavioural and psychophysiological tools. *Exercise and Sport Sciences Reviews, 39,* 85–92.

Conson, M., Sarà, M., Pistoia, F., & Trojano, L. (2009). Action observation improves motor imagery: Specific interactions between simulative processes. *Experimental Brain Research, 199,* 71–81.

Crisp, R. J., Birtel, M. D., & Meleady, R. (2011). Mental simulation of social thought and action: Trivial tasks or tools for transforming social policy? *Current Directions in Psychological Science, 20,* 261–264.

Cumming, J., & Ramsey, R. (2009). Imagery interventions in sport. In Mellalieu, S. D., & Hanton, S. (Eds.), *Advances in applied sport psychology: A review* (pp. 5–36). Oxford: Routledge.

Decety, J., & Ingvar, D. H. (1990). Brain structures participating in mental simulation of motor behaviour: A neuropsychological interpretation. *Acta Psychologica, 73,* 13–34.

de Lange, F. P., Roelofs, K., & Toni, I. (2008). Motor imagery: A window into the mechanisms and alterations of the motor system. *Cortex, 44,* 494–506.

Denis, M. (1985). Visual imagery and the use of mental practice in the development of motor skills. *Canadian Journal of Applied Sports Science, 10,* 4–16.

Denis, M., & Carfantan, M. (1985). People's knowledge about images. *Cognition, 20,* 49–60.

Di Pellegrino, G., Fadiga, L., Fogassi, L., Gallese, V., & Rizzolatti, G. (1992). Understanding motor events: A neurophysiological study. *Experimental Brain Research, 91,* 176–180.

Driskell, J. E., Copper, C., & Moran, A. P. (1994). Does mental practice enhance performance? *Journal of Applied Psychology, 79,* 481–492.

Fadiga, L., Fogassi, L, Pavesi, G., & Rizzolatti G. (1995). Motor facilitation during action observation: A magnetic stimulation study. *Journal of Neurophysiology, 73,* 2608–2611.

Farah, M. J. (1984). The neurological basis of mental imagery: A componential analysis. *Cognition, 18*, 245–272.

Fattapposta, F., Amabile, G., Cordischi, M. V., Di Venanzio, D., Foti, A., Pierelli, F., & Morrocutti, C. (1996). Long-term practice effects on a new skilled motor learning: an electrophysiological study. *Electroencephalography and Clinical Neurophysiology, 99*, 495–507.

Feltz, D. L., & Landers, D. M. (1983). The effects of mental practice on motor skill learning and performance: A meta-analysis. *Journal of Sport Psychology, 2*, 211–220.

Finke, R. A. (1979). The functional equivalence of mental images and errors of movement. *Cognitive Psychology, 11*, 235–264.

Gentili, R., Papaxanthis, C., & Pozzo, T. (2006). Improvement and generalization of arm motor performance through motor imagery practice. *Neuroscience, 137*, 761–772.

Goss, S., Hall, C., Buckolz, E., & Fishburne, G. (1986). Imagery ability and the acquisition and retention of movements. *Memory & Cognition, 14*, 469–477.

Grèzes, J., & Decety, J. (2001). Functional anatomy of execution, mental simulation, observation, and verb generation of actions: A meta-analysis. *Human Brain Mapping, 12*, 1–19.

Guillot, A., & Collet, C. (2005). Duration of mentally simulated movement: A review. *Journal of Motor Behavior, 37*, 10–20.

Guillot, A., Collet, C., Nguyen, V. A., Malouin, F., Richards, C., & Doyon, J. (2009). Brain activity during visual versus kinaesthetic imagery: An fMRI study. *Human Brain Mapping, 30*, 2157–2172.

Guillot, A., Hoyek, N., Louis, M., & Collet, C. (2012). Learning by thinking: Review and future directions for the timing of imagined movements. *International Review of Sport and Exercise Psychology, 5*, 3–22.

Guillot, A., Lebon, F., Rouffet, D., Champely, S., Doyon, J., & Collet, C. (2007). Muscular responses during motor imagery as a function of muscle contraction types. *International Journal of Psychophysiology, 66*, 18–27.

Guillot, A., Louis, M., & Collet, C. (2010). Neurophysiological substrates of motor imagery ability. In Guillot, A., & Collet, C. (Eds.), *The neurophysiological foundations of mental and motor imagery* (pp. 109–124). Oxford: Oxford University Press.

Hardy, L., Jones, G., & Gould, D. (1996). *Understanding psychological preparation for sport: Theory and practice of elite performers*. Chichester: John Wiley.

Hatta, A., Nishihira, Y., Higashiura, T., Kim, S. R., & Kaneda, T. (2009). Long-term motor practice induces practice-dependent modulation of movement-related cortical potentials (MRCP) preceding a self-paced non-dominant handgrip movement in kendo players. *Neuroscience Letters, 459*, 105–108.

Heremans, E., Smits-Engelsman, B., Caeyenberghsm, K., Vercruysse, S., Nieuwboer, A., Feys, P., & Helsen, W. F. (2011). Keeping an eye on imagery: The role of eye movements during motor imagery training. *Neuroscience, 195*, 37–44.

Holmes, P. (2007). Theoretical and practical problems for imagery in stroke rehabilitation: An observational study. *Rehabilitation Psychology, 52*, 1–10.

Holmes, P., & Calmels, C. (2008). A neuroscientific review of imagery and observation use in sport. *Journal of Motor Behavior, 40*, 433–445.

Holmes, P., & Calmels, C. (2011). Mental practice: Neuroscientific support for a new approach. In Collins, D., Button, A., & Richards, H. (Eds.), *Performance psychology: A practitioner's guide* (pp. 231–244). Oxford: Churchill Livingstone.

Holmes, P., & Collins, D. (2001). The PETTLEP approach to motor imagery: A functional equivalence model for sport psychologists. *Journal of Applied Sport Psychology, 13*, 60–83.

Holmes, P., Cumming, J., & Edwards, M. G. (2010). Movement imagery, observation, and skill. In Guillot, A., & Collet, C. (Eds.), *The neurophysiological foundations of mental and motor imagery* (pp. 253–269). Oxford: Oxford University Press.

Isaac, A., Marks, D., & Russell, E. (1986). An instrument for assessing imagery of movement: The Vividness of Movement Imagery Questionnaire (VMIQ). *Journal of Mental Imagery*, *10*, 23–30.

Jacobson, E. (1932). Electrophysiology of mental activities. *American Journal of Psychology*, *44*, 677–694.

James, W. (1890). *Principles of psychology*. New York: Holt, Rinehart & Winston.

Jeannerod, M. (1994). The representing brain: Neural correlates of motor intention and imagery. *Behavioral and Brain Sciences*, *17*, 187–245.

Jeannerod, M. (2001). Neural simulation of action: A unifying mechanism for motor cognition. *NeuroImage*, *14*, 103–109.

Johnson, R. B. (2011). Musical tempo stability in mental practice: A comparison of motor and non-motor imagery techniques. *Research Studies in Music Education*, *33*, 3–30.

Kosslyn, S. M. (1994). *Image and brain: The resolution of the imagery debate*. Cambridge, MA: MIT Press.

Kozhevnikov, M., Kosslyn, S. M., & Shephard, J. M. (2005). Spatial versus object visualizers: A new characterization of visual cognitive style. *Memory and Cognition*, *33*, 710–726.

Lang, P. J. (1979). A bio-informational theory of emotional imagery. *Psychophysiology*, *17*, 495–512.

Loporto, M., McAllister, C., Hardwick, R., Williams, J., & Holmes, P. S. (2011). Transcranial magnetic stimulation as a technique for investigating action observation in sport, exercise and rehabilitation settings. *Journal of Motor Behavior*, *43*, 361–373.

MacIntyre, T., & Moran, A. (2007a). A qualitative investigation of imagery use and meta-imagery processes among elite canoe-slalom competitors. *Journal of Imagery Research in Sport and Physical Activity*, *2*, article 3. doi: 10.2202/1932-0191.1009.

MacIntyre, T., & Moran, A. (2007b). A qualitative investigation of meta-imagery processes and imagery direction among elite athletes. *Journal of Imagery Research in Sport and Physical Activity*, *2*(1), article 4. doi: 10.2202/1932-0191.1022.

MacIntyre, T., & Moran, A. (2010). Meta-imagery processes among elite sports performers. In Guillot, A., & Collet, C. (Eds.), *The neurophysiological foundations of mental and motor imagery* (pp. 227–244). Oxford: Oxford University Press.

MacIntyre, T., Moran, A., & Jennings, D. (2002). Is controllability of imagery related to canoe-slalom performance? *Perceptual and Motor Skills*, *94*, 1245–1250.

Macuga, K. L., & Frey, S. H. (2012). Neural representations involved in observed, imagined, and imitated actions are dissociable and hierarchically organized. *NeuroImage*, *59*, 2798–2807.

Malouin, F., Richards, C., Duran, A., & Doyon. J. (2009). Added value of mental practice combined with a small amount of physical practice on the relearning of rising and sitting post-stroke: A pilot study. *Journal of Neurologic Physical Therapy*, *33*, 195–202.

Martin, K. A., Moritz, S. E., & Hall, C. (1999). Imagery use in sport: A literature review and applied model. *Sport Psychologist*, *13*, 245–268.

McCormick, S., Causer, J., & Holmes, P. S. (under review). Eye gaze metrics reflect a shared motor representation for action observation and movement imagery. *Behavioural Brain Research*.

Moran, A. P. (1993). Conceptual and methodological issues in the measurement of mental imagery skills in athletes. *Journal of Sport Behaviour*, *16*, 156–170.

Moran, A. P. (2002). In the mind's eye. *The Psychologist, 15*, 414–415.

Moran, A. P. (2012). *Sport and exercise psychology: A critical introduction* (2nd edn.), London: Routledge.

Moran, A. P., & MacIntyre, T. (1998). "There's more to an image than meets the eye": A qualitative study of kinaesthetic imagery among elite canoe-slalomists. *Irish Journal of Psychology, 19*, 406–423.

Moran, A., Guillot, A., MacIntyre, T., & Collet, C. (in press). Re-imagining motor imagery: Building bridges between cognitive neuroscience and sport psychology. *British Journal of Psychology.* doi: 10.1111/j.2044-8295.2011.02068.x.

Morris, T. (1997). *Psychological skills training in sport: An overview* (2nd edn.). Leeds: National Coaching Foundation.

Morris, T., Spittle, M., & Watt, A. P. (2005). *Imagery in sport.* Champaign, IL: Human Kinetics.

Munroe, K. J., Giaccobi, P. R., Jr., Hall, C. R., and Weinberg, R. (2000). The four W's of imagery use: Where, when, why, and what. *Sport Psychologist, 14*, 119–137.

Munroe-Chandler, K., & Morris, T. (2011). Imagery. In Morris, T., & Terry, P. C. (Eds.), *The new sport and exercise psychology companion* (pp. 275–308). Morgantown, WV: Fitness Information Technology.

Munzert, J., Lorey, B., & Zentgraf, K. (2009). Cognitive motor processes: The role of motor imagery in the study of motor representations. *Brain Research Reviews, 60*, 306–326.

Nilsen, D. M., Gillen, G., & Gordon, A. M. (2010). Use of mental practice to improve upper-limb recovery after stroke: A systematic review. *American Journal of Occupational Therapy, 64*, 695–708.

Olsson, C. J., Jonsson, B., & Nyberg, L. (2008) Internal imagery training in active high jumpers. *Scandinavian Journal of Psychology, 49*, 133–140.

Page, S. J., Levine, P., & Leonard, A. C. (2007). Mental practice in chronic stroke: Results of a randomized, placebo-controlled trial. *Stroke, 38*, 1293–1297.

Pearson, J., Rademaker, R. L., & Tong, F. (2011). Evaluating the mind's eye: The metacognition of visual imagery. *Psychological Science, 22*, 1535–1542.

Phelps, M. (with Abrahamson, A.) (2008a). *No limits: The will to succeed.* New York: Free Press.

Phelps, M. (2008b). Why pain and disorder led to an iron will to win. *The Guardian* (Sport), 13 December, p. 10.

Ram, N., Riggs, S. M., Skaling, S., Landers, D. M., & McCullagh, P. (2007). A comparison of modelling and imagery in the acquisition and retention of motor skills. *Journal of Sports Sciences, 25*, 587–597.

Ramsey, R., Cumming, J., & Edwards, M. G. (2008). Exploring a modified conceptualisation of imagery direction and golf putting performance. *International Journal of Sport and Exercise Psychology, 6*, 207–223.

Reiser, M., Büsch, D., & Munzert, J. (2011). Strength gains by motor imagery with different ratios of physical to mental practice. *Frontiers in Psychology, 2*, article 194. doi: 10.3389/fpsyg.2011.00194.

Roberts, R., Callow, N., Hardy, L., Markland, D., & Bringer, J. (2008). Movement imagery ability: Development and assessment of a revised version of the Vividness of Movement Imagery Questionnaire. *Journal of Sport & Exercise Psychology, 30*, 200–221.

Robin, N., Dominique, L., Toussaint, L., Blandin, Y., Guillot, A., & Le Her, M. (2007). Effects of motor imagery training on service return in tennis: The role of imagery ability. *International Journal of Sport & Exercise Psychology, 2*, 175–186.

Roosink, M., & Zijdewind, I. (2010). Corticospinal excitability during observation and imagery of simple and complex hand tasks: Implications for motor rehabilitation. *Behavioural Brain Research, 213*, 35–41.

Schuster, C., Hilfiker, R., Amft, O., Scheidhauer, A., Andrews, B., Butler, J., Kischka, U., & Ettlin, T. (2011). Best practice for motor imagery: A systematic literature review on motor imagery training elements in five different disciplines. *BMC Medicine, 9*, 75. doi: 10.1186/1741-7015-9-75

Shibasaki, H., & Hallett, M. (2006). What is the Bereitschaftspotential? *Clinical Neurophysiology, 117*, 2341–2356.

Smith, D., Collins, D. J., & Holmes, P. S. (2003). Impact and mechanism of mental practice effects on strength. *International Journal of Sport and Exercise Psychology, 1*, 293–306.

Smith, D. Wright, C. J., Allsopp, A., & Westhead, H. (2007). It's all in the mind: PETTLEP-based imagery and sports performance. *Journal of Applied Sport Psychology, 19*, 80–92.

Taylor, M. K., Gould, D., & Rolo, C. (2008). Performance strategies of US Olympians in practice and competition. *High Ability Studies, 19*, 19–36.

Uithol, S., van Rooij, I., Bekkering, H., & Haselager, P. (2011). Understanding motor resonance. *Social Neuroscience, 6*, 388–397. doi: 10.1080/17470919.2011.559129.

Vandenberg, S., and Kuse, A. R. (1978). Mental rotations: A group test of three-dimensional spatial visualization. *Perceptual and Motor Skills, 47*, 599–604.

Weinberg, R. S. (2008). Does imagery work? Effects on performance and mental skills. *Journal of Imagery Research in Sport and Physical Activity, 3*, article 1. doi: 10.2202/1932-0191.1025.

Welfringer, A., Leifert-Fiebach, G., Babinsky, R., & Brandt, T. (2011). Visuomotor imagery as a new tool in the rehabilitation of neglect: A randomsed controlled study of feasibility and efficacy. *Disability and Rehabilitation, 33*, 2033–2043.

Williams, J., Pearce, A., Loporto, M., Morris, T., & Holmes, P. S. (2012). The relationship between corticospinal excitability during motor imagery and motor imagery ability. *Behavioural Brain Research, 226*, 369–375.

Wright, D. J., Holmes, P. S., DiRusso, F., Loporto, M., & Smith, D. K. (2011). Differences in cortical activity related to motor planning between experienced and novice musicians during guitar playing. *Human Movement Science*. doi: org/10.1016/j.humov.2011.07.001.

7 Ecological dynamics and motor learning design in sport

Keith Davids, Duarte Araújo, Robert Hristovski, Pedro Passos and Jia Yi Chow

We outline an ecological dynamics approach to motor learning that identifies the learner–environment relationship as the basis for learning design in sport. The relevant scale of analysis for understanding how to design tasks for motor learning and practice is to consider how each learner interacts with the environment. This approach to learning design captures intentionality and perception and action as intertwined processes underpinning individual differences in movement behaviour. During learning, the role of movement pattern variability is fundamental in supporting the exploratory behaviours needed to seek and establish functional movement solutions by each learner. Learning is enhanced by a strategy of locating the learner in the meta-stable region of the perceptual–motor workspace. In this region the learner does not act in a manner that is either completely independent or completely dependent on the environment. In this context, numerous rich and creative adaptive actions emerge from the task constraints. We discuss the implications of these ideas for a non-linear pedagogy after providing a brief explanation of key ideas in ecological dynamics.

Ecological dynamics

The ecological approach to learning (e.g. J. Gibson & E. Gibson, 1955; E. Gibson & Pick, 2000) originated as an alternative to enrichment theories of learning (more recently exemplified in the ACT-R model, Anderson et al., 2004). In enrichment theories, environmental stimuli are ambiguous and individuals resolve this ambiguity by enriching information-poor stimuli through inferential processes or internal knowledge structures. The emergence of expertise with learning and experience is believed to occur through an increase in the sophistication of enriched internalized processes and structures (Jacobs & Michaels, 2007).

In contrast, ecological dynamics advocates that the relevant scale of analysis for understanding behaviour is the functionality of the individual–environment relationship (Araújo, Davids & Hristovski, 2006). The mutuality and reciprocity of performers and their environments can result in an enhanced coupling of perception and action subsystems through learning. The acquisition of skill emerges as a consequence of indeterminate interactions between learners and the environment (Barab & Kirshner, 2001; Chow, Davids, Hristovski, Araújo & Passos, 2011; Davids,

Button & Bennett, 2008). During their interactions with other individuals and key objects, surfaces and events when practising, each individual learns to perceive the surrounding layout of the environment in the scale of his or her body and action capabilities (Turvey & Shaw, 1999). Learning leads to changes in environmental properties to which a learner's perceptual system becomes attuned, captured by key events, objects and inter-individual interactions (Jacobs & Michaels, 2007). Ecological dynamics attempts to explain how learners become adept at exploiting available sources of information for regulating performance.

The sophistication of skilled performance derives from the functionality of the improved fit between experts and their performance environments (Araújo & Davids, 2011). Performance and learning are constrained by key features of the performer–environment system including characteristics of the environment, the biomechanics, physiology and morphology of the individual, and task-specific constraints. Functionally adaptive, goal-directed behaviours emerge as learners attempt to satisfy these interacting constraints (Araújo et al., 2006; Chow et al., 2011; Davids et al., 2008). Proponents of ecological dynamics argue that explanations of learning should be aimed at 'phenomena within the organism–environment synergy rather than within the organism per se' (Beek & Meijer, 1988, p. 160). Understanding of movement skill acquisition may be enhanced as a result of an ecological dynamics focus, with its emphasis on the learner–environment relationship.

Skill acquisition in ecological dynamics

Successful performance in sport is characterized by reproducible low-dimensional patterns of behaviour, which are functional, consistent with respect to performance outcomes and resistant to perturbation (Warren, 2006). Low-dimensional patterns of behaviour are relatively stable and coordinated movements that have been well practised. They are less complex to perform since motor system degrees of freedom have been integrated into a functionally coherent and organized action, characteristic of a skilled athlete. Skilled performers are not locked into rigidly stable solutions (e.g. technical, tactical), but can modulate their behaviours to achieve consistent performance outcome goals, a capacity termed 'dexterity' (Bernstein, 1967, 1996; see also Davids et al., 2008). Successful performers are able to adapt their actions to dynamically shifting environments that characterize competitive sport. For example, there will probably be variability in the distance between the gymnast–beam 'system' before a vault is performed, or variability in the gymnast–floor (or bar) system when a vault in the air is performed. Such performance conditions require some level of compensatory movement pattern variability even in the most stable of athlete–environment relations.

Such adaptive flexibility in motor performance is tailored to current environmental conditions and task demands and implicates ongoing perceptual regulation of action. This idea was exemplified by Araújo et al. (2006) in studies of different sports including sailing, basketball and boxing. Changes in behaviours emerged during the action, such as a change in direction when dribbling past an opponent in basketball, or selecting a jab instead of a hook in boxing. From several available performance solutions, a decision emerged based on an athlete's perceptual attunement to key information sources such as time needed to close a gap with an opponent (i.e. a defender in basketball or adversary in boxing). During sport performance, if more functional movement patterns emerge to fit changing environmental circumstances due to performance fluctuations created by dynamic instabilities in the performer–environment system, the performer will be helped to discover and explore those functional movement patterns. However, fluctuations in the movement patterns themselves may or may not be functional. Fluctuations in the conditions of the performance environment can play a role in learning by helping individuals to search for more varied and effective movement solutions to fit the task dynamics.

Stable behavioural solutions correspond to attractors (i.e. preferred states) in the behavioural dynamics of the performer–environment system (Warren, 2006). Transitions between stable behavioural patterns correspond to bifurcations (or changes in behaviours). To illustrate, consider an attacker and defender engaged in a dyad in a team sport such as rugby union. Patterns of attack and defence in team games can be shaped by fluctuations caused by local interactions of individual attackers and defenders in game subphases (Passos et al., 2009). The interactions of opposing players in team games can be characterized as fluctuations of different magnitudes that can provide a measure of the stability of an attacker–defender dyad. The moment that this equilibrium is broken a system bifurcation emerges; for example, the attacker emerges as the player closest to the try line or the defender successfully rips the ball from an attacker in a tackle. System bifurcations can provide a mechanism for athletes 'deciding' when one mode of behaviour is no longer functional (Kelso & Engström, 2006). Such instabilities do not exist a priori in a performance context in sport but are emergent and dynamic, shaped by the specific confluence of task and environmental constraints. These ideas are congruent with Gibson's (1979) proposition that control in human behaviour lies in the actor–environment system, not solely within the individual.

For each learner, the task in sport is to exploit physical (i.e. mechanical) and informational (i.e. patterns in the distribution of stimulus energy) constraints to stabilize an intended behaviour. An emergent performance solution may rely more or less upon physical or informational regularities, depending on the task. There are typically a limited number of varied but stable performance solutions that can be achieved for a desired outcome. In a team ball game such as volleyball, an individual may have several options for attacking the ball at the net. The most functional option at any moment will emerge dependent on the state of the environment (e.g. positioning of defenders on the court, height and location of the ball with respect to the net, and how many touches are left for the attacking side).

Representative learning design

Brunswik (1956) advocated the investigation of performer–environment interactions in psychological research using the concept of 'representative experimental design'. Perceptual variables incorporated into experimental designs should be sampled from the performer's typical performance environment, to which behaviour is intended to be generalized. In motor learning, design of learning tasks should represent the task constraints of the performance environment. In representative design there is a strong emphasis on the specificity of the relations between the individual and the environment, which is often neglected in traditional approaches to behavioural sciences (Dunwoody, 2006).

Generalizability is central to Brunswik's (1956) notion of representative experimental design. Brunswikian concepts in ecological psychology are harmonious with Gibson's (1979) emphasis on the reciprocal relations between perception and action. In studies of motor learning in sport, 'representative learning design' implies the generalization of learning task constraints to the task constraints encountered during performance, for example when perceiving the actions of a 'live' opponent in a study of anticipation (Araújo et al., 2006; Pinder, Davids, Renshaw & Araújo, 2011). An important pedagogical principle in sport is the need to ensure that there is adequate 'sampling' of information from the performance environment in a teaching task, ensuring that modified games will provide a close representation of an actual game so that important sources of information are present (Tan, Chow & Davids, in press). The criteria to develop an operational definition of 'representative learning design' (Araújo, Davids & Passos, 2007; Pinder et al., 2011) are synthesized in Table 7.1.

In cricket, batting against a bowling machine is not representative of batting against a real bowler (Pinder et al., 2011). There were clear distinctions in emergent movement patterns under the two conditions. Against the ball projection machine, batters could use only ball flight information. Therefore, the tendency to design simplistic and controlled practice drills may not accomplish the requisite level of representative design to enhance learning in specific sports.

Non-linear pedagogy and the role of constraints in facilitating learning

Conceptualizing humans as belonging to a class of non-linear dynamical systems has led to the development of a *non-linear pedagogy* (Chow, Davids, Button & Koh, 2006; Renshaw, Chow, Davids & Hammond, 2010). It has been argued that the learning process can be guided by manipulating key constraints acting on each individual (Davids, Button & Bennett, 2008). Newell (1986) classified three categories of constraints: task, organismic and environmental. These constraints do not influence the learning process independently, but rather form complex interacting configurations that shape *the perceptual–motor landscape* of each learner (Davids et al., 2008; Chow et al., 2011). The perceptual–motor landscape of a learner forms a kind of workspace in which all potential movement solutions for an individual learner may exist. In non-linear neurobiological systems, constraint configurations do not prescribe each learner's behaviour but simply guide it.

In the theory of 'direct' learning (Jacobs & Michaels, 2007), information from the environment, in the form of ambient energy arrays, is critical in channelling learners to acquire movement skills. Jacobs and Michaels described learning as the process of change in the relevant informational parameters that informs action and

Table 7.1 Criteria, description and examples for 'representative learning design'

Criteria	Description	Examples
Design complex tasks	Provide learners with opportunities to explore a variety of task solutions	Challenge learners to practise under different task constraints in which information or goals are changed
Provide access to relevant sources of information	Create tasks that specify properties of interest for learners. Allow them to make reliable judgements and actions based on relevant patterns in the environment	Perceptual judgements and actions of an advanced tennis player will be improved at a faster rate if he or she is required to hit a ball that comes from the actions of an opponent rather than from a ball projection machine
Use dynamic tasks	Include tasks that evolve over time	Playing small-sided games (2v1 or 3v3) encourages learners to understand where to move in order to perform an action. This opportunity for establishing a relationship between movement and action may not be afforded in static practice drills
Allow for active perception	Enable learners to act in context in order to perceive informational variables that support achievement of their goals	Movement interactions between an attacker and a defender allow perception of informational variables such as interpersonal distance and the time to close the space between players
Set achievable goals	Design tasks in which goals can always be achieved with different degrees of success (e.g. more quickly or slowly, in a bigger or smaller area)	In a tennis practice game when an advanced player plays with a novice, the task of the advanced player might be to place the ball into certain restricted areas of the court, and the task of the novice is simply to return the ball to the other side

learning. Direct learning is aligned with the theory of direct perception, according to which perception *is* the detection of information (Michaels & Carello, 1981), avoiding the need to assume different internal processes from the detection of information. In the theory of direct learning, perceptual information is directly mapped to action and the information for learning is directly perceived by individuals.

Individual differences in learning

It is unsurprising that the non-linear interactions of key constraints lead to individual differences in how learners assemble movement solutions. This is an important advance in understanding since many traditional theories of learning recognize the existence of individual differences, but fail to provide an analysis of how these may be designed into learning programmes. A non-linear pedagogical approach provides a principled, theoretical framework for understanding individuality and applying the ideas in learning design. Even if task and environmental constraints were considered as constant, the learning dynamics of each individual would be different. The distinctive configurations of constraints between learners are manifest in how each individual attempts to satisfy specific task constraints during practice. It is futile to try and identify a common, idealized motor pattern towards which all learners should aspire (e.g. learning a 'classical' technique for an action). Individual learners can often experience discontinuous, qualitative changes in performance due to the presence of instabilities in their perceptual–motor landscape. These instabilities may be due to growth, maturation and learning. The perceptual–motor landscape may undergo changes in stability, requiring learners to adapt quickly to a newly emerged stable movement solution (i.e. on a much shorter timescale than the long-term learning process itself). For example, during adolescence, sudden growth spurts may alter limb properties, requiring learners to recalibrate their movement responses. Similarly, changes to functional performance characteristics due to influences of training may lead to muscle asymmetries, with concomitant effects on motor performance. Non-linear pedagogy highlights the individuality of learning pathways and individuality of performance solutions. Constraints can act on learners along different timescales, from the immediate (at the timescale of perception and action) to the more long-term (at the timescale of developmental change over months and years).

The role of behavioural variability in learning

The 'search and assemble' process that characterizes learning in each individual can be enhanced by system variability, which amplifies exploratory activity and guides discovery of individualized functional solutions (Newell, Liu & Mayer-Kress, 2008; Schöllhorn, Mayer-Kress, Newell & Michelbrink, 2009). Intrinsic movement variability enlarges the area of solution search in the learner's phase space, that is the conceptual space of all possible movement solutions.

The positive role that system variability can play in facilitating adaptive behaviours is a feature of neurobiological learning in general. Although the mechanics of ball passing between players in team games can be deterministically modelled, the trajectory of the ball after only a few passes cannot be deterministically predicted due to its sensitivity to small differences in trajectory variations r. This may be considered an example of the so-called 'Sinai billiards dynamics' (see, for example, Rozikov, 2007), in which chaotic ball trajectories are formed from minute variations that accumulate. Non-deterministic processes, however, do not signify the absence of predictability. For example, when boxers practise punching against a heavy bag or opponent, the hand-striking sequences tend to show different degrees of influence of previous strikes on subsequent sequences of action (Hristovski, Davids & Araújo, 2009). The non-deterministic nature of the boxer–target system means that, although subsequent changes in the system's state cannot be predicted with perfect probability, emerging system states are somewhat correlated. Perturbations are usually composed of influences that are external to the system (e.g. the presence of significant others) and that make the system drift from its stationary state. This contrasts with fluctuations that signify drifts from the stationary state generated by intrinsic system disturbances (such as when interpersonal distance between an attacker and a marking defender causes fluctuations in the balance of an attacker–defender dyad in team sports).

These ideas suggest that adaptive variability in neurobiological systems has a functional role in producing subtle variations and adaptive patterns of behaviour in ever-changing environments. Schöllhorn and colleagues have advocated a 'Differential Learning' approach, in which learners experience a variety of movement patterns (thus providing a 'noisy' learning environment), to encourage development of an individualized movement pattern that best fits the task dynamics of the context. Schöllhorn, Beckman, Michelbrink, Sechelmann and Davids (2006) studied the acquisition of dribbling and passing skills in association football. Participants were exposed to continuous changes in movement execution, avoidance of repetitions, absence of corrective instructions and a focus on exploratory practice. This group showed stronger learning effects than other participants exposed to a traditional teaching approach that emphasized repetition of a putative optimal technique. In summary, challenging individuals to perform different variations of a skill can be beneficial since learners can be engaged to search for functional movement solutions by adding movement variability to a target skill (see also Frank, Michelbrink, Beckmann & Schöllhorn, 2008; Schöllhorn et al., 2009).

The differential learning findings demonstrated how the introduction of movement variability during learning can support transitions from one pattern to a new adaptive pattern. Clearly, not all variability is beneficial (Hamill, Haddad, Heiderscheit, Emmerik & Li, 2006) and a key challenge is to design variability strategically into a learning task to encourage functional and adaptive learning behaviours.

Constrained variability, coloured noise and meta-stability in learning designs

The amount and type of noise present in learning environments can constrain the behaviours emerging from learners. In multi-stable, dynamical systems, such as human movement systems, noise can play a functional role by enhancing the probability of transition between the multiple states of the system. The interjection of noise or signal variability can contribute to the exploration of task solutions.

Coaches can harness these ideas to constrain learning environments by understanding how to structure variability. Noise is white when all its components can contribute equally to the overall power of the noise, as in white light, whose different colours contribute equally to the spectrum. With coloured noise, some, usually lower-frequency (e.g. red), components contribute more than others, thereby containing variable structure rather than randomness. Coloured (i.e. correlated) noise has structure to it and, from a learning perspective, it stimulates movement system variability. This type of variability could be achieved through carefully considered manipulations to specific task and environmental constraints. In learning environments in which the noise added by a teacher or coach is white, learners are left to their own devices to explore system multi-stability and discover movement solutions themselves. When adding coloured noise, pedagogists implement processes of guided discovery. This constrains a learner to search in specific, meta-stable regions of the perceptual–motor performance workspace. In this region a learner will be poised at the edge of instability to facilitate possible transitions between movement behaviours that could be effective for changing performance situations. The learner cannot act completely independently of environmental constraints, nor in a fully dependent manner (waiting for information to act).

These ideas were illustrated by Hristovski, Davids and Araújo (2006), who investigated the impact of target distance on action patterns of boxers. No specific instructions were given to boxers on how to hit a heavy punch bag. The distance between the boxers and the punching bag was manipulated. Different scaled-body distances afforded the emergence of different movement patterns (e.g. hooks, jabs, uppercuts). At a critical scaled-body distance (0.6), boxers were in a maximal meta-stability state in which they could flexibly switch between any of the boxing action modes. The scaled-body distance value of 0.6 was critical in pushing the boxer's movement system to the edge of instability, from where each punching mode could be spontaneously activated under the task and the environmental constraints. At other values of scaled distance this level of flexibility in emergent actions was not observed.

Why is meta-stability so important for learning design? Meta-stable states have been defined as 'dynamically stable', allowing systems to remain balanced in readiness for transitions (Kelso, 1995). In the meta-stable state, small fluctuations can push it towards a specific action path. Rich interactions can spontaneously emerge within complex systems when previously uncorrelated system components or processes suddenly become interconnected under constraints (Guerin & Kunkle, 2004; Juarrero, 1999).

A good example of system meta-stability was observed in the contextual dependency that emerged between attackers and defenders in rugby union dyads (Passos et al., 2009). As interpersonal distance decreased, the attacker–defender system entered a meta-stable region of performance, signifying that there was a balance in the readiness of the system to transit between multiple attractors. Within certain values of interpersonal distance, three possible outcomes exerted influence on the system: (1) an effective tackle could occur; (2) a tackle could occur but the attacker could pass the defender; or (3) the attacker could avoid physical contact with the defender and run towards the try line. The emergence of one of these outcomes was due to the level of coupling among system components. When the attacker and defender entered a meta-stable region (due primarily to decreasing interpersonal distance) the components of the dyadic system became more or less coupled. If an attacker and defender became coupled, then a tackle was more likely to occur, whereas a try was more likely when they were not coupled.

Meta-stable states in complex neurobiological systems are ideal for learning because varied and creative patterns of behaviour can arise (Hristovski et al., 2006; Hristovski, Davids, Araújo & Passos, 2011). In some contexts such as ice climbing or kayaking, discovery learning based on random variability (i.e. white noise) may not have desirable consequences for learners, because of obvious health and safety issues. In these circumstances, the difference between random fluctuations and constrained fluctuations in learners needs to be recognized.

The coupling that emerges between a learner and the environment in team games during learning implies that it is important to discern the dynamics induced by the co-adaptive movements of attackers and defenders. Different types of environmental information variability could have profound effects on success. In other sciences it has been shown that coloured noise enhances the switching rate between stable modes of behaviour more successfully than uncorrelated (white) noise (Wio, 2005). Adding structured variability to the practice environments of attackers and defenders in small-sided team games can help individual learners discover and explore the range of decisions and actions available to them in specific game subphases. Switching between different modes of behaviour can provide the adaptive variability needed to perform successfully in team games.

These findings illustrate why, more recently, there has been much greater emphasis on exploring how variability can be infused in the motor learning process (e.g. Schöllhorn et al., 2009).The variability added through learning design requires more options to be created for advanced learners (at the control stage of learning) and fewer options for novice learners (at the coordination stage). At the control stage, more advanced learners have more relatively stable patterns of movement coordination available (e.g. volleyballers who can successfully perform a defensive dig with two arms). More practice variability can be added to the learning environments of these players in order to 'perturb' them from their stable skill base. Space and time manipulations during practice can lead these players to explore and acquire other skills for defending an attack, perhaps involving one arm as well as two. On the other hand, beginners in volleyball are seeking to establish more stable movement patterns for defending and need less variability (see also Newell, 1985). Pedagogists need to infuse a relevant amount and type of noise to place learners in the meta-stable region, with an emphasis on individual differences in learning.

During motor learning when noise can be incorporated, free competition between particular solutions can occur, and coaches or trainers should not be too prescriptive in directing learners to find functional performance solutions (Chow et al., 2011). Learning to find performance solutions is predicated on the education of intention (i.e. converging task goals with the performer's goals), attunement (i.e. the appropriate perception and use of key sources of information), calibration (i.e. scaling movement to the key information sources) (Fajen, Riley & Turvey, 2009; Jacobs & Michaels, 2007) and the functional reorganization of perceptual–motor degrees of freedom (Newell, 1985; Savelsbergh & Van der Kamp, 2000) (see Table 7.2). Next we discuss how these learning processes contribute to three possible phases of skill development: (1) exploration, (2) discovery and stabilization and (3) exploitation.

How manipulating constraints can enhance skill acquisition in sport

Goal constraints can be considered *extraordinary* in comparison with physical constraints, regulating action if a specific performance outcome is intended. Intentional constraints shape actions to change current information into information that is specific in supporting an intended outcome (Shaw & Turvey, 1999). This argument implies that the first step in the learning process is the 'education

Table 7.2 Phases of the development of skill and related learning processes

Phases of skill development	Main learning processes
Exploration of degrees of freedom to achieve a task goal: searches the internal and external system degrees of freedom to find a way to achieve a certain goal	Education of intention: converging task goals with learner's goals
Exploring task solutions and stabilizing them: identifies tentative performance solutions and attempts to reproduce them during goal-directed behaviour	Attunement: the appropriate perception and use of sources of information
Exploiting perceptual–motor degrees of freedom: immediate adaptation to situational demands and effective goal achievement	Calibration: scaling action to the information

of intention' (Jacobs & Michaels, 2007), which will initiate the process of exploring system degrees of freedom.

Changing constraints shape emerging behaviours, and interactions between an individual performer, environment and task over time can produce a particular function of behavioural change. The relative impact of constraints changes with time can be visualized in Figure 7.1, showing how constraints channel a learning system to define a specific path to an intended goal. Figure 7.1 depicts a convergence between the degrees of freedom bounded by the environment and the individual. During learning these become constrained to form links (synergies) that allow goal achievement. The more specifically defined is the goal path, the more do functional constraints and task constraints specify the behaviours for achieving that goal.

The closer the performer is to actual performance, the more he or she is sensitive to momentary variations and is constrained by past events. This is why Figure 7.1

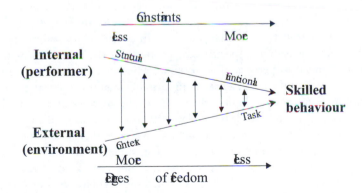

Figure 7.1 A schematic showing that to learn action solutions is to influence the convergent interactions of a performer with the environment in goal-directed activity. The degrees of freedom are reduced in the same proportion as there are more constraints to channel behaviour.

shows that, near the moment when skilled behaviour emerges, functional characteristics of the individual (e.g. fatigue, emotions, concentration) become more influential. However, during learning, at a longer timescale than that of performance, the individual's structural characteristics (e.g. height, limb length) may be more influential.

In seeking solutions to behavioural task goals, the performer is attempting to discover the dynamic characteristics of a system defined over the individual performer, environment and task.

Exploring degrees of freedom to achieve a task goal

Intentional constraints shape perception–action couplings. In certain situations, particular perceptions and actions are more functional than others and, with experience, learners get better at choosing the perceptions and actions they can use to achieve task goals. Different intentions organize perceptual–motor systems in distinct ways. Educating the intentions of learners influences which particular informational variable needs to be perceived.

The education of intention is not just an information-guiding process. Intention plays its role by priming a perceptual system to be attuned to information appropriate for specific perceptions and actions. In other words, intentions direct the attention of a learner and performer. Intentions motivate exploratory behaviours that constrain perception, which further constrains action, and so on. In a one-against-one basketball game close to the basket, it can be assumed that attackers with the ball intend to dribble past the defender and to shoot, rather than simply to maintain possession of the ball. Such assumptions are necessary because of the intertwined relations between intentions, perceptions and actions.

This aspect of learning design is also impacted by Bernstein's (1967) insights on how individual degrees of freedom are regulated. When the intentions of a performer correspond with a task goal there is a need to establish basic relationships with the environment to acquire minimum control over the system (e.g. what to attend to, what movements and postures are involved). At this stage, movement may be coupled to a specific source of information that supports action, but it does not mean that it specifies the property of the environment that the performer intended to perceive. For example, when a goal tender in ice hockey attempts to intercept the puck, a specifying variable might be the trajectory of the puck. Information from the flight of the puck will specify when and where the goal tender's intercepting limb needs to be placed in space to successfully parry a shot. The term *non-specifying variable* is reserved for a variable that does not specify the property that a perceiver intends to perceive (e.g. a player attempting to perceive the trajectory of a puck despite the deceptive movements of an opponent striking it). Skilled athletes can orient their bodies to hit a shot in one corner of a goal while shooting at the opposite corner to provide non-specifying information to confuse a goal tender. The term *specifying variable* is used only for a variable that specifies the property that a perceiver intends to perceive (e.g. the focus of expansion of the puck on a goal tender's retina specifies the speed of approach of the puck for interception).

Exploring task solutions and stabilizing them

Later in learning, the performer identifies tentative performance solutions and attempts to reproduce them during goal-directed behaviour by reorganizing the previously exaggerated constriction of degrees of freedom (Vereijken, van Emmerik, Whiting & Newell, 1992). New action possibilities start to be identified (e.g. when an informational variable is not useful). Perceptual attunement is the process of learning which sources of information to attend to in which situations and when. With practice, learners converge from sources of information that may be only partly useful in one situation (i.e. non-specifying) to sources of information that are more useful (i.e. specifying), under a variety of circumstances. The stabilization of discovered solutions, as well as exploration of the limits of these solutions, and the search for new, specifying information–action couplings, form the dominant characteristics of this phase. In catching a fly ball in baseball, the information a novice picks up may be the peak optical velocity or the maximum height of the ball. These sources of information do not exactly specify the direction and speed with which a fielder should run to intercept the ball. Only during later phases of skill development can the individual converge on other more specifying variables such as vertical optical acceleration (Michaels & Oudejans, 1992).

Exploiting perceptual–motor degrees of freedom

Specifying information sources tend to be regularly used by skilled athletes because they have searched for and discovered these during extensive practice. The exploitation of motor and perceptual degrees of freedom is a characteristic of skilled behaviour in sport and allows adaptation to situational demands and effective goal achievement. At this stage, athletes achieve attunement to a wider range of spatial and temporal variables and greater sensitivity to the contextual consequences of their actions (Araújo, Davids & Serpa, 2005). System degeneracy, or the ability of elements that are structurally different to perform a similar function or yield a similar output, is an essential feature of skilled behaviour. It enhances the flexibility of athletes in competitive performance environments (Davids, Button, Araújo, Renshaw & Hristovski, 2006). Exploiting neurobiological degeneracy is a key aspect of skilled behaviour in sport because performance is not limited to a restricted movement pattern or just a few perceptual variables to make decisions and to regulate actions.

A relevant process at this stage is that of calibration or scaling of the perceptual-motor system to information. Specifying information can appropriately constrain a perception or action. Body dimensions and action capabilities are not fixed, but often change on account of development, ageing and training. When these change, actions that were once possible may become impossible (or vice versa, Fajen et al., 2009). For example, players' effective body dimensions are altered by use of implements such as racquets, roller blades and sticks. Calibration and recalibration are necessary to establish and update the mapping between the units in which the relevant properties of the world are perceived and the units in which the action is realized.

For a properly calibrated performer, body-scaled and action-scaled affordances can be directly and reliably perceived by simply picking up the relevant sources of information (Fajen et al., 2009). Although recalibration occurs quite rapidly, it is likely that continued experience leads to further refinement. Affordances that are both body- and action-scaled may be prevalent in sports. The development of motor skill is not a homogeneous process, and idiosyncratic manifestations are expected (Newell et al., 2008). Processes such as education of intention, attunement and calibration can occur in all the three phases. In addition, learners may benefit from some kinds of enrichment, most obviously through physical conditioning and regular access to high-quality equipment and practice facilities (such as a diving pool and a springboard in learning to dive). This enrichment does not theoretically explain the learning process, since it merely facilitates learning.

In summary, intentions, perceptions and actions are intertwined processes that benefit from the education of intention, attunement to key perceptual variables in the performance environment and calibration as the system changes as a result of processes such as development and maturation. Learning environments need to be carefully designed in order to facilitate appropriate interactions between these. A major concept in ensuring a functional learning design is *representative learning design* (Pinder et al., 2011), predicated on Brunswik's (1956) representative task design.

Designing learning contexts in sport

In the study of perception and action, representative design (Brunswik, 1956) has been acknowledged as the generalization of task constraints in experimental designs to the constraints encountered in specific performance environments, such as sport (Araújo et al., 2006; Davids, 2008). Ensuring that task constraints are representative is not a trivial matter since, in sport studies, small changes in task constraints can lead to substantial changes in performance outcomes and movement responses (Hristovski et al., 2006). In fact, task sensitive bifurcations naturally partition the continuum of actions (individual or collective) into discrete, qualitatively distinct 'typical situations' (see Figure 7.2) of any representative learning design (Hristovski et al., 2011). For example, in boxing, the clench situation is qualitatively different from that of close-distance fighting because of the *number* and the *types* of actions that boxers can use. Similarly, close-distance fighting differs from half-distance and long-distance fighting, making them all different typical performance situations. The borders between qualitatively different typical situations are defined by the abrupt change of the number and the type of affordable actions (i.e. opportunities for action). Typical performance situations are performer-dependent and should be defined with respect to body- or action-scaled possibilities.

By directing attention to these qualitative changes when individually defined situations emerge or cease to exist, that is, training at the very borders of different typical performance situations in sport, may prove to be useful. Whereas training 'inside' the regions of typical situations may stabilize the afforded actions and their coupling, training at the bifurcation points offers acquisition of qualitatively different performer–environment interactions and sensitization to qualitative situation changes in competition.

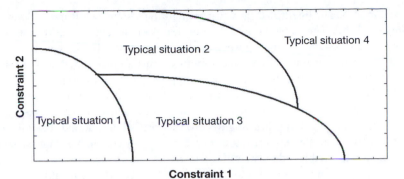
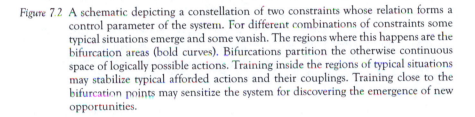

Figure 7.2 A schematic depicting a constellation of two constraints whose relation forms a control parameter of the system. For different combinations of constraints some typical situations emerge and some vanish. The regions where this happens are the bifurcation areas (bold curves). Bifurcations partition the otherwise continuous space of logically possible actions. Training inside the regions of typical situations may stabilize typical afforded actions and their couplings. Training close to the bifurcation points may sensitize the system for discovering the emergence of new opportunities.

Pedagogists need to appreciate fully the major constraints of a particular performance environment and how the design of practice tasks and interventions may support the maintenance of coupled perception and action processes, which reflect the functional behaviours of athletes. The ubiquitous practice of decomposing tasks into smaller, putatively more manageable parts needs to be considered since a coach may be interfering with the acquisition of an important perception–action coupling. *Representative learning design* is a new term which theoretically captures how motor learning theorists and pedagogues might use insights from ecological dynamics, such as perception–action coupling, emergence under constraints, self-organization, task simplification, movement pattern variability and neurobiological system degeneracy, to ensure that practice and training task constraints are representative of the context towards which they are intended to generalize (Pinder et al., 2011).

The constraints of training and practice need to replicate the performance environment adequately so that they are not too static, allowing learners to detect affordances and couple actions to key information sources. Learners need to move in order to learn how to pick up information successfully to regulate their actions, which support the perception of further specifying variables to coordinate movements in a cyclical manner (Gibson, 1979). This critical requirement was highlighted in a recent study examining the effectiveness of dynamic versus static training drills designed to replicate the lower-limb coordination patterns in the sport of triple jumping (Wilson, Simpson, Van Emmerik & Hamill, 2008). Static tests lack functionality because they typically restrict the exploratory processes of a learner and do not represent the constraints of performance. This criticism was directed at a new soccer skills test comprising passing and shooting tasks that required players to kick a moving ball, delivered at a constant speed, towards one of four randomly determined targets (identified by a custom lighting system, see Russell, Benton & Kingsley, 2010). The static nature of cones, for example, allows a performer to be completely in control of the interpersonal distance and relative velocity that has been shown to constrain successful dribbling against a moving defender (Passos et al., 2008). By neglecting the active role of opponents in task design, Russell et al. (2010) did not reproduce the dynamic nature of the football performance environment, which would impact on the functionality of the skills' evaluation test.

To attain representative learning design, theorists should design dynamic interventions that consider interacting constraints on movement behaviours, sample informational variables adequately and ensure the *functional* coupling between perception and action processes (Pinder et al., 2011). Functionality would ensure that (1) the degree of success of a performer's actions are controlled for, and compared between contexts, and (2) performers are able to achieve specific goals by regulating actions in learning contexts (movement responses, decision-making) with comparable information to that existing in the performance environment.

In order to examine empirically the degree of association between behaviours in a learning task with that of a performance setting, the importance of Stoffregen, Bardy, Smart and Pagulayan's (2003) concept of *action fidelity* needs to be recognized (Araújo et al., 2007). Stoffregen et al. proposed that fidelity exists when there is a transfer of performance. Practice, training and learning tasks are simulations of the performance environment that need to be high in action fidelity (in much the same way that video designs in studies of anticipation are intended as simulations of a performance context that is the subject of generalization, e.g. Araújo et al., 2005). The degree of action fidelity can be measured by analysing task performance in detail. For example, measures of task performance in sport, such as time taken to complete a task and observed kinematic (coordination) data during performance, would provide means to assess action fidelity (Araújo et al., 2007).

Conclusions and implications for practice

According to the ecological dynamics approach, the training of motor skill should be based on organizing practice conditions that promote the development of expertise, even in non-experts (Araújo, 2007). We concur with Klein's (1997) view that a solution is to teach performers to learn like experts, and to gain expertise autonomously when practising in training sessions or in competitions. There is no general 'optimal organization' for designing practices. The organization of training practices that are useful (i.e. to develop sport expertise) is that which is relevant to improve performance of a specific individual athlete, or groups of athletes, in a certain context learning a certain task (Davids, Button & Bennett, 2008).

Successful learning design is based on a sound understanding of (1) the expertise level of the performer on the task, (2) the functions (goals) to be trained and (3) the primary constraints on behaviour (organismic, task and environmental) to be manipulated or taken into account during learning. The key to assisting learners in acquiring functional movement behaviours comes about through presenting the relevant constraints during the different phases of skill development.

Coaches are typically more concerned with manipulating task constraints, since they are open to control and provide a direct channel to shape the progression of an athlete. A major challenge is to consider the functional representativeness of training exercises. Rules, instructions and equipment can be manipulated to narrow the search within the perceptual–motor workspace such that effective actions can be made.

Personal constraints should be intimately related with task constraints. Therefore, interventions may occur by selecting or transforming aspects of the task in order to facilitate a specific impact on an individual athlete, for example to select athletes differing in height to play one-on-one near the basket in basketball. Some interventions (e.g. induction of fatigue, thermal conditions of specific performance environments, changes in emotional state, inducing variability) may be appropriate to facilitate coping skills in individual learners. Designing these critical features of performance into learning programmes makes practice more representative. For example, adding variability into movement patterns has been shown to help learners differentiate actions during learning, allowing them to become more functionally adaptive in their movements (see Schöllhorn et al., 2006). Environmental constraints cannot be easily manipulated, but they may be considered to promote a better adaptation of the performer to the performance context.

References

Anderson, J. R., Bothell, D., Byrne, M.-D., Douglass, S., Lebiere, C., & Qin, Y. (2004). An integrated theory of the mind. *Psychological Review, 111*(4), 1036–1060.

Araújo, D. (2007). Promoting ecologies where performers exhibit expert interactions. *International Journal of Sport Psychology, 38*, 73–77.

Araújo, D., & Davids, K. (2011). What exactly is *acquired* during skill acquisition? *Journal of Consciousness Studies, 18*, 7–23.

Araújo, D., Davids, K., & Hristovski, R. (2006). The ecological dynamics of decision making in sport. *Psychology of Sport and Exercise, 7*, 653–676.

Araújo, D., Davids, K., & Passos, P. (2007). Ecological validity, representative design and correspondence between experimental task constraints and behavioral settings. *Ecological Psychology, 19*, 69–78.

Araújo, D., Davids, K., & Serpa, S. (2005). An ecological approach to expertise effects in decision-making in a simulated sailing regatta. *Psychology of Sport and Exercise, 6*(6), 671–692.

Barab, S. A., & Kirshner, D. (2001). Guests editors' introduction: Rethinking methodologies in the learning sciences. *Journal of the Learning Sciences, 10*(1&2), 5–15.

Beek, P. J., & Meijer, O. G. (1988). On the nature of the motor-action controversy. In Meijer, O. G., & Roth, K. (Eds.), *Complex movement behavior: The motor-action controversy.* Amsterdam: North-Holland.

Bernstein, N. (1967). *The co-ordination and regulation of movements.* Oxford: Pergamon Press.

Bernstein, N. (1996). On dexterity and its development. In Latash, M., & Turvey, M. T. (Eds.), *On dexterity and its development* (pp. 3–24), Mahwah, NJ: Erlbaum.

Brunswik, E. (1956). *Perception and the representative design of psychological experiments* (2nd edn.). Berkeley: University of California Press.

Chow, J. Y., Davids, K., Button, C., & Koh, M. (2006). Organisation of motor system degrees of freedom during the soccer chip: An analysis of skilled performance. *International Journal of Sport Psychology, 37*, 207–229.

Chow, J. Y., Davids, K., Hristovski, R., Araújo, D., & Passos, P. (2011). Nonlinear pedagogy: Learning design for self-organizing neurobiological systems. *New Ideas in Psychology, 29,* 189–200.

Davids, K. (2008). Designing representative task constraints for studying visual anticipation in fast ball sports: What we can learn from past and contemporary insights in neurobiology and psychology. *International Journal of Sport Psychology, 39,* 166–177.

Davids, K., Button, C. Araújo, D., Renshaw, I., & Hristovski, R. (2006). Movement models from sports provide representative task constraints for studying adaptive behavior in human motor systems. *Adaptive Behavior, 14,* 73–95.

Davids, K., Button, C., & Bennett, S. (2008). *Dynamics of skill acquisition: A constraints-led approach.* Champaign, IL: Human Kinetics.

Dunwoody, P. T. (2006). The neglect of the environment by cognitive psychology. *Journal of Theoretical and Philosophical Psychology, 26,* 139–153.

Fajen, B., Riley, M., & Turvey, M. (2009). Information, affordances and the control of action in sport. *International Journal of Sport Psychology, 40,* 79–107.

Frank, T. D., Michelbrink, M., Beckmann, H., & Schöllhorn, W. I. (2008). A quantitative dynamical systems approach to differential learning: Self-organization principle and order parameter equations. *Biological Cybernetics, 98*(1), 19–31.

Gibson, J. J. (1979). *The ecological approach to visual perception.* Hillsdale, NJ: Lawrence Erlbaum Associates.

Gibson, J., & Gibson, E. (1955). Perceptual learning: Differentiation or enrichment? *Psychological Research, 62,* 32–41.

Gibson, E. J., & Pick, A. D. (2000). *An ecological approach to perceptual learning and development.* New York: Oxford University Press.

Guerin, S., & Kunkle, D. (2004). Emergence of constraint in self-organizing systems. *Nonlinear Dynamics, Psychology, and Life Sciences, 8,* 131–146.

Hamill, J., Haddad, J. M., Heiderscheit, B. C., Emmerik, R. E. A., & Li, L. (2006). Clinical relevance of variability in coordination. In Davids, K., Bennett, S., & Newell, K. M. (Eds.), *Movement system variability* (pp. 153–165). Champaign, IL: Human Kinetics.

Hristovski, R., Davids, K., & Araújo, D. (2006). Affordance-controlled bifurcations of action patterns in martial arts. *Nonlinear Dynamics, Psychology & the Life Sciences, 10,* 409–444.

Hristovski, R., Davids, K., & Araújo, D. (2009). Information for regulating action in sport: Metastability and emergence of tactical solutions under ecological constraints. In Araujo, D., Ripoll, H., & Raab, M. (Eds.), *Perspectives on cognition and action in sport* (pp. 43–57). Hauppauge, NY: Nova Science Publishers.

Hristovski, R., Davids, K., Araújo, D. & Passos, P. (2011). Constraints-induced emergence of functional novelty in complex neurobiological systems: A basis for creativity in sport. *Nonlinear Dynamics, Psychology and the Life Sciences, 15,* 175–206.

Jacobs, D., & Michaels, C. (2007). Direct learning. *Ecological Psychology, 19,* 321–349.

Juarrero, A. (1999). *Dynamics in action: Intentional behavior as a complex system.* Cambridge, MA: MIT Press.

Kelso, J. S. (1995). *Dynamic patterns: The self-organization of brain and behaviour.* Cambridge, MA: MIT.

Kelso, J., & Engstrom, D. (2006). *The complementary nature.* Cambridge, MA: MIT Press.

Klein, G. (1997). Developing expertise in decision making. *Thinking and Reasoning, 3*(4), 337–352.

Michaels, C. F., & Carello, C. (1981). *Direct perception.* Englewood Cliffs, NJ: Prentice Hall.

Michaels, C. F., & Oudejans, R. R. D. (1992). The optics and actions of catching fly balls: Zeroing out optical acceleration. *Ecological Psychology, 4,* 199–222.

Newell, K. (1985). Coordination, control, and skill. In Goodman, D., Wilberg, R., & Franks, I. (Eds.), *Differing perspectives in motor learning, memory and control* (pp. 295–317). Amsterdam: North-Holland.

Newell, K. M. (1986). Constraints on the development of coordination. In Wade, M. G., & Whiting, H. T. A. (Eds.), *Motor development in children: Aspects of coordination and control* (pp. 341–360). Dordrecht, Netherlands: Martinus Nijhoff.

Newell, K. M., Liu, Y.-T., & Mayer-Kress, G. (2008). Landscapes beyond the HKB Model. In Fuchs, A., & Jirsa, V. K. (Eds.), *Coordination: Neural, behavioral and social dynamics*. Berlin: Springer Verlag.

Passos, P., Araújo, D., Davids, K., Gouveia, L., Serpa, S., & Milho, J. (2008). Information governing dynamics of attacker–defender interactions in youth level rugby union. *Journal of Sports Sciences, 26*, 1421–1429.

Passos, P., Araújo, D., Davids, K., Gouveia, L., Serpa, S., Milho, J., & Fonseca, S. (2009). Interpersonal pattern dynamics and adaptive behavior in multi-agent neurobiological systems: A conceptual model and data. *Journal of Motor Behavior, 41*(5), 445–459.

Pinder, R., Davids, K., Renshaw, I., & Araújo, D. (2011). Representative learning design and functionality of research and practice in sport. *Journal of Sport & Exercise Psychology, 33*, 146–155.

Renshaw, I., Chow, J. Y., Davids, K., & Hammond, J. (2010). A constraints-led perspective to understanding skill acquisition and game play: A basis for integration of motor learning theory and physical education praxis? *Physical Education & Sport Pedagogy*. doi: 10.1080/17408980902791586

Rozikov, U. A. (2007). What is mathematical billiards? *Math Track, 3*, 56–65.

Russell, M., Benton, D., & Kingsley, M. (2010). Reliability and construct validity of soccer skills tests that measure passing, shooting, and dribbling. *Journal of Sports Sciences, 28*(13), 1399–1408.

Savelsbergh, G., & Van der Kamp, J. (2000). Information in learning to coordinate and control movement: Is there a need for specificity of practice? *International Journal of Sport Psychology, 31*, 467–484.

Schöllhorn, W. I., Beckmann, H., Michelbrink, M., Sechelmann, M., Trockel, M., & Davids, K. (2006). Does noise provide a basis for the unification of motor learning theories? *International Journal of Sport Psychology, 37*, 1–21.

Schöllhorn, W. I., Mayer-Kress, G., Newell, K. M., & Michelbrink, M. (2009). Time scales of adaptive behavior and motor learning in the presence of stochastic perturbations. *Human Movement Science, 28*(3), 319–333.

Shaw, R., & Turvey, M. (1999). Ecological foundations of cognition II: Degrees of freedom and conserved quantities in animal-environment systems. *Journal of Consciousness Studies, 6*(11–12), 111–123.

Stoffregen, T. A., Bardy, B. G. Smart, L. J., & Pagulayan, R. J. (2003). On the nature and evaluation of fidelity in virtual environments. In Hettinger, L. J., & Haas, M. W. (Ed.), *Virtual and adaptive environments: Applications, implications, and human performance issues* (pp. 111–128). Mahwah, NJ: Lawrence Erlbaum Associates.

Tan, C. W. K., Chow, J. Y., & Davids, K. (in press). "How does TGfU work?": Examining the relationship between learning design in TGfU and a nonlinear pedagogy. *Physical Education and Sport Pedagogy*.

Turvey, M. T., & Shaw, R. (1999). Ecological foundations of cognition I: Symmetry and specificity of animal–environment systems. *Journal of Consciousness Studies, 6*(11–12), 95–110.

Vereijken, B., van Emmerik, R. E., Whiting, H. T., & Newell, K. (1992). Free(z)ing degrees of freedom in skill acquisition. *Journal of Motor Behavior, 24*, 133–142.

Warren, W. (2006). The dynamics of perception and action. *Psychological Review, 113,* 358–389.

Wilson, C., Simpson, S. E., Van Emmerik, R. E. A., & Hamill, J. (2008). Coordination variability and skill development in expert triple jumpers. *Sports Biomechanics, 7*(1), 2–9.

Wio, H. (2005). Noise induced phenomena and nonextensivity. *Europhysics News, 36*(6), 197–201.

8 The representation, production, and transfer of simple and complex movement sequences

Charles H. Shea and David L. Wright

Introduction

Understanding the processes involved in fluent production of sequential movements such as those involved in daily life, sports, and work activities (e.g., speech, handwriting, typing, playing a musical instrument, driving an automobile, or operating complex equipment) has been the focus of research for a number of theoretical and applied reasons. Theoretically, sequential movements are thought to be initially composed of a number of relatively independent elements that, through practice, are organized into what appear to be a smaller number of subsequences (Park & Shea, 2003b; termed *motor chunks* by Verwey, 1994). Moreover, the sequences are coded in one of two coordinate systems. One coordinate system is based on Cartesian coordinates of the visual–spatial movement space and the other is based on motor coordinates, such as sequential joint angles or muscle activation patterns. Further, the coordinate system used by a participant to code or represent sequence information appears to play an important role in determining how effectively it can be produced under various retention and transfer conditions. From a practical standpoint, the study of sequential movements is important because this type of movement comprises a significant proportion of our skilled movement repertoire and often represents some of the most complicated and difficult movements we wish to acquire and execute. Improved understanding of the processes involved in the performance, learning, and transfer of movement sequences should lead to the design of more effective and efficient training procedures that exploit the way we structure and represent sequence information in memory.

In the following sections we briefly review traditional theoretical perspectives on sequence representation and production. These perspectives provide important clues to the ways in which movement sequences can be adapted to novel movement demands. For example, novice soccer players experience some difficulty during practice when different types of passes are required from attempt to attempt (random practice), which could be eliminated by asking them to practice the same pass over and over before moving to different type of pass (blocked practice). However, a large body of research has demonstrated that the variability introduced in random practice conditions results in better learning and transfer than in the blocked practice conditions. Next, we describe research that illustrates how movement sequences are structured and represented in memory. We describe online enhancements that arise from various changes in practice composition (e.g., observing modeled behaviors) and schedule (e.g., changes in the practice order of to-be-learned actions) and offline enhancement that can accrue through the memory-consolidation process (such as rest or sleep). We introduce one theoretical perspective that focuses on the coding of sequence information (e.g., the features of to-be-learned movements that are stored in memory) and summarize a series of recent experiments that illustrate how the coordinate system used to code sequence information plays a critical role in the transfer of that sequence (Hikosaka et al., 1999).

Traditional theoretical perspectives for movement sequence acquisition

Lashley (1951) proposed that sequential actions are structured such that the order of the movement elements is determined independent of the nature of the individual movement elements (Nissen & Bullemer, 1987; Povel & Collard, 1982). For example, when pianists play a piece of music from memory, they do not begin by retrieving from memory the entire set of commands required to play the piece of music. Rather they appear to retrieve one subsequence at a time and while playing that subsequence they retrieve and ready the next subsequence for execution. This process is similar to the way a skilled typist produces the key strokes when typing a paper. This notion of independent or hierarchical control of movement sequences was further developed as a result of a series of experiments proposed by Rosenbaum and colleagues (e.g., Rosenbaum, Kenny, & Derr, 1983; Rosenbaum & Saltzman, 1984). Hierarchical control of movement sequences was conceptualized as an inverted tree/branch metaphor such that higher levels (nodes), which were thought to transmit sequence order information, branched into lower levels, where specific effector information was stored (Nissen & Bullemer, 1987). The memorial representation of this information was thought to be retrieved, unpacked, parameterized, and/or edited (depending on the theoretical model adopted) before execution so as to meet the specific environmental demands. These models seemed to account fairly well for the time delays between the executions of the discrete individual and/or grouped elements in the sequence.

The emergence of a structure for movement sequences during acquisition

The serial reaction time task (SRTT) has been one of the most frequent methods used to study sequential movements over the last 40 years (e.g., Nissen & Bullemer, 1987; Povel & Collard, 1982). When performing the SRTT, participants initially react to visual signals with predetermined key presses, as they would in a choice reaction time paradigm. If the stimuli are presented in a repeating sequence the participant begins to anticipate the upcoming stimuli and as a result reduces the time to respond to each signal. As the sequence order is learned, the time required to complete the series of key presses is significantly reduced. Importantly, with sufficient practice, the participants become less reliant on the presence of the visual stimulus, while still exhibiting accurate and rapid response production.

The process of movement sequence acquisition was illustrated in work by Park and Shea (2003a, 2005) during which participants moved a lever in an attempt to "hit" sequentially illuminated targets projected onto a table top (Figure 8.1a). When a participant moved the cursor into the target area, the illumination was turned off and the next target in the sequence was presented. A 16-element movement sequence was practiced repeatedly (16 blocks of 10 repetitions), although participants were not informed of the presence of a sequence. Participants were simply instructed to move the lever from target to target as quickly and smoothly as possible. Figure 8.1b provides an example of the average duration for each of the 16 elements in the sequence for the first (filled circles) and fifth (open circles) blocks of practice. The movement sequence on average is produced more quickly on Block 5 than on Block 1. More importantly, the pattern of element durations that emerged during Block 5 suggested that a structure had been imposed on the sequential behavior. This can be seen by comparing individual element durations in Block 1 and Block 5. The differences in time required to complete each of the 16 individual elements were relatively small on the first block of practice. However, by Block 5 participants began to decrease the duration of some elements, but not others. This difference arose because participants began grouping elements into functional subsequences.

Subsequences within a movement sequence are typically characterized by a relatively slow response to one element followed by a faster response to one or more subsequent elements. The first element is thought to be slowed because of the additional processing required to retrieve, organize, process, and initiate the subsequence, but the subsequent elements were produced more rapidly because the processing and articulatory activities required for their execution were completed

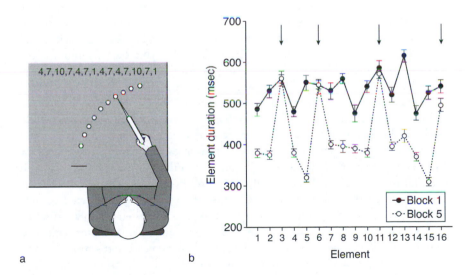

a   b

Figure 8.1 Illustration of the arm used and direction of movement during acquisition (a). Note that the targets were arbitrarily labeled 1–10 starting from the start position (bottom of the illustration). The sequence order is provided above. Element durations on Block 1 (filled circles) and Block 5 (open circles) are presented (b). Arrows mark the first element in each subsequence (adapted from Park & Shea, 2005)

in advance. In Figure 8.1b Elements 3, 6, 11, and 16 in Block 5 were produced more slowly than one or more of the following elements and these elements had not improved much over practice. The major decrease in element duration accrued from the elements within a subsequence and not from the elements that marked the beginning of the subsequences. Note that in this paradigm the participants responded to the 16-element repeated sequence continuously for 10 repetitions within each block. This procedure allowed participants to group elements from the end of the sequence with elements at the beginning of the sequence. This appears to account for Elements 16, 1, and 2 being grouped together in a single chunk. Remarkably, many participants impose similar structures on a given movement sequence when the practice conditions are the same, suggesting that there are general constraints operating on the imposition of structure. Nonetheless, there is also a degree of between-participant variability, suggesting that there is some flexibility in the representation of sequence knowledge (Verwey & Eikelboom, 2003).

Movement structure will be impacted by practice extent

It seems reasonable to assume that performance improvements that are concomitant with changes in movement structure are intimately related to the quantity of practice experienced by the learner. The previous section described how ordinal structure (i.e., serial order) emerged as the learner was exposed to greater practice extent during the learning of a movement sequence (Park & Shea, 2005). Recall, that the transition points within the sequence changed across practice suggesting that the learner adapted the manner in which they parsed the entire action to accomplish an overall faster production of the task. The formation and reorganization of motor chunks have been described as a fundamental strategy used to facilitate early improvement in the performance of complex serial behaviors and considered central to motor skill learning (Sakai, Hikosaka & Nakamura, 2004; Sakai, Kitaguchi, & Hikosaka, 2003; Verwey & Eikelboom, 2003). Moreover, the particular manner in which the movement is parsed plays a critical role in the generalizability or transfer of components of that action.

For example, in keeping with the previous discussion of Park and Shea's work, Sakai revealed that participants who practiced a 10-item sequence, using trial and error, performed the action as clusters of responses (i.e., chunks) separated by longer time transitions. In a subsequent transfer test the learned sequence was split such that these acquired clusters or chunks were preserved or destroyed. Transfer performance on the task that merely shuffled the originally constructed clusters was more accurate and fluent than on the task that consisted of only partial or disrupted clusters. These findings intimate that (1) acquired visuo-motor sequences are represented as subsequences or motor chunks that emerge across practice, and (2) these subsequences have functional significance in transfer to novel situations (Panzer, Wilde, & Shea, 2006).

These findings have interesting implications for sequential actions in sport. For example, one could envision that in diving, dance, or gymnastics, when the performer first constructs a routine, the individual movement elements (e.g., a back somersault in a floor routine) constitute independent motor elements. With more practice, actions initially represented as individual elements might be integrated (consolidated) together to form a subsequence or a motor chunk. Of greatest importance is that the new, more integrated subsequences each involving multiple elements would theoretically be available to utilize anywhere within larger routines and be performed as effectively as in their original locus in the routine.

Evidence for continued change in movement structure with increasing practice extent, beyond those associated with an action's serial order, can be found elsewhere. Whitacre and Shea (2005) had individuals exert force on a transducer in an attempt to match a force–time waveform displayed on a computer monitor. The task variations that were practiced, for either 20 or 200 trials, involved the same relative force and time structure as well as a fixed absolute time across trials, but differed with respect to the overall force demanded for each task variation. With minimal practice the acquisition of accurate relative time and force profiles was achieved and remained stable across a 24-hour delayed retention period. In contrast, the ability to scale the behavior precisely with respect to the correct amount of force demanded more moderate as opposed to minimal practice. Even with 200 trials of practice, no change was evident in the learner's ability to scale the absolute time feature of this sequential task adequately. These data suggest that movement structure undergoes significant change early in practice. Modifications of relative and absolute time features of the movement representation proceed at different rates, highlighted by specific improvements being manifest at different junctures during a bout of practice.

An extension of the findings reported in the previous paragraph is related to a common belief that broad transfer is less likely when the learner has been exposed to increasingly large amounts of practice of any specific task. For example, there is a growing body of experimental evidence indicating that, early in practice, effector-independent behavior is observed, but greater practice extent often leads to effector-dependent constraints (Jordan, 1995; Park & Shea, 2005; Verwey & Wright, 2004) as participants refine the movement by optimizing the characteristics of the specific effectors being used. This finding has very important implications for individuals who are exposed to extensive sport training and have achieved a high level of expertise. Specifically, instructors working with such individuals need to be very aware that, as performers approximate an elite performance level following long-term training, their capacity to adapt such well honed skills may be reduced. Note, however, that many of the experiments that reported increasing specificity resulting from extended practice did not provide participants with variability during practice. Presumably, variability introduced during practice, although it may reduce the ultimate level of skill achieved for a specific task, may provide the flexibility in performance required in many sport situations.

Movement structure can be impacted by practice schedule

Although the amount of practice experienced by the learner has been described as a crucial factor in establishing very high levels of performance (see Ericsson, Krampe,

& Tesch-Romer, 1993), there is ample evidence that the schedule for each bout of practice plays an important role in maximizing the utility of training. We offer a couple of examples from our work addressing contextual interference to illustrate that practice schedule can impact the evolution of movement structure and the resultant performance. Wilde, Magnuson, and Shea (2005) required individuals to practice three similar six-element key press sequences in a blocked (participants finished practice for one sequence before practicing the next sequence) or random (intermingling practice of each of the three sequences throughout the training phase) practice format. The sequences used in this experiment had previously been used by Povel and Collard (1982). What was interesting about these sequences was that the second sequence was constructed from the first sequence by merely moving the first element to the end of the sequence and the third sequence was constructed by moving the first element of the second sequence to the end. Thus, although the three sequences were very similar, Povel and Collard found that, when practicing them independently, participants tended to structure two of the sequences similarly whereas a third was structured in a different manner. In the Wilde et al. experiment, performance on subsequent retention and transfer tests revealed that the practice format to which the learner was initially exposed (either blocked or random) had an important influence on the manner in which the sequences were structured. Random practice resulted in the development of a uniform response structure for all sequences (i.e., similar element durations). In contrast, blocked practice resulted in the construction of different movement structures that were best suited to meeting the requirements of each unique response. Thus, random practice, which is typically viewed as being more effective in terms of learning and transfer than blocked practice, hindered the learner's ability to detect a unique solution to a particular sequence that was detected during blocked practice. Despite this shortcoming, random practice does provide the opportunity to identify commonalities between actions, which plays a role in enhancing transfer performance. The flexibility provided through random practice may play an important role in training for many sports.

In a similar study, Wright, Black, Immink, Brueckner, and Magnuson (2004) included random and blocked practice of either simple or complex timing sequences. In this case, the interest was not only on the emerging structure of the sequence but also on the latencies that were involved in initiating the movement sequence. Their findings indicated that the resiliency of the structure supporting response production, that is the relative timing between keys on delayed retention and transfer tests, was superior following random as opposed to blocked practice. The differences in the conclusions reached from these two studies might be explained by practice distribution effects. Although these studies involved roughly the same amount of practice, Wright et al. presented the practice trials over four days as opposed to within one training session, possibly taking advantage of benefits from the well-documented distribution of practice benefits (e.g., Shea, Lai, Black, & Park, 2001; Tsutsui, Lee, & Hodges, 1998). In addition to developing a more adaptable movement sequence structure following random practice, this training format afforded faster access to the structure for the purpose of implementation, as evidenced by the consistently shorter study and reaction times, argued to be indices of different features of motor preparation (see also Immink & Wright, 2001; Klapp, 1995).

In summary, we have highlighted the importance of considering both practice quantity and practice quality when attempting to understand the development of movement sequence representation and its generalization. Teachers and instructors cannot ignore the critical contribution of both practice composition and scheduling to motor learning and memory. We used a well-examined practice-scheduling phenomenon, contextual interference, to illustrate this point. These data indicated that, although random and blocked practice formats can both provide benefits for general outcome-based measures of performance, random practice is particularly useful for successful acquisition of a movement's global requirements (relative time structure), which is likely to contribute to this practice format's efficacy in supporting transfer to new movements that share similar features.

Movement structure can be influenced by non-practice factors

Thus far, we have considered only contributions of practice per se to retention and transfer of sequential behaviors. An interesting development in recent years has focused on performance enhancements from non-practice behaviors such as sleep. These benefits have been referred to as "offline" improvements because they are above and beyond those that can be accounted for by the practice itself. Walker, Brakefield, Hobson, and Stickgold (2003) reported significant offline facilitation for accuracy and speed of simple finger-sequencing actions. The important manipulation in this work was a test that was administered following a 12-hour delay during which participants either stayed awake or slept. When they were given the opportunity to sleep, performance, in terms of both accuracy and speed, improved by as much as 20% compared with an equivalent time spent awake. This finding has been replicated numerous times and underscores (1) the potential contributions available for movement sequence performance from non-practice factors (e.g., sleep), and (2) the existence of significant latent enhancements that can occur outside the common practice environment.

At least a part of the offline enhancements revealed by Walker and colleagues (e.g., Walker, 2005; Walker & Stickgold, 2006) has been attributed to a continued re-parsing of the movement structure during sleep. Using finger-sequencing tasks, Wright, Rhee, and Vaculin (2010) replicated earlier findings from Kuriyama, Stickgold, and Walker (2004), which revealed that individual transitions within a practiced motor sequence performed most slowly at the end of a period of practice exhibited about twice as much improvement overnight as that observed for the transitions performed most rapidly at the end of training (see Figure 8.2). They argued that latent sleep-dependent improvements amalgamate separate motor chunks into larger, more unitary, functional units that are easily transferred either within or across other movement sequences. Since this amalgamation process is assumed to occur across the normal course of practice, it appears that memory consolidation instigated during the act of practice either continues for a substantial amount of time after training is complete or is re-engaged during sleep.

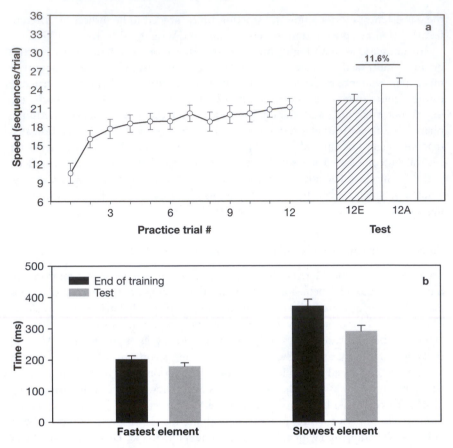

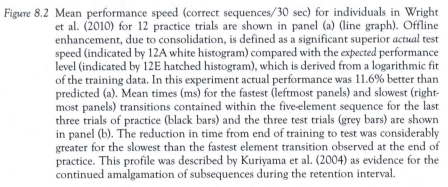

Figure 8.2 Mean performance speed (correct sequences/30 sec) for individuals in Wright et al. (2010) for 12 practice trials are shown in panel (a) (line graph). Offline enhancement, due to consolidation, is defined as a significant superior *actual* test speed (indicated by 12A white histogram) compared with the *expected* performance level (indicated by 12E hatched histogram), which is derived from a logarithmic fit of the training data. In this experiment actual performance was 11.6% better than predicted (a). Mean times (ms) for the fastest (leftmost panels) and slowest (right-most panels) transitions contained within the five-element sequence for the last three trials of practice (black bars) and the three test trials (grey bars) are shown in panel (b). The reduction in time from end of training to test was considerably greater for the slowest than the fastest element transition observed at the end of practice. This profile was described by Kuriyama et al. (2004) as evidence for the continued amalgamation of subsequences during the retention interval.

Continued offline improvements were also shown following further practice in the study by Wright et al., but these benefits were not associated with reorganization of the movement structure. These data suggest that additional memory operations, beyond those needed to amalgamate motor chunks, are also susceptible to memory consolidation.

Two candidate processes responsible for the aforementioned offline improvement in Wright et al. (2010) is concatenation (Verwey, 1994) and coactivation (Jordan, 1995). Concatenation is the process of forming movement subsequences by combining individual movement elements together, and coactivation indicates that participants begin processing the next subsequence while the current subsequence is being executed. In the work of Park and Shea (2005) participants first developed a movement structure whereby individual elements in the sequence were grouped into subsequences and then participants began to reduce the time required to transition more smoothly from one subsequence to the next. This process is thought to occur because participants, after structuring the sequence, can reallocate processing resources during the production of one subsequence to the processing of the subsequent subsequence. The result is a relatively smooth and seamless response production. The concatenation process could be viewed as further consolidation of the subsequences into a single chunk; however, on an effector transfer test the subsequences again emerged, suggesting that concatenation had minimized the transition time between subsequences.

In this section we have outlined our current thinking, not only in terms of the nature and organization of knowledge that is stored about sequential actions, but also how such knowledge is garnered through practice and experience. Obviously, as the learner is exposed to practice, not only is more knowledge acquired but its representational form and relationship to other knowledge change. It is often hard to look beyond the noted importance of practicing with greater frequency. There is heightened consideration of this perspective in both the scientific (Ericsson et al., 1993) and lay (Gladwell, 2008) literature. Nonetheless, it is critical to be aware that the format of practice, in terms of what is actually practiced and how practice is structured, will play a role in determining what is eventually learned and when. It is incumbent on the instructor or coach to understand the potentially powerful influence that non-practice factors might have on the rate and nature of skill acquisition and transfer capacity. Sleep was used for the purpose of illustration in this section but other factors such as exercise and fitness are quickly becoming areas of interest as a means of enhancing declarative and procedural skill learning (Cotman & Berchtold, 2002).

Coordinate systems used during the acquisition of motor sequences

A number of researchers have proposed that sequential tasks are represented in relatively abstract, effector-independent forms (Grafton, Hazeltine, & Ivry, 1998; Schmidt, 1975; van Mier & Petersen, 2006; Verwey & Clegg, 2005; Willingham, Wells, Farrell, & Stemwedel, 2000). Recall that this position is congruent with the claim that one should gain some advantage in the form of positive transfer when faced with learning a new movement performed with a relatively unused effector (e.g., non-kicking foot in soccer) if the learner has been exposed to significant practice with another effector (e.g., kicking foot in soccer). However, there is research consistent with the notion that movement sequences are represented in more effector-specific forms, which optimize the neurological and anatomical properties of a specific effector system during practice in order to refine response production (Jordan, 1995; Park & Shea, 2003a, 2003b, 2005).

A model put forward by Hikosaka et al. (1999; also see Bapi, Doya, & Harner, 2000; Verwey & Wright, 2004) proposes that the learning of movement sequences involves both a fast-developing, effector-independent component represented in visual–spatial coordinates (e.g., spatial locations of end effectors and/or sequential target positions), and a slower-developing, effector-dependent component represented in motor coordinates (e.g., activation patterns of the agonist/antagonist muscles and/or achieved joint angles). Hikosaka et al. (1999; Hikosaka, Nakamura, Sakai, & Nakahara, 2002) suggested that the representation for a given sequence is distributed in the brain in different forms (i.e., visual–spatial and motor) with distinct neural networks supporting production of the movement. According to Hikosaka, early in acquisition, the sequence is executed in a discrete manner whereby each element in the sequence is produced independently. With additional practice, the reliance on serial sensorimotor processes diminishes and new connections are formed between the individual elements (see also Bapi, Miyapuram, Graydon, & Doya, 2006). Initially, a sequence is coded in visual–spatial coordinates that rely on attention, explicit knowledge, and working memory. The visual–spatial representation is thought to be abstract, and thus is transferable to an unpracticed set of effectors resulting in relatively good performance of a novel task variation that has the same visual/spatial characteristics. In parallel another code represented in motor coordinates (e.g., sequential pattern of muscle activation and/or joint angles) also develops. Codes represented in motor coordinates are more effector-specific (Hikosaka et al., 2002) given that anatomical and neurological properties of the specific effector used during practice are being exploited to improve performance (Park & Shea, 2005). Thus, transfer to the same activation pattern of homologous muscles is supported, but transfer to non-homologous muscles or different activation patterns with homologous muscles is limited. For example, transferring an extension–flexion–extension movement using the bicep and triceps of the right arm to the left arm, where the same pattern of muscle activation would be required, would be considered homologous muscle activation. The model proposed by Hikosaka et al. (1999, 2002) was developed based largely on findings from multi-element keypressing tasks of varying length and structure. This model predicts that the reliance on the visual–spatial representation will gradually decrease over practice. Later in practice, the production of sequential movements is believed to rely more heavily on the motor representation, which allows a more rapid and precise execution of the sequence.

Recently, experiments utilizing (1) inter-manual transfer (e.g., Kovacs, Boyle, Grutmatcher, & Shea, 2010; Kovacs, Han, & Shea, 2009; Kovacs, Muehlbauer & Shea, 2009), whereby participants practice with one limb and are later tested on the contralateral limb, (2) inter-manual practice (e.g., Panzer, Muehlbauer, et al., 2009, 2011), whereby participants practice with both the left and right limbs, and (3) observational practice (e.g., Boutin, Fries, Panzer, Blandin, & Shea, 2010; Grutmatcher, Panzer, Blandin, & Shea, 2011) in the performance and learning of simple and complex movement sequences have been interpreted in terms of the Hikosaka model (codes developed in visual–spatial and motor coordinates). As discussed below, results from these experiments suggest modifications to the Hikosaka model, particularly with respect to the presumed later reliance on motor codes for performance following practice, irrespective of the type of response required (see Shea, Kovacs, & Panzer, 2011, for review).

Coding of simple and complex movement sequences

Kovacs, Muehlbauer, et al. (2009) conducted three experiments in which the amount of practice was manipulated using a task requiring the learning of a complex, 14-element, dynamic movement sequence, similar to that illustrated in Figure 8.3a. In each experiment participants practiced the movement sequence with either the left or right limb for 1, 4, or 12 days (Experiments 1–3 respectively). A delayed retention test and two effector transfer tests (visual–spatial and motor) were administered (Figure 8.3b–d). In the visual–spatial transfer test the visual–spatial coordinates were reinstated, so that participants moved to the same spatial locations as during acquisition, but used the unpracticed limb. Because the contralateral limb was used, a new unpracticed pattern of muscle activation (i.e., non-homologous flexion and extension) and joint angles was needed. The motor transfer test also involved the unpracticed limb but with a mirror presentation of the target positions. The motor test required the same pattern of homologous muscle activation and the achievement of the same relative joint angles as during practice, but the spatial locations were altered. Thus, during the motor transfer test, the motor coordinates were reinstated and the visual–spatial coordinates were altered, whereas during the

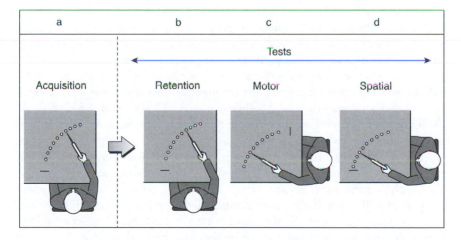

Figure 8.3 Illustration of the experimental setup during acquisition of a 14-element dynamic movement sequence (a), and on the retention (b, same conditions) and motor (c) and spatial (d) effector transfer tests. Note that the participant started the movement from the start line and that the pattern of target illumination was determined from that position. (Adapted from Kovacs, Muehlbauer, et al., 2009.)

spatial transfer test the visual–spatial coordinates were reinstated and the motor coordinates were altered. The Hikosaka et al. (1999, 2002) model would predict an increased reliance on codes formulated in motor coordinates as practice continues, which in turn would lead to better transfer performance on the motor versus spatial task.

After 1, 4, and 12 days of practice participants performed substantially better on the spatial transfer test than on the motor transfer test. Although performance on the motor transfer tests showed significant improvements after 12 days of prac-tice, transfer performance when the spatial coordinates were reinstated was still significantly faster than when the motor coordinates were reinstated. Although it is possible that practice beyond 12 days may eventually result in better motor transfer than spatial transfer, these results suggest, at a minimum, that the amount of practice required to develop salient motor codes may increase dramatically when the complexity of the movement sequence increases. It appears possible that for some complex tasks spatial coordinates may provide the optimal metric from which to develop movement codes independent of the amount of practice. In support of this supposition one might consider the problem faced by dancers when practicing complex dance routines in preparation for an impending performance. In cases where similar features of the routine must be performed in different directions, orientations, or locations on the floor, one would assume that for skilled dancers motor codes for the various dance elements would be available for use. For example, the assumed low attentional cost associated with using a motor code would presum-ably be very advantageous to successful performance. However, it is common, even for skilled dancers, to practice the required components in several directions or orientations during their preparations. In this case, one might argue that spatial codes are critical to either supplement or replace the motor codes for the dancer to implement the required series of actions during these routines.

Note that Hikosaka et al., using a five-element key press task, found that partici-pants performed transfer tests best early in practice when spatial coordinates were reinstated, but later in practice participants responded substantially better on the transfer test when the motor coordinates were reinstated. These findings coupled with the results of extended practice on the complex 14-element movement sequence led Shea and colleagues (Kovacs, Muehlbauer, et al., 2009; Panzer, Krueger, et al., 2009) to hypothesize that relatively simple motor tasks may be coded, even follow-ing relatively little practice, in motor coordinates. To test this notion, Kovacs, Han, and Shea (2009) had participants practice either a relatively simple and slightly more complex movement sequence (Figure 8.4) for one practice session (99 trials). The simple sequence (S1) involved three movement reversals with a movement duration of 1200 ms and the more complex movement sequence (S2) involved five movement reversals with a movement duration of 2000 ms. Importantly, both movement sequences were constructed by summing two sine-waves such that the first 1200 ms of the longer sequences (S2) was the same as the shorter duration sequence (S1). They hypothesized that the increased functional difficulty of S2 may result in participants more effectively coding the sequence using spatial coordinates

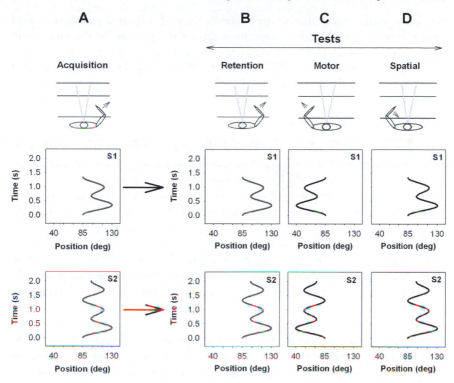

Figure 8.4 Illustration of the experimental setup during acquisition (a), and on the retention (b) and motor (c) and spatial (d) effector transfer tests for sequences S1 (simple) and S2 (complex). (Adapted from Kovacs, Han, et al., 2010.)

following only 99 trials of practice whereas the S1 may be more effectively coded at this stage of practice using motor coordinates.

The results confirmed these predictions. Participants who practiced the simple sequence (S1) performed the motor transfer test with homologous muscles of the contralateral limb as effectively as they performed the retention test, which was conducted under the same conditions and with the same limb as during practice. Performance on the visual–spatial transfer test was poorer than on either the motor transfer test or the retention test. Conversely, participants who practiced the more complex sequence (S2) performed the spatial transfer test, in which the spatial coordinates were reinstated, as well as the retention test. Performance on the motor transfer test was poorer than that on either the visual–spatial transfer test or the retention test. These findings provide strong support for the notion that the coordinate system used to code movement sequences and the manner in which participants respond on transfer tests is influenced by the characteristics of the movement (also see Panzer, Krueger, et al., 2009, 2011). However, the kinematics for S1 were consistent with those typically found for pre-planned movements (i.e., no online corrections), whereas the kinematics for S2 indicated participants used online control to make subtle corrections during the progress of the movement. This caused Kovacs et al. (2010) to hypothesize that the coordinate system used to code sequence information may be dependent on the control processes used rather than the sequence characteristics per se.

Pre-planned and online control

Recent experimental evidence suggests that the pattern of inter-manual transfer for rapid movement sequences differs from that found for longer duration, multi-element sequences. Kovacs et al. (2010) hypothesized that the production of rapid, less complex movements, which are thought to be controlled by pre-planned processes, may develop reliance on motor coordinates earlier in practice than longer-duration movement sequences. These latter sequences, which appear to be structured into a series of subsequences, are thought to require online control for the activation of the successive subsequences (e.g., Braden, Panzer, & Shea, 2008; Park & Shea, 2005; Wilde & Shea, 2006). Kovacs et al. (2010) utilized a sequential movement with three reversals with 1300 ms duration. In one condition before and during the movement participants were provided with a template indicating the goal pattern and a cursor indicating the current position of their movement. The presentation of the cursor and template during the movement were designed to increase the likelihood that participants would engage in online control. A second acquisition condition was designed so that participants could view the goal movement template before responding but the template was removed as soon as movement began. This condition was designed to encourage participants to pre-plan the movement because extrinsic information was withdrawn during response production, making online control difficult. Note that participants in both conditions were asked to produce the same movement during acquisition and were given the same number of practice trials. In addition, the retention and transfer tests for the two groups were conducted in the same manner.

Consistent with predictions, participants in the online condition (template during) transferred better when the spatial coordinates were reinstated on the transfer test than when the motor coordinates were reinstated. Participants in the pre-planned condition (no template) produced enhanced transfer when the motor coordinates were reinstated. These results provide strong evidence that the control system used during response production plays a role in determining the optimal coordinate system used to code the movement sequence. Thus, it appears that task characteristics and the associated control processes play an important role. It is also interesting to note that pre-planning and online control of movement sequences have been shown to utilize different information and rely on different neural pathways (e.g., Glover, 2004; Hikosaka et al., 2002). Furthermore, pre-planning determines the initial kinematic characteristics of the movement including timing and velocity whereas the online control system monitors and occasionally adjusts movement progress "in flight" but these adjustments are limited to the spatial characteristics of the movement (Glover, 2004). In other words, shorter-duration movements, with few elements, predominantly rely on pre-planning whereas longer-duration movements with more elements have an initial pre-planned component after which movement control is gradually taken over by the online contro

Development of movement codes during observation

Not all forms of practice include execution of the to-be-learned action. There is an abundance of experimental work on the efficacy of imagery and observation as tools for facilitating motor learning. Learning thorough observation is particularly interesting because of the central nature of its practical analog, the demonstration. There is currently debate about whether observational practice promotes the development of motor codes during observation (Maslovat, Hodges, Krigolson, & Handy, 2010; Ong & Hodges, 2010; also see Mattar & Gribble, 2005). The inter-manual practice paradigm, described earlier as a means to determine the coordinate system used to code movements sequences, might provide some insight into the nature of learning through observation. Boutin et al. (2010), for example, looked at the coding of a complex 14-element movement sequence following physical practice and action observation. An observer was paired with a physical practice performer who had not been exposed to the task before (often termed a learning model) and was privy to all instructions, observation of the movement and extrinsic feedback provided to the physical practice performer. As previously shown (e.g., Kovacs, Muehlbauer, et al., 2009), the physical practice participants performed the spatial transfer test as effectively as the retention test. Performance on the motor transfer test was significantly poorer. The observers, although not permitted prior physical practice, performed the retention test as rapidly as the physical practice participants and also performed the spatial transfer test as effectively as the retention test. For the observers, performance on the motor test was also significantly poorer than that on the retention and spatial test. In a similar experiment, Grutmatcher et al. (2011) investigated physical and observational practice with the simple waveform reproduction task used earlier by Kovacs, Han, et al. (2009). Recall that Kovacs et al. revealed that participants performed better on the motor transfer test than the visual after only one practice session. If motor information can be extracted through demonstrations then observers should also initially code this response in motor coordinates. Contrary to this prediction and different from the physical practice group, the observers performed the spatial test better than the motor test. There was no difference between the observers' performance on the spatial test and the physical practice participants' performance on the spatial test. This difference may help explain why observation for some tasks results in retention and transfer performance that is as effective as that exhibited by physical practice participants whereas in other experiments observers perform more poorly than participants allowed physical practice. These results are in accordance with other experiments that have failed to demonstrate the development of motor codes through observation (Maslovat et al., 2010; Ong & Hodges, 2010). In an earlier section it was suggested that the development of motor codes occurs as a result of the learner taking advantage of the characteristics of the specific effectors being used to more effectively produce the sequence. It appears that exposure to only demonstration or other forms of observational learning will limit the participant's ability to develop codes in motor coordinates and ultimately limit potential improvement.

Summary

The present findings illustrate that during the learning of movement sequences the performer imposes a structure on the individual elements that compose the movement sequence. This structure greatly reduces the processing demands associated with production of the movement and increases the rapidity and fluidity with which the sequence can be produced. The development of the sequence structure is clearly influenced by the practice schedule and appears to involve both online and offline consolidation processes. The coding of the sequence information occurs in a coordinate system (motor or visual–spatial) that appears to be related to the complexity of the movement sequence and the control processes used to produce the sequence, and ultimately dictates the participant's ability to transfer to new unpracticed conditions. This information should be quite useful in the design of new movement training and retraining protocols particularly when the learned sequences must be performed with either hand or when the ability to transfer to unpracticed conditions is an important feature of learning. Future research, however, is required to determine the optimal coordinate system for various tasks and how practice can be manipulated to enhance coding and ultimately consolidation in that coordinate system.

References

Bapi, R. S., Doya, K., & Harner, A. M. (2000). Evidence for effector independent and dependent representations and their differential time course of acquisition during motor sequence learning. *Experimental Brain Research, 132*(2), 149–162.

Bapi, R. S., Miyapuram, K. P., Graydon, F. X., & Doya, K. (2006). fMRI investigation of cortical and subcortical networks in the learning of abstract and effector-specific representations of motor sequences. *Neuroimage, 32*(2), 714–727.

Boutin, A., Fries, U., Panzer, S., Blandin, Y., & Shea, C. H. (2010). Role of action observation and action in sequences learning and coding. *Acta Psychologica, 135*, 240–251.

Braden, H., Panzer, S. & Shea, C. H. (2008). The effects of sequence difficulty and practice on proportional and non-proportional transfer. *Quarterly Journal of Experimental Psychology, 61*, 1321–1339.

Cotman, C. W., & Berchtold, N. C. (2002). Exercise: A behavioral intervention to enhance brain health and plasticity. *Trends in Neurosciences, 25*(6), 295–301.

Ericsson, K. A., Krampe, R. T., & Tesch-Romer, C. (1993). The role of deliberate practice in the acquisition of expert performance. *Psychological Review, 100*, 363–406.

Gladwell, M. (2008). *Outliers: The story of success.* New York: Little, Brown.

Glover, S. (2004). Separate visual representations in the planning and control of action-response. *Behavioral and Brain Sciences, 27*(1), 57–78.

Grafton, S. T., Hazeltine, E., & Ivry, R. B. (1998). Abstract and effector-specific representations of motor sequences identified with PET. *Journal of Neuroscience, 18*(22), 9420–9428.

Gruetzmacher, N., Panzer, S., Blandin, Y., & Shea, C. H. (2011). Observation and physical practice: Coding of simple motor sequences. *Quarterly Journal of Experimental Psychology, 64*, 1111–1123.

Hikosaka, O., Nakahara, H., Rand, M. K., Sakai, K., Lu, X. F., Nakamura, K., et al. (1999). Parallel neural networks for learning sequential procedures. *Trends in Neurosciences, 22*(10), 464–471.

Hikosaka, O., Nakamura, K., Sakai, K., & Nakahara, H. (2002). Central mechanisms of motor skill learning. *Current Opinion in Neurobiology, 12*(2), 217–222.

Immink, M. A., & Wright, D. L. (2001). Motor programming during high and low contextual interference practice conditions. *Journal of Experimental Psychology: Human Perception and Performance, 27*, 423–437.

Jordan, M. I. (1995). The organization of action sequences: Evidence from a relearning task. *Journal of Motor Behavior, 27*(2), 179–192.

Klapp, S. T. (1995). Motor response programming during simple and choice reaction time: The role of practice. *Journal of Experimental Psychology: Human Perception and Performance, 21*, 1015–1027.

Kovacs, A. J., Boyle, J., Grutmatcher, N., & Shea, C. H. (2010). Coding of on-line and pre-planned movement sequences. *Acta Psychologica, 133*, 119–126.

Kovacs, A. J., Han, D-W., & Shea, C. H. (2009). The representation of movement sequences is related to task characteristics. *Acta Psychologica, 132*, 54–61.

Kovacs, A.J, Muehlbauer, T., & Shea, C. H. (2009). The coding and effector transfer of movement sequences. *Journal of Experimental Psychology: Human Perception and Performance, 35*(2), 390–407.

Kuriyama, K., Stickgold, R., & Walker, M. P. (2004). Sleep dependent learning and motor-skill complexity. *Learning & Memory, 11*, 705–713.

Lashley, K. S. (1951). The problem of serial order in behavior. In Jeffress, L. A. (Ed.), *Cerebral mechanisms in behavior* (pp. 112–136). New York: Wiley.

Maslovat, D., Hodges, N. J., Krigolson, O. E., & Handy, T. C. (2010). Observational practice benefits are limited to perceptual improvements in the acquisition of a novel coordination skill. *Experimental Brain Research, 204*(1), 119–130.

Mattar, A. A.G., & Gribble, P. L. (2005). Motor learning by observing. *Neuron, 46*(1), 153–160.

Nissen, M. J., & Bullemer, P. (1987). Attentional requirements of learning-evidence from performance-measures. *Cognitive Psychology, 19*(1), 1–32.

Ong, N. T., & Hodges, N. J. (2010). Absence of after-effects for observers after watching a visuomotor adaptation. *Experimental Brain Research, 205*(3), 325–334.

Panzer, S., Gruetzmacher, N., Fries, U., Kruger, M., & Shea, C. H. (2011). Age related effects in interlimb practice on coding complex movement sequences. *Human Movement Science, 30*, 459–474.

Panzer, S., Krueger, M., Muehlbauer, T., Kovacs, A. J., Shea, C. H. (2009). Inter-manual transfer and practice: Coding of simple motor sequences. *Acta Psychologica, 131*(2), 99–109.

Panzer, S., Muehlbauer, T., Krueger, M., Buesch, D., Naundorf, F., & Shea, C. H. (2009). Effects of interlimb practice on coding and learning of movement sequences. *Quarterly Journal of Experimental Psychology, 62*(7), 1265–1276.

Panzer, S., Wilde, H., & Shea, C. H. (2006). The learning of similar complex movement sequences: Proactive and retroactive effects on learning. *Journal of Motor Behavior, 38*, 60–70.

Park, J. H., & Shea, C. H. (2003a). Effect of practice on effector independence. *Journal of Motor Behavior, 35*(1), 33–40.

Park, J.-H., & Shea, C. H. (2003b). The independence of sequence structure and element production in timing sequences. *Research Quarterly for Exercise and Sport, 74*, 401–420.

Park, J. H., & Shea, C. H. (2005). Sequence learning: Response structure and effector transfer. *Quarterly Journal of Experimental Psychology, 58*(3), 387–419.

Povel, D., & Collard, R. (1982). Structural factors in patterned finger tapping. *Acta Psychologica, 52*, 107–123.

Rosenbaum, D. A., Kenny, S., & Derr, M. A. (1983). Hierarchical control of rapid movement sequences. *Journal of Experimental Psychology: Human Perception and Performance, 9*, 86–102.

Rosenbaum, D. A., & Saltzman, E. (1984). A motor-program editor. In Prinz, W., and Sanders, A. (Eds.), *Cognition and motor processes VIII* (pp. 93–106). Berlin: Springer.

Sakai, K., Hikosaka, O., & Nakamura, K. (2004). Emergence of rhythm during motor learning. *Trends in Cognitive Science, 8*(12), 547–553.

Sakai, K., Kitaguchi, K., & Hikosaka, O. (2003). Chunking during human visuomotor sequence learning. *Experimental Brain Research, 152*, 229–242.

Schmidt, R. A. (1975). Schema theory of discrete motor skill learning. *Psychological Review, 82*(4), 225–260.

Shea, C. H., Kovacs, A. J., & Panzer, S. (2011). The coding and transfer of movement sequences. *Frontiers in Movement Science and Sports Psychology*. doi 10.3389 fpsyg.

Shea, C. H., Lai, Q., Black, C., & Park, J.-H. (2001). Spacing practice sessions across days benefits the learning of motor skills. *Human Movement Science, 19*, 737–760.

Tsutsui, S., Lee, T. D., & Hodges, N. J. (1998). Contextual interference in learning new patterns of bimanual coordination. *Journal of Motor Behavior, 30*(2), 151–167.

van Mier, H. I., & Petersen, S. E. (2006). Intermanual transfer effects in sequential tactuomotor learning: Evidence for effector independent coding. *Neuropsychologia, 44*(6), 939–949.

Verwey, W. B. (1994). Evidence for the development of concurrent processing in a sequential key pressing task. *Acta Psychologica, 85*(3), 245–262.

Verwey, W. B., & Clegg, B. A. (2005). Effector dependent sequence learning in the serial RT task. *Psychological Research – Psychologische Forschung, 69*(4), 242–251.

Verwey, W. B., & Eikelboom, T. (2003). Evidence for lasting sequence segmentation in the discrete sequence production task. *Journal of Motor Behavior, 35*, 171–181.

Verwey, W. B., & Wright, D. L. (2004). Effector-independent and effector-dependent learning in the discrete sequence production task. *Psychological Research, 68*, 64–70.

Walker, M. P. (2005). A refined model of sleep and the time course of memory formation. *Behavioral Brain Science, 28*, 51–64.

Walker, M. P., Brakefield, T., Hobson, J. A., & Stickgold, R. (2003). Dissociable stages of human memory consolidation and reconsolidation. *Nature, 425*, 616–620.

Walker, M. P., & Stickgold, R. (2006). Sleep, memory, and plasticity. *Annual Review of Psychology, 57*, 139–166.

Wilde, H., Magnuson, C., & Shea, C. H. (2005). Random and blocked practice of movement sequences: Differential effects on response structure and movement speed. *Research Quarterly for Exercise and Sport, 76*, 416–425.

Wilde, H. & Shea, C. H. (2006). Proportional and non-proportional transfer of movement sequences. *Quarterly Journal of Experimental Psychology, 59*, 1626–1647.

Willingham, D. B., Wells, L. A., Farrell, J. M., & Stemwedel, M. E. (2000). Implicit motor sequence learning is represented in response locations. *Memory & Cognition, 28*(3), 366–375.

Wright, D. L., Black, C. B., Immink, M. A., Brueckner, S., & Magnuson, C. (2004). Long-term motor programming improvements occur via concatenating movement sequences during random but not blocked practice. *Journal of Motor Behavior, 36*, 39–50.

Wright, D. L., Rhee, J., & Vaculin, A. (2010). Enhancement consolidation is not restricted to improving motor sequence learning by establishing motor chunks. *Journal of Motor Behavior, 42*(5), 319–326.

9 Physical guidance research

Assisting principles and supporting evidence

Nicola J. Hodges and Paul Campagnaro

When teaching a new motor skill, it is not uncommon for the instructor to take hold of the learner and physically guide him or her through the movement. Some examples include a golf instructor demonstrating a "correct" swing by placing a hand over the learner's hand or a tennis instructor taking a learner, in slow motion, through a backhand volley. Physical guidance might also include active assist exercises, typically performed by rehabilitation therapists, but more commonly with various robotic devices that physically interact with a patient or an experimental participant.

In this chapter we review evidence regarding the effectiveness of various guidance techniques in motor-related tasks. We focus on the mechanisms that underlie physical guidance and detail the conditions that appear necessary for it to positively impact learning. There are a limited number of sport-related studies and what exists in the literature is quite dated. Perhaps not surprisingly, rehabilitation and associated areas, in which recovery following disease or injury is the primary goal, have dominated this field of research in the past decade. In some ways there is a circular pattern of dependence developing between this rehabilitation-focused research and motor learning. Marchal-Crespo and Reinkensmeyer (2009, p. 2), who are leading researchers in the field of rehabilitation and robotic therapy, conclude that "Robotic therapy control algorithms have . . . been designed on an *ad hoc* basis, usually drawing on some concepts from the rehabilitation, neuroscience and motor learning literature." In this chapter we attempt to bind research and theory together to provide guidance for motor learning researchers and theorists, as well as practitioners in sports and rehabilitation.

We start by defining physical guidance, and then continue by reviewing some historical literature and associated ideas on this topic. We consider the implications of this research for mechanisms of physical guidance and motor learning theory. We then discuss more current empirical research, and attempt to evaluate and recommend methods of physical guidance that appear to show promise for promoting learning and briefly discuss some unresolved issues.

What is physical guidance?

There does not appear to be one clear definition of physical guidance. At the time of writing, there was not even an entry for *physical guidance* in Wikipedia.

It is, however, mentioned within the term *indexing*, an engineering term used in reference to motion meaning "is moving (or being moved) into a new position or location quickly and easily but also precisely" (www.wikipedia.org). Physical guidance, as researchers refer to it in reference to motor learning, embodies part of this definition, that is "moving or *being moved* [italics added] into a new position or location," although physical guidance can involve techniques that are not always quick and easy to administer, nor necessarily precise. The term *physical* in front of *guidance* has been necessary to distinguish this type of guidance from that which is informational in nature. There is a considerable body of research showing that instructions, feedback, or demonstrations can play a strong guiding role in leading people to correct performance.

In the past, "physical guidance" typically referred to the manual moving of a part of a person, such as their arm, from one position to another (e.g., Holding & Macrae, 1964). This has also been referred to as passive guidance in as much as the person being moved is not expected to be actively involved in sending motor commands and associated self-generated, feedforward (or predictive) processes needed to initiate and execute an action. Manual guidance is probably a common teaching technique in many sport skills (such as a baseball swing or swimming stroke) and is frequently used in rehabilitation therapy in which the patient is guided through a desired or functional movement trajectory (e.g., the Bobath concept, also known as NeuroDevelopmental Therapy, http://en.wikipedia.org/wiki/Bobath_concept). Another term used to describe this type of physical guidance is *haptic guidance* (e.g., Feygin, Keehner & Tendick, 2002). The emphasis is on the sense of touch or position that is typically afforded by some mechanical device or robot. Haptic training and associated research has tended to be the language of use in mechanical engineering with particular relevance to the design of simulators or virtual environments, as might be used in (micro)surgery or aircraft control. In Table 9.1 we highlight some key research studies in the areas of physical guidance along with the terminology (and learning outcomes) that has accompanied this research.

Although passive guidance methods are common and have received considerable research attention, physical guidance has been studied with respect to techniques and devices that act to assist only part of the movement. These have included mechanical stops to indicate a target location (Holding & Macrae, 1964) or devices that serve a similar purpose to training wheels on a bike, such as a handrails or ski poles to aid balance when learning slalom movements on a ski simulator (Wulf, Shea, & Whitacre, 1998; Wulf & Toole, 1999). In rehabilitation environments this type of guidance is sometimes referred to as "active assist" (e.g., Lum, Burgar, Shor, Majmundar & Van der Loos, 2002). These techniques are common among therapist and patient interactions, in which both individuals share the effort to complete a movement, with the therapist providing a physically supportive role (such as supporting a limb that has poor muscle tone). These types of manual guidance are also popular in sports such as gymnastics in which the risk of injury is high and a desired movement, rather than outcome, is the primary goal (Arkaev & Suchilin, 2004).

With the advent of more sophisticated technology for sports and rehabilitation, manual guidance may be substituted by potentially more efficient technical or robotic guidance. These robotic assistive therapies have met with similar successes

Table 9.1 A summary of physical guidance research with respect to the terminology, authors, and general effects as a function of the time of measurement

Guidance technique terminology	Authors	ST benefits	Learning efficacy
Forced response	Waters (1930)	✓	–
	Melcher (1934)	✓	–
	Macrae & Holding (1966)	✓	–
Terminal-error elimination	Holding & Macrae (1964)	✓	–
Slaved guidance	Baker (1968)	✓	✗
Passive (mechanical) guidance	Armstrong (1970)	✓	✗
Constraining endpoint error	Winstein, Pohl, & Lewthwaite (1994)	✓	✗
Partial and passive guidance	Feijen, Hodges, & Beek (2010)	✓	✗
Assistive conditions	Domingo & Ferris (2009)	✗	–
Physical guidance (poles)	Wulf, Shea, & Whitacre (1998)	✓	✓
Haptic (force) guidance	Yang, Bischof, & Boulanger (2008)	✗	✗
Position haptic guidance	Feygin et al. (2002)	✓ (timing)	–
Force haptic guidance	Bluteau, Coquillart, Payan, & Gentaz (2008)	✓ (fluidity)	–
Error reduction (adaptive guidance)	Marchal-Crespo & Reinkensmeyer (2008)	✓	–
	Marchal-Crespo, McHughen, Cramer, & Reinkensmeyer (2010)	✓	✓
Performance-based progressive therapy	Ferraro et al. (2003)	(stroke)	✓
Haptic tracking (light touch)	Rosenbaum, Dawson, & Challis (2006)	✓	–

ST, short term or learning efficacy referring to testing beyond a 24-hour interval; ✓, positive compared with other conditions; ✗, negative compared with other conditions; –, not evaluated

to therapist-driven interventions, in as much as encouraging use of an injured limb (e.g., Kahn, Zygman, Rymer, & Reinkensmeyer, 2006; Lum et al., 2002), but benefits are typically apparent only if the learner or patient is actively involved in initiating the movement. A common argument underlying the potential effectiveness of physical guidance is that it allows a person to "feel" a movement that cannot already be performed. Guidance techniques also restrict errors through limiting or eliminating incorrect movements (Howard, 2003), such that they can provide a necessary safety role, one of avoiding falls or injury. Intuitively, the concept of physical guidance seems to make a lot of sense, especially in cases where the learner may have difficulty viewing his or her own movement and visual demonstrations are potentially of limited value. Experimental results, however, suggest that physical guidance is not necessarily a good teaching tool when used frequently without considerable input (cognitive, sensory, and emotional) from the learner.

Physical guidance research . . . a look back

Physical guidance leads to generally excellent performance during the training/ acquisition phase. Almost by definition, guidance procedures are intended to restrict error and hence outcome success is expected. For motor learning to be inferred, however, it is necessary to measure whether this error reduction translates into performance gains during retention, when the physical guidance is no longer present. Early research was often difficult to interpret where this question was concerned, hampered also by different definitions of physical guidance (Howard, 2003; see also Table 9.1).

In some early research, experimental participants gripped a handle as it was moved correctly by the experimenter through a hidden maze (Melcher, 1934; Waters, 1930). The participant's limb was passively conducted through the required movement, termed *forced response*. This initial guidance had positive benefits when the participants subsequently moved through the maze, suggesting that this guidance aided learning. However, these tests were performed over a limited time period and arguably participants were picking up more explicit, strategic knowledge (such as directions), rather than learning movements per se. Holding and Macrae (1964) employed a *passive guidance* task similar to the above. In this experiment, however, the task was a simple linear movement: participants grasped a knob attached to a sleeve that was moved along a rod for a required distance. *Terminal error elimination* form of guidance was provided on another version of their task in which participants produced the linear movement actively, but a terminal stop ensured that the movement ended precisely. Although positive benefits for both were found (in comparison with no-practice controls), and for complex tracking in comparison with trial and error practice when transfer without the guidance was assessed (Macrae & Holding, 1966), no long-term effects were studied (e.g., retention tests conducted 24 hours or more later).

Long-term retention was evaluated in two subsequent studies. Baker (1968) had participants grasp a *slaved* joystick in a pursuit-tracking task that was connected to movements made by an unguided physical practice person. Although this guided group performed well in early unguided tests of performance (as well as or better than the unguided *master* group) in a 6-week retention test, this *slaved* guidance group performed worse than the unguided group and no better than a group who had never practiced but just watched. However, in Baker's study, no attempt was made to ensure that participants were not trying to "correct" the errors of their unguided partner (referred to as *stick fighting*) and hence both the experience of errors and opportunities to actively apply forces might have added to initial gains. This was one of the first studies to employ a delayed retention test to measure learning. Although the authors were unable at the time to explain these decrements in retention associated with guidance conditions, the reduced experience (and effort) detecting and correcting errors appeared to have hampered the cognitive and sensory processes involved in long-term retention.

Practice effects as a result of physical guidance were also found to be relativity temporary by Armstrong (1970; who incidentally provided an excellent review of early guidance research). In his experiment, participants practiced a complex spatio-temporal pattern with their elbow. In one group a mechanical movement device controlled the movement and prevented "mistakes." During practice this group performed well because errors were restricted, but when the device was removed performance deteriorated significantly, such that no learning was said to occur in this *passive guidance* group.

A form of physical guidance like that described above was later defined by Winstein, Pohl, and Lewthwaite (1994) as *constraining endpoint error*. In addition to testing the potential negative effects of physical guidance, they manipulated the availability of information to determine how different sources of information that guide performance, but have been shown to negatively impact retention, interact. Participants were required to rotate a lever through various angles to a predetermined radial position to a block that acted as physical guidance ensuring the correct endpoint. As predicted, combining a physical guidance condition with a high frequency of feedback resulted in the poorest retention.

In summary, physical guidance aids performance during acquisition and typically immediate retention, but it is detrimental to learning (i.e., delayed retention and transfer) when the guidance is no longer available. The logic is that, when present, guidance ensures that the task is performed with little or no error. However, when it is present on every trial, the learner becomes dependent upon it, failing to acquire an internal, self-generated reference of what correct performance looks and feels like. Therefore, physical guidance during practice hampers the error detection processes necessary to perform the task without guidance (Schmidt, 1991). More effective learning is the result when guidance is given less frequently (e.g., in a fading schedule) (Winstein et al., 1994). In this situation there is a balance between the potential beneficial effects of guidance (e.g., establishing what a correct movement feels like), and those afforded by practicing without guidance on some trials (e.g., developing intrinsic error detection capabilities and being actively involved in the sensorimotor decision processes).

How does physical guidance work and why does it not?

Overdependence and the guidance hypothesis

According to the guidance hypothesis (Schmidt, 1991), external feedback (such as knowledge of results from a coach about the speed or accuracy of a throw) provides useful information that helps to correct errors and improve subsequent performance. However, too much feedback can be detrimental to long-term storage and retention, as it disrupts critical between-trial processing. Therefore, feedback is said to contain guiding properties (Schmidt, 1991). Frequent feedback has been thought of as analogous to a crutch (Salmoni, Schmidt, & Walter, 1984), effectively aiding the learner (to walk) when present, but preventing or hampering performance if absent. If you never drop the crutch you will never be able to walk without it; practice has to take place in the absence of the crutch if the goal is non-assisted walking. This illustration shows how feedback guidance effects are exemplified (and magnified) when considered in the context of an actual physical device rather than just feedback. Not only do learners fail to engage in the processing activities required for successful learning after a trial, but they do not need to engage in processing of the feedback during execution either.

Reference of correctness

The importance of gaining sensory experience of a correct movement was integral to Adams's (1971) closed-loop theory of motor learning. This "correct" experience of sensory feedback was thought to aid learning through the development of a *perceptual trace*. This trace acts as a reference-of-correctness to guide movements in a closed-loop fashion, such that movements can be adjusted based on perceived error between actual and desired perceptual consequences. However, learning does not proceed well without errors, and experiences of actions outside a specific desired action can aid long-term learning (e.g., Shapiro & Schmidt, 1982). Schmidt explicitly took this important point into account when proposing the *recognition schema* and associated ideas of *generalized motor programs* in his schema theory of learning (Schmidt, 1975, 1976). Of particular importance was the experience of sensory consequences related to a desired movement (e.g., kicking a ball from various distances towards the goal in soccer), but not an exact "copy" (just kicking from the penalty spot). Schemas were seen more as abstract concepts storing generalized rules of behavior. In this way, the constrained type of learning typical of physical guidance would inhibit rather than aid motor learning.

Specificity of practice

The idea that learning must, in some ways, be specific to the desired action did resurface some years later under the title of *specificity of practice* (Khan & Franks, 2004; Proteau, 1992). Although it bears similarities to other important theories of learning in psychology, what was highlighted was that optimal learning occurs when the sensory conditions of practice match those experienced in a later test or transfer phase. Therefore, changing the sensory experiences between practice and testing, which would be the case when guidance or an assistive device is removed (such as removing a float when swimming), will result in poor transfer. People come to show dependence on the primary source(s) of information available during practice as well as the relationship between these different types of sensory feedback.

Efferent and feedforward processes

One of the important features missing from passive guidance conditions is self-generation of movement and the sending of motor commands. In the absence of this efferent process (i.e., movement initiation and the active correction of errors), actions and motor learning will be impaired (e.g., Schmidt & White, 1972). What is also missing, and what has begun to receive considerably more attention in computational (or internal) models of motor control, is a feedforward process assumed to be responsible for the (implicit) prediction of sensory consequences. The idea is that when we move we simultaneously send a copy of this motor command to a forward model in terms of an *efference copy* (like a photocopy of our intended action). Based on this command (and what we plan to do), there is the (automatic) expectation of what the movement will feel and look like. This mechanism allows us to determine what actions are self-generated and saves time in enabling fast corrections of errors, without the need for actual feedback (Bays & Wolpert, 2007; Wolpert & Ghahramani, 2000). Therefore passive physical guidance conditions downplay not only efference, with respect to the sending of motor commands, but potentially afference, associated with the prediction of what the movement should feel like.

Sensory dominance and perceptual representations

The idea that actions are planned in terms of their anticipated sensory consequences was first entertained by James (1890/1981) and later refined by Hommel, Prinz, and colleagues (e.g., Hommel, Müsseler, Aschersleben, & Prinz, 2001). Distal sensory effects of an action could act to prime the selection of a related action. Motor commands are selected based on their expected sensory consequences. This emphasis on the sensory effects of an action, rather than the actual motor commands in terms of initiating and planning, has implications for the effectiveness of guidance techniques. The experience of the sensory consequences would allow for a representation of the desired motor commands to develop somewhat as a consequence of this sensory experience. Indeed, Mechsner, Kerzel, Knoblich, & Prinz (2001, p. 69) concluded that 'voluntary movements are organized by the way of a representation of the perceptual goals whereas the corresponding motor activity, of sometimes high complexity, is spontaneously and flexibly tuned in'. These theoretical ideas contrast with other frameworks discussed so far in as much as physical guidance conditions would not necessarily be expected to result in impoverished learning.

Constraints

Physical devices act as constraints on action and we often think of constraints as potentially negative. However, constraints do not need to act on the actual movement. Moreover, the idea that the movement is a potential desired and emergent consequence of constraints typifies a model of learning based on a more positive role that (physical) constraints play in shaping and teaching movements. According to Newell (1986), environmental, person, and task-related constraints determine the patterns of movement that will emerge. The challenge therefore is one of knowing and imposing the necessary constraints to encourage the desired action, not of knowing the desired action or movement pattern in advance and teaching this action.

What is required when setting up for effective guidance is to optimize the constraints such that the target movement or task is achieved without physically controlling the movement. What remains when the guidance is removed is an emergent (or stable) pattern of movement that accomplishes the task goal successfully. For example, if the goal is to perform a chip shot in soccer (one that requires the ball to lift to clear an object) then the placement of an object in front of the kicker will encourage this desired movement (Hodges, Hayes, Breslin, & Williams, 2005). Importantly, the physical constraint in this example is not one that directs what the movement should look like or feel like, but rather one that directs task selection and encourages processes associated with planning and execution (also Davids, Button, & Bennett, 2008).

Constraint-based techniques for teaching racket sport skills have been reviewed by Kernodle and Turner (1998). These include the use of rubber tubing on the arms or legs to restrict swing and/or encourage the fast return to a previous spot on the court, or cone-shaped hats (halos) to encourage the racket trajectory to scale the perimeter of the hat during high shots (such as drives and smashes in badminton). A desired movement is brought about in an active manner as a solution to a problem (constraint). The question of whether the subsequent removal of these constraints affects later performance has, however, received little attention. We would suspect that the guidance properties of these constraints would covary in direct proportion to how restrictive they are and whether they directly affect the produced movement.

Physical guidance research: now and the future

Given some outstanding issues concerning how physical guidance works, the seeming necessity of this technique for the learning/relearning of particular motor skills (where safety and injury are potential problems), and technological advances in assistive devices (e.g., Riener, Nef, & Colombo, 2005), there has been a resurgence of interest in the mechanisms and potential effectiveness of physical guidance.

Active movement guidance

For physical guidance to work, the learner needs to have some active involvement in the learning process, rather than passively receiving sensory input only. However, on the basis of three experiments showing that visual–spatial, rather than motor- or efferent-related, constraints were more important for the stability of dual-limb coordination, Mechsner et al. (2001) claimed that the brain does not need to consider the muscle commands necessary for particular movements. In support, Atchy-Delama, Zanone, Peper, and Beek (2005) showed that mere experience of the sensory consequences (i.e., visual and proprioceptive feedback) was sufficient for learning a new coordination movement. In this experiment, the congruence between motor commands and sensory consequences was broken in one group by means of a physical weight added to one of the limbs (see Figure 9.1). This allowed the person to produce a challenging movement, which required an asynchrony between the arms, by intending to make symmetrical flexion/extension movements (i.e., in-phrase). This could be seen as analogous to arm actions in juggling. Once the weight was removed this partial physical guidance group showed positive transfer in that they were better able to perform the asynchronous movement than before practice (and now to produce the appropriate, asynchronous motor commands even though these had never been practiced).

Therefore it appears that experience of how the movement looks and feels is potentially sufficient for learning. However, the learners in Atchy-Delama et al.'s experiment were still actively involved in producing the sensory consequences, and this active involvement would still promote the updating of an internal (forward) model. If it is mere experience of the sensory consequences that is important, then passive learning conditions (typical of past guidance research) should result in the same positive effects. As expected, in a partial replication of this study, passive guidance achieved by a robotic-type set-up involving servo-motors (see schematic in Figure 9.2), did not aid learning (Feijen, Hodges, & Beek, 2010). Although we replicated the findings of Atchy-Delama and colleagues showing positive transfer for the partial guidance, hand-weighted condition (see Figure 9.3), when we studied durations within a trial spent performing the asynchronous movement, this weighted group spent less time performing the correct movemet than an "active" group who practiced without any guidance. Therefore, active experience of the "correct" sensory consequences through partial guidance (such as weighting a limb to achieve a desired golf swing) does not make up for the additional experiences gained through trial-and-error physical practice.

Figure 9.1 A picture showing the weights used to create spatially incongruent movements in the study by Feijen et al. (2010; similar methods were used originally by Atchy-Delama et al., 2005).

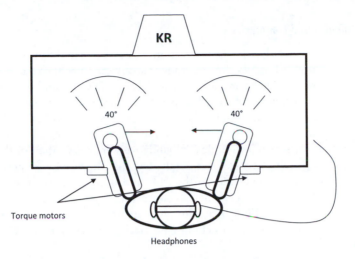

Figure 9.2 A schematic diagram of the physical set-up used to perform and learn bimanual coordination movements (e.g., Feijen et al., 2010). Participants rested their forearms on the platforms (manipulanda) and produced flexion and extension movements about the elbow joint. In physical guidance conditions, torque motors under the table top controlled the movements of the platforms in order to physically guide the participant to make 30° relative phase movements. In this experiment the desired movement goal was alerted by auditory metronomes (through headphones).

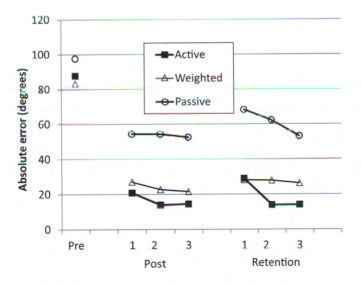

Figure 9.3 Average absolute error values for three groups (Active physical practice without guidance, Partial physical guidance through the use of weights and Passive guidance through the use of guiding motors) practicing a 30° relative phase movement. Data are shown for one trial before practice manipulations and for three trials immediately after practice (post-test) as well as in a delayed retention test. These data are adapted from Feijen et al. (2010).

Task difficulty and complexity

There appears to be task-difficulty interactions with respect to the effects of various physical guidance techniques. In one study that involved healthy volunteers walking on a narrow or wide beam, Domingo and Ferris (2009) found that "assistive" conditions (i.e., a stabilizing device) hampered pre–post test improvements in comparison with non-assistive conditions (see also Domingo & Ferris, 2010). However, task difficulty moderated these effects such that, when it was low (as with the wide beam), the costs associated with physical guidance were *greater* than in the harder condition. This finding occurred despite the fact that the number of performance failures per minute did not differ in the wide and narrow groups. Therefore, the harder the task, the more likely that guidance will be helpful, or at least not as negative in consequence. Similar conclusions were made by Singer (1977) based on his review of response-directed (including physical guidance) versus trial-and-error learning.

Further support for skill complexity underpinning the potential effectiveness of guidance methods was shown by Wulf, Shea, and Whitacre (1998). Although these authors did not manipulate task difficulty, they argued that the positive effects of ski-pole use when learning how to ride a ski simulator were related to the many degrees of freedom required for successful control. They argued that, as movement complexity increases, physical guidance may be beneficial because it allows the learner to feel the correct movement early in practice. Similar rationale has been presented for the use of stabilizer or training wheels on a bike. However, it is possible that the success of guidance in this ski example was more related to the type of guidance provided (i.e., stability poles), rather than complexity. For example, Sidaway et al. (2008) found that manual guidance at the hips failed to help healthy people learn an asymmetrical weight-bearing balance task. Wulf et al. (1998) also attributed the success of the ski poles to the fact that their use did not dictate how errors should be reduced (or performance improved) and thus they did not become a "crutch" for performance. This factor is likely to be a critical feature for effective guidance in that it allows exploration of the task and a feel of what is correct, but also allows errors to be made and encourages self-generated performance solutions.

With respect to learning to ride a bicycle, it appears that most trainers believe that training wheels do not teach a person to ride a bicycle, most importantly because they do not teach the rider how to balance. This is supported by the success of small bicycles without pedals that allow children to "ride" at an early age through the practice of balance control. Unlike training wheels, the ski poles used in the study by Wulf and colleagues could be used or relied on more or less when needed and thus they still allowed errors and balance practice. When we tried to uncover empirical data on training wheels, despite not uncovering any research, we found numerous patented aids that had in common the ability to allow the child to balance and just receive guidance when needed (such as retractable wheels, performance-dependent sensors, or clamps). As we detail below, the emotional guidance from these aids could also partially explain their widespread use.

Robot guidance and task complexity

In mechanical engineering there has been considerable interest in the use of haptics (i.e., touch or force-guidance) to aid motor learning, with somewhat mixed results. For example, in a letter-drawing task using a position-dependent robot, there were no benefits following either single or repeated (4 days) training (Yang, Bischof, & Boulanger, 2008). It appears that the potential benefits of haptic guidance are greatest for teaching temporal/rhythmic aspects of a task or motor skill, especially when used in combination with other types of sensory feedback (e.g., Feygin, Keehner, & Tendick, 2002; Morris, Tan, Barbagli, Chang, & Salisbury, 2007). Arguably, these are the aspects of a motor skill that are difficult to impart to a learner strategically and are not particularly amenable to observational practice (e.g., Blandin, Lhuisset, & Proteau, 1999; Maslovat, Hodges, Krigolson, & Handy, 2010). Although relatively simple timing aspects might be amenable to training, as with sequence-learning tasks, for coordination skills, where the timing between hands for example is critical (such as juggling or cricket bowling), passive guidance does not seem to be effective (Feijen et al., 2010; Tsutsui & Imanaka, 2003).

There have been differences in these studies with respect to training of forces or position. In force guidance, the experience is one of forces that would be exerted by an expert or teacher as they make a particular movement, whereas position guidance can be thought of as more like a constant spring acting to bring about a desired position. For the training of novel letter writing, force guidance has been shown to be preferable to position guidance for improvement of movement fluidity (Bluteau, Coquillart, Payan, & Gentaz, 2008). However, only short-term tests of retention were used. Although force guidance training has potential applications for sports that require a certain amount of force applied to a known mass, such as when putting in golf (Huang, Kunkel, Brindza, & Kuchenbecker, 2011) or throwing the rock to the button in curling, for these techniques to be effective in the long term, the physical guidance in general should be limited, such that the learner experiences more than a correct or desired movement, as we elaborate below.

Functional task difficulty and adaptive guidance

There is evidence that the potential benefits to be gained from physical guidance are dependent on the performer's skill level. Marchal-Crespo, McHughen, Cramer, and Reinkensmeyer (2010) used a robot (force-controlled) device to help guide steering corrections during a driving simulation on a curved path, particularly with respect to when the wheel should be turned. Participants with more errors early in practice benefited more from guidance than participants with lower errors. This makes sense when one considers that, if the task is already low in error, reducing error further will either not aid or potentially hamper performance or learning. These effects are consistent with the challenge point framework (Guadagnoli & Lee, 2004). Accordingly, information should be provided to meet the demands of the task for the learner (i.e., functional task difficulty) optimally. Too much information, whether externally provided feedback or physical guidance, for a proficient performer, or for an easy task, would not be a useful teaching method, as little engagement would be fostered in order to retain the skills. In contrast, if the learner finds the task difficult or the task is complex, then methods of simplifying learning are more likely to be beneficial. Importantly, techniques that dynamically capture the learner's current capabilities will be the best methods for learning.

Similar benefits for *error reduction* techniques for less skilled participants, in comparison with benefits for *error amplifying* techniques for more skilled participants have been shown (e.g., Milot, Marchal-Crepo, Green, Cramer, & Reinkensmeyer, 2010). The idea that increased errors or variability in the movement will aid learning stands in stark contrast to the techniques that have typically been explored to aid learning through guidance and error reduction (see Reinkensmeyer & Patton, 2009). Although these error amplification methods are starting to receive attention in rehabilitation and in sports (e.g., Schöllhorn et al., 2006), in our laboratory we have not found these forced-error techniques to benefit learning among novices learning to produce novel coordination movements (Edwards & Hodges, in press). It could be that neither forced errors nor error reduction techniques, both ends of the error and error-free continuum, are useful learning aids and that methods that optimally balance errors with correct performance will be most effective for learning (see also van Asseldonk, Wessels, Stienen, van der Helm, & van der Kooij, 2009).

An important component of the steering guidance techniques that have been used by Reinkensmeyer and colleagues is that the guidance "kicked in" only when needed and the amount of guidance decreased as practice increased (like bandwidth methods of feedback provision, e.g., Lee & Maraj, 1994). Marchal-Crespo and Reinkensmeyer (2008) found that this adaptive method of providing guidance was more effective than a fixed method when the steering guidance was subsequently removed. Similar performance-dependent methods of administering physical guidance using robotic interfaces have been developed (e.g., Ferraro et al., 2003; Krebs et al., 2003), under the term *Performance Based Progressive Therapy* (see Hogan et al., 2006, for a review). In this, robotic therapy is designed to assist or resist movements only when needed (via an impedance controller) or to help patients improve on specific aspects of their reach as needed, such as speed or accuracy. The therapy can also be programmed to respond to changes in muscle activation. Positive benefits of this type of therapy for patients after stroke have been quite promising. With respect to sport, it might be possible to imagine such a system that can act to guide a person through an action (such as a tennis serve or golf swing) based only on certain desired parameters. This procedure would ensure that the learner is an active participant and that guidance is given only for selected parts of the movement.

Self-scheduled guidance

Another way that the learner can become more engaged in learning, but benefit from guidance, is to give the learner control over when to receive guidance. Wulf and Toole (1999) gave participants control over when to use the ski poles on the previously discussed ski simulator task. These learners were compared with a group who had no choice, but were matched (yoked) with respect to the trials on which the poles were allowed. Although the groups did not differ in practice, the self-control group outperformed the yoked group in retention without the poles with respect to movement amplitude. Therefore, not only is it beneficial to limit guidance during practice, it is useful to engage the learner in determining on which trials support is needed. In view of the benefits of adaptive practice schedules, at least part of these benefits is likely to be a result of guidance when needed. Whether these effects are moderated by motivational factors remains to be tested.

Physical guidance and positive affect

There have been attempts to determine whether physical guidance has motivational or related competency effects on performance and learning, which might justify its use beyond outcome measures. McAuley (1985) taught gymnasts to perform a mount from a springboard onto a balance beam with and without guidance. The guided gymnasts scored higher on an immediate post-practice test and showed higher perceptions of competence. Despite this positive effect, Wulf and Toole (1999) did not find differences in measures of self-efficacy or fear of injury with self-directed guidance, and mixed results were found in a study involving two gymnastic skills (Heinen, Pizzera, & Cottyn, 2009). Although manual guidance positively aided acquisition and transfer for one skill (a fast somersault dismount), guidance did not alleviate fear more than no-guidance conditions. For two slower skills (cartwheel and slower somersault), manual guidance did not affect performance, but did lead to higher ratings of efficacy and reduced fear of injury.

It appears that guidance conditions are only moderately affected by perceptions of ability and related affect (if at all). It might be that guidance conditions have differential effects on individuals, in some cases acting to increase feelings of competence, but in others decreasing confidence (owing to dependencies that might develop).

Tactile guidance

Light touch, or what has been termed haptic tracking, has received some attention of late as a method to teach people to perform what would be otherwise difficult movements. Participants learn to track another's actions by very lightly staying in contact with the other person. Rosenbaum, Dawson, and Challis (2006) have likened this to slow dancing with a partner. There is evidence that light touch onto a surface can aid balance (e.g., Jeka, 1997; Jeka & Lackner, 1994), and thus this type of "light" physical guidance might have potential benefits for the acquisition of motor skills, without negative consequences associated with its removal. Indeed, Jeka (1997) showed that light touch engages different processes from that engendered from force contact (in which a person actually leans on something or someone for support). Although this hypothesis was not directly tested, Rosenbaum and colleagues showed that light touch by a partner who moved another person's hands bimanually and without vision, encouraged desired, asynchronous, and independent movements of the person's limbs. Even when the hands were guided to make incongruent movements (e.g., a circle and a square), participants showed no difficulty being guided. Haptic tracking facilitated interlimb independence arguably because it obviated the need for high-level, attentional control. However, no attempts were made to measure transfer of learning in the absence of this haptic tracking.

There is some unsubstantiated evidence that passively feeling the oscillatory movements of a hand-held rollerball before physical practice (a vibrating, spinning device whose axis of rotation moves inside a plastic shell, such as the Powerball©, DynaFlex, 2009) helps the learner acquire the specific wrist motions needed to pick up speed and get the rollerball moving (D. Goodman, personal communication). The learner still has to figure out what to do, but the tactile (haptic) feedback appears to impart knowledge of the actual voluntary movements required to keep the ball in motion (see also Liu, Luo, Mayer-Kress, & Newell, 2012). This task might be akin to knowing or feeling what it is like to perform the Middle-Eastern dance move called a "shimmy," whereby the dancer's body vibrates as a result of an apparent tensing and relaxing of targeted muscles to create the impression that the body is vibrating or shimmying. This type of move is difficult to pick up from watching and takes practice in order to feel a "correct" shimmy. Indeed, physical guidance might work by helping the learner appreciate what not to do as much as what they should do, in order that it can be differentiated and organized (Gentile, 1972). If it were possible to find a way to share these desired vibro-tactile consequences of an expert with a learner then arguably learning would be enhanced (one technique is for the learner to stand behind a "teacher" and place their hands on their hips, although the success of this method is unclear). Interestingly, there are robotic devices (e.g., MIME, Mirror-Image Movement Enabler) that allow the learner to experience motions of the opposite arm (through calculations of inverse force dynamics) and this technique has recently been used effectively to provide a reference for the hemiparetic limb in training arm motions after stroke (e.g., Burgar et al., 2011; see Figure 9.4). These robotic techniques might prove useful in training the non-preferred limb for sport-related tasks such as throwing.

Summary, outstanding issues, and conclusions

In summary, we advocate the use of physical guidance techniques that (1) are administered in a faded schedule, or at least not on every trial; (2) are determined based on an individual's needs, with more guidance being appropriate for more complex tasks and for individuals with lower initial performance; and (3) encourage active involvement from the learner. This last use of the term *active* refers to both the self-generation of movement (i.e., the physical aspect) as well as person-appropriate processing activities that are necessary before and after a movement, to ensure optimal learning.

Guidance probably has real value in situations where the task is difficult and/or dangerous to perform, such as in diving, trampolining, or ski-jumping. It allows the novice to "try the task" and "get a feel for it" in a safe and non-threatening environment. Similarly, if the task is relatively complex, requiring unusual movements or a particular fluid or rhythmic movement, guidance may allow for exploration of the

Figure 9.4 Illustration of a person moving with the MIME robot like that used in the study by Burgar et al. (2011; VA Palo Alto Heath Care System, Rehabilitation R&D Service, US Dept. of Veterans Affairs).

task, a process which can arguably lead to more effective learning (e.g., Wulf et al., 1998). The important issue then becomes one of determining the critical point to remove guidance. How do we know when that point is reached? That assist-as-need techniques positively impact short-term and long-term learning speaks to the idea that (a reduction in) errors should drive this selection process.

One potential problem with evaluating the effectiveness of guidance-based techniques or therapies, particularly as they relate to robotic guidance, is that there appear to be so many different control strategies (Marchal-Crespo & Reinkensmeyer, 2009). Rarely, if ever, are two or more robotic control strategies (such as force and position controllers, or different types of normative movements) compared directly with each other (cf. Bluteau et al., 2008). Constraints-based models of control are based on the assumption that "normal" or "optimal" patterns of movement do not exist (e.g., Davids, Button, & Bennett, 2008). Therefore, passive guidance techniques seem to be the antithesis of this approach, given that they are based on "normative" or "optimal" trajectories. However, where constraints-based models in sport have been studied, the focus has typically been on the development of movement skills for expert performance, whereas the challenge for a physical therapist is merely to achieve functional (rather than skilled) behavior.

If we conclude that physical guidance can be beneficial to motor learning, if given sparingly, and we conclude that it primarily hampers learning through the restriction or prevention of errors, how are we to reconcile some recent findings in the motor learning literature showing that techniques that restrict errors (so termed errorless learning, though strictly speaking they are never completely errorless) have potentially beneficial effects in retention and transfer tests than "errorful" conditions (e.g., Poolton, Masters, & Maxwell, 2005)? Perhaps there are optimal amounts of error that need to be experienced and too much (completely unguided) is as bad as too little. These ideas marry with the challenge point framework (Guadagnoli & Lee, 2004) and the need to match information to the learner's level of skill and hence the task's functional difficulty.

Physical guidance is a technique, at least in some degree, that is of considerable demand in sports and other settings. As we have shown, it can positively aid both short-term performance and learning if used sparingly, based on a person's current and ever-changing level of performance, and if used in such a way that the movement is steered to the "correct" or desired path, rather than directly guided. We know why it works, and why it does not, but there are still questions to be asked about potential affective responses to physical guidance as well as the general role of errors and variability in learning and how these are best optimized to bring about learning and transfer.

References

Adams, J. A. (1971). A closed-loop theory of motor learning. *Journal of Motor Behavior, 3,* 111–150.

Armstrong, T. R. (1970). *Training for the production of memorized movement patterns* (Tech. Rep. NO. 26). Ann Arbor, MI: University of Michigan, Department of Psychology.

Arkaev, L. I., & Suchilin, N. G. (2004). *How to create champions: The theory & methodology of training top-class gymnasts.* Oxford: Meyer & Meyer Sport.

Atchy-Delama, P., Zanone, P. G., Peper, C. E., & Beek, P. J. (2005). Movement-related sensory feedback mediates the learning of a new bimanual relative phase pattern. *Journal of Motor Behavior, 37,* 186–196.

Baker, C. H. (1968). An evaluation of guidance in learning a motor skill. *Canadian Journal of Psychology, 22,* 217–227.

Bays, P. M., & Wolpert, D. M. (2007). Computational principles of sensorimotor control that minimize uncertainty and variability. *Journal of Physiology, 578,* 387–396.

Blandin, Y., Lhuisset, L., & Proteau, L. (1999). Cognitive processes underlying observational learning of motor skills. *Quarterly Journal of Experimental Psychology, 52,* 957–979.

Bluteau, J., Coquillart, S., Payan, Y., & Gentaz, E. (2008). Haptic guidance improves the visuo-manual tracking of trajectories. *PLoS ONE 3:* e1775.

Burgar, C. G., Lum, P. S., Scremin, A. M.E., Garber, S. L., Van der Loos, H. F.M., Kenney, D., & Shor, P. (2011). Robot-assisted upper-limb therapy in acute rehabilitation setting following stroke: Department of Veterans Affairs multisite clinical trial. *Journal of Rehabilitation Research & Development, 48,* 445–58.

Davids, K., Button, C., & Bennett, S. (2008). *The dynamics of skill acquisition.* Chicago: Human Kinetics.

Domingo, A., & Ferris, D. P. (2009) Effects of physical guidance on short-term learning of walking on a narrow beam. *Gait & Posture, 30,* 464–468.

Domingo, A., & Ferris, D. P. (2010). The effects of error augmentation on learning to walk on a narrow balance beam. *Experimental Brain Research, 206,* 359–370.

DynaFlex. (2009). *Powerball.* Retrieved March 8, 2012, from http://iprs.cbp.gov/index.asp?action=detail&id=105377&searchArg=CHENG&page=1

Edwards, C. A. L., & Hodges, N. J. (in press). Acquiring a novel coordination movement with non-task related variability. *Open Sports Science Journal.*

Feijen, L., Hodges, N. J., & Beek, P. (2010). Acquiring a novel coordination skill without practicing the desired motor commands. *Journal of Motor Behavior, 42*, 295–306.

Ferraro, M., Palazzolo, J. J., Krol, J., Krebs, H. I., Hogan, N., & Volpe, B. T. (2003). Robot-aided sensorimotor arm training improves outcome in patients with chronic stroke. *Neurology, 61*, 1604–1607.

Feygin, D., Keehner, M., & Tendick, F. (2002). Haptic guidance: Experimental evaluation of a haptic training method for a perceptual motor skill. *Proceedings of the 10th Symposium on Haptic Interfaces for Virtual Environments & Teleoperator Systems* (HAPTICS, 2002). doi: 10.1109/HAPTIC.2002.998939

Gentile, A. M. (1972). A working model of skill acquisition with application to teaching. *Quest, 17*, 3–23.

Guadagnoli, M., & Lee, T. (2004). Challenge point: A framework for conceptualizing the effects of various practice conditions in motor learning. *Journal of Motor Behavior, 36*, 212–224.

Heinen, T., Pizzera, A., & Cottyn, J. (2009). When is manual guidance effective for the acquisition of complex skills in gymnastics? *International Journal of Sport Psychology, 40*, 1–22.

Hodges, N. J., Hayes, S. J., Breslin, G., & Williams, A. M. (2005). An evaluation of the minimal constraining information during movement observation and reproduction. *Acta Psychologica, 119*, 264–282.

Hogan, N., Krebs, H. I., Rohrer, B., Palazzolo, J. J., Dipietro, L., Fasoli, S. E., et al. (2006). Motions or muscles? Some behavioral factors underlying robotic assistance of motor recovery. *Journal of Rehabilitation Research & Development, 43*, 605–618.

Holding, D. H., & Macrae, A. W. (1964). Guidance, restriction and knowledge of results. *Ergonomics, 9*, 289–295.

Hommel, B., Müsseler, J., Aschersleben, G., & Prinz, W. (2001). The Theory of Event Coding (TEC): A framework for perception and action planning. *Behavioral & Brain Sciences, 24*, 849–937.

Howard, J. T. III. (2003). *Physical guidance in motor learning*. Unpublished master's thesis, Queensland University of Technology, Brisbane, Australia.

Huang, P. Y., Kunkel, J. A., Brindza, J., & Kuchenbecker, K. J. (2011). Haptically assisted golf putting through a planar four-cable system. *World Haptics Conference, IEEE*, 191–196. doi: 10.1109/WHC.2011.5945484.

James, W. (1890/1981) *The principles of psychology, vol. I.* Cambridge, MA: Harvard University Press.

Jeka, J. J. (1997). Light touch contact as a balance aid. *Physical Therapy, 77*, 476–487.

Jeka, J. J., & Lackner, J. R. (1994). Fingertip contact influences human postural control. *Experimental Brain Research, 100*, 495–502.

Kahn, L. E., Zygman, M. L., Rymer, W. Z., & Reinkensmeyer, D. J. (2006). Robot-assisted reaching exercise promotes arm movement recovery in chronic hemiparetic stroke: A randomized controlled pilot study. *Journal of NeuroEngineering & Rehabilitation, 3*, 12. Retrieved April, 2012, from http://www.jneuroengrehab.com/content/3/1/12

Kernodle, M. W., & Turner, E. T. (1998). The effective use of guidance technique in teaching racquet sports. *Journal of Physical Education, Recreation & Dance, 69*, 49–54.

Khan, M. A., & Franks, I. M. (2004). The utilization of visual feedback in the acquisition of motor skills. In Williams, A. M., & Hodges, N. J. (Eds.), *Skill acquisition in sport: Research, theory and practice* (pp. 121–144). New York: Routledge.

Krebs, H. I., Volpe, B. T., Aisen, M. L., Hening, W., Adamovich, S., Poizner, H., Subrahmanyan, K., & Hogan, N. (2003). Robotic applications in neuromotor rehabilitation. *Robotica, 21*, 3–11.

Lee T. D., & Maraj, B. K. (1994). Effects of bandwidth goals and bandwidth knowledge of results on motor learning. *Research Quarterly for Exercise & Sport, 65,* 244–249.

Liu, Y.-T., Luo, Z.-Y., Mayer-Kress, G., & Newell, K. M. (2012). Self-organized criticality and learning a new coordination task. *Human Movement Science, 31,* 40–54.

Lum, P. S., Burgar, C. G., Shor, P. C., Majmundar, M., & Van der Loos, M. (2002). Robot-assisted movement training compared with conventional therapy techniques for the rehabilitation of upper-limb motor function after stroke. *Archives of Physical Medicine & Rehabilitation, 83,* 952–959.

Macrae, A. W., & Holding, D. H. (1966). Transfer of training after guidance or practice. *Quarterly Journal of Experimental Psychology, 18,* 327–333.

Marchal-Crespo, L., McHughen, S., Cramer, S. C., & Reinkensmeyer, D. J. (2010). The effect of haptic guidance, aging, and initial skill level on motor learning of a steering task. *Experimental Brain Research, 201,* 209–220.

Marchal-Crespo, L., & Reinkensmeyer, D. J. (2008). Haptic guidance can enhance motor learning of a steering task. *Journal of Motor Behavior, 40,* 545–557.

Marchal-Crespo, L., & Reinkensmeyer, D. J. (2009). Review of control strategies for robotic movement training after neurologic injury. *Journal of Neuroengineering and Rehabilitation, 16,* 20.

Maslovat, D., Hodges, N. J., Krigolson, O., & Handy, T. (2010). Observational practice benefits are limited to perceptual improvements in the acquisition of a novel coordination skill. *Experimental Brain Research, 204,* 119–130.

McAuley, E. (1985). Successes and causality in sport: The influence of perception. *Journal of Sport Psychology, 7,* 13–22.

Mechsner, F., Kerzel, D., Knoblich, G., & Prinz, W. (2001). Perceptual basis of bimanual coordination. *Letters to Nature, 414,* 69–73.

Melcher, R. T. (1934). Children's motor learning with and without vision. *Child Development, 5,* 315–350.

Milot, M. H., Marchal-Crespo, L., Green, C. S., Cramer, S. C., & Reinkensmeyer, D. J. (2010). Comparison of error-amplification and haptic-guidance training techniques for learning of a timing-based motor task by healthy individuals. *Experimental Brain Research, 201,* 119–131.

Morris, D., Tan, H., Barbagli, F., Chang, T., & Salisbury, K. (2007). Haptic feedback enhances force skill learning. In *Proceedings of EuroHaptics Conference and Symposium on Haptic Interfaces for Virtual Environment and Teleoperator Systems* (pp. 21–26).

Newell, K. M. (1986). Constraints on the development of coordination. In Wade, M. G., and Whiting, H. T. A. (Eds.), *Motor development in children: Aspects of coordination and control* (pp. 341–360). Boston: Martinus Nijhoff.

Poolton, J. M., Masters, R. S. W., & Maxwell, J. P. (2005). The relationship between initial errorless learning conditions and subsequent performance. *Human Movement Science, 24,* 362–378.

Proteau, L. (1992). On the specificity of learning and the role of visual information for movement control. In Proteau, L., & Elliott, D. (Eds.), *Vision and motor control* (pp. 67–103). Amsterdam: North-Holland.

Reinkensmeyer, D. J., & Patton, J. L. (2009). Can robots help the learning of skilled actions? *Exercise and Sport Science Reviews, 37,* 43–51.

Riener, R., Nef, T., & Colombo, G. (2005). Robot-aided neurorehabilitation of the upper extremities. *Medicine, Biological Engineering & Computing, 43,* 2–10.

Rosenbaum, D. A., Dawson, A. M., & Challis, J. H. (2006). Haptic tracking permits bimanual independence. *Journal of Experimental Psychology: Human Perception & Performance, 32,* 1266–1275.

Salmoni, A. W., Schmidt, R. A., & Walter, C. B. (1984). Knowledge of results and motor learning: A review and critical reappraisal. *Psychological Bulletin, 95*, 355–386.

Schmidt, R. A. (1975). A schema theory of discrete motor skill learning. *Psychological Review, 82*, 225–226.

Schmidt, R. A. (1976). The schema as a solution to some persistent problems in motor learning theory. In Stelmach, G. E. (Ed.), *Motor control: Issues and trends* (pp. 41–65). New York: Academic.

Schmidt, R. A. (1991). Frequent augmented feedback and degrade learning: Evidence and interpretations. In Stelmach, G. E., & Requin, J. (Eds.), *Tutorials in motor neuroscience* (pp. 59–75). Dordrecht, Netherlands: Kluwer Academic Publishers.

Schmidt, R. A., & White, J. L. (1972). Evidence for an error detection mechanism in motor skills: A test of Adams' closed-loop theory. *Journal of Motor Behavior, 4*, 143–153.

Schöllhorn, W., Michelbrink, M., Beckmann, H., Sechelmann, M., Trockel, M., & Davids, K. (2006). Does noise provide a basis for the unification of motor learning theories? *International Journal of Sport Psychology, 37*, 186–206.

Shapiro, D. C., & Schmidt, R. C. (1982). The schema theory: Recent evidence and developmental implications. In Kelso, J. A. S., & Clark, J. E. (Eds.), *The development of movement control and coordination* (pp. 113–150). New York: John Wiley.

Sidaway, B., Ahn, S., Boldeau, P., Griffin, S., Noyes, B., Pelletier, K. (2008). A comparison of manual guidance and knowledge of results in the learning of a weight-bearing skill. *Journal of Neurolology and Physical Therapy, 32*, 32–38.

Singer, R. N. (1977). To err or not to err: A question for the instruction of psychomotor skills. *Review of Educational Research, 47*, 479–498.

Tsutsui, S., & Imanaka, K. (2003). Effect of manual guidance on acquiring a new bimanual coordination pattern. *Research Quarterly for Exercise & Sport, 74*, 104–109.

van Asseldonk, E. H. F., Wessels, M., Stienen, A. H. A., van der Helm, F. C. T., & van der Kooij, H. (2009). Influence of haptic guidance in learning a novel visuomotor task. *Journal of Physiology, 103*, 276–285.

Waters, R. H. (1930). The influence of large amounts of manual guidance upon human maze learning. *Journal of Genetic Psychology, 4*, 213–228.

Winstein, C. J., Pohl, P. S., & Lewthwaite, R. (1994). Effects of physical guidance and knowledge of results on motor learning: Support for the guidance hypothesis. *Research Quarterly for Exercise and Sport, 65*(4), 316–323.

Wolpert, D. M., & Ghahramani, Z. (2000). Computational principles of movement neuroscience. *Nature Neuroscience, 3*, 1212–1217.

Wulf, G., Shea, C. H., & Whitacre, C. A. (1998). Physical-guidance benefits in learning a complex motor skill. *Journal of Motor Behavior, 30*, 367–380.

Wulf, G., & Toole, T. (1999). Physical assistance devices in complex motor skill learning, benefits of a self controlled practice schedule. *Research Quarterly for Exercise & Sport, 70*, 265–272.

Yang, X-D., Bischof, W. F., & Boulanger, P. (2008). Validating the performance of haptic motor skill training. *Proceedings of HAPTICS, 978*. 29–135.

Part III
Issues in motor learning

10 Motor learning through a motivational lens

Rebecca Lewthwaite and Gabriele Wulf

Introduction

Practice is generally considered one of the most critical contributors to motor learning in most domains of human activity, including sports (Schmidt & Lee, 2005). However, in addition to the sheer number of practice trials, other factors (e.g., instructions, feedback, movement demonstrations, imagery, action observation) have been shown to influence the extent and rate of learning. In the research literature, these factors are often considered on the basis of the information they convey to the learner. Yet human learners are more than neutral processors of information, and there is accumulating evidence to suggest that learning is optimized by practice conditions that account for motivational factors.

Motivation, *movement*, and *motor* share the same Latin root (*movere*, to move). On some level, to move implies that one is motivated, and to be motivated implies that one moves toward (or away from) something. Scientifically, the term *motivation* is used in different ways: (1) as a description of the drive toward some goal, usually in terms of level of intensity and direction of movement; (2) as a field of study or an umbrella concept encompassing not only that drive, but its causes and consequences. The former use is more in keeping with a behaviorist tradition in which behavior is assumed to be reinforced by the outcome of that behavior or the extent to which reward or punishment occurs with the behavior. The latter, more cognitive, conceptualization is most prominent in social and sport psychology and accounts for the study of social-cognitive constructs such as goal orientations, self-efficacy, attitudes, intentions, and emotional and affective states as they relate to motor performance and motor behavior. With some exceptions, researchers examining personality dispositions, social-cognitive variables (cognitions such as self-efficacy affected by social influences present or perceived), or social processes have assumed until recently that these motivational factors exert their influence on motor learning through longer-term pathways that engage interest and encourage continued practice.

A second body of work developing in motivation and motor learning is grounded in neuroscience. This more recent work stems from animal and human studies in motor neurophysiology (D. Brooks, 2001; V. Brooks, 1986), human neuroclinical populations (such as Parkinson's disease; Rowe et al., 2008; Schmidt et al., 2008), and recently neurocomputational modeling of systems and processes involved in reward and memory (Abe et al., 2011). Relative to the role of motivation in motor learning, these studies suggest linkages between motivation – often in the forms of food or monetary rewards – affective experience (Siessmeier et al., 2006), dopamine release in the corticostriatal system, and modulation or reinforcement of motor learning. Furthermore, the relatively recent discovery of the mirror neuron system that ties motor and premotor neural networks to language, movement, and social behavior has implications for the association of action observation and action execution, a relationship with relevance to motor learning and motivation (Lewthwaite & Wulf, 2010a). We expect that soon there will be a stronger connection with the emerging field of social-cognitive-affective neuroscience as it pertains to movement phenomena. We limit our discussion of the motivation–motor learning neuroscience evidence here and turn to the focus of this chapter on behavioral research that supports a stronger role for motivation than most perspectives on motor learning have recognized.

An integration of these varying scientific traditions with relevance to motor learning has not yet been sufficiently attempted, let alone accomplished. In this chapter, we focus on the behavioral literature relating social-cognitive factors to motor learning. We utilize a meta-theoretical framework on fundamental psychological needs (e.g., Deci & Ryan, 2000, 2008; Ryan & Deci, 2007) as a means to organize our discussion of motivation in the context of motor learning research. We chose this motivational framework for consideration of motor learning research because of the range of factors considered, which may fit well, if loosely, with available literature describing motivational influences. In contrast to the neurophysiologic and neurocomputational research that emanates from animal research origins and generally utilizes extrinsic forms of motivation such as external rewards, the motivation of interest in the psychological needs and self-determination framework centers on intrinsic sources of motivation. Intrinsic motivation refers to an "inherent tendency to seek out novelty and challenges, to extend and exercise one's capacities, to explore, and to learn" (Ryan & Deci, 2000, p. 70). In choosing the psychological needs framework, we do not imply that the enhancement of learning is fueled by intrinsic forms of motivation alone, as the discussion of the neuroscientific literature above would refute. However, although extrinsically induced motivational neuromodulation can affect motor learning in the short term, the literature described below would suggest that social-cognitive influences of a more intrinsic nature can serve this function as well. Persistence in movement behavior – a requirement for expertise and skill development over the longer term – appears to be importantly dependent upon intrinsic forms of motivation (e.g., Pelletier, Fortier, Vallerand, & Briere, 2001).

The fundamental psychological needs framework, and particularly the related Self-Determination Theory (Ryan & Deci, 2000), have been deployed broadly to examine determinants of health and behavioral outcomes, including sport, physical activity, and exercise adherence (e.g., Adie, Duda, & Ntoumanis, 2008; Duncan, Hall, Wilson, & O, 2010; Williams, Niemiec, Patrick, Ryan, & Deci, 2009). Providing evidence that such needs are truly innate or fundamental is beyond the scope of this chapter, and indeed taxes claims for most biological and psychological notions of essential elements, though scholars periodically attempt the task (e.g., Corning, 2000; White, 1959). However, Deci and Ryan's conceptualization of psychological needs provides a useful framework for contemplating categories of motivational variables in social-psychological research. This framework may help readers recognize motivational influences on motor learning. Furthermore, a motivational framework may partially account for a variety of conditions of practice that characterize research in motor learning.

Psychological well-being and optimal functioning and learning in a broad range of domains appear to depend on support for, or satisfaction of, basic needs: competence, autonomy, and social relatedness (e.g., Deci & Ryan, 2000, 2008). These needs have ramifications for the survival and development of living beings. It would be hard to imagine that the pursuit of increasing competence, sufficient autonomy in one's actions, and connectedness to others, who ensure from birth that we can survive and thrive, would not be of fundamental benefit to humans and animals alike. The need for competence refers to the need to experience oneself as capable and competent, whereas autonomy is related to the need to control or actively participate in determining one's own actions and behavior. Social relatedness describes the need to feel connected with others or to experience satisfaction in one's involvement with the social world. For example, greater levels of reported need satisfaction have been found to predict intrinsic motivation in physical education settings (Standage, Duda, & Ntoumanis, 2005), and positive affect in vocational dancers (Quested & Duda, 2010). We contend that psychological needs must be met in order to optimize the learning of sport skills. In this chapter, we review factors that have been demonstrated to enhance motor learning – presumably by addressing or supporting one or more of the basic psychological needs.

Competence

If the behavior of living beings is fueled in part by the need to maintain and enhance competence (e.g., Deci & Ryan, 2000; White, 1959), sport provides many opportunities to build skills as well as the associated perceptions or beliefs that one can overcome challenge, become skilled, or improve skills. Practically speaking, it is hard to separate performance capacity itself from the perceptions that one is capable, as they generally develop in concert. Theoretically (e.g., Bandura, 1977) and experimentally, though, the perception of competence (and related sense of confidence) is separable from the possession of competence and the former may be of greater consequence in motor learning.

Sport is a field in which performance and learning typically take place in public arenas. Skill learning often occurs in groups, and performances frequently happen in the certain or potential presence of other performers, competitors, and audiences. Such venues provide plenty of opportunity for formal and informal feedback, including social comparison: providing individuals with almost instant and often implicit feedback regarding their competence level relative to others. In addition, feedback about their performance or improvement is provided through many sources, including coaches, parents, or fellow athletes. Moreover, sport is a domain in which good or poor performance is often attributed to an inherent ability, talent, or lack thereof. All of these factors not only provide individuals with a certain sense of competence (or lack of competence), but may also influence the interpretation of their competence (e.g., as being a function of practice, effort, and learning, or inherited abilities).

As we will argue in this section, loss of confidence, concerns about capabilities, and feelings of embarrassment are not conducive to the activities and practice that promote learning. By creating conditions that enhance the learner's feelings of competence, instructors or coaches can speed the learning process and enhance performance. Such conditions involve positive feedback about the learner's performance and information affecting learners' conceptions of ability. Furthermore, conditions that reliably affect skill acquisition itself, such as external attentional focus instructions (e.g., Wulf, 2007a) or modeling (e.g., Clark & Ste-Marie, 2007; Maslovat, Hayes, Horn, & Hodges, 2010), would be expected to contribute indirectly to perceptions of competence.

Positive feedback

In the motor learning literature, most researchers over the past 40 years have been concerned with the informational function of feedback, that is, its role in providing information about an individual's performance in relation to the task goal (for reviews, see Swinnen, 1996; Wulf & Shea, 2004). Similarly, practitioners often see performance feedback from this perspective. A track and field coach, for instance, might identify deviations in throwers' or runners' movement patterns from the optimal technique and instruct them about how to change their movement patterns (i.e., a kind of prescriptive form of feedback). Although prescriptive feedback can play an important role in any learning process, a somewhat underappreciated aspect of feedback by learning researchers has been its influence on the performer's motivational state. In fact, a recent study by Mouratidis, Lens, and Vansteenkiste (2010) demonstrated that the way in which potentially threatening corrective feedback (i.e., information about how to improve performance) is provided by a coach has an important influence on motivation. The perception of such feedback as autonomy-supportive was positively related to the athletes' intrinsic motivation, which, in turn, was positively related to their intentions to persist as well as their well-being (see also the "Autonomy" section below). Recent studies in the motor learning domain provide converging evidence that positive (or negative) feedback affects not only an individual's motivation but also, and arguably not coincidentally, his or her skill learning.

In a series of studies, it was found that providing learners with feedback after "good" trials, compared with "poor" trials, resulted in more effective learning (e.g., Chiviacowsky & Wulf, 2007; Chiviacowsky, Wulf, Wally, & Borges, 2009). In those studies, feedback about task performance (i.e., accuracy of throwing an object at a target) was provided after each block of six practice trials. However, it was provided on only half of those trials. Unbeknownst to the learners, one group of participants was given feedback about their three best trials in that block, whereas another group was provided with feedback on their three worst trials. Participants receiving feedback after their best trials demonstrated more effective learning. This effect was seen not only in young adults (Chiviacowsky & Wulf, 2007) (see Figure 10.1), but also in older (65 years, on average) unimpaired adults (Chiviacowsky et al., 2009). Thus, feedback emphasizing successful performance, while ignoring less successful attempts, benefited learning. A subsequent study linked this effect to participants' enhanced intrinsic motivation when they received feedback after good trials (Badami, VaezMousavi, Wulf, & Namazizadeh, 2011). These researchers found that intrinsic motivation, in general, and perceived competence, in particular, increased with feedback after good trials. Given that learners often have a relatively good feel for how they perform (Chiviacowsky & Wulf, 2002), instructor feedback indicating errors not only may be superfluous, but can also irritate some people or heighten concerns about the self that may hamper learning (Wulf & Lewthwaite, 2010). Deliberately choosing to frame feedback around available positive aspects of performance, or to precede critique with acknowledgment of positive assets, might be expected to enhance the learning of motor skills. Evaluation of these "emphasize the positive" approaches for motor skill learning would be an important area for future systematic investigations.

Self-related concerns or worries may be induced by feedback about learners' capabilities relative to others, or their improvements relative to themselves or others. In experimental studies, the effects of normative feedback – which involves norms such as a peer group's actual or false average performance or improvement scores – have been examined. Information about relative performance may be provided in addition to a participant's personal performance score (Bandura & Jourden, 1991; Johnson, Turban, Pieper, & Ng, 1996). Providing individuals with normative information, such as the "average" scores of learners on a given motor task, can therefore be a potent basis for evaluation of personal performance. Favorable

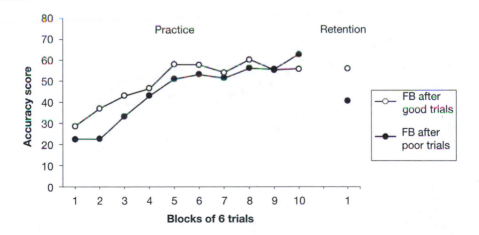

Figure 10.1 Accuracy scores of the groups receiving feedback (FB) after good versus poor trials in the study by Chiviacowsky and Wulf (2007).

comparisons with others result in perceptions of competence, increased self-efficacy (situation-specific self-confidence), and motivation to exert effort or practice a skill (Kavussanu & Roberts, 1996), whereas negative comparisons have the opposite effect (Hutchinson, Sherman, Martinovic, & Tenenbaum, 2008; Johnson et al., 1996).

Recently, researchers have demonstrated experimentally that motor learning can be enhanced by (false) positive normative feedback (Wulf, Chiviacowsky, & Lewthwaite, 2010; Lewthwaite & Wulf, 2010b). In one study, two groups of participants practicing a balance task were given normative feedback, in addition to veridical feedback about their performance, after each trial (Lewthwaite & Wulf, 2010b). Participants in the "Better" group were led to believe that their performance was better than average, whereas the opposite was the case for "Worse" group participants. The Better group demonstrated more effective learning than both the Worse and Control groups, whereas there were no differences between the last two conditions (see Figure 10.2). Positive normative feedback not only led to better outcome scores, but produced qualitative differences in participants' control of movements as well: individuals who received feedback indicating that they performed above average exhibited greater automaticity in movement control. Thus, the mere conviction of being "good" at a particular task, or showing "better" improvement (Wulf et al., 2010), facilitated the learning process. Interestingly, no comparison information (control condition) resulted in similar performance and learning to negative normative feedback – perhaps for different reasons or because both conditions trigger thoughts about the self and ensuing self-regulatory activities that hamper learning of the primary task (Wulf & Lewthwaite, 2010). Some might

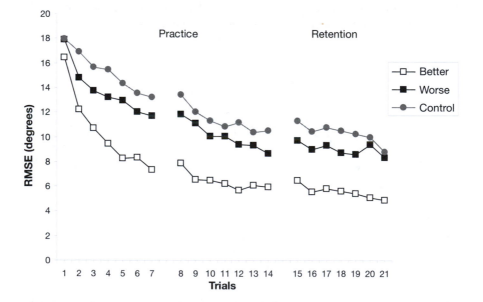

Figure 10.2 Deviations of the balance platform from the horizontal in Better, Worse, and Control groups in the study by Lewthwaite and Wulf (2010b).

wonder if the literature on the effects of normative comparisons and the use of false feedback argues for these kinds of manipulations in practical settings. On ethical grounds, of course, it does not. Furthermore, we would suggest that it is the environmental availability of information implying that one is an effective performer, or the provision of positive, competence-affirming, feedback in conditions of learning, that is critical. This provision is something many practitioners intuitively do, but others may be more focused on correcting errors per se, with unintended impacts on the motivational and thus learning consequences.

It appears that people who are at the initial stages of learning of a new motor task, and express low confidence in their ability to acquire a task, quickly benefit from positive feedback (Wulf & Bragg, 2010). Whereas low confidence was indeed associated with dampened improvement across practice and learning of a balance (stabilometer) task, feedback (falsely) suggesting that performance was above average resulted in performance that was no different from that of participants with initially high confidence in their ability to learn the task quickly. Positive feedback appears to increase the performer's sense of competence – even in those with low confidence or self-efficacy – reducing self-related concerns and facilitating enhanced task-related attention and learning.

Conceptions of ability

Talented and *gifted* are attributes that are often ascribed to athletes. Irrespective of the extent to which motor performance is based on inherent factors rather than practice and effort, researchers have shown that people's conceptions of or beliefs regarding the nature of key abilities affect their motivation and performance. Specifically, people's view of their abilities – or competencies – as something that reflects a fixed capacity versus something that is amenable to change with practice influences their level of achievement in given activities (e.g., Dweck & Leggett, 1988; Mangels, Butterfield, Lamb, Good, & Dweck, 2006). In general, people tend to differ in their beliefs about whether abilities are generally stable and fixed, or learnable and malleable (e.g., Dweck, 1999; Dweck & Leggett, 1988). People in the former group tend to be concerned with proving their ability by outperforming others. Negative feedback is perceived by them as a threat to the self because it reveals an available level of ability that is less than optimal. As a consequence, they show less effort and persistence in difficult situations that may reveal the limits of their ability. Entity theorists, that is people who believe that abilities are fixed, may avoid situations in which they do not perform well. In contrast, people who subscribe to incremental theories (i.e., that abilities are changeable or malleable) are more focused on learning and improving their performance on a given task. They tend to be more intrinsically motivated and to seek challenging situations. When confronted with difficulties, they try to overcome those by increasing their effort. Well-known examples of individuals whose hard work made them world-class athletes – despite initial setbacks – include Michael Jordan (who was cut from his high school basketball team), Jackie Joyner Kersee (who did not win any races for a long time in her early career), and Wilma Rudolph (who had a partially paralyzed leg due to polio). As Rudolph once said, "Some might attribute my transformation to the laws of heredity . . . But I think it was my reward for all those hours of work on the bridle path, the neighborhood sidewalks and the schoolhouse corridors" (see Dweck, 2006, p. 88).

Research related to conceptions of ability has important implications for learning and performance in sports. Even though most people already have certain ability conceptions, these can be influenced by the instructions or information conveyed to them by coaches or parents. Some researchers have manipulated ability conceptions to assess their influence on individuals' motivation and performance of motor skills (e.g., Belcher, Lee, Solmon, & Harrison, 2003; Jourden, Bandura, & Banfield, 1991; Li, Lee, & Solmon, 2005, 2008). For example, Jourden et al. (1991) used a pursuit rotor task, requiring participants to track a moving cursor with a stylus. They told participants in an inherent aptitude condition that the apparatus measured their natural capacity for processing dynamic information. In the acquirable-skill condition, participants were informed that the task represented a learnable skill. Those in the latter group showed greater self-efficacy and more positive affective self-reactions, and expressed greater interest in the task. Moreover, individuals in the acquirable-skill group demonstrated a greater improvement across trials than did those in the inherent aptitude group.

In a more recent study, Wulf and Lewthwaite (2009) examined more permanent (i.e., learning) effects of instructionally induced conceptions of ability. Participants in their study practiced a balance task, and ability conceptions were induced through instructions depicting performance on the task as something that reflected either an inherent ability for balance or an acquirable skill. Participants in the acquirable-skill group showed a greater improvement in balance performance across retention trials, as well as demonstrating greater automaticity in the control of their movements (i.e., frequency of movement adjustments) than did those in the inherent-ability group. Thus, instructions portraying the task as an acquirable skill resulted in more effective learning than did instructions intimating that performance reflected an inherent capacity. Similarly to other variables discussed in this section (e.g., positive performance feedback), people's conception of their abilities or competencies appear to affect the extent to which they become self-conscious – with concomitant effects on motor performance and learning. Individuals who view a task as a reflection of an inherent ability presumably approach practice situations with more apprehension than those who see task performance as an acquirable skill with opportunities to improve. Fixed-attribute beliefs, in turn, may hinder the learning process, compared with beliefs that skill is malleable and in which errors or incapacity are seen as temporary and part of the learning. In summary, feelings of competence – one of the basic psychological needs (Deci & Ryan, 2008; White, 1959) – can be enhanced or compromised in many situations that occur in a sports context. Preserving or restoring a sense of competence is important, not only to enhance motivation and general well-being, but to facilitate continued skill learning. This aim can be achieved in various ways. For example, one should keep in mind that, pragmatically, motivational and informational aspects of feedback are often intertwined. Feedback will almost certainly convey significance for learners' motivational states as well as carrying other information relevant to task performance. It is common for instructors to bring their expertise to bear with a focus on optimizing the movement technique, which can be interpreted by some to be a form of (unintended) negative feedback, rather than to acknowledge explicitly a performer's movement or personal assets for success. It may be tempting to provide immediate feedback when an error occurs. However, error information not only may be superfluous, as learners may already have a good feel for how well they performed (e.g., Chiviacowsky & Wulf, 2002), but has the potential to be perceived as negative, demoralizing in impact, and perhaps indicative of less than desirable levels of personal autonomy. Feedback indicating that performance is below expectations – especially when presented repeatedly – may have immediately as well as ultimately negative effects on learning. Furthermore, people's conceptions of ability can influence the learning of motor skills. Individuals who view a task as an acquirable skill presumably approach the learning situation with less apprehension than those who see task performance as a reflection of a fixed (lack of) ability. Experimental instructions are able to override dispositional conceptions of ability that participants may hold. Certainly, practitioners should eschew insinuations of fixed abilities. It would seem advantageous to ensure explicitly that problematic assumptions that change is not likely, or difficult to achieve, be explored, discussed, and challenged as part of the training and learning process. Furthermore, instructions or feedback should focus on a performer's improvements or effort invested in practice. Even simple differences in wording can have an important influence on individuals' motivation and continued interest in a movement task (Cimpian, Arce, Markman, & Dweck, 2007).

Autonomy

Autonomy refers to people's basic need to determine and have control of their own behavior. In the past few years, a number of researchers have shown that motor skill learning can be enhanced by giving the learner some control over practice conditions (for a review, see Wulf, 2007b) – that is by satisfying their need for autonomy. This contrasts with many practical settings, including sports practice, in which some instructors and coaches may prescribe the task they want an athlete to perform, the order of different tasks, and the number of sets and repetitions for each. Some practitioners may provide feedback to the learner about correct or incorrect parts of the movement, and may give demonstrations of the goal movement pattern. Thus, while instructors control almost all aspects of the training sessions, the performer assumes a relatively passive role. There is ample evidence to suggest that granting the learner some autonomy in the training process can significantly enhance learning. In this section, we review studies that have examined learner control or self-control with respect to the delivery of feedback, augmented information, the use of physical assistance devices, and demonstrations of the goal movement.

Feedback

Studies examining effects of self-control usually involve a yoking procedure, in which each participant in a self-control group is paired with another participant in a yoked group. A participant in the yoked group would receive feedback, for example, on the same trials on which his or her counterpart in the self-control group had requested feedback. The purpose of such a yoking procedure is to control for the amount and timing of feedback (or whatever factor is controlled by the learner). Because the average frequency and time of feedback delivery are identical in the self-control and yoked groups, any group differences that emerge on retention or transfer tests can be attributed to the fact that one group had control over a certain variable, whereas the other group did not.

Learning advantages for self-controlled feedback schedules have been found with various movement tasks. For example, some studies have used throwing tasks, in which feedback was provided about movement form (e.g., Janelle, Barba, Frehlich, Tennant, & Cauraugh, 1997) or the accuracy of the throws (Chiviacowsky, Wulf, Laroque de Medeiros, Kaefer, & Tani, 2008). Furthermore, self-controlled concurrent feedback has been shown to enhance the learning of perceptual invariants (i.e., adjusting walking speed when walking through virtual opening and closing doors) (Huet, Camachon, Fernandez, Jacobs, & Montagne, 2009) and learning to land a virtual aircraft (Huet, Jacobs, Camachon, Goulon, & Montagne, 2009). Other researchers have found learning advantages of self-controlled feedback for timing tasks (Chen, Hendrick, & Lidor, 2002; Chiviacowsky & Wulf, 2002; Patterson & Carter, 2010). Chiviacowsky and Wulf (2002) asked participants to press certain keys on a numeric keypad with prescribed time intervals between key presses. On a transfer test with novel goal movement times, the self-controlled feedback group outperformed the yoked group, demonstrating that self-controlled feedback can enhance *transfer* to novel variations of the skill (see Figure 10.3). In addition, the learning advantages of self-controlled feedback have been shown to generalize to situations in which multiple tasks with different timing goals have to be learned (Patterson & Carter, 2010).

An interesting aspect of some studies (e.g., Chiviacowsky & Wulf, 2002; Patterson & Carter, 2010) was questionnaire results which indicated that self-control learners requested feedback mainly after they thought they had had a "good" trial (and that yoked learners would have preferred to receive feedback after good trials). This finding suggests that one reason for the effectiveness of self-controlled feedback may be that it has the potential to enhance learners' feeling of competence (see above).

The percentage of practice trials on which self-control learners requested feedback varied widely between studies, ranging from 11% (Janelle et al., 1997) to 97% (Chen et al., 2002; Chiviacowsky & Wulf, 2002: 35%; Chiviacowsky et al., 2008: 28%). The frequency of feedback requests might depend on the nature of the task, the type of feedback provided or otherwise available to the learner, or on the exact instructions given to participants (i.e., to what extent they encourage the learner to ask for feedback). Yet, it appears that the feedback frequency is less important than the learner's opportunity to choose or not to choose feedback. Otherwise, it would be difficult to see why learning advantages for self-controlled feedback occurred when the feedback frequency was almost 100% (Chen et al., 2002). This finding suggests that learners' need for autonomy plays an important role in this context.

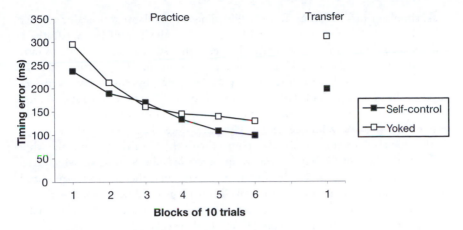

Figure 10.3 Timing errors of the self-control and yoked groups during practice and transfer in the study by Chiviacowsky and Wulf (2002).

Augmented task information

Sometimes information, or reminders, about the movement pattern to be executed are provided to the learner. This process would occur primarily in situations in which remembering the correct sequence of movement elements is challenging, for example, when learning dance routines, the manual gestures of sign language, or a typographical script. Patterson and Lee (2010) used a Graffiti language-learning task that involved entering symbols into a personal digital assistant (PDA) when prompted by the English-script cue. A group, allowed to decide when they wanted to view the correct pairing of the English cue and respective symbol, as well as the viewing duration, before entering the symbol, outperformed both a yoked group and a group presented with the correct pairing before each practice trial on a recall test. That is, the "self-regulated" group recalled more symbols than the other two groups. This group also showed equivalent recall to groups (self-regulated, yoked, every-trial) that were presented the pairings *after* the respective practice trials, providing them with the opportunity to engage in memory retrieval practice. Thus, when the presentation of augmented task information prior to movement execution was controlled by the learner, it did not result in the typically seen detrimental effects due to strong guidance or dependency.

Assistive devices

Self-controlled practice advantages have also been seen when learners are given control over the use of physical assistive devices (Hartman, 2007; Wulf, Clauss, Shea, & Whitacre, 2001; Wulf & Toole, 1999). In one study, participants practiced a ski-simulator task (Wulf & Toole, 1999). The ski-simulator consists of a pair of bowed rails and a platform on wheels attached to the end of the apparatus by rubber belts. The platform, on which the performer stands, can be made to move sideways on the rails by making slalom-type movements. The participant's task was to produce the largest possible amplitudes. The physical assistance devices used in the Wulf and Toole (1999) study were ski poles. These generally facilitate the maintenance of balance and have been shown to enhance the learning of this task (Wulf, Shea, & Whitacre, 1998). The poles were placed on the floor in front of the ski-simulator and remained in contact with the floor throughout the whole trial. Participants in the self-control group were allowed to choose on which trials they wanted to use the poles during practice. Although there were no amplitude differences between this group and a yoked control group during practice, the self-control participants showed more effective learning, as measured by performance on a retention test without the poles, than did their yoked counterparts.

In another study, Hartman (2007) used another balance task (stabilometer) and allowed one group of participants to decide on which trial they wanted to use poles as assistive devices. He found that the self-controlled use of poles again significantly enhanced the learning of this task compared with a yoked condition. This finding is particularly interesting because, in a pilot study, Hartman did not find advantages of using the poles for the learning of this task. This finding suggests that control over an assistive device can have a beneficial effect on learning, even if that device in and of itself is relatively ineffective. To our knowledge, no person has yet examined _____ control over the use of a device or technique (e.g., an internal _____ known to be detrimental to performance to determine the rela- _____ two conditions.

Movement demonstrations

Learning through observation, or modeling, is a commonly used technique when it comes to teaching motor skills (for reviews, see Maslovat, Hayes, Horn, & Hodges, 2010; McCullagh & Weiss, 2001). This includes sport settings, in which an instructor might demonstrate the goal movement to the learner. In one study, Wulf, Raupach, and Pfeiffer (2005) examined whether model presentations provided at the learners' request would enhance learning, compared with providing them without consideration for their preferences. Participants practiced a complex motor skill (basketball jump shot) and a video of a skilled model either could be requested (self-control) or was provided at the same respective times (yoked) during the practice phase. After a 7-day retention interval, the self-control group had significantly higher form scores than the yoked group (shot accuracy did not differ between groups). Interestingly, the differential learning effects occurred despite a relatively low frequency of model presentations (5.8% of the practice trials).

The picture that emerges from self-control studies is that practice conditions that meet people's needs for autonomy by allowing them to exert some control over the practice situation benefit learning. It should be pointed out that the benefits of self-controlled practice are not always apparent immediately. In many experimental studies, performance differences between self-control and yoked groups did not occur until retention or transfer testing at a later time. Thus, it appears that self-control and yoked conditions have different effects on practice performance versus learning (retention/transfer). As self-controlled practice presumably involves continuous assessments of one's performance and decision-making processes regarding feedback or movement demonstrations, for example, it might make practice more "difficult," temporarily depressing performance. Instructors (and learners) should be aware of the fact that the beneficial effects of self-controlled practice may be latent and delayed, and any lack of immediate performance enhancement should not deter them from relinquishing some control over the practice conditions to the performers.

Social relatedness

A performer's basic psychological need to experience satisfaction in interactions with others (social relatedness; Deci & Ryan, 2008; Ryan & Deci, 2007) may to some extent be met through interactions with other learners, teammates, or coaches (e.g., Cox, Duncheon, & McDavid, 2009). A few researchers have shown that participants who practiced motor skills with another learner demonstrated advantages compared with those who practiced individually (e.g., Granados & Wulf, 2007; Shea, Wulf, & Whitacre, 1999). For example, in one study, a dynamic balance task was used to compare the effectiveness of dyad practice (i.e., practice in pairs) versus individual practice (Shea et al., 1999). Participants in the dyad group took turns during practice, such that one partner performed a trial while the other observed, and vice versa. In addition to the opportunity to observe the other person, participants were encouraged to give each other feedback or share certain movement strategies they might have found helpful during the rest intervals. Participants who practiced with a partner (dyad group) learned the task more effectively and were subsequently superior to participants in another group who practiced individually when tested (individually) one day later (see Figure 10.4).

Practice in dyads presumably has several advantages that contribute to its learning benefits. One of those factors is learning through observation. Research has shown that observational practice can make unique and important contributions to learning especially when observation is combined with physical practice (Shea, Wright, Wulf, & Whitacre, 2000; Shebilske, Regian, Arthur, & Jordan, 1992). Neuroimaging experiments suggest that a set of common neural structures are activated during both action production and action observation (Gallese & Goldman, 1998; Grezes & Decety, 2001; Jeannerod, 1994).

However, practicing together with another learner most likely has beneficial effects on learning that go beyond those related to observation per se. Learning benefits of dyad practice are presumably also a result of enhanced motivation, resulting perhaps from comparison with the partner, the setting of higher goals, or the loss of self-consciousness as people fulfill interdependent dyadic roles and find another in the same learning boat. It is perhaps not coincidental that participants in collaborative or cooperative learning situations often anecdotally report more enjoyment

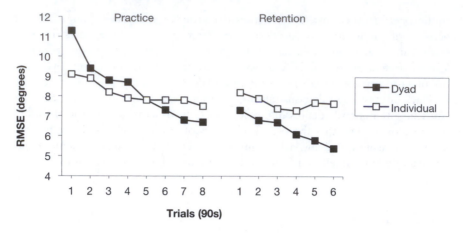

Figure 10.4 Deviations of the balance platform from the horizontal in dyad-practice and individual-practice groups in the study by Shea, Wulf, and Whitacre (1999).

than they have experienced learning alone (Mueller, Georges, & Vaslow, 2007). It is probably also not coincidental that findings regarding the mirror neuron system continue to link action observation, movement production, and social insight (Gallese & Goldman, 1998).

In summary, practice settings that take into account learners' need for social relatedness, for example by providing them with the opportunity to interact and practice with another learner, may be particularly effective, thanks to various direct and indirect effects on the patient's motivation. Such opportunities may also increase the accrual of practice trials beyond those accomplished with the teacher's assistance.

Conclusions and future directions

The findings reviewed here provide evidence of the importance of motivational influences on motor learning, potentially suggesting that factors heretofore presumed to play task-informational roles may operate at least partially through motivational channels. Fundamental psychological needs related to perceptions of competence, autonomy, and social relatedness may govern many of these motivational effects. Just which and how many conventional "conditions of practice" in the motor learning literature may owe some or all of their impacts to motivation is one of the most interesting and potentially important lines of inquiry in future research on motor learning. Instructions and feedback that convey positive messages regarding the learner and the value of effort and practice, or portray abilities and skills as acquirable, can help increase individuals' feelings of competence and optimize the conditions for motor learning. It is worth noting that both animal and human studies have found positive learning impacts with more positive reinforcement or augmented feedback (e.g., more food, money, perceptions of greater competence); negative circumstances have not reduced learning below control conditions. As criticism and negative feedback, and the concomitant efforts at self-regulation of thoughts and emotions, abound in real-life performance and instruction setting, it is important to continue to pursue the existence and nature of this possible positive advantage.

Recognizing individuals' need for autonomy and granting them some control over the practice conditions should further enhance their motivation and learning. Competence and autonomy (and social relatedness) needs and satisfying conditions operate concurrently, and supporting one could affect another, positively or negatively. That is, facilitating more athlete autonomy could be done in the context of supporting competence perceptions or deflating them. With awareness and practice, coaches and instructors can provide choices and opportunities for expressing opinions and preferences (i.e., autonomy support) that enhance competence or are within the bounds of athletes' and learners' present (perceptions of) competence level. Providing choices of practice activities or strategies well beyond or below current (perceived) competencies may support one need (autonomy) to the detriment of another (competence).

Finally, the need for social relatedness is presently under-studied but it is arguably richly relevant in any sport or movement endeavor. Appreciating the dimensions of this amorphous motivational category is important. Furthermore, critical tests of whether fostering (presumably competence-affirming) interactions with other performers results in beneficial learning effects or not are warranted.

One of the challenges for practitioners in movement skill settings is to balance support of multiple motivational and task-specific informational needs at once. The work described above argues for generally stronger recognition of motivational needs within an optimal learning equation. Whether motivational needs can be effectively supported depends in part on astute recognition that it is the meaning of conditions of practice or communications within the practice setting that determines how learners and athletes will experience them. Although there are common motivational effects (e.g., positive normative feedback, self-control) to be employed in the experimental study of motivational impacts on learning, many other effects of the social environment of motor skills will be more individual in nature and based on the implications of conditions for a given learner's needs for competence, autonomy, or social relatedness or other rewarding conditions. Broader use of questionnaire assessments of subjective cognitive and affective experience, as well as physiological and neuroimaging methods (e.g., Carlson, Greenberg, Rubin, & Mujica-Parodi, 2011) for understanding experienced thoughts and emotions will support motivational inquiries in motor learning.

References

Abe, M., Schambra, H., Wassermann, E. M., Luckenbaugh, D., Schweighofer, N., & Cohen, L. G. (2011). Reward improves long-term retention of a motor memory through induction of offline memory gains. *Current Biology.* doi: 10.1016/j.cub.2011.02.030.

Adie, J., Duda, J. L., & Ntoumanis, N. (2008). Autonomy support, basic need satisfaction and the optimal functioning of adult male and female sport participants: A test of basic needs theory. *Motivation and Emotion, 32,* 189–199.

Badami, R., VaezMousavi, M., Wulf, G., & Namazizadeh, M. (2011). Feedback after good trials enhances intrinsic motivation. *Research Quarterly for Exercise and Sport, 82,* 360–364.

Bandura, A. (1977). Self-efficacy: Toward a unifying theory of behavioral change. *Psychological Review, 84,* 191–215.

Bandura, A., & Jourden, F. J. (1991). Self-regulatory mechanisms governing the impact of social comparison on complex decision making. *Journal of Personality and Social Psychology, 60,* 941–951.

Belcher, D., Lee, A. M., Solmon, M. A., & Harrison, L., Jr. (2003). The influence of gender-related beliefs and conceptions of ability on women learning the hockey wrist shot. *Research Quarterly for Exercise and Sport, 74,* 183–192.

Brooks, D. J. (2001). Functional imaging studies on dopamine and motor control. *Journal of Neural Transmission, 108,* 1283–1298.

Brooks, V. B. (1986). How does the limbic system assist motor learning? A limbic comparator hypothesis. *Brain Behavior and Evolution, 29,* 29–53.

Carlson, J. M., Greenberg, T., Rubin, D., & Mujica-Parodi, L. R. (2011). Feeling anxious: Anticipatory amygdalo-insular response predicts the feeling of anxious anticipation. *Social Cognitive Affective Neuroscience, 6,* 74–81.

Chen, D. D., Hendrick, J. L., & Lidor, R. (2002). Enhancing self-controlled learning environments: The use of self-regulated feedback information. *Journal of Human Movement Studies, 43,* 69–86.

Chiviacowsky, S., & Wulf, G. (2002). Self-controlled feedback: Does it enhance learning because performers get feedback when they need it? *Research Quarterly for Exercise and Sport, 73,* 408–415.

Chiviacowsky, S., & Wulf, G. (2007). Feedback after good trials enhances learning. *Research Quarterly for Exercise and Sport, 78,* 40–47.

Chiviacowsky, S., Wulf, G., Laroque de Medeiros, F., Kaefer, A., & Tani, G. (2008). Learning benefits of self-controlled knowledge of results in 10-year old children. *Research Quarterly for Exercise and Sport, 79,* 405–410.

Chiviacowsky, S., Wulf, G., Wally, R., & Borges, T. (2009). KR after good trials enhances learning in older adults. *Research Quarterly for Exercise and Sport, 80,* 663–668.

Cimpian, A., Arce, H.-M., Markman, E. M., & Dweck, C. S. (2007). Subtle linguistic cues affect children's motivation. *Psychological Science, 18,* 314–316.

Clark, S. E., & D. M. Ste-Marie (2007). The impact of self-as-a-model interventions on children's self-regulation of learning and swimming performance. *Journal of Sports Sciences, 25,* 577–586.

Corning, P. A. (2000). Biological adaptation in human societies: A "basic needs" approach. *Bioeconomics, 2,* 41–86.

Cox, A., Duncheon, N., & McDavid, L. (2009). Peers and teachers as sources of relatedness perceptions, motivation, and affective responses in physical education. *Research Quarterly for Exercise and Sport, 80,* 765–773.

Deci, E. L., & Ryan, R. M. (2000). The "what" and "why" of goal pursuits: Human needs and the self-determination of behavior. *Psychological Inquiry, 11,* 227–268.

Deci, E. L., & Ryan, R. M. (2008). Self-determination theory: A macrotheory of human motivation, development, and health. *Canadian Psychology, 49,* 182–185.

Duncan, L. R., Hall, C. R., Wilson, P. M., & O, J. (2010). Exercise motivation: A cross-sectional analysis examining its relationships with frequency, intensity, and duration of exercise. *International Journal of Behavioral Nutrition and Physical Activity.* doi: 10.1186/1479-5868-7-7

Dweck, C. S. (1999). *Self-theories: Their role in motivation, personality, and development.* Philadelphia, PA: Psychology Press.

Dweck, C. S. (2006). *Mindset: The new psychology of success.* New York: Random House.

Dweck, C. S., & Leggett, E. L. (1988). A social-cognitive approach to motivation and personality. *Psychological Review, 95,* 256–273.

Gallese V, & Goldman, A. (1998). Mirror neurons and the simulation theory of mind-reading. *Trends in Cognitive Sciences, 2,* 493–501.

Granados, C., & Wulf, G. (2007). Enhancing motor learning through dyad practice: Contributions of observation and dialogue. *Research Quarterly for Exercise and Sport, 78,* 197–203.

Grezes, J., & Decety, J. (2001). Functional anatomy of execution, mental simulation, observation, and verb generation of actions: A meta-analysis. *Human Brain Mapping, 12,* 1–19.

Hartman, J. M. (2007). Self-controlled use of a perceived physical assistance device during a balancing task. *Perceptual and Motor Skills, 104,* 1005–1016.

Huet, M., Camachon, C., Fernandez, L., Jacobs, D. M., & Montagne, G. (2009). Self-controlled concurrent feedback and the education of attention towards perceptual invariants. *Human Movement Science, 28,* 450–467.

Huet, M., Jacobs, D. M., Camachon, C., Goulon, C., & Montagne, G. (2009). Self-controlled concurrent feedback facilitates the learning of the final approach phase in a fixed-base flight simulator. *Human Factors, 51,* 858–871.

Hutchinson, J. C., Sherman, T., Martinovic, N., & Tenenbaum, G. (2008). The effect of manipulated self-efficacy on perceived and sustained effort. *Journal of Applied Sport Psychology, 20,* 457–472.

Janelle, C. M., Barba, D. A., Frehlich, S. G., Tennant, L. K., & Cauraugh, J. H. (1997). Maximizing performance effectiveness through videotape replay and a self-controlled learning environment. *Research Quarterly for Exercise and Sport, 68,* 269–279.

Jeannerod, M. (1994). The representing brain: Neural correlates of motor intention and imagery. *Behavioral and Brain Sciences, 17,* 326–338.

Johnson, D. S., Turban, D. B., Pieper, K. F., & Ng, Y. M. (1996). Exploring the role of normative- and performance-based feedback in motivational processes. *Journal of Applied Social Psychology, 26,* 973–992.

Jourden, F. J., Bandura, A., & Banfield, J. T. (1991). The impact of conceptions of ability on self-regulatory factors and motor skill acquisition. *Journal of Sport & Exercise Psychology, 8,* 213–226.

Kavussanu, M., & Roberts, G. C. (1996). Motivation in physical activity contexts: The relationship of perceived motivational climate to intrinsic motivation and self-efficacy. *Journal of Sport & Exercise Psychology, 18,* 264–280.

Lewthwaite, R., & Wulf, G. (2010a). Grand challenge for movement science and sport psychology: Embracing the social-cognitive-affective-motor nature of motor behavior. *Frontiers in Psychology.* doi: 10.3389/fpsyg.2010.00042.

Lewthwaite, R., & Wulf, G. (2010b). Social-comparative feedback affects motor skill learning. *Quarterly Journal of Experimental Psychology, 63,* 738–749.

Li, W., Lee, A. M., & Solmon, M. A. (2005). Examining the relationship among dispositional ability conceptions, intrinsic motivation, perceived competence, experience, and performance. *Journal of Teaching in Physical Education, 24,* 51–65.

Li, W., Lee, A. M., & Solmon, M. A. (2008). Effects of dispositional ability conception, manipulated learning environments, and intrinsic motivation on persistence and performance: An interaction approach. *Research Quarterly for Exercise and Sport, 79,* 51–61.

Mangels, J. A., Butterfield, B., Lamb, J., Good, C., & Dweck, C. S. (2006). Why do beliefs about intelligence influence learning success? A social cognitive neuroscience model. *Social Cognitive and Affective Neuroscience, 1,* 75–86.

Maslovat, D., Hayes, S. J., Horn, R., & Hodges, N. J. (2010). Motor learning through observation. In Elliott, D., & Horn, M. A. (Eds.), *Vision and goal-directed movement: Neurobehavioral perspectives* (p. 315–340). Champaign, IL: Human Kinetics.

McCullagh, P., & Weiss, M. (2001). Modeling: Considerations for motor skill performance and psychological responses. In Singer, R. N., Hausenblas, H. A., & Janelle, C. M. (Eds.), *Handbook of sport psychology* (pp. 205–238). New York: Wiley.

Mouratidis, A., Lens, W., & Vansteenkiste, M. (2010). How you provide corrective feedback makes a difference: The motivating role of communicating in an autonomy-supporting way. *Journal of Sport & Exercise Psychology, 32*, 619–637.

Mueller, D., Georges, A., & Vaslow, D. (2007). Cooperative learning as applied to resident instruction in radiology reporting. *Academic Radiology, 14*, 1577–1583.

Patterson, J. T., & Carter, M. (2010). Learner regulated knowledge of results during the acquisition of multiple timing goals. *Human Movement Science, 29*, 214–227.

Patterson, J. T., & Lee, T. D. (2010). Self-regulated frequency of augmented information in skill learning. *Canadian Journal of Experimental Psychology, 63*, 33–40.

Pelletier, L. G., Fortier, M. S., Vallerand, R. J., & Briere, N. M. (2001). Associations among perceived autonomy support, forms of self-regulation, and persistence: A prospective study. *Motivation and Emotion, 25*, 279–306.

Quested, E., & Duda, J. L. (2010). Exploring the social-environmental determinants of well- and ill-being in dancers: A test of basic needs theory. *Journal of Sport & Exercise Psychology, 32*, 39–60.

Rowe, J. B., Hughes, L., Ghosh, B. C., Eckstein, D., Williams-Gray, C. H., Fallon, S., Barker, R. A., & Owen, A. M. (2008). Parkinson's disease and dopaminergic therapy: Differential effects on movement, reward and cognition. *Brain, 131*, 2094–2105.

Ryan, R. M., & Deci, E. L. (2000). Self-determination theory and the facilitation of intrinsic motivation, social development, and well-being. *American Psychologist, 55*, 68–78.

Ryan, R. M., & Deci, E. L. (2007). Active human nature: Self-determination theory and the promotion and maintenance of sport, exercise, and health. In Hagger, M. S., & Chatzisarantis, N. L. D. (Eds.), *Intrinsic motivation and self-determination in exercise and sport* (p. 1–19). Champaign, IL: Human Kinetics.

Schmidt, R. A., & Lee, T. D. (2005). *Motor learning and control* (4th edn.). Champaign, IL: Human Kinetics Publishers.

Schmidt, L., d'Arc, B. F., Lafargue, G., Galanaud, D., Czernecki, V., Grabli, D., et al. (2008). Disconnecting force from money: Effects of basal ganglia damage on incentive motivation. *Brain, 131*, 1303–1310.

Shea, C. H., Wulf, G., & Whitacre, C. (1999). Enhancing training efficiency and effectiveness through the use of dyad training. *Journal of Motor Behavior, 31*(2), 119–125.

Shea, C. H., Wright, D. L., Wulf, G., & Whitacre, C. (2000). Physical and observational practice afford unique learning opportunities. *Journal of Motor Behavior, 32*, 27–36.

Shebilske, W. L., Regian, J. W., Arthur, W., & Jordan, J. A. (1992). A dyadic protocol for training complex skills. *Human Factors, 34*, 369–374.

Siessmeier, T., Kienast, T., Wrase, J., Larsen, J. L., Braus, D. F., Smolka, M. N., et al. (2006). Net influx of plasma 6-[1-sup-8F] fluoro-L-DOPA (FDOPA) to the ventral striatum correlates with prefrontal processing of affective stimuli. *European Journal of Neuroscience, 24*, 305–313.

Standage, M., Duda, J. L., & Ntoumanis, N. (2005). A test of self-determination theory in school physical education. *British Journal of Educational Psychology, 75*, 411–433.

Swinnen, S. P. (1996). Information feedback for motor skill learning: A review. In Zelaznik, H. N. (Ed.), *Advances in Motor Learning and Control* (p. 37–66). Champaign, IL: Human Kinetics.

White, R. W. (1959). Motivation reconsidered: The concept of competence. *Psychological Review, 66*, 297–333.

Williams, G. C., Niemiec, C. P., Patrick, H., Ryan, R. M., & Deci, E. L. (2009). The importance of supporting autonomy and perceived competence in facilitating long-term tobacco abstinence. *Annals of Behavioral Medicine, 37*, 315–324.

Wulf, G. (2007a). *Attention and motor skill learning*. Champaign, IL: Human Kinetics.

Wulf, G. (2007b). Self-controlled practice enhances motor learning: Implications for physiotherapy. *Physiotherapy, 93*, 96–101.

Wulf, G., & Bragg, K. (2010). Unpublished data. University of Nevada, Las Vegas.

Wulf, G., Chiviacowsky, S., & Lewthwaite, R. (2010). Normative feedback effects on the learning of a timing task. *Research Quarterly for Exercise and Sport, 81*, 425–431.

Wulf, G., Clauss, A., Shea, C. H., & Whitacre, C. (2001). Benefits of self-control in dyad practice. *Research Quarterly for Exercise and Sport, 72*, 299–303.

Wulf, G., & Lewthwaite, R. (2009). Conceptions of ability affect motor learning. *Journal of Motor Behavior, 41*, 461–467.

Wulf, G., & Lewthwaite, R. (2010). Effortless motor learning? An external focus of attention enhances movement effectiveness and efficiency. In Bruya, B. (Ed.), *Effortless attention: A new perspective in attention and action* (p. 75–101). Cambridge, MA: MIT Press.

Wulf, G., Raupach, M., & Pfeiffer, F. (2005). Self-controlled observational practice enhances learning. *Research Quarterly for Exercise and Sport, 76*, 107–111.

Wulf, G., & Shea, C. H. (2004). Understanding the role of augmented feedback: The good, the bad, and the ugly. In Williams, A. M., & Hodges, N. J. (Eds.), *Skill acquisition in sport: Research, theory and practice* (pp. 121–144). London: Routledge.

Wulf, G., Shea, C. H., & Whitacre, C. A. (1998). Physical guidance benefits in learning a complex motor skill. *Journal of Motor Behavior, 30*, 367–380.

Wulf, G., & Toole, T. (1999). Physical assistance devices in complex motor skill learning: Benefits of a self-controlled practice schedule. *Research Quarterly for Exercise and Sport, 70*, 265–272.

11 Motor skill consolidation

Maxime Trempe and Luc Proteau

Introduction

Physical practice has long been regarded as the single most determinant factor of motor skill acquisition, and early models of motor skill learning advocated this position (Adams, 1971; Crossman, 1959; Fitts, 1964; Schmidt, 1975). Often expressed by the old adage "practice makes perfect," this idea easily relates to the common observation that extensive practice is necessary to master a complex motor skill. Although the importance of physical practice of motor skills is undeniable, recent evidence demonstrates that the neurobiological changes that constitute the foundation of learning do not occur during physical practice. Specifically, the pioneering works of Merzenich (Merzenich, Kaas, Nelson, Sur, & Felleman, 1983) and Taub (1980) on brain plasticity provided clear demonstrations that learning modifies neuronal connections within the adult brain. Physical practice has been associated with the enlargement of specific cortical motor maps (Karni et al., 1995; Pascual-Leone et al., 1995) and the recruitment of different brain networks (Doyon & Benali, 2005). However, these changes require significant synaptic reorganization that involves the expression of specific genes and the creation of new proteins (Kandel, 2001; McGaugh, 2000). Just as Rome was not built in a day, this neuronal reorganization requires time to be completed and is therefore likely to extend beyond practice sessions.

The idea that some "learning" processes remain active after physical practice was first demonstrated in animal studies. In an experiment typical of these studies, rodents were administered a protein synthesis inhibitor before acquiring a certain behavior (McGaugh, 2000). Although the animals had no difficulty acquiring the correct behavior, retention was strongly impaired when the animals were retested the following day. This finding suggests that the drug disrupted important processes normally occurring *after* the acquisition phase. Moreover, the observation that only retention, not acquisition, was impaired provided compelling evidence that the processes responsible for retention differ from those serving acquisition. This finding suggests a two-stage model in which memories are first acquired and then stored for long-term retention. These post-acquisition processes are essential to memory formation and have been grouped under the term *consolidation* (Krakauer & Shadmehr, 2006; Robertson, Pascual-Leone, & Miall, 2004; Stickgold & Walker, 2007).

A growing body of evidence demonstrates that consolidation processes are crucial for motor skill learning. For example, repetitive transcranial magnetic stimulation (TMS) applied over the primary motor cortex, immediately after participants had practiced a fast ballistic pinch of the index finger and thumb, impaired retention of the motor skill (Muellbacher et al., 2002; see also Baraduc, Lang, Rothwell, & Wolpert, 2004). No impairment was observed if the same stimulation was applied to control sites (occipital cortex and dorsolateral prefrontal cortex) or 6 hours after practice ended (Muellbacher et al., 2002; see also Kantak, Sullivan, Fisher, Knowlton, & Winstein, 2010), suggesting that consolidation processes are both localized within specific brain networks and time-dependent. Similar observations have been reported for participants learning to adapt their movements to compensate for a perturbation of visual feedback (visuomotor rotation) or to external forces applied against their hand (dynamic adaptation). Although participants adapted their movements to compensate for such perturbations within one practice session, retention was impaired if a second and opposed perturbation (Task B) was practiced immediately after the first one (Task A). In contrast, retention was hardly affected if Tasks A and B were practiced several hours apart (Brashers-Krug, Shadmehr, & Bizzi, 1996; Krakauer, Ghilardi, & Ghez, 1999). In both these examples, the disruption of the consolidation processes (with repetitive TMS or by practicing a conflicting task) had a significant effect on learning.

Performance stabilization

Previous research on memory consolidation has demonstrated that retention can be impaired if an interfering agent (e.g., drugs, electroshock, protein synthesis inhibitor) is administered soon after the acquisition of a new memory (McGaugh, 2000). Similarly, practicing two different tasks successively has been found to impair retention (Brashers-Krug et al., 1996; Krakauer et al., 1999; Walker, Brakefield, Hobson, & Stickgold, 2003), whereas no such interference is observed when the interfering agent or the second task is experienced several hours after initial acquisition. Consolidation therefore plays a protective role for newly developed memory representations by transitioning them from a labile, interference-susceptible state to a more stable, interference-resistant state (see Figure 11.1, left panel).

The observation that retention is impaired when two tasks are practiced successively implies that it may be impossible to consolidate two different motor skills simultaneously. This conclusion is somewhat difficult to reconcile with the common observation that motor skills are rarely learned in complete isolation from one another; consolidation may not always be subject to interference. When participants learn to adapt their movements to compensate for a 30° counterclockwise rotation of visual feedback, retention is impaired when a second rotation is practiced immediately after the first one (Krakauer et al., 1999), regardless of the size (in degrees) of the second interfering rotation (Hinder, Walk, Wooley, Riek, & Carson, 2007). Interference has also been reported when participants successively learned two distinct sequences of finger movements (Walker, Brakefield, Hobson, et al., 2003). In contrast, no interference occurred when the second visuomotor rotation

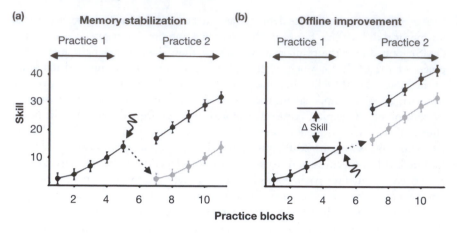

Figure 11.1 The two most common behavioural outcomes of consolidation: performance stabilization (a) and offline learning (b). (a) An interfering agent administered soon after the acquisition of a motor skill (lightning arrow) impairs retention such that performance returns to initial level when practice is resumed (gray line). No performance loss occurs if the interfering agent is administered several hours after acquisition (black line). (b) When two practice sessions are spaced by sufficient time, performance spontaneously increases at the beginning of the second session (black line). An interfering agent administered soon after the acquisition of a motor skill (lightning arrow) causes the skill to be only maintained. From Robertson & Cohen (2006, p. 264), copyright © 2006 (SAGE Publications). Reprinted by permission of SAGE Publications.

was replaced by a dynamic adaptation task in which participants had to adjust their movements to compensate for a force pulling on their arm (Krakauer et al., 1999). Similarly, Balas, Roitenberg, Giladi, and Karni (2007) reported interference when participants wrote a few words in their native language after practicing a sequence of finger movements, whereas no interference was observed when the writing task was performed with the other hand (Balas, Netser, Giladi, & Karni, 2007) or when participants wrote the same words using an unfamiliar script (Balas, Roitenberg, et al., 2007).

One current hypothesis is that interference between two tasks depends on the degree to which their memory representations conflict in working memory (Bays, Flanagan, & Wolpert, 2005). Shadmehr and Holcomb (1999) observed interference when two skills activated the same brain network (i.e., when the neuronal representations of the two skills overlapped) as if the memory representation of the second task overwrote the first one and erased the performance gains resulting from practice. This hypothesis leads to the prediction that interchanging the execution of two skills every few trials should produce massive interference between the skills and result in poor learning. However, this prediction finds little experimental support. In contrast, a large body of research on *contextual interference* has shown that random practice (i.e., interchanging the execution of two skills from trial to trial) consistently results in better retention than a schedule in which two skills are practiced separately in a blocked manner, one after the other. The beneficial effect of random practice on motor learning has been associated with the increased cognitive effort imposed by this type of schedule (Lee & Magill, 1983; Shea & Morgan, 1979). One possibility to reconcile these two ideas is that by interchanging the tasks constantly during practice (random practice), the learner gains awareness of the different nature of the tasks and is able to form a specific memory representation for each task. Because the two tasks are then clearly dissociated, interference is decreased (Bays et al., 2005). In contrast, a blocked practice schedule, in which the two skills are practiced one after the other, may not facilitate such dissociation and the same memory representation may be reactivated during practice of the second skill, thus causing interference and resulting in impaired retention.

In sum, when two different motor skills have to be learned, optimal learning may be achieved by practicing the second skill several hours after the first one, that is when the first skill has become consolidated. Whenever this schedule is not possible, coaches and instructors should structure the practice session to favor a clear dissociation between the skills (for example, by changing the exercises or the context of the exercises), thus ensuring minimal interference between the two skills.

The case of offline learning

In addition to performance stabilization, consolidation has been associated with offline learning, which is a spontaneous improvement in performance without practice (Robertson et al., 2004; Walker, 2005). This behavioral outcome was first observed using a perceptual learning task in which participants had to identify the orientation of a briefly presented set of bars (Karni & Sagi, 1993; Stickgold, James, & Hobson, 2000). With practice, participants improved their discrimination skill. When retested the following day, participants performed significantly better than at the end of the initial practice session, even though they received no additional training (Karni & Sagi, 1993). This result generated great enthusiasm in the research community as it ran against the old adage "practice makes perfect" and indicated that the simple passage of time could be sufficient to improve one's performance (see Figure 11.1, right panel). Since then, other procedural tasks have been used to determine if the passage of time could also be beneficial to motor skill learning. Among the different tasks used, the finger sequence task and the serial reaction time task (SRTT) have been the two most common.

The finger sequence task consists of producing a sequence of finger movements as quickly and accurately as possible. In typical experiments, participants are first taught a five-element sequence before practicing it for 12 blocks of 30 seconds each, with each block separated by a 30-second pause. This practice session is then followed several hours later by a retention test (three blocks). Consolidation intervals ranging from 8 to 24 hours led to significant increases in the number of sequences performed during each block, ranging from 18% (Korman, Raz, Flash, & Karni, 2003; Kuriyama, Stickgold, & Walker, 2004; Walker, Brakefield, Morgan, Hobson, & Stickgold, 2002) to 34% (Fischer, Hallschmid, Elsner, & Born, 2002). In some instances, these gains were accompanied by an increase in the number of correct movements per block (Fischer et al., 2002; Korman et al., 2003; Kuriyama et al., 2004). As with the visual discrimination task, these gains occurred although no practice took place between the practice and retest sessions. No significant offline learning was observed when the consolidation interval was shorter than 5 hours (Korman et al., 2003; Walker et al., 2002).

Similar results have been reported with the SRTT, in which participants had to respond quickly and accurately to one of four stimuli presented on a computer screen. Unknown to the participants, in some conditions the stimuli presentation followed a pre-determined sequence (usually made of 12 elements). After a single practice session, reaction times were shorter when the stimuli were presented in the pre-determined sequence rather than randomly, indicating that the participants had learned the sequence. Because participants were usually unable to evoke the sequence order explicitly, learning was thought to occur implicitly. When re-tested 12 hours after the initial practice session, with no additional practice between the sessions, the participants' reaction time "spontaneously" decreased (Press, Casement, Pascual-Leone, & Robertson, 2005).

These results show that motor skill learning progresses even when the learner is not actively practicing the task. Similar observations have been reported with an auditory discrimination task (Gaab, Paetzold, Becker, Walker, & Schlaug, 2004) and a visuomotor adaptation task (Doyon, et al., 2009; Huber, Ghilardi, Massimini, & Tononi, 2004; Trempe & Proteau, 2010). Although there is no doubt that consolidation is beneficial to memory retention, the question of whether consolidation truly *improves* performance remains open for debate, specifically because it is often difficult to isolate offline learning from other confounding factors. For example, offline learning should not be confused with the simple dissipation of the fatigue caused by massed practice. Fatigue impairs performance and can mask the true learning that occurs during a practice session. Therefore, a rest interval sufficiently long for participants to recover would result in a spontaneous increase in performance (see Rickard, Cai, Rieth, Jones, & Colin Ard, 2008, for a discussion). Additionally, one should be particularly cautious with experiments in which learning is assessed by averaging several practice trials together. This procedure is common in the SRTT literature, in which as many as 15 repetitions of the learned sequences are used to evaluate retention (180 movements; see, for example, Press et al., 2005), as well as in the finger sequence task, in which as many as three blocks of 30 seconds are averaged (Fischer et al., 2002; Walker et al., 2002). It is difficult to determine whether the spontaneous increase in performance observed in retention originates from consolidation or is simply due to continued learning *during* retention (see also Robertson et al., 2004, for a similar discussion). This pitfall could be avoided by considering only the first few movements of the re-test session. However, these trials are often contaminated by a "warm-up decrement" (i.e., a small and short-lived decrease in performance at the beginning of a practice session; see Schmidt & Lee, 2005, p. 448) that potentially masks offline learning. Alternatively, offline and online learning could be dissociated by comparing the performance of a consolidation group with the performance of a control group performing as many trials without a chance to consolidate the new skill. Assuming that control participants did not suffer from fatigue (by the use of short training sessions, for example), their performance should indicate the amount of improvement that can be expected solely from physical practice. Unfortunately, this control condition is far too often lacking.

One idea that is particularly appealing for offline learning is that the learner may gain an "insight" between practice sessions regarding the execution of the motor task, thus improving his or her performance. Most of us have had the experience of finding the solution to a difficult problem after putting it is aside for a while, giving rise to the popular expression *sleep on it*. In a clever experiment, Wagner, Gais, Haider, Verleger, and Born (2004) empirically tested this idea by asking participants to find the answer to long sequences of mental calculations. Unknown to the participants, all sequences were governed by a specific rule that provided the final answer without having to do all the calculations. Participants who benefited from a night of sleep between the practice and retest sessions were significantly more likely to discover the rule than those who did not sleep, supporting the popular conception that insight can arise when a problem is left aside. Although this effect may occur when learning a motor skill, experimental evidence is still needed.

Underlying processes

Extensive work has been done to characterize the processes of consolidation and identify the molecular substrates of memory. James McGaugh (2000) and the Nobel laureate Eric Kandel (2000) have led this field of research and demonstrated how memory formation produces long-lasting changes within different neuronal networks. Recently, attention has been directed at the finding that memories acquired during practice are replayed during subsequent rest intervals, with (Ji & Wilson, 2007; Wilson & McNaughton, 1994) or without sleep (Hoffman & McNaughton, 2002). When a rodent moves within its environment, "place cells" located in the hippocampus fire selectively with the specific positions occupied by the animal (O'Keefe & Nadel, 1978). Each path followed by the animal is associated with a specific activation sequence of hippocampal neuronal ensembles. Wilson and McNaughton (1994) were the first to report that the activation sequence elicited during practice was later reactivated during rest, suggesting that the memory representation was being replayed and further processed after the practice session. A similar reactivation of the hippocampus has been reported after practice sessions of a route-learning task in humans (Peigneux et al., 2004). Brain activity during rest periods is therefore influenced by prior waking experiences, arguing that consolidation may not be limited to a "construction" process based on synaptic modification but may include further information processing.

The latter idea is consistent with the results of neuroimaging studies that report that consolidation is associated with a shift of the brain networks solicited during practice (Karni et al., 1995; Shadmehr & Holcomb, 1997; Walker, Stickgold, Alsop, Gaab, & Schlaug, 2005). Shadmehr and Holcomb (1997) reported a reduction in the activation of the prefrontal cortex when participants resumed practice after 5.5 hours of consolidation and an increase in the activation of the contralateral dorsal premotor, contralateral posterior parietal, and ipsilateral anterior cerebellar cortex. Similarly, experiments involving rodents demonstrate that memories that were initially hippocampus-dependent gradually evolved to become hippocampus-independent after consolidation, indicating that the memory trace was transferred to different brain structures during consolidation (Tse et al., 2007). These results suggest that consolidation may play an important role in integrating new memories into pre-existing networks (Walker & Stickgold, 2010).

The observations that consolidation has localized (modification of specific synapses) and widespread (interaction between large networks) effects argues that consolidation may comprise two distinct processes: first, a "synaptic consolidation" process involving the formation of new synapses or the modification of existing ones by molecular mechanisms, and, second, a "system consolidation" process by which memory representations are further processed and integrated with existing memories (Diekelmann & Born, 2007, 2010). Although it may be tempting to associate these two processes with the two behavioral outcomes presented above (i.e., performance stabilization and offline learning), experimental evidence is still required.

The role of sleep in memory consolidation

A large amount of research has been dedicated to the role of sleep in memory consolidation. Because of the brain's reduced capability to process exteroceptive information during sleep (Rama, Cho, & Kushida, 2006), the sleeping state seems particularly well suited for large scale reorganization of neuronal connections. Although this hypothesis is both plausible and appealing, conclusions are controversial (Cai & Rickard, 2009; Rickard et al., 2008; Vertes, 2004; Vertes & Siegel, 2005). For example, offline learning following an initial practice session of the finger sequence task has been reported to occur with (Fischer et al., 2002; Walker et al., 2002) or without (Fischer et al., 2002) sleep, whereas some authors reported no offline learning at all (Cai & Rickard, 2009). When sleep-dependent gains were observed, they could be correlated with the amount of time spent either in slow-wave sleep (Walker et al., 2002) or in REM (random eye movement) sleep (Fischer et al., 2002). Moreover, the observation that brain reactivation occurs while awake (Hoffman & McNaughton, 2002) or sleeping (Ji & Wilson, 2007; Wilson & McNaughton, 1994) suggests that some processes could take place regardless of the brain state. Those seeking a more in-depth discussion of the importance of sleep in memory consolidation are referred elsewhere (Diekelmann & Born, 2010; Vassalli & Dijk, 2009; Vertes, 2004; Walker, 2005).

Consolidation and motor skill learning

There is now ample evidence supporting the position that consolidation is an important process in motor skill learning. However, *what* is learned or stabilized during consolidation remains largely speculative. One current view proposes that consolidation leads to the automatization of the new motor skill (Walker & Stickgold, 2006). This hypothesis originates from the results of Kuriyama et al. (2004), who used a finger sequence task to demonstrate that gains in speed after consolidation were larger for the transitions that were performed slowly during acquisition, whereas fast and easy transitions showed only minimal improvement. This finding was interpreted as evidence that participants initially learned the sequence by "chunking" or grouping certain segments together (Rosenbloom & Newell, 1987) and that consolidation allowed participants to incorporate the smaller memory units (chunks) into a larger, single memory representation. Consolidation would therefore promote the "unitization" of distinct memory units into a global schema or motor program (Walker & Stickgold, 2010). Support for this hypothesis was provided by recent results showing that, after extensive practice and consolidation, the elements of a sequence become so firmly linked together that asking participants to modify the last elements of the sequence slowed down performance of the entire sequence (Rozanov, Keren, & Karni, 2010). This "unitization" may therefore free some attentional resources, making the execution of the skill more automatic.

The automatization hypothesis finds support in previous neuroimaging studies. Shadmehr and Holcomb (1997) reported that, when participants adapted their movements to a velocity-dependent force field (dynamic adaptation), a consolidation interval resulted in a shift of the brain activation pattern from regions involved in the cognitive processing of information to regions regulating automated movements. Using a finger sequence task, Walker et al. (2005) reported activation increases in the cerebellum and primary motor cortex following consolidation.

Because consolidation had been linked to the development of a global motor program, we recently conducted an experiment to determine which specific aspects of the motor program are consolidated and stored in long-term memory (Trempe, Mackrous, & Proteau, unpublished data). Participants practiced a sequence of back and forth planar movements toward three different targets while the normal dynamics of their movement were modified by the lateral attachment of a 1-kg mass to their forearm. The task required that participants (1) learn the relative timing of the movement sequence to perform each segment in the prescribed intermediate time (the invariant of the motor program); (2) learn to complete the entire movement sequence in a prescribed total movement time (the parameter of the motor program); and (3) reach the targets as accurately as possible. After completing an initial training session in which visual and temporal feedback were provided, participants performed immediate and 24-hour no-feedback retention tests. The precision and variability of the relative timing were maintained closer to the levels obtained during the immediate retention test in the 24-hour retention test, indicating that the structure of the motor program had been consolidated and stored in memory (see Figure 11.2a). These results support the idea that consolidation promotes the formation of a generalized motor program. Interestingly, participants showed a significant decrease in spatial accuracy when retested 24 hours post acquisition compared with the immediate retention test (see Figure 11.2b). This observation suggests that the response specification relating to spatial accuracy may

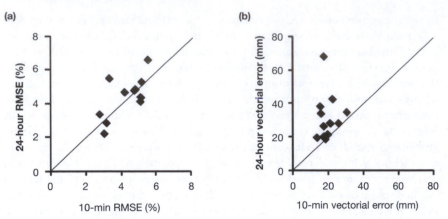

Figure 11.2 Participants practiced a sequence of back and forth planar movements toward three different targets and had to perform each segment in a prescribed movement time while being spatially accurate. Participants were retested without visual feedback, 10 minutes and 24 hours later. Each symbol represents the participants' mean error 10 minutes (x axis) and 24 hours (y axis) after acquisition. Data illustrated close to the identity line indicate good retention and above the identity line indicate impaired retention. There was good retention of the structure of the motor program (RMSE) 24 hours after acquisition (a). However, participants failed to retain the response specification relating to spatial accuracy, as shown by a decrease in the vectorial error 24 hours after acquisition (b).

not be consolidated between training sessions and may need to be recalibrated at the beginning of each session. This result is in line with many reports showing that performance usually suffers from a short-lived "warm-up decrement." It seems therefore advisable for coaches and instructors to provide their athletes/students with the opportunity to rehearse and recalibrate the consolidated motor skill before a competition event or practice session.

Time course of motor skill consolidation

Memory consolidation is, by definition, time-dependent. As time passes, the memory trace of the motor skill becomes stable and resistant to interference. Surprisingly, the relationship between time and consolidation remains poorly understood. Brashers-Krug et al. (1996) tested the effects of several between-session time intervals (from no break to 4 hours) on memory consolidation. Although statistical comparisons were not designed to contrast the different time intervals, their data revealed a trend for better retention following longer consolidation (see Figure 11.3). Similarly, in a study conducted by Press et al. (2005), longer consolidation intervals were associated with greater gains in performance (for a 4- versus 12-hour interval).

The observation that consolidation progresses with the passage of time raises two important questions, namely, "Is there a minimal amount of time required?" and

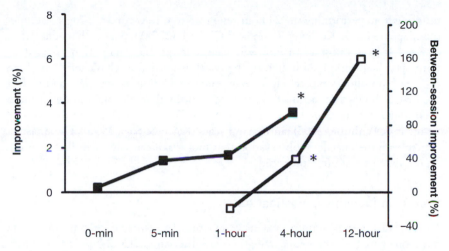

Figure 11.3 When participants had to adapt their movements to two different visuomotor rotations (Tasks A and B), there was impaired retention of Task A when the second task (Task B) was experienced immediately after Task A (0-min group). Increasing the between-task interval resulted in progressively better retention. However, only a 4-hour between-task interval allowed participants to perform significantly better in retention than in acquisition (adapted from Brashers-Krug et al., 1996, filled squares, left y axis). When participants learned to produce a sequence of finger movements, longer between-session intervals (4- and 12-hour) resulted in greater performance gains than a 1-hour interval (adapted from Press et al., 2005, open squares, right y axis).

"Is there a maximum time beyond which no more gain will occur?" The first question appears particularly important for optimizing motor skill learning as it defines the minimal time window during which memories should be protected from interfering agents. Unfortunately, no clear answer can be found in the current literature, mostly because the statistical comparisons rarely have the necessary power to detect the small differences occurring after short consolidation intervals. Nonetheless, a trend for consolidation gain has been observed after 5 minutes (Brashers-Krug et al., 1996), 30 minutes (Hotermans, Peigneux, Maertens de Noordhout, Moonen, & Maquet, 2006), and 2 hours (Walker, et al., 2002), although no gain was reported after 1 hour by Press et al. (2005).

A similar difficulty arises when assessing whether there is an upper time limit to memory consolidation. Although higher gains have been observed with longer consolidation intervals, it seems unlikely that these gains would grow indefinitely. For participants learning a finger sequence task, 72 hours of consolidation resulted in greater performance gains than 24 hours (Walker, Brakefield, Seidman, et al., 2003). Similarly, Korman et al. (2003) reported slightly larger gains for a 48-hour retention interval than a 24-hour interval. However, because the authors used a repeated measures design, it is difficult to determine whether these additional gains were related to the prolonged consolidation period or to the additional practice resulting from performing the 24-hour retention test. In contrast, using a visuomotor adaptation task, Krakauer, Ghez, and Ghilardi (2005) reported that adaptation assessed 48 hours post acquisition was slightly lower than adaptation assessed 24 hours post acquisition. Although further work is needed to characterize the time course of consolidation precisely, it seems safe to state that most gains occur within the first 24 hours after acquisition. It is noteworthy that consolidation gains have been found to persist for 1 month (Penhune & Doyon, 2002), 2 months (Savion-Lemieux & Penhune, 2005), and even 3 years (Karni & Sagi, 1993). These results concur with the anecdotal observation that motor skills are never really forgotten, even if they are not often practiced.

Factors influencing consolidation

Motor skill expertise requires extensive practice. In favorable circumstances, the more one practices, the better one gets. Does the same relation apply to the consolidation processes? Does more practice result in a better or perhaps deeper reorganization of the memory trace? Using a finger sequence task, Walker, Brakefield, Seidman, et al. (2003) reported that doubling the amount of practice from 12 to 24 blocks of 30 seconds had no significant impact on between-session improvement (see also Wright, Rhee, & Vaculin, 2010), suggesting no relation between the quantity of practice and consolidation. In contrast, Krakauer et al. (2005) reported that, although doubling the amount of initial practice in a visuomotor adaptation task (from 264 to 528 trials) did not lead to better performance during acquisition, it did prevent the interfering effect of practicing a second and conflicting rotation 5 minutes after the acquisition of the first rotation. Thus, extensive practice may not result in additional consolidation gains, but it does seem to influence the stability of the new memory representation.

Alternatively, it has been suggested that consolidation may depend not on the amount of practice per se, but rather on the attainment of a certain performance level (Hauptmann & Karni, 2002). Using a word-counting task, Hauptmann and Karni (2002) reported that consolidation resulted in performance gains only when asymptotic performance (the leveling off or saturation of within-session improvement) had been reached during the initial practice session (see also Korman et al., 2003, for a similar discussion), regardless of the amount of initial practice (Hauptmann, Reinhart, Brandt, & Karni, 2005). Using a visuomotor adaptation task, we also observed that participants who attained a performance close to perfect during acquisition had difficulty in de-adapting their movement following consolidation. No such difficulty was observed when participants did not benefit from consolidation or did not attain close to perfect performance during acquisition (Trempe & Proteau, 2010). In experiments involving rodents (Kleim et al., 2004) and humans (Karni et al., 1995) evidence is presented to suggest that a reorganization of the primary motor cortex occurs when performance reaches an asymptote. Some consolidation processes are performance-dependent in that a certain level of performance must be attained to trigger the resource- and energy-consuming process of plasticity.

How is this performance level determined? We recently suggested that the feedback received by the learner during acquisition might act as an important signal to trigger specific consolidation processes (Trempe, Sabourin, & Proteau, 2012, in press). Two groups of participants performed an initial practice session of a visuomotor adaption task before being retested the following day. The practice and re-test sessions were identical for both groups with the exception of the feedback given to the participants during the first session. One group received positive feedback that led the participants to feel successful, whereas the other group received feedback that led them to believe they did not do very well. The participants did not differ in performance during acquisition. However, when re-tested 24 hours later, participants who were led to feel successful during acquisition showed better retention than those who were led to feel less successful. The "successful" participants even outperformed another group who were led to feel successful during practice, but were not allowed a consolidation interval, indicating that the increased performance in retention was not simply caused by higher motivation (see Figure 11.4). We concluded that feedback is not only used to modify movements from trial to trial, but also serves an important role in memory formation. Further evidence supporting the role of feedback for memory formation is provided by a recent report (Hadipour-Niktarash, Lee, Desmond, & Shadmehr, 2007) in which a TMS stimulation applied over the primary motor cortex immediately after movement execution (the moment when the learner receives feedback) impaired retention. The same stimulation applied 700 ms after movement completion had no effect on retention. At the neurophysiological level, the feedback treatment is associated with a modulation of the EEG signal over the frontal cortex (Holroyd, Pakzad-Vaezi, & Krigolson, 2008) that is believed to be elicited by the anterior cingulate cortex, a major output of the mesencephalic dopaminergic system (Holroyd & Coles, 2002). The important role of dopamine in memory formation (Jay, 2003) suggests

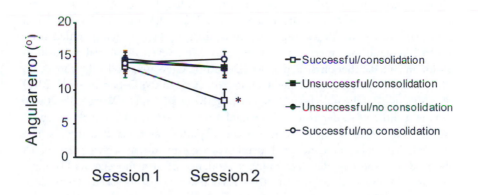

Figure 11.4 Mean angular error of participants who adapted to a rotation of visual feedback. Although the participants' adaptation did not differ during the first practice session, participants who felt successful and benefited from a consolidation interval showed better retention during the second practice session (adapted from Trempe, Sabourin & Proteau, 2012).

that positive feedback acts as a reward signal that triggers specific consolidation processes.

Whether there is a minimal quantity or frequency of successful feedback to trigger these consolidation processes is still an open question. Anecdotal evidence from everyday life indicates that some experiences need only to occur once to be remembered for the rest of our lives, indicating that certain types of memory do not necessitate a critical amount of repetition or reward to be remembered. No convincing evidence indicates whether there is a minimum frequency or occurrence of successful feedback that must be experienced to consolidate a motor skill. The observation that participants can learn a timed motor sequence with as little as one block of trials (2 min and 12 s of practice; Savion-Lemieux & Penhune, 2005) or a visuomotor rotation with only 24 trials (for a total practice time of 6 s; Trempe & Proteau, 2010) suggests that, if a minimum exists, it seems to be quite low.

It is advisable for coaches and instructors to avoid rewarding incorrect movements for the sake of increasing the learner's motivation. Such inappropriate reinforcement may lead the learner to consolidate faulty movements that will inevitably have to be corrected in future practice sessions. A specific and measurable objective to be achieved during the practice session should be established with the learner (Kyllo & Landers, 1995) and opportunities to evaluate performance in relation with the objective should be provided. Thus, only successful movements (i.e., movements that attained the objective) are rewarded and consolidated.

Observation and consolidation

In most reports, consolidation has been studied using physical practice tasks, thus raising the possibility that it may be a prerequisite for motor skill consolidation. Four reports have investigated the consolidation processes following either observation (Van Der Werf, Van Der Helm, Schoonheim, Ridderikhoff, & Van Someren, 2009) or motor imagery (Debarnot, Creveaux, Collet, Doyon, & Guillot, 2009; Debarnot, Creveaux, Collet, Gemignani, et al., 2009; Debarnot, Maley, De Rossi, & Guillot, 2010). In all these reports, a consolidation interval that included sleep resulted in significant increases in performance. However, the initial acquisition session included either physical practice (Debarnot, Creveaux, Collet, Doyon, et al., 2009; Debarnot, Creveaux, Collet, Gemignani, et al., 2009; Debarnot et al., 2010) or contractions of the muscles used to perform the task (Van Der Werf et al., 2009), making it difficult to determine if consolidation was triggered uniquely by observation/motor imagery. To determine if consolidation takes place in the absence of physical practice, we conducted a series of experiments in which participants observed an expert model performing a sequence of arm movements (Trempe, Sabourin, Rohbanfard, & Proteau, 2011). Participants who were asked to reproduce the sequence 24 hours after observation performed no better than participants who reproduced the sequence 5 minutes after observation, indicating that a prolonged retention interval did not result in offline learning. However, the results of a second experiment demonstrated that the memory representation of the sequence learned by observation was stabilized during retention and interfered with the learning of a second sequence observed 8 hours later. No such interference occurred when the two sequences were observed 5 minutes apart. This result is contrary to what is typically reported when tasks are physically practiced (Brashers-Krug et al., 1996; Krakauer et al., 1999) and suggests that consolidation processes take place after observation learning and differ from those taking place after physical practice.

Interestingly, observation resulted in better learning when the two tasks were observed 5 minutes apart. Coaches and instructors wishing to demonstrate two different skills during a practice session may optimize their athlete's/student's learning by demonstrating the two skills in close succession. This presentation schedule allows the learner to form a clear representation for each skill and decreases potential interference between the two skills.

Reconsolidate the consolidated memories

Once consolidated, memories are not forever protected against interference. Walker, Brakefield, Hobson, et al. (2003) demonstrated that the memory representation of a finger movement sequence could be disrupted by a second interfering sequence even after it had been consolidated. Specifically, participants learned a first sequence (Sequence A) on day 1 and demonstrated offline learning when retested on day 2. Then, if participants practiced a second sequence (Sequence B) immediately after recall of Sequence A on day 2, retention of Sequence A was impaired when retested 24 hours later (on day 3). No such impairment was observed if Sequence B was practiced on day 2 without recall of Sequence A. The authors concluded that the reactivation of Sequence A on day 2 returned its memory representation to a labile state that was susceptible to interference from Sequence B. Without recall, the memory representation remained in a stable form and was not subject to interference. This finding suggests that, once reactivated, memories need to go through another consolidation phase, or "reconsolidation," to regain a stable form (for reviews see Alberini, 2005; Nader & Hardt, 2009). Learning could then be seen as a cycle of destabilization–reconsolidation. According to Alberini (2005), the stability of a memory representation depends on the number of destabilization–reconsolidation cycles experienced. Every time memories are destabilized and reconsolidated, they become more stable and less susceptible to disruption, explaining the notorious difficulty of getting rid of an old habit when performing a motor skill.

Results from reconsolidation experiments provide valuable guidance for learners wishing to modify a deeply anchored, incorrect technical execution. Because memory traces become labile once again upon rehearsal, an effective training method may consist of deliberately rehearsing the incorrect execution at the beginning of the practice session before attempting to perform the correct movement. The destabilized memory representation associated with the incorrect execution may then be subject to interference from the correct movement and eventually be overwritten by the desired memory trace. This appealing hypothesis will, however, benefit from experimentations to evaluate its promises.

Conclusion

Although early models of motor skill learning have traditionally seen physical practice as the most important factor, researchers have recently highlighted the important role of consolidation processes for motor skill learning. During consolidation, the memory representation for the skill undergoes further processing to become integrated into existing brain networks and kept in long-term memory, a dynamic process that is repeated every time the memory representation is rehearsed. Although practice still makes perfect, consolidation ensures that perfection is maintained.

References

Adams, J. A. (1971). A closed-loop theory of motor learning. *Journal of Motor Behavior, 3,* 111–150.

Alberini, C. M. (2005). Mechanisms of memory stabilization: are consolidation and reconsolidation similar or distinct processes? *Trends in Neurosciences, 28*(1), 51–56.

Balas, M., Netser, S., Giladi, N., & Karni, A. (2007). Interference to consolidation phase gains in learning a novel movement sequence by handwriting: Dependence on laterality and the level of experience with the written sequence. *Experimental Brain Research, 180,* 237–246.

Balas, M., Roitenberg, N., Giladi, N., & Karni, A. (2007). When practice does not make perfect: Well-practiced handwriting interferes with the consolidation phase gains in learning a movement sequence. *Experimental Brain Research, 178,* 499–508.

Baraduc, P., Lang, N., Rothwell, J. C., & Wolpert, D. M. (2004). Consolidation of dynamic motor learning is not disrupted by rTMS of the primary motor cortex. *Current Biology, 14,* 252–256.

Bays, P. M., Flanagan, J. R., & Wolpert, D. M. (2005). Interference between velocity-dependent and position-dependent force-fields indicates that tasks depending on different kinematic parameters compete for motor working memory. *Experimental Brain Research, 163,* 400–405.

Brashers-Krug, T., Shadmehr, R., & Bizzi, E. (1996). Consolidation in human motor memory. *Nature, 382,* 252–254.

Cai, D. J., & Rickard, T. C. (2009). Reconsidering the role of sleep for motor memory. *Behavioral Neuroscience, 123*(6), 1153–1157.

Crossman, E. R. F. W. (1959). A theory of the acquisition of speed skill. *Ergonomics, 2,* 153–166.

Debarnot, U., Creveaux, T., Collet, C., Doyon, J., & Guillot, A. (2009). Sleep contribution to motor memory consolidation: A motor imagery study. *Sleep, 32*(12), 1559–1565.

Debarnot, U., Creveaux, T., Collet, C., Gemignani, A., Massarelli, R., Doyon, J., et al. (2009). Sleep-related improvements in motor learning following mental practice. *Brain and Cognition, 69*(2), 398–405.

Debarnot, U., Maley, L., De Rossi, D., & Guillot, A. (2010). Motor interference does not impair the memory consolidation of imagined movements. *Brain and Cognition, 74,* 52–57.

Diekelmann, S., & Born, J. (2007). One memory, two ways to consolidate? *Nature Neuroscience, 10*(9), 1085–1086.

Diekelmann, S., & Born, J. (2010). The memory function of sleep. *Nature Reviews Neuroscience, 11,* 114–126.

Doyon, J., & Benali, H. (2005). Reorganization and plasticity in the adult brain during learning of motor skills. *Current Opinion in Neurobiology, 15,* 161–167.

Doyon, J., Korman, M., Morin, A., Dostie, V., Tahar, A., Benali, H., et al. (2009). Contribution of night and day sleep vs. simple passage of time to the consolidation of motor sequence and visuomotor adaptation learning. *Experimental Brain Research, 195*(1), 15–26.

Fischer, S., Hallschmid, M., Elsner, A. L., & Born, J. (2002). Sleep forms memory for finger skills. *Proceedings of the National Academy of Sciences of the United States of America, 99*(18), 11987–11991.

Fitts, P. M. (1964). Perceptual–motor skills learning. In Melton, A. W. (Ed.), *Categories of human learning* (pp. 243–285). New York: Academic Press.

Gaab, N., Paetzold, M., Becker, M., Walker, M. P., & Schlaug, G. (2004). The influence of sleep on auditory learning: A behavioral study. *Neuroreport, 15*(4), 731–734.

Hadipour-Niktarash, A., Lee, C. K., Desmond, J. E., & Shadmehr, R. (2007). Impairment of retention but not acquisition of a visuomotor skill through time-dependent disruption of primary motor cortex. *Journal of Neuroscience, 27*(49), 13413–13419.

Hauptmann, B., & Karni, A. (2002). From primed to learn: The saturation of repetition priming and the induction of long-term memory. *Cognitive Brain Research, 13,* 313–322.

Hauptmann, B., Reinhart, E., Brandt, S. A., & Karni, A. (2005). The predictive value of the leveling off of the within-session performance for the procedural memory consolidation. *Cognitive Brain Research, 24,* 181–189.

Hinder, M. R., Walk, L., Wooley, D. G., Riek, S., & Carson, R. G. (2007). The interference effects of non-rotated versus counter-rotated trials in visuomotor adaptation. *Experimental Brain Research, 180,* 629–640.

Hoffman, K. L., & McNaughton, B. L. (2002). Coordinated reactivation of distributed memory traces in primate neocortex. *Science, 297,* 2070–2073.

Holroyd, C. B., & Coles, M. G. H. (2002). The neural basis of human error processing: Reinforcement learning, dopamine, and the error-related negativity. *Psychological Review, 109*(4), 679–709.

Holroyd, C. B., Pakzad-Vaezi, K. L., & Krigolson, O. E. (2008). The feedback correct-related positivity: Sensitivity of the event-related brain potential to unexpected positive feedback. *Psychophysiology, 45,* 688–697.

Hotermans, C., Peigneux, P., Maertens de Noordhout, A., Moonen, G., & Maquet, P. (2006). Early boost and slow consolidation in motor skill learning. *Learning and Memory, 13,* 580–583.

Huber, R., Ghilardi, M. F., Massimini, M., & Tononi, G. (2004). Local sleep and learning. *Nature, 430,* 78–81.

Jay, T. M. (2003). Dopamine: A potential substrate for synaptic plasticity and memory mechanisms. *Progress in Neurobiology, 69,* 375–390.

Ji, D., & Wilson, M. A. (2007). Coordinated memory replay in the visual cortex and hippocampus during sleep. *Nature Neuroscience, 10*(1), 100–107.

Kandel, E. R. (2000). Cellular mechanisms of learning and the biological basis of individuality. In Kandel, E. R., Schwartz, J. H., & Jessell, T. M. (Eds.), *Principles of neural science* (4th edn., pp. 1247–1279). New York: McGraw-Hill.

Kandel, E. R. (2001). The molecular biology of memory storage: A dialogue between genes and synapses. *Science, 294,* 1030–1038.

Kantak, S. S., Sullivan, K. J., Fisher, B. E., Knowlton, B. J., & Winstein, C. J. (2010). Neural substrates of motor memory consolidation depend on practice structure. *Nature Neuroscience, 13*(8), 923–925.

Karni, A., Meyer, G., Jezzard, P., Adams, M. M., Turner, R., & Ungerleider, L. G. (1995). Functional MRI evidence for adult motor cortex plasticity during motor skill learning. *Nature, 377*, 155–158.

Karni, A., & Sagi, D. (1993). The time course of learning a visual skill. *Nature, 365*, 250–252.

Kleim, J. A., Hogg, T. M., VanderBerg, P. M., Cooper, N. R., Bruneau, R., & Remple, M. (2004). Cortical synaptogenesis and motor map reorganization occur during late, but not early, phase of motor skill learning. *Journal of Neuroscience, 24*(3), 628–633.

Korman, M., Raz, N., Flash, T., & Karni, A. (2003). Multiple shifts in the representation of a motor sequence during the acquisition of skilled performance. *Proceedings of the National Academy of Sciences of the United States of America, 100*(21), 12492–12497.

Krakauer, J. W., Ghez, C., & Ghilardi, M. F. (2005). Adaptation to visuomotor transformations: Consolidation, interference, and forgetting. *Journal of Neuroscience, 25*(2), 473–478.

Krakauer, J. W., Ghilardi, M. F., & Ghez, C. (1999). Independent learning of internal models for kinematic and dynamic control of reaching. *Nature neuroscience, 2*(11), 1026–1031.

Krakauer, J. W., & Shadmehr, R. (2006). Consolidation of motor memory. *Trends in Neurosciences, 29*(1), 58–64.

Kuriyama, K., Stickgold, R., & Walker, M. P. (2004). Sleep-dependent learning and motor-skill complexity. *Learning & Memory, 11*(6), 705–713.

Kyllo, L. B., & Landers, D. M. (1995). Goal setting in sport and exercise: A research synthesis to resolve the controversy. *Journal of Sport and Exercise Psychology, 17*(2), 117–137.

Lee, T. D., & Magill, R. A. (1983). The locus of contextual interference in motor-skill acquisition. *Journal of Experimental Psychology Learning Memory and Cognition, 9*(4), 730–746.

McGaugh, J. L. (2000). Memory: A century of consolidation. *Science, 287*, 248–251.

Merzenich, M. M., Kaas, J. H., Nelson, R. J., Sur, M., & Felleman, D. (1983). Topographic reorganization of somatosensory cortical areas 3b and 1 in adult monkeys following restricted deafferentation. *Neuroscience, 8*(1), 33–55.

Muellbacher, W., Ziemann, U., Wissel, J., Dang, N., Kofler, M., Facchini, S., et al. (2002). Early consolidation in human primary motor cortex. *Nature, 415*, 640–644.

Nader, K., & Hardt, O. (2009). A single standard for memory: The case for reconsolidation. *Nature Reviews Neuroscience, 10*, 224–234.

O'Keefe, J., & Nadel, L. (1978). *The hippocampus as a cognitive map.* Oxford: Clarendon Press.

Pascual-Leone, A., Dang, N., Cohen, L. G., Brasil-Neto, J. P., Cammarota, A., & Hallett, M. (1995). Modulation of muscle responses evoked by transcranial magnetic stimulation during the acquisition of new fine motor skills. *Journal of Neurophysiology, 74*(3), 1037–1045.

Peigneux, P., Laureys, S., Fuchs, S., Collette, F., Perrin, F., Reggers, J., et al. (2004). Are spatial memories strengthened in the human hippocampus during slow wave sleep? *Neuron, 44*, 535–545.

Penhune, V. B., & Doyon, J. (2002). Dynamic cortical and subcortical networks in learning and delayed recall of timed motor sequences. *Journal of Neuroscience, 22*(4), 1397–1406.

Press, D. Z., Casement, M. D., Pascual-Leone, A., & Robertson, E. M. (2005). The time course of off-line motor sequence learning. *Cognitive Brain Research, 25*(1), 375–378.

Rama, A. N., Cho, S. C., & Kushida, C. A. (2006). Normal human sleep. In Lee-Chiong, T. (Ed.), *Sleep: A comprehensive handbook* (pp. 3–9). Hoboken, NJ: John Wiley & Sons.

Rickard, T. C., Cai, D. J., Rieth, C. A., Jones, J., & Colin Ard, M. (2008). Sleep does not enhance motor sequence learning. *Journal of Experimental Psychology: Learning, Memory, and Cognition, 34*(4), 834–842.

Robertson, E. M., & Cohen, D. A. (2006). Understanding consolidation through the architecture of memories. [review]. *Neuroscientist, 12*(3), 261–271.

Robertson, E. M., Pascual-Leone, A., & Miall, R. C. (2004). Current concepts in procedural consolidation. *Nature Reviews Neuroscience, 5*(7), 576–582.

Rosenbloom, P., & Newell, A. (1987). Learning by chunking: A production system model of practice. In Klahr, D., Langley, P., & Neches, R. T. (Eds.), *Production system models of learning and development* (pp. 221–286). Cambridge, MA: MIT Press.

Rozanov, S., Keren, O., & Karni, A. (2010). The specificity of memory for a highly trained finger movement sequence: Change the endings, change all. *Brain Research, 1331*, 80–87.

Savion-Lemieux, T., & Penhune, V. B. (2005). The effects of practice and delay on motor skill learning and retention. *Experimental Brain Research, 161*, 423–431.

Schmidt, R. A. (1975). A schema theory of discrete motor skill learning. *Psychological Review, 82*(4), 225–260.

Schmidt, R. A., & Lee, T. D. (2005). *Motor control and learning: A behavioral emphasis* (4th edn.). Champaign, IL: Human Kinetics.

Shadmehr, R., & Holcomb, H. H. (1997). Neural correlates of motor memory consolidation. *Science, 277*, 821–825.

Shadmehr, R., & Holcomb, H. H. (1999). Inhibitory control of competing motor memories. *Experimental Brain Research, 126*, 235–251.

Shea, J. B., & Morgan, R. L. (1979). Contextual interference effects on the acquisition, retention, and transfer of a motor skill. *Journal of Experimental Psychology: Human Learning and Memory, 5*(2), 179–187.

Stickgold, R., James, L. T., & Hobson, J. A. (2000). Visual discrimination learning requires sleep after training. *Nature Neuroscience, 3*(12), 1237–1238.

Stickgold, R., & Walker, M. P. (2007). Sleep-dependent memory consolidation and reconsolidation. *Sleep Medicine, 8*, 331–343.

Taub, E. (1980). Somatosensory deafferentation research with monkeys: Implications for rehabilitation medicine. In Ince, L. P. (Ed.), *Behavioral Psychology in Rehabilitation Medicine: Clinical Applications* (pp. 371–401). New York: Williams & Wilkins.

Trempe, M., & Proteau, L. (2010). Distinct consolidation outcomes in a visuomotor adaptation task: Off-line leaning and persistent after-effect. *Brain and Cognition, 73*(2), 135–145.

Trempe, M., Sabourin, M., & Proteau, L. (2012). Success modulates consolidation of a visuomotor adaptation task. *Journal of Experimental Psychology: Learning, Memory, and Cognition, 38*(1), 52–60.

Trempe, M., Sabourin, M., Rohbanfard, H., & Proteau, L. (2011). Observation learning versus physical practice leads to different consolidation outcomes in a movement timing task. *Experimental Brain Research, 209*(2), 181–192.

Tse, D., Langston, R., Kakeyama, M., Bethus, I., Spooner, P. A., Wood, E. R., et al. (2007). Schemas and memory consolidation. *Science, 316*, 76–82.

Van Der Werf, Y. D., Van Der Helm, E., Schoonheim, M. M., Ridderikhoff, A., & Van Someren, E. J. W. (2009). Learning by observation requires an early sleep window. *Proceedings of the National Academy of Sciences of the United States of America, 106*(45), 18926–18930.

Vassalli, A., & Dijk, D. J. (2009). Sleep function: Current questions and new approaches. *European Journal of Neuroscience, 29*, 1830–1841.

Vertes, R. (2004). Memory consolidation in sleep: Dream or reality. *Neuron, 44*, 135–148.

Vertes, R., & Siegel, J. (2005). Time for the sleep community to take a critical look at the purported role of sleep in memory processing. *Sleep, 28*(10), 1228–1229.

Wagner, U., Gais, S., Haider, H., Verleger, R., & Born, J. (2004). Sleep inspires insight. *Nature, 427*, 352–355.

Walker, M. P. (2005). A refined model of sleep and the time course of memory formation. *Behavioral and Brain Sciences, 28*, 51–104.

Walker, M. P., Brakefield, T., Hobson, J. A., & Stickgold, R. (2003). Dissociable stages of human memory consolidation and reconsolidation. *Nature, 425,* 616–620.

Walker, M. P., Brakefield, T., Morgan, A., Hobson, J. A., & Stickgold, R. (2002). Practice with sleep makes perfect: Sleep-dependent motor skill learning. *Neuron, 35,* 205–211.

Walker, M. P., Brakefield, T., Seidman, J., Morgan, A., Hobson, J. A., & Stickgold, R. (2003). Sleep and the time course of motor skill learning. *Learning & Memory, 10*(4), 275–284.

Walker, M. P., & Stickgold, R. (2006). Sleep, memory, and plasticity. *Annual Review of Psychology, 57,* 139–166.

Walker, M. P., & Stickgold, R. (2010). Overnight alchemy: Sleep-dependent memory evolution. *Nature Reviews Neuroscience, 11,* 218.

Walker, M. P., Stickgold, R., Alsop, D., Gaab, N., & Schlaug, G. (2005). Sleep-dependent motor memory plasticity in the human brain. *Neuroscience, 133*(4), 911–917.

Wilson, M. A., & McNaughton, B. L. (1994). Reactivation of hippocampal ensemble memories during sleep. *Science, 265*(5172), 676–679.

Wright, D. L., Rhee, J.-H., & Vaculin, A. (2010). Offline improvement during motor sequence learning is not restricted to developing motor chunks. *Journal of Motor Behavior, 42*(5), 317–324.

12 Critical periods, sensitive periods, and readiness for motor skill learning

David I. Anderson, Richard A. Magill, and Regis Thouvarecq

When should a child be exposed to learning a new skill? Is there an optimum age? Will the optimum age vary from skill to skill? Is there a danger of initiating learning too early? Will ultimate proficiency be compromised if learning is initiated too late? These questions stem from a deep-rooted conviction that experiences can have a greater influence at some times during life than at others and that such times must be exploited for optimum skill development. Although these questions appear centrally relevant to skill acquisition theorists and practitioners, they have been the subject of surprisingly little research. Far more attention has been devoted to the host of variables known to influence skill acquisition once the learning process has been initiated. However, motor skill learning must ultimately be considered within a developmental context if it is to be fully understood.

The question of *when* to initiate learning has traditionally been discussed in the context of critical periods and readiness for learning. The critical period concept is ubiquitous in the developmental neuroscience literature and the readiness concept is equally prevalent in the developmental and educational psychology literatures. Nevertheless, our understanding of when children are best prepared to profit from specific experiences and how to create that preparation is poor. In this chapter, we discuss how the critical period and readiness concepts have been or could be applied to motor skill learning. Although clear answers to the questions posed in the opening paragraph are difficult to provide, we highlight the range of factors that need to be considered in providing plausible answers.

The critical period concept

Myrtle McGraw (1935) was the first to use the *critical period* label in the context of motor skill acquisition. McGraw observed the twin boys Johnny and Jimmy in her laboratory for the first 22 months of their lives. During this time, Johnny was challenged by a variety of stimulating motor activities while Jimmy was left to play with a few toys in his crib. When the twins were 22 months old, Jimmy was given an intense 2.5 months of practice in the same activities that Johnny had practiced earlier. Johnny's early exposure was beneficial for the development of some skills such as climbing, swimming, and rollerskating, but had no effect on skills such as crawling and walking and appeared detrimental for others such as tricycling when compared with Jimmy's later exposure. McGraw argued that there were critical periods for learning motor skills (McGraw, 1935, 1939, 1985).

The critical period concept originated in the field of embryology, where the embryo's ultimate form was shown to be exquisitely sensitive to the timing of developmental disruptions (e.g., Spemann, 1938). Critical periods are now well-established phenomena in embryological development and nearly every parent is familiar with the notion that teratogens (external agents) will have widely different effects depending on the timing of exposure. The period of most rapid growth or differentiation of an organ or system is generally considered the most susceptible time (Moore & Persaud, 1998).

The most widely cited example of a critical period in mammalian development concerns the visual system. Hubel and Wiesel demonstrated that surgical closure of one eye during a brief period after birth causes a severe visual impairment in species such as cats and monkeys when the eye is later reopened (Hubel & Wiesel, 1970). Critical periods have been demonstrated for auditory development, tactile development, and motor and neuromuscular development in the rat (Jamon & Serradj, 2009). A special issue of *Developmental Psychobiology* indicated that critical periods in human sensory development are pervasive (Maurer, 2005).

Konrad Lorenz's work on imprinting has had the most significant and enduring effect on the study of critical periods in the acquisition of new behaviors. Imprinting describes the tendency for certain species of birds to fixate and follow the first moving object they see. Lorenz noted that the process of imprinting was confined to a very short period early in life and that once accomplished it was irreversible (Lorenz, 1937). These characteristics – short duration, early in life, irreversible – came to characterize critical period discussions during the decades of research that followed (for recent examples, Bolhuis, Okanoya, & Scharff, 2010; Habib & Besson, 2009).

Critical periods or sensitive periods?

Volumes of published research since Lorenz's early work have shown that critical periods are rarely brief and sharply defined, and rarely are their effects irreversible (see Anderson, 2002; Bruer, 2001; Hensch, 2004). Many have challenged the relevance of the critical period concept for human behavioral development (e.g., Bruer, 1999; Thelen & Smith, 1998), noting, for example, that children can recover dramatically from years of severe deprivation (Clarke & Clarke, 1976). Even kittens deprived of visual experience during the critical period defined by Hubel and Wiesel (1970) can make substantial improvements in visual functioning if subsequently forced to use the deprived eye in visual training tasks (Harwerth, Smith, Crawford, & van Noorden, 1989).

Unfortunately, misapplication of Lorenz's narrowly defined critical period concept to a sweeping range of developmental phenomena created considerable confusion and controversy over the value of the concept in behavioral development.

Many researchers now prefer to use the term *sensitive phase* or *sensitive period* when referring to heightened periods of susceptibility to environmental input in behavioral and perceptual development. Knudsen (2004) has provided a particularly good distinction between critical periods and sensitive periods:

> When the effect of experience on the brain is particularly strong during a limited period in development, this period is referred to as a sensitive period . . . When experience provides information that is essential for normal development and alters performance permanently, such sensitive periods are referred to as critical periods. (p. 1412)

Knudsen's definition permits differentiation between the development of behavior, which is well known to exhibit considerable plasticity across the lifespan (e.g., Greenough, Black, & Wallace, 1987), and the development of the neural circuitry underlying behavior, which can show marked reductions in plasticity across the lifespan (Hensch, 2004; Johnson, 2005). Windows of opportunity and vulnerability in the skill acquisition process are best described as sensitive periods.

What determines the start and end of a sensitive period?

Contemporary thinking suggests that sensitive periods can be understood only within the complex web of constraints that govern all developmental changes. Because numerous factors have been shown to modify the onsets, offsets, durations, and potency of sensitive periods (Bornstein, 1989; Hensch, 2004), it is helpful to think of these more globally as periods of heightened plasticity. Systems are more plastic (easier to shape) during their early phase of organization or when they are undergoing transitions. However, neuroscientists have found a number of ways to enhance plasticity in biological systems across their lifespan and many changes that were once considered irreversible are open to change (Hensch, 2004; Knudsen, 2004). For example, blindfolding an adult for as little as 45–60 min can enhance visual cortex excitability (plasticity), as demonstrated by neuroimaging and neuro-activation devices (functional magnetic resonance imaging, fMRI, and transcranial magnetic stimulation, TMS, respectively; Sathian, 2005).

According to Scott and colleagues, sensitive periods for learning will most often occur during the early phase of the learning process, when the system is less stable and mechanized (Scott, 1962; Scott, Stewart, & De Ghett, 1974). The system's learning potential is much greater when the system is in a relatively undifferentiated or unstable state. Thelen (1995) has captured the importance of this notion for behavioral development in the following way: "Knowing when systems are in transition is important because theory predicts that interventions can only be effective when the system has sufficient flexibility to explore and select new solutions" (p. 94).

Sensitive periods for learning are now believed to result from the learning process itself. The sensitive period opens when learning a new skill begins and terminates when learning is complete. This view has been supported by evidence showing that the periods can be extended and are self-terminating. For example, Cynader, Timney, and Mitchell (1980) have shown that kittens dark-reared for longer than normal remain highly sensitive to the effects of monocular deprivation, and Chang and Merzenich (2003) have shown that rats prevented from hearing patterned sounds have immature tone-based brain maps. According to Knudsen (2004), absence of the relevant stimulation prevents neural circuits from being adequately activated, thus preventing the cellular and molecular processes that strengthen and consolidate synapses.

In his *interactive specialization* hypothesis, Johnson (2005) argues that brain development reflects changes in the interrelations among neural networks in different brain regions that compete with each other. Plasticity is reduced when the functional specialization of a region is completed. Changes at the neural circuit level might be irreversible because certain synapses are committed to a particular pattern of organization, and synapses that could have subserved alternative patterns have been lost for lack of reinforcement (Greenough et al., 1987). However, irreversible changes in a neural circuit do not automatically lead to irreversible changes in behavior. Higher-level circuits, which remain plastic for longer periods, can compensate for aberrant circuits at lower levels in the hierarchy or higher-level circuits can derive information from alternative pathways (Knudsen, 2004).

The first three years of life appear to be the period during which experience plays a fundamental role in organizing the brain systems that underlie human perception. Event-related potential (ERP) experiments on adults have shown that auditory stimuli elicit large responses over the brain's temporal cortex, but little to no response over the visual cortex. In contrast, large responses are seen over the auditory and visual cortices in a 6-month-old infant. The auditory responses over the visual area gradually decline over the ensuing months until they are no longer present at approximately 36 months (Neville & Bruer, 2001). Thus, the neural substrate that underlies perception (and presumably action) seems relatively undifferentiated early in life and becomes progressively more differentiated and committed to specific functions with experience.

Sensitive periods for language and music acquisition

The existence of sensitive periods for the acquisition of complex behaviors such as language and music remains controversial. Many researchers consider it inappropriate to speak about sensitive periods for language or musical acquisition even though there may be sensitive or even critical periods for the component subsystems that contribute to these skills (Neville & Bruer, 2001). Nevertheless, it is useful to consider the evidence that has been put forward in favor of sensitive periods for language and music to provoke further thinking on the relevance of the sensitive period hypothesis for motor skill learning.

Lenneberg (1967) was the first to propose a critical period for language development, which occurred between the ages of 2 years and puberty. He assumed that language acquisition was impossible before 2 because of maturational factors and after puberty because of lack of cerebral plasticity resulting from lateralization of the language function. Subsequently, researchers have argued that there are probably sensitive periods for each of the component subsystems from which language is constructed (Bortfield & Whitehouse, 2001).

One of the most fascinating examples of a sensitive period in language acquisition concerns the rapid decline in sensitivity to non-native phonological speech contrasts between 6 and 12 months of age (Werker & Tees, 1984). Before 6 months, infants are capable of discriminating all of the speech sounds that constitute all spoken languages. The decline in sensitivity is considered a classic example of loss of skill through lack of practice. The early plasticity is gradually lost as the neurological substrate available for phonological processing is recruited to enhance sensitivity to the language that is most frequently heard. Werker and Tees (2005) have argued that the declines in sensitivity are not absolute. Continuous exposure to speech contrasts during the first 2 years of life, followed by complete lack of exposure when children are adopted into families that speak a different language, appears sufficient to accelerate the relearning of the original speech contrasts during adulthood (Werker & Tees, 2005). Occasional exposure to a language after 12 months of age appears sufficient to maintain phonemic discrimination (Werker & Tees, 2005).

The ability of infants to distinguish speech contrasts is curiously similar to their ability to recognize chimpanzee faces: a skill that can be done with ease before 6 months of age, but which seems to disappear after 9 months (Pascalis, de Haan, & Nelson, 2002). In both cases, the infant possesses a remarkable early capacity for pattern recognition, which becomes increasingly specific to the most frequently experienced patterns. Johnson and Newport (1989) reported one of the most well-known studies of sensitive periods for second language acquisition. They studied the English grammatical comprehension of Chinese and Korean immigrants whose first exposure to English occurred some time between the ages of 3 and 39 years, but who all had 10 years of exposure to the language. The group who arrived between 3 and 7 years of age were indistinguishable from native speakers, whereas a significant decline in comprehension with age occurred for all others in the study.

The age of 7 years has also been deemed critical for exposure to music if one is to gain the proficiency of an expert musician (Habib & Besson, 2009). The argument is based on the number of differences in brain responses to auditory stimuli observed in musicians who were exposed to musical training before or after the age of 7 years. Watanabe, Savion-Lemieux, and Penhune (2007) have provided the most convincing evidence for an early sensitive period in the motor component of musical training. They matched two groups of musicians who had started practice before or after the age of 7 on years of musical experience, years of formal training, and hours of current practice. Both groups were compared on their ability to learn a rapid, finger sequencing, visual tracking task. As shown in Figure 12.1, clear differences were seen on the rate and level of learning achieved on the task in favor of the group who had begun practice before 7 years, though the authors were quick to point out the considerable overlap in performance. So, early training was important, but it was not the only factor that contributed to adult performance (see also Bailey & Penhune, 2010).

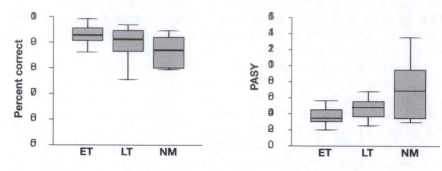

Figure 12.1 Average percentage correct and percentage response asynchrony (PASY) for early
trained (ET), late trained (LT), and non-musicians (NM) across 5 days of learning
of a finger sequencing task that required synchronization with a visual stimulus. Though the ET musicians were less asynchronous than the LT musicians
overall, there was considerable overlap between the two groups. Adapted from
Watanabe, Savion-Lemieux, & Penhune (2007).

Critical sequences within the learning process

In development, Schneirla and Rosenblatt (1963) have argued instead for the
importance of critical *sequences* in development. They showed that social development in the kitten was heavily dependent upon the kitten receiving experiences in
a particular order. If one phase within the sequence was skipped, the next phase
would not begin. Similarly, Sosniak (1985) has argued that acquiring expertise in
sports, music, arts, mathematics, and science may be critically dependent on experiencing learning phases in a particular sequence. The sequence most commonly
associated with success was one in which the individual was informally exposed to
the activity through play, then worked hard to develop technical skill, and finally
was encouraged to express his or her own personality and creativity through the
activity.

Some researchers have shown that later phases within motor learning can be
more sensitive to perturbation than earlier phases. Temporarily paralyzing the vocal
muscles of song birds during early development had no effect on adult song production, but paralysis later in development, when the adult song was emerging, resulted
in permanent motor deficits (Pytte & Suthers, 2000). These authors suggest that
the late sensorimotor integration phase of practice is a sensitive period for song
development, but also for motor development in general. For example, infants with
long-term tracheotomies that prevent vocalization show more rapid recovery in
vocal development when the disruption is early in the babbling phase rather than
later, at word production onset. This may reflect the diminished plasticity available
during this phase of learning.

In summary, although sensitive periods are well established in embryological
development and early sensory development, their relevance for motor skill learning is questionable. The capacity to achieve similar outcomes from different starting
points is a hallmark of behavioral development and plasticity is apparent across
the lifespan. Nevertheless, research in language and music acquisition suggests that

exposure to a skill before the age of 7 years might lead to neurological changes that markedly enhance the potential for performance or learning of the skill later in life. That said, receiving experiences in a particular sequence within the learning process might be more important than the age of exposure to a new skill, and disruption of the later consolidation phase of learning can be more detrimental than disruption of earlier phases.

The readiness concept

Readiness versus sensitive periods

The notion that sequences within the learning process are important (and perhaps even critical) provides an appropriate transition to thinking about readiness for learning motor skills. It is difficult to define the term *readiness* precisely because the concept is used broadly and frequently in a wide variety of contexts. To complicate matters, researchers have used the terms *readiness*, *critical periods*, and *sensitive periods* interchangeably to account for rapid changes in learning.

Despite the confusion, the readiness concept is based on a simple premise: that learning and development are constructive, stage-like processes characterized by the hierarchical integration and coordination of component subskills and processes. Hierarchical integration and coordination are features of nearly every modern theory of development (Fischer & Bidell, 2006). Gagné (1968) has described the constructive nature of development most cogently by stating that the "child progresses from one point to the next in his development . . . because he learns an ordered set of capabilities which build upon each other in progressive fashion through the process of differentiation, recall, and transfer of learning" (p. 181).

Readiness for learning implies then that children have acquired the simpler prerequisite skills that will enable them to acquire more complex skills (Bruner, 1966; Fischer, 2009; Kagan, 1990). Mastering prerequisites early in learning is presumed to have a positive effect on the quality and rate of learning. Although this simple notion is one of the cornerstones of contemporary educational practice and curriculum design, translating it into clear guidelines for practice has proved difficult.

Examples of readiness for learning motor skills

McGraw's research on Johnny and Jimmy was introduced at the beginning of the chapter as one of the earliest demonstrations of critical periods for learning motor skills. McGraw spoke about critical periods, yet her observations were more pertinent to the readiness concept. For example, Johnny was given considerable practice on tricycle riding when he was 11 months old, whereas Jimmy was not exposed to tricycling until he was 22 months. Johnny struggled for 8 months before showing any improvement whereas Jimmy, despite his later exposure, mastered the task rapidly. McGraw (1939) claimed that for Johnny "activity was initiated before his neuro-muscular mechanisms were ready for such a performance" (p. 3) and that it is simply wasted effort to begin training before adequate "neural readiness."

Gesell and Thompson (1929) reached a similar conclusion in their study of identical twin girls. One twin was given special training between the ages of 46 and 52 weeks in locomotor activities related to stair climbing. The other twin did not receive training until 53 weeks of age. At 53 weeks, the untrained twin did not climb the stairs as well as the trained twin. However, following only 2 weeks of training, 5 weeks less than the previously trained twin, the untrained twin surpassed her sister in climbing the stairs. Gesell and Thompson concluded that better learning with less training results when the child's maturation level is adequate for the skill

Since the early work in the 1920s and 1930s, there has been a paucity of research on readiness for learning motor skills. Arend (1980a, 1980b) contributed to the theoretical discussion by attempting to identify the physical, cognitive, perceptual, and perceptual–motor substrates of skillful movement and suggested ways in which those substrates could be developed before practice of the whole skill. However, Blanksby and colleagues have provided the only tangible evidence that initiating learning at different ages influences the rate at which motor skills are acquired (Blanksby, Parker, Bradley, & Ong, 1995; Parker & Blanksby, 1997). The records of 326 children from a swim school were analyzed with respect to the age at which they had started instruction, the number of lessons, and the age at which they were able to swim 10 m while coordinating arms, legs, and breathing (Level 3, Australian competency; Blanksby et al., 1995). The later the age of first introduction to swim instruction, the fewer lessons and less time it took to achieve the target competency. The optimum starting age for acquiring competency was 5.5 years, though the number of lessons required to reach the competency continued to decline at 6, 7, and 8 years of age (see Table 12.1). Thus, an earlier introduction to swimming lessons failed to translate into significantly earlier swimming competence. The optimum starting age of 5.5 years for swim instruction is remarkably similar to starting ages reported for expert performers in other sports and activities. For example,

Table 12.1 Average number of lessons, age, and duration to reach Level 3 swimming proficiency for children starting swimming lessons at different ages

Starting age (years)	Number of participants	Number of lessons to reach Level 3	Age at Level 3 (years)	Duration to Level 3 (months)
2.7	24	110.6	5.6	36.1
3.5	39	84.3	5.6	25.2
4.5	60	54.1	5.8	15.5
5.4	74	38.6	6.3	9.9
6.5	64	28.7	7.1	7.5
7.4	42	18.0	7.8	4.6
8.4	23	14.7	8.6	3.0

Source: Adapted from Table 2 in Blanksby, Parker, Bradley, & Ong (1995).

Starkes, Deakin, Allard, Hodges, and Hayes (1996) remarked how similar the starting ages for Ericsson, Krampe, and Tesch-Römer's (1993) expert pianists (5.8 years) and "highest" violinists (5.0 years) were to the mean starting age (5.3 years) of the elite figure skaters they studied. In a subsequent section we will consider whether children younger than 5 years of age learn differently from older children.

Determining readiness

It is troubling that researchers have provided so little insight into how to determine readiness for motor skill learning or when learning should be initiated (Haubenstricker & Seefeldt, 2002). Our poor understanding of the relation between prerequisite skills and later learning is partially responsible for this situation. The relationship between prerequisites and later learning is far less intuitive than it appears. For example, basic skills and capacities are poor predictors of later performance (Ericsson et al., 1993; Ericsson & Lehmann, 1996). Similarly, early learning (Magill, 2010) and early performance of fundamental motor skills (Haubenstricker & Seefeldt, 1986) are poor predictors of later learning and performance. Early and later learning appear to depend on very different types of capacities and abilities (Ackerman, 1988).

Bidell and Fischer (1997) have blamed our past tendency to view development through a linear and reductionist lens for our inability to conceptualize how development can proceed through the hierarchical integration of component skills. We expect to see simple relations between isolated skills and more complex behaviors; however, contemporary theories of development suggest that the relations among variables are profoundly non-linear and context dependent (Thelen & Smith, 1998). Moreover, the self-organizing nature of development leads to co-actions among component skills (Gottlieb, 1997). Co-action means that independent skills can literally transform each other when they are integrated into the larger whole. Consequently, any given skill might function quite differently when viewed in isolation (or in a different context) than when viewed within the context of a broader skill.

Further complication arises when one considers that prerequisite skills can be consequences or antecedents of the learning process. For example, researchers have revealed clear improvements in reading ability following training in the skill of segmenting speech into phonemes – a classic example of how building prerequisites can facilitate learning. However, the greatest changes in phonemic segmentation result from formal reading instruction in first-grade (Morrison, McMahon-Griffith, & Frazier, 1996). Thus, reading contributes to the development of one of the prerequisite skills, showing that one does not have to wait for prerequisite skills to emerge before skill introduction.

Early versus delayed exposure to learning

The critical period and readiness concepts suggest that early learning provides the foundation for later learning. This idea is important because it means that the quality of early learning is critical. It also means that early learning could facilitate or hinder later learning. Many researchers have advocated that children should be exposed to a wide diversity of movement experiences early in life to develop the perceptual–motor capacities that will facilitate the subsequent learning of more advanced skills. Bernstein (1996) noted that a person who had established what he referred to as a *better collection of background corrections* (acquired mechanisms that compensate for errors in movement execution) would be better equipped to find quick solutions for new motor problems. Bernstein also assumed that a wide range of movement experiences was necessary to establish a broad collection of background corrections.

Early learning experiences can also create difficulties for later learning. Second-language learning is thought to be more difficult than first-language learning because of interference caused by the first language. Werker and Tees (2005) have proposed a cascade model of language learning that is consistent with the principles of hierarchical integration. Lower-level units in the hierarchy, such as phoneme discrimination, are recruited and reinforced by higher-level units as language skill develops. As a result, the lower-level units become highly resistant to change and can interfere with second-language learning. Interference from earlier learning has also been proposed to account for the difficulty of learning perfect pitch after the age of 6 because once the relative features of a melody are noticed it is very difficult to distinguish absolute features (Takeuchi & Hulse, 1993).

The acquisition of bad habits is a potential negative consequence of initiating learning too early. Because prerequisites cannot always be developed during prac-tice of the whole skill, the child may compensate inappropriately for the essential prerequisites that are missing. Bad habits can develop because children lack the strength to appropriately manipulate the sporting equipment they are provided with (Ward & Groppel, 1980) or because they come to rely on perceptual (Woollacott, Debû, & Shumway-Cook, 1987) or cognitive strategies (McGraw, 1939) that are inappropriate at a later stage. Early mistakes, frustrations, or failures that result from exposing children to skills at too early an age could have profound negative consequences for long-term learning if they create a negative attitude toward learn-ing (Weiss & Ferrer-Caja, 2002). For example, Gesell and Ilg (1946) have noted that children worry about making mistakes and are careful not to expose themselves to criticism at around 5 to 6 years of age.

Do younger and older children learn differently?

Bernstein (1996) suggested that children can learn some skills more easily than adults. For example, he stated that "skills like swimming take much more time and more effort to become automated in adults than in children, because in children such skills are immediately put under the control of the level of space" (p. 182). In contrast, the inhibiting centers that prevent clumsy movements are already strongly developed in adults, such that control is assigned to a higher, more strategic level.

Bernstein's suggestion is intriguing when considered in relation to Blanksby et al.'s (1995) conclusion that 5.5 years of age is optimum for introducing children to instruction in the front crawl. The 5- to 7-year shift was first officially labeled by Sheldon White (1965), although Piaget (1950) is best known for making this shift central in his theory of cognitive development. It is generally after the age of 7 years that children shift from pre-operational thinking to concrete operational thinking. They perform less egocentrically, focus less on the individual aspects of a situation when problem solving, and come to realize that other minds can have different views from their own. The 5-year-old child in Figure 12.2 is entering a phase in which she will be able to simultaneously contemplate more facets of the game of badminton than simply hitting the birdie.

Important changes in perceptual and motor performance also occur between 5 and 7 years. Children shift from considering the individual dimensions of weight and distance to considering both together when solving balance scale problems (Siegler, 1996). An interesting dissociation has been shown between 5-year-olds' explicit and implicit understanding of a throwing task (Krist, Fieberg, & Wilkening, 1993). Five-year-olds performed a throwing task accurately (appropriately modulated force according to launch height and target distance), but took only target distance into account in a force judgment version of the task. In contrast, many 10-year-olds and most adults took both into account in the judgment task. Discontinuities in performance between 6 and 7 years of age have also been reported in a study of sequential finger pointing. Children at this age were able to use strategies consistent with those of older children when the task was easy; however, when the task was

Figure 12.2 The child playing badminton has just entered the 5- to 7-year shift.

difficult they used strategies that were more similar to those of younger children (Badan, Hauert, & Mounoud, 2000). Noticeable changes in task strategies and motor performance have been documented after the age of 5 years for a range of different tasks, including lifting objects, visuomanual tracking, target pointing, drawing, and writing (Mounoud, 1996). Children also show a decrease in mirror movements (unwanted movements of the opposite limb) after the age of 7 years (Garvey et al., 2003). In addition, the speed of information processing, as revealed by decreased reaction times to pre-cued information, shows major improvements between 6 and 8 years (Olivier, Ripoll, & Audiffren, 1997). Finally, changes in children's ability to switch flexibly between or integrate visual, vestibular, and somatosensory information have been proposed to account for regressions followed by improvements in postural control strategies around 6 years (Woollacott et al., 1987).

In summary, children below the age of 5 years might learn quite differently from children over the age of 7 years and adults. Children become increasingly adult-like in their approach to problem solving after 7 years. It is not clear exactly what implications this idea has for the age at which children should be exposed to motor skills, particularly as children vary greatly at any given age on account of prior learning experiences and the range of intrinsic and extrinsic factors that modulate growth and maturation as well as motor and psychological development. Nevertheless, a profitable direction for future research would be to more closely examine changes in motor performance and learning that occur between 5 and 7. It is plausible that very different learning strategies would be most appropriate for children at either side of this age period.

Conclusions and future directions

Considerable research is required to answer the questions posed at the outset of this chapter. The critical period and readiness concepts inform our understanding of when to initiate learning; however, the concepts have not yet led to the development of specific guidelines. In the final section of this chapter, we outline a framework to guide future research.

The most definitive evidence for sensitive periods in human development has been provided by embryologists and those who study the early development of sensory systems. Embryological and early sensory development occur over considerably shorter timescales than behavioral development and are more amenable to experimental manipulation and animal modeling. In contrast, the typical study of sensitive periods in human behavioral development uses a quasi-experimental approach, focused on naturally occurring populations that have had similar experiences (often atypical ones) at different times in their lives. Potential confounding factors are numerous in such designs.

Convincing evidence for sensitive periods in sport skill development requires that researchers use true experimental designs in which participants are randomly assigned to treatments. The ideal design systematically varies the age at which a child is exposed to a sport while keeping the duration of exposure constant or systematically varying the duration of exposure (Bruer, 2001) (see Figure 12.3).

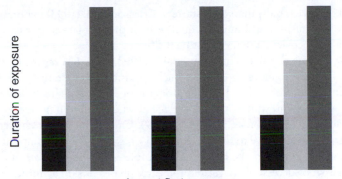

Figure 12.3 Schematic of an ideal design for the experimental study of sensitive periods in sport skill acquisition. The age at which the child is exposed to the sport and the duration of exposure (indicated by the different colored bars) should be manipulated systematically. The children should be assessed on the same outcomes and the assessments should be conducted immediately after each exposure period and again after a delay.

Systematically varying the duration of exposure enables one to establish whether age and duration of exposure interact in interesting ways. In addition, the age of exposure must vary widely to ensure that the entire duration of a sensitive period is identified and to establish whether any benefits associated with a later exposure are a function of differential readiness rather than a sensitive period.

Such experimental designs are clearly effortful and time-consuming and they may be impractical when cultural pressures make it impossible to control the age of initial exposure. However, this limitation can be overcome by conducting research with cultural groups that are not typically exposed to the skill of interest. The school setting is likely to be the most practical arena in which to conduct experimental research on sensitive periods and readiness because teachers can dedicate units of study to learning a particular skill while carefully monitoring instruction and duration.

Quasi-experimental research designs can still make an important contribution to our understanding of sensitive periods and readiness in sport skill acquisition and they may represent the best approach when resources are limited. The paradigm used to study expertise in sport offers an excellent starting point. Researchers have already addressed whether practice undertaken early in an athlete's career makes a contribution to ultimate skill proficiency equivalent to that of practice undertaken later in the career. However, the findings are equivocal and seem to depend on the nature of the sport under investigation (Hodges, Kerr, Starkes, Weir, & Nananidou, 2004). Ericsson and colleagues (Ericsson et al., 1993) have argued forcefully that the amount of deliberate practice is a far better predictor of expertise than the age at which an individual begins practice. Early-starting experts typically outperform later-starting experts when compared at a particular age because they have accumulated more deliberate practice. While acknowledging that later starters may initially learn a skill more rapidly than early starters, Ericsson et al. (1993) maintain that the rate of skill acquisition will quickly equalize such that the late starter typically ends up with a practice deficit that cannot be made up.

It may be time to subject Ericsson et al.'s (1993) assertion regarding the downsides of a late start to more rigorous testing by paying greater attention to the ages at which experts are first exposed to their domain of expertise. This has already been done, to some extent, with respect to the age at which children decide to specialize in sport (e.g., Côté, Lidor, & Hackfort, 2009). One of the major challenges with assessing start ages relative to the development of expertise is the sampling bias that results from studying experts. Because the sample of experts consists of only those individuals who successfully navigated the early phases of skill acquisition, we gain no insight into how practice histories influence those individuals who dropped out. Sensitive periods and readiness are as important for the latter groups as they are for experts (and potentially more important).

In addition to research on experts, researchers should consider the quasi-experimental design used by Blanksby et al. (1995) to study the influence of start age on the development of swimming proficiency. The Blanksby design is unusual relative to the typical design used to study sensitive periods because experience is measured rather than manipulated. Many schools, clubs, and centers must have records that could be used to assess age effects in sport skill development.

Many opportunities exist to contribute to this exciting and intriguing area of research and one hopes that the limitations in our current understanding of opportune times to initiate motor skill learning will inspire further research. Studying readiness and sensitive periods in the development of sport skills is a challenging enterprise, but one that could also be enormously rewarding. Framing the study of learning within a developmental context could markedly enhance our understanding of how to facilitate skill acquisition.

References

Ackerman, P. L. (1988). Determinants of individual differences during skill acquisition: Cognitive abilities and information processing. *Journal of Experimental Psychology: General, 117*, 288–318.

Anderson, D. I. (2002). Do critical periods and readiness determine when to initiate sport skill learning? In Smoll, F. L., and Smith, R. E. (Eds.), *Children and youth in sport: A biopsychosocial perspective* (2nd edn., pp. 105–148). Dubuque, IA: Kendall/Hunt.

Arend, S. (1980a). Developing the substrates of skillful movement. *Motor Skills: Theory into Practice, 4*, 3–10.

Arend, S. (1980b). Developing perceptual skills prior to motor performance. *Motor Skills: Theory into Practice, 4*, 11–17.

Badan, M., Hauert, C. A., & Mounoud, P. (2000). Sequential pointing in children and adults. *Journal of Experimental Child Psychology, 75*, 43–69.

Bailey, J. A., & Penhune, V. B. (2010). Rhythm synchronization performance and auditory working memory in early- and late-trained musicians. *Experimental Brain Research, 204*, 91–101.

Bernstein, N. A. (1996). On dexterity and its development. In Latash, M. L., & Turvey, M. T. (Eds.), *Dexterity and its development* (pp. 3–244). Mahwah, NJ: Lawrence Erlbaum.

Bidell, T. R., & Fischer, K. W. (1997). Between nature and nurture: The role of human agency in the epigenesis of intelligence. In Sternberg, R. J., & Grigorenko, E. (Eds.), *Intelligence, heredity, and environment* (pp. 193–242). Cambridge: University of Cambridge Press.

Blanksby, B. A., Parker, H. E., Bradley, S., & Ong, V. (1995). Children's readiness for learning front crawl swimming. *Australian Journal of Science and Medicine in Sport, 27,* 34–37.

Bolhuis, J. J., Okanoya, K., & Scharff, C. (2010). Twitter evolution: Converging mechanisms in birdsong and human speech. *Nature Reviews: Neuroscience, 11,* 747–759.

Bornstein, M. H. (1989). Sensitive periods in development: Structural characteristics and causal interpretations. *Psychological Bulletin, 105,* 179–197.

Bortfield, H., & Whitehouse, G. J. (2001). Sensitive periods in first language acquisition. In Bailey, D. B., Bruer, J. T., Symons, F. J., & Lichtman, J. W. (Eds.), *Critical thinking about critical periods* (pp. 173–192). Baltimore, MD: Paul H. Brookes.

Bruer, J. T. (1999). *The myth of the first three years: A new understanding of early brain development and lifelong learning.* New York: Free Press.

Bruer, J. T. (2001). A critical and sensitive period primer. In Bailey, D. B., Bruer, J. T., Symons, F. J., & Lichtman, J. W. (Eds.), *Critical thinking about critical periods* (pp. 3–26). Baltimore, MD: Paul H. Brookes.

Bruner, J. S. (1966). *Toward a theory of instruction.* Cambridge, MA: Harvard University Press.

Chang, E. F., & Merzenich, M. M. (2003). Environmental noise retards auditory cortical development. *Science, 300,* 498–502.

Clarke, A. M., & Clarke, A. D. B. (Eds.) (1976). *Early experience: Myth and evidence.* New York: Free Press.

Côté, J., Lidor, R., & Hackfort, D. (2009). ISSP position stand: To sample or to specialize? Seven postulates about youth sport activities that lead to continued participation and elite performance. *International Journal of Sport and Exercise Psychology, 9,* 7–17.

Cynader, M., Timney, B. N., & Mitchell, D. E. (1980). Period of susceptibility of kitten visual cortex to the effects of monocular deprivation extends beyond six months of age. *Brain Research, 191,* 545–550.

Ericsson, K. A., Krampe, R. T., & Tesch-Römer, C. (1993). The role of deliberate practice in the acquisition of expert performance. *Psychological Review, 100,* 363–406.

Ericsson, K. A, & Lehmann, A. C. (1996). Expert and exceptional performance: Evidence of maximal adaptation to task constraints. *Annual Review of Psychology, 47,* 273–305.

Fischer, K. W. (2009). Mind, brain, and education: Building a scientific groundwork for learning and teaching. *Mind, Brain, and Education, 3,* 3–16.

Fischer, K. W., & Bidell, T. R. (2006). Dynamic development of action and thought. In Damon, W., & Lerner, R. (Eds.), *Handbook of Child Psychology* (6th edn.), *Vol. I: Theoretical models of human development* (pp. 313–399). Hoboken, NJ: John Wiley & Sons.

Gagné, R. M. (1968). Contributions of learning to human development. *Psychological Review, 75,* 177–191.

Garvey, M. A., Ziemann, U., Bartko, J. J., Denckla, M., Barker, C. A., & Wassermann, E. M. (2003). Cortical correlates of neuromotor development in healthy children. *Clinical Neurophysiology, 114,* 1662–1670.

Gesell, A., & Ilg, F. (1946). *The child from five to ten.* New York: Harper & Row.

Gesell, A., & Thompson, H. (1929). Learning and growth in identical infant twins: An experimental study by the method of co-twin control. *Genetic Psychology Monographs, 6,* 1–124.

Gottlieb, G. (1997). *Synthesizing nature–nurture: Prenatal roots of instinctive behavior.* Mahwah, NJ: Lawrence Erlbaum Associates.

Greenough, W. T., Black, J. E., & Wallace, C. S. (1987). Experience and brain development. *Child Development, 58,* 539–559.

Habib, M., & Besson, M. (2009). What do music training and musical experience teach us about brain plasticity? *Music Perception, 26,* 279–285.

Harwerth, R. S., Smith, E. L. III, Crawford, M. L. J., & van Noorden, G. K. (1989). The effects of reverse monocular deprivation in monkeys I: Psychophysical experiments. *Experimental Brain Research, 74,* 327–337.

Haubenstricker, J. L., & Seefeldt, V. (1986). Acquisition of motor skills during childhood. In Seefeldt, V. (Ed.), *Physical activity and well-being* (pp. 41–102). Reston, VA: AAHPERD.

Haubenstricker, J. L., & Seefeldt, V. (2002). The concept of readiness applied to the acquisition of motor skills. In Smoll, F. L., and Smith, R. E. (Eds.), *Children and youth in sport: A biopsychosocial perspective* (2nd edn., pp. 61–81). Dubuque, IA: Kendall/Hunt.

Hensch, T. K. (2004). Critical period regulation. *Annual Review of Neuroscience, 27,* 549–579.

Hodges, N. J., Kerr, T., Starkes, J. L., Weir, P. L., & Nananidou, A. (2004). Predicting performance times from deliberate practice hours for triathletes and swimmers: What, when, and where is practice important? *Journal of Experimental Psychology: Applied, 10,* 219–237.

Hubel, D. H., & Wiesel, T. N. (1970). The period of susceptibility to the physiological effects of unilateral eye closure in kittens. *Journal of Physiology, 206,* 419–436.

Jamon, M., & Serradj, N. (2009). Ground-based researches on the effects of altered gravity on mice development. *Microgravity Science and Technology, 21,* 327–337.

Johnson, M. H. (2005). Sensitive periods in functional brain development: Problems and prospects. *Developmental Psychobiology, 46,* 287–292.

Johnson, J. S., & Newport, E. L. (1989). Critical period effects in second language learning: The influence of maturational state on the acquisition of English as a second language. *Cognitive Psychology, 21,* 60–99.

Kagan, S. L. (1990). Readiness 2000: Rethinking rhetoric and responsibility. *Phi Delta Kappa International, 72,* 272–279.

Knudsen, E. I. (2004). Sensitive periods in the development of brain and behavior. *Journal of Cognitive Neuroscience, 16,* 1412–1425.

Krist, H., Fieberg, E. L., & Wilkening, F. (1993). Intuitive physics in action and judgment: The development of knowledge about projectile motion. *Journal of Experimental Psychology: Learning, Memory, and Cognition, 19,* 952–966.

Lenneberg, E. (1967). *Biological foundations of language.* New York: John Wiley & Sons.

Lorenz, K. (1937). The companion in the bird's world. *The Auk, 54,* 245–273.

Magill, R. A. (2010). *Motor learning and control: Concepts and applications* (9th edn.). New York: McGraw-Hill.

Maurer, D. (2005). Introduction to the special issue on critical periods reexamined: Evidence from human sensory development. *Developmental Psychobiology, 46,* 155.

McGraw, M. B. (1935). *Growth: A study of Johnny and Jimmy.* New York: Appleton-Century.

McGraw, M. B. (1939). Later development of children specially trained during infancy: Johnny and Jimmy at school age. *Child Development, 10,* 1–19.

McGraw, M. B. (1985). Professional and personal blunders in child development research. *Psychological Record, 35,* 165–170.

Moore K. L., & Persaud T. V. N. (1998). *The developing human: Clinically oriented embryology* (6th edn.). Philadelphia: W. B. Saunders.

Morrison, F. J., McMahon-Griffith, E., & Frazier, J. A. (1996). Schooling and the 5 to 7 shift: A natural experiment. In Sameroff, A. J., & Haith, M. M. (Eds.), *The five to seven year shift: the age of reason and responsibility* (pp. 161–186). Chicago, IL: University of Chicago Press.

Mounoud, P. (1996). A recursive transformation of central cognitive mechanisms: The shift from partial to whole representations. In Sameroff, A. J., & Haith, M. M. (Eds.), *The five to seven year shift: the age of reason and responsibility* (pp. 85–110). Chicago, IL: University of Chicago Press.

Neville, H. J., & Bruer, J. T. (2001). Language processing: How experience affects brain organization. In Bailey, D. B., Bruer, J. T., Symons, F. J., & Lichtman, J. W. (Eds.), *Critical thinking about critical periods* (pp. 151–172). Baltimore, MD: Paul H. Brookes.

Olivier, I., Ripoll, H., & Audiffren, M. (1997). Age differences in using precued information to pre-program interception of a ball. *Perceptual and Motor Skills, 85,* 123–127.

Parker, H. E., & Blanksby, B. A. (1997). Starting age and aquatic skill learning in young children: Mastery of prerequisite water confidence and basic aquatic locomotion skills. *Australian Journal of Science and Medicine in Sport, 29,* 83–87.

Pascalis, O., de Haan, M., & Nelson, C. A. (2002). Is face processing species-specific during the first year of life? *Science, 296,* 1321–1323.

Piaget, J. (1950). *The psychology of intelligence.* London: Routledge and Kegan Paul.

Pytte, C. L., & Suthers, R. A. (2000). Sensitive period for sensorimotor integration during vocal motor learning. *Journal of Neurobiology, 42,* 172–189.

Sathian, K. (2005). Visual cortical activity during tactile perception in the sighted and the visually deprived. *Developmental Psychobiology, 46,* 279–286.

Schneirla, T. C., & Rosenblatt, J. S. (1963). "Critical periods" in the development of behavior. *Science, 139,* 1110–1115.

Scott, J. P. (1962). Critical periods in behavioral development. *Science, 138*(3544), 949–958.

Scott, J. P., Stewart, J. M., & De Ghett, V. J. (1974). Critical periods in the organization of systems. *Developmental Psychobiology, 7,* 489–513.

Siegler, R. S. (1996). Unidimensional thinking, multidimensional thinking, and characteristic tendencies of thought. In Sameroff, A. J., & Haith, M. M. (Eds.), *The five to seven year shift: the age of reason and responsibility* (pp. 63–84). Chicago, IL: University of Chicago Press.

Sosniak, L. A. (1985). Phases of learning. In Bloom, B. S. (Ed.), *Developing talent in young people* (pp. 409–438). New York: Ballantine Books.

Spemann, H. (1938). *Embryonic development and induction.* New Haven, CT: Yale University.

Starkes, J. L., Deakin, J. M., Allard, F., Hodges, N. J., & Hayes, A. (1996). Deliberate practice in sports: What is it anyway? In Ericsson, K. A. (Ed.), *The road to excellence: The acquisition of expert performance in the arts and sciences, sports, and games* (pp. 81–106). Mahwah, NJ: Lawrence Erlbaum.

Takeuchi, A. H., & Hulse, S. H. (1993). Absolute pitch. *Psychological Bulletin, 113,* 345–361.

Thelen, E. (1995). Motor development: A new synthesis. *American Psychologist, 50,* 79–95.

Thelen, E., & Smith, L. B. (1998). Dynamic systems theories. In Damon, W. (Series Ed.) & Lerner, R. M. (Vol. Ed.), *Handbook of child psychology* (5th edn., vol. 1, pp. 563–634). New York: John Wiley & Sons.

Ward, T., & Groppel, J. (1980). Sport implement selection: Can it be based upon anthropometric indicators? *Motor Skills: Theory into Practice, 4,* 103–110.

Watanabe, D., Savion-Lemieux, T., & Penhune, V. B. (2007). The effect of early musical training on adult motor performance: Evidence for a sensitive period in motor learning. *Experimental Brain Research, 176,* 332–340.

Weiss, M. R., & Ferrer-Caja, E. (2002). Motivational orientations and sport behaviors. In Horn, T. S. (Ed.), *Advances in sport psychology* (pp. 101–184). Champaign, IL: Human Kinetics.

Werker, J. F., & Tees, R. C. (1984). Cross-language speech perception: Evidence for perceptual reorganization during the first year of life. *Infant Behavior and Development, 7*, 49–63.

Werker, J. F. & Tees, R. C. (2005). Speech perception as a window for understanding plasticity and commitment in language systems of the brain. *Developmental Psychobiology, 46*, 233–251.

White, S. H. (1965). Evidence for hierarchical arrangement of learning processes. In Lipsitt, L. P., & Spiker, C. C. (Eds.), *Advances in child development and behavior* (pp. 187–220). New York: Academic Press.

Woollacott, M. H., Debû, B., & Shumway-Cook, A. (1987). Children's development of posture and balance control: Changes in motor coordination and sensory integration. In Gould, D., & Weiss, M. R. (Eds.), *Advances in pediatric sport sciences: Behavioral issues, vol. 2* (pp. 211–233). Champaign, IL: Human Kinetics.

13 Mechanisms of skilled joint action performance

Terry Eskenazi, Robrecht Van Der Wel, and Natalie Sebanz

Introduction

Joint actions are building blocks of our social life; examples range from two friends walking together to construction workers building a skyscraper. They are actions that individuals need to, or prefer to, perform with others. We call it a joint action when two or more people coordinate their actions in space and time to bring about a change in the environment (Sebanz, Bekkering, & Knoblich, 2006) Team sports form a clear case of joint action in which often very fine-grained coordination is required. Take the alley-oop example in basketball. One player throws the ball toward the basket while a teammate jumps up near it, catches the ball midair, and immediately scores. Each player needs to anticipate the other's move, and to perform his or her own move at the exact correct moment to be able to score. What are the essential cognitive and motor mechanisms that make such joint actions possible? How are joint skills, be they basketball or ballroom dancing, acquired?

Whereas initial interest in joint action centered on philosophical questions about the nature of shared intentions (Clark, 1996), over the last few years a growing number of empirical studies have enhanced our understanding of the mechanisms underlying interpersonal coordination. Acknowledging that the mechanisms that make acting jointly possible may, at least to some extent, be irreducible to the mechanisms individuals rely on when acting alone, researchers have focused on individuals acting in a variety of joint settings. A range of mechanisms operating at different levels have been targeted, from the planning of actions, including the representations underlying jointly performed tasks, to the mechanisms supporting real-time coordination. We provide an overview of some of the basic mechanisms that make joint action possible. In particular, we focus on evidence for perception–action couplings between individuals, on how these couplings are mediated by higher-level planning processes, and on the role of shared task representations. Implications for joint skill learning are discussed throughout the chapter.

Perception–action links

Direct links: entrainment

Entrainment is a widely studied social motor coordination process (Schmidt, Fitzpatrick, Caron, & Mergeche, in press) that leads to temporal coordination of two actors' behavior, even in the absence of a direct mechanical coupling. It can be considered a form of emergent coordination (Knoblich, Butterfill, & Sebanz, 2011) in that it happens regardless of whether or not an intention to coordinate is present. In this sense, it is said to be "direct." In dynamical systems theory, entrainment is thought to reflect the coupling of rhythmic oscillators (Schmidt & Richardson, 2008). It is observed in both mechanical systems, such as when two pendulum clocks placed on a wall become synchronized (Huygens, 1673/1986), and in biological systems, such as when the hand movements of a person performing bimanual actions synchronize (e.g., Haken, Kelso, & Bunz, 1985), as would be the case in jump-rope skipping or rowing.

Ecological psychologists have studied entrainment in an interpersonal (i.e., between different people) context to determine whether dynamical principles of intrapersonal (i.e., within a person) coordination also hold for the interpersonal case (Marsh, Richardson, & Schmidt, 2009). It has been shown that the joint movements of different people follow the same dynamical principles as the joint movements of an individual's limbs. This has been shown, for example, when people walk together (Van Ulzen, Lamoth, Daffertshofer, Semin, & Beek, 2008), swing pendulums (Amazeen, Schmidt, & Turvey, 1995; Richardson, Marsh, & Schmidt, 2005; Schmidt, Bienvenu, Fitzpatrick, & Amazeen, 1998) or their legs (Schmidt, Carello, & Turvey, 1990), or rock in rocking chairs alongside each other (Richardson, Marsh, Isenhower, Goodman, & Schmidt, 2007). Furthermore, entrainment occurs in a wide range of social contexts, including the synchronization of body sway during conversation (Shockley, Santana, & Fowler, 2003), and in larger groups of people, such as a theatre audience clapping in unison (Néda, Ravasz, Brechet, Vicsek, & Barabási, 2000).

Clearly, entrainment contributes to joint task performance in which synchronization is part of the goal of the joint action, such as synchronized swimming or dancing. Interestingly, the tendency to entrain seems to be preserved even under unfavorable conditions. Richardson and colleagues (2007) found that people sitting in rocking chairs next to each other fell into synchrony even when the eigenfrequency of the two rocking chairs differed. This tendency to entrain may come at the cost of increased energy expenditure. In a recent study, participants walking on a treadmill were found to spend more energy when they were visually coupled with the image of a body walking in anti-phase (i.e., contralateral arm and leg) than with the image of a body walking in phase (i.e., mirror image of ipsilateral arm and leg; Eaves, Hodges, & Williams, 2008).

There is some evidence to suggest that entrainment aids cooperation beyond synchronization. Being synchronized has been shown to have positive effects on other aspects of joint performance including language comprehension (Richardson & Dale, 2005) and the ability to cooperate (Valdesolo, Ouyang, & DeSteno, 2010). Furthermore, synchronization seems to foster group cohesion. Participants reported liking a task partner more when they had performed a tapping task in synchrony with their partner than when they had tapped at a different tempo, even though they knew that external signals determined the tempo (Hove & Risen, 2009). Participants who had walked in step in groups of three made more cooperative choices in a subsequent coordination game than participants who had not walked in step (Wiltermuth & Heath, 2009). The synchronized walking group also reported feeling more connected and trusted each other more. These findings suggest that entrainment or synchronization plays an important part in increasing group cohesion.

Finally, an interesting hypothesis to be explored is that entrainment in the context of joint practice aids in the learning of individual tasks that require precise timing. According to this hypothesis, novices joining a group of more experienced individuals should be pulled towards particular dynamics, which may help them improve their performance at a faster rate than practicing alone. For instance, a beginner at juggling might be able to decrease the spatiotemporal variability of his throwing patterns at a faster rate when practicing amongst a group of more experienced jugglers whose actions provide a useful attractor toward expert dynamics (Huys, Daffertshofer, & Beek, 2004; Santvoort & Beek, 1999).

Common coding: perception–action matching and motor simulation

Whereas some researchers claim direct links between perception and action that do not involve mental representations (e.g. Gibson, 1979; Marsh, Richardson, & Schmidt, 2009), other researchers postulate that perception and action are tightly linked through common underlying representations (Jeannerod, 2001; Prinz, 1997), which may help to mimic, predict, and understand the actions of others. The term *perception–action matching* refers to the finding that when we observe somebody acting this activates a corresponding representation of the action in our own motor system.

According to the common coding theory (Hommel, Müsseler, Aschersleben, & Prinz, 2001; Prinz, 1997), actions are coded in terms of their distal perceptual consequences. For example, when kicking a football, the kicking action is specified in terms of the visual consequence of the action (the ball trajectory) rather than in terms of the particular muscles to be moved (Ford, Hodges, Huys, & Williams, 2006, 2009; Ford, Hodges, & Williams, 2007). From the assumption that actions are coded in terms of their effects, it follows that perceived actions and the actions we produce ourselves can be represented in the same format (e.g., a ball trajectory can be represented in the same way regardless of whether I am planning to kick the ball or you have kicked it). This "common coding" creates an interface between action execution and action observation, because similar motor representations are activated for actions we observe and for actions we are capable of producing (Bach & Tipper, 2007; Brass, Bekkering, & Prinz, 2001).

Supporting evidence from behavioral studies (Brass et al., 2001; Kilner, Paulignan, & Blakemore, 2003) shows that people are faster at performing a particular movement (e.g., lifting their finger) when they concurrently see a corresponding movement (watching someone lifting a finger) than when they see the opposite movement (watching someone moving a finger down). A growing body of evidence from neurophysiology shows how the coupling between perception and action is implemented at a neuronal level. Single-cell studies in monkeys led to the discovery of mirror neurons in motor cortices of the macaque monkey (Di Pellegrino, Fadiga, Fogassi, Gallese, & Rizzolatti, 1992; Gallese, Fadiga, Fogassi, &

Rizzolatti, 1996). These mirror neurons fire not only when the monkey performs an action, but also when the monkey observes the same action performed by someone else (for a recent review, Rizzolatti & Sinigaglia, 2010). A range of neurophysiological studies (e.g., Fadiga, Craighero, & Olivier, 2005; Hamilton & Grafton, 2007) indicate the presence of an analogous mirroring circuitry in the human brain. The human mirror system, which comprises motor areas underlying action execution (pre-motor cortex, inferior parietal lobule), similarly responds to observation of corresponding actions (e.g., Calvo-Merino, Glaser, Grèzes, Passingham, & Haggard, 2005; Hamilton & Grafton, 2007; Kilner, Neal, Weiskopf, Friston, & Frith, 2009).

If action perception and action execution activate common motor representations, one's level of expertise should influence the extent to which action-related brain regions respond to observed actions. For example, watching a figure skater perform a triple somersault should activate a corresponding motor representation in other figure skaters, but less so in speed skaters. Researchers have employed neuroimaging techniques to show increased activity of the mirror circuitry when people observed movements they were able to perform compared with movements that were not in their motor repertoire. In a study involving the use of functional magnetic resonance imaging (fMRI), Calvo-Merino and colleagues (2005) recorded brain activation when expert ballet and capoeira dancers watched ballet and capoeira moves. Higher activation in the observers' mirroring areas was recorded when they watched movements in which they had expertise. Ballet dancers showed more neural activity in action-related regions when watching ballet moves than when watching capoeira moves, and vice versa for capoeira dancers (Figures 13.1 and 13.2). In another fMRI study Cross, Hamilton, and Grafton (2006) monitored changes in mirroring activity as expert dancers learned novel dance sequences over the course of 5 weeks. A higher activation of the mirror circuitry was elicited when

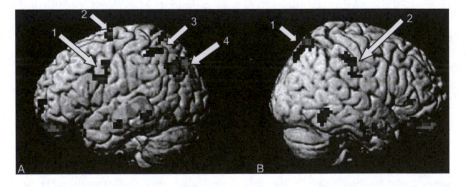

Figure 13.1 Significant neural activations, revealed by the interaction between group (ballet dancers, capoiera dancers, novices) and stimulus (ballet or capoiera moves), are found in areas identified as part of the human mirror system. Panel A: Left hemisphere (1) ventral pre-motor cortex, (2) dorsal pre-motor cortex, (3) intra-parietal sulcus (IPS), and (4) posterior superior temporal sulcus (pSTS). Panel B: Right hemisphere (1) superior parietal lobule (SPL) and (2) IPS. Taken from Calvo-Merino et al. (2005).

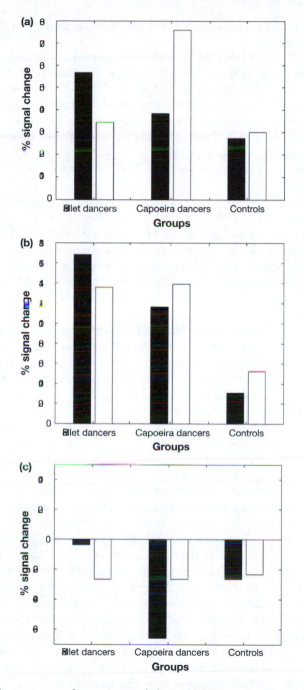

Figure 13.2 Change in neural activity recorded in specific areas that are found significant in the three experimental groups: (a) left premotor cortex, (b) left intra-parietal sulcus (IPS), and (c) left posterior superior temporal sulcus (pSTS). Black bars reflect activations for ballet stimulus and white bars reflect activations for capoeira stimulus. Taken from Calvo-Merino et al. (2005).

the dancers watched sequences that they had learned than when they watched unfamiliar sequences.

It has been proposed that the match between perceived and performed actions allows the observer to simulate observed actions as they unfold in real time (Wilson & Knoblich, 2005; Wolpert, Doya, & Kawato, 2003). The motor system of the observer runs these simulations using internal models, which comprise one's bodily mechanics and previously learned links between actions and their consequences (Wolpert et al., 2003). Simulation theorists posit that the same internal models that guide execution of actions are put into use when observing actions, and these internal models serve predictions about the likely outcomes of the observed actions (Knoblich, 2008).

Studies on motor laws in perception provide evidence for this claim. If the motor system runs simulations of the observed actions, then the motor laws that govern execution of actions should govern their perception in similar ways. For example, Fitts's law (Fitts, 1954), which formulates the speed–accuracy constraints in biological movements, applies to perception of movements as well (Eskenazi, Grosjean, Humphreys, & Knoblich, 2009; Grosjean, Shiffrar, & Knoblich, 2007). Similarly, if internal models are applied to the observed actions, one should be better at predicting the outcome of recordings of one's own actions than at predicting the outcomes of others' actions. This is expected because the match between the observed action effects and the corresponding motor program of the observer is highest when one perceives one's own action effects. A range of studies investigating identification of one's previously recorded actions, for example, clapping (Flach, Knoblich, & Prinz, 2004), dart throwing (Knoblich & Flach, 2001), and piano performance (Repp & Knoblich, 2004), have supported this hypothesis.

The notion of internal models also predicts that sports experts should be better than novices at predicting the outcomes of actions that are part of their action repertoire. Sports experts should even do better than visual experts, such as sports reporters, who have watched particular movements countless times, but are not experts at performing them. To explore this possibility, Aglioti, Cesari, Romani, and Urgesi (2008) compared the ability of professional basketball players and basketball reporters to predict the success of basketball shots. The former group, who had the motor skills required in the action observed, were better at predicting the outcomes of the shots than the reporters who were only visually familiar with basketball moves. Thus, the type of expertise (visual only in reporters versus visual and motor in players) influenced prediction accuracy in action observation (Figure 13.3). A study on deception detection in basketball (Sebanz & Shiffrar, 2007) showed that motor expertise in basketball also helped to infer a player's intention. Basketball experts could tell passes from fakes even when they were only provided with kinematic information about a basketball player's movements through point-light displays. In contrast, novices, who tended to rely on static features such as the position of particular body parts, performed no better than chance on this task.

Internal models may not only serve to predict what others are going to do next, but also help to predict the timing of others' actions, which is crucial for joint action (Sebanz & Knoblich, 2009). The predictive mechanisms people use when

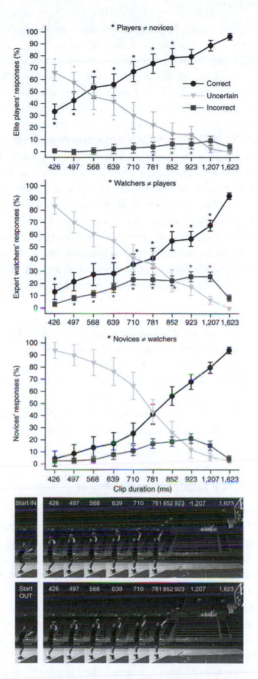

Figure 13.3 Percentages of uncertain, correct, and incorrect responses made by the elite players, expert watchers, and novice groups at different clip durations. Asterisks indicate significant comparisons between elite athletes and novices (upper graph), between expert watchers and elite players (center graph), and between novices and expert watchers (lower graph). Taken from Aglioti et al. (2008).

they perform an action could be used to predict the actions of others, and aid temporal coordination of one's own actions with those of others. An indirect way to test this is to investigate whether people are better able to synchronize with their own earlier actions (as these are the best fit with their internal models) than with the actions of others. To test this idea, expert pianists were asked to perform parts of duet pieces (Keller, Knoblich, & Repp, 2007). The pianists were then asked to coordinate with previously recorded pieces, performed either by themselves or by another pianist. As predicted, the synchronization accuracy was best when the pianists performed a duet with their own recordings, suggesting that it is easier to coordinate with people who are similar to oneself in terms of motor performance. This finding would imply that athletes might achieve better coordination when playing with team members who are at a comparable skill level, and who have learned to perform particular movements in a similar way.

Interpersonal coordination does not necessarily require specific predictions about the actions of others. Actors may also generate predictions about the consequences of the combined effects of their own actions and the actions of others on the environment (Knoblich & Jordan, 2003; Sebanz & Knoblich, 2009). To illustrate, a team of rowers may learn to coordinate strokes by learning to anticipate the combined consequences of their strokes on the movement of the boat, rather than making specific predictions about each other's strokes. This process involves the acquisition of new predictive models during joint practice. A study by Knoblich and Jordan (2003) provides evidence that, through training, it is possible to integrate predictions about one's own actions and the actions of others. Two people coordinating their actions to control a moving object became as coordinated as single individuals performing the same task bimanually, provided there was an opportunity to learn about the consequences of their own and their partner's actions.

Interplay between action simulation and planning

Perception–action matching and action simulation are often considered to be automatic processes. However, researchers have provided evidence that the mechanisms operating when observing another person in action are modulated by the social context. If an observer believes that an action is not produced voluntarily, the tendency to mimic that action, which is taken as a marker for perception–action matching, disappears (Kilner et al., 2003; Liepelt, von Cramon, & Brass, 2008). Liepelt and colleagues (2008) compared mimicry during observation of intended and unintended movements. The observed finger movements were mimicked less when controlled by an external device than when generated voluntarily. In another study, perceptually identical movements interfered with observers' simultaneous movements only when the observers believed they were seeing human movements (Stanley, Gowe, & Miall, 2007; but see Bouquet, Gaurier, Shipley, Toussaint, & Blandin, 2007, for the role of biological motion).

In some cases, the intentions ascribed to individuals can prevail over the tendency to mimic an observed movement. When observing actions incongruent with the intention of an observed actor, people inadvertently perform compensatory movements. In one study, participants were asked to track a ball moving towards a goal on the computer screen, similar to seeing a football approaching the goal (De Maeght & Prinz, 2004). When the ball went too far to the right the participants were found to sway towards the left. In another study, when watching a person balancing on a wobbly surface, participants tilted their bodies in the opposite direction to where the actor was bending (Sebanz & Shiffrar, 2007). This tendency to perform compensatory movements is widespread in fans trying to "push" the ball in the net when watching soccer or ice hockey.

Furthermore, planning to perform a joint action in a complementary context can overrule the tendency to mimic observed actions. In team sports, for example, when one teammate throws the ball at another, the latter does not repeat the throwing action, but executes a complementary action to catch the ball. Van Schie, Van Waterschoot, and Bekkering (2008) studied this in an experimental setup in which participants were asked to perform either an identical or a complementary grasping action. If they saw someone grasping an object at the top with a precision grip, their task could be either to do the same, or to grasp the object at its base with a power grip, as if taking it over from the other person. Under certain conditions, participants showed a tendency to prepare for complementary movements even when they were instructed to imitate the observed movement. This tendency probably reflects our life-long practice of engaging in complementary joint actions such as passing objects to each other. In sport settings, training specific kinds of complementary actions such as a particular throw to a teammate in ball sports, may lead to these complementary actions becoming the "default."

Finally, there is evidence to suggest that the social relation between actor and observer constrains motor simulation. Kourtis, Sebanz, and Knoblich (2010) reported that neural markers reflecting anticipatory motor activation (the late part of the contingent negative variation and the suppression of oscillatory activity in the beta rhythm) were more pronounced when participants were anticipating the action of their interaction partner than when they anticipated the same action to be performed by a third person with whom they never interacted. For a sports context, this implies that the motor system might be especially sensitive to upcoming actions to be performed by teammates with whom one is trying to cooperate.

The nature of the interaction context (cooperative or competitive) may also affect the way in which different cues about an interaction partner's actions are attended to. In a recent study, Streuber, de la Rosa, Knoblish, Sebanz, and Buelthoff (in press) varied the visibility of different sources of visual information and showed that this modulated table tennis performance differently when players played cooperatively or competitively. Participants played table tennis in a dark room with only the ball, net, and table visible while the other's body and/or racket were rendered visible by means of self-glowing markers. In the cooperative condition seeing the other player's racket led to the largest performance increase, whereas in the competitive condition seeing the opponent player's body resulted in the largest performance increase. This indicates that, in a cooperative context, it may be sufficient to rely on ball trajectories (which can be derived from seeing the racket) whereas in a competitive context, in which deception is a possibility, the motor system may be used to simulate the opponent's bodily movements.

Shared task representations

Perception–action coupling is an important component of joint action. However, it does not fully account for performing a joint action successfully. Often, it is necessary to know what a partner's task is and to make predictions about his or her actions based on this knowledge rather than waiting until an action has been initiated. To illustrate with an example from soccer, when the goalkeeper throws a ball to players of his or her own team, the keeper will consider the specific role of the player (defense or attack) towards whom he or she is directing the ball.

Studies on joint task performance suggest that individuals form representations detailing not only their own tasks, but also the task of their interaction partners, even when this is not strictly necessary. One of the initial studies (Sebanz, Knoblich, & Prinz, 2003) demonstrating this used a variant of a spatial compatibility paradigm, known as the Simon paradigm (Simon, 1990; Simon, Hinrichs, & Craft, 1970). In the classical Simon task, the participant is asked to respond to one of two stimulus features, for example the color of the ring on a finger pointing left or right. If the ring is red, a left key press is required; if the ring is green, a right key press is required. The other stimulus feature, the

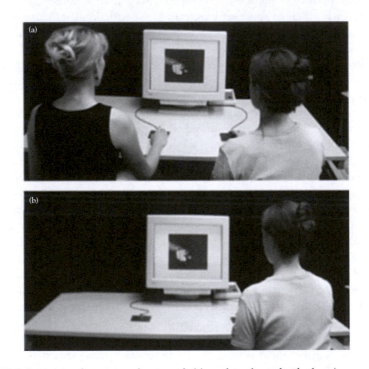

Figure 13.4 Setting in the joint go/no-go task (a), and in the individual go/no-go task (b). Taken from Sebanz et al. (2003).

pointing direction of the finger, is irrelevant to the task. The general finding is that participants are nevertheless slower in responding with the left key when the finger is pointing to the right, and vice versa. Such a compatibility effect occurs because the spatial stimulus feature (pointing direction) automatically activates the spatially corresponding response, which interferes with the correct response as stipulated by the task rules.

In a social version of the Simon paradigm, the authors found the same compatibility effect (Figures 13.4 and 13.5). Two participants performed the task together, and each participant was required to respond to only one of the two colors of the ring placed on the finger. The participant sitting on the left was to respond with the left key press to red, and the one sitting on the right with the right key press to green. In this go/no-go task, the irrelevant stimulus feature (i.e., direction of the pointing finger) still interfered with the participants' response. Importantly, the effect was observed only when participants performed the task with another person. When they performed the same half of the task on their own, the compatibility effect did not occur (Figures 13.4 and 13.5).

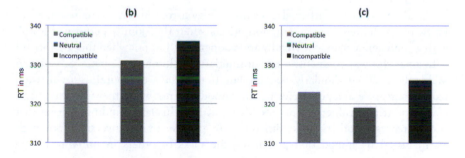

Figure 13.5 Mean reaction times on compatible, neutral, and incompatible trials in (a) the two-choice condition, in which one person performed the whole task, (b) the joint go/no-go condition, in which two people shared the task, and (c) the individual go/no-go condition, in which one person performed one half of the task. Taken from Sebanz et al. (2003).

The above finding indicates that, when performing the task together, participants represented their co-actor's task. This "task sharing" or "task co-representation" effect has been replicated in a number of studies using the same (Sebanz, Knoblich, & Prinz, 2005; Tsai, Kuo, Jing, Hung, & Tzeng, 2006; Welsh, Higgins, Ray, & Weeks, 2007) as well as different paradigms (e.g., SNARC paradigm; Atmaca, Sebanz, Prinz, & Knoblich, 2008). It has been shown that co-representation does not require the actual presence of an interaction partner; the mere belief that another person is performing a particular task is sufficient for representing their task (Tsai et al., 2006). However, when participants were told that a computer was taking care of the other task, this task was not represented (ibid.). Furthermore, a recent study showed that a partner's task is represented only when the partner acts intentionally and not when a machine is controlling his or her actions (Atmaca, Sebanz, & Knoblich, 2011). This may have implications for virtual video games in which people play against another person or a computer.

Besides the perceived intentionality of the co-actor, several other factors have been shown to modulate task co-representation. First, the context in which a social interaction takes places has implications for task performance. Some findings suggest that individuals represent the tasks of their interaction partners in both cooperative and competitive situations as long as their performance is interdependent (de Bruijn, de Lange, von Cramon, & Ulsperger, 2009; Ruys & Aarts, 2010). In an auditory version of the social Simon paradigm (Ruys & Aarts, 2010) a larger effect was found in social contexts where the individual goal to receive a monetary reward was linked to one's task partner (regardless of whether people were cooperating with or competing against the task partner), compared with a context in which individuals' goals were independent of their partner's goals. This finding suggests that task co-representation is not restricted to joint action, but serves a general role in generating predictions about others' actions, be they teammates or opponents. However, there are recent findings to suggest that another's task is represented only in a cooperative setting, but not in a competitive setting (Iani, Anelli, Nicoletti, Arcuri, & Rubichi, 2011).

As a second factor, affect also seems to play a role in task co-representation. Participants showed co-representation effects when they jointly performed a task with a confederate who was friendly and cooperative, but not when they performed with one who was competitive and intimidating (Hommel, Colzato, & van den Wildenberg, 2009). Similarly, co-representation effects were found to occur when participants were in a positive or neutral mood and not when they were in a negative mood (Kuhbandner, Pekrun, & Maier, 2010). This latter finding suggests that people represent others' tasks differently in positive or negative situations with an increased likelihood of representing the tasks of others in non-threatening situations.

Task co-representation may also allow us to monitor others' performance and notice mistakes committed by our interaction partners. It has been shown that processes involved in monitoring our behavior are also involved when observing others. Van Schie, Mars, Coles, and Bekkering (2004) examined the neural mechanisms underlying observation of erroneous actions by means of human event-related potentials (ERP) and reported that observing another's errors elicited a modulation of the same ERP component (error-related negativity, ERN) that is commonly elicited by self-generated errors. In a similar vein, Schuch and Tipper (2007) showed that people become slower and more accurate in their subsequent actions not only following their own errors, but also following an interaction partner's errors. However, error-monitoring processes during observation seem to depend on the relation between actor and observer. In a recent study (de Bruijn et al., 2009) participants were asked to play a computerized game with another person, either together (i.e., cooperation) or against one another (i.e., competition). The authors found that observing others' errors during competition activated reward-related brain regions in the observer.

Although there is much evidence to suggest that similar representations and processes underlie individual and joint task performance, it is important to keep in mind potential differences and limitations. Although representing a co-actor's task leads to the activation of action representations in line with the task to be performed, this does not imply that the actions to be performed by the co-actor are specified all the way in terms of the motor commands to be executed. Rather, task co-representation may be restricted to a higher level of action planning, such that co-representing the other's task would activate the action plan needed to achieve particular effects. This would imply that there may be important differences between individual and joint performance.

In line with this view, researchers investigating transfer effects from individual to joint task performance and vice versa found an interesting asymmetry (Milanese, Iani, & Rubichi, 2010). Practicing the social version of the Simon task together with a co-actor modulated performance on a subsequent joint task. Practicing the whole task alone led to the same modulation in the subsequently performed joint task. However, following joint practice, there was no transfer effect on individual performance of the whole task. This observation suggests that in some ways task representations governing joint actions are different from representations governing individual actions. This conclusion may have important implications for skill learning, suggesting that jointly acquired skills cannot be transferred directly to solo performance. To illustrate, a singles tennis player might be able to transfer his or her skills to a double, whereas someone trained only to play doubles might have difficulties playing singles.

Summary and conclusions

We have reviewed research on basic mechanisms underlying the ability to engage in joint action. Entrainment leads to synchronization of behaviors even in the absence of an intention to coordinate, thus constituting a form of emergent coordination. Apart from fostering synchronization, it may serve joint action by increasing group cohesion. A common coding of perceived and performed actions provides a basis for predicting others' actions by means of motor simulation, with internal models playing an important role in facilitating temporal coordination. The activation of corresponding actions through action perception is modulated by various factors, including the social relation between actor and observer. Finally, the tendency to represent co-actors' tasks serves to predict and monitor their performance.

Team sports form a hallmark case of joint action for which understanding coordination mechanisms bears special significance. Some kinds of sports demand strict synchronization, such as synchronized swimming or high diving. In such cases, emergent coordination could play a central role in the success of joint action. Other kinds of team sports require coordinating the onset of discrete events and anticipating others' actions, such as making a pass in soccer or basketball. In such situations, task co-representation and motor simulation may play a key role because being synchronized is not sufficient. Much is still to be explored to understand how different coordination mechanisms interact for successful joint performance, and to test the extent to which findings from tightly controlled laboratory studies can be generalized to joint action in situ.

Although only a few joint action studies investigated learning processes directly, the research discussed here has several implications for skill acquisition. First, teaching of skills is a social activity in which observational learning and imitation play a big part. The teaching/learning situation shares many elements with joint action (and can even be construed as a particular kind of joint action), involving, for example, shared task and action representations. Considering the impact of interpersonal and inter-group relations on basic processes such as motor simulation and imitation may be useful both when considering teacher–student interactions and when considering exercises to be performed amongst students. To give a concrete example, research on joint task performance has shown that groups mimic actions performed by other groups much more readily than actions performed by single individuals (Tsai, Sebanz, & Knoblich, 2011). This finding suggests that teaching a joint skill is best accomplished through joint demonstration (a practice that of course already exists, for instance, in ballroom dancing). Second, research on transfer effects between different social settings suggests that tasks acquired together may be represented in fundamentally different ways from tasks acquired alone. This observation has implications for designing individual and group exercises, as well as for the training of team sports. Finally, joint action research highlights the importance of studying how groups of individuals learn to coordinate their actions. So far, research suggests that learning joint skills may involve acquiring internal models that specify how one's own actions in the context of others' lead to particular changes in the environment. Further research on joint skill acquisition will help us to better understand the mechanisms underlying the precise interpersonal coordination that is required for many joint actions, be it basketball, acrobatics, or rowing.

References

Aglioti, S. M., Cesari, P., Romani, M., & Urgesi, C. (2008). Action anticipation and motor resonance in elite basketball players. *Nature Neuroscience, 11*(9), 1109–1116.

Amazeen, P. G., Schmidt, R. C., & Turvey, M. T. (1995). Frequency detuning of the phase entrainment dynamics of visually coupled rhythmic movements. *Biological Cybernetics, 72*(6), 511–518.

Atmaca, S., Sebanz, N., & Knoblich, G. (2011). The joint Flanker effect. *Experimental Brain Research, 211*, 371–385.

Atmaca, S., Sebanz, N., Prinz, W., & Knoblich, G. (2008). Action co-representation: The joint SNARC effect. *Social Neuroscience, 3*, 410–420.

Bach, P., & Tipper, S. P. (2007). Implicit action encoding influences personal-trait judgments. *Cognition, 102*, 151–178.

Bouquet, C. A., Gaurier, V., Shipley, T., Toussaint, L., & Blandin, Y. (2007). Influence of the perception of biological or non-biological motion on movement execution. *Journal of Sports Sciences, 25*, 519–530.

Brass, M., Bekkering, H., & Prinz, W. (2001). Movement observation affects movement execution in a simple response task. *Acta Psychologica, 106*, 3–22.

Calvo-Merino, B., Glaser, D., Grèzes, J., Passingham, R., & Haggard, P. (2005). Action observation and acquired motor skills: An fMRI study with expert dancers. *Cerebral Cortex, 15*, 1243–1249.

Clark, H. H. (1996). *Using language.* Cambridge, UK: Cambridge University Press.

Cross, E. S., Hamilton, A. F., & Grafton, S. T. (2006). Building a motor simulation de novo: Observation of dance by dancers. *Neuroimage, 31*, 1257–1267.

de Bruijn, E. R.A., de Lange, F.P, von Cramon, D. Y., & Ulsperger, M. (2009). When errors are rewarding. *Journal of Neuroscience, 29*(39), 12183–12186.

De Maeght, S., & Prinz, W. (2004) Action induction through action observation. *Psychological Research, 68*(2–3), 97–114.

Di Pellegrino, G., Fadiga, L., Fogassi, L., Gallese, V., & Rizzolatti, G. (1992). Understanding motor events: A neurophysiological study. *Experimental Brain Research, 9*, 176–180.

Eaves, D., Hodges, N. J., & Williams, A. M. (2008). Energetic costs of incidental visual coupling during treadmill running. *Medicine & Science in Sports & Exercise, 40*, 1506–1514.

Eskenazi, T., Grosjean, M., Humphreys, G., & Knoblich, G. (2009). The role of motor simulation in action perception: A neuropsychological case study. *Psychological Research, 73*(4), 477–485.

Fadiga, L., Craighero, L., & Olivier, E. (2005). Human motor cortex excitability during the perception of others' action. *Current Opinion in Neurobiology, 15*, 213–218.

Fitts, P. M. (1954). The information capacity of the human motor system in controlling the amplitude of movement. *Journal of Experimental Psychology, 47*(6), 381–391.

Flach, R., Knoblich, G., & Prinz, W. (2004). The two-thirds power law in motion perception: When do motor anticipations come into play? *Visual Cognition, 11*, 461–481.

Ford, P., Hodges, N. J., Huys, R., & Williams, A. M. (2006). The role of external action-effects in the execution of a soccer kick: A comparison across skill-level. *Motor Control, 10*, 386–404.

Ford, P., Hodges, N. J., Huys, R., & Williams, A. M. (2009). Evidence for end-point trajectory planning during a kicking action. *Motor Control, 13*, 1–24.

Ford, P., Hodges, N. J., & Williams, A. M. (2007). Examining the role of action-effects in the execution of a skilled soccer kick through erroneous feedback. *Journal of Motor Behavior, 39*, 481–490.

Gallese, V., Fadiga, L., Fogassi, L., & Rizzolatti, G. (1996). Action recognition in the premotor cortex. *Brain, 119*, 593–609.

Gibson, J. J. (1979). *An ecological approach to visual perception.* Boston: Houghton Mifflin.

Grosjean, M., Shiffrar, M., & Knoblich, G. (2007). Fitts's law holds for action perception. *Psychological Science, 18*(2), 95–99.

Haken, H., Kelso, J. A. S., & Bunz, H. (1985). A theoretical model of phase transitions in human hand movements. *Biological Cybernetics, 51*(5), 347–356.

Hamilton, A., & Grafton, S. (2007). The motor hierarchy: From kinematics to goals and intentions. In Haggard, P., Rosetti, Y., & Kawato, M. (Eds.), *Sensorimotor Foundations of*

Higher Cognition: Attention and Performance, XXII (pp. 381–408). Oxford, UK: Oxford University Press.

Hommel, B., Colzato, L. S., & van den Wildenberg, W. P. M. (2009). How social are task representations? *Psychological Science, 20*, 794–798.

Hommel, B., Müsseler, J., Aschersleben, G., & Prinz, W. (2001). The theory of event coding (TEC): A framework for perception and action. *Behavioral and Brain Sciences, 24*, 849–937.

Hove, M. J., & Risen, J. L. (2009). It's all in the timing: Interpersonal synchrony increases affiliation. *Social Cognition, 27*(6), 947–960.

Huygens, C. (1673/1986). *The pendulum clock or geometrical demonstrations concerning the motion of pendula as applied to clocks.* (Blackwell, R. J., Trans.) Ames: Iowa State University Press.

Huys, R., Daffertshofer, A., & Beek, P. J. (2004). Multiple time scales and multiform dynamics in learning to juggle. *Motor Control, 8*, 188–212.

Iani, C., Anelli, F., Nicoletti, R., Arcuri, L. & Rubichi, S. (2011). The role of group membership on the modulation of joint action. *Experimental Brain Research, 211*, 439–445.

Jeannerod, M. (2001). Neural simulation of action: A unifying mechanism for motor cognition. *NeuroImage, 14*, S103–S109.

Keller, P. E., Knoblich, G., & Repp, B. H. (2007). Pianists duet better when they play with themselves: On the possible role of action simulation in synchronization. *Consciousness and Cognition, 16*(1), 102–111.

Kilner, J. M., Neal, A., Weiskopf, N., Friston, K. J., & Frith, C. (2009). Evidence of mirror neurons in human inferior frontal gyrus. *Journal of Neuroscience, 29*(32), 10153–10159.

Kilner, J. M., Paulignan, Y., & Blakemore, S. J. (2003). An interference effect of observed biological movement on action. *Current Biology, 13*, 522–525.

Knoblich, G. (2008). Bodily and motor contributions to action perception. In Klatzky, R. L., MacWhinney, B., & Behrmann, M. (Eds.), *Embodiment, ego-space, and action* (pp. 45–78). Pittsburgh, PA: Psychology Press.

Knoblich, G., Butterfill, S., & Sebanz, N. (2011). Psychological research on joint action: Theory and data. *Psychology of Learning and Motivation, 54*, 59–101.

Knoblich, G. & Flach, R. (2001). Predicting the effects of actions: Interactions of perception and action. *Psychological Science, 12*, 467–472.

Knoblich, G. & Jordan, S. (2003). Action coordination in groups and individuals: Learning anticipatory control. *Journal of Experimental Psychology: Learning, Memory, & Cognition, 29*, 1006–1016.

Kourtis, D., Sebanz, N., & Knoblich, G. (2010). Favouritism in the motor system: Social interaction modulates action simulation. *Biology Letters, 6*, 758–761.

Kuhbandner, C., Pekrun, R., & Maier, M. (2010) The role of negative affect in the "mirroring" of other person's actions. *Cognition & Emotion, 24*(7), 1182–1990.

Liepelt, R., von Cramon, D. Y., & Brass, M. (2008). What is matched in direct matching? Intention attribution modulates motor priming. *Journal of Experimental Psychology: Human Perception and Performance, 34*(3), 578–591.

Marsh, K. L., Richardson, M. J., & Schmidt, R. C. (2009). Social connection through joint action and interpersonal coordination. *Topics in Cognitive Science, 1*(2), 320–339.

Milanese, N., Iani, C., & Rubichi, S. (2010). Shared learning shapes human performance: Transfer effects in task sharing. *Cognition, 116*(1), 15–22.

Néda, Z., Ravasz, E., Brechet, T., Vicsek, T., & Barabási, A.-L. (2000). Self organizing processes: The sound of many hands clapping. *Nature, 403*, 849–850.

Prinz, W. (1997). Perception and action planning. *European Journal of Cognitive Psychology, 9*, 129–154.

Repp, B. H., & Knoblich, G. (2004). Perceiving action identity: How pianists recognize their own performances. *Psychological Science, 15*, 604–609.

Richardson, D. C., & Dale, R. (2005). Looking to understand: The coupling between the speakers' and listeners' eye movements and its relationship to discourse comprehension. *Cognitive Science, 29*, 1045–1060.

Richardson, M. J., Marsh, K. L., Isenhower, R., Goodman, J., & Schmidt, R. C. (2007). Rocking together: Dynamics of intentional and unintentional interpersonal coordination. *Human Movement Science, 26*, 867–891.

Richardson, M. J., Marsh, K., & Schmidt, R. C. (2005). Effects of visual and verbal interaction on unintentional interpersonal coordination. *Journal of Experimental Psychology: Human Perception and Performance, 31*(1), 62–67.

Rizzolatti, G., & Sinigaglia, C. (2010). The functional role of the parieto-frontal mirror circuit: Interpretations and misinterpretations. *Nature Reviews Neuroscience, 11*, 264–274.

Ruys, K. I., & Aarts, H. (2010). When competition merges people's behavior: Interdependency activates shared action representations. *Journal of Experimental Social Psychology, 46*(6), 1130–1133.

Santvoort, A. A. M., & Beek, P. J. (1999). Spatiotemporal variability in cascade juggling. *Acta Psychologica, 91*, 131–151.

Schmidt, R. C., Bienvenu, M., Fitzpatrick, P. A., & Amazeen, P. G. (1998). A comparison of within- and between-person coordination: Coordination breakdowns and coupling strength. *Journal of Experimental Psychology: Human Perception and Performance, 24*, 884–900.

Schmidt, R. C., Carello, C., & Turvey, M. T. (1990). Phase transitions and critical fluctuations in the visual coordination of rhythmic movements between people. *Journal of Experimental Psychology: Human Perception and Performance, 16*, 227–247.

Schmidt, R. C., Fitzpatrick, P., Caron, R., & Mergeche, J. (2011). Understanding social motor coordination. *Human Movement Science, 30*(5), 834–845.

Schmidt, R. C., & Richardson, M. J. (2008). Dynamics of interpersonal coordination. In Fuchs, A., & Jirsa, V. (Eds.), *Coordination: Neural, Behavioral and Social Dynamics* (vol. 17, pp. 267–292). Berlin: Springer.

Schuch, S., & Tipper, S. P. (2007). On observing another person's actions: Influences of observed inhibition and errors. *Perception & Psychophysics, 69*, 828–837.

Sebanz, N., & Knoblich, G. (2009). Prediction in joint action: What, when, and where. *Topics in Cognitive Science, 1*, 353–367.

Sebanz, N., Bekkering, H., & Knoblich, G. (2006). Joint action: Bodies and minds moving together. *Trends in Cognitive Science, 10*(2), 70–76.

Sebanz, N., Knoblich, G., & Prinz, W. (2003). Representing others' actions: Just like one's own? *Cognition, 88*, B11–B21.

Sebanz, N., Knoblich, G., & Prinz, W. (2005). How two share a task. *Journal of Experimental Psychology: Human Perception and Performance, 31*(6), 1234–1246.

Sebanz, N., & Shiffrar, M. (2007). Bodily bonds: Effects of social context on ideomotor movements. In Haggard, P., Rossetti, Y., & Kawato, M. (Eds.), *Sensorimotor Foundations of Higher Cognition: Attention and Performance, XXII* (pp. 267–292). Oxford, UK: Oxford University Press.

Shockley, K., Santana, M. V., & Fowler, C. A. (2003). Mutual interpersonal postural constraints are involved in cooperative conversation. *Journal of Experimental Psychology: Human Perception and Performance, 29*(2), 326–332.

Simon, J. R. (1990). The effects of irrelevant directional cue on human information processing. In Proctor, R. W., & Reeve, T. G. (Eds.), *Stimulus–response compatibility* (pp. 31–86). North Holland: Elsevier Science Publishers.

Simon, J. R., Hinrichs, J. V., & Craft, J. L. (1970). Auditory S–R compatibility: Reaction time as a function of ear–hand correspondence and ear–response–location correspondence. *Journal of Experimental Psychology, 86*(1), 97–102.

Stanley, J., Gowen, E., & Miall, R. C. (2007). Effects of agency on movement interference during observation of a moving dot stimulus. *Journal of Experimental Psychology: Human Perception and Performance, 33*(4), 915–992.

Streuber, S., Knoblich, G., Sebanz, N. Buelthoff, H. H., & de la Rosa, S. (2011). The effect of social context on the use of visual information. *Experimental Brain Research, 214*(2), 273–284.

Tsai, C.-C., Kuo, W.-J., Jing, J.-T., Hung, D. L., & Tzeng, O. J.-L. (2006). A common coding framework in self–other interaction: Evidence from joint action task. *Experimental Brain Research, 175*, 353–362.

Tsai, J. C., Sebanz, N., & Knoblich, G. (2011). The GROOP effect: Groups mimic group actions. *Cognition, 118*(1), 135–140.

Valdesolo, P., Ouyang, J., & De Steno, D. (2010). The rhythm of joint action: Synchrony promotes cooperative ability. *Journal of Experimental Psychology, 46*(4), 693–695.

Van Schie, H. T., Mars, R. B., Coles, M. G. H., & Bekkering, H. (2004). Modulation of activity in medial frontal and motor cortices during error observation. *Nature Neuroscience, 7*(5), 549–554.

Van Schie, H. T., Van Waterschoot, B. M., & Bekkering, H. (2008). Understanding action beyond imitation: Reversed compatibility effects of action observation in imitation and joint action. *Journal of Experimental Psychology: Human Perception and Performance, 34*(6), 1493–1500.

Van Ulzen, N. R., Lamoth, C. J., Daffertshofer, A., Semin, G. R., & Beek, P. J. (2008). Characteristics of instructed and uninstructed interpersonal coordination while walking in pairs. *Neuroscience Letters, 432*(2), 88–93.

Welsh, T., Higgins, L., Ray, M., & Weeks, D. (2007) Seeing vs. believing: Is believing sufficient to activate the processes of response co-representation? *Human Movement Science, 26*(6), 853–866.

Wilson, M., & Knoblich, G. (2005). The case for motor involvement in perceiving conspecifics. *Psychological Bulletin, 131*, 460–473.

Wiltermuth, S. S., & Heath. C. (2009). Synchrony and cooperation. *Psychological Science, 20*(7), 904–911.

Wolpert, D. M., Doya, K., & Kawato, M. (2003). A unifying computational framework for motor control and interaction. *Philosophical Transactions of the Royal Society of London B, 358*, 593–602.

14 Motor skill learning and its neurophysiology

Katie P. Wadden, Michael R. Borich, and Lara A. Boyd

Introduction

An explosion of research over the past decade has clearly established that changes in both brain physiology and anatomy underpin the learning of new, and the modification of existing, motor skills. Although we are still discovering precisely what changes in the brain are associated with specific motor behaviors, the concept of a dynamically changing or "neuroplastic" brain that supports motor learning is now unquestioned. In this chapter we highlight key discoveries in neurophysiology that elucidate how brain function shapes motor learning; these discoveries span animal models to human research. We focus on three main areas of work that have particular relevance for the acquisition of motor skill in sport. First, we discuss the physiological mechanisms involved in the induction of long-term changes in the brain that enable us to store and retrieve memories for later use. Second, we review the neurophysiology associated with short-term, within-session change in motor behavior (i.e., performance) and long-term, more permanent change in the capability for responding (i.e., motor learning). In conjunction with this discussion, we consider what neural regions are associated with the varied stages of motor learning. Finally, we take into account how networks of brain regions act in concert to support motor skill learning.

Motor learning and neuroplasticity

Motor learning is the acquisition of a new behavior through skilled practice, resulting in a relatively permanent change in the ability of an individual to perform a movement (Salmoni, Schmidt, & Walter, 1984; Schmidt & Lee, 2011). Once a skilled movement is learned, the ability to perform the skill should be robust and stable. Experience, practice, or change in behavior stimulates the brain to reorganize; this process is known as "neuroplasticity" (Nudo, 2006). Neuroplasticity, in the context of motor learning, refers to changes in neural organization associated with skilled practice or modifications of movement patterns (Berlucchi & Buchtel, 2009). When a skill is repeatedly practiced, neural changes occur as a result of functional reorganization across many brain regions (Karni et al., 1998). This process enables athletes to not just maintain, but also improve, skilled movement. Neuroplastic changes in the brain may occur at the molecular, cellular, synaptic, network, and/or regional levels of the brain.

Synaptic plasticity

The idea of neuroplasticity is not new and was first discussed by William James in 1890 (James, 1890). Charles Scott Sherrington (Sherrington, 1897) introduced the concept that within the neural pathways of the central nervous system the terminal element of a neuron, called a synapse, transmits a signal that can be altered by experience. The theory of neuroplasticity was furthered by Ramón y Cajal (1909–1911), who first proposed the concept of a dynamic nervous system. Nearly 40 years passed before Hebbian learning (Hebb, 1949) was outlined, stipulating that the connectivity between two neurons is strengthened when they are activated simultaneously (Bi & Poo, 2001). The direct relationships among changes in synapses, patterns of activity across the whole brain, and behavior have remained elusive, largely owing to the difficulty of studying synaptic activity in the mammalian brain.

One model for investigating changes in synaptic connections associated with learning has been the gill- and siphon-withdrawal reflex of *Aplysia californica*. Study of this adult sea slug revealed that both pre- and post-synaptic changes occur between sensory and motor neuron connections during motor learning; this provides direct evidence that experience-dependent neuroplasticity contributes to learning (Antonov, Antonova, Kandel, & Hawkins, 2003). Through the *Aplysia* model it was discovered that synaptic connections between the neuron strengthen as a result of behavioral experience (Antonov, Kandel, & Hawkins, 2010).

Long-term potentiation and depression

Lasting changes in synaptic strength result from repetitive stimulation of excitatory synapses (Bliss & Lomo, 1973). This process is known as long-term potentiation (LTP). Synaptic strengthening also results from associated activity across connected neurons. When a neuron is stimulated it excites adjacent neurons; in this fashion, patterns of coordinated activity induce synaptic strengthening within neuronal networks (Sjostrom, Rancz, Roth, & Hausser, 2008). The first experiments identifying LTP were performed using granule cells of the hippocampus (a structure required for conscious memory formation for facts and events); brief trains of high-frequency stimulation to excitatory pathways in anaesthetized animal, or in the in-vitro hippocampal slice preparation, cause a sustained increase in synaptic transmission (Bliss & Collingridge, 1993).

Following initial potentiation, LTP induces an early phase that lasts for 1–3 hours and a later phase that involves both intracellular gene translation and protein transcription (Reymann & Frey, 2007). In the early phase, following high-frequency stimulation of synapses, release of the neurotransmitter glutamate binds on two different postsynaptic receptors (N-Methyl-D-asparate [NMDA] and α-amino-3-hydroxyl-5-methyl-4-isoxazolepropionic acid [AMPA]). LTP is rapidly triggered when the NMDA receptor is activated by the depolarization of the postsynaptic cell. In rodents, blocking NMDA receptors induces spatial learning deficits, providing evidence that synaptic plasticity is an important component in memory formation (Morris, 1989).

The inverse of LTP, long-term depression (LTD), is a weakening of the net efficacy of a synapse due to the repetitive unsuccessful firing of a pre-synaptic neuron on a post-synaptic neuron. The effect can lead to a lasting experience-dependent decrease in synaptic efficacy (Mulkey & Malenka, 1992). LTD may underlie the process of "forgetting" and/or the removal of certain behaviors. It may also serve as a homeostatic mechanism; if LTP strengthens synapses then a reverse mechanism, LTD, must act to weaken synaptic activity to maintain a balance between potentiation and depression. This adaptation prevents the experience-dependent saturation of synapses during learning over time (Cooke & Bliss, 2006).

The LTP correlates with growth of new projections, or dendritic spines, at the post-synaptic neuron. The expansion of dendritic spines associated with skilled practice strengthens neural pathways and promotes long-term memory formation by increasing the efficacy of pre-synaptic activity on post-synaptic behavior (Lamprecht & LeDoux, 2004). The LTP induces changes in the dendrites, including altering the numbers and shapes of their spines (Harris, 1999; Yu & Zuo, 2011). Morphological changes in the dendrites are associated with opening of NMDA and AMPA channels following LTP, whereas synaptic depression associated with LTD causes dendritic spine shrinkage and retraction (Dur-e-Ahmad, Imran, & Gul, 2010). This process can occur rapidly; 30 minutes of LTP can result in measurable morphological changes in dendritic spines (Engert & Bonhoeffer, 1999).

Motor learning in rodents also leads to structural modifications of the neuron including increases in dendritic branching and in the number of synapses per neuron (Greenough, Larson, & Withers, 1985; Kleim, Hogg, VandenBerg, Cooper, Bruneau, & Remple, 2004). In particular, motor learning strengthens connections between neurons within the primary motor cortex (Harms, Rioult-Pedottie, Carter, & Dunaevsky, 2008). The motor cortex is a brain area that controls movement of the body; importantly it is organized somatotopically (an ordered representation of body region). Skill learning leads to expansions in the size of cortical representations of the body part being used for a specific movement (Monfils & Teskey, 2004). For example, skilled violinists have large finger representations in the motor cortex (Elbert, Pantev, Wienbruch, Rockstroh, & Taub, 1995). This expansion is attributed to the formation of new synapses in the motor cortex associated with extensive, skilled motor practice (Kleim et al., 2004).

Critically, neuroplastic change in the brain is extremely dependent upon practice of skilled movements (Nudo, 2006). Changes in cortical representation of body parts and the induction of LTP/LDP are distinctively driven by the type of skilled motor practice and do not simply result from repetitive or increased general motor use of a body part (Boyd, Vidoni, & Wessel, 2010; Kleim et al., 2004). Thus, neuroplasticity in the brain is dependent on both skill and learning. Given this, any intervention designed to facilitate sport performance must be focused on skilled movement; repetitive or non-specific use alone is not likely to facilitate long-term changes in the underlying neuroanatomical or neurophysiological systems.

Experience-dependent plasticity

In humans, changes in brain in response to skill training can be measured by advanced neuroimaging techniques, such as functional magnetic resonance imaging (fMRI) and electroencephalography (EEG), that reflect learning-related reorganization of patterns of brain activity. Tools that index brain excitability (i.e., transcranial magnetic stimulation, TMS; see Figure 14.1) also assess learning-dependent changes in brain behavior. These approaches can provide unique insights into brain behavior associated with motor learning.

An athlete often demonstrates significant within-session improvements when practicing a new skill. Termed "fast learning" (Doyon & Benali, 2005), the rate of change within a session can be impressive; however, this does not necessarily translate to maintained improvements in motor skill. With practice across training sessions, improvement commonly plateaus and the slope of change associated with learning is reduced (Karni et al., 1998). This "slow learning" phase (Doyon & Benali, 2005) can continue for long periods of time. Following the conclusion of a practice session, motor memories may be strengthened or enhanced by an offline process known as *consolidation*, referring to the process of memory stabilization, and in some cases enhancement, that allows successful skill retrieval at a later date and resistance to interference from competing memories (Brashers-Krug et al., 1996). A key question centers on why the speed of change associated with motor skill acquisition varies within and across practice sessions. Neurophysiology provides the answer. Rapid changes in the amount and location of neurotransmitters, within and between the neurons of the brain, support fast learning (Nudo, 2006); whereas the structural modifications enabling new contacts between neurons underpin slow

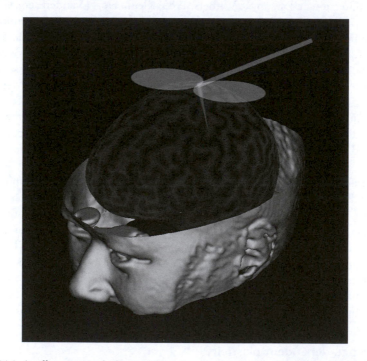

Figure 14.1 An illustration of a figure-eight transcranial magnetic stimulation (TMS) coil positioned over the left primary motor cortex (pointer) of a magnetic resonance imaging (MRI)-generated three-dimensional curvilinear reconstruction of the brain.

learning (Kleim et al., 2004). Because altering neuron structure requires more time than does reallocating neurotransmitters, rates of change in behavior associated with learning vary between early and late learning (Karni et al., 1998).

Importantly, different networks of brain regions appear to support fast and slow learning, as well as the intermediate step of consolidation. When an athlete begins initial skill acquisition during the fast learning phase, the cortico-striatal and cortico-cerebellar anatomical systems are primarily recruited (Doyon & Benali, 2005). With practice, the athlete enters the slow phase of learning and these two systems contribute equally to different aspects of skilled performance (Orban et al., 2010). At this time, the neural correlates of memory consolidation are less clear.

Neural correlates of motor learning

When a coach begins to teach a new skill to an athlete, it may be initially practiced as a series of isolated components that, with practice, are combined to form a complete sequence of movements. This process is known as *sequence learning*. If the coach instructs the athlete to modify an aspect of the skill, the athlete must change his or her motor commands to adapt to changes in motor output and sensory input known as *sensorimotor adaptation* (Seidler, 2010). Different motor commands are required for kicking a rolling ball with an increased force output toward a long-range target in comparison with kicking a stationary ball with reduced force output toward a short-range target. In this chapter we use sequence learning and sensorimotor adaptation as examples of the skill acquisition process. Sequence skill learning and sensorimotor adaptation occur through distinct neural processes, which are further segregated depending on the phases of learning as illustrated in Figure 14.1.

Frontal cortex

During the initial stages of motor skill learning, the athlete uses a significant amount of cognitive resources that are reflected in brain activity patterns. The frontal cortex is associated with attention to motor action; this region is highly active in early learning when the athlete relies on the processing of visual and proprioceptive sensory information for correct motor performance (Debaere, Wenderoth, Sunaert, van Hecke, & Swinnen, 2004; Meehan, Randhawa, Wessel, & Boyd, 2011). With practice, the athlete eventually combines distinct, individual movements into single behavioral units known as motor chunks. Chunking allows for faster, more efficient movements because only one motor plan has to be operationalized (Sakai, Hikosaka, & Nakamura, 2004). As motor chunks are formed, the frontal cortex initiates working-memory processes within subcortical areas to facilitate storage of these units of movements for later retrieval (McCarthy et al., 1994). The frontal cortex is also activated early in sensorimotor adaptation, as the athlete relies on cognitive processes associated with spatial attention and spatial working memory (Seidler, 2010). Comparing brain areas associated with the pre-performance of an archery routine between world-class archers and non-athletes showed that the frontal cortex was significantly more active in non-athletes during aiming (Kim et al.,

2008). With practice, as movements become more automatic, brain activity shifts from the frontal cortex to subcortical brain areas such as the basal ganglia (Jenkins, Brooks, Nixon, Frackowiak, & Passingham, 1994).

Basal ganglia

The basal ganglia are made of up several subcortical brain areas including the caudate nucleus, putamen, globus pallidus, substantia nigra, and subthalamic nucleus. These structures are key for motor learning, sending direct output to the motor cortical regions (Middleton & Strick, 2000). The basal ganglia are critical for switching among different motor responses, an essential function for sequence learning (Harrington & Haaland, 1991). Several lines of evidence demonstrate that the basal ganglia are integrally involved in the advanced preparation of plans, or programs, for movement (Jennings, 1995; Stelmach, Worringham, & Strand, 1987). Activity in the basal ganglia has been associated with motor learning during a continuous implicit motor sequence task (Boyd et al., 2009; Boyd & Winstein, 2004).

Cerebellum

Another key region for motor skill acquisition is the cerebellum. It has been postulated that the role of the cerebellum is in the development of predictive models of movement that detect discrepancies between planned and actual sensory feedback resulting from a movement (Wolpert, Miall, & Kawato, 1998); these functions are key for sensorimotor adaptation. Cerebellar activity is largely absent when sensory feedback is unavailable during imagined movements, but is present when actual movement occurs (Nair, Purcott, Fuchs, Steinberg, & Kelso, 2003). Altering the control parameters to produce unexpected discrepancies between predicted and actual movement during visuomotor tracking increases cerebellar activation (Flament, Ellermann, Kim, Ugurbil, & Ebner, 1996).

Primary motor cortex

The primary motor cortex is capable of rapid and long-lasting reorganization of representations (Hess & Donoghue, 1994). The primary motor cortex has been shown to be highly influenced by experience-dependent inputs known to induce physiologic reorganization of limb representation in cortical tissue that correlate with improvements in motor function (Nudo, Milliken, Jenkins, & Merzenich, 1996). Recruitment of additional synapses enlarges the cortical region involved in controlling skilled movements, and these expansions have been observed both anatomically and physiologically (Kleim, 2011). Novelty and complexity of movement are key factors driving learning-dependent changes. For example, long-term cortical synaptogenesis and motor map reorganization were observed following repetitive training of a complex motor task involving skilled reaching movements, but not general increases in motor activity (Kleim et al., 2004; Kleim, Lussnig, Schwartz, Comery, & Greenough, 1996). During the initial phase of learning, it is believed that altering the effectiveness of existing synapses via increases in neuronal excitability supports neuroplasticity (Rioult-Pedotti, Friedman, Hess, & Donoghue, 1998). Changes in synaptic number follow later; when the rate of gain in performance is much lower (Kleim et al., 2004). In the later stages of learning dendritic growth and enhanced synaptic responses occur within the forelimb representation of the motor cortex generating morphological changes and training-induced alterations in synaptic efficacy (Monfils & Teskey, 2004).

Non-invasive TMS can be used to study neuroplasticity in humans through activation of the primary motor cortex using a brief high-current pulse sent through a magnetic coil placed above the scalp (Barker, Jalinous, & Freeston, 1985; see Figure 14.2). This technique trans-synaptically activates cortical outputs, producing a muscle response known as a motor-evoked potential (MEP), a common measure of cortical excitability (Rothwell, 1997). Cortical excitability increases in elite basketball players and expert basketball spectators while they observe a video of basketball shots, compared with when they watch static images of basketball players or videos of soccer kicks, and in comparison with novice spectators (Aglioti, Cesari, Romani, & Urgesi, 2008). Thus, task-specific learning associated with extensive practice may fine-tune the motor system in elite athletes (Aglioti et al., 2008). It appears that motor cortex reorganization supporting motor learning requires linkage of the sensory and motor experience. Electrically induced sensory feedback (peripheral stimulation of the muscle) accompanied by passive movements does not stimulate neuroplastic change (Ziemann, Muellbacher, Hallett, & Cohen, 2001), whereas cortical excitability and reorganization of muscle representation maps within the primary motor cortex have been demonstrated after skilled motor training in humans (Classen, Leipert, Wise, Hallett, & Cohen, 1998). Individuals who practiced a one-handed, five-finger exercise on the piano had significantly greater enlargements in the cortical representations of finger flexor and extensor muscles than control participants who increased hand use without specific skill learning (Pascual-Leone, Wassermann, Sadato, & Hallett, 1995). Similarly, comparing muscle representations in elite volleyball players to runners revealed larger cortical representations of the shoulder muscles (Tyc, Boyadjian, & Devanne, 2005). Runners showed no significant difference in hemisphere representation of the motor cortex whereas the volleyball players had larger representational maps for their dominant striking limb.

Currently, extensive evaluation of an athlete's cardiovascular fitness, muscular strength, coordination, balance, flexibility, and sport-specific skill are performed. Soon it may be possible that neuroimaging of the brain will provide elite athletes with a new assessments of skill learning and performance. Could future work allow the evaluation of changes in cortical representation and excitability following training? Neurophysiology and sport is an exciting and expanding field showing great promise for the advancement of elite athletic evaluation.

Although a number of brain areas are associated with distinct phases and task-specific modes of motor learning, they rarely operate in isolation but rather act together as networks of activity. Therefore, we will now focus on the roles of two key networks known to be important for motor learning: the cortico-striatal and cortico-cerebellar systems (Figure 14.3).

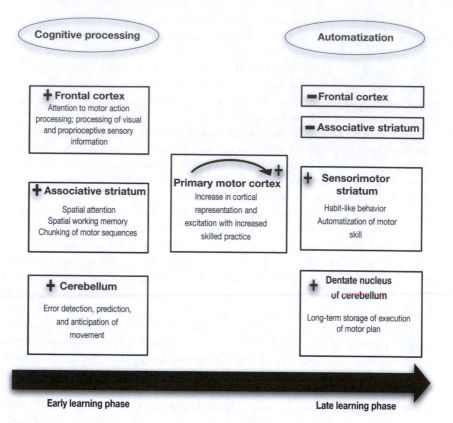

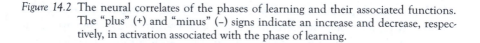

Figure 14.2 The neural correlates of the phases of learning and their associated functions. The "plus" (+) and "minus" (–) signs indicate an increase and decrease, respectively, in activation associated with the phase of learning.

Plasticity of the cortico-striatal pathway

The striatum is a subcortical structure within the basal ganglia receiving cortical inputs consisting of (1) the *associative striatum*, which receives input from the temporal lobes and prefrontal cortex and includes the caudate nucleus and the anterior putamen, and (2) the *sensoriomotor striatum*, which receives input from the parietal lobes, and motor and pre-motor cortex, and includes all of the putamen except the anterior portion (Ashby, Turner, & Horvitz, 2010). During early performance, the athlete engages in goal-directed behavior whereby the motor actions are consciously performed to achieve desirable goals (e.g., serving a tennis ball inside the service area) or to avoid undesirable outcomes (such as hitting the ball into the net). Extensive practice of the skill allows for a level of automaticity whereby the athlete now has the ability to perform consistently with limited variability, although this may have associated costs as discussed below.

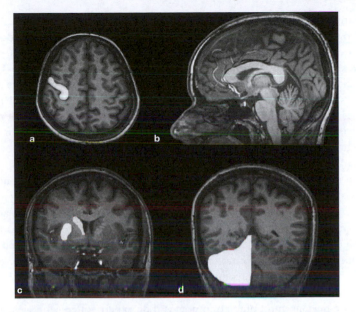

Figure 14.3 Anatomical MRI images with region of interest (ROI) drawings in radiological space. (a) ROI of the right primary motor cortex in the transverse view. (b) Mid-sagittal view of the brain. (c) ROI of the right caudate (medial) and putamen (lateral) in the coronal view. (d) ROI of the right cerebellum in the coronal view.

The associative striatum (dorsomedial; mainly located in the caudate nucleus) has increased activation during early learning relative to late (Lehericy et al., 2005). This change probably supports cognitive strategies and working memory (Jueptner et al., 1997). The sensoriomotor striatum (dorsolateral; mainly located in the putamen) supports habit-like behaviors and appears to reorganize dynamically to enable long-term representation of skilled actions (Lehericy et al., 2005). The sensorimotor striatum receives direct projections from the pre-motor and primary motor cortex and, thus, increased activation in this region with practice may be a direct result of the integration of signals associated with goal-directed learning (Ashby et al., 2010).

Changes in cortico-striatal synaptic efficacy are important for the regulation of excitatory input to the basal ganglia, playing a key role in long-term synaptic plasticity (Partridge, Tang & Lovinger, 2000; Spencer & Murphy, 2000). During learning the striatum releases the neurotransmitter dopamine, which affects neuronal firing patterns and allows for cortico-striatal plasticity by stimulating LTP or LTD (Centonze, Saulle, Bernardi, & Calabresi, 2001).

During motor learning, the dopaminergic system plays a role in the selection and execution of movements, and in the process of shifting a behavior toward becoming automatic (Badgaiyan, Fischman, & Alpert, 2007; Tremblay et al., 2010). The dopamine-mediated reward system contributes to fine-tuning readjustments in the intermediate phase of learning, facilitating new and adaptable control of movements (Paquet et al., 2008). Following repeated practice, the dopamine-mediated reward signals strengthen active cortico-striatal synapses by increases in dopamine neurotransmitter discharge rates in response to conditioned rewards such as feedback (Doya 2007; Schultz 2002). When these rewards are removed, dopamine signals are depressed and, as a result, activated cortico-striatal synapses undergo LTD, weakening synaptic strength (Wickens, Horvitz, Costa, & Killcross, 2007). Thus, striatal cells that undergo LTP associated with successful behaviors produce a highly selective activation pattern within specific networks of striatal neurons (Ashby et al., 2010). Over the duration of goal-directed learning the number of active striatal neurons decreases as their activity becomes focused within a select group whose activation is time-locked to task-related events (Barnes, Kubota, Hu, Jin, & Graybiel, 2005).

When an athlete learns a new skill it is important that the dopamine-mediated reward system be active during the new sequence of movements. By using feedback regarding the outcome of actions, such as accurately hitting a target, an athlete is able to associate the correct action with success. This change leads to increased neural signaling within the dopaminergic system. The sensory, motor, and higher-level association areas are connected to both the frontal cortex and the striatum, which in turn are highly interconnected with each other (Petrides & Pandya, 2006; Wise, Murray, & Gerfen, 1996). In an fMRI study, greater activation was noted in the caudate nucleus and putamen in novice than expert golfers who were asked to actively plan and imagine performing a pre-shot routine (Milton, Solodkin, Hlustik, & Small, 2007). The authors proposed that, even when mentally performing, the novice golfers' imagined movements were in the early phase of learning whereas the experts had already automatized their pre-shot routine (Milton et al., 2007). Active planning for novice athletes appears to be more cognitive and demands greater activation of the associative striatum than for expert athletes. Similarly, the volume of striatum (putamen and caudate nucleus) in elite basketball players is significantly greater than it is in non-athletes matched for height (Park et al., 2010). As expert athletes continuously rely on shifting from acquiring new skills to automaticity of practiced skills, one would expect greater morphological change due to plasticity. In an unpublished study, we have shown that implicit sequence motor learning is associated with greater activation of the caudate nucleus following 5 days of tracking practice among older adults (Figure 14.4). These data support the idea that the striatum is central for learning and automatization of skills that require repetitive practice. A key input for the reorganization of the cortical-striatal system is feedback regarding performance during skilled practice and may be particularly important during early learning.

Plasticity of the cortico-cerebellar pathway

The role of the cerebellum during motor learning has been closely associated with the early phase of learning. Cerebellar activity decreases with practice as the sequence of movements becomes more automated (Doyon et al., 1998). However, the dentate nucleus, a portion of the cerebellum that is connected to the primary motor cortex, has been shown to be active in the slow phase of learning (Doyon et al., 2002). This is an example of the complex network of processes involved in

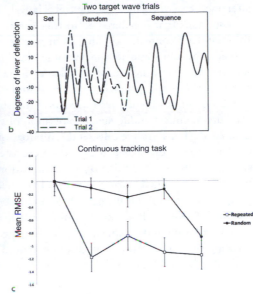

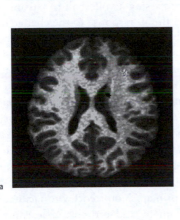

Figure 14.4 Neural correlates of implicit sequence specific learning in older adults. Unpublished data from the Boyd lab (2011). (a) fMRI of the brain. The arrow pointing to the blackened area indicates significant increased activation of the caudate nuclei during implicit sequence specific learning in older adults. (b) The continuous tracking task performed across multiple days of practice. The task involved the tracking of a repeated and random sequence with a joystick. (c) For normalized mean RMSE, greater improvements in performance during repeated compared with random sequence tracking were shown (p = 0.05).

learning whereby differential processing roles exist even within the homogeneous structure of the cerebellum. Previously, it was thought that the cortico-striatal and cortico-cerebellar system worked in parallel but contributed uniquely to motor sequence learning and motor adaptation (Doyon, Penhune, & Ungerleider, 2003). However, we now understand that both the basal ganglia and the cerebellum have recurrent projections to overlapping cortical areas. It is believed that these parallel channels work in a complementary fashion (Doya, 2000).

Learning is initiated in the cerebellar cortex by recognition of cell-firing patterns and then proceeds into the deeper nuclei, where long-term storage by means of plasticity occurs (Jorntell & Hansel, 2006). Numerous paradigms support this notion, including studies of adaptation of eye reflexes that stabilize gaze by countering movement of the head (Maekawa & Simpson, 1972) and classical eye-blink conditioning (Mauk, Steinmetz, & Thompson, 1986). Plasticity and memory in the cerebellum result from LTD in the Purkinje cell synapses (Ito, Sakurai, & Tongroach, 1982). The Purkinje cells in the cerebellum receive two types of excitatory neuronal inputs: parallel and climbing fibers. Climbing fibers send input signals to depress simultaneously active Purkinje cells in the cerebellum in response to error or to alter motor performance (Jorntell & Hansel, 2006). Parallel fibers are activated by a stimulus that is habituated to trigger a response (Thompson & Kim, 1996). In an athletic context, switching from practicing passing a volleyball to passing a basketball would stimulate the climbing fibers to fire in response to the change in sensory input (i.e., the weight and shape of the ball). Motor learning occurs as the climbing fibers and parallel fibers fire simultaneously on the Purkinje cells. This process continuously depresses synaptic transmission from the parallel fibers to the Purkinje fibers, inducing reorganization of the neuronal network through LTD (Ito, 2000). The Purkinje cells send inhibitory output signals to the deep cerebellar nuclei to refine the signals necessary to execute a motor program. The inhibitory signals are based on prediction or anticipation derived from past experience of the behavior formed during practice. This mechanism allows the cerebellum to proactively send inhibitory signals to modify behavior prior to skilled movement production (Koziol, Budding, & Chidekel, 2010).

The striatum and cerebellum work with the primary motor cortex to facilitate learning of skilled movement through reinforcement and error-based learning. Expert rugby and basketball players have been shown to be superior to novices in detecting deceptive actions when an attacking player fakes a cut or when a player fakes a pass (Jackson, Warren, & Abernethy, 2006). It is hypothesized that during action observation the athlete's motor system may become active as a predictive mechanism to anticipate the opponent's intentions (Sebanz & Shiffrar, 2009). Of future interest would be the evaluation of brain activation in these areas during action observation of correct and incorrect sport performance in the various phases of learning. Is activity in the striatum during a well-executed movement correlated significantly with real-life athletic performance in athletes? Do athletes who show more activity in the cerebellum during incorrect execution of a motor skill perform better in real life? These are a few of the questions that might be considered by merging the fields of neurobiology and motor learning in athletes.

Pathways for research in sport

Much of our understanding of how the brain functions during learning comes from controlled laboratory settings. For researchers, coaches, and athletes in the area of elite sport performance, the question of ecological validity arises. How well can we transfer models of neural processes involved in "theoretical" motor learning with that involved in elite athletic training? It is well known that the psychological processes of elite athletes differ greatly from that of amateur and novice athletes when practicing their domain specific motor skills (Baker, Cote, & Abernethy, 2003). For example, in the later phase of learning, automatization of motor skills is associated with an overall reduction in cortical activation that has been suggested to reveal experience-related improvements in processing efficiency (Gobel, Parrish, & Reber, 2011). According to the theory of deliberate practice proposed by Ericsson, Krampe, and Tesch-Romer (1993), athletes who become experts in their domain actively seek ways to resist the development of automaticity in order to continuously enhance their performance. Expert athletes strive to increase speed, accuracy, and control of their motor skills, raising their performance standards (Ericsson, 2008). In contrast, amateur athletes who participate in sport for enjoyment may not seek out improvement strategies as readily and thus will remain in the automatization stage. It has been shown that amateur singers use less concentration and focus during a singing lesson than expert singers, who actively increase their concentration (Grape, Sandgren, Hansson, Ericson, & Theorell, 2003). This strategy may be key for the continued refinement of motor skills. Active engagement in a task maintains a high level of neural engagement, stimulating synaptic plasticity (Kimberley et al., 2008).

In future, researchers interested in the neurophysiology of motor skill acquisition in sport should begin to investigate differences in neural networks associated with novice and expert performance in real-world domain-related activities in concert with the phase of learning. When a decrease in cortical activation is evident the athlete is likely to be entering the automatization stage and motor learning has potentially plateaued. Thus the next phase in the exploration of skill acquisition in athletic performance is the optimization of practice paradigms driven by measures of cortical activation. As cortical activation decreases there should be an increase in the complexity of the task in order to resist automatization of motor learning both behaviorally and neurologically. However, as stated by Ericsson (2008), there should be limits on the amount of deliberate practice (cognitively demanding practice) an athlete incorporates into his or her training regime. Athletes report not being able to participant in deliberate practice if they are incapable of sustaining a level of concentration needed for the cognitively demanding training. Investigating the neural networks and cortical activation levels associated with cognitively demanding training (frequency, intensity, time, type) that yield optimal performance outcomes compared with excessive demands that may lead to "burnout," or minimal demands that do not improve performance, would be of interest. With advancements in neurophysiology techniques, supplementary information may become available that can complement other measures of performance such as cardiovascular fitness, muscular strength, and endurance.

Conclusions

Repeatedly performing motor skills in practice and game settings stimulates experience-dependent plasticity throughout the brain. These changes are the result of alterations in the brain behavior at the cellular, synaptic, and regional levels of organization. Critically, neuroplastic change to support motor learning at all levels of expertise and performance is stimulated by experience and practice that is skill-specific and mediated by feedback and reward systems. Changes in the neural structures that support learning and athletic performance do not occur without specific skilled behavioral practice. Discoveries about the neural underpinnings of how elite athletes learn will continue to advance our understanding of the impact of highly repetitive motor training on an extremely adaptable nervous system. Furthermore, this work may help reveal how elite athletes consistently and successfully perform highly skilled, complex movements during competition. As advanced techniques used to image brain behavior continue to be refined, the neural processes underlying sport-specific performance are increasingly available for inquiry. These advances will offer novel breakthroughs for future training and evaluation strategies aimed at maximizing sport-specific skill learning.

References

Aglioti, S. M., Cesari, P., Romani, M., & Urgesi, C. (2008). Action anticipation and motor resonance in elite basketball players. *Nature Neuroscience, 11*, 1109–1116.

Antonov, I., Antonova, I., Kandel, E. R., & Hawkins, R. D. (2003). Activity-dependent presynaptic facilitation and hebbian LTP are both required and interact during classical conditioning in *Aplysia*. *Neuron, 37*, 135–147.

Antonov, I., Kandel, E. R., & Hawkins, R. D. (2010) Presynaptic and postsynaptic mechanisms of synaptic plasticity and metaplasticity during intermediate-term memory formation in *Aplysia*. *Journal of Neuroscience, 30*, 5781–5791.

Ashby, F. G., Turner, B. O., & Horvitz, J. C. (2010) Cortical and basal ganglia contributions to habit learning and automaticity. *Trends in Cognitive Sciences, 14*, 208–215.

Badgaiyan, R. D., Fischman, A. J., & Alpert, N. M. (2007). Striatal dopamine release in sequential learning. *Neuroimage, 38*, 549–556.

Baker, J., Cote, J., & Abernethy, B. (2003). Learning from the experts: Practice activities of expert decision makers in sport. *Research Quarterly for Exercise & Sport, 74*, 342–347.

Barker, A. T., Jalinous, R., & Freeston, I. L. (1985). Non-invasive magnetic stimulation of human motor cortex. *The Lancet, 1*, 1106–1107.

Barnes, T. D., Kubota, Y., Hu, D., Jin, D. Z., & Graybiel, A. M. (2005). Activity of striatal neurons reflects dynamic encoding and recoding of procedural memories. *Nature, 437*, 1158–1161.

Berlucchi, G., & Buchtel, H. A. (2009). Neuronal plasticity: Historical roots and evolution of meaning. *Experimental Brain Research/Experimentelle Hirnforschung/Experimentation cerebrale, 192*, 307–319.

Bi, G., & Poo, M. (2001). Synaptic modification by correlated activity: Hebb's postulate revisited. *Annual Review of Neuroscience, 24*, 139–166.

Bliss, T. V., & Collingridge, G. L. (1993). A synaptic model of memory: Long-term potentiation in the hippocampus. *Nature, 361*, 31–39.

Bliss, T. V., & Lomo, T. (1973). Long-lasting potentiation of synaptic transmission in the dentate area of the anaesthetized rabbit following stimulation of the perforant path. *Journal of Physiology, 232*, 331–356.

Boyd, L. A., Edwards, J. D., Siengsukon, C. S., Vidoni, E. D., Wessel, B. D., & Linsdell, M. A. (2009). Motor sequence chunking is impaired by basal ganglia stroke. *Neurobiology of Learning and Memory, 92*, 35–44.

Boyd, L. A., Vidoni, E. D., & Wessel, B. D. (2010). Motor learning after stroke: Is skill acquisition a prerequisite for contralesional neuroplastic change? *Neuroscience Letters, 482*, 21–25.

Boyd, L. A., & Winstein, C. J. (2004). Providing explicit information disrupts implicit motor learning after basal ganglia stroke. *Learning & Memory, 11*, 388–396.

Brashers-Krug, T., Shadmehr, R., & Bizzi, E. (1996). Consolidation in human motor memory. *Nature, 382*, 252–255.

Centonze, D., Saulle, E., Bernardi, G., & Calabresi, P. (2001). Receptor and post-receptor mechanisms of ischemic long-term potentiation in the striatum. *Functional Neurology, 16*, 149–152.

Classen, J., Liepert, J., Wise, S. P., Hallett, M., & Cohen, L. G. (1998). Rapid plasticity of human cortical movement representation induced by practice. *Journal of Neurophysiology, 79*, 1117–1123.

Cooke, S. F., & Bliss, T. V. (2006). Plasticity in the human central nervous system. *Brain, 129*, 1659–1673.

Debaere, F., Wenderoth, N., Sunaert, S., Van Hecke, P., & Swinnen, S. P. (2004). Cerebellar and premotor function in bimanual coordination: parametric neural responses to spatiotemporal complexity and cycling frequency. *Neuroimage, 21*, 1416–1427.

Doya, K. (2000). Complementary roles of basal ganglia and cerebellum in learning and motor control. *Current Opinion in Neurobiology, 10*, 732–739.

Doya, K. (2007). Reinforcement learning: Computational theory and biological mechanisms. *HFSP Journal, 1*, 30–40.

Doyon, J., & Benali, H. (2005). Reorganization and plasticity in the adult brain during learning of motor skills. *Current Opinion in Neurobiology, 15*, 161–167.

Doyon, J., Laforce, R., Jr., Bouchard, G., Gaudreau, D., Roy, J., Poirier, M., et al. (1998). Role of the striatum, cerebellum and frontal lobes in the automatization of a repeated visuomotor sequence of movements. *Neuropsychologia, 36*, 625–641.

Doyon, J., Penhune, V., & Ungerleider, L. G. (2003). Distinct contribution of the cortico-striatal and cortico-cerebellar systems to motor skill learning. *Neuropsychologia, 41*, 252–262.

Doyon, J., Song, A. W., Karni, A., Lalonde, F., Adams, M. M., & Ungerleider, L. G. (2002). Experience-dependent changes in cerebellar contributions to motor sequence learning. *Proceedings of the National Academy of Sciences of the United States of America, 99*, 1017–1022.

Dur-e-Ahmad, M., Imran, M., & Gul, A. (2010). Calcium dynamics in dendritic spines: A link to structural plasticity. *Mathematical Biosciences, 230*, 55–66.

Elbert, T., Pantev, C., Wienbruch, C., Rockstroh, B., & Taub, E. (1995). Increased cortical representation of the fingers of the left hand in string players. *Science, 270*, 305–307.

Engert, F., & Bonhoeffer, T. (1999). Dendritic spine changes associated with hippocampal long-term synaptic plasticity. *Nature, 399*, 66–70.

Ericsson, K. A. (2008). Deliberate practice and acquisition of expert performance: A general overview. *Academic Emergency Medicine, 11*, 988–994.

Ericsson, K. A., Krampe, R. T., & Tesch-Romer, C. (1993). The role of deliberate practice in the acquisition of expert performance. *Psychological Review, 100*(3), 363–406.

Flament, D., Ellermann, J. M., Kim, S. G., Ugurbil, K., & Ebner, T. J. (1996). Functional magnetic resonance imaging of cerebellar activation during the learning of a visuomotor dissociation task. *Human Brain Mapping, 4*, 210–226.

Gobel, E. W., Parrish, T. B., & Reber, P. J. (2011). Neural correlates of skill acquisition: Decreased cortical activity during a serial interception sequence learning task. *Neuroimage, 58*, 1150–1157.

Grape, C., Sandgren, M., Hansson, L. O., Ericson, M., & Theorell, T. (2003). Does singing promote well-being?: An empirical study of professional and amateur singers during a singing lesson. *Integrative Physiological and Behavioral Science, 38*, 65–74.

Greenough, W. T., Larson, J. R., & Withers, G. S. (1985). Effects of unilateral and bilateral training in a reaching task on dendritic branching of neurons in the rat motor-sensory forelimb cortex. *Behavioral and Neural Biology, 44*, 301–314.

Harms, K. J., Rioult-Pedotti, M. S., Carter, D. R., & Dunaevsky, A. (2008). Transient spine expansion and learning-induced plasticity in layer 1 primary motor cortex. *Journal of Neuroscience, 28,* 5686–5690.

Harrington, D. L., & Haaland, K. Y. (1991). Sequencing in Parkinson's disease: Abnormalities in programming and controlling movement. *Brain: A Journal of Neurology, 114*(1A), 99–115.

Harris, K. M. (1999). Structure, development, and plasticity of dendritic spines. *Current Opinion in Neurobiology, 9,* 343–348.

Hebb, D. O. (1949). *The organization of behavior.* New York: Wiley & Sons.

Hess, G., & Donoghue, J. P. (1994). Long-term potentiation of horizontal connections provides a mechanism to reorganize cortical motor maps. *Journal of Neurophysiology, 71,* 2543–2547.

Ito, M. (2000). Mechanisms of motor learning in the cerebellum. *Brain Research, 1–2,* 237–245.

Ito, M., Sakurai, M., & Tongroach, P. (1982). Climbing fibre induced depression of both mossy fibre responsiveness and glutamate sensitivity of cerebellar Purkinje cells. *Journal of Physiology, 324,* 113–134.

Jackson, R. C., Warren, S., & Abernethy, B. (2006). Anticipation skill and susceptibility to deceptive movement. *Acta Psychologica (Amsterdam), 123,* 355–371.

James, W. (1890). *The principles of psychology, vol. 1.* New York: Henry Holt.

Jenkins, I. H., Brooks, D. J., Nixon, P. D., Frackowiak, R. S., & Passingham, R. E. (1994). Motor sequence learning: A study with positron emission tomography. *Journal of Neuroscience, 14,* 3775–3790.

Jennings, P. J. (1995). Evidence of incomplete motor programming in Parkinson's disease. *Journal of Motor Behavior, 27,* 310–324.

Jorntell, H., & Hansel, C. (2006). Synaptic memories upside down: Bidirectional plasticity at cerebellar parallel fiber–Purkinje cell synapses. *Neuron, 52,* 227–238.

Jueptner, M., Stephan, K. M., Frith, C. D., Brooks, D. J., Frackowiak, R. S., & Passingham, R. E. (1997). Anatomy of motor learning. I: Frontal cortex and attention to action. *Journal of Neurophysiology, 77,* 1313–1324.

Karni, A., Meyer, G., Rey-Hipolito, C., Jezzard, P., Adams, M. M., Turner, R., & Ungerleider, L. G. (1998). The acquisition of skilled motor performance: Fast and slow experience-driven changes in primary motor cortex. *Proceedings of the National Academy of Sciences of the United States of America, 95,* 861–868.

Kim, J., Lee, H. M., Kim, W. J., Park, H. J., Kim, S. W., Moon, D. H., et al. (2008). Neural correlates of pre-performance routines in expert and novice archers. *Neuroscience Letters, 445,* 236–241.

Kimberley, T. J., Lewis, S. M., Strand, C., Rice, B. D., Hall, S., & Slivnik, P. (2008). Neural substrates of cognitive changes during a motor task in subjects with stroke. *Journal of Neurologic Physical Therapy, 32,* 110–117.

Kleim, J. A. (2011). Neural plasticity and neurorehabilitation: Teaching the new brain old tricks. *Journal of Communication Disorders, 44,* 521–528.

Kleim, J. A., Hogg, T. M., VandenBerg, P. M., Cooper, N. R., Bruneau, R., & Remple, M. (2004). Cortical synaptogenesis and motor map reorganization occur during late, but not early, phase of motor skill learning. *Journal of Neuroscience, 24,* 628–633.

Kleim, J. A., Lussnig, E., Schwarz, E. R., Comery, T. A., & Greenough, W. T. (1996). Synaptogenesis and Fos expression in the motor cortex of the adult rat after motor skill learning. *Journal of Neuroscience, 16,* 4529–4535.

Koziol, L. F., Budding, D. E., & Chidekel, D. (2010). Adaptation, expertise, and giftedness: towards an understanding of cortical, subcortical, and cerebellar network contributions. *Cerebellum, 9,* 499–529.

Lamprecht, R., & LeDoux, J. (2004). Structural plasticity and memory. *Nature Reviews Neuroscience, 5,* 45–54.

Lehericy, S., Benali, H., Van de Moortele, P. F., Pelegrini-Issac, M., Waechter, T., Ugurbil, K., & Doyon, J. (2005). Distinct basal ganglia territories are engaged in early and advanced motor sequence learning. *Proceedings of the National Academy of Sciences of the United States of America, 102,* 12566–12571.

Maekawa, K., & Simpson, J. I. (1972). Climbing fiber activation of Purkinje cells in the flocculus by impulses transferred through the visual pathway. *Brain Research, 39,* 245–251.

Mauk, M. D., Steinmetz, J. E., & Thompson, R. F. (1986). Classical conditioning using stimulation of the inferior olive as the unconditioned stimulus. *Proceedings of the National Academy of Sciences of the United States of America, 83,* 5349–5353.

McCarthy, G., Blamire, A. M., Puce, A., Nobre, A. C., Bloch, G., Hyder, F., et al. (1994). Functional magnetic resonance imaging of human prefrontal cortex activation during a spatial working memory task. *Proceedings of the National Academy of Sciences of the United States of America, 91,* 8690–8694.

Meehan, S. K., Randhawa, B., Wessel, B., & Boyd, L. A. (2011). Implicit sequence-specific motor learning after subcortical stroke is associated with increased prefrontal brain activations: an fMRI study. *Human Brain Mapping, 32,* 290–303.

Middleton, F. A., & Strick, P. L. (2000). Basal ganglia and cerebellar loops: Motor and cognitive circuits. *Brain Research: Brain Research Reviews, 31,* 236–250.

Milton, J., Solodkin, A., Hlustik, P., & Small, S. L. (2007). The mind of expert motor performance is cool and focused. *Neuroimage, 35,* 804–813.

Monfils, M. H., & Teskey, G. C. (2004). Skilled-learning-induced potentiation in rat sensorimotor cortex: A transient form of behavioural long-term potentiation. *Neuroscience, 125,* 329–336.

Morris, R. G. (1989). Synaptic plasticity and learning: Selective impairment of learning rats and blockade of long-term potentiation in vivo by the N-methyl-D-aspartate receptor antagonist AP5. *Journal of Neuroscience, 9,* 3040–57.

Mulkey, R. M., & Malenka, R. C. (1992). Mechanisms underlying induction of homosynaptic long-term depression in area CA1 of the hippocampus. *Neuron, 9,* 967–975.

Nair, D. G., Purcott, K. L., Fuchs, A., Steinberg, F., & Kelso, J. A. (2003). Cortical and cerebellar activity of the human brain during imagined and executed unimanual and bimanual action sequences: a functional MRI study. *Brain Research Cognitive Brain Research, 15,* 250–260.

Nudo, R. J. (2006). Plasticity. *NeuroRx: The Journal of the American Society for Experimental NeuroTherapeutics, 3,* 420–427.

Nudo, R. J., Milliken, G. W., Jenkins, W. M., & Merzenich, M. M. (1996). Use-dependent alterations of movement representations in primary motor cortex of adult squirrel monkeys. *Journal of Neuroscience, 16,* 785–807.

Orban, P., Peigneux, P., Lungu, O., Albouy, G., Breton, E., Laberenne, F., et al. (2010). The multifaceted nature of the relationship between performance and brain activity in motor sequence learning. *Neuroimage, 49,* 694–702.

Paquet, F., Bedard, M. A., Levesque, M., Tremblay, P. L., Lemay, M., Blanchet, P. J., et al. (2008). Sensorimotor adaptation in Parkinson's disease: Evidence for a dopamine dependent remapping disturbance. *Experimental Brain Research, 185,* 227–236.

Park, I. S., Lee, K. J., Han, J. W., Lee, N. J., Lee, W. T., Park, K. A., & Rhyu, I. J. (2010). Basketball training increases striatum volume. *Human Movement Science, 30*, 56–62.

Partridge, J. G., Tang, K. C., & Lovinger, D. M. (2000). Regional and postnatal heterogeneity of activity-dependent long-term changes in synaptic efficacy in the dorsal striatum. *Journal of Neurophysiology, 84*, 1422–1429.

Pascual-Leone, A., Wassermann, E. M., Sadato, N., & Hallett, M. (1995). The role of reading activity on the modulation of motor cortical outputs to the reading hand in Braille readers. *Annals of Neurology, 38*, 910–915.

Petrides, M., & Pandya, D. N. (2006). Efferent association pathways originating in the caudal prefrontal cortex in the macacque monkey. *The Journal of Comparative Neurology, 498*, 227–251.

Ramón y Cajal, S. (1909–1911). Histologie du systeme nerveux de l'homme et des vertebres. Maloine: Paris.

Reymann, K. G., & Frey, J. V. (2007). The late maintenance of hippocampal LTP: Requirements, phases, "synpatic tagging", "late associativity" and implications. *Neuropharmacology, 52*, 24–40.

Rioult-Pedotti, M. S., Friedman, D., Hess, G., & Donoghue, J. P. (1998). Strengthening of horizontal cortical connections following skill learning. *Nature Neuroscience, 1*, 230–234.

Rothwell, J. C. (1997). Techniques and mechanisms of action of transcranial stimulation of the human motor cortex. *Journal of Neuroscience Methods, 74*, 113–122.

Sakai, K., Hikosaka, O., & Nakamura, K. (2004). Emergence of rhythm during motor learning. *Trends in Cognitive Sciences, 8*, 547–553.

Salmoni, A. W., Schmidt, R. A., & Walter, C. B. (1984). Knowledge of results and motor learning: A review and critical reappraisal. *Psychological Bulletin, 95*, 355–386.

Schmidt, R. A., & Lee, T. D. (2011). *Motor control and learning: A behavioral emphasis* (5th edn.). Champaign, IL: Human Kinetics.

Schultz, W. (2002). Getting formal with dopamine and reward. *Neuron, 36*, 241–263.

Sebanz, N., & Shiffrar, M. (2009). Detecting deception in a bluffing body: The role of expertise. *Psychonomic Bulletin and Review, 16*, 170–175.

Seidler, R. D. (2010). Neural correlates of motor learning, transfer of learning, and learning to learn. *Exercise and Sport Sciences Reviews, 38*, 3–9.

Sherrington, C. S. (1897). *The central nervous system* (7th edn.). Part III (Foster, M., Ed.). London: Macmillan.

Sjostrom, P. J., Rancz, E. A., Roth, A., & Hausser, M. (2008). Dendritic excitability and synaptic plasticity. *Physiological Reviews, 88*, 769–840.

Spencer, J. P., & Murphy, K. P. (2000). Bi-directional changes in synaptic plasticity induced at corticostriatal synapses in vitro. *Experimental Brain Research, 135*, 497–503.

Stelmach, G. E., Worringham, C. J., & Strand, E. A. (1987). The programming and execution of movement sequences in Parkinson's disease. *International Journal of Neuroscience, 36*, 55–65.

Thompson, R. F., & Kim, J. J. (1996). Memory systems in the brain and localization of a memory. *Proceedings of the National Academy of Sciences of the United States of America, 93*, 13438–13444.

Tremblay, P. L., Bedard, M. A., Langlois, D., Blanchet, P. J., Lemay, M., & Parent, M. (2010). Movement chunking during sequence learning is a dopamine-dependant process: A study conducted in Parkinson's disease. *Experimental Brain Research, 205*, 375–385.

Tyc, F., Boyadjian, A., & Devanne, H. (2005). Motor cortex plasticity induced by extensive training revealed by transcranial magnetic stimulation in human. *European Journal of Neuroscience, 21*, 259–266.

Wickens, J. R., Horvitz, J. C., Costa, R. M., & Killcross, S. (2007). Dopaminergic mechanisms in actions and habits. *Journal of Neuroscience, 27,* 8181–8183.

Wise, S. P., Murray, E. A., & Gerfen, C. R. (1996). The frontal cortex–basal ganglia system in primates. *Critical Reviews in Neurobiology, 10,* 317–356.

Wolpert, D. M., Miall, R. C., & Kawato, M. (1998). Internal models in the cerebellum. *Trends in Cognitive Sciences, 2,* 338–347.

Yu, X., & Zuo, Y. (2011). Spine plasticity in the motor cortex. *Current Opinion in Neurobiology, 21,* 169–174.

Ziemann, U., Muellbacher, W., Hallett, M., & Cohen, L. G. (2001). Modulation of practice-dependent plasticity in human motor cortex. *Brain: A Journal of Neurology, 124,* 1171–1181.

Part IV

Skilled performance

15 The development of skill in sport

Jean Côté, Jennifer Murphy-Mills, and Bruce Abernethy

In this chapter we contrast two approaches to talent development in sport. The first approach is centered on a deliberate practice-oriented model in which early specialization in one sport is the main feature of talent development. The second approach is centered on a late specialization model that considers the interaction of skill development with psychosocial variables and the sampling of various sports during childhood. We draw a working distinction between learning activities that are typically regarded as *practice or training* and those that may be more accurately regarded as *play*, and draw a contrast between the concepts of *early specialization* and *early sampling* for the acquisition of skill in sport.

Practice and play

We have used the term *practice* for organized activities in which the principal focus is on skill development and performance enhancement and the term *play* to describe activities undertaken primarily for intrinsic enjoyment, but which may nevertheless ultimately contribute to the acquisition of skills (Côté, Baker, & Abernethy, 2007). Although practice is uniformly regarded in the motor learning literature as the variable having the greatest singular influence on skill acquisition, there remains a host of unanswered questions about how much and what type of practice is necessary and/or is best for the development of expertise. Much of the experimental work on the relationship between practice conditions, learning, and performance has been conducted using laboratory tasks in which the changes in performance are recorded over a relatively small number of trials of practice in which untrained individuals (novices) are used as participants. Such approaches have proven useful in addressing motor learning of new skills (see Lee, Chamberlin & Hodges, 2001), yet they have contributed less to the understanding of the long-term development of sport skills. This relative lack of impact is largely because the acquisition and performance of sport skills may require literally millions of trials and typically a decade or more of regular, sustained practice to acquire. Because experimental work examining the acquisition of skills in a prospective, longitudinal manner is fraught with logistical difficulties, the bulk of knowledge regarding the relationship between practice quantity and type has come, by necessity, from studies in which the practice histories of experts are determined retrospectively. Much of this work has been profoundly influenced by the conceptualization of deliberate practice as the single type of activity leading to elite performance in sport (Ericsson, Krampe, & Tesch-Römer, 1993).

Ericsson and colleagues (1993) produced a seminal paper on the role of practice and expert development that shaped a great deal of the research that followed. Their position (based on work of Simon & Chase, 1973, and others) was that with due attention to what they called "deliberate practice" one could prevent performance improvements from leveling off, thus circumventing the asymptotic effects that underpin the power law of practice. Deliberate practice was operationalized as any training activity (1) undertaken with the specific purpose of increasing performance (e.g., not for enjoyment or external rewards); (2) requiring cognitive and/or physical effort; and (3) relevant to promoting positive skill development. Ericsson et al. (1993) suggested, on the basis of an intensive examination of the training and performance of elite musicians, that the relationship between time spent in deliberate practice and performance was monotonic (i.e., linear) rather than a power function. Moreover, they contended that the primary factor distinguishing performers at different skill levels was the number of hours spent in deliberate practice, thus attributing it a causal role in the attainment of expertise. For instance, in their examination of violinists, experts had accumulated over 7,400 hours of deliberate practice by 18 years of age, compared with 5,300 hours for intermediate-level performers and 3,400 hours for lower-level performers.

Although the original data and conceptual arguments were based on work with musicians, Ericsson and his colleagues have repeatedly contended that it also applies to the development of expertise in other domains, including sport. There is a body of evidence to support this contention (e.g., Deakin & Cobley, 2003; Helsen, Starkes, & Hodges, 1998; Hodges & Starkes, 1996; Starkes, Deakin, Allard, Hodges, & Hayes, 1996). There is, however, some controversy about definitional aspects of deliberate practice, especially in relation to the contention that practice must be deliberate in order to be beneficial, and to the proposition that practice alone rather than in combination with other activities or hereditary factors sets the limits to performance (see, for example, Abernethy, Farrow, & Berry, 2003; Baker & Horton, 2004; Sternberg, 1996).

Recognizing that athletes tend to first experience sport through fun and playful games, Côté (1999) coined the term *deliberate play* to characterize a form of sporting activity that involves early developmental physical activities that are intrinsically motivating, provide immediate gratification, and are specifically designed to maximize enjoyment. Deliberate play activities, such as street hockey or backyard soccer, are regulated by rules adapted from standardized sport rules and are set up and monitored by the participants themselves. It is a form of sport activity that differs from (1) the physical play activities of infancy and early childhood (Denzin, 1975; Pellegrini & Smith, 1998; Piaget, 1962); (2) the specific pedagogical games/play designed to improve performance (Griffin & Butler, 2005; Launder, 2001); (3) the structured practice activities typical of organized sport; and (4) deliberate practice activities (Ericsson et al., 1993).

Practice and play activities in youth sport can be conceptualized along a continuum that shows how much instruction and input is vested by the adult (i.e., coach) versus the youth. At one end of the continuum are sport activities in which adults have minimal roles in providing instructions, as in play activities. At the other end are sport activities in which adults set the direction and provide the instruction in a structured environment, such as the structured practices and competitions of organized sport.

Early specialization and sampling

The early specialization approach to talent development has gained popularity in the last few years because of the work of Ericsson and colleagues (1993) on deliberate practice. In their original study, Ericsson et al. (1993) proposed that non-expert violinists could not catch up to expert violinists since the latter group had started deliberate practice at an earlier age and had accumulated more total hours of deliberate practice throughout development. Furthermore, Ericsson and colleagues (1993) proposed that violinists need to accumulate approximately 10,000 hours of deliberate practice to become experts. Those who advocate early specialization believe that investment in deliberate practice in one activity from a young age distinguishes future experts from non-experts. Advocates of early specialization within the sport domain also propose that the timing at which deliberate practice begins is imperative for elite performance since some skills and movements (e.g., extending the back when pitching in baseball) are best developed before the body physiologically matures (e.g., bones calcify; Ericsson, 2003). It is apparent that commitment to large quantities of deliberate practice in one sport from a young age (early specialization) is one approach to developing elite athletes. For example, researchers (Helsen, Hodges, Van Winckel, & Starkes, 2000; Helsen et al., 1998; Ward, Hodges, Williams, & Starkes, 2004) have found support for the relationship between the amount of deliberate practice and the attainment of expertise across a variety of sports.

A number of researchers, however, have demonstrated that some athletes who had diversified sport backgrounds and engaged in deliberate play during childhood still reached an elite level in sport (e.g., Baker, Côté, & Abernethy, 2003b; Baker, Côté, & Deakin, 2005; Berry, Abernethy, & Côté, 2008; Bloom, 1985; Carlson, 1988; Soberlak & Côté, 2003). Early *sampling* was defined as participation in a wide variety of sports that involve high levels of deliberate play and low levels of deliberate practice (Côté, Baker, & Abernethy, 2003; Côté, Baker, & Abernethy, 2007). A diversified approach to early athlete development may not be at odds with monotonic or power profiles of the practice/proficiency relationship. During the initial stages of development, increases in performance occur on account of rapid improvement in general capabilities. With prolonged practice and training over time, improvements become much more specific and more difficult to attain. During the initial exposure to the task, however, the same general adaptations may be produced through similar activities that share the same elements. For instance, Abernethy, Baker, and Côté (2005) showed that experts from different sports consistently outperformed non-experts in their recall of defensive player positions, suggesting that some selective transfer of pattern recall skills may be possible. From a physical conditioning point of view, childhood involvement in running or cycling will produce the same general physiological adaptations (e.g., increases in blood volume and maximal cardiac output) as sport-specific involvement. Once general cognitive or physical adaptations have been made through play and involvement in various sport activities during childhood, training should become more specific.

When considering the dichotomy of early specialization and sampling, it is apparent that both approaches can lead to expertise development under optimal conditions. Although experts typically accumulate more hours of sport-specific practice than non-experts by the time they reach national level competition as adults, some retrospective studies have indicated that these differences between elite and less elite athletes do not occur until adolescence (Baker et al., 2003a; Berry, Abernethy, & Côté, 2008; Hodges & Starkes, 1996). On the other hand, other retrospective studies (Helsen et al., 1998; Ward, Hodges, Starkes, & Williams, 2007) showed that the accumulated amount of structured practice discriminated between soccer players' skill levels in Europe as early as age 7. Higher amounts of training at earlier ages are also a discriminator between elite and less elite athletes in sports in which peak performance occurs before biological maturation or adulthood, such as women's gymnastics (Law, Côté, & Ericsson, 2007) and women's figure skating (Deakin & Cobley, 2003). However, as will be indicated later, this level of involvement during early periods of development can have significant negative consequences for continued sport participation and can ultimately affect the number of prospects available for talent development programs.

Athlete development models

Over the last three decades, a number of athlete development models that integrate the concepts of practice/play and early specialization/sampling have been proposed. Alfermann and Stambulova (2007) highlighted and reviewed five research-based models (Bloom, 1985; Côté, 1999; Salmela, 1994; Stambulova, 1994; Wylleman & Lavallee, 2004). More recently, Bruner, Erickson, Wilson, and Côté (2010) conducted a citation network analysis and revealed two additional models published in peer-reviewed journals (Abbott & Collins, 2004; Bailey & Morley, 2006).

One of the earliest models of expertise development emerged from Bloom's (1985) examination of experts in disciplines such as mathematics, art, science, and sport. Bloom utilized qualitative, retrospective interviews to describe the life story of these talented individuals. A general pattern of development was inferred to be characterized by three stages: (1) initiation stage, in which the individual becomes involved in the activity and is identified as talented; (2) development stage, in which the individual becomes committed to the activity and the levels of training and specialization are increased; and (3) perfection stage, in which the activity becomes the center of the individual's life and the individual reaches his or her highest level of proficiency. The existence of such stages suggests that individuals must tackle the unique challenges associated with each stage and successfully transfer between stages. Although Bloom's (1985) model does not specifically focus on sport, the influence of this early model can still be seen today, as a recent citation analysis found that Bloom's (1985) *Developing Talent in Young People* is the most prominently cited text within the athlete development literature (Bruner, Erickson, McFadden, & Côté, 2009).

Building upon the work of Bloom (1985), the athlete development models proposed by Salmela (1994), Stambulova (1994), and Wylleman and Lavallee (2004) provide complementary ways of conceptualizing the pathway to athletic excellence. Salmela (1994) and Wylleman and Lavallee (2004) identified normative transitions occurring between the stages of initiation, development, perfection, and discontinuation. The model put forth by Stambulova (1994) suggests that the athletic career is characterized by five stages: (1) preparatory stage; (2) beginning of specialization; (3) intensive training in chosen sport; (4) culmination stage; and (5) the final stage, followed by discontinuation. Whereas all three models were designed to characterize the different stages of athlete development, Stambulova's (1994) and Wylleman and Lavallee's (2004) models were constructed to depict key transitions in an athlete's career. Wylleman and Lavallee's (2004) developmental model also integrates athlete development with three other levels of development: (1) psychological; (2) psychosocial; and (3) academic-vocational, to encourage researchers to take into account athletes' demands and transitions outside the sport environment.

The models proposed by Abbott and Collins (2004) and Bailey and Morley (2006) challenge researchers to broaden the conceptualization of athlete development. Abbott and Collins (2004) emphasize the influence of psychosocial behaviors in facilitating successful transitions. According to Abbott and Collins (2004), an athlete's ability to travel along the talent development pathway is shaped by the development and application of mental skills such as goal setting and imagery. They suggest that psychomotor (e.g., hand–eye coordination, balance) and physical (e.g., height, muscle composition) factors can either facilitate or inhibit an athlete's ability to successfully negotiate developmental transitions, but that it is crucial to place early and continual emphasis on the development of key psycho-behavioral strategies.

The model proposed by Bailey and Morley (2006) was derived from empirical research investigating the processes of talent development within the physical education, rather than sport, setting (e.g., Bailey, Dismore, & Morley, 2009; Bailey, Tan, & Morley, 2004). These authors sought to gain a greater understanding of the perspectives of teachers, students, and policymakers regarding the nature, content, and character of the talent development process in physical education and to identify the strategies used to foster development. Based on a series of studies, three main hypotheses have been put forward. The first relates to the differentiation between potential and performance. Like Abbott and Collins (2002), the authors contend that current performance is a poor indicator of ability since it can be mediated by a myriad of other influences, such as inherited abilities, training, support, parental investment, and social values. The second hypothesis is that talent development needs to be viewed as a multi-dimensional construct that stems from the emergence of a wide range of abilities (including interpersonal, intrapersonal, cognitive, and creative ability). The third hypothesis is that practice plays an important role in fostering talent development.

Although all these models provide a wealth of insightful information regarding athlete development, it is important to outline their limitations. First, the majority of these models fail to provide testable tenets that can enhance our understanding of athlete development. For instance, there is a lack of information relating to the quantifiable components that characterize each stage of development. Second, several of the models encompass variables that are difficult to test retrospectively, such as psychosocial behaviors (Abbott & Collins, 2004) or an athlete's potential (Bailey & Morley, 2006). A third limitation is that many of the stage-based models (e.g., Bloom, 1985; Stambulova, 1994) comprise qualitative stages that are hard to define. For example, although Stambulova (1994) suggests that athletic careers are characterized by five stages, it is unclear what indicators could be employed to track transitions between these stages. Thus, these development models have been atheoretical or descriptive in nature, providing no account of individual differences in attained performance among top-level athletes with similar developmental opportunities. As a result, the knowledge base would greatly benefit from models that address how changes in athlete development can be tracked over time. The ability to quantitatively chronicle the transitions of athletes along the talent development pathway holds significant potential. There is consequently a need for quasi-experimental research designs that contrast pathways of development of experts and less expert athletes by tracking variables that are known to make a difference to long-term performance achievement.

One model that has attempted to address these limitations is the Developmental Model of Sport Participation (DMSP; Côté, 1999; Côté et al., 2007). Recent citation analysis studies (Bruner et al., 2009; Bruner et al., 2010) have found the DMSP to be the most prominent conceptualization of athletes' development within the sport literature. It is a conceptual framework that integrates the developing person and their environment. As illustrated in Figure 15.1, the DMSP has three sport participation trajectories: (1) recreational participation through early sampling and deliberate play; (2) elite performance through early sampling and deliberate play; and (3) elite performance through early specialization and deliberate practice. The different stages within a trajectory are based on changes in the type and amount of involvement in sport, play, and practice and are linked to specific outcomes in terms of long-term performance, continued participation, and personal development.

The DMSP has been developed and refined over the last 10 years and presents a set of concepts and variables about the development of athletes that are quantifiable and testable. An advantage of this model is that the stages of the DMSP are identified by clear indicators that are consistent with both sport-specific and general theories of child and adolescent development. Furthermore, research conducted with the DMSP has been guided by a unique methodology that can be effectively used to empirically test the propositions of this athlete development model.

The DMSP was developed in four steps. The first step involved an initial conceptualization of athletes' development resulting from interviews with parents, coaches, and athletes (Côté, 1999). This original model was in line with results from other qualitative studies of athletic development (e.g., Bloom, 1985; Carlson, 1988)

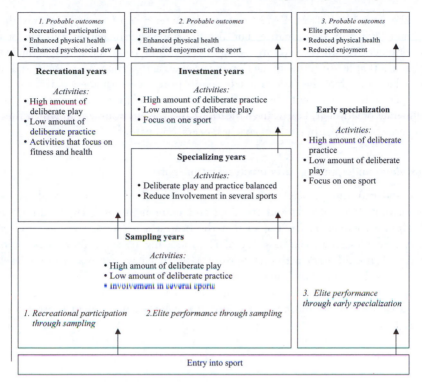

Figure 15.1 The Developmental Model of Sport Participation. Adapted from Côté, Baker, & Abernethy (2007).

while providing explicit and original propositions that could be quantified and tested empirically. In a second step, a quantitative, retrospective methodology was developed over several years (Côté, Ericsson, & Law, 2005) to test the main assumptions of the DMSP. Using this methodology, a series of studies were conducted to compare groups of expert and non-expert athletes to refine the DMSP and provide clarity on its different processes, outcomes, and trajectories (e.g. Baker, Côté, & Abernethy, 2003a, 2003b; Berry et al., 2008; Law et al., 2007). Third, the retrospective method was adapted and used to test the DMSP in terms of other outcomes associated with sport involvement (i.e., personal development, dropout, and continued participation; e.g., Fraser-Thomas, Côté, & Deakin, 2008a; Strachan, Côté, & Deakin, 2009b; Wall & Côté, 2007). This holistic approach was further substantiated with new qualitative studies with athletes who have achieved various outcomes in sport (Fraser-Thomas & Côté, 2009; Strachan, Côté, & Deakin, 2009a). A final fourth step involved the refinement of the DMSP through the writing of theoretical papers and the creation of seven postulates related to the process variables inherent to the different pathways of the DMSP and its various outcomes (Côté et al., 2007; Côté, Lidor, & Hackfort, 2009).

The postulates of the DMSP feature characteristics of sport programs that promote not only performance, but also continued participation and personal development for all involved in sport. The DMSP is based on a developmental approach that features the interaction of variables across time. The DMSP and its postulates integrate the various outcomes of sport – performance, participation, and personal development – by focusing on key proximal processes (deliberate play, deliberate practice, and early diversification) and the environment in which these processes are happening (role of coaches, peers, and parents).

Postulates underpinning early involvement in sport

The underpinning principle of sport programs for children is to provide space, opportunities for playing and training, and equipment for a large number of children across various sports, so that the best athletes among a large pool of motivated adolescents can be selected. The following are seven postulates associated with the different pathways of the DMSP that have received various levels of empirical support (see Table 15.1). The postulates highlight the efficiency of sport programs based on early sampling (postulates 1, 2, and 3), deliberate play (postulates 4 and 5) and key transitions throughout development (postulates 6 and 7).

Table 15.1 Seven postulates about youth sport activities

Postulate 1	Early diversification (sampling) does not hinder elite sport participation in sports in which peak performance is reached after maturation
Postulate 2	Early diversification (sampling) is linked to a longer sport career and has positive implications for long-term sport involvement
Postulate 3	Early diversification (sampling) allows participation in a range of contexts that most favorably affects positive youth development
Postulate 4	High amounts of deliberate play during the sampling years build a solid foundation of intrinsic motivation through involvement in activities that are enjoyable and promote intrinsic regulation
Postulate 5	A high amount of deliberate play during the sampling years establishes a range of motor and cognitive experiences that children can ultimately bring to their principal sport of interest
Postulate 6	Around the end of primary school (about age 13 years), children should have the opportunity either to choose to specialize in their favorite sport or to continue in sport at a recreational level
Postulate 7	Late adolescents (around age 16 years) have developed the physical, cognitive, social, emotional, and motor skills needed to invest their effort into highly specialized training in one sport

Postulate 1: Early diversification (sampling) does not hinder elite sport participation in sports in which peak performance is reached after maturation

There is a common belief that, in order to become elite, athletes must specialize in their sport from an early age (Côté & Fraser-Thomas, 2011). However, evidence exists to suggest that early involvement in a variety of sports can also lead to elite performance. Studies of elite athletes in several sports, including ice hockey (Soberlak & Côté, 2003), field hockey, basketball, and netball (Baker et al., 2003b), baseball (Hill, 1993), tennis (Carlson, 1988; Côté, 1999; Monsaas, 1985), triathlon (Baker et al., 2005), Australian rules football (Berry et al., 2008), and rowing (Côté, 1999) demonstrate that elite performance in these sports is usually preceded by a period of sampling various sports and often includes early participation in the specializing sport. A common characteristic of these sports is that the age of peak performance usually occurs after the athlete has fully matured, generally in the late twenties or early thirties. Typically, athletes in these sports will specialize in their main sport around age 13–15 years and fully invest in their training around age 16 years.

Nonetheless, in sports such as women's gymnastics or women's figure skating, in which peak performance usually occurs before full maturation, athletes do not appear to benefit from a period of sampling or diversification. Studies of gymnasts (Law et al., 2007) and figure skaters (Starkes et al., 1996) suggest that early specialization is a strong predictor of elite performance. However, it is important to keep in mind that peak performance in these sports generally occurs in the middle and late teens, thus indicating the value of early specialization.

Postulate 2: Early diversification (sampling) is linked to a longer sport career and has positive implications for long-term sport involvement

Current research suggests that engaging in a variety of sports may help to promote long-term sport participation. For example, in their study of Russian swimmers, Barynina and Vaitsekhovskii (1992) found that athletes who began specialized training in swimming around age 12–13 years spent a longer time on the national team and ended their sport careers later than swimmers who specialized at around age 9–10 years. The results of this study are congruent with the work of Baker and colleagues (2005), whose study of Master triathletes showed that sampling a range of sports during childhood was associated with sport participation that extended into late adulthood. Previous studies have also indicated that early specialization may have detrimental effects on athletes' sport careers. Gould, Udry, Tuffey, and Loehr's (1996) study of burnout in elite tennis players demonstrated that a sole focus on tennis at a young age led to more youth sport dropout/burnout. Furthermore, intense and repeated training in one sport at a young age has been associated with higher rates of injury (Law et al., 2007), which ultimately has an effect on the length of a sport career. Two recent studies show that sport programs that focus on large amounts of deliberate practice during childhood are more likely to lead to dropout (Fraser-Thomas et al., 2008a; Wall & Côté, 2007). These results, along with qualitative data of dropout and burnout athletes (e.g., Carlson, 1988; Fraser-Thomas, Côté, & Deakin, 2008b), indicate that sport programs that focus solely on the accumulation of vast amounts of deliberate practice during childhood may have more psychological and physical costs than childhood sport programs that focus on deliberate play and sampling.

Therefore, early specialization has been shown to shorten peak performance, increase dropout/burnout, and increase injuries in young athletes in some sports. Athletes in sports in which peak performance is reached after maturation generally have a longer career than athletes from sports in which early specialization is the norm, such as women's gymnastics and figure skating. Given the various costs associated with early specialization and the possible benefits of early diversification, in postulate 2 we suggest that early diversification may be a more favorable pathway to elite performance.

Postulate 3: Early diversification (sampling) allows participation in a range of contexts that most favorably affects positive youth development

It is clear that different sports offer distinct social contexts and opportunities for socialization. For example, a tennis player may spend a greater amount of one-on-one quality time with an adult (i.e., coach) than a basketball player. On the other hand, the broader social system of a basketball team may provide learning experiences that are not available in an individual sport such as tennis. Even sports that are similar in terms of structure (e.g., soccer and field hockey) can result in very different types of experiences because of the unique context (e.g., different teammates and coaches) in which they take place. Therefore, it is suggested that early diversification has the potential to promote a broader spectrum of developmental experiences and outcomes than early specialization. Wright and Côté (2003), in their examination of university-level athletes, reported that diversified sport experiences during childhood fostered positive peer relationships and leadership skills. Additionally, several longitudinal studies indicate that young people who are involved in varied activities score more favorably on personal and social outcome measures such as well-being (Busseri, Rose-Krasnor, Willoughby, & Chalmers, 2006) and positive peer relationships (Fredricks & Eccles, 2006) than those who specialize in one activity. The underlying assumption of this postulate is that early diversification between the ages of 6 and 12 years is an important contributor to the physical, cognitive, social, and emotional development of elite athletes.

Postulate 4: High amounts of deliberate play during the sampling years build a solid foundation of intrinsic motivation through involvement in activities that are enjoyable and promote intrinsic regulation

From a motivational perspective, children become involved in deliberate play because of their own interest in the activity, as opposed to external reasons such as improving performance or winning medals (Soberlak & Côté, 2003). Since deliberate play activities tend to be freely chosen and directed by children, they will ensure that deliberate play sessions are enjoyable (Lester & Russell, 2008). This type of early involvement in sport may help children become more self-directed toward their participation in sport (Ryan & Deci, 2000; Vallerand, 2001). This contention is supported by the tenets of self-determination theory, which predict that early intrinsically motivating behaviors (e.g., deliberate play) will have a positive effect over time on an individual's overall motivation and ultimately the individual's willingness to engage in more externally controlled activities (e.g., deliberate practice). Furthermore, promoting a deliberate play environment during the sampling years is closely linked to creating a "mastery" or "task" climate in sport that will ultimately foster children's motivation for sport (Biddle, 2001; Treasure, 2001).

Self-control is a dimension that clearly differentiates between deliberate practice and deliberate play. Because deliberate play is freely chosen and not prescribed by an adult, it can be quickly changed by the children involved to maximize enjoyment. Whereas several studies show that deliberate practice could be perceived as enjoyable (e.g., Hodges, Kerr, Starkes, Weir, & Nananidou, 2004; Ward, Hodges, Williams, & Starkes, 2004; Young & Salmela, 2002), deliberate play, by definition, is enjoyable and intrinsically motivating. By exercising this free choice and self-direction, children ensure that the overall course of an active play or deliberate play session is enjoyable (Lester & Russell, 2008). If they lack ownership of control, as is the case in deliberate practice, children are not able to continuously structure and direct their own participation toward intrinsically motivated forms in the same manner. Viewed from this perspective, deliberate play can therefore become an activity in childhood that may help promote the development of children's harmonious passion towards sport. According to Vallerand and colleagues (2007), harmonious passion results from the autonomous internalization of an activity. This occurs when an activity that an individual enjoys and engages in on a regular basis becomes internalized to the extent that it is highly valued. Given that deliberate play is an activity that children tend to enjoy, value, and freely choose to engage in, it is evident that deliberate play may play an important role in fostering harmonious passion. This may be beneficial since harmonious passion has been linked with both performance attainment in sport (Vallerand et al., 2007) and positive sport experiences (Vallerand et al., 2006).

Postulate 5: A high amount of deliberate play during the sampling years establishes a range of motor and cognitive experiences that children can ultimately bring to their principal sport of interest

Deliberate play serves as a way for youth to explore their physical capacities in various contexts and at a minimal cost in terms of resources. Qualitative analyses of children's early involvement in sports such as tennis (Carlson, 1988; Côté, 1999), rowing (Côté, 1999), and baseball (Hill, 1993) showed that deliberate play-like activities were important in the first few years of elite athletes' engagement in sport. Soberlak and Côté (2003) showed that elite hockey players spent slightly more time in deliberate play activities than deliberate practice activities before age 20 years.

Berry et al. (2008), in a study of elite Australian football players, found that both the amount of time invested in structured practice activities in invasion-type sports and the amount of time spent in deliberate play of the same types of sports were significantly greater for players classified by coaches as exceptional decision-makers than ones classified as poor decision-makers. In this study, the amount of experience accumulated in the playing of invasion-type sport activities rather than the specific intent of the activity (play or practice) appeared to be the most crucial factor for the eventual emergence of expert perceptual and decision-making skills.

Although the majority of coaches continue to use explicit instruction to guide a developing athlete's attention to a specific aspect of his or her performance, research examining the concept of implicit learning shows that a significant degree of learning can occur in situations where attention is not directed consciously to the mechanics of movement production. Implicit learning may be therefore more likely to occur in deliberate play activities than it is in deliberate practice in which conscious attention to error correction is the principal focus. For long-term skill acquisition, there is evidence that tasks learned implicitly are more resistant to performance-related pressure than explicitly learned skills (Reber, 1989).

Deliberate play activities involve an engagement of time in physical activities that is difficult to match with any kind of structured practice. When children play one-on-one basketball, for fun, in a driveway for 2 hours, there are few periods of waiting like those found in structured practice. Since deliberate play provides young people with the opportunity to generate and experiment with new skills, they can learn how to adapt to novel and uncertain situations (e.g., Lester & Russell, 2008; Memmert & Roth, 2007; Pellegrini, Dupuis, & Smith, 2007). In doing so, authors have suggested that play activities and deliberate play may help foster skill innovation, creativity, and flexibility (Côté et al., 2007; Lester & Russell, 2008; Pellegrini et al., 2007). Therefore, although there are obvious advantages to having a coach available to provide feedback during practice, monitor success, and provide instruction, it is unclear if, during early stages of development, the benefits of organized practice are superior to the benefits gained from engagement in deliberate play.

Postulate 6: Around the end of primary school (about age 13 years), children should have the opportunity either to choose to specialize in their favorite sport or to continue in sport at a recreational level

Early adolescence (i.e., ages 13–15) is an important period for the development of psychological processes, such as identity and competence (Lerner, Freund, De Stefanis, & Habermas, 2001). MacPhail, Gorely, and Kirk (2003) conducted an 18-month-long ethnographic study of an English athletic club and noted a shift of position of its members from sampler to specializer in the age range 12–15 years. During that period, the young athletes decided to focus their energy and resources on specific sporting activities in order to develop competence and achieve a higher level of performance in fewer selected sports. According to Horn and Harris (2002), it is only at about the age of 12 or 13 years that children are able to fully understand the effects that effort, practice, and ability have on their competence and performances. Therefore, the quality of early learning experiences through sampling and play during childhood develops perceptions of competence, which in turn leads to motivation for continued participation during adolescence (Kirk, 2005). The important characteristics that mark the transition between the sampling and the specializing or recreational phases in early adolescence include a reduction in the number of sporting activities, an increase in practice hours and/or intensity of practice, a greater emphasis on competition and success, and more support provided by the family, school, and club (MacPhail & Kirk, 2006).

Postulate 7: Late adolescents (around age 16 years) have developed the physical, cognitive, social, emotional, and motor skills needed to invest their effort into highly specialized training in one sport

Professional ice hockey players from the age of 6 to 20 years had accumulated 3,072 hours of sport-specific practice (including organized hockey practice, power skating, hockey school, and dry-land/weight training), of which an average of 459 hours was accumulated during the sampling years (ages 6–12 and representing 10% of the total hours invested; Soberlak & Côté, 2003). Conversely, an average of 2,215 hours of sport-specific practice occurred during the investment years (ages 16–20, representing 56% of the total hours invested). These findings support evidence from previous studies (e.g., Baker et al., 2003b; Bloom, 1985; Côté, 1999; Helsen et al., 1998), identifying the investment years as the period in which elite athletes are devoted to specialized training. In a review of developmental factors that affect sport participation, Patel, Pratt, and Greydanus (2002) suggest that late adolescents have the psychological, social, emotional, and physical maturity to meet the demands of competitive sports. Individuals at this stage of development also have the capacity to understand the benefits and costs of intense focus on one sport and are able to make an independent decision about investing in a particular sport.

Conclusions

The postulates and models of athlete development reviewed in this chapter highlight that the achievement of expertise in sport is not the result of a particular physical, psychological, or sociological factor; rather, it is the integration of factors from the individual and the context. The DMSP (Côté et al., 2007) provides a comprehensive framework that outlines different pathways of involvement in sport. Early sampling can lead to either recreational participation or elite performance in sport and is based on two main elements of childhood sport participation: (1) involvement in various sports; and (2) participation in deliberate play. Early specialization implies a focused involvement in only one sport and a high amount of deliberate practice activities with the goal of improving skills and performance in this sport during childhood. This pathway is likely to lead to elite performance, but also to more overuse injuries and dropout.

The seven postulates associated with the DMSP highlight the benefits of early sampling for continued sport participation, elite performance, and personal development through sport. Through early sampling and deliberate play, children have the opportunity to learn emotional, cognitive, and motor skills in several contexts that will be important in their later participation or investment in sport. By the time athletes reach adolescence, they will have learned a variety of fundamental movement skills during the sampling years and will have the experiential base to develop more mature cognitive and emotional skills. The decision to choose an early sampling or early specialization pathway involves several trade-offs. Accordingly, before embarking on a specific type of activity and training, athletes, parents, and coaches should weigh the potential health, psychological, sociological, and motor benefits and risks associated with early sampling or early specialization in children aged 6–12 years.

When coaches develop activities for youth practices and when sport organizations design youth sport programs, they should consider the seven postulates of the DMSP and the outcomes associated with certain sport development pathways. In particular, coaches and practitioners must consider the differing implications of deliberate play, deliberate practice, sampling, and early specialization. This chapter has showed that young people's health, psychosocial development, and motor skill development should and must be considered as a whole, instead of as separate entities, by youth sport programmers. Young people should be encouraged to participate in diverse sports and extracurricular activities that focus on fun, play, excitement, recreation, personal involvement, games, friendships, variety, and choice. Activities and contexts that promote regular participation, enjoyment, and skill acquisition are the building blocks of all effective youth sport programs.

References

Abbott, A., & Collins, D. (2002). A theoretical and empirical analysis of a "state of the art" talent identification model. *High Ability Studies, 13*, 157–178.

Abbott, A., & Collins, D. (2004). Eliminating the dichotomy between theory and practice in talent identification and development: Considering the role of psychology. *Journal of Sport Sciences, 22*, 395–408.

Abernethy, B., Baker, J., & Côté, J. (2005). Transfer of pattern recall skills as a contributor to the development of sport expertise. *Applied Cognitive Psychology, 19*, 705–718.

Abernethy, B., Farrow, D., & Berry, J. (2003). Constraints and issues in the development of a general theory of expert perceptual–motor performance. In Starkes, J. L., and Ericsson, K. A. (Eds.), *Expert performance in sports: Advances in research on sport expertise* (pp. 349–369). Champaign, IL: Human Kinetics.

Alfermann, D., & Stambulova, N. (2007). Career transitions and career termination. In Tenenbaum, G., & Eklund, R. C. (Eds.), *Handbook of sport psychology* (pp. 712–733). Hoboken, NJ: John Wiley & Sons.

Bailey, R. P., Dismore, H., & Morley, D. (2009). Talent development in physical education: A national survey of practices in England. *Physical Education and Sport Pedagogy, 14*, 59–72.

Bailey, R. P., & Morley, D. (2006). Towards a model of talent development in physical education. *Sport, Education, and Society, 11*, 211–230.

Bailey, R. P., Tan, J., & Morley, D. (2004). Talented pupils in physical education: Secondary school teachers' experiences of identifying talent within the "Excellence in Cities" scheme. *Physical Education and Sport Pedagogy, 9*(2), 133–148.

Baker, J., Côté, J., & Abernethy, B. (2003a). Learning from the experts: Practice activities of expert decision makers in sport. *Research Quarterly for Exercise and Sport, 74*, 342–347.

Baker, J., Côté, J., & Abernethy, B. (2003b). Sport specific training, deliberate practice and the development of expertise in team ball sports. *Journal of Applied Sport Psychology, 15*, 12–25.

Baker, J., Côté, J., & Deakin, J. (2005). Expertise in ultra-endurance triathletes: Early sport involvement, training structure and the theory of deliberate practice. *Journal of Applied Sport Psychology, 17*(1), 64–78.

Baker, J., & Horton, S. (2004). A review of primary and secondary influences on sport expertise. *High Ability Studies, 15*, 211–228.

Barynina, I. I., & Vaitsekhovskii, S. M. (1992, August). The aftermath of early sports specialization for highly qualified swimmers. *Fitness and Sports Review International, 132*–133.

Berry, J., Abernethy, B., & Côté, J. (2008). The contribution of structured practice and deliberate play to the development of expert perceptual and decision-making skill. *Journal of Sport and Exercise Psychology, 30*, 685–708.

Biddle, S. J. H. (2001). Enhancing motivation in physical education. In Roberts, G. C. (Ed.), *Advances in motivation in sport and exercise* (pp. 101–128). Champaign, IL: Human Kinetics.

Bloom, B. S. (Ed.). (1985). *Developing talent in young people*. New York: Ballantine.

Bruner, M. W., Erickson, K., McFadden, K. K., & Côté, J. (2009). Tracing the origins of athlete development models in sport: A citation path network analysis. *International Review of Sport and Exercise Psychology, 2*, 23–37.

Bruner, M. W., Erickson, K., Wilson, B., & Côté, J. (2010). An appraisal of athlete development models through citation network analysis. *Psychology of Sport and Exercise, 11*, 133–139.

Busseri, M. A., Rose-Krasnor, L., Willoughby, T., & Chalmers, H. (2006). A longitudinal examination of breadth and intensity of youth activity involvement and successful development. *Developmental Psychology, 42*, 1313–1326.

Carlson, R. C. (1988). The socialization of elite tennis players in Sweden: An analysis of the players' backgrounds and development. *Sociology of Sport Journal, 5*, 241–256.

Côté, J. (1999). The influence of the family in the development of talent in sports. *Sport Psychologist, 13*, 395–417.

Côté, J., Baker, J., & Abernethy, B. (2003). From play to practice: A developmental framework for the acquisition of expertise in team sports. In Starkes, J., & Ericsson, K. A. (Eds.), *Expert performance in sports: Advances in research on sport expertise* (pp. 89–110). Champaign, IL: Human Kinetics.

Côté, J., Baker, J., & Abernethy, B. (2007). Practice and play in the development of sport expertise. In Eklund, R., & Tenenbaum, G. (Eds.), *Handbook of sport psychology* (3rd edn., pp. 184–202). Hoboken, NJ: Wiley.

Côté, J., & Fraser-Thomas, J. (2011). Youth involvement and positive development in sport. In Crocker, P. (Ed.)., *Sport psychology: A Canadian perspective* (2nd edn., pp. 226–242). Toronto: Pearson.

Côté, J., Ericsson, K. A., & Law, M. (2005). Tracing the development of athletes using retrospective interview methods: A proposed interview and validation procedure for reported information. *Journal of Applied Sport Psychology, 17*, 1–19.

Côté, J., Lidor, R., & Hackfort, D. (2009). To sample or to specialize? Seven postulates about youth sport activities that lead to continued participation and elite performance. *International Journal of Sport and Exercise Psychology, 9*, 7–17.

Deakin, J. M., & Cobley, S. (2003). An examination of the practice environments in figure skating and volleyball: A search for deliberate practice. In Starkes, J., & Ericsson, K. A.

(Eds.), *Expert performance in sports: Advances in research on sport expertise* (pp. 90–113). Champaign, IL: Human Kinetics.

Denzin, M. K. (1975). Play, games and interaction: The contexts of childhood interaction. *Sociological Quarterly, 16*, 458–476.

Ericsson, K. A. (2003). Development of elite performance and deliberate practice: An update from the perspective of the expert performance approach. In Starkes, J. L., & Ericsson, K. A. (Eds.), *Expert performance in sports: Advances in research on sports expertise* (pp. 49–81). Champaign, IL: Human Kinetics.

Ericsson, K. A., Krampe, R. T., & Tesch-Römer, C. (1993). The role of deliberate practice in the acquisition of expert performance. *Psychological Review, 100*, 363–406.

Fraser-Thomas, J., & Côté, J. (2009). Understanding adolescents' positive and negative developmental experiences in sport. *Sport Psychologist, 23*, 3–23.

Fraser-Thomas, J., Côté, J., & Deakin, J. (2008a). Examining adolescent sport dropout and prolonged engagement from a developmental perspective. *Journal of Applied Sport Psychology, 20*, 318–333.

Fraser-Thomas, J., Côté, J., & Deakin, J. (2008b). Understanding dropout and prolonged engagement in adolescent competitive sport. *Psychology of Sport and Exercise, 9*, 645–662.

Fredricks, J. A., & Eccles, J. S. (2006). Extracurricular involvement and adolescent adjustment: Impact of duration, number of activities, and breadth of participation. *Applied Developmental Science, 10*, 132–146.

Gould, D., Udry, E., Tuffey, S., & Loehr, J. (1996). Burnout in competitive junior tennis players. 1: A quantitative psychological assessment. *Sport Psychologist, 10*, 322–340.

Griffin, L. L., & Butler, J. I. (Eds.). (2005). *Teaching games for understanding: Theory, research, and practice.* Champaign, IL: Human Kinetics.

Helsen, W. F., Hodges, N. J., Van Winckel, J., & Starkes, J. L. (2000). The roles of talent, physical precocity and practice in the development of soccer expertise. *Journal of Sport Sciences, 18*, 727–736.

Helsen, W. F., Starkes, J. L., & Hodges, N. J. (1998). Team sports and the theory of deliberate practice. *Journal of Sport & Exercise Psychology, 20*, 12–34.

Hill, G. M. (1993). Youth participation of professional baseball players. *Sociology of Sport Journal, 10*, 107–114.

Hodges, N. J., Kerr, T., Starkes, J. L., Weir, P. L., & Nananidou, A. (2004). Predicting performance times from deliberate practice hours for triathletes and swimmers: What, when, and where is practice important? *Journal of Experimental Psychology: Applied, 10*, 219–237.

Hodges, N. J. & Starkes, J. L. (1996). Wrestling with the nature of expertise: A sport specific test of Ericsson, Krampe and Tesch-Römer's (1993) theory of "deliberate practice." *International Journal of Sport Psychology, 27*, 400–424.

Horn, T. S., & Harris, A. (2002). Perceived competence in young athletes: Research findings and recommendations for coaches and parents. In Smoll, F. L., & Smith, R. E. (Eds.), *Children and youth in sport: A biopsychosocial perspective* (2nd edn., pp. 435–464). Dubuque, IA: Kendall-Hunt.

Kirk, D. (2005). Physical education, youth sport and lifelong participation: The importance of early learning experiences. *European Physical Education Review, 11*, 239–255.

Launder, A. G. (2001). *Play practice: The games approach to teaching and coaching sports.* Champaign, IL: Human Kinetics.

Law, M., Côté, J., & Ericsson, K. A. (2007). The development of expertise in rhythmic gymnastics. *International Journal of Sport and Exercise Psychology, 5*, 82–103.

Lee, T. D., Chamberlin, C. J., & Hodges, N. J. (2001). Practice. In Singer, R. N., Hausenblas, H. A., & Janelle, C. M. (Eds.), *Handbook of sport psychology* (2nd edn., pp. 115–143). New York: Wiley.

Lerner, R. M., Freund, A. M., De Stefanis, I., & Habermas, T. (2001). Understanding developmental regulation in adolescence: The use of the selection, optimization, and compensation model. *Human Development, 44,* 29–50.

Lester, S., & Russell, W. (2008) *Play for a change: Play, policy and practice: A review of contemporary perspectives – Summary report.* Play England. Retrieved December 3, 2010, from http://www.playengland.org.uk/resources/play-for-a-change-symmary.pdf.

MacPhail, A., Gorely, T., & Kirk, D. (2003). Young people's socialization into sport: A case study of an athletics club. *Sport Education and Society, 8,* 251–267.

MacPhail, A., & Kirk, D. (2006). Young people's socialization into sport: Experiencing the specializing phase. *Leisure Studies, 25,* 57–74.

Memmert, D., & Roth, K. (2007). The effects of non-specific and specific concepts on tactical creativity in team ball sports. *Journal of Sport Sciences, 25,* 1423–1432.

Monsaas, J. A. (1985). Learning to be a world-class tennis player. In Bloom, B. S. (Ed.), *Developing talent in young people* (pp. 211–269). New York: Ballantine.

Patel, D. R., Pratt, H. D., & Greydanus, D. E. (2002). Pediatric neurodevelopment and sports participation: When are children ready to play sports? *Pediatric Clinics of North America, 49,* 505–531.

Pellegrini, A. D., Dupuis, D., & Smith, P. K. (2007). Play in evolution and development. *Developmental Review, 27,* 261–276.

Pellegrini, A. D., & Smith, P. K. (1998). Physical activity play: The nature and function of neglected aspect of play. *Child Development, 69,* 577–598.

Piaget, J. (1962). *Play, dreams, and imitation in childhood.* New York: W. W. Norton.

Reber, A. S. (1989). Implicit learning and tacit knowledge. *Journal of Experimental Psychology: General, 118,* 219–235.

Ryan, R. M., & Deci, E. L. (2000). Self-determination theory and the facilitation of intrinsic motivation, social development, and well being. *American Psychologist, 55,* 68–78.

Salmela, J. H. (1994). Stages and transitions across sports careers. In Hackfort, D. (Ed.), *Psycho-social issues and interventions in elite sports* (pp. 11–28). Frankfurt: Lang.

Simon, H. A., & Chase, W. G. (1973). Skill in chess. *American Scientist, 61,* 394–403.

Soberlak, P., & Côté, J. (2003). The developmental activities of elite ice hockey players. *Journal of Applied Sport Psychology, 15,* 41–49.

Stambulova, N. B. (1994). Developmental sports career investigations in Russia: A post perestroika analysis. *Sport Psychologist, 8,* 221–237.

Starkes, J. L., Deakin, J. M., Allard, F., Hodges, N. J., & Hayes, A. (1996). Deliberate practice in sports: What is it anyway? In Ericsson, K. A. (Ed.), *The road to excellence: The acquisition of expert performance in the arts, sciences, sports and games* (pp. 81–106). Mahwah, NJ: Erlbaum.

Sternberg, R. J. (1996). Costs of expertise. In Ericsson, K. A. (Ed.), *The road to excellence: The acquisition of expert performance in the arts and sciences, sports, and games* (pp. 347–354). Mahwah, NJ: Erlbaum.

Strachan, L., Côté, J., & Deakin, J. (2009a). An evaluation of personal and contextual factors in competitive youth sport. *Journal of Applied Sport Psychology, 21,* 340–355.

Strachan, L., Côté, J., & Deakin, J. (2009b). "Specializers" versus "samplers" in youth sport: Comparing experiences and outcomes. *Sport Psychologist, 23,* 77–92.

Treasure, D. C. (2001). Enhancing young people's motivation in youth sport: An achievement goal approach. In Roberts, G. C. (Ed.), *Advances in motivation in sport and exercise* (pp. 79–100). Champaign, IL: Human Kinetics.

Vallerand, R. J. (2001). A hierarchical model of intrinsic and extrinsic motivation in sport and exercise. In Roberts, G. C. (Ed.), *Advances in motivation in sport and exercise* (pp. 263–319). Champaign, IL: Human Kinetics.

Vallerand, R. J., Rousseau, F. L., Gouzet, F. M. E., Dumais, A., Grenier, S., & Blanchard, C. M. (2006). Passion in sport: A look at determinants and affective experiences. *Journal of Sport & Exercise Psychology, 28,* 454–478.

Vallerand, R. J., Salvy, S. J., Mageau, G. A., Elliot, A. J., Denis, P. L., Gouzet, F. M. E., & Blanchard, C. (2007). On the role of passion in performance. *Journal of Personality, 75,* 505–533.

Wall, M., & Côté, J. (2007). Developmental activities that lead to drop out and investment in sport. *Physical Education & Sport Pedagogy, 12,* 77–87.

Ward, P., Hodges, N. J., Starkes, J. L., & Williams, A. M. (2007). The road to excellence: Deliberate practice and the development of expertise. *High Abilities Studies, 18,* 119–153.

Ward, P., Hodges, N. J., Williams, A. M., & Starkes, J. L. (2004). Deliberate practice and expert performance: Defining the path to excellence. In Williams, A. M., & Hodges, N. J. (Eds.), *Skill acquisition in sport: Research theory and practice* (pp. 231–258). New York: Routledge.

Wright, A. D., & Côté, J. (2003). A retrospective analysis of leadership development through sport. *Sport Psychologist, 17,* 268–291.

Wylleman, P., & Lavallee, D. (2004). A developmental perspective on transitions faced by athletes. In Weiss, M. R. (Ed.), *Developmental sport and exercise psychology: A lifespan perspective* (pp. 507–527). Morgantown, WV: FIT.

Young, B. W., & Salmela, J. H. (2002). Perceptions of training and deliberate practice of middle distance runners. *International Journal of Sport Psychology, 33,* 167–181.

16 Anticipatory behavior and expert performance

Bruce Abernethy, Damian Farrow, Adam D. Gorman, and David L. Mann

Two complementary but fundamentally different approaches can be employed when attempting to understand how skill in sport is acquired. One approach, which has been the historically dominant one within the motor learning field, involves tracing the development of particular skills and control processes in untrained participants as they are given carefully controlled schedules (and combinations) of practice, instruction and feedback (e.g., Adams, 1987; Schmidt & Lee, 2011). Such an approach can be instructive with respect to changes that occur early in the learning process although the (relatively) short-term nature of the practice interventions that are achievable under typical laboratory conditions, and the generally simplistic nature of the skills that have been examined in this way, can make inference to skill learning as it occurs in the sport domain problematic. The alternative approach – the expertise approach – involves making comparisons between experts in the sports domain with less skilled and less highly practiced individuals. These contrasts, from different ends of the skill spectrum, can be used both to ascertain the nature of the expert advantage and to identify the key processes that are refined and modified as a functional adaptation to years of practice and domain-specific experience (e.g., Abernethy, Burgess-Limerick, & Parks, 1994; Starkes & Ericsson, 2003).

In this chapter, we provide a brief overview of the expert performance approach to skill acquisition. The first section of the chapter presents a general introduction to expert performance, examining, among other things, why the study of expertise is important, what is known about the defining characteristics of expert performance of sports skills, and the types of methods and levels of evidence and analysis used to study expertise. One of the quintessential characteristics of expert performance across a range of sports, and within numerous different tasks within sports, is the enhanced capability of experts to use anticipation to deal with the inherent time constraints that competition places upon perceiving and acting. In the second section of this chapter, we review some of the evidence in relation to expert anticipation as it pertains to performance in situations, such as striking sports, that require the precise execution of interceptive movements. In the third section of the chapter, we review evidence in relation to expert anticipation as it occurs in situations, common in many team ball sports, that require complex patterns of movement of multiple players to be recognized and interpreted in order to make appropriate response-selection decisions. The final section of the chapter builds on the knowledge gleaned from studies of expertise in anticipation to illustrate how this knowledge can, and might, be used to develop improved approaches to skill learning or, in other words, approaches that can help make non-experts more expert-like more rapidly.

An introduction to the study of expertise

Experts are those people who consistently display exceptional levels of performance in a particular domain. In sport, as in other domains of human performance, expertise is highly valued because it is unusual and it is not readily acquired, generally requiring a decade or more (and literally millions of trials) of purposeful practice. Any means that can be found to uncover the keys to expert performance and through this accelerate the normal rate of acquisition of expertise would be particularly advantageous. To develop an evidence-based approach to skill acquisition based on an understanding of expert performance, it is necessary to know the answers to a number of key questions. These include:

1　What specific attributes are essential for expert performance?
2　How do experts differ from non-experts in their learning and control of these essential skill attributes?
3　How do experts become expert (and, relatedly, what essential conditions must be present during the developing years to improve the probability of expertise being developed)?

Research on sport expertise is progressively supplying information on a number of these fundamental questions (for a summary, see Abernethy, 2008).

In relation to the first question regarding attributes, it is now apparent that the expert superiority, as far as perceptual-cognitive skill is concerned, is primarily limited to processes that require the encoding, synthesis, and interpretation of domain-specific information, such as selective attention, pattern recall, and recognition. Expert superiority is less apparent or non-existent on more generalized attributes (such as visual acuity and reflex latency). Experts also show superior performance to non-experts under multi-tasking situations, suggesting that the primary movement control of experts is less attention demanding (and hence more automatic) than that of non-experts (Gabbett, Wake, & Abernethy, 2011; Schneider, 1985). Evidence of systematic differences between experts and non-experts now exists not only at the behavioral level but also increasingly from psychophysiological (e.g., Taliep et al., 2008) and neuro-anatomical levels of analysis (e.g., Wright, Bishop, Jackson, & Abernethy, 2010).

In relation to the second question concerning how experts differ from non-experts, the accumulated evidence suggests that a key contributing factor to the experts' superiority on selective aspects of perceiving and acting is their capability to pick up information from cues or sources of information to which non-experts are not attuned. Experts in various sports tasks have been shown to be able to pick up information from features of the task that less skilled individuals either do not attend to or lack the requisite knowledge to be able to use effectively. For example, in a study of expert and less proficient badminton players, in which select combinations of postural cues from an opponent were presented using point-light displays, Abernethy and Zawi (2007) demonstrated that the expert players were able to pick up useful advance information to predict stroke direction from the independent motion of the opponent's lower body and racket, whereas less skilled players could not.

In relation to the third question regarding the achievement of expertise, engagement in extensive amounts of both incidental and deliberate practice over an extended period of time appears a necessary condition for expertise to emerge. Both practice done with the intentional purpose of skill progression, what Ericsson, Krampe, and Tesch-Römer (1993) have termed *deliberate practice*, and practice undertaken as an incidental consequence of sport play, what Côté (1999) has termed *deliberate play*, differentiate sports experts from non-experts.

In primarily cognitive tasks (such as solving problems in physics) that have few, if any, time constraints on responding, an identifying characteristic of the experts is their capacity to perform faster, and with less error, than non-experts (Glaser & Chi, 1988). In sport tasks, in which the time for responding can be extremely limited, the capacity of the highly skilled athlete to perform the requisite skills in a precise but apparently unhurried manner is an even more compelling feature of expertise. The capacity to make accurate perceptual judgments based on early information, accurate response choices based on only partial information, and precisely timed movement responses through early preparation suggests that the use of anticipation and control based on prediction of future states is one of the fundamental elements upon which expert performance is based (Yarrow, Brown, & Krakauer, 2009). The enhanced capability of the expert to predict future events from early or partial information offers a plausible explanation of the phenomenological impression created by experts of "having all the time in the world" and being able to "read the play" in a way that the less skilled cannot. In the sections that follow, we briefly review some of the empirical evidence that supports anticipation as a key element of expert performance and as one of the fundamental changes in perceptual–motor control that accompanies high levels of skill learning in sport.

Experts have "all the time in the world": anticipatory behavior in interceptive tasks

Expert performers from a wide variety of sports consistently demonstrate a domain-specific ability to predict (or *anticipate*) event outcomes based on observation of their opponent's movement pattern and especially the basic biomechanical (kinematic) properties of the movement pattern. These anticipatory skills may be necessary to overcome the extreme temporal demands inherent in many sporting tasks, particularly in interceptive (hitting) skills that occur in sports such as badminton, squash, tennis, cricket, and baseball. In these sports the expert performer is able to anticipate certain characteristics of the target to be intercepted (usually a ball) through the judicious examination of the pre-ball-flight information contained within the kinematics of the opposition player's movements. Anticipation has traditionally been examined experimentally using *temporal occlusion*, whereby vision of an opposing player is occluded at a key moment in the movement sequence to test if the observer is able to predict the ensuing event outcome. For example, vision (typically video footage) of a tennis serve shown from the perspective of a receiver may be shown up to the point of racket–ball contact, after which the display is occluded and the observer predicts the direction in which the ball was served. Whereas the temporal occlusion approach has been used for over 30 years to demonstrate that expert performers across a wide range of sports out-perform novices when anticipating movement outcomes (e.g., Jones & Miles, 1978), more recent research has built on these original findings to better understand the nature and sources of information used by skilled performers to facilitate improved interceptive performance.

Progressive temporal occlusion

The progressive temporal occlusion approach has been used to establish how early in the event sequence expert performers are able to anticipate event outcomes. Anticipation is tested across a series of experimental trials, with the moment of occlusion systematically manipulated (Figure 16.1). Experts are better able to predict event outcomes and do so based on information presented earlier in the event sequence (e.g., Abernethy & Russell, 1987a; Farrow, Abernethy, & Jackson, 2005). This finding has been evident across a wide range of sports including ice hockey, field hockey, tennis, badminton, squash, soccer, cricket, baseball, handball, and volleyball.

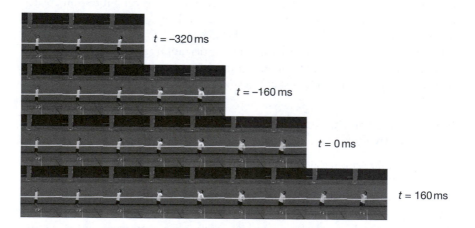

Figure 16.1 A schematic demonstration of the progressive temporal occlusion method. Video footage is selectively edited to show a movement sequence up to a given moment in time. In this example, footage of a badminton stroke is edited with images depicting every second frame of video footage. Occlusion points are shown from 320 ms prior to 160 ms after contact with the shuttlecock.

Spatial occlusion

The systematic occlusion of display features has been used in combination with temporal occlusion to establish the specific *locations* of the information expert performers rely on to underpin their superior anticipation. *Spatial occlusion* allows researchers to make inferences about the relative importance of different information sources (typically body segments or hitting implements) by examining the decrease in anticipatory performance when vision of these specific features is denied. Video footage of an event sequence is usually relied on to occlude information spatially; early studies masked limbs or hitting implements (Abernethy, 1990a; Abernethy & Russell, 1987a; Williams & Davids, 1998), whereas a more recent approach has been to remove this information using advanced video-editing software (Müller, Abernethy, & Farrow, 2006). Whereas these studies rely on video editing to occlude spatial information from the observer, Panchuk and Vickers (2009) recently examined the in situ anticipatory ability of ice hockey goaltenders by using a physical screen to occlude specific segments of a shooting player and his or her stick. Their manipulation demonstrated that selective removal of vision of the stick, but not of either the upper or lower body, significantly impaired performance compared with a control condition with no occlusion. Spatial occlusion studies have typically shown that expert performers, in comparison with their less skilled counterparts, are able to pick up information that is more remote from the end effector. For example, a skilled tennis player looking to anticipate the direction of a serve may rely on information from the racket and hitting arm of the server, whereas a player of lesser skill may rely on the racket alone. Skilled performers also appear more capable of eliciting movement outcomes from the relative movement of adjacent body segments (Müller et al., 2006); for example, the hand position in relation to the position of the forearm rather than simply the wrist or the forearm alone in the case of cricket bowling. As the movement of segments located more proximal to the body core will precede the movement of more distal ones, providing relatively earlier information about movement outcomes, these findings are consistent with the proposition that skilled players are more able to pick up useful information (and, in turn, make better response-selection decisions) earlier in the movement sequence.

Point-light displays

Point-light displays (Johansson, 1973) replace the object of interest (e.g., a tennis server) with a series of isolated points of light located on key biomechanical elements of the movement pattern (e.g., on the joint centers of the tennis server's upper body). These displays allow the essential kinematic information purveying the underlying movement pattern to remain, while contextual information such as figural and facial cues, shape, contour, and color are all removed. The point-light method, when combined with temporal occlusion, has provided a powerful and convenient means of better understanding the kinematic basis for skilled anticipation (Figure 16.2).

The expert advantage for anticipation has typically been found to remain when

Figure 16.2 An example of a point-light display, in which significant biomechanical sources of information are replaced by points of light. In this example, images of a tennis serve are shown with the point-light equivalent below.

a video display is replaced by a point-light display (e.g., Abernethy, Gill, Parks, & Packer, 2001; Abernethy & Zawi, 2007; Ward, Williams, & Bennett, 2002), suggesting that experts rely on kinematic rather than contextual information to underpin their anticipatory advantage. These findings have led to the use of point-light displays as a powerful and controllable means of *manipulating* displays to understand better how expert performers extract meaningful information from movement patterns (e.g., Huys, Smeeton, Hodges, Beek, & Williams, 2008; Pollick, Fidopiastis, & Braden, 2001). Studies using point-light displays have shown similarities between expert prediction of movement and expert production of the same movement, suggesting that common processing may be involved (Abernethy, Zawi, & Jackson, 2008). This conclusion has also been recently supported by more direct evidence from studies using functional magnetic resonance imaging (fMRI) in conjunction with point-light displays. For example, Wright et al. (2010) have shown greater involvement of the mirror neuron system – a collection of neurons in the brain active in both perception and action – in the anticipatory behavior of experts than in non-experts.

Visual search

The registration of visual search (gaze) behaviors provides another (supplementary) means of gaining evidence on the key sources of information that expert performers rely on to anticipate event outcomes. In general, findings have supported those found using spatial occlusion, with expert performers spending more time than novices fixating upon events and segments that occur earlier in the kinematic chain. For example, more time is spent by a skilled soccer goalkeeper observing the non-kicking leg rather than the kicking leg of a penalty taker (Savelsbergh, van der Kamp, Williams, & Ward, 2005; Savelsbergh, Williams, van der Kamp, & Ward, 2002), or by a skilled tennis player observing the shoulder rather than the racket of a server (Goulet, Bard, & Fleury, 1989; Williams, Ward, Knowles, & Smeeton, 2002).

A long-standing limitation for the registration of gaze behaviors is the inability to understand the role of peripheral vision in skilled anticipation. Although central vision is clearly the key source of information used for most conscious decisions in sport, it is questionable whether gaze behavior accurately reflects information pickup (Williams, Janelle, & Davids, 2004). To this end, it is noteworthy that the expert advantage in anticipation is not always supported by differences in patterns of gaze (e.g., Abernethy, 1990b; Abernethy & Russell, 1987b). Gaze-contingent displays, in which the content of the video display shown to the participant is dependent on the location of gaze, provide a promising means of clarifying the role of peripheral vision in the future (e.g., Hagemann, Schorer, Canal-Bruland, Lotz, & Strauss, 2010).

Laboratory versus in situ studies

What is known about expert anticipation in sport has in large part come from studies in which video displays are used to simulate the displays normally found in the natural setting. In using these displays, though, two particular assumptions have been made: (1) that a video simulation will accurately convey the same information that is available in situ, and (2) that the perceptual responses (verbal or pen-and-paper) made by participants will accurately reflect the movement responses produced in the performance environment. Perceptual judgments made in response to video simulations may fail to accurately represent the true nature of the expert advantage in anticipation. In this sense, one expectation is that the size of the expert advantage will increase as the experimental task more closely represents the real-life one (Abernethy, Thomas, & Thomas, 1993). Liquid crystal occlusion goggles (Milgram, 1987) have allowed experimenters to temporally occlude the vision of participants in real-life scenarios to confirm the expert advantage in anticipation when an in situ display is used (e.g., Abernethy et al., 2001; Starkes, Edwards, Dissanayake, & Dunn, 1995). There is now a growing body of evidence that, when a movement response is incorporated to more closely represent that produced in real life, there is a further improvement in the anticipatory performance of skilled observers beyond that possible when making a verbal response (Farrow & Abernethy, 2003; Mann, Abernethy, & Farrow, 2010). These findings are consistent with the incorporation of movement making use of the dorsal vision-for-action pathway that is implicated in online interceptive actions, of the type needed in many sporting tasks (Milner & Goodale, 1995). Van der Kamp, Rivas, van Doorn, & Savelsbergh (2008) have put forward a compelling argument that many of the existing laboratory-based studies of anticipation are likely to have elicited responses of the ventral vision-for-perception pathway, with in situ studies required to better understand the interaction of the two pathways most likely relied on in the performance environment.

Experts can "read the play": anticipatory behavior in pattern recognition tasks

The ability to perceive information rapidly and accurately from a complex and structured team-sport pattern, colloquially referred to as "reading the play," has been shown to be a defining characteristic of sporting expertise. Research from a range of different sports including soccer (Williams & Davids, 1995), volleyball (Borgeaud & Abernethy, 1987), handball (Tenenbaum, Levy-Kolker, Bar-Eli, & Weinberg, 1994), and basketball (Starkes, Allard, Lindley, & O'Reilly, 1994) has consistently revealed that, when expert sports performers are briefly shown a pattern of play from their domain, they are able to recall the inherent features within the pattern with greater accuracy than their less skilled counterparts.

One of the earliest studies to examine team-sport patterns was conducted by Allard, Graham, and Paarsalu (1980). Experienced and inexperienced basketball players were presented with static slides showing structured and unstructured patterns of play. The structured images showed situations in which one team was clearly on the offensive, whereas the unstructured slides showed situations in which the ball had just changed possession or was in dispute. Participants were asked to recall the locations of all players in the images immediately after viewing each slide for 4 seconds. The more experienced players were better able to recall the locations of players from the images, but this advantage was apparent only when the patterns were presented as structured situations. This selective expert advantage on only structured display presentations has been shown to persist when the test patterns are presented as dynamic video images (Borgeaud & Abernethy, 1987), or even when the information is displayed as dynamic sequences from a dance routine (Deakin & Allard, 1991), and has important theoretical implications concerning the underlying mechanisms that contribute to expert pattern perception in sport and other domains.

Theories of expert pattern perception

The findings reported by Allard et al. (1980) for recall by basketball experts essentially mirrored those found earlier in a landmark study of chess players by Chase and Simon (1973). Chase and Simon showed that master players were able to accurately recall the locations of more chess pieces than less skilled players only when the pieces were arranged in typical game configurations. When the pieces were randomly arranged on the boards, the performance of the expert players deteriorated to a level commensurate with that of a beginner. Chase and Simon (1973) concluded that the superiority of the master players was not due to an oversized memory capacity for information of all types, but rather the source of the advantage must be an enhanced ability to store and retrieve domain-specific information. More specifically, they believed that the experts were able to group the chess pieces into meaningful chunks and, in doing so, mitigate the demands on short-term memory capacity. This subsequently led to the development of the "chunking theory" of expert memory.

One of the limitations of the chunking theory was the inability to explain research showing that expert chess players could continue to recall large amounts of information, even when an interference task was inserted between the presentation and recall of the patterns (Charness, 1976; Gobet & Simon, 1998). Gobet and Simon (1996) asked players to recall up to five different chess boards and found that experienced players could recall 15 chunks at a time, thus clearly exceeding the well-established capacity of short-term memory. These studies therefore provided evidence to suggest that long-term memory structures were also an important contributor to expert recall performance. Gobet and Simon (1996) consequently developed the "template theory" to provide a link between the chunking theory and long-term memory retrieval structures. They proposed that, after extended practice, chunks develop into more complex structures called "templates," which are essentially large chunks of information that possess "slots" that can be filled rapidly when viewing new chess positions. These templates also contain information on plans, moves, and tactical concepts, thereby providing a theoretical basis for a predictive component in expert pattern perception.

The anticipatory nature of expert pattern perception

One of the key questions surrounding the investigation of pattern perception in the sporting domain is the extent to which recall tasks are representative of the functional requirements of performance in the natural setting. Although an expertise effect exists for the recall of structured sporting patterns, 4-second recall tasks are rarely, if ever, a core requirement of normal game play. Researchers have therefore questioned whether the superiority of experts is a by-product of task familiarity and experience or it is a genuine constituent of skilled performance (Allard, Deakin, Parker, & Rodgers, 1993; Williams & Davids, 1995).

To address this question, Williams and Davids (1995) examined the perceptual-cognitive skill of a group of highly skilled soccer players and compared their results with lower-skilled players and physically disabled spectators. All three groups had comparable levels of exposure to the sport but, importantly, the physically disabled participants had acquired their experience solely through observation. The results from recall, recognition, and anticipation tests showed that the highly skilled players demonstrated a larger and more elaborate task-specific knowledge base than the other two groups, suggesting that the perceptual-cognitive superiority of experts is a core constituent of expertise that is acquired through direct participation in the sport, rather than through observation alone. Superior anticipation and superior recall and recognition frequently co-exist in sports, suggesting that the encoding and structuring of representations of movement in memory may play an important functional role in decision-making and prediction (North, Ward, Ericsson, & Williams, 2011; North, Williams, Hodges, Ward, & Ericsson, 2009; Starkes et al., 1994). For successful participation in a dynamic team-sport environment, players must be able to identify structures and understand the relative meaning of certain player locations within the complex array (Starkes et al., 1994). The ability to extract large quantities of perceptual information in a relatively brief time period may enable experts to predict the evolution of the pattern and may therefore provide the basis for prediction (Williams & Davids, 1995).

More direct evidence of the predictive nature of pattern perception in team sports has been recently reported using a different (recognition) paradigm. Didierjean and Marmèche (2005) used short-term and long-term recognition tasks in which participants of varying skill levels from basketball were asked to differentiate between previously presented schematic configurations and new configurations. Experienced basketball players were more likely to anticipate the subsequent movement of the players in the patterns and this made it difficult for them to differentiate accurately between patterns previously seen and patterns that were further advanced in the direction of the normal temporal evolution of the pattern. Gorman, Abernethy, and Farrow (2011) used a similar approach, but found that, when the images were presented as moving videos, both expert and recreational players tended to predict the evolution of the patterns. This finding suggested that the addition of movement in the video images provided sufficient information to allow the less skilled players also to predict the subsequent movements of players. This study also showed that the tendency of experienced players to predict future events and apply an anticipatory encoding process (typically referred to as *representational momentum*) is not limited to static patterns but also occurs in more dynamic situations typical of the actual performance environment of competitive sport. In pattern recall and recognition, as in anticipation for interception, predictive behavior appears to be a fundamental contributor to skilled performance (Figure 16.3).

Transfer of pattern perception skills

The extent to which an expert performer in a particular sport can successfully transfer his or her perceptual and anticipatory skill from one sport to another is an interesting, yet rarely investigated, question within the study of skill acquisition. Allard and Starkes (1991) were the first to highlight the potential for transfer between sports when they reported the results of an unpublished study comparing the recall performance of ice hockey and basketball players. Both groups were better able to recall patterns from their preferred sport, but recall performance for the patterns from the other (unfamiliar) sports was also relatively high. Smeeton, Ward, and Williams (2004) compared recognition performance across two sports deemed to be structurally similar (soccer and field hockey) and one that was presumed to be structurally dissimilar (volleyball). They found that the soccer and field hockey players did not differ in their recognition of stimuli drawn from both soccer and field hockey, suggesting that the structural, relational, and tactical similarities between the two sports may have facilitated positive transfer of skill between the two tasks. As expected, the volleyball players were able to successfully retrieve perceptual information from their own sport, but they were unable to transfer this ability to the dissimilar sports.

The transfer of pattern perception skill may be limited to specific elements within the pattern. Abernethy, Baker, and Côté (2005) used a recall task to compare transfer of perceptual skill between netball, basketball, and field hockey patterns.

(a)

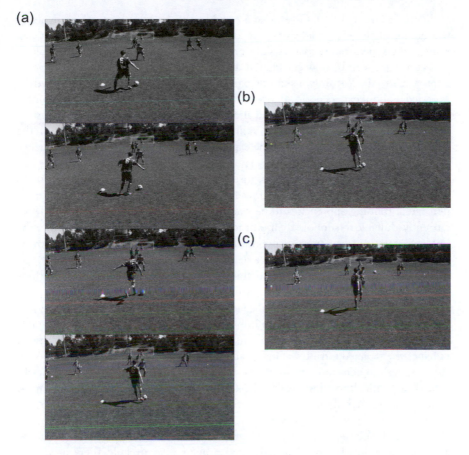

(b)

(c)

Figure 16.3 A demonstration of the anticipatory nature of pattern perception. When asked
to recall the pattern of players shown at the conclusion of a movement sequence
(depicted in panel a), rather than recalling the position of players at the end of
the sequence (shown in panel b), observers will tend to anticipate the future
location of players (shown in panel c).

Experts from other sports performed at or near the level of sport-specific experts on
the recall of defensive player positions, despite little direct experience in the sport.
These findings provided evidence to suggest that positive transfer in pattern perception may occur primarily in the recognition of defensive structures. The notion of
positive transfer is appealing from both a theoretical and a practical perspective but
further research is required to confirm and extend these findings.

Using knowledge about expertise to guide skill learning practices

It has been argued that an increased understanding of expertise is essential to
develop new and improved means of fostering skill learning (Abernethy, 1996;

Williams & Grant, 1999). Given that a considerable amount is now known about the nature of the expert advantage in different sports tasks, especially as it pertains to the superior anticipatory skills of experts, it would not be unreasonable to expect to have seen by now substantial development of systematic, evidence-based approaches to the learning of skills of experts. Unfortunately, despite the growth of knowledge about expert performance and a demand for evidence-based recommendations from practitioners in the field about how to train skills such as anticipation, the emergence of new approaches to skill learning has been slow. In relation to the learning of the perceptual skills of the experts by non-experts, the existing evidence suggests that knowledge and passive exposure to the informational sources used by expert performers is, in and of itself, insufficient to guarantee skill acquisition. To understand why this is the case requires the claims and underlying assumptions of perceptual training approaches to be examined relative to the empirical evidence currently available to support their efficacy. Other outstanding issues related to the implementation of new training approaches also need to be considered to provide a platform for positive future advancements.

In order for any visual-perceptual training approach to work effectively, three essential conditions must be met (Abernethy & Wood, 2001). First, the perceptual skill to be developed must be a limiting factor to sport performance (and ideally one that is reliably less well developed in non-experts than in experts). Second, suitable training regimes must be found that supplement physical practice and selectively enhance the targeted attribute. Finally, any improvements in this attribute through the training program must translate to improved sport performance. Historically, it has been difficult to address all of these questions satisfactorily because of limitations in the research designs employed to examine skill learning. In particular, the historical reliance on laboratory-based testing, the approach of using short acquisition periods focused on untrained participants, and a lack of suitable placebo and control groups for many years limited progress. Fortunately, there have been significant improvements in research design and methodology over the last decade that have helped provide some new insights into the applications and limits of perceptual training in "real-world" settings. Research on experts suggests that, to realize perceptual improvement of a kind that is likely to benefit the performer, the content of the perceptual training needs to be context-sensitive rather than generic in nature (Abernethy, 1996). With this principle in mind, a number of different perceptual training approaches have been developed over the past decade and their efficacy examined. Some researchers have used repetitive exposure to sport-specific patterns in combination with occlusion techniques, others have sought to teach the eye movement patterns of experts to the learners or have highlighted key information sources in an effort to guide the attention of the learner, and others have manipulated the instructions provided to promote implicit rather than explicit processing of the key information. Implicit processing is that which occurs without the concurrent accumulation of explicit/verbalizable knowledge (Maxwell, Masters, & Eves, 2000). The majority of these training studies have demonstrated improvements in the speed and/or accuracy of perceptual skill following training. However, the improvements in perceptual skill are often only assessed in laboratory settings and, where they are examined in situ, the degree of transfer to the "real-world" setting has been disappointingly small.

Ensuring learning benefits that apply in situ

Although the question of laboratory-to-field transfer has been a persistent one since early research efforts (e.g., Starkes & Lindley, 1994), recently some researchers have been successful in demonstrating that perceptual training provides a significant benefit to performance in the natural setting that is not merely the result of test familiarity or expectancy. Williams, Ward, and Chapman (2003) provided video-based perceptual training to enhance the ability of a group of novice field hockey goalkeepers to anticipate the location of a penalty flick at goal. Results from a field test that required participants to move in response to "live" penalty flicks at goal indicated that the perceptual skill developed through the video-based training had successfully transferred to actual on-field performance. Hopwood, Mann, Farrow, and Nielsen (2011) examined whether video-based perceptual training that required cricket fielders to perform a shadow movement in response to temporally occluded strokes from a batsman could augment significant physical practice of the skill when transferred to the performance setting (Figure 16.4). The cricketers drawn from a high-performance training academy demonstrated enhanced speed and appropriateness of movement initiation when fielding in a temporally demanding position close to the batsmen. This improvement was beyond that obtained through their significant engagement in fielding practice as part of regular training. Since these performers were already highly skilled, these findings further strengthen the argument that video-based perceptual training may be a valuable accelerator of skill acquisition.

If perceptual skills such as anticipation can be improved through video-based training methods, an associated issue relates to how this improved perceptual skill is integrated with the motor skills needed to produce successful actions, such as the interception needed in many striking sports. Although advocates of perceptual training have long highlighted the importance of recalibrating new perceptual learning with the action response, there has, to date, been relatively little effort to examine this issue theoretically or practically. Milner and Goodale's (1995) conceptualization of the existence of two functionally different visual systems involved in perceptual–motor responses (a ventral "vision-for-perception" system and a dorsal "vision-for-action" system) offers a theoretical framework from which to examine this issue further, and the continued evolution of virtual reality (VR) applications may offer an appropriate training platform. VR has the potential to afford researchers the best of both worlds in terms of a controllable, realistic, interactive stimulus display linked to a naturalistic response. Methods such as VR may permit a more systematic investigation of the issue of perception–action coupling as well as the underlying mechanisms of visual perception although use of VR in promoting the acquisition of expertise in sport is still in its infancy.

(a)

(b)

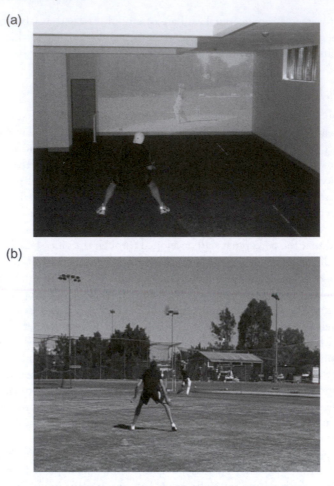

Figure 16.4 Skilled cricketers taking part in (a) a perceptual training program to improve fielding skill, and (b) a test of on-field skill transfer. Reproduced with permission from Hopwood et al. (2011).

Broadening the focus on acquiring anticipation skills

A limitation of the extant perceptual training literature has been the predominant focus on training performers to anticipate likely events based on an opponent's postural orientation. For instance, researchers have trained performers to anticipate the direction of a tennis serve based on the kinematics of the server (Farrow & Abernethy, 2002) and similarly others have examined situations such as defending a soccer penalty kick or hockey shot on goal (e.g., Williams et al., 2003). In contrast, relatively few have attempted to enhance the ability of performers to recognize and respond to the invariant patterns of play, such as a zone defense or press, that occur in team sports such as basketball and football (for exceptions, see Christina,

Barresi, & Shaffner, 1990; Starkes & Lindley, 1994). Given the evidence presented in the previous section of this chapter regarding the central role that anticipatory behavior plays in expert performance in these situations, this dearth of perceptual training approaches in team sports is surprising. Developing and assessing the efficacy of perceptual training regimes in these settings would appear to offer fertile research opportunities given the myriad of theoretical and applied issues that can be addressed in such settings.

The influence of learner awareness on skill-learning efficacy

A conceptual understanding of how learning, especially learning of expert perception, might evolve is important for advancing skill acquisition for sport at both a theoretical and a practical level. In this respect the distinction drawn between implicit and explicit learning is important. Although only a handful of researchers have examined perceptual training using an implicit learning approach (i.e., an approach that seeks to promote learning without the concurrent development of verbalizable knowledge about the task), the evidence in relation to the efficacy of the approach is encouraging. Farrow and Abernethy (2002) perceptually trained intermediately skilled tennis players to anticipate the direction of tennis serves occluded at racket–ball contact. One group was instructed to estimate the speed of the serve. This instruction was designed to draw the players' attention implicitly to key kinematic information in the service action but without any accompanying verbalizable knowledge. A second group was explicitly told what key kinematic parameters to attend to in order to anticipate service direction. Results revealed that, although the implicit training group acquired fewer explicit rules about how to anticipate service direction than the explicit group, its members displayed superior anticipatory performance. Other researchers have manipulated the visual display rather than the instructions and have demonstrated that a group given color cues to help with orienting attention to important information sources produced superior learning to a group given explicit instruction about the location of the key cues (Hagemann, Strauss, & Cañal-Bruland, 2006). Furthermore, consistent with implicit motor learning research, Smeeton, Williams, Hodges, and Ward (2005) have demonstrated implicit perceptual training's robustness under anxiety-provoking conditions, although the efficacy of the implicit approach may be dependent upon the level of complexity inherent in the sport task. Raab (2003) found that implicit learning was advantageous in low-complexity situations (i.e., situations in which the tactical options available to a player in a team-sport context were few) where relatively simple "if–then" decision-making rules could be applied. For example, in a situation when a basketball player may decide to shoot depending only on the positioning of his immediate defender, implicit learning may be beneficial. However, when the complexity of the tactical situation was increased by manipulating perceptual and cognitive aspects of the display through the use of more elaborate defensive formations, where mapping to an immediate defender was not possible, explicit learning enhanced performance.

Conclusions

Studying experts in sport, and contrasting their performance with that of people of less skill from within the same domain, provides an important window into the understanding of skill learning. It has been now well established, from studies both within and beyond the sport domain, that the expert advantage is not evident across all tasks and processes but is selective to those tasks that require the pick-up, analysis, and subsequent utilization for action of domain-specific information. In sport tasks, one of the most consistent and persistent aspects of the expert's advantage is the capability to anticipate, using partial information picked up early in the temporal evolution of the task for the prospective control of action. Both in the anticipation of the actions of opponents in one-on-one situations and in the rapid recognition of complex patterns in team sports, the capability of experts to anticipate effectively is a defining feature of their differentiation from non-experts. Armed with this knowledge, approaches are now being developed that attempt to accelerate the acquisition of these critical aspects of expert performance amongst non-experts. The value of such training approaches may well be dependent upon establishing learning states in which the usual coupling of perception and action can be preserved in as natural a fashion as possible and anticipatory skill can be acquired in a relatively implicit way.

References

Abernethy, B. (1990a). Anticipation in squash: Differences in advance cue utilization between expert and novice players. *Journal of Sports Sciences, 8,* 17–34.

Abernethy, B. (1990b). Expertise, visual search and information pick-up in squash. *Perception, 19,* 63–77.

Abernethy, B. (1996). Training the visual-perceptual skills of athletes: Insights from the study of motor expertise. *American Journal of Sports Medicine, 24*(6), S89–S92.

Abernethy, B. (2008). Developing expertise in sport: How research can inform practice. In Farrow, D., Baker, J., & MacMahon, C. (Eds.), *Developing elite sports performers: Lessons from theory and practice* (pp. 1–14). London: Routledge.

Abernethy, B., Baker, J., & Côté, J. (2005). Transfer of pattern recall skills may contribute to the development of sport expertise. *Applied Cognitive Psychology, 19,* 705–718.

Abernethy, B., Burgess-Limerick, R. J., & Parks, S. (1994). Contrasting approaches to the study of motor expertise. *Quest, 46,* 186–198.

Abernethy, B., Gill, D. P., Parks, S. L., & Packer, S. T. (2001). Expertise and the perception of kinematic and situational probability information. *Perception, 30,* 233–252. doi: 10.1068/p2872.

Abernethy, B., & Russell, D. G. (1987a). Expert–novice differences in an applied selective attention task. *Journal of Sport Psychology, 9,* 326–345.

Abernethy, B., & Russell, D. G. (1987b). The relationship between expertise and visual search in a racquet sport. *Human Movement Science, 6*(4), 283–319.

Abernethy, B., Thomas, K. T., & Thomas, J. R. (1993). Strategies for improving understanding of motor expertise. In Starkes, J. L., & Allard, F. (Eds.), *Cognitive issues in motor expertise* (pp. 317–356). Amsterdam: Elsevier Publishers.

Abernethy, B., & Wood, J. M. (2001). Do generalized visual training programmes for sport really work? *Journal of Sports Sciences, 19,* 203–222.

Abernethy, B., & Zawi, K. (2007). Pickup of essential kinematics underpins expert perception of movement patterns. *Journal of Motor Behavior, 39*(5), 353–367.

Abernethy, B., Zawi, K., & Jackson, R. C. (2008). Expertise and attunement to kinematic constraints. *Perception, 37*(6), 931–948.

Adams, J. A. (1987). Historical review and appraisal of research on the learning, retention, and transfer of human motor skills. *Psychological Bulletin, 101*, 41–74.

Allard, F., Deakin, J., Parker, S., & Rodgers, W. (1993). Declarative knowledge in skilled motor performance: Byproduct or constituent? In Starkes, J. L., & Allard, F. (Eds.), *Cognitive issues in motor expertise* (pp. 95–107). Amsterdam: Elsevier Science.

Allard, F., Graham, S., & Paarsalu, M. E. (1980). Perception in sport: Basketball. *Journal of Sport Psychology, 2*, 14–21.

Allard, F., & Starkes, J. L. (1991). Motor-skill experts in sports, dance, and other domains. In Ericsson, K. A., & Smith, J. (Eds.), *Toward a general theory of expertise: Prospects and limits* (pp. 126–152). Cambridge: Cambridge University Press.

Borgeaud, P., & Abernethy, B. (1987). Skilled perception in volleyball defense. *Journal of Sport Psychology, 9*, 400–406.

Charness, N. (1976). Memory for chess positions: Resistance to interference. *Journal of Experimental Psychology: Human Learning and Memory, 2*, 641–653.

Chase, W. G., & Simon, H. A. (1973). Perception in chess. *Cognitive Psychology, 4*, 55–81.

Christina, R. W., Barresi, J. V., & Shaffner, P. (1990). The development of response selection accuracy in a football linebacker using video training. *Sport Psychologist, 4*, 11–17.

Côté, J. (1999). The influence of the family in the development of talent in sports. *Sport Psychologist, 13*, 395–417.

Deakin, J. M., & Allard, F. (1991). Skilled memory in expert figure skaters. *Memory and Cognition, 19*, 79–86.

Didierjean, A., & Marmèche, E. (2005). Anticipatory representation of visual basketball scenes by novice and expert players. *Visual Cognition, 12*, 265–283.

Ericsson, K. A., Krampe, R. T., & Tesch-Römer, C. (1993). The role of deliberate practice in the acquisition of expert performance. *Psychological Review, 100*, 363–406.

Farrow, D., & Abernethy, B. (2002). Can anticipatory skills be learned through implicit video-based perceptual training? *Journal of Sports Sciences, 20*, 471–485.

Farrow, D., & Abernethy, B. (2003). Do expertise and the degree of perception–action coupling affect natural anticipatory performance? *Perception, 32*, 1127–1139.

Farrow, D., Abernethy, B., & Jackson, R. C. (2005). Probing expert anticipation with the temporal occlusion paradigm: Experimental investigations of some methodological issues. *Motor Control, 9*, 332–351.

Gabbett, T., Wake, M., & Abernethy, B. (2011). Use of dual-task methodology for skill assessment and development: Examples from rugby league. *Journal of Sports Sciences, 29*, 7–18.

Glaser, R., & Chi, M. T. H. (1988). Overview. In Chi, M. T. H., Glaser, R., & Farr, M. J. (Eds.), *The nature of expertise* (pp. xv–xxviii). Hillsdale, NJ: Erlbaum.

Gobet, F., & Simon, H. A. (1996). Templates in chess memory: A mechanism for recalling several boards. *Cognitive Psychology, 31*, 1–40.

Gobet, F., & Simon, H. A. (1998). Expert memory: Revisiting the chunking hypothesis. *Memory, 6*, 225–255.

Gorman, A. D., Abernethy, B., & Farrow, D. (2011). Investigating the anticipatory nature of pattern perception in sport. *Memory & Cognition, 39*, 894–901.

Goulet, C., Bard, C., & Fleury, M. (1989). Expertise differences in preparing to return a tennis serve: A visual information processing approach. *Journal of Sport & Exercise Psychology, 11*, 382–398.

Hagemann, N., Schorer, J., Canal-Bruland, R., Lotz, S., & Strauss, B. (2010). Visual perception in fencing: Do the eye movements of fencers represent their information pickup? *Attention, Perception, & Psychophysics, 72,* 2204–2214.

Hagemann, N., Strauss, B., & Cañal-Bruland, R. (2006). Training perceptual skill by orienting visual attention. *Journal of Sport & Exercise Psychology, 28,* 143–158.

Hopwood, M., Mann, D. L., Farrow, D., & Nielsen, T. (2011). Does visual-perceptual training augment the fielding performance of skilled cricketers? *International Journal of Sports Science & Coaching, 6,* 523–536.

Huys, R., Smeeton, N. J., Hodges, N. J., Beek, P. J., & Williams, A. M. (2008). On the dynamic information underlying visual anticipation skill. *Perception & Psychophysics, 70,* 1217–1234.

Johansson, G. (1973). Visual perception of biological motion and a model for its analysis. *Perceptual Psychophysics, 14,* 201–211.

Jones, C. M., & Miles, T. R. (1978). Use of advanced cues in predicting the flight of a lawn tennis ball. *Journal of Human Movement Studies, 4,* 231–235.

Mann, D. L., Abernethy, B., & Farrow, D. (2010). Action specificity increases anticipatory performance and the expert advantage in natural interceptive tasks. *Acta Psychologica, 135*(1), 17–23.

Maxwell, J. P., Masters, R. S.W., & Eves, F. F. (2000). From novice to no know-how: A longitudinal study of implicit motor learning. *Journal of Sports Sciences, 18, 111–120.*

Milgram, P. (1987). A spectacle-mounted liquid-crystal tachistoscope. *Behavior Research Methods, Instruments & Computers, 19,* 449–456.

Milner, A. D., & Goodale, M. A. (1995). *The visual brain in action.* Oxford: Oxford University Press.

Müller, S., Abernethy, B., & Farrow, D. T. (2006). How do world-class cricket batsmen anticipate a bowler's intention? *Quarterly Journal of Experimental Psychology, 59,* 2162–2186.

North, J. S., Ward, P., Ericsson, A., & Williams, A. M. (2011). Mechanisms underlying skilled anticipation and recognition in a dynamic and temporally constrained domain. *Memory, 19,* 155–168.

North, J. S., Williams, A. M., Hodges, N., Ward, P., & Ericsson, K. A. (2009). Perceiving patterns in dynamic action sequences: Investigating the processes underpinning stimulus recognition and anticipation skill. *Applied Cognitive Psychology, 23,* 878–894.

Panchuk, D., & Vickers, J. N. (2009). Using spatial occlusion to explore the control strategies used in rapid interceptive actions: Predictive or prospective control? *Journal of Sports Sciences, 27*(12), 1249–1260.

Pollick, F. E., Fidopiastis, C., & Braden, V. (2001). Recognising the style of spatially exaggerated tennis serves. *Perception, 30,* 323–338.

Raab, M. (2003). Decision making in sports: Influence of complexity on implicit and explicit learning. *International Journal of Sport & Exercise Psychology, 1,* 406–433.

Savelsbergh, G. J. P., van der Kamp, J., Williams, A. M., & Ward, P. (2005). Anticipation and visual search behaviour in expert soccer goalkeepers. *Ergonomics, 48*(11–14), 1686–1697.

Savelsbergh, G. J. P., Williams, A. M., van der Kamp, J., & Ward, P. (2002). Visual search, anticipation and expertise in soccer goalkeepers. *Journal of Sports Sciences, 20,* 279–287.

Schmidt, R. A., & Lee, T. D. (2011). *Motor control and learning: A behavioral emphasis* (5th edn.). Champaign, IL: Human Kinetics.

Schneider, W. (1985). Towards a model of attention and the development of automatic processing. In Posner, M. I., & Marin, O. (Eds.), *Attention and performance XI* (pp. 475–492). Hillsdale, NJ: Erlbaum.

Smeeton, N. J., Ward, P., & Williams, A. M. (2004). Do pattern recognition skills transfer across sports? A preliminary analysis. *Journal of Sports Sciences, 22*, 205–213.

Smeeton, N. J., Williams, A. M., Hodges, N. J., & Ward, P. (2005). The relative effectiveness of various instructional approaches in developing anticipation skill. *Journal of Experimental Psychology: Applied, 11*, 98–110.

Starkes, J., Allard, F., Lindley, S., & O'Reilly, K. (1994). Abilities and skill in basketball. *International Journal of Sport Psychology, 25*, 249–265.

Starkes, J. L., Edwards, P., Dissanayake, P., & Dunn, T. (1995). A new technology and field test of advance cue usage in volleyball. *Research Quarterly for Exercise & Sport, 66*, 162–167.

Starkes, J. L. & Ericsson, K. A. (Eds.) (2003). *Expert performance in sports: Advances in research on sport expertise.* Champaign, IL: Human Kinetics.

Starkes, J. L., & Lindley, S. (1994). Can we hasten expertise by video simulations? *Quest, 46*, 211–222.

Taliep, M. S., St Clair Gibson, A., Gray, J., van der Merwe, L., Vaughan, C. L., Noakes, T. D., et al. (2008). Event-related potentials, reaction time and response selection of skilled and less-skilled cricket batsmen. *Perception, 37*, 96–105.

Tenenbaum, G., Levy-Kolker, N., Bar-Eli, M., & Weinberg, R. (1994). Information recall of younger and older skilled athletes: The role of display complexity, attentional resources and visual exposure duration. *Journal of Sports Sciences, 12*, 529–534.

van der Kamp, J., Rivas, F., van Doorn, H., & Savelsbergh, G. J. P. (2008). Ventral and dorsal contributions in visual anticipation in fast ball sports. *International Journal of Sport Psychology, 39*(2), 100–130.

Ward, P., Williams, A. M., & Bennett, S. J. (2002). Visual search and biological motion perception in tennis. *Research Quarterly for Exercise & Sport, 73*, 107–112.

Williams, M., & Davids, K. (1995). Declarative knowledge in sport: A by-product of experience or a characteristic of expertise? *Journal of Sport & Exercise Psychology, 17*, 259–275.

Williams, A. M., & Davids, K. (1998). Visual search strategy, selective attention, and expertise in soccer. *Research Quarterly for Exercise & Sport, 69*, 111–128.

Williams, A. M., & Grant, A. (1999). Training perceptual skill in sport. *International Journal of Sport Psychology, 30*, 194–220.

Williams, A. M., Janelle, C. M., & Davids, K. (2004). Constraints on the search for visual information in sport. *International Journal of Sport & Exercise Psychology, 2*, 301–318.

Williams, A. M., Ward, P., & Chapman, C. (2003). Training perceptual skill in field hockey: Is there transfer from the laboratory to the field? *Research Quarterly for Exercise and Sport, 74*, 98–103.

Williams, A. M., Ward, P., Knowles, J. M., & Smeeton, N. J. (2002). Anticipation skill in a real-world task: Measurement, training, and transfer in tennis. *Journal of Experimental Psychology: Applied, 8*(4), 259–270.

Wright, M. J., Bishop, D., Jackson, R. C., & Abernethy, B. (2010). Functional MRI reveals expert–novice differences during sport-related anticipation. *NeuroReport, 21*, 94–98.

Yarrow, K., Brown, P., & Krakauer, J. W. (2009). Inside the brain of an elite athlete: The neural processes that support high achievement in sports. *Nature Reviews Neuroscience, 10*, 585–596.

17 Perceptual expertise

What can be trained?

Joe Causer, Christopher M. Janelle, Joan N. Vickers and A. Mark Williams

An extensive body of research suggests that vision is the dominant sensory system underpinning human function (Williams, Davids & Williams, 1999). As a consequence, researchers have attempted to enhance understanding of how vision contributes to performance in many areas of activity (see Harris & Jenkins, 2010; Land & Tatler, 2009). In the domain of sport, a particular interest has been to ascertain how experts and novices use the visual system differently to allocate attention and guide performance. Mann, Williams, Ward and Janelle (2007) conducted a meta-analysis of nearly three decades of empirical work in this area. The review highlighted some of the key skill-based differences that have been reported in regard to both how performers allocate limited attention resources within the visual field and the manner in which the different components of the visual system (i.e. the fovea, parafovea and periphery) are employed to capture relevant information to guide action. As our knowledge of the mechanisms underpinning the effective use of vision has developed, there has been increased interest in exploring whether and how training programmes can be designed to facilitate performance across numerous domains (Abernethy, Wann & Parks, 1998; Williams et al., 1999).

In this chapter, we review two related bodies of research work that have explored whether training programmes can be developed to improve visual perception in sport. First, we present an overview of research that has examined whether the use of vision can be improved in perceptual–motor tasks that involve an aiming component, such as in archery, shotgun shooting, and the basketball free throw. In particular, we overview contemporary work on the *quiet eye period*. We highlight recent attempts to enhance this variable through systematic training interventions. In the second half of the chapter, we explore the perceptual-cognitive skills that underpin anticipation and decision-making in racquet sports and team ball games such as tennis and soccer. We briefly highlight key perceptual-cognitive skills and review research that has examined how their acquisition may be facilitated through systematic training interventions.

The quiet eye period and training interventions

The *quiet eye period* was initially identified by Vickers (1996c). She examined the gaze behaviours of national-level players when they were performing basketball free throw shots. The expert players employed a longer duration of final fixation before initiation of movement than less expert players. This final fixation on the target during the preparatory phase of movement was defined as the quiet eye period. More specifically, the quiet eye (QE) is defined as the final fixation or tracking gaze that is located on a specific location or object in the visuomotor workspace within 3° of visual angle (or less) for a minimum of 100 ms (Vickers, 2007). The QE period appears to functionally represent the time needed to organize the neural networks and visual parameters responsible for the orienting and control of visual attention (Vickers, 2007). The onset of QE occurs before the final movement, and the offset when gaze deviates off the location or object. The QE period is presumed to be associated with the amount of cognitive programming required for successful aiming (Williams, Singer & Frehlich, 2002).

Quiet eye and performance

Quiet eye has been shown to be a characteristic of high-level performance in a variety of sporting contexts, including aiming at a fixed target (Harle & Vickers, 2001; Janelle et al., 2000; Oudejans, Koedijker, Bleijendaal & Bakker, 2005; Oudejans, van de Langernberg & Hutter, 2002; Vickers, 1996a, 1996b, 1996c; Vickers & Williams, 2007) or at a moving/abstract target (Causer, Bennett, Holmes, Janelle & Williams, 2010; Vickers, 1992, 2004; Williams, Singer et al., 2002) and in interceptive timing tasks (Adolphe, Vickers & LaPlante, 1997; McPherson & Vickers, 2004; Panchuck & Vickers, 2006; Williams, Vickers & Rodrigues, 2002). Experts exhibit both an earlier onset and longer duration of QE than non-experts in various sporting tasks such as tennis (Singer et al., 1998), ice hockey (Martell & Vickers, 2004; Panchuck & Vickers, 2006), soccer (Nagano, Kato & Fukuda, 2006; Williams & Davids, 1998), volleyball (McPherson & Vickers, 2004; Vickers & Adolphe, 1997), basketball free throws (Vickers, 1996a, 1996c), baseball batting (Radlo, Janelle, Barba & Frehlich, 2001), shooting (Causer et al., 2010; Vickers & Williams, 2007) and ballet (Panchuck & Vickers, 2011).

The QE duration has been found to increase with target difficulty, with skilled billiard players employing fixations of longer duration as the difficulty of the shot increases (Williams, Singer & Frehlich, 2002). In comparison with less skilled players, the skilled players were more efficient in their eye movements, exhibiting longer but fewer fixations on both the cue and target balls. It is widely accepted that more complex motor responses require longer pre-programming times (Henry, 1980; Henry & Rogers, 1960; Klapp, 1977) and hence longer QE durations would be predicted for more complex shots according to a programming explanation for the QE phenomenon.

The QE has been associated with spectral indices (alpha and beta power) of cortical activation among elite and sub-elite marksmen (Janelle et al., 2000). The elite shooters employed longer QE periods and exhibited pronounced hemispheric asymmetry. More specifically, greater right relative to left hemisphere activation was identified among elite than less elite shooters. A quieting of the left hemisphere was reported, implying a reduction in verbal analytical processing, relative to the visuospatially dominant right hemisphere. These findings suggest that a relationship exists between the QE period and cerebral efficiency, but the association between the QE and spectral asymmetry was not reported and would not likely emerge given the nature of spectral EEG in particular (Fabiani, Gratton & Coles, 2000).

The use of event-related potentials (ERP) has been reported in various psychophysiological investigations that have examined attentional processes involved prior to task execution. The ERP is derived from the average of multiple responses and represents the temporal relationship of cortical activation to a specific event, thereby providing a time-locked index of the psychological correlates of performance (Fabiani et al., 2000). The *Bereitschaftspotential* (BP) is a class of ERP that is of particular interest when studying the preparatory period preceding task execution. The BP is a negative potential that precedes an actual, intended, or imagined event by 1–1.5s and indexes anticipatory attention and movement preparation (Simonton, 2004). Mann, Coombes, Mousseau, and Janelle (2011) explored the association of the *Bereitschaftspotential* (BP) and QE period in high- and low-handicap golfers during execution of a golf putt. The low-handicap golfers were more accurate and less variable in their performance than the high-handicap golfers. Systematic differences in QE duration and *Bereitschaftspotential* were observed, with experts exhibiting a prolonged QE period and greater cortical activation in the right-central region than non-experts. A significant association between cortical activation and QE duration was noted, longer QE being positively correlated with the magnitude (negativity) of the BP.

Quiet eye training interventions

Although there has been significant growth in research on the QE period, few researchers have used this knowledge to develop training interventions. However, there are a handful of exceptions. The efficacy of a 6-week visual skills training programme was investigated by Adolphe et al. (1997) using a group of elite volleyball players. Participants received video feedback in relation to their gaze behaviour when passing the ball to the setter area, followed by five training sessions on court. These sessions consisted of viewing their gaze behaviours on video and participating in a progression of exercises designed to improve visual tracking and performance, such as tracking a tennis ball, or detecting the ball coming from behind a barrier. Participants who completed the intervention demonstrated an earlier tracking onset and longer duration of QE. The small sample size (only three receivers were included in the pre- to post- analysis) and lack of a placebo or control group were significant limitations.

Harle and Vickers (2001) investigated whether these short-term enhancements could be sustained over an extended period. A specialized QE training intervention was employed in university-level basketball players over two seasons. Players in the intervention team received QE training during free throw shooting, whereas a control group received no training. The intervention involved video modelling and feedback to help athletes develop QE characteristics that had been robustly observed in elite performers. During the training sessions, athletes were shown their own gaze behaviour on video, which was then compared with that of an elite model. They were also given a pre-shot routine to follow while undertaking the free throw task. Participants in the experimental group improved their free throw accuracy by more than 22% compared with a control group, and training QE led to a longer duration of QE and a faster shot movement time. Unfortunately, only the intervention group participated in the pre- and post-test measures of gaze behaviour. Any improvements in gaze behaviour may therefore have been due to familiarization or a number of other factors that were not controlled in this study.

In an effort to overcome perceived deficiencies with previous work, Causer, Holmes and Williams (2011) designed and implemented a more controlled experiment, which attempted to improve the efficiency of both gaze and motor behaviours in elite, international-level skeet shooters. The shooters were assigned to two matched-ability groups. Participants in the control group completed a pre- and post-test only. Participants in the training group underwent an 8-week intervention consisting of eight training sessions and three video feedback sessions. In weeks 1, 3 and 6 both groups received a 30-minute video feedback session of their performance, along with a video model of an 'expert shooter'. The training group received feedback on their QE characteristics in relation to the expert model. Video feedback emphasized the need for earlier target detection and a prolonged period of tracking in order to accurately 'programme' an appropriate response. This strategy was reinforced by comparing onset and duration of QE on successful and unsuccessful trials, and then comparing these with the expert model. Participants in the control group received videos of both their performances and that of the 'expert shooter' without any feedback or instruction in relation to QE characteristics. As a measure of transfer, scores from the three competitions directly preceding and succeeding the training intervention were compared.

Participants in the training group improved their QE durations and employed an earlier onset of QE on the pre- compared with the post-test (see Figure 17.1). However, the control group showed no change in either of these gaze characteristics. Furthermore, the training group increased shooting accuracy from 63% in the pre-test to 77% in the post-test, whereas for the control group no significant changes in performance from pre- (63%) to post-test (61%) were reported (see Figure 17.1). The improved accuracy scores transferred into competition, with the training group scoring higher in competitions post- than pre-intervention. Findings highlight the potential effectiveness of QE training in guiding attention allocation and the efficiency of motor execution.

Stress, performance and quiet eye training

Gaze characteristics have been employed as indicators of visual attention (e.g. Behan & Wilson, 2008; Nieuwenhuys, Pijpers, Oudejans & Bakker, 2008; Wilson, Wood & Vine, 2009). An increase in stress, particularly through heightened levels of anxiety, has been reported to reduce the efficiency of gaze behaviour in a multitude of perceptual–motor tasks (Janelle, 2002) as indexed by higher search rates (Williams, Vickers et al., 2002), an inefficient use of the fovea (Williams &

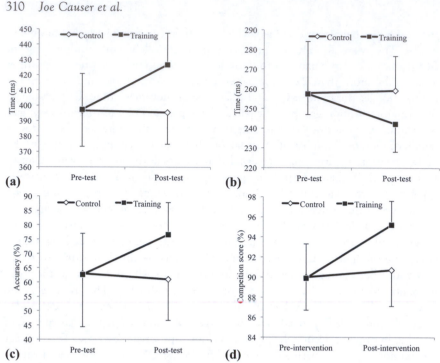

Figure 17.1 (a) The mean QE duration (ms) in the pre-test and post-test for control and training groups. (b) The mean onset of QE duration (ms) in the pre-test and post-test for control and training groups. (c) The mean performance accuracy (%) of the control and training groups in the pre-test and post-test. (d) The mean competition scores (%) of the control and training groups in three competitions before and after the training intervention. (Adapted from Causer, Holmes & Williams, 2011.)

Elliott, 1999) and shorter QE durations (Behan & Wilson, 2008; Causer, Holmes, Smith & Williams, 2011). Stressful situations are likely to reduce QE duration as a result of less efficient processing, leading to more fixations of shorter duration (see Williams & Elliott, 1999). A longer QE period would prevent the eye from fixating on irrelevant areas insulating the performer from the negative effects of stress.

An illustration of the effects of stress on QE characteristics was reported by Vickers and Williams (2007). They tested the gaze behaviours of elite biathlon shooters under high- and low-stress conditions, with the conditions being differentiated based on levels of competitive anxiety and physical workload (i.e. variations in power output levels). Shooters who did not 'choke' (fail to perform up to whatever level of skill and ability the person had at the time) employed a longer QE period during the high- than low-stress condition. Participants who choked (showed performance decrements) demonstrated a decrease in QE duration under high stress. The authors concluded that, for some performers at high levels of stress, visual attention remains directed externally to critical task information, which appears to protect athletes from choking. Findings have been corroborated in other tasks such as shotgun shooting (Causer, Holmes, Smith et al., 2011), simulated archery (Behan & Wilson, 2008) and basketball (Wilson, Vine & Wood, 2009).

In an effort to mediate any potentially negative effects of anxiety, Vine and Wilson (2011) examined the efficacy of a training intervention designed to improve QE characteristics in basketball free throws. They examined whether such training would protect participants against disruptions in attention when anxious. Novice participants were allocated to either a control or QE training group, with the latter receiving a 360-trial training period. The training group performed more accurately than a control group across retention tests, under 'normal' conditions. Under increased anxiety, the control group performed worse than in the pre-test, whereas the QE training group maintained their levels of performance (see also Vine & Wilson, 2010).

To examine the extent to which training benefits transfer to the competitive setting, Vine, Moore and Wilson (2011) examined the effect of a QE training programme on putting performance in elite golfers when anxious, and evaluated them in practice and in competition. Participants were randomly assigned to a control or training group, both of which received video feedback relating to gaze behaviours. The training group received additional instructions to maintain longer QE periods. Putting performance in 10 subsequent competitions was then recorded. A laboratory-based retention test was performed at the conclusion of the study. Regression analysis revealed that the QE duration predicted 43% of the variance in putting performance in the test phase. Participants in the training group were able to maintain QE duration under pressure that was similar to the low-anxiety condition, whereas the control group showed a reduction in QE duration (see Figure 17.2). These performance differences transferred into competition. The training group made 1.9 fewer putts per round than pre-intervention, whereas the control

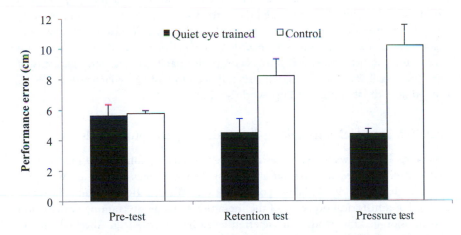

Figure 17.2 Putting performance error (cm) for QE-trained and control groups across pre-test, retention test and pressure test conditions (standard error) (adapted from Vine et al., 2011).

group showed no pre- to post-test differences. The authors did not record gaze behaviour during the competitions and therefore could not directly attribute the increased performance to preservation of the QE period.

Further research is needed to enhance understanding of QE and associated perceptual training programmes, particularly given that the underlying mechanism(s) responsible for the phenomenon are still unknown. The application of neuroscience techniques and methods may help to address gaps in knowledge. Electroencephalography (EEG), functional magnetic resonance imaging (fMRI) and transcranial magnetic stimulation (TMS) offer great promise for delineating the brain processes associated with changes to QE. As discussed previously, Mann et al. (2011) employed EEG in an investigation of the QE period in golfers. Systematic differences in, and an association between, QE and BP across skill level were observed. Additional work is needed to determine how anxiety affects the efficiency of the neural networks in such tasks. TMS could be used to interfere temporarily with function in particular cortical areas, which would allow an insight into the time course of involvement as well as the functional connectivity of areas active during preparation and execution of complex movement plans, including neural circuits involved with emotional reactivity and regulation (see Coombes et al., 2009). Functional imaging during manipulations of QE could help identify the loci of cortical and subcortical structural involvement, which may offer evidence towards resolution of the continuing debate concerning the motor programming and/or emotion regulation functions afforded by an extended QE period. An increased understanding of underlying processes during QE will allow more effective training programmes to evolve, increasing the potential for performance improvement.

In summary, we have demonstrated that the QE period is related to higher levels of skill and/or performance in a wide range of aiming tasks. We have highlighted that the QE period can be detrimentally affected by stressors such as physiological workload and anxiety, but that lengthening the QE period may be a compensatory strategy that mediates any negative effects on performance. We explored how training interventions that promote the maintenance or elongation of the QE duration can reduce the negative effects of stress on performance. The general plasticity of perceptual skill was supported, with several accounts of QE characteristics being trained in both laboratory and real-world settings.

Anticipation, decision-making and training perceptual skills

Several recent reviews have synthesized current understanding of the mechanisms that permit effective anticipation and decision-making (e.g. Causer & Williams, 2012; Williams, 2009; Williams, Ford, Eccles & Ward, 2010; Williams & Ward, 2007). For a historical overview of the literature focusing on training anticipation and decision-making, readers are referred to earlier reviews (e.g. Abernethy et al., 1998; Ward & Williams, 2003; Ward, Williams & Hancock, 2006; Williams & Grant, 1999; Williams, Ward & Smeeton, 2004). We begin with a brief synopsis of the perceptual-cognitive skills underpinning anticipation and decision-making.

Perceptual-cognitive expertise

In recent years, researchers have attempted to identify skill-based differences in perceptual-cognitive expertise in sport (see Hodges, Huys & Starkes, 2007; Williams & Abernethy, 2012; Williams et al., 2010). Several distinct perceptual-cognitive skills are thought to precipitate anticipation and decision-making judgments (Williams, 2009). In sport, these perceptual-cognitive skills include: (1) greater efficiency and effectiveness in moving the eyes around the display in an effort to extract information from relevant display areas (see Roca, Ford, McRobert & Williams, 2011; Vaeyens, Lenoir, Philippaerts & Williams, 2007; Vaeyens, Lenoir, Williams, Mazyn & Philippaerts, 2007; Williams, Ward, Smeeton & Allen, 2004); (2) the ability to pick up advance information from an opponent's postural orientation prior to a key event such as ball release or racquet–ball contact (see Müller, Abernethy & Farrow, 2006; Ward, Williams & Bennett, 2002); (3) a capacity to identify familiar patterns or sequences of play within dynamic team sports (see North, Williams, Hodges, Ward, & Ericsson 2009; Williams, Hodges, North & Barton, 2006); and (4) the capability to engage in forward thinking and to accurately predict the likely choice options open to an opponent at any given moment (see McRobert, Ward, Eccles & Williams, 2011).

There have been few attempts to examine the relative importance of these different perceptual-cognitive skills and how this may vary as a function of the specific task, situation or context (Williams, 2009). More importantly, given our focus on training interventions, it remains unclear if developing each of these skills in isolation leads to changes in performance, or if meaningful transfer can only be achieved if these skills interact in a dynamic manner during training so as to mimic the demands of the competition. In the remainder of this section, we review much of the work focusing on training interventions, with a particular focus on research that has emerged over the past decade.

Perceptual-cognitive skills and training interventions

The majority of researchers in sport have used video-based simulations coupled with instruction and varying amounts of feedback in an effort to facilitate the acquisition of perceptual-cognitive skill. These training programmes have typically highlighted the links between important display (postural) cues and eventual outcome (Christina, Barresi & Shaffner, 1990; Singer et al., 1994; Williams & Burwitz, 1993). Williams and Burwitz (1993) reported improved anticipation skill among novice soccer goalkeepers when the relationship between important postural cues and the outcome of penalty kicks was highlighted using video-based simulation training. A similar approach was employed by Savelsbergh, van Gastel and van Kampen (2010), who required novice goalkeepers to anticipate penalty kick direction by moving a joystick in response to video clips projected onto a screen. A perceptual learning group viewed clips that highlighted key information from the run-up sequence, a training group viewed unedited videos and a control group simply performed pre- and post-tests. Visual search behaviours changed from pre- to post-test in the perceptual training group, leading to earlier initiation of the joystick movement after the intervention. This earlier initiation coincided with the timing of the most important visual information and led to better performance than observed in the training and control groups. Similar techniques have been employed with varying degrees of success in tennis (Farrow, Abernethy & Jackson, 2005; Williams, Ward, Knowles & Smeeton, 2002), badminton (Abernethy & Russell, 1987; Hagemann, Strauss & Cañal-Bruland, 2006) and basketball (Farrow & Fournier, 2005; Gorman & Farrow, 2009).

A number of shortcomings with previous research have been noted (Williams & Grant, 1999), including the absence of placebo and/or control groups. Any improvements in performance, therefore, may be due to conformational bias or increased familiarization with the task, rather than to the intervention itself. Furthermore, suitable transfer and/or retention tests have not been employed to examine whether training facilitated performance in the real-world context or if these improvements were maintained in the long term.

Some of the above issues have been addressed in a training programme to improve anticipation in the penalty flick in field hockey (Williams, Ward & Chapman, 2003). Laboratory- and field-based measures of anticipation were recorded in training, placebo and control groups. The training group was exposed to video simulation training whereby the key informational cues underlying anticipation were highlighted. Participants who underwent the training programme improved their performance beyond that of a placebo group and a no-training control group in both the laboratory- and field-based tests of anticipation. Findings suggest that interventions which highlight the most informative cues and corresponding action requirements, whether by video simulation or instruction in situ, appear to have practical utility in facilitating perceptual-cognitive expertise in sport (Williams & Ward, 2003).

Although training interventions that emphasize critical cues associated with performance have been reported to be beneficial for novice and sub-elite athletes, the benefits of these interventions for elite athletes is less clear. Hagemann and colleagues (2006) examined the effectiveness of training anticipation for differing skill levels in badminton by orientating attention toward key stimuli. Novice and expert athletes were shown a sequence of 84 video clips before, immediately after, and 7 days subsequent to a training programme. Novice and expert participants were split into three groups. In the attention-orienting training groups, attention was drawn to key stimuli (as determined by a pre-study) through a transparent red patch. Non-attention orienting groups watched the same video sequences without the red patch. The two training groups were compared with no-training controls. The novice players in the video alone and attention-training group improved anticipation skill in the post-test compared with the controls (see Figure 17.3), with this effect being maintained on the retention test. The training programme had no effect on expert players, suggesting that video-based visual training to improve anticipation may be more beneficial for novice than expert players. A ceiling effect may be partly responsible for the observed findings, with the expert players already demonstrating high levels of performance prior to the intervention.

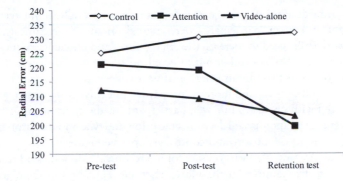

Figure 17.3 Changes in prediction skills in the three novice groups over the pre-, post- and retention tests (adapted from Hagemann et al., 2006).

Smeeton, Williams, Hodges and Ward (2005) reported improvements in antici-pation skill on laboratory- and field-based tests following video-based training with junior, intermediate-level tennis players. Players who were provided with explicit instruction (prescriptive information on the location of key postural cues and their relevance to successful performance) or guided discovery training (told location of the advance cues and encouraged to work out the relationship between various bodily orientations and shot outcome) improved their performance during acquisi-tion at a faster rate than non-instructed players (i.e. discovery learning). However, in a delayed retention test, in which players performed under much higher levels of anxiety, the group trained using explicit instruction showed a decline in decision times compared with groups who either received guided discovery instruction or were left to engage in discovery learning. No changes in response accuracy were reported. Although all three methods of training facilitated anticipation skill, guided discovery methods afforded quicker learning and demonstrated greater resilience under pressure.

It is clear from the studies above that perceptual-cognitive training interventions can enhance the performance of developing athletes in many tasks. What is less clear is whether these improvements can be extended to other populations, such as older generations of performers (50+ years). It is suggested that, although physical abilities decline with the deterioration in muscle size and strength, bone density, joint and muscular flexibility and aerobic capacity, adaptations in perceptual-cognitive skills may be able to compensate for motor deficiencies (Starkes, Cullen & MacMahon, 2004). Caserta, Young and Janelle (2007) examined whether multi-dimensional perceptual-cognitive skills training, including situational awareness, anticipation and decision-making, improves on-court tennis performance in older adults in comparison with a physical training programme. Participants were split into three groups: perceptual-cognitive skill training; technique-footwork training; and a control. In the perceptual-cognitive training group, participants received information on the importance of situational awareness, the key cues that provide the most information during several tennis shots, how to anticipate ball direction and the advantages of making the correct decisions during a rally. In the technique-footwork training group, participants were trained on specific technical and on-court footwork drills used to increase the effectiveness and efficiency of movement during match play. The control group received no training or instruction. In the post-test, participants played four games against an expert tennis player. The training group responded faster and more accurately to shots hit during matches played post- compared with pre-test. Moreover, participants in the training group made a higher percentage of appropriate decisions regarding the type and direction of shots hit than the technique-footwork and control groups (see Figure 17.4).

Coaches predominantly focus on developing technical skill and tend to neglect perceptual-cognitive training. Furthermore, when perceptual training programmes are utilized they tend to be employed in an isolated manner and not integrated into a holistic approach. Technical and perceptual training interventions should not be seen as mutually exclusive, and the benefit of combining the two methods can potentially enhance skill acquisition. Raab, Masters and Maxwell (2005) compared the effectiveness of decision training and behavioural methods ('how' decisions) when attempting to enhance decision-making ('what' decisions) in elite table tennis players. The behavioural group received technical training at regular intervals emphasizing targeting accuracy in the forehand and backhand strokes. The decision group received a combination of training. In the first 4 weeks, participants underwent the same training as the behavioural group. However, the remaining 5 weeks consisted of transition training between forehand and backhand ('what' training), which consisted of video feedback and modelling orientated toward improving their transitions from backhand to forehand. The two groups were assessed on how well they performed strokes technically and their ability to make the best tactical decisions in competitive game situations. The decision group recorded higher ratings of performance than the behaviour group. The results suggest that a combination of behavioural and decision training can improve the performance of elite players compared with behavioural training alone.

More recently, researchers have examined whether the negative effects of anxiety can be mediated through perceptual-cognitive training (Behan & Wilson, 2008; Causer, Holmes, Smith, et al., 2011; Nieuwenhuys et al., 2008; Wilson, Wood et al., 2009). Nieuwenhuys and Oudejans (2011) used a novel method to train police officers' shooting behaviour under conditions of high stress and anxiety. In simulated scenarios, police officers executed a shooting exercise against an opponent that did (high anxiety) or did not (low anxiety) shoot back using coloured soap cartridges. Using a pre-test, post-test and 4-month retention interval they reported that positive changes in movement speed and accuracy of response could be explained only by changes in gaze behaviour. When compared with a control group, officers who were trained under high anxiety developed gaze characteristics that were relatively calm and characterized by long final fixations on target-related locations (the target at which participants were supposed to shoot), which indicated control of goal-directed attention after training. When performance was poor, this was accompanied by relatively short final fixations on the target-related locations, indicating that goal-directed attentional control was not achieved to the same degree.

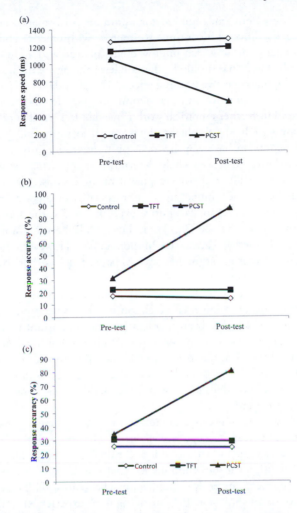

Figure 17.4 (a) Mean response speed (ms). (b) Response accuracy (%). (c) Performance decision-making (%) as a function of training group and pre-/post-test. Notes: PCST = perceptual-cognitive skills training; TFT = technical-footwork training. (Adapted from Caserta et al., 2007.)

Much scope remains for researchers interested in examining the effectiveness of perceptual-cognitive training programmes. The question of how practice should be structured for effective learning has always been a fruitful area for debate in the motor skills literature (see Lee, Chamberlin & Hodges, 2001). The consensus is that variability of practice and high contextual interference conditions are beneficial for skill acquisition. In contrast, researchers have not examined whether similar principles apply in the learning of perceptual-cognitive skills. Furthermore, the optimal frequency and duration of perceptual-cognitive training sessions have yet to be determined. Several unanswered questions remain pertaining to the scheduling and type of training environment required for optimum performance enhancement: Does perceptual-cognitive skill continue to improve with practice and training, or is there an optimal point at which improvements plateau and additional training benefits are negligible? What should be the skill level and age of the learner in order to optimize perceptual-cognitive training effects? The abundance of motor learning literature dealing with practice and instruction can provide guidance for some of the above issues, but further empirical work is needed to identify optimal practice conditions relating to the development of perceptual-cognitive skill.

A recent development has been the focus on trying to identify the antecedents of perceptual-cognitive expertise to help determine what practice activities athletes should engage in to facilitate the development of these skills. Several researchers have suggested that the accumulation of sport-specific, deliberate practice is key to the development of perceptual-cognitive expertise within the sport (see Baker, Côté & Abernethy, 2003a, 2003b; Ford, Low, McRobert & Williams, 2010; Weissensteiner, Abernethy, Farrow & Müller, 2008). However, there has also been the suggestion that engagement in a diversity of sports that share common characteristics and components may be equally beneficial in positively transferring across sports (Berry, Abernethy & Côté, 2008). The engagement in sport-specific deliberate play, for instance informal neighbourhood pick-up games such as street soccer or backyard cricket, has been highlighted as an important precursor to the development of perceptual-cognitive expertise (Williams, Ford & Ward, in press). These deliberate play environments may provide an opportunity for players to solve problems through trial and error and discovery learning, necessitating that perceptual, cognitive and motor skills are engaged interactively in solving problems in a dynamic, adaptive manner.

Another issue worthy of investigation relates to the role of meta-cognitive skills in the development of perceptual-cognitive expertise. Meta-cognition is "the ability to reflect upon, understand, and control one's learning" (Schraw & Dennison, 1994, p. 460). Meta-cognition can be "thinking of what one knows (i.e., meta-cognitive knowledge), what one is currently doing (i.e., meta-cognitive skill) or what is one's current cognitive or affective state (i.e., meta-cognitive experience)" (Hacker, 1998, p. 3). It involves reflecting on one's own thoughts, perceptions and movements. It is suggested that meta-cognitive activities can stimulate learning and problem-solving processes (Davidson & Sternberg, 1998; Malpass, O'Neil & Hocevar, 1999; Swanson, 1992). Are those individuals who possess more refined perceptual-cognitive skills more likely to engage in meta-cognitive thought processes? It is possible that those who demonstrate exceptional levels of perceptual-cognitive expertise engage in more extensive meta-cognitive thought processes before, after and during training and match play. These processes may facilitate the more rapid acquisition of the knowledge structures underpinning anticipation and decision-making skill and may be particularly important when acquiring new skills or transferring existing skill sets to unfamiliar environments (Howard, McGee, Hong & Shia, 2000).

In summary, we have reviewed the literature on training perceptual expertise. We described the QE period, outlined its influence on performance, and evaluated whether training interventions can be developed to modify QE characteristics in sport. Several studies were reviewed to highlight the plasticity of the QE period and to illustrate how maintaining or elongating its duration can enhance performance. Furthermore, interventions that modify QE behaviour can mediate the negative effects of stressors such as physiological workload and anxiety on performance. In the second half of the chapter, we identified the perceptual-cognitive skills that underpin anticipation and decision-making. We provide evidence that video-based simulation training can be utilized to highlight critical environmental cues and their relation to eventual outcome. Furthermore, field-based training interventions can be employed with athletes taking part in interventions in situ to facilitate transfer of skills into the real-world setting. The potential for training perceptual-cognitive skills is wide and unrestricted by age, skill or sport type. We highlighted how training under high-anxiety conditions can mediate negative effects on performance in competition. The literature clearly supports the suggestion that perceptual-cognitive skills can be trained under various conditions and that these improvements can be transferred into real-world settings. In conclusion, we have presented compelling evidence that performance in a wide range of sports and tasks can be improved through implementation of systematic perceptual skills training programmes. Further research will aid in creating training recommendations that are best tailored to meet the specific needs of learners in order to maximise programme effectiveness.

References

Abernethy, B., & Russell, D. G. (1987). The relationship between expertise and visual search strategy in a racquet sport. *Human Movement Science, 6*, 283–319.

Abernethy, B., Wann, J. P., & Parks, S. (1998). Training perceptual–motor skills for sport. In Elliott, B. C. (Ed.), *Training in sport: Applying sport science* (pp. 1–68). Chichester: Wiley.

Adolphe, R. M., Vickers, J. N., & LaPlante, G. (1997). The effects of training visual attention on gaze behaviour and accuracy: A pilot study. *International Journal of Sports Vision, 4*(1), 28–33.

Baker, J., Côté, J., & Abernethy, B. (2003a). Learning from the experts: Practice activities of expert decision makers in sport. *Research Quarterly for Exercise & Sport, 74*(3), 342–347.

Baker, J., Côté, J., & Abernethy, B. (2003b). Sport-specific practice and the development of expert decision-making in team ball sports. *Journal of Applied Sport Psychology, 15*, 12–25.

Behan, M., & Wilson, M. (2008). State anxiety and visual attention: The role of the quiet eye period in aiming to a far target. *Journal of Sports Sciences, 26*(2), 207–215.

Berry, J., Abernethy, B., & Côté, J. (2008). The contribution of structured activity and deliberate play to the development of expert perceptual and decision-making skill. *Journal of Sport & Exercise Psychology, 30*, 685–708.

Caserta, R. J., Young, J., & Janelle, C. M. (2007). Old dogs, new tricks: Training the perceptual skills of senior tennis players. *Journal of Sport & Exercise Psychology, 29*, 479–497.

Causer, J., Bennett, S. J., Holmes, P. S., Janelle, C. M., & Williams, A. M. (2010). Quiet eye duration and gun motion in elite shotgun shooting. *Medicine & Science in Sports & Exercise, 42*(8), 1599–1608.

Causer, J., Holmes, P. S., Smith, N. C., & Williams, A. M. (2011). Anxiety, movement kinematics, and visual attention in elite-level performers. *Emotion, 11*(3), 595–602.

Causer, J., Holmes, P. S., & Williams, A. M. (2011). Quiet eye training in a visuomotor control task. *Medicine & Science in Sports & Exercise, 43*(6), 1042–1049.

Causer, J., & Williams, A. M. (2012). Decision making in sport. In O'Donoghue, P., Sampaio, J., & McGarry, T. (Eds.), *The Routledge handbook of sports performance analysis*. London: Routledge.

Christina, R. W., Barresi, J. V., & Shaffner, P. (1990). The development of response selection accuracy in a football linebacker using video training. *Sport Psychologist, 4*, 11–17.

Coombes, S. A., Tandonnet, C., Fujiyama, H., Janelle, C. M., Cauraugh, J. H., & Summer, J. J. (2009). Emotion and motor preparation: a transcranial magnetic stimulation study of corticospinal motor tract excitability. *Cognitive, Affective and Behavioral Neuroscience, 9*(4), 380–388.

Davidson, J. E., & Sternberg, R. J. (1998). Smart problem solving: How metacognition helps. In Hacker, D. J., Dunlosky, J., & Graesser, A. C. (Eds.), *Metacognition in educational theory and practice* (pp. 47–68). Mahwah, NJ: Lawrence Erlbaum Associates.

Fabiani, M., Gratton, G., & Coles, M. G. H. (2000). Event related brain potentials: Methods, theory, and applications. In Cacioppo, J. T., Tassinary, L. G., & Berntson, G. G. (Eds.), *Handbook of psychophysiology* (pp. 53–84). Cambridge: Cambridge University Press.

Farrow, D., Abernethy, B., & Jackson, R. C. (2005). Probing expert anticipation with the temporal occlusion paradigm: Experimental investigations of some methodological issues. *Motor Control, 9*, 332–351.

Farrow, D., & Fournier, J. (2005). Training perceptual skill in basketball: Does it benefit the highly skilled? Paper presented at the Proceedings of the 11th World Congress of Sport Psychology: Promoting Health & Performance for Life International Society of Sport Psychology, Sydney, Australia.

Ford, P. R., Low, J., McRobert, A. P., & Williams, A. M. (2010). Developmental activities that contribute to high or low performance by elite cricket batters at recognizing type of delivery from advanced postural cues. *Journal of Sport & Exercise Psychology, 32*, 638–654.

Gorman, A. D., & Farrow, D. (2009). Perceptual training using explicit and implicit instructional techniques: Does it benefit skilled performers? *International Journal of Sports Science & Coaching, 4*, 193–208.

Hacker, D. J. (1998). Definitions and empirical foundations. In Hacker, D. J., Dunlosky, J., & Graesser, A. C. (Eds.), *Metacognition in educational theory and practice* (pp. 1–23). Mahwah, NJ: Lawrence Erlbaum Associates.

Hagemann, N., Strauss, B., & Cañal-Bruland, R. (2006). Training perceptual skill by orienting visual attention. *Journal of Sport & Exercise Psychology, 28*, 143–158.

Harle, S. K., & Vickers, J. N. (2001). Training quiet eye improves accuracy in the basketball free throw. *Sport Psychologist, 15*, 289–305.

Harris, L., & Jenkins, M. (2010). *Vision in 3D environments*. New York: Cambridge University Press.

Henry, F. M. (1980). Use of simple reaction time in motor programming studies: A reply to Klapp, Wyatt and Lingo. *Journal of Motor Behavior, 12*, 163–168.

Henry, F. M., & Rogers, D. E. (1960). Increased response latency for complicated movements and a "memory drum" theory of neuromotor reaction. *Research Quarterly, 31*, 448–458.

Hodges, N. J., Huys, R., & Starkes, J. L. (2007). Methodological review and evaluation of research in expert performance in sport. In Tenenbaum, G., & Ecklund, R. (Eds.), *Handbook of sport psychology* (pp. 161–183). New York: Wiley.

Howard, B. C., McGee, S., Hong, N., & Shia, R. (2000). *The influence of metacognition on problem-solving in computer-based science inquiry*. Paper presented at the American Educational Research Association.

Janelle, C. M. (2002). Anxiety, arousal and visual attention: A mechanistic account of performance variability. *Journal of Sports Sciences, 20*, 237–251.

Janelle, C. M., Hillman, C. H., Apparies, R. J., Murray, N. P., Meili, L., Fallon, E. A., et al. (2000). Expertise differences in cortical activation and gaze behavior during rifle shooting. *Journal of Sport & Exercise Psychology, 22*, 167–182.

Klapp, S. T. (1977). Reaction time analysis of programming control. *Exercise & Sport Sciences Reviews, 5*, 231–253.

Land, M. F., & Tatler, B. W. (2009). *Looking and acting: Vision and eye movements in natural behaviour.* Oxford: Oxford University Press.

Lee, T. D., Chamberlin, C. J., & Hodges, N. J. (2001). Practice. In Singer, R. N., Hausenblas, H. A., & Janelle, C. M. (Eds.), *Handbook of sport psychology* (pp. 115–143). New York: Wiley.

Malpass, J. R., O'Neil, H. F., & Hocevar, D. (1999). Self-regulation, goal orientation, self-efficacy, worry, and high-stakes math achievement for mathematically gifted high school students. *Roeper Review, 21*(4), 281–288.

Mann, D. T. Y., Coombes, S. A., Mousseau, M. B., & Janelle, C. M. (2011). Quiet eye and the Bereitschaftspotential: Visuomotor mechanisms of expert motor performance. *Cognitive Processing, 12*(3), 223–234.

Mann, D. T. Y., Williams, A. M., Ward, P., & Janelle, C. M. (2007). Perceptual-cognitive expertise in sport: A meta-analysis. *Journal of Sport & Exercise Psychology, 29*, 457–478.

Martell, S. G., & Vickers, J. N. (2004). Gaze characteristics of elite and near-elite athletes in ice hockey defensive tactics. *Human Movement Science, 22*, 689–712.

McPherson, S. L., & Vickers, J. N. (2004). Cognitive control in motor expertise. *International Journal of Sport & Exercise Psychology, 2*, 274–300.

McRobert, A. P., Ward, P., Eccles, D. W., & Williams, A. M. (2011). The effect of manipulating context-specific information on perceptual-cognitive processes during a simulated anticipation task. *British Journal of Psychology, 102*(3), 519–534.

Müller, S., Abernethy, B., & Farrow, D. (2006). How do world-class cricket batsmen anticipate a bowler's intention? *Quarterly Journal of Experimental Psychology, 59*(12), 2162–2186.

Nagano, T., Kato, T., & Fukuda, T. (2006). Visual behaviors in soccer players while kicking with the inside of the foot. *Perceptual & Motor Skills, 102*, 147–156.

Nieuwenhuys, A., & Oudejans, R. R. D. (2011). Training with anxiety: short- and long-term effects on police officers' shooting behavior under pressure. *Cognitive Processing, 12*(3), 277–288.

Nieuwenhuys, A., Pijpers, J. R., Oudejans, R. R. D., & Bakker, F. C. (2008). The influence of anxiety on visual attention in climbing. *Journal of Sport & Exercise Psychology, 30*, 171–185.

North, J. S., Williams, A. M., Hodges, N. J., Ward, P., & Ericsson, K. A. (2009). Perceiving patterns in dynamic action sequences: Investigating the processes underpinning stimulus recognition and anticipation skill. *Applied Cognitive Psychology, 23*, 878–894.

Oudejans, R. R. D., Koedijker, J. M., Bleijendaal, I., & Bakker, F. C. (2005). The education of attention in aiming at a far target: Training visual control in basketball jump shooting. *International Journal of Sport & Exercise Psychology, 3*, 197–221.

Oudejans, R. R. D., van de Langernberg, R. W., & Hutter, R. I. (2002). Aiming at a far target under different viewing conditions: Visual control in basketball jump shooting. *Human Movement Science, 21*, 457–480.

Panchuck, D., & Vickers, J. N. (2006). Gaze behaviors of goaltenders under spatial-temporal constraints. *Human Movement Science, 25*, 733–752.

Panchuck, D., & Vickers, J. N. (2011). Effect of narrowing the base of support on the gait, gaze and quiet eye of elite ballet dancers and controls. *Cognitive Processing, 12*(3), 267–276.

Raab, M., Masters, R. S. W., & Maxwell, J. P. (2005). Improving the 'how' and 'what' decisions of elite table tennis players. *Human Movement Science, 24*, 326–344.

Radlo, S. J., Janelle, C. M., Barba, D. A., & Frehlich, S. G. (2001). Perceptual decision making for baseball pitch recognition: Using P300 latency and amplitude to index attentional processing. *Research Quarterly for Exercise & Sport, 72*(1), 22–31.

Roca, A., Ford, P. R., McRobert, A. P., & Williams, A. M. (2011). Identifying the processes underpinning anticipation and decision-making in a dynamic time-constrained task. *Cognitive Processing, 12*(3), 301–310.

Savelsbergh, G. J. P., van Gastel, P. J., & van Kampen, P. M. (2010). Anticipation of penalty kicking direction can be improved by directing attention through perceptual learning. *International Journal of Sport Psychology, 41*(4), 24–41.

Schraw, G., & Dennison, R. S. (1994). Assessing metacognitive awareness. *Contemporary Educational Psychology, 19*, 460–475.

Simonton, D. K. (2004). *Creativity in science: Chance, logic, genius, and Zeitgeist*. Cambridge: Cambridge University Press.

Singer, R. N., Cauraugh, J. H., Chen, D., Steinberg, G. M., Frehlich, S. G., & Wang, L. (1994). Training mental quickness in beginning/intermediate tennis players. *Sport Psychologist, 8*, 305–318.

Singer, R. N., Williams, A. M., Frehlich, S. G., Janelle, C. M., Radlo, S. J., Barba, D. A., et al. (1998). New frontiers in visual search: An exploratory study in live tennis situations. *Research Quarterly for Exercise & Sport, 69*(4), 290–296.

Smeeton, N. J., Williams, A. M., Hodges, N. J., & Ward, P. (2005). The relative effectiveness of various instructional approaches in developing anticipation skill. *Journal of Experimental Psychology: Applied, 11*(2), 98–110.

Starkes, J. L., Cullen, J. D., & MacMahon, C. (2004). A life-span model of the acquisition and retention of expert perceptual–motor performance. In Williams, A. M., & Hodges, N. J. (Eds.), *Skill acquisition in sport: Research, theory and practice*. New York: Routledge.

Swanson, H. L. (1992). The relationship between metacognition and problem solving in gifted children. *Roeper Review, 20*, 4–9.

Vaeyens, R., Lenoir, M., Philippaerts, R. M., & Williams, A. M. (2007). Mechanisms underpinning successful decision making in skilled youth soccer players: An analysis of visual search behaviors. *Journal of Motor Behavior, 39*(5), 395–408.

Vaeyens, R., Lenoir, M., Williams, A. M., Mazyn, L., & Philippaerts, R. M. (2007). The effects of task constraints on visual search behavior and decision-making skill in youth soccer players. *Journal of Sport & Exercise Psychology, 29*, 147–169.

Vickers, J. N. (1992). Gaze control in putting. *Perception, 21*, 117–132.

Vickers, J. N. (1996a). Control of visual attention during basketball free throw. *American Journal of Sports Medicine, 3*, 93–97.

Vickers, J. N. (1996b). Location of fixation, landing position of the ball and accuracy during the free throw. *International Journal of Sports Vision, 3*(1), 54–60.

Vickers, J. N. (1996c). Visual control while aiming at a far target. *Journal of Experimental Psychology: Human Perception & Performance, 22*, 342–354.

Vickers, J. N. (2004). The quiet eye: it's the difference between a good putter and a poor one. *Golf Digest, January*, 96–101.

Vickers, J. N. (2007). *Perception, cognition and decision training: The quiet eye in action*. Champaign, IL: Human Kinetics.

Vickers, J. N., & Adolphe, R. A. (1997). Gaze behaviour during a ball tracking and aiming skill. *International Journal of Sports Vision, 4*, 18–27.

Vickers, J. N., & Williams, A. M. (2007). Performing under pressure: The effects of physiological arousal, cognitive anxiety, and gaze control in biathlon. *Journal of Motor Behavior, 39*(5), 381–394.

Vine, S. J., Moore, L. J., & Wilson, M. (2011). Quiet eye training facilitates competitive putting performance in elite golfers. *Frontiers in Psychology, 2*, 1–9.

Vine, S. J., & Wilson, M. (2010). Quiet eye training: Effects on learning and performance under pressure. *Journal of Applied Sport Psychology, 22*, 361–376.

Vine, S. J., & Wilson, M. (2011). The influence of quiet eye training and pressure on attention and visuo-motor control. *Acta Psychologica, 136*, 340–346.

Ward, P., & Williams, A. M. (2003). Perceptual and cognitive skill development in soccer: The multidimensional nature of expert performance. *Journal of Sport & Exercise Psychology, 25*(1), 93–111.

Ward, P., Williams, A. M., & Bennett, S. J. (2002). Visual search and biological motion perception in tennis. *Research Quarterly for Exercise & Sport, 73*(1), 107–112.

Ward, P., Williams, A. M., & Hancock, P. A. (2006). Simulation for performance and training. In Ericsson, K. A., Charness, N., Feltovich, P. J., & Hoffman, R. R. (Eds.), *The Cambridge handbook of expertise and expert performance* (pp. 243–262). Cambridge: Cambridge University Press.

Weissensteiner, J., Abernethy, B., Farrow, D., & Müller, S. (2008). The development of anticipation: A cross-sectional examination of the practice experiences contributing to skill in cricket batting. *Journal of Sport & Exercise Psychology, 30*, 663–684.

Williams, A. M. (2009). Perceiving the intentions of others: How do skilled performers make anticipation judgments? *Progress in Brain Research, 174*, 73–83.

Williams, A. M., & Abernethy, B. (2012). Anticipation and decision-making: Skills, methods, and measures. In Tenenbaum, G., & Ecklund, R. (Eds.), *Handbook of measurement in sport and exercise psychology* (pp. 191–202). Champaign, IL: Human Kinetics.

Williams, A. M., & Burwitz, L. (1993). Advance cue utilization in soccer. In Reilly, T., Clarys, J., & Stibbe, A. (Eds.), *Science and football II* (pp. 239–243). London: E & FN Spon.

Williams, A. M., & Davids, K. (1998). Visual search strategy, selective attention and expertise in soccer. *Research Quarterly for Exercise & Sport, 69*, 111–128.

Williams, A. M., Davids, K., & Williams, J. G. (1999). *Visual perception and action in sport.* London: E & FN Spon.

Williams, A. M., & Elliott, D. (1999). Anxiety, expertise and visual search strategy in karate. *Journal of Sport & Exercise Psychology, 21*, 362–375.

Williams, A. M., Ford, P. R., Eccles, D. W., & Ward, P. (2010). Perceptual-cognitive expertise in sport and its acquisition: Implications for applied cognitive psychology. *Applied Cognitive Psychology, 25*(3), 432–442.

Williams, A. M., & Grant, A. (1999). Training perceptual skill in sport. *International Journal of Sport Psychology, 30*, 194–220.

Williams, A. M., Hodges, N. J., North, J. S., & Barton, G. (2006). Perceiving patterns of play in dynamic sport tasks: Investigating the essential information underlying skilled performance. *Perception, 35*, 317–332.

Williams, A. M., Singer, R. N., & Frehlich, S. G. (2002). Quiet eye duration, expertise, and task complexity in near and far aiming tasks. *Journal of Motor Behavior, 34*(2), 197–207.

Williams, A. M., Vickers, J. N., & Rodrigues, S. T. (2002). The effects of anxiety on visual search, movement kinematics, and performance in table tennis: A test of Eysenck and Calvo's processing efficiency theory. *Journal of Sport & Exercise Psychology, 24*, 438–455.

Williams, A. M., & Ward, P. (2003). Perceptual expertise: Development in sport. In Starkes, J. L., & Ericsson, K. A. (Eds.), *Expert performance in sports* (pp. 219–249). Champaign, IL: Human Kinetics.

Williams, A. M., & Ward, P. (2007). Perceptual-cognitive expertise in sport: Exploring new horizons. In Tenenbaum, G., & Ecklund, R. (Eds.), *Handbook of sport psychology* (pp. 203–223). New York: Wiley.

Williams, A. M., Ward, P., Bell-Walker, J., & Ford, P. (2011). Discovering the antecedents of anticipation and decision making skill. *British Journal of Psychology.* doi:
10.1111/j.2044-8295.2011.02081.x.

Williams, A. M., Ward, P., & Chapman, C. (2003). Training perceptual skill in field hockey:
Is there transfer from the laboratory to the field? *Research Quarterly for Exercise & Sport,*
74(1), 98–103.

Williams, A. M., Ward, P., Knowles, J. M., & Smeeton, N. J. (2002). Anticipation skill in
a real-world task: Measurement, training, and transfer in tennis. *Journal of Experimental
Psychology: Applied, 8*(4), 259–270.

Williams, A. M., Ward, P., & Smeeton, N. J. (2004). Perceptual and cognitive expertise
in sport: Implications for skill acquisition and performance enhancement. In Williams,
A. M., & Hodges, N. J. (Eds.), *Skill acquisition in sport: Research, theory, and practice*
(pp. 328–348). London: Routledge.

Williams, A. M., Ward, P., Smeeton, N. J., & Allen, D. (2004). Developing anticipation skills
in tennis using on-court instruction: Perception versus perception and action. *Journal of
Applied Sport Psychology, 16,* 350–360.

Wilson, M., Vine, S. J., & Wood, G. (2009). The influence of anxiety on visual attentional
control in basketball free throw shooting. *Journal of Sport & Exercise Psychology, 31,* 152–168.

Wilson, M., Wood, G., & Vine, S. J. (2009). Anxiety, attentional control, and performance
impairment in penalty kicks. *Journal of Sport & Exercise Psychology, 31,* 761–775.

18 Embodied cognition

From the playing field to the classroom

Carly Kontra, Neil B. Albert and Sian L. Beilock

Experience acting in the world is ubiquitous, and thus we may sometimes take for granted the profound effect it has on our perception of the world around us. Consider for a moment simple everyday actions such as reaching for and grasping objects. As an infant develops the necessary skill to perform these actions, his or her ability to interpret others' movement in a social context develops too (Woodward, 2009). Now consider a world-class athlete who spends many thousands of hours practising a set of skills (say, a jump shot in basketball or a 3-foot putt in golf). The process of accumulating a lot of specific motor experience, such as the practice needed to acquire athletic or musical expertise, can have a sizeable effect on both brain structure and function. Moreover, over time, practice changes the way our brain interprets and responds to relevant stimuli in the environment. Expert performers (e.g. athletes, musicians, dancers) represent the extreme of accumulated specific action experience and have thus been an important focus for the study of practice-related neural and cognitive changes. They are also an integral piece of the investigation into how people's action experience carries implications beyond their own performance, altering how they perceive the world around them.

In the current chapter we focus on structural and functional neural changes that accompany specific sensory and motor (sensorimotor) experience. Furthermore, we consider the effects that experience acting in the world can have on the perception of others' actions. The idea that sensorimotor experience impacts how we perceive information – even when we have no intention to act – begs the investigation of other situations in which action experience might affect cognition. In the final section of this chapter, we discuss some of the varied ways in which action impacts high-level cognitive activities. We discuss the potential for use of specific sensorimotor experience to drive learning within the realm of education, using literatures relating to embodied cognition and expertise in motor skills as a springboard. In particular, we explore how we might leverage sensorimotor learning to deepen comprehension of action-related concepts in the classroom.

Practice-related changes in neural structure and function

Within his model of expertise, Ericsson argues that deliberate practice produces physiological changes that are the building blocks of expertise (Ericsson, Krampe

& Tesch-Römer, 1993; Ward, Hodges, Starkes & Williams, 2007). These physiological changes most certainly occur in the body (e.g. muscles develop mass, speed improves), but they are seen in the brain as well. Neural changes underlying performance are thought to separate experts from less skilled individuals. These changes affect how the brain supports exceptional performance, and can be borne out in brain structure and/or function.

The classic example of structural changes associated with experience is the case of London cab drivers. London cab drivers develop extensive knowledge of the intricate metropolitan streets and how to navigate them ('The Knowledge' takes years of training and is a requirement for city taxi licensing). Maguire et al. (2000) showed that the posterior hippocampus, a cortical area important for navigating and recalling complex routes, is enlarged in London cabbies compared with non-drivers. The more convincing finding in connecting the role of practice with neural change is the significant positive correlation between the size of a cab driver's posterior hippocampus and the number of years spent behind the wheel. The longer a London cab driver has been on the streets (the more experience accumulated), the larger the part of his hippocampus involved in successfully finding a route becomes (Maguire et al., 2000). Similarly, mastering the art of juggling has been found to be associated with changes in grey matter density. Draganski et al. (2004) found that, after several months of practice at juggling, participants showed an increase in grey matter (where cell bodies of neurons are housed) density in areas of the brain involved with motion perception. This phenomenon generally indicates greater communication among neurons. When participants stopped their intensive juggling practice, density in those motion perception regions decreased; plasticity in neural structure relates to sensorimotor experience over time.

Practice-related effects have been studied extensively in musicians as well. One advantage of studying musical expertise is that experiments testing the abilities of musicians can independently focus on sensory or motor skill, and this level of control has led to some interesting observations. One remarkable sensory skill is absolute or perfect pitch, which is associated with early musical (e.g. piano, violin) training. Absolute pitch – the ability to name the exact note one hears, regardless of changes in other factors that typically affect pitch perception – is associated with an increased engagement of dorsolateral pre-frontal cortex during pitch discrimination tasks (Zatorre, Perry, Beckett, Westbury & Evans, 1998). This pattern of neural functioning goes hand-in-hand with marked changes in anatomical connections within the auditory system. Specifically, people with absolute pitch show greater connectivity between the primary auditory cortex and other brain regions that support the processing of sounds (Loui, Li, Hohmann & Schlaug, 2011). The relationship between early musical training and the attainment of absolute pitch suggests that absolute pitch is not simply an innate sensory skill, but one that is attained through specific (in this case, early) sensorimotor experience (for a review, see Münte, Altenmüller & Jäncke, 2002).

Numerous other researchers have substantiated expertise-related physiological and anatomical differences in musicians and connected these changes to training and experience (for a review, see Peretz & Zatorre, 2005). Using voxel-based morphometry, it has been demonstrated that higher-level brain areas with functions related to the motor system (e.g. Broca's area and superior parietal cortex) are better developed in expert musicians than in non-musicians (Gaser & Schlaug, 2003; Sluming, Brooks, Howard, Downes & Roberts, 2007). For instance, Gaser and Schlaug (2003) demonstrated that the extent of structural enrichment is related to measures of musical expertise and daily practice duration. More playing experience was related to increased grey matter density in primary motor and somatosensory areas, premotor areas, anterior superior parietal areas and the inferior temporal gyrus (Gaser & Schlaug, 2003).

The examples given above suggest that, across domains of expertise, the same deliberate sensorimotor practice that supports performance also invokes our inherent neural plasticity. Next we will move beyond the neural changes thought to support expert performance in order to investigate some of the less direct consequences of specialized action experience. These indirect consequences will be the impetus behind our proposed use of sensorimotor skill in an educational context. First, however, we introduce the theoretical framework that underlies this reasoning.

Embodied effects of sensorimotor experience on the observation of others' actions

Much of cognitive psychology regards the mind as an abstract information processor. However, work in the domain of embodied cognition strives to take into account the importance of interaction with one's environment; this tradition dates back to Gibson (1979), who espoused the evolutionary relevance of perception in service of action. Various theories of embodied cognition have emerged over the past few decades (see Barsalou, 1999; Niedenthal, 2007; Zwaan, 1999). Wilson (2002) summarized six prevalent viewpoints inherent in most concepts of embodied cognition, one of which she described as the idea that 'offline cognition is body-based' (p. 626). The brain inherently resides in a physical body, and is thus constantly exposed to perceptual information. During activation of mental representations that are allegedly abstract and decoupled from sensorimotor inputs, brain systems that evolved for perception and action may be co-opted to support cognition. In this way, sensorimotor resources can covertly affect high-level cognition even when there is no explicit intent to act. Support for this particular view of embodied cognition drives much of the research documented in the current chapter. Specifically, in terms of the investigation of action experience, these embodied views suggest that experience-dependent neural changes not only support the execution of actions, but play an important role in how expert performers understand and react to the actions of others.

How might one's experience performing a specific action change the neural activity underlying observation of that action? In one of the first studies to address this question, Calvo-Merino, Glaser, Grezes, Passingham and Haggard (2005) recruited participants with a range of experience performing classical ballet and capoeira (a Brazilian art form that combines elements of dance and martial arts). Calvo-Merino et al. used functional magnetic resonance imaging (fMRI) to study differences in neural activation when individuals watched actions in which they were skilled compared with actions in which they were not skilled. First, participants passively observed videos of the two movement styles in the scanner. Next, neural activity when participants observed their own dance style was compared with neural activity when they watched the other, unfamiliar dance style (e.g. ballet dancers watching ballet versus ballet dancers watching capoeira). When experts viewed the familiar versus unfamiliar movements, a network of brain regions thought to support both the observation and production of action elicited greater activation (e.g. bilateral activation in premotor cortex and intraparietal sulcus, right superior parietal lobe and left posterior superior temporal sulcus; Rizzolatti, Fogassi & Gallese, 2001).

In order to explore whether the specific experience of doing (as opposed to seeing) the actions within a domain was responsible for their effects, Calvo-Merino, Grèzes, Glaser, Passingham and Haggard (2006) examined neural activation in male and female ballet dancers. Classical ballet exemplifies codified movements that differ by gender. Because male and female ballet dancers train together, they have extensive experience seeing (but not doing) many gender-specific movements. Thus, ballet dancers represent an ideal group to test the relationships between motor experience, observation, and action perception. Calvo-Merino and colleagues found greater premotor, parietal, and cerebellar activity when dancers viewed movement from their own repertoire than movement performed by the opposite gender. Having previously produced specific actions affected the way the dancers subsequently perceived those actions, supporting the embodied hypothesis that systems involved in action production can also underlie action perception.

In another study with expert dancers, Cross, Hamilton and Grafton (2006) set out to 'build a motor simulation de novo' by training a specific set of movements and testing neural activity in response to seeing those movements before and after training. In doing so, Cross and colleagues provided some of the most compelling evidence to date for the experience-dependence of observational embodied effects. At initial testing, expert dancers' brain activity was recorded while they watched novel sequences of dance movements. Over the next 5 weeks, these dancers practised some of the novel sequences of movements but not others. After training, participants showed greater 'motor resonance', or neural re-instantiation of motor plans, when observing trained movement sequences than untrained movement sequences. In addition, neural activity was correlated with the dancers' ratings of their own ability to perform the various sequences. These data support the idea that our previous action experience impacts our ability to perceive the actions of others through a re-activation of some of the same sensorimotor brain areas we have used to act.

Finally, another example of the impact of doing (rather than seeing) on the observation of others' actions comes from work by Casile and Giese (2006). These researchers demonstrated that even a small amount of specific motor experience can enhance individuals' ability to make fine perceptual discriminations. Typically, human gait patterns are characterized by a phase difference of approximately 180° between the two opposite arms and the two opposite legs. Casile and Giese trained individuals to perform an unusual gait pattern: arm movements that matched a phase difference of 270° (rather than the typical 180°). Participants were trained while blindfolded, and given only minimal verbal and haptic feedback from the experimenter. Before and after training, participants performed a visual discrimination task in which they were presented with consecutive pairs of point-light walkers. Participants were asked to determine whether the gait patterns of the point-light walkers were the same or different. Within each pair, one of the walker's gait patterns corresponded to a phase difference of 180°, 225° or 270°. The other point-light walker either matched the first exactly, or moved with a phase difference shifted slightly away from each of the three prototypes.

As one might expect, before motor training, participants performed at a high level of accuracy on the 180° discriminations, as these are the gait patterns most similar to what people see and do on a daily basis. In contrast, participants' discrimination ability was poor for the two unusual gait patterns (225° and 270°). After motor training, participants' performance on the 180° and 225° discriminations remained unchanged (relatively high and low accuracy, respectively). Importantly, discrimination performance significantly improved for the 270° displays: the gait pattern with which participants had been given sensorimotor experience. Moreover, the more accurately participants had learned to perform the 270° gait pattern during training, the better their post-test performance increase on the 270° discrimination trials. These data suggest a direct influence of learning a motor sequence on the ability to perceive slight variations in that sequence – an influence that does not depend on visual learning, as individuals were blindfolded during motor skill acquisition. Even brief motor training seems to have reorganized participants' representation of one specific gait pattern, integrating sensorimotor experience within that representation and thereby grounding visual discrimination performance in the sensorimotor systems of the brain.

One of the themes present in the above-mentioned findings is that areas of the brain typically associated with sensorimotor skill execution are recruited under circumstances where people are observing but not performing the action(s) in question. The results of these studies extend our understanding of the embodied theory that 'offline cognition is body-based' (Wilson, 2002, p. 626). When we observe others performing actions with which we are familiar, we experience increased motor resonance even when we have no intent to act (Aglioti, Cesari, Romani & Urgesi, 2008; Calvo-Merino et al., 2005, 2006; Cross et al., 2006). Moreover, the extent to which someone recruits sensorimotor processes during observation seems to be tightly linked to that individual's ability to perform the actions he or she is observing.

These embodied findings seem applicable to coaching methods; they suggest that, although observational training can sometimes be effective in terms of boosting performance, observation will be most effective when it integrates sensorimotor experience. Moreover, the idea that action experience changes not only domain-specific behavioural performance, but the neural basis of action observation, suggests that experience acting in the world may facilitate understanding of abstract conceptual information – for example, action-related language. At its core, this idea provides strong evidence for the potential value of athletic training far beyond the playing field. Whereas most arguments for physical education focus on benefits such as learning teamwork, maintaining cardiovascular health, learning to live a healthy and active lifestyle, and the expansion of executive function abilities, it may be the case that a breadth of sensorimotor experiences leaves students with a greater expanse of the brain available to support subsequent conceptual representation. If embodied representations can support higher-level conceptual processing, it stands to reason that this could be a useful framework for efforts toward educational interventions and improved achievement. In the next section, we explore the idea that the neural processes which typically underlie our ability to act also come to subserve our ability to understand.

Applying sensorimotor experience in the classroom

Work by Glenberg and colleagues (Glenberg, Brown & Levin, 2007; Glenberg, Gutierrez, Levin, Japuntich & Kaschak, 2004) presents evidence for the potential educational value of an embodied cognition framework. Glenberg et al. explored language comprehension in young children in both formal and informal learning environments. Students worked in action and non-action reading groups. In an action reading group, each student read a sentence aloud and then acted out the events of the sentence using objects mentioned in the text. In the non-action group, students simply read the sentence aloud and then repeated it. On a subsequent comprehension test, students who had acted out the sentences' events showed significantly greater understanding and retention than those who had read the sentences repeatedly (Glenberg et al., 2004, 2007). Sensorimotor experience with the sentence content enhanced students' understanding and, also importantly, their retention of the learned information.

Why would this sensorimotor experience be beneficial for understanding high-level concepts? One potential theory is that physical experience is beneficial merely because it serves to engage students with the activity in question. Students may devote more attention to the entire learning experience and thus understand and remember more content. However, from an embodied cognition perspective the more interesting claim is that students' experiences acting out the events in each sentence allowed them to call upon a rich set of sensorimotor experiences when they were later being tested for comprehension. Perhaps this second mechanism lies behind the action reading group's enhanced understanding and retention of the material. Support for the latter idea comes from related work out of our laboratory.

Beilock, Lyons, Mattarella-Micke, Nusbaum and Small (2008; see also Holt & Beilock, 2006) used a case of athletic expertise to test the transfer of embodied effects to language comprehension. Beilock et al. (2008) recruited expert and novice ice hockey players for a behavioural and neuroimaging study. In the scanner, participants passively listened to sentences depicting hockey-specific actions (e.g. 'The hockey player finished the stride') and everyday actions (e.g. 'The individual pushed the cart'). Later, all participants completed a comprehension test outside the scanner that gauged their understanding of the sentences they had heard.

The comprehension task involved the auditory presentation of each sentence (hockey-specific or everyday action) followed by the presentation of a picture (Figure 18.1). Participants were asked to judge whether the actor in the picture had been mentioned in the sentence. In some pictures, the actor performed the action described in the sentence; in some, the actor performed an action not mentioned in the sentence; and, in some, the actor pictured was not mentioned at all in the sentences (these were included as fillers). If participants comprehend the actions described in the sentences they hear, they should be faster to correctly identify a match between the actor in the picture and the actor mentioned in the sentence when that actor is pictured performing an action that matches the action described in the sentence (compared with when that actor is pictured performing an action that does not match the action described in the sentence).

As expected, all participants regardless of hockey experience performed well on the everyday action sentences. However, behavioural performance for the hockey-specific action sentences was correlated with hockey experience such that the experts exhibited greater comprehension than novices (see Beilock et al., 2008).

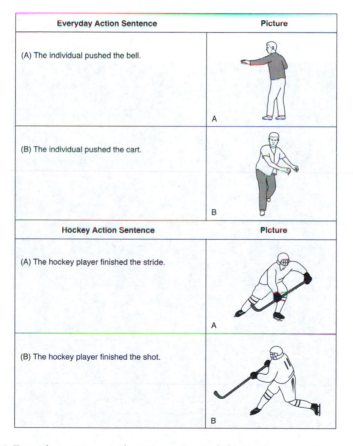

Figure 18.1 Example sentences and pictures presented during the comprehension task in Beilock et al. (2008). Adapted with permission.

Most interestingly, the neural data collected when individuals merely listened to the hockey action sentences explained the relationship between hockey experience and sentence comprehension. In particular, activity in the left dorsal premotor cortex (dPMc, Figure 18.2) fully mediated (or accounted for) the relationship between action experience and comprehension. The more extensive an individual's hockey experience, the greater the neural activation in left dPMc for hockey-specific language and the better an individual's hockey specific language comprehension. These data support the hypothesis that our understanding of language describing action is driven by experience-dependent activation of dPMc, a region thought to support the selection of well-learned action plans and procedural knowledge (Grafton, Fagg, & Arbib 1998; O'Shea, Sebastian, Boorman, Johansen-Berg & Rushworth, 2007; Toni et al., 2002).

This work with hockey players exemplifies how sensorimotor experience can lead to the recruitment of brain areas not typically associated with the cognitive task at hand (e.g. language processing). This recruitment was shown to be beneficial for comprehension of action language and probably explains why Glenberg et al. (2004, 2007) found improved story comprehension for children who had acted out the events in the stories in question. We propose here a theoretical leap in the

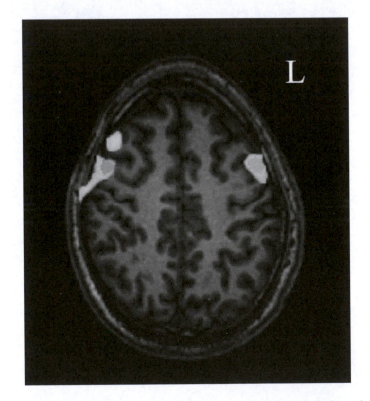

Figure 18.2 Visualization of dorsal premotor regions implicated in Beilock et al. (2008). Reprinted with permission.

application of this finding; namely, a place for specific sensorimotor experience to support learning in the classroom. Consider a college-level course in physics as an example. Introductory physics courses traditionally begin with topics in mechanics, and it is here that students first encounter the challenging concept of vector quantities such as velocity, force, torque and angular momentum. These quantities exhibit a salient relationship between concept and action, and lend themselves well to sensorimotor experiences in the classroom/laboratory environment during which the student takes on an active role.

Of course we do not mean to suggest that the general idea of learning from experience is a novel one. In fact, science education commonly includes a laboratory-based component built out of models of experiential learning (e.g. Kolb, 1984). However, these experiences can vary widely both in design and in execution. For instance, laboratory sessions are typically completed in small groups of students who will take a more or less active role. Even within the category of active laboratory experiences, activities can range from the observation of physical phenomena to the measurement of outcomes to the diagrammatical depiction of invisible physical forces. From the perspective of embodied cognition, one could argue that rich sensorimotor experience tightly linked to the concept in question will drive learning most effectively. This scenario predicts the formation of a representation in the student's sensorimotor system that will come to underlie his or her conceptual representation.

We have begun to test these predictions in the laboratory, using mechanical physics as a conceptual test-bed for other educational applications. Undergraduates at the University of Chicago who had no college-level physics experience participated in pairs. Each participant was randomly assigned to either the Action or the Observation group. During a 10-minute training session, participants felt (Action) and/or saw (Observation) a series of trials involving two bicycle wheels on an axle. The wheels were used to demonstrate various factors that change the angular momentum of a physical system, and thus affect torque when the wheels' axle is tilted through space (Figure 18.3). As Action participants tilted the axle of the spinning wheels, they felt a resistance that indicated the magnitude and direction of torque for each trial. Observation participants received visual information about the magnitude and direction of torque for each trial via a laser pointer mounted in the axle (see Kontra, Beilock & Fischer, in preparation).

Before and after training, participants completed a computerized torque judgment task (TJT) to assess comprehension. They were asked to compare videos of two avatars, each tilting a set of bicycle wheels on an axle just like the ones used during training. Factors such as the moment of inertia, angular speed, direction of spin and rate of tilt were varied from trial to trial. Participants had to determine which of the two avatars was experiencing more torque (or resistance), or alternatively if the two avatars were experiencing the same amount of torque.

The Action and Observation groups did not differ in accuracy on the pre-test TJT. However, at post-test the Action group showed a 10% improvement in performance above the Observation group. This improvement seems to have been driven mainly by increased comprehension of the concept of vector cancellation, or the

Figure 18.3 Schematic of an Action participant manipulating bicycle wheels on an axle.

idea that angular momentum and torque are vector quantities with both magnitude and direction and can therefore cancel and sum to zero. The Action participants seemed to be integrating their specific sensorimotor experience with the bicycle wheels with their subsequent performance on our physics comprehension task. After just 10 minutes of specific action experience linked to the concepts of torque and angular momentum, participants were better able to make judgments about the magnitude of torques within a physical system. [Within this work we are not yet able to parse the relative contributions of creating the torque (tilting the axle) and feeling the torque (experiencing resistance, or deflection of the axle, while tilting).] During post-test, Action participants may be relying on a re-instantiation of motor areas of the brain to support learning. We are currently testing this idea using fMRI.

These findings support the notion that, beyond implications for performance and the observation of others' actions, sensorimotor experience can impact high-level cognitive activities such as comprehension of action language or physics concepts. Although more work needs to be done in order to investigate which concepts will benefit most from sensorimotor training, and what aspects of sensorimotor experience are most effective in driving learning, our findings represent an exciting application of embodied cognition within the educational realm.

Summary and conclusions

We have discussed various examples of neural and behavioural evidence that demonstrate changes resulting from motor experience and the attainment of skill expertise. As in the examples of navigational and musical expertise, experience changes the brain both in structure and in function. These changes carry implications for performance. However, beyond implications for performance within a domain, a hallmark of these experience-dependent changes is that offline cognition relating to the learned skills becomes body-based. Re-instantiation of previous sensorimotor experience can affect the perception of others' actions, as we saw above in the examples of ballet dancers and capoeira experts. Furthermore, because sensorimotor experience impacts perception by the recruitment of neural regions involved in action instantiation, it seems that motor experience can impact higher-level cognitive activities (e.g. language and physics comprehension) when one is merely thinking about the concepts in question. This idea carries strong educational implications.

In our opinion, recent work in the embodied cognition literature provides an avenue for investigation into methods of educational intervention. The theoretical framework we have discussed has already been shown to be influential in the realm of sensorimotor skill acquisition, as well as in providing a general neural mechanism for effects of expertise on action observation. Perhaps we can revisit decades of fascinating motor learning research with an eye toward driving educational improvement. There is considerable basic research to form the foundation of an applied agenda, and the time may be right to see those basic science efforts extended into an educational context.

References

Aglioti, S. M., Cesari, P., Romani, M., & Urgesi, C. (2008). Action anticipation and motor resonance in elite basketball players. *Nature Neuroscience, 11*, 1109–1116.

Barsalou, L. W. (1999). Perceptual symbol systems. *Behavioral and Brain Sciences, 22*, 577–609.

Beilock, S. L., Lyons, I. M., Mattarella-Micke, A., Nusbaum, H. C., & Small, S. L. (2008). Sports experience changes the neural processing of action language. *Proceedings of the National Academy of Sciences of the United States of America, 105*, 13269–13273.

Calvo-Merino, B., Glaser, D. E., Grezes, J., Passingham, R. E., & Haggard, P. (2005). Action observation and acquired motor skills: An fMRI study with expert dancers. *Cerebral Cortex, 15*, 1243–1249.

Calvo-Merino, B., Grèzes, J., Glaser, D. E., Passingham, R. E., & Haggard, P. (2006). Seeing or doing? Influence of visual and motor familiarity in action observation. *Current Biology, 16*, 1905–1910.

Casile, A., & Giese, M. A. (2006). Nonvisual motor training influences biological motion perception. *Current Biology, 16*, 69–74.

Cross, E. S., Hamilton, A. F. D. C., & Grafton, S. T. (2006). Building a motor simulation de novo: Observation of dance by dancers. *NeuroImage, 31*, 1257–1267.

Draganski, B., Gaser, C., Busch, V., Schuierer, G., Bogdahn, U., May, A. (2004). Changes in grey matter induced by training: Newly honed juggling skills show up as transient feature on a brain-imaging scan. *Nature, 427*, 311–312.

Ericsson, K. A., Krampe, R. T., & Tesch-Römer, C. (1993). The role of deliberate practice in the acquisition of expert performance. *Psychological Review, 100*, 363–406.

Gaser, C., & Schlaug, G. (2003). Brain structures differ between musicians and non-musicians. *Journal of Neuroscience, 23*, 9240–9245.

Gibson, J. J. (1979). *The ecological approach to visual perception.* Boston, MA: Houghton Mifflin.

Glenberg, A. M., Brown, M., & Levin, J. R. (2007). Enhancing comprehension in small reading groups using a manipulation strategy. *Contemporary Educational Psychology, 32,* 389–399.

Glenberg, A. M., Gutierrez, T., Levin, J. R., Japuntich, S., & Kaschak, M. P. (2004). Activity and imagined activity can enhance young children's reading comprehension. *Journal of Educational Psychology, 96,* 424–436.

Grafton, S., Fagg, A., & Arbib, M. (1998). Dorsal premotor cortex and conditional movement selection: A PET functional mapping study. *Journal of Neurophysiology, 79,* 1092–1097.

Holt, L. E. & Beilock, S. L. (2006). Expertise and its embodiment: Examining the impact of sensorimotor skill expertise on the representation of action-related text. *Psychonomic Bulletin & Review, 13,* 694–701.

Kolb, D. A. (1984). *Experiential learning: Experience as the source of learning and development.* Englewood Cliffs, NJ: Prentice-Hall.

Kontra, C., Beilock S. L., & Fischer, S. (in preparation). Embodied physics learning.

Loui, P., Li, H. C., Hohmann, A., & Schlaug, G. (2011). Enhanced cortical connectivity in absolute pitch musicians: A model for local hyperconnectivity. *Journal of Cognitive Neuroscience, 23,* 1015–1026.

Maguire, E. A., Gadian, D. G., Johnsrude, I. S., Good, C. D., Ashburner, J., Frackowiak, R. S.J., & Frith, C. D. (2000). Navigation-related structural change in the hippocampi of taxi drivers. *Proceedings of the National Academy of Sciences, 97,* 4398–4403.

Münte, T. F., Altenmüller, E., & Jäncke, L. (2002). The musician's brain as a model of neuroplasticity. *Nature Reviews Neuroscience, 3,* 473–478.

Niedenthal, P. M. (2007). Embodying emotion. *Science, 316,* 1002–1005.

O'Shea, J., Sebastian, C., Boorman, E. D., Johansen-Berg, H., & Rushworth, M. F. S. (2007). Functional specificity of premotor–motor cortical interactions during action selection. *European Journal of Neuroscience, 26,* 2085–2095.

Peretz, I., & Zatorre, R. (2005). Brain organization for music processing. *Annual Review of Psychology, 56,* 89–114.

Rizzolatti, G., Fogassi, L., & Gallese, V. (2001). Neurophysiological mechanisms underlying the understanding and imitation of action. *Nature Reviews Neuroscience, 2,* 661–670.

Sluming, V., Brooks, J., Howard, M., Downes, J. J., & Roberts, N. (2007). Broca's area supports enhanced visuospatial cognition in orchestral musicians. *Journal of Neuroscience, 27,* 3799–3806.

Toni, I., Shah, N. J., Frink, G. R., Thoenissen, D., Passingham, R. E., & Zilles, K. (2002). Multiple movement representations in the human brain: An event-related fMRI study. *Journal of Cognitive Neuroscience, 14,* 769–784.

Ward, P., Hodges, N. J., Starkes, J. L., & Williams, M. A. (2007). The road to excellence: Deliberate practice and the development of expertise. *High Ability Studies, 18,* 119–153.

Wilson, M. (2002). Six views of embodied cognition. *Psychonomic Bulletin & Review, 9,* 625–636.

Woodward, A. L. (2009). Infants' grasp of others' intentions. *Current Directions in Psychological Science, 18,* 53–57.

Zatorre, R. J., Perry, D. W., Beckett, C. A., Westbury, C. F., and Evans, A. C. (1998) Functional anatomy of musical processing in listeners with absolute pitch and relative pitch. *Proceedings of the National Academy of Sciences (U.S.A.), 95,* 3172–3177.

Zwaan, R. A. (1999). Embodied cognition, perceptual symbols, and situation models. *Discourse Processes, 28,* 81–88.

19 Especial skills

Generality and specificity in motor learning

Gavin Breslin, Richard A. Schmidt, and Timothy D. Lee

Introduction

In studies involving the performance of expert basketball players executing the set shot from different distances, Keetch, Schmidt, Lee, and Young (2005) found that success was negatively related to the distance of the shooter to the basket; as the distance from the basket increased, accuracy declined. This finding is not new, of course, as numerous principles of motor control predict this result (e.g., Schmidt, Zelaznik, Hawkins, Frank, & Quinn, 1979). However, a rather unexpected finding was that, when the shot was taken from one specific location 15 ft from the basket, performance was considerably more accurate than the accuracy predicted from surrounding locations (i.e., 9, 11, 13, 17, 19, and 21 ft).

Figure 19.1 contains a plot of the accuracy of set-shot performance (percentage correct shots) as a function of the distance from the basket. Individual regression analyses using the shortest three distances (9, 11, and 13 ft) and the longest three distances (17, 19, and 21 ft) yielded the line of best fit illustrated in Figure 19.1. The value predicted for the 15-ft shot was interpolated from these analyses. As represented in the figure, the actual performance at the 15-ft distance was considerably (and significantly) more proficient than performance predicted from the regression analyses.

Keetch et al. (2005) argued that there is a relatively simple explanation for this finding. As all basketball players know, the 15-ft. distance to the basket represents the free throw line (or foul line): the location from which a player may take an undefended set shot after being fouled during play (i.e., with no defensive player, almost always using a shot in which the feet do not leave the floor). Moreover, since "foul shots" occur frequently during a basketball game, and often play an important role in the outcome of a contest, there is usually considerable emphasis placed on taking foul shots during practice. During practice, these set shots are taken almost exclusively from the 15-ft distance, which is the same as during a game. Moreover, set shots are almost never taken in the regular flow of play (because the shot would be relatively easy to block). Thus, the set shot is a particular skill that is practiced with the intent of being used for one specific aspect of basketball play only: taking a foul shot.

The participants studied by Keetch et al. were basketball experts (collegiate-level players). So, during their skill development they had no doubt accumulated massive

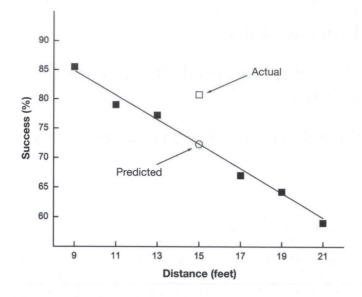

Figure 19.1 Accuracy of set-shot performance (percentage correct shots) as a function of the distance from the basket for experienced basketball players. A regression analysis using the shortest three distances (9 ft, 11 ft, and 13 ft) and the longest three distances (17 ft, 19 ft, and 21 ft) yielded the line of best fit shown. Also shown are the predicted and actual values for performance at 15 ft. (Adapted from Keetch, Schmidt, Lee, & Young, 2005.)

amounts of practice at performing set shots taken only from the foul-line distance. Therefore, the findings from these initial experiments suggested two important features underlying the set-shot skill: (1) that the set-shot representation in memory was sufficiently *general* to allow set shots to be taken from many different distances, with highly predictable results (as revealed by the fit of the regression analyses); and (2) that the memory representation had a *specific* component such that an advantage in outcome accuracy was obtained whenever a set shot was attempted from a distance of 15 ft from the basket. Keetch et al. termed this latter type of memorial representation an "especial skill": a highly specific skill embedded within a more general class of skills or, as a dictionary definition would suggest, an exception to the rule. Our goals in this chapter are to review the research on especial skills and then to present some new data that extend our understanding of the phenomenon.

Several experiments have been conducted since the original work by Keetch et al. (2005; see Figure 19.1). One important first step was to replicate the especial effect with different players, which was successful (in this case, with women collegiate players; see Keetch et al., 2005, Exp. 2; Keetch, Lee, & Schmidt, 2008). The next step was to extend the especial-skill effect. In Keetch et al. (2005, Exp. 2), the visual cues from the surrounding environment (i.e., the painted markings on the court) were covered for the purpose of assessing whether the visual context formed a part of the memory representation for the especial skill. If covering the lines on the court diminished or eliminated the advantage seen at the foul line, this finding could be used as evidence to argue that the contextual information formed part of the memory representation. However, the results revealed no decrement in performance when the visual cues were removed, and the especial-skill effect remained intact, whereby the accuracy at 15 ft was systematically greater than that predicted by the regression analysis.

Generality and specificity in learning

The observation of a general, linear relationship in the performance of the set shots at the non-15-ft locations, as well as other findings of generalizability in motor control, are accounted for by Schmidt's (1975) schema theory. According to the theory, a single motor program controls action at all of these various distances. This program is generalizable, however, such that providing overall-force and overall-timing parameters allows shots from any (reasonable) distance. Observations such as these are consistent with a view that the memory representation underlying motor skills must be sufficiently general in order to combat two potential problems in motor control: (1) the storage problem, which is related to the vast size of memory that would be required if every conceivable type of motor-control solution were based on a specific, stored memory representation; and (2) the novelty problem, which is conceptualized as the ability to use a stored memory representation to generate a skillfully executed yet previously unpracticed movement. According to schema theory, the generalizable quality of the motor program solves both of these limitations.

Nevertheless, research has shown that specificity effects exist and must be accounted for in motor-control theory. According to a specificity view, each learned motor skill is represented in memory along with the sensorimotor information that was present during initial practice (e.g., Proteau, 1992; Wright & Shea, 1994). Published reports focusing on the performance and learning of sensorimotor skills have revealed that the specific information (such as visual and motor feedback information) acquired during many trials of practice becomes critical to sustain performance in tests of retention. In contrast, performance is no longer sustained with the same levels of accuracy when this information is removed in retention tests, or when additional types of information (i.e., "normally" beneficial for performance) are inserted instead.

Although there is considerable evidence demonstrating the presence of specificity effects in movement control, there is only one theory that details a specificity process in motor learning. According to Adams (1971), the feedback (e.g., proprioceptive) resulting from goal-directed movements is stored in memory for the actions actually performed. These representations accumulate with additional practice attempts, resulting in a type of frequency histogram that changes shape as practice continues. During practice with knowledge of results, the memory representation for the dominant (correct) action is strengthened while the perceptual traces for non-dominant (or incorrect actions) are not. Skilled movement results when a single feedback representation dominates all others in memory, with the isolated "modal" representation of the correct movement being the specific memory basis for an accurate performance of this movement. In this view, the learner moves in such a way that the feedback generated by the action matches the feedback representation contained in the perceptual trace. Adams argued that the movement was controlled in a closed-loop way, using the currently produced feedback evaluated in terms of the perceptual trace. Presumably, all skilled movements would be represented by a single, specific, modal perceptual trace.

From research presented on the generality and specificity of practice, it is clear that at present no single general theory of motor control/learning can account for both types of findings in the especial-skills studies. In particular, the specific enhanced performance outcome of the especial-skill effect (Keetch et al., 2005) cannot be explained by generality alone, and the regularity of the distance/accuracy relationship cannot be accounted for by the specificity view alone. As a result, renewed interest in generality and specificity of practice has emerged, using the paradigm and analyses developed by Keetch et al. (2005) in their original study (e.g., Breslin, Hodges, Kennedy, Hanlon, & Williams, 2010; Breslin, Hodges, Steenson, & Williams, 2012; Keetch et al., 2008; Simons, Wilson, Wilson, & Theall, 2009).

Experiments exploring the especial-skill effect

We mentioned earlier the results of a study wherein the visual cues from the surrounding environment were removed without a resulting decrement in performance; that is, the especial-skill effect remained intact (Keetch et al., 2005, Exp. 2). The authors hypothesized that the enhanced performance of the set shot at the foul line could be a result of either specificity in visual aspects of the task (related to the perceived distance and location of the player from the basket) or enhanced parameter selection (Keetch et al., 2005).

To this point in the development of the research, the especial-skill effect had been shown only in basketball, leading another group of researchers to explore the especial-skill effect in baseball. Simons et al. (2009), adopting a research method similar to the protocol used in Keetch et al. (2005), explored whether the especial-skill effect would emerge at the 60.5-ft distance: the regulation distance for pitching in baseball. Experienced college-level baseball pitchers were studied under conditions in which most contextual cues of the "real-world" task of baseball were removed: the study was completed in a gymnasium to eliminate the context of the baseball field and associated cues, and there was no facsimile of the "home plate"; only a target was presented. Pitchers performed 18 randomized throws to targets ranging in distance from 36.5 to 84.5 ft. Of critical importance to the experimental design, the regulation pitching distance (60.5 ft.) was accompanied by two other distances that were only 1 ft shorter (59.5 ft) and 1 ft longer (61.5 ft) than the regulation distance respectively.

Consistent with previous studies involving basketball, the results indicated a significant negative trend between accuracy and distance for all non-regulation distances in baseball (see Figure 19.2). Furthermore, pitching at 60.5 ft was significantly more accurate than predicted (based on the regressed distance/accuracy performance relationship), supporting the presence of an especial skill. A particularly interesting finding was that the especial-skill effect was seen only if the pitchers threw from this exact location, but not if the pitchers threw from just 1 ft in front of or 1 ft behind the location where massive amounts of practice had been acquired. Thus, the evidence suggested that extended practice at the specific distance and/or the visual angle from the target was critical for this task, and was what probably led to the enhanced performance characteristic associated with the especial-skill effect.

To test whether the especial-skills phenomenon was, in fact, a property of the sensorimotor conditions afforded at this specific location over others, Breslin et al. (2010) included a group of novice participants in their study design of the basketball set shot (see Figure 19.3). This novice group had no advantage at the 15-ft free-throw line (i.e., there was no evidence of an especial-skill effect) compared with the other distances from the basket when participants performed with a regular basketball. The set-shot performance of the novice group followed a linear relationship; that is, when a line of "goodness of fit" was applied to the novices' data, a linear trend was shown between accuracy and distance (R^2 = 0.92). When a similar calculation was performed for an expert group, the R-squared value was lower than that for novices (R^2 = 0.81). These findings support the view that the especial skill is a result of massive amounts of practice for the expert group, but not for novices.

Explanations of the especial-skill effect

Several explanations have been proposed to account for the uniqueness of the especial-skill effect: (1) the visual-context hypothesis; (2) the learned-parameters hypothesis; and (3) the specific-motor-program hypothesis (Breslin et al., 2010; Keetch et al., 2008). We review evidence supporting or refuting these hypotheses in the next sections.

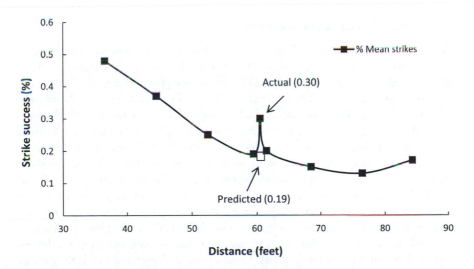

Figure 19.2 Mean group accuracy scores (percent "strikes") as a function of distance from the target. The difference between predicted and actual accuracy are shown. (From Simons, Wilson, Wilson, & Theall, 2009.)

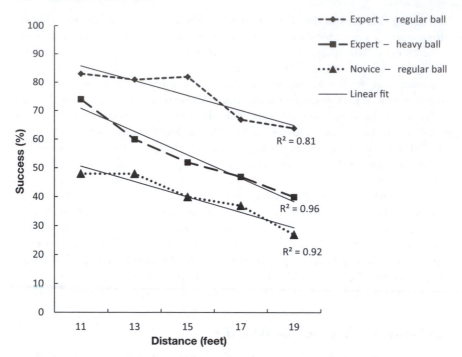

Figure 19.3 Accuracy of set-shot performance (percent correct shots) as a function of distance to the basket for novice and expert players as a function of ball weight. A regression analysis using the shortest three distances (9 ft, 11 ft, and 13 ft) and the longest three distances (17 ft, 19 ft, and 21 ft) yielded the lines of best fit shown. (Adapted from Breslin, Hodges, Kennedy, Hanlon, & Williams, 2010.)

Hypothesis 1: Visual-context hypothesis

Almost every skilled basketball player takes his or her free-throw shots at an angle that is perpendicular to the basketball backboard (i.e., shots are taken from locations directly in front of the basket). Therefore, one plausible explanation for the development of an especial skill is that the shot is always performed in the context of nearly identical visual surroundings because of the constant visual angle experienced in practice. To examine this hypothesis, Keetch et al. (2008) manipulated the horizontal visual angle at which the expert basketball players viewed the basket by having the athletes take set shots at seven different locations, all from distances of 15 ft. The "normal" free throw was taken at an angle directly perpendicular to the backboard. The other six positions included three locations to the left of this normal foul-line position (at 45°, 60°, and 75° to the basket) and three locations to the right of the normal foul shot position (at 105°, 120°, and 135°). Performance at the foul line was significantly more accurate than shots taken from the left or right of the foul line (see Figure 19.4). The decrement in performance at the various locations (relative to the 90° location) was attributed to a change in the visual angle between the player and the basket, providing support for the prediction made by the "visual-context" hypothesis.

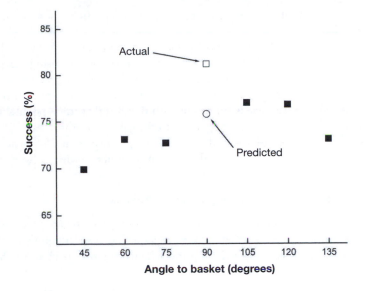

Figure 19.4 Percentage correct shots taken at different visual angles (45, 60, 75, 90, 105, 120, and 135 degrees) relative to the basket for experienced basketball players (from Keetch, Lee, & Schmidt, 2008).

Hypothesis 2: Learned-parameters hypothesis

An alternative view, the "learned-parameters" hypothesis, suggests that what is learned after massive amounts of practice at one distance is the capability to select a nearly optimal, specific set of parameters for the generalized set-shot program (see Schmidt, 1975) that will propel the ball the correct distance to the basket. Presumably, such a set of specific parameters was not learned for the other distances because very little practice had been experienced. In the Keetch et al. (2008) study (see Figure 19.4), the shots were taken at different angles to the basket, but all maintained a constant distance of 15 ft. Thus, the learned-parameters hypothesis predicted that the same parameters could have been used at all the positions with equivalent accuracy. The finding presented in Figure 19.4 appears to argue against a learned-parameters hypothesis for the especial-skill effect and, thus, in favor of a visual-context explanation.

Although there is no evidence to suggest that parameter-scaling processes play a role in the establishment of the especial-skill effect in this earlier study by Keetch et al. (2005), Breslin et al. (2010) tested the learned-parameters hypothesis by using a non-standard basketball. This allowed direct manipulation of the force- and time-scaling aspects of the basketball set shot at the foul line. In their study experienced players performed shots at varying distances from the basket (11 ft, 13 ft, 15 ft, 17 ft, and 19 ft). Half of the shots were taken with a regulation basketball and the other half were taken with a heavier ball. The weight of the ball was increased 2.3-fold without affecting the size or surface feel of the ball. The ball-weight manipulation would alter the absolute-force output characteristics of the movement, requiring the player to select different movement parameters (force) from those used with the regulation ball.

The findings from Breslin and colleagues are also presented in Figure 19.3. An especial-skill effect was observed again for the expert players using a regulation basketball, but the use of an overweight ball with the same players eliminated the effect (i.e., there was no advantage at the 15-ft free-throw distance with the heavy ball). This lack of advantage is consistent with the idea that the especial-skill effect is the result of massive amounts of practice in the *specific* free-throw task. Of course, because the experienced players had essentially no practice at the 15-ft position with a weighted ball, there should be no advantage at the foul line with the weighted ball.

Hypothesis 3: The specific-motor-program hypothesis

The third hypothesis is that, when set shots from the foul line are practiced extensively, the learner acquires a new motor program that is specific only to that one task. That is, the learner does not use the schema-rule that is used for the other distances, but rather creates a special motor program to handle only the one free-throw task that is called for so often in the game of basketball. Several of the predictions from this hypothesis are straightforward. If the learner develops a new motor program only for the especial skill, one should be able to observe differences in the movement patterning of the especial skill compared with the patterning of the shots taken at adjacent distances, which are presumably controlled by a generalized motor program (GMP) and used for the remainder of the distances (i.e., for 9, 11, 13, 17, 19, and 21 ft).

Breslin et al. (2010) examined this hypothesis by conducting a kinematic analysis of the set shots with the regular and the weighted basketballs across the various distances (11, 13, 15, 17, and 19 ft). By measuring the elbow angle throughout the shot, the authors were able to compute elbow angular velocity and angular acceleration using samples recorded during the two kinds of shots (i.e., the kinematics of the set shot at 15 ft versus the kinematics of set shots at other distances). These kinematic variables were selected for analysis based on previous research showing that, of the various joints used in this action, the elbow had the greatest angular range of motion during the propulsion phase of the set-shot movement (Button, MacLeod, Coleman, & Sanders, 2003). Five distinct landmarks were identified, using the methods employed by Schneider and Schmidt (1995). These kinematic landmarks were labeled A–E (See Figure 19.5 and Table 19.1) and corresponded to peaks in flexion, angular velocity, and angular acceleration. Also calculated were the times to reach these points as a function of the overall movement duration. Furthermore, a measure of inter-joint-coordination strength (that is, the correlation computed [with zero time lag] within-subjects, over trials) was calculated for the shoulder–elbow and elbow–wrist joint-pairs (de Oliveira, Oudejans, & Beek, 2009). Coordination between joints was assessed in both the anterior–posterior (y) and vertical (z) axes, as these are the axes in which the set-shot motion primarily occurs.

The specific-motor-program hypothesis predicts that, if the relative timing of the set shot at the foul line (15 ft) is different from the relative timing observed at nearer (11 and 13 ft) and farther distances (17 and 19 ft), this would indicate that a

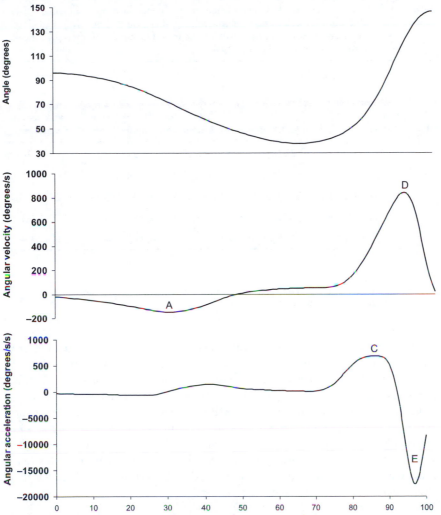

Figure 19.5 Exemplar angle–time, angular-velocity–time, and angular-acceleration–time series for a single subject at the 15-ft line. The temporal locations of landmarks A–E are shown.

distinct and separate memory representation was created for the especial skill. In other words, a memory representation that differs from similar movements belonging to the same class of actions exists (i.e., separate from the GMP). The findings showed that the relative timing at the 15-ft distance was not significantly different from other near and far distances (with the exception of the 19-ft distance; see Table 19.1). The (almost complete) absence of differences across the distances provided no evidence that the especial skill at the free-throw line was governed by a separate motor program. Furthermore, there was no indication that the shoulder–elbow

Table 19.1 Relative timing (time to kinematic landmark divided by movement time × 100) for elbow angle (peak flexion), elbow velocity (negative and positive), and elbow acceleration (positive and negative) for the expert group for different distances from the basket with the regular ball

	Kinematic landmarks				
Distance (ft)	A peak negative velocity	B peak flexion	C peak positive acceleration	D peak positive velocity	E peak negative acceleration
11	34.71 (7.98)	61.22 (8.02)	83.69 (2.08)	90.27 (1.78)	97.78 (0.91)
13	35.4 (9.33)	63.04 (7.45)	83.36 (2.30)	90.04 (1.77)	97.60 (1.03)
15	34.02 (6.27)	60.27 (7.58)	82.20 (3.15)	89.47 (2.24)	97.24 (1.06)
17	34.09 (11.98)	62.47 (8.11)	82.22 (2.54)	89.51 (1.74)	97.11 (1.18)
19	37.82 (11.53)	65.73 (8.46)*	83.00 (2.53)	89.98 (1.90)	97.11 (1.43)

Notes
*$p < 0.01$
SD values are in parentheses. Columns appear in chronological order corresponding to when in the execution of the set-shot the landmarks are evidenced.

or elbow–wrist couplings changed with distance. These findings lend support to a conclusion that the outcome properties of the especial skill are not the result of the formation of a "new," specific motor program for the free-throw shot, but rather result from improved capabilities to scale the GMP. Therefore, for an especial skill, this may suggest that the same GMP is applied for performing all set shots (11, 13, 15, 17, and 19 ft), yet with massive amounts of practice a more accurate or "refined" parameter selection is implemented through the recall schema. The absence of evidence for a unique GMP at the 15-ft line strengthens our belief in the learned-parameters explanation for the especial-skill effect that is perhaps additionally moderated by the visual sensory context.

Creating an especial skill effect through practice

Until recently, little was known about how early or late in practice the especial-skill effect emerged, and whether or not the especial-skill effect actually is a result of massive amounts of practice (Breslin et al., 2010; Keetch et al., 2005). With the exception of one previous study (Breslin et al., 2010; see Figure 19.3 here) in which a novice group of participants was studied, the type of practice needed for novices to develop an especial skill had not been explored. Breslin, Hodges, Steenson, and Williams (2012) manipulated the nature of practice, that is, variable- or constant-practice conditions. In a pre-test, across a number of distances, presumably performance at 15 ft would be based on the selection of parameters for the GMP governing the larger class of set shots. However, after 300 trials of practice, the reliance on parameter selection would remain for the variable practice group who practiced the set shot across each of the various distances (11, 13, 15, 17, and 19 ft). This selection mechanism might break down for a group practicing under constant practice (i.e., having practice only at the 15-ft distance). In view of the variability-of-practice literature (Shea & Kohl, 1990, 1991), there might even be reason to suspect that the variable group would be more accurate at the free-throw line in a post-test than the constant-practice group. The reason for better accuracy for the variable practice could be attributed to the player's being able to rely on the relative strength of the GMP through practice at the near and far distances and the 15-ft line as opposed to relying only on practice at the 15-ft distance line that would be attributed by specificity of practice views.

Shot accuracy (at the 15-ft distance), for both groups, did not differ statistically. However, on the post-test, there was a significant difference between the actual and expected scores for the constant-practice group, but not for the variable-practice group, with the constant group showing improved accuracy on the actual shot compared with predicted. This finding provided evidence that an effect similar to the especial-skill effect emerged as a result of constant practice at the free-throw line, but not for variable practice. It is worth noting, however, that no significant main effect for group nor a group by distance interaction was reported in the study. This suggests that one type of practice was no better or worse than the other in enhancing learning, but paradoxically a difference between expected versus actual scores for the constant group at the 15-ft line was present. From these data, it appears that there is some reason to think that the especial-skill effect is brought about by constant practice conditions. If this were the case, then it might be possible to study reasons for the especial-skills effect using a learning paradigm by manipulation of the sensorimotor conditions coupled with measurement of movement kinematics. Importantly, massive amounts of practice were not required to show the difference between actual and predicted scores at the 15-ft distance.

Implications for theory development and directions for future research

The findings presented have implications both for furthering understanding of the especial-skill effect and for theories of motor learning. These findings seem to support a specificity interpretation while at the same time, which may seem contradictory, they are in line with schema-theory predictions. Briefly, schema theory would suggest that no single action within a class of actions should be any more refined than others within the same class. Instead of a new motor program for the especial skill, schema theory would hold that one GMP is used for all of the members of the class (for a review, see Schmidt & Lee, 2005; see also Keetch et al., 2008), but that the 15-ft distance enjoyed a benefit in terms of parameter selection. Certainly, more work is needed to unravel these issues. In future researchers could explore the emergence of the especial effect across different tasks, in the form of learning studies employing measures of visual attention and full-body movement kinematics. The types of tasks that could be explored include serving an ace ball in tennis or volleyball, scoring triple 20 in a game of darts, or hitting the middle target in archery across varying distances. It is not clear whether the automaticity of the especial skill effect is resilient to the effect of fatigue, distraction, competitive pressure, or performance anxiety, so the application of especial skills remains unclear. Work is currently being untaken in our laboratories to explore some of these potential effects.

Summary and conclusion

The advantage in performance at the foul line in basketball led Keetch and colleagues (2005) to the label of "especial skill." Various research groups have replicated the especial-skill findings and offered explanations of why it occurred. It seems that both the visual-context (Keetch et al., 2008) and learned-parameters hypotheses (Breslin et al., 2010) provide plausible explanations for the memory representation that governs especial skills. Our bias is to favor the learned-parameters hypothesis, as the visual-context hypothesis does not really provide an explanation for especial skills; it simply isolates certain visually based factors that influence performance. Based on kinematic evidence from one study (Breslin et al., 2010), there seems to be no evidence that the especial skill is based on a unique motor program learned for the foul shot only. However, this conclusion is relatively weak and requires further exploration, as it is based on null effects in the kinematic analyses. Certainly more work is needed to unravel these issues.

References

Adams, J. A. (1971). A closed-loop theory of motor learning. *Journal of Motor Behavior, 3,* 111–150.

Breslin, G., Hodges, N, J., Kennedy, R., Hanlon, M., & Williams, A. M. (2010). An especial skill: Support for a learned parameters hypothesis. *Acta Psychologica, 134,* 55–60.

Breslin, G., Hodges, N, J., Steenson, A., & Williams, A. M. (2012). Constant or variable practice: Recreating the especial skill effect. *Acta Psychologica.* doi: 10.1016/j.actpsy.2012.04.002.

Button, C., Macleod, M., Coleman, S., & Sanders, R., (2003). Examining movement variability in the basketball free-throw action at different skill levels. *Research Quarterly for Exercise and Sport, 74,* 257–269.

de Oliveira, R. F., Oudejans, R. D., & Beek, P. J. (2009). Experts appear to use angle of elevation information in basketball shooting. *Journal of Experimental Psychology: Human Perception and Performance, 35,* 750–761.

Keetch, K. M., Schmidt, R. A., Lee, T. D., & Young, D. E. (2005). Especial skills: Their emergence with massive amounts of practice. *Journal of Experimental Psychology: Human Perception and Performance, 31,* 970–978.

Keetch, K. M., Lee, T. D., & Schmidt, R. A. (2008). Especial skills: Specificity embedded within generality. *Journal of Sport & Exercise Psychology, 30,* 723–736.

Proteau, L. (1992). On the specificity of learning and the role of visual information for movement control. In Proteau, L., & Elliott, D. (Eds.), *Vision and motor control* (pp. 67–103). Amsterdam: Elsevier.

Schmidt, R. A. (1975). A schema theory of discrete motor skill learning. *Psychological Review, 82,* 225–260.

Schmidt, R. A., & Lee, T. D. (2005). *Motor control and learning: A behavioral emphasis* (5th edn.). Champaign, IL: Human Kinetics.

Schmidt, R. A., Zelaznik, H. N., Hawkins, B., Frank, J. S., & Quinn, J. T. (1979). Motor-output variability: A theory for the accuracy of rapid motor acts. *Psychological Review, 86,* 415–451.

Schneider, D. M., & Schmidt, R. A. (1995). Units of action in motor control: Role of response complexity and target speed. *Human Performance, 8,* 27–49.

Shea, C. H., & Kohl, R. M. (1990). Specificity and variability of practice. *Research Quarterly for Exercise and Sport, 61,* 169–177.

Shea, C. H., & Kohl, R. M. (1991). Composition of practice: Influence on the retention of motor skills. *Research Quarterly for Exercise and Sport, 62,* 187–195.

Simons, J. P., Wilson, J., Wilson, G., & Theall, S. (2009). Challenges to cognitive bases for an especial motor skill at the regulation baseball pitching distance. *Research Quarterly for Exercise and Sport, 80*(3), 469–479.

Wright, D. L., & Shea, C. H. (1994). Cognition and motor skill acquisition: Contextual dependencies. In Reynolds, C. R. (Ed.), *Cognitive assessment: A multidisciplinary perspective* (pp. 89–106). New York: Plenum Press.

Part V

Research, theory and practice

Challenges and solutions

20 Translating theory into practice

Working at the 'coal face' in the UK!

A. Mark Williams, Paul Ford, Joe Causer, Oliver Logan and Stafford Murray

Introduction

Research in the area of skill acquisition has a long history, dating back at least as far as the work of Bryan and Harter (1897, 1899). The application of scientific findings from this field had a significant impact on policy and practice in human factors and ergonomics in the second half of the twentieth century (Summers, 2004). However, there has been limited application of the principles of skill acquisition in elite sport (Williams, 2006). This latter observation is surprising given the corresponding investment in scientific support in high-performance sport over the last two decades in many countries, particularly in exercise physiology, performance analysis and sport psychology. It appears that few scientists in the area of skill acquisition are engaging with practitioners. The prevailing tendency is for scientists to be less concerned about how knowledge generated could have translational impact and more occupied with the need to achieve traditional academic markers of impact and esteem. These latter motives are without doubt worthy and necessary benchmarks of academic excellence and career progression. However, there is increasing awareness that all fields of science must impact broadly on society by influencing public policy and behaviour. An enhanced focus on translational impact has resulted in renewed (or new) efforts to bridge the gap between theory and applied practice in the field of skill acquisition in sport (Williams & Ford, 2009; Williams & Hodges, 2005).

In this chapter, we describe recent attempts at the English Institute of Sport to forge closer links between scientists with a background in skill acquisition, and its cognate discipline areas of cognitive psychology, motor behaviour, motor control, motor learning and behavioural neuroscience, and those involved in high-performance sport. Our intention is to present a record of these recent developments in the hope that this is helpful to others in the area of skill acquisition who may be attempting to forge links with external stakeholders, particularly in the area of elite sport. In the first section, we outline how the partnership was initiated and how this has developed over time. In the second section, we provide an illustration of some of the work completed through reference to two case study examples involving elite performers in archery and shooting. These case studies illustrate how scientific principles from the skill acquisition literature may be applied at the 'coal face'. In the final section, we highlight some challenges and suggestions of how these links may be fostered by others in the future so that the area of skill acquisition may develop into a more vibrant field for applied practice over coming years. Although there has been steady progress in integrating theory and practice in this field, it should be acknowledged that there remains much work to be done. As an illustration, the English Institute of Sport currently employs about 50 strength and conditioning specialists, 20 exercise physiologists, 20 performance lifestyle advisors, 20 performance analysts and 14 sport psychologists. It does not currently employ a full-time skill acquisition specialist, although one of the co-authors (Logan) fulfils the role of National Lead for Skill Acquisition on a part-time basis.

Building partnerships: engagement with practitioners

Traditionally, issues related to skill acquisition have been assumed to fall under the remit of the coach. In recent years there is growing interest from practitioners at the English Institute of Sport in exploring how skill acquisition specialists can work with coaches and other practitioners to enhance the processes underpinning elite athlete development. Contemporary literature on expertise and skill learning is now widely available through traditional scientific outlets (e.g. Davids, Button & Bennett, 2008; Farrow, Baker & MacMahon, 2009; Hodges & Williams, 2007), as well as popular science books (e.g. Coyle, 2009; Gladwell, 2008; Syed, 2009). As a result of this growth in interest, and prior to the recruitment of one of the co-authors (Logan) as National Lead for Skill Acquisition, the lead author (Williams) was invited by the National Lead for Performance Analysis (Murray) to deliver a series of workshops to illustrate what skill acquisition had to offer this cohort of practitioners in their work with elite athletes. These talks were largely based around recent scientific papers (see Williams & Ford, 2009; Williams & Hodges, 2005). The sessions included discussion around a range of themes related to anticipation and decision-making; visual gaze during aiming tasks; structuring practice; conveying information to athletes (instruction and feedback); deliberate practice; and models and systems for talent identification and development.

As a follow up to these didactic, seminar and discussion sessions, efforts were made to interview all 20 of the Performance Analysts employed by the English Institute of Sport in order to (1) identify their experiential background in the area of skill acquisition; (2) ascertain whether, or how, they were using skill acquisition principles in their working practices; and (3) identify potential areas where support from skill acquisition specialists could most benefit their current practice. At the time of the survey, the 20 Performance Analysts employed by the English Institute of Sport completed a questionnaire survey and participated in a 45-minute interview session conducted by two of the co-authors (Williams, Ford). The average length of service of the analysts in the English Institute of Sport system was 23.5 months (range = 2 to 66 months). These individuals were working with a total of 19 different high-performance sports. The survey identified that additional understanding of skill acquisition principles would assist both practitioners and the coaches and athletes with which they work. All were motivated to learn more about this area and to work with a specialist or group of specialists with a background in skill acquisition.

After this interview phase, efforts were made to undertake field visits to examine the current working practices of Performance Analysts and to ascertain whether, or how, they may be improved through closer integration with skill acquisition specialists. Funding for this initiative was provided by UK Sport. A number of 1-day field visits were undertaken over a 6-week period. Two of the co-authors (Williams, Ford) shadowed a sample of eight Performance Analysts as they carried out their routine, day-to-day work with Olympic sports. The first half of the visit involved observation of current practice, whereas in the second half of each visit efforts were made to engage with the Performance Analysts to ascertain the aims and objectives of the work and explore potential areas in which skill acquisition input could impact on performance. The Performance Analysts were working with national teams in the following sports: archery; badminton; boxing; canoeing; diving; gymnastics; field hockey; handball; sailing; shooting; squash; and taekwondo. The reported observations corroborated those that emerged from the earlier questionnaire/interview phase, with few documented examples of skill acquisition theory and research being applied in daily work practices. However, several potential areas for intervention were identified across these sports. These areas are identified in Table 20.1.

The potential avenues for interventions were evaluated on a range of factors, such as the level of interest demonstrated by coaches and analysts and the potential impact of the work in regards to increasing the chances of success at international level (i.e. podium positions). We report by way of illustration two such case studies in the next section of the chapter involving interventions in archery and shooting respectively.

Table 20.1 Potential areas for intervention using skill acquisition theory as identified following site visits and discussions with Performance Analysts

Number of sports interested	Topic areas
9	Testing and training anticipation and decision-making
7	Enhancing feedback provision
3	Training quiet eye
2	Developing external focus of attention
2	Identifying the conditions underpinning deliberate practice
2	Specificity of practice environment and transfer to competition
1	Identifying the effects of stress on performance

Putting theory into practice: illustrations of applied interventions

Case study 1: 'You can teach an old dog a new trick!'

In the winter of 2009, a new Head Coach for Great Britain's archery squad was employed; he was very interested in applying principles of skill acquisition theory in practice. As a result of the new coach's initial assessment of the strengths and weaknesses of athletes in the squad, it was decided that some major technical changes were required. The main reason for this perceived need to change technique was to improve performance consistency particularly under pressure in competition. Some of the athletes were adopting what was considered an older-style technique and the new coach felt that these athletes should change to a newer and superior technique. The coach was particularly interested in accelerating learning of the new technique and ensuring that the control processes were seemingly automatic for the athlete in order to reduce any negative impact during the competition season. An initial difficulty was encountered in the lack of scientific literature on how people re-learn or modify already acquired skills (for exceptions, see, for example, Hodges & Franks, 2002; Zanone & Kelso, 1997) or on how elite athletes learn (Williams & Ericsson, 2008).

The new technique required athletes to draw the bow using more of the scapular musculature (i.e. mid trapezius and rhomboids), so that the whole of the shoulder complex moves around the ribcage (see Figure 20.1). This technical change was thought to be more effective and efficient biomechanically than the older technique, thanks to greater alignment of forces through the joints and skeletal system of the upper limbs (Lin et al., 2010). The new technique required strength and endurance of the upper body, in particular the forearm and shoulder girdle (Ertan, Kental, Tumer & Korkusuz, 2003). In contrast, the old style has an over-reliance on the posterior deltoid and upper trapezius muscles in the draw phase, which calls for more muscular strength and is less efficient. The differences between the new and old technique are shown in Figure 20.1.

A framework for technical change was developed based on motor learning theory and research. In particular, this framework was designed to take advantage of the benefits of fading feedback to prevent guidance effects (e.g. Winstein & Schmidt, 1990) and bringing in challenge points at an optimal time in the learning process (Guadagnoli & Lee, 2004). A particular concern was to try and prevent athletes from reverting to earlier stages of skill learning by focusing attention internally on technical aspects of performance, rather than externally on performance effects and outcome (see Masters & Maxwell, 2004). In an effort to modify technique with minimal cognitive engagement, task constraints were modified while retaining a relationship with the fundamental movement.

In the very early stages, the new movement pattern was learnt with a Theraband© rather than with a bow, as this was perceived to be the easiest method for training the movement in archery. Discovery-based learning processes were encouraged to

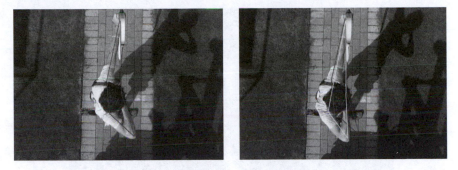

Figure 20.1 An overhead view of the change in draw technique. The old technique is shown on the left and the new technique on the right.

promote active learning and self-regulation of feedback (i.e. awareness of errors and how to correct them), while simultaneously de-emphasizing rules or internal body-focused instruction. Skills learnt in this manner may be performed better in front of an audience, create less interference when the performer has a complex decision to make, and appear more resistant to physiological fatigue (Masters, Poolton & Maxwell 2008). Although the coach had a goal movement pattern in mind, the athlete was allowed as much freedom as possible to explore the movement through self-discovery. During this initial phase, their practice was sometimes supported by video feedback viewed from overhead and side-on perspectives.

In addition, the coach provided physical guidance in order to convey the feel of the movement and promote self-awareness. The coach worked on the principle that guidance should be used infrequently with the least physical restraint possible. It was considered important to provide some hands-on instruction for the athletes to keep them motivated, as well as to help the coach feel involved in the learning process. A balance was struck between the level of explicit instruction provided by the coach and the need for the archers to develop self-awareness of how the new technique differed from the old one, while maintaining an external focus on the target and task goal.

A number of approaches were used to reduce the dependency on extrinsic feedback from the coach and/or video screen: delayed feedback (e.g. summary-trials feedback); bandwidth feedback; and the use of self-selected feedback schedules (see Chapter 1). These approaches enabled the archer to practise the movement, to focus on processing intrinsic feedback and to cross-reference this information against either the visual feedback provided on the video screens or verbal feedback from the coach. The feedback, when provided, was typically qualitative in nature. The athlete was provided with feedback only when deemed absolutely necessary by the coach in order to encourage the athletes to develop their intrinsic feedback mechanisms (e.g. Swinnen, Schmidt, Nicholson & Shapiro, 1990). An example of an archer receiving delayed visual feedback is presented in Figure 20.2.

When the athletes became more skilled at the movement such that the level of

Figure 20.2 An elite archer receiving delayed video feedback.

difficulty associated with the changes decreased, the 'challenge point' was raised during practice (Guadagnoli & Lee, 2004). A number of task constraints were manipulated to increase difficulty, notably varying the 'weight' or force necessary to draw the bow string back, varying the distance from the target (e.g. from 70 m to 90 m) and decreasing the size of the target area. In order to mimic the variability inherent in competition, anxiety (e.g. by creating head-to-head matches with financial incentives), fatigue (i.e. by testing at the start and the end of a training session), distracters (e.g. crowd noise and loud music) and environmental conditions (i.e. shooting arrows indoors and outdoors) were manipulated. The intention was to ensure that the athletes practised under the full range of conditions that would be experienced in actual competition. In order to encourage a more external focus on the target, different pictorial features were introduced on the face of the target. The archers were required to identify specific changes to target features, constraining them to attend to the movement dynamics externally rather than internally.

When the archers were able to shoot using the new technique from the competition distance of 70 m, with draw forces nearing competition levels, a quantitative biomechanical analysis was undertaken. The consistency of execution of the shot was viewed as a key performance indicator between a successful and unsuccessful archer and when comparing successful archers on hits and misses. The archers were tested in both low-intensity shooting conditions (i.e. normal individual practice) and high-intensity practice (i.e. competitive shooting for a financial prize). Kinematic data were analysed to assess how the increased constraints of a pressurized environment affected execution.

Six months post intervention, all four archers involved in the technical modifications were shooting scores equal to or higher than those recorded pre-intervention.

Three of the four athletes were successful in selection for the 2010 Commonwealth Games and all three won silver medals in these games. Two of the three athletes set new competition personal bests 9 months post-intervention, whereas the third athlete was judged by the Head Coach to have a much more consistent competition performance in the knockout rounds. The fourth athlete, who was a junior at the time of intervention, set a new junior British record in competition 15 months post intervention. All four athletes can now use bows with a greater draw force than pre-intervention thanks to increased biomechanical alignment and efficiency.

Case study 2: 'Keep your eye on the target!'

At the start of a 4-year Olympic cycle, Great Britain Shooting commissioned a 3-year project in the area of skill acquisition with the goal of improving performance at its highest level, specifically in the Olympic shotgun disciplines of skeet, trap and double trap. A number of initial meetings were conducted to engage coaches, athletes, support staff and managerial staff with the programme of work. Several small-group and one-to-one meetings took place to ensure the research staff and applied practitioners knew their responsibilities and to encourage transparency between parties. The meetings enabled detailed and accurate timetables to be developed in order to organize test sessions and feedback opportunities. As the athletes were at the highest level in their sport, they were regularly taking part in competitions both nationally and internationally, so communication and organization between groups was imperative.

The project was split into three main phases designed to (1) determine critical performance variables that are characteristic of successful and less successful shooters; (2) examine how competitive anxiety influences performance variables; and (3) evaluate whether these variables can be modified through applied interventions in an effort to increase performance. Although these goals were ultimately concerned with performance improvement, there was significant scope to explore the skill acquisition and motor behaviour theories of attentional control, anxiety, gaze behaviours and motor skill learning.

A paucity of literature on shotgun shooting existed coupled with conflicting anecdotal evidence in regard to the optimal strategies underlying superior performance. In the initial phase (Causer, Bennett, Holmes, Janelle & Williams, 2010), gaze behaviours and gun barrel kinematics were collected from elite and sub-elite shooters in their natural environment. An eye movement registration system was used to measure visual characteristics during the shooting task, while two external video cameras collected kinematic variables from the gun barrel, such as acceleration, velocity profiles and displacement metrics. The intention was to identify critical differences in movement characteristics and visual behaviours between elite and sub-elite shooters, as well as successful and unsuccessful shots. In particular, the focus was to identify how expertise is developed and to capture empirically subtle differences in behaviour that lead to small mistakes at the top level (i.e. differentiating a podium from non-podium finish). An example of the set-up used to collected data in situ with elite shooters is presented in Figure 20.3.

Figure 20.3 (a) A shooter wearing the Mobile Eye system; (b) the view from the eye movement system camera with a red dot indicating point of gaze; and (c) the eye with the three harmless near infra-red (IR) lights that are used to measure movements.

The visual behaviour known as *quiet eye* (QE; Vickers, 1996; see Chapter 17, this book) was of particular interest. The QE is defined as the final fixation or tracking gaze that is located on a specific location/object (in this case the clay target) in the visual display for a minimum of 100 ms. An earlier onset and longer duration of QE have been reported to be markers of expertise and successful performance in a range of aiming and interceptive actions (Vickers, 2007). It is suggested that the QE period functionally represents the time needed to organize the neural networks and visual parameters responsible for the orienting and control of visual attention (Vickers, 1996). The onset of QE occurs prior to the final movement of the task, and the offset occurs naturally when the gaze deviates off the location or object. The key principle is that QE duration is associated with the amount of cognitive programming required for successful aiming.

An earlier onset and longer duration of QE differentiated shots by elite and sub-elite athletes across all disciplines, as well as when comparing the same shooter on successful and unsuccessful shots. An earlier fixation on the clay, followed by a prolonged tracking of the target, appeared to enable shooters to more accurately process the trajectory, direction and speed of the clay in relation to the gun barrel before selecting the correct response characteristics. The analysis of the gun barrel kinematics revealed specific variations in techniques across disciplines depending on temporal demands. However, generally more spatial and temporally efficient gun barrel movements were evident for the elite than sub-elite shooters, as well as between successful and unsuccessful shots.

This initial phase provided a baseline for future interventions and helped identify the critical variables that directly influence performance. The next phase (Causer, Holmes, Smith & Williams, 2011) involved identifying how anxiety affected performance. As shooters compete at World Championships, World Cups, Olympic Games and other prestigious events they are inevitably faced with high-anxiety situations. In these situations, the ability to maintain performance under stress is vital. Anxious competitors frequently worry about the threat to a current goal and attempt to develop strategies to reduce any negative effects. Attention is diverted away from task-relevant stimuli and toward task-irrelevant stimuli, irrespective of whether these stimuli are internal (e.g. worrisome thoughts) or external (e.g. environmental distracters). According to attentional control theory (ACT; Eysenck, Derakshan, Santos & Calvo, 2007), anxiety disrupts the balance between the two attentional systems, namely, goal-directed (top-down control) and stimulus-driven (bottom-up control) (Corbetta & Shulman, 2002). An increase in anxiety is associated with greater influence of the stimulus-driven attentional system and a decrease in involvement of the goal-directed attentional system. However, anxiety does not normally impair performance effectiveness if compensatory strategies can be applied, such as enhanced effort and encouraging use of auxiliary processing resources.

The intention was to examine whether anxiety influenced performance effectiveness (i.e. outcome) and efficiency (i.e. the amount of resources or effort needed to complete the task) for Olympic skeet shooting. A group of elite shooters were tested under low-anxiety (normal training) and high-anxiety (competition environment; selection coaches present; financial incentives) conditions measuring the same variables as in initial phase. Self-report measures of anxiety indicated that the participants were significantly more anxious in the high- than low-anxiety condition. In high-anxiety conditions the shooters demonstrated shorter QE durations, increased gun barrel movement variability and less efficient gun motion, as indexed by increases in both gun barrel displacement and peak velocity, along with a decreased performance outcome (fewer successful trials) compared with low-anxiety conditions. As shooters became more anxious, they allocated more attention to determining and coping with stressors, leaving fewer resources available for the shooting task, as evidenced by shorter QE periods under high levels of anxiety.

In the third phase (Causer, Holmes & Williams, 2011) a training intervention was implemented to extend the QE period and expedite the onset of QE in order to enhance performance and increase resilience in competition. A four-step pre-shot routine was developed (see Table 20.2). This routine was designed to increase attention on the task and promote earlier fixation and longer tracking phases on the target. The routine was practised in the training sessions. Video feedback sessions were used to compare gaze characteristics between successful and unsuccessful shots. The importance of the QE period was highlighted and the benefits of the four-step routine reinforced. Video and gaze behaviours of an expert model were used to compare behaviours in order to identify the ideal visual technique.

Participants were tested pre- and post-intervention and the results compared against a control group. The intervention group significantly increased its mean QE duration, employed an earlier onset of QE and displayed greater shooting accuracy from pre- to post-intervention. The intervention group significantly reduced gun barrel displacement and peak velocity on the post- compared with the pre-test, even though neither variable was overtly trained. The shooters' scores in competition pre- and post-intervention were used to determine whether the training transferred to performance in actual competition setting. The intervention group significantly improved its shooting accuracy from pre- to post-intervention. No pre- to

Table 20.2 Pre-shot routine used to train QE

Step	Instruction
1	Stand at the station with the gun in the hold position (in a location you are able to replicate with little variability and where there will be minimum horizontal gun barrel displacement; rotate your head toward the high tower, and direct your gaze to a suitable target pick-up point position
2	Using your normal routine, when ready, call for the targets
3	Direct eye focus to the first target as quickly as possible and track the target continuously until you pull the trigger. After the execution of the first shot, become visually aware of the second target and direct your eye focus to it. Continually track the target, making sure that the target is in visual focus before shooting
4	Use a stable and consistent gun motion throughout the task, trying to keep the gun barrel at a constant velocity with no periods of high acceleration

Source: Causer, Holmes & Williams (2011).

post-test differences were observed for the control group on the measures reported. Importantly, after only an 8-week intervention, the shooting performance of elite athletes improved by 8%. A gold medal at the Olympics is normally achieved with a score of around 121 out of 125 targets, suggesting that this type of intervention can have a significant impact on the ability to win medals and gain podium places at the elite level.

Challenges, future directions and potential evolution of the field

Working as a skill acquisition specialist in elite sport is a rewarding experience. The opportunity to interact with some of the best athletes, coaches and practitioners in the world in an effort to make discernible differences to their chances of medal success is fulfilling and enjoyable. However, there are many challenges, not least the difficulties involved in attempting to produce good-quality science (or work that passes peer-review scrutiny from academics) while at the same time providing information that impacts on elite athlete development. The need to achieve an effective balance between scientific and translational impact/value presents the greatest challenge for academics working at the 'coal face'. However, there is much to be gained if an effective balance can be reached since working at the 'coal face' presents opportunities to learn more about the demands inherent in performing at the highest levels, which in turn can help define meaningful questions for scientists to answer (Ericsson & Williams, 2007; Vernig, 2007).

The process of working as a skill acquisition specialist in elite sport has presented other, albeit slightly more peripheral, challenges that merit documentation. The role of a skill acquisition specialist is potentially more closely aligned and even intertwined with that of the coach than other sports science disciplines, since both are interested in developing practices and instructional methods that facilitate athlete development. It is crucial that skill acquisition specialists see themselves not as coaches per se, but as support staff that can work closely with coaches in an effort to refine aspects of behaviour related to skill development. The role of a coach is much more wide-ranging than that of a skill acquisition specialist (e.g. Ford, Coughlan & Williams, 2009). Coaches have a broader skill set and more refined and specific professional and craft knowledge of their sport. Skill acquisition specialists should help coaches develop their understanding of the scientific principles that underpin effective learning and how these may be translated into effective coach behaviours. These two roles should be viewed as complementary and any perceived criticism or challenge to current coaching practices may not be helpful in initial meetings or during conversations with staff working in the sports.

Other challenges are presented by the nature of elite sport. The environment is extremely dynamic and fast-paced, with coaches and athletes trying to optimise the time available for practice. Skill acquisition specialists have to be seen to be interested, engaged and willing to invest a lot of time in the athletes and coaches to build the trust and understanding. Practitioners in elite sport work long and anti-social hours, so specialists need to understand and work within these behaviour patterns. Moreover, the athletes in elite sport are elite and they do not fall into the normal cross-section of society. If the athlete is a consistent medal winner at major championships, then he or she is by definition unique and the data produced are likely to fall outside any established norms. Often interventions will be focused on a single athlete and consequently it may be difficult to run statistical analyses or publish any of the data collected.

Williams and Ford continue to have adjunct positions at the English Institute of Sport while simultaneously retaining their roles as full-time academics. In September 2011, a full-time Research Assistant was appointed in this area at Liverpool John Moores University, funded by the English Institute of Sport. Initially, the appointment is for 12 months with the intention of securing further funding through to the Olympics in Brazil 2016. This Research Assistant is engaged in applied projects involving Great Britain Taekwondo and Badminton. The former organization is interested in developing interventions that mediate any negative effects of stress on performance, whereas the latter is interested in developing methods to improve anticipation and the ability to deceive opponents. These projects are ongoing and it is envisaged that both will have an influence on performance ahead of the London Olympics.

In the medium term, the intention is to continue to build a stronger case for investment within the English Institute of Sport in skill acquisition support. Such an argument will require evidence that contemporary research in the area of skill acquisition can impact on performance at the elite level (e.g. through documented case studies). A difficulty is that the overriding majority of published literature has examined the process of learning using novel tasks and novice learners over relatively short practice periods (Williams & Ericsson, 2008). In contrast, at the elite level in sport, coaches are interested in identifying methods that can improve performance of already well-learnt skills using highly trained athletes. Although it may be relatively easy to argue that research on skill acquisition can have an impact across the skill continuum, the case that this body of work can make the difference between a gold and silver medal in the cauldron of elite sport has yet to be made in a compelling manner. The availability of such data will make it easier to justify any additional investment of resources.

It is hoped that all the Home Countries (England, Northern Ireland, Scotland and Wales) Institutes of Sport will develop and invest in skill acquisition in the next Olympic cycle. This investment should extend to ensure that support is provided to winter as well as summer sports and to Paralympic in addition to Olympic athletes. A systematic education programme is required to ensure that practitioners with a background in other sport science subdisciplines such as performance analysts, bio mechanists, sport psychologists and exercise physiologists, as well as coaches and administrators, have an increased awareness and understanding of skill acquisition principles and how they can help facilitate elite athlete development. The majority of these practitioners employ skill acquisition theory in their daily practices, without necessarily having a formal knowledge of the underlying principles. For example, nearly all are engaged in providing feedback, albeit few are likely to appreciate that there exists an extensive literature base to guide this process in the area of skill acquisition. The principles that emerge from the learning sciences are essential to many facets of activity related to elite athlete development.

The application of principles emerging from skill acquisition research is gathering pace in many of the professional sports beyond the remit of the English Institute of Sport. For example, the English Cricket Board now employs a Skill Acquisition Lead on a full-time basis and has clear links with academic departments working in the area. The transfer of knowledge between academics and those involved in elite sport including those at the English Institute of Sport has also gathered pace. The Expertise and Skill Acquisition Network (ESAN) was established in October 2010. The main mission of ESAN is to provide opportunities for scientists and those working as practitioners and coaches in the field of elite sport to network and engage in knowledge transfer activities that positively impact on elite athlete development. A group of almost 30 people attended the inaugural meeting at the National Cricket Performance Centre, Loughborough University. The second meeting of ESAN occurred in April 2011, hosted by Loughborough University, and attracted almost 50 delegates. The next scheduled meeting is in April 2012, hosted by Liverpool John Moores University. In 2011, ESAN was recognized by the British Psychological Society as a Special Interest Group, thereby providing a platform for continued professional development of the field. In the future, it is hoped that ESAN will create links with other similar networks in Australia and North America in order to transfer knowledge at a global level.

Our intention in this chapter was to illustrate how theory can translate into applied practice in elite sport. It was not our intention to present a definitive framework of best practice or to propose a model for others to follow. Our intention was to document a recent journey that we have made, as well as the potential direction of travel in the future, in the hope that such information will help others in the area of skill acquisition who are motivated to follow a similar pathway. The chapter largely presents a descriptive account of our experiences in trying to build bridges between the often disparate worlds of academia and elite-level sport. We illustrated through two case studies how research in the area of skill acquisition can have translational impact at the 'coal face' in elite sport. Some challenges that we have faced along the way were highlighted. We appreciate that much work needs be done if this area is to develop and impact on athlete development in a similar manner to other more established sport science subdisciplines such as exercise physiology, biomechanics and sport psychology. However, we remain optimistic that the field of skill acquisition can develop into an established area of applied practice to complement its existing strengths in traditional academic fields. In order to have meaningful translational impact, greater efforts are needed to promote a bidirectional dialogue and stronger interactions between scientists, coaches and practitioners.

References

Bryan, W. L., & Harter, N. (1897). Studies in the physiology and psychology of the telegraphic language. *Psychological Review, 4*(1), 27–53.

Bryan, W. L., & Harter, N. (1899). Studies on the telegraphic language: The acquisition of a hierarchy of habits. *Psychological Review, 6*, 345–375.

Causer, J., Bennett, S. J., Holmes, P. S., Janelle, C. M., & Williams, A. M. (2010). Quiet eye duration and gun motion in elite shotgun shooting. *Medicine & Science in Sports & Exercise, 42*(8), 1599–1608.

Causer, J., Holmes, P. S., Smith, N. C., & Williams, A. M. (2011). Anxiety, movement kinematics, and visual attention in elite-level performers. *Emotion, 11*(3), 595–602.

Causer, J., Holmes, P. S., & Williams, A. M. (2011). Quiet eye training in a visuomotor control task. *Medicine & Science in Sports & Exercise, 43*(6), 1042–1049.

Corbetta, M., & Shulman, G. L. (2002). Control of goal-directed and stimulus driven attention in the brain. *Nature Reviews Neuroscience, 3*, 201–215.

Coyle, D. (2009). *The talent code.* New York: Bantam.

Davids, K., Button, C., & Bennett, S. J. (2008). *Dynamics of skill acquisition: A constraints-led approach.* Champaign, IL: Human Kinetics.

Ericsson, K. A., & Williams, A. M. (2007). Capturing naturally occurring superior performance in the laboratory: Translational research on expert performance. *Journal of Experimental Psychology: Applied, 13*, 115–123.

Ertan, H., Kental, B., Tumer, S. T., & Korkusuz, F. (2003). Activation patterns in forearm muscles during archery shooting. *Human Movement Science, 22*, 37–45.

Eysenck, M. W., Derakshan, N., Santos, R., & Calvo, M. G. (2007). Anxiety and cognitive performance: Attentional control theory. *Emotion, 7*, 336–353.

Farrow, D., Baker, J., & MacMahon, C. (2009). *Developing elite sports performers: Lessons from theory and practice.* London: Routledge.

Ford, P. R., Coughlan, E., & Williams, A. M. (2009). The expert-performance approach as a framework for understanding and enhancing coaching performance, expertise and learning. *International Journal of Sports Science & Coaching, 4*(3), 451–463.

Gladwell, M. (2008). *Outliers.* London: Allen Lane.

Guadagnoli, M. A., & Lee, T. D. (2004). Challenge point: A framework for conceptualizing the effects of various practice conditions in motor learning. *Journal of Motor Behavior, 36*, 212–224.

Hodges, N. J., & Franks, I. M. (2002). Modelling coaching practice: The role of instruction and demonstration. *Journal of Sports Sciences, 20*, 793–811.

Hodges, N. J., & Williams, A. M. (2007). Current status of observational learning research and the role of demonstrations in sport. *Journal of Sports Sciences, 25*(5), 495–496.

Lin, J.-J., Hung, C.-J., Yang, C.-C., Chen, H.-Y., Chou, F.-C., & Lu, T.-W. (2010). Activation and tremor of the shoulder muscles to the demands of an archery task. *Journal of Sports Sciences, 28*(4), 415–421.

Masters, R., & Maxwell, J. P. (2004). Implicit motor learning, reinvestment and movement disruption. What you don't know won't hurt you? In Williams, A. M., & Hodges, N. J. (Eds.), *Skill acquisition in Sport: Research, theory and practice* (pp. 207–228). London: Routledge.

Masters, R., Poolton, J. M., & Maxwell, J. P. (2008). Stable implicit motor processes despite aerobic locomotor fatigue. *Consciousness and Cognition, 17*(1), 335–338.

Summers, J. (2004). A historical perspective on skill acquisition. In Williams, A. M., & Hodges, N. J. (Eds.), *Skill acquisition in sport: Research, theory and practice* (pp. 7–26). London: Routledge.

Swinnen, S. P., Schmidt, R. A., Nicholson, D. E., & Shapiro, D. C. (1990). Information feedback for skill acquisition: Instantaneous knowledge of results degrades learning. *Journal of Experimental Psychology: Learning, Memory and Cognition, 16*, 706–716.

Syed, M. (2009). *Bounce.* New York: HarperCollins.

Vernig, P. M. (2007). From science to practice: Bridging the gap with translational research. *APS Observer, 20*, 29–30.

Vickers, J. N. (1996). Visual control while aiming at a far target. *Journal of Experimental Psychology: Human Perception & Performance, 22*, 342–354.

Vickers, J. N. (2007). *Perception, cognition and decision training: The quiet eye in action.* Champaign, IL: Human Kinetics.

Williams, A. M. (2006) What ever happened to motor behavior? The missing ingredient in the recipe for Olympic success. *Sport and Exercise Scientist, June, 22–23.

Williams, A. M., & Ericsson, K. A. (2008). From the guest editors: How do experts learn? *Journal of Sport & Exercise Psychology, 30*, 1–11.

Williams, A. M., & Ford, P. R. (2009). Promoting a skills-based agenda in Olympic sports: The role of skill-acquisition specialists. *Journal of Sports Sciences, 27*(13), 1381–1392.

Williams, A. M., & Hodges, N. J. (2005). Practice, instruction and skill acquisition in soccer challenging tradition. *Journal of Sports Sciences, 23*, 637–650.

Winstein, C. J., & Schmidt R. A. (1990). Reduced frequency of knowledge of results enhances motor skill learning. *Journal of Experimental Psychology: Learning, Memory and Cognition, 16*, 677–691.

Zanone, P.-G., & Kelso, J. A. S. (1997). The coordination dynamics of learning and transfer: Collective and component levels. *Journal of Experimental Psychology: Human Perception and Performance, 23*, 1454–1480.

21 Working in the field (Southern Hemisphere)

Chris Button and Damian Farrow

Introduction

In the Southern Hemisphere, the number of skill acquisition researchers who are working in the field is few in comparison with other sport science disciplines (such as physiology, strength and conditioning, and sport psychology). Arguably this situation has developed from the lack of a dedicated accreditation pathway for skill acquisition within professional bodies such as Sport and Exercise Science New Zealand (SESNZ) and Exercise and Sports Science Australia (ESSA). It is also likely that many academics perceive research, theory and practice to be an awkward *menage-à-trois* to combine effectively, dissuading them from leaving the relative comfort of the classroom or laboratory. However, although fundamental motor learning research dates back to the late 1800s, it is still a relatively young and evolving sports science discipline. Skill acquisition has made considerable strides in recent times with notable developments in research techniques, theory, practical implications and technology. In fact, the arrival of the new millennium seems to have heralded a new dawn for skill acquisition as a discipline. In Australia and New Zealand in particular, there appears to be increasing recognition of its role and potential value for high-performance sports. For example, new support positions for skill acquisition specialists have been created within the Australian Institute of Sport (AIS), and New Zealand's equivalent body (NZ Academy of Sport) appears keen to follow this lead. Specific skills development-focused coaching jobs have appeared in many of our most popular sports such as rugby, soccer, cricket and Australian rules football. The formation of the Australasian Skill Acquisition Research Group (ASARG) in 2007, which has since met on a yearly basis to discuss practice and promote the discipline, is further evidence of the critical mass of skill acquisition specialists who are currently working in the Southern Hemisphere. Between 20 and 50 researchers and practitioners have regularly attended ASARG since its formation.

The first author (Button) has worked as a skill acquisition lecturer for over 10 years in New Zealand and previously the UK. On a regular basis over this period he has consulted, and conducted applied research, with several high-performance sports including badminton, cricket, motorsport, football and netball. Much of Button's research and consultancy work has been influenced by ecological theories of motor learning (see Davids, Button & Bennett, 2008). This author works at the University of Otago in New Zealand and maintains a productive working relationship with the NZ Academy of Sport, the organization that administers sport science services for elite athletes. The second author (Farrow) is a motor learning lecturer, having been the inaugural skill acquisition specialist at the AIS in 2002. In 2010 he took up a conjoint appointment between Victoria University and the AIS in an applied research role in which he attempts to forge strategic research partnerships between sports scientists, coaches and academics.

In this chapter, we provide brief case studies from two sports, badminton (Button) and swimming (Farrow), to illustrate the kind of support activities that we have been involved with in recent years. Thereafter, we reflect on the challenges faced in trying to satisfy the often competing demands of service support, applied research and academic expectations. We offer some of the solutions that have worked effectively for us, and finally signpost directions in which the professional practice of skill acquisition needs to develop in future. What the future holds for skill acquisition as a discipline remains to be seen, although, in our opinion, the recent signs in Australasia at least are very promising.

Case studies

Badminton

In one of my (Button) first experiences of applied work, I spent 3 years assisting the national coach of a high-performance senior badminton squad. For the first year, I was mentored by a senior skill acquisition colleague and for the remaining time I worked alone or occasionally alongside a Performance Analyst. This initial period of mentorship, although brief, was extremely valuable and helped me to feel more at ease in an environment with which I had little familiarity. I typically attended one training session per week (approximately 3 hours) at a large sports hall and occasionally travelled to competitions, primarily to film the players and later generate feedback and notational analysis. The training sessions that I attended had a primary emphasis on technique and skills development, although, as with all of the athletes' training, there was a significant game-like physical intensity to the practice activities.

At our first meeting with the coach, we introduced some key skill acquisition themes (see checklist in Table 21.1) and it was established that the coach was keen to receive advice about issues such as practice scheduling, altering well-established coordination patterns and training anticipation. We also conducted individual interviews with the players to explain our roles and then assessed their perceived needs and compared them with the coach's views.

In relation to the first issue highlighted by the coach (i.e. practice scheduling) it became clear that many of his drills were developed to address one or two key issues. As such the practice activities seemed heavily technique focused and repetitive, although still quite demanding. For example, in one drill the coach would stand on a bench at the baseline and smash consecutive shuttles to the receiving

Table 21.1 Key themes of skill acquisition introduced/discussed with coach and players

Topics	Relevant chapters in this book	Who requested further information
Communication		
Instructional effectiveness	2, 4	Coach + 1 player
Feedback provision	1, 3, 10	1 player
Coach–athlete/athlete–athlete relationships	13, 15	7 players
Development of skill		
Changing skilled movement	7	Coach + 10 players
Skill development and periodization	15	Coach + 1 player
Postural development for performance	–	4 players
Improving balance/proprioception	–	3 players
Recognizing skill development and planning	12	–
Optimizing pre-performance preparation	6	–
Development of speed		
Speed–accuracy development	–	3 players
Reaction and movement time development	–	5 players
Perceptual awareness of key information	7, 16	1 player
Anticipation training	17	Coach + 4 players
Retention		
Understanding practice structure	8, 11, 19	Coach
Perception–action development	13	4 players
Optimizing design of practice environment	5, 9	2 players
Effective practice for competition transfer	4, 8	3 players
Understanding internal and external factors affecting skilled performance		
Constraints analysis of athlete performance	7	8 players
Identification of strengths and weaknesses	–	1 player

player's forehand or backhand with only a brief delay between smashes to allow the player to reset his or her position. Then during breaks the coach would provide feedback to help improve the player's body position, footwork, and racket carriage. The coach explained that the rationale for this activity was to allow him to mimic the speed and intensity of attacking play in a game situation while training the player's ability to return fast smashes under pressure and recover quickly. After the session, discussions arose with the coach about how the scheduling of practice can affect skill retention and transfer (e.g. Ollis, Button & Fairweather, 2005) and how such drills can alter the typical perceptual demands inherent in game play (e.g. Wilson, Simpson & Hamill, 2009). It was agreed together that a more effective way to implement this practice activity was to design a two-versus-one drill, in which the doubles team adopted an attacking 'front–rear'-style formation. The role of the rear court player was mainly to smash to the single player's forehand and backhand court (as the coach had been doing from the bench) whereas the forecourt doubles player might engage in a net rally or play a defensive clear shot. By mixing up the delivery of shots for the receiving singles player, yet keeping a one-player advantage for the doubles team, it was possible to maintain the playing intensity of the drill and game-like perceptual demands while still focusing upon training the ability to retrieve a smash.

The coach and several players themselves expressed interest in the issue of how to adjust well-established coordination patterns. Although most of the players were still young they had been playing competitively for at least 5 years and consequently they had all developed strong preferences and styles of playing. For example, we spent several sessions together exploring how the players could develop their technique for one of the most potent shots in badminton, the smash. Video analysis revealed that many of the players relied mainly on their upper body to generate power when smashing. We felt that, by initiating the kinetic chain earlier in their hips followed by their trunk and shoulders, these players could generate an even more powerful and effective action (B. K. Lee, 1993).

Some of the skill acquisition-specific strategies that we used included:

- providing video feedback of technique/movement in breaks;
- asking the players to vary the amplitude and timing of movement (related to the scaling of key control parameters, a concept used to probe the dynamics of skilled performance; Davids et al., 2008);
- getting the players to smash when playing with their non-dominant hand, thereby causing a sufficiently large disturbance to established, stable movement patterns to encourage exploration (Button, Chow & Rein, 2008); and
- applying elastic resistance with straps wrapped around the hips to promote earlier and stronger involvement of proximal segments in the kinetic chain.

In brief, the rationale for each activity was to challenge the player to relearn elements of the skill and explore the optimal timing and sequencing of actions to develop speed and accuracy in the shot (Lee, 1993). Inevitably, the players reported making more mistakes and that their action felt very strange during this period of exploration. However, it was reinforced to them (and the coach) that some variability in performance outcomes is likely, even necessary, to accompany any alterations to stable coordination patterns (Davids, Glazier, Araújo & Bartlett, 2003).

Badminton is a very fast sport that presents players with considerable perceptual demands. Several players indicated that their anticipation could be improved and that they needed to develop perceptual awareness. Once more, in this situation we experimented with a few practice activities. Being aware of previous research using video occlusion techniques in racket sports (Farrow, Abernethy & Jackson, 2005), I created edited video footage for each player in which other players were filmed from the receiver's perspective playing a range of shots (i.e. smash, clear, cut and drop). The footage was occluded at the point of racquet–shuttle contact and the players had to anticipate the likely direction of the shot. Although I felt this strategy was initially helpful in terms of educating players about relevant kinematic information that may be present in their opponent's action, I was not sure that the players were able to apply the information well on court. Therefore, I created a game-like practice activity in which the players had to react to shots from a player in the rear court using darkened shuttles (dyed green). Against a dark background the dark shuttle was difficult to see and hence players were forced to rely more on anticipatory information to predict how to respond. Feedback later from the players suggested that they enjoyed this kind of game specific practice despite the increased perceptual challenge. In fact, one player said that, when returning to a normal white shuttle after practising this drill, it felt as if he were watching in slow motion, which I took to be a positive sign!

By now you should be asking yourselves how I evaluated whether these new practice interventions were effective. In fact, this is one of the issues which I have found most challenging and frustrating with regard to applied work. Perhaps surprisingly, getting objective evidence (data) to test the effectiveness of an intervention is not always easy. In some sports, such as rifle shooting, there are quite simple ways to monitor performance effectiveness (e.g. shooting accuracy) and to relate that to an athlete's behaviours. However, in complex, dynamic sports such as badminton, relating performance to behaviour is not as straightforward. One obvious strategy might be to examine the players' game performance before and after the new intervention. However, with no control condition or group to compare against and a multitude of extraneous variables in competition it is impossible to establish whether it was the intervention itself that led to any changes. Occasionally, technology may provide solutions, for example when trying to measure a change in response time through high-speed video (Kwan, Andersen, Cheng, Tang & Rasmussen, 2011) or alternatively the speed of a smash with a speed gun. On reflection, the strategy I most often turned to in practice was to regularly conduct semi-qualitative analyses of video footage. This helped me and the coach to establish directly whether certain changes in movement patterns resulted from the interventions and whether they persisted from one situation or training session to the next. As we discuss later in the chapter, evaluating the effectiveness of practice activities will be an important issue for future practitioners.

To summarize, it may be of interest to reflect upon how my research and applied work experiences have influenced each other. I would suggest that the former (research) has had a more direct and obvious influence upon the latter (applied work); indeed I would not contemplate working in a high-performance environment without confidence in my theoretical knowledge. However, the extent to which applied work has influenced subsequent research is less obvious to me. I have always found most satisfaction in using sport as a task vehicle to test theory, so I do not attribute this trend in my research to consultancy work. However, I do admit to a growing interest in research topics such as automaticity and decision making, and feel sure that this subtle change in research emphasis has been prompted by many of the inspiring athletes and coaches I have worked with.

Swimming

After I (Farrow) completed my doctoral work examining perceptual skill in time-stressed interceptive sports, it was a rude awakening when I accepted a role with the AIS Swimming Program. In Australia, swimming is a high-profile sport and the predominant disciplines in relation to sports science application have been biomechanics and physiology, with a liberal dose of nutrition and psychology. However, the coach determined that there was something missing between the application of his coaching skills and the information provided by the biomechanist. Perceptively, the coach viewed a skill acquisition specialist as the missing ingredient and hence sought a meeting with myself to see what I had to offer.

Servicing sports programmes and specifically coaches, and to a lesser extent the athletes, is all about building relationships. I have found the completion of a practice analysis is a valuable strategy in establishing a foundation for future servicing. Practice analysis involves attending a range of practice sessions and objectively analysing them relative to the established principles of skill acquisition. In particular, I evaluate the structure and organization of practice and the coach's instruction and feedback relative to the drill/session objective when expressed as a learning or performance goal. Often the very simplest observations are the most telling, particularly when you are not familiar with the sport, as was the case for me with swimming. Frequently, I found myself challenging the practice/coaching traditions of the sport built around experiential knowledge "how I learnt or was coached" compared with the empirical evidence on which my evaluation was predominantly based. This is an important issue that will be discussed in great detail in a later section; the best science is created by the merging of the two viewpoints through constant collaboration.

The practice analysis with swimming highlighted a range of classic skill acquisition issues. First, it was evident that the differentiation between learning and performance is not something that is actively considered in the macro- and micro-planning of a swimming programme and its sessions. The programme is typically arranged in 14- to 16-week training blocks that lead to a competition phase, followed by a 2-week recovery period. This process is generally repeated over the 4-year cycle between Olympic campaigns. Obviously certain events are more important than others, particularly as the cycle gets closer to Olympic trials and then the main event. Initially, I contextualized learning and performance in relation to swimming, highlighting that learning sessions tend to encourage trial and error, a focus on technical skill production and an accompanying de-emphasis on recording results/times. In particular, I reinforced to the coach that observable change in behaviour may not be immediately apparent. In contrast, performance sessions should encourage technical excellence and fast times: essentially a test of how the swimmer is performing at present (Schmidt & Lee, 1999). We then developed together some examples of practice goals. For example, learning-focused sessions included:

- Sessions when no lap times were recorded; I asked the coach how his athletes would respond if he arrived on pool deck without a stopwatch.
- Swimmers reporting their own stroke rates, but not given feedback until a block of efforts were completed. We discussed the notion of faded feedback and strategies to delay/summarize the resultant information to encourage the swimmers to work on developing their own error detection and correction system (Lavery, 1962; Salmoni, Schmidt & Walter, 1984; Sherwood, 1988). Consequently, the coach began to ask swimmers to report on how they felt a particular technical element was completed rather than always starting a conversation with an athlete with an observation or suggestion (Chambers & Vickers, 2006).

For sessions, or indeed specific sets within a session, designed to have a performance focus we trialled the following:

- Requiring a single race effort at the end of a session; lap time and stroke rate are reported and a qualitative rating of technical success is documented through video analysis of the performance. This method was used to allow the athlete to recalibrate their practice repetitions within the context of performance, and ascertain what practice effects (technical foci) could be maintained under more competition-like conditions (much like a post-test condition).
- A strong integration of all elements of a swim race, for example, when each effort started with a dive start rather than the typical push off the wall from within the pool. This was consistent with notions of transfer-appropriate processing in which the value of any practice completed needs to be examined on the basis of how the skill is performed in a test context (Bransford, Franks, Morris & Stein, 1979; T. D. Lee, 1988).

Closely related to the overarching learning and performance objectives of a session was the need for the coach to consider the practice structure and organization of the drills he was asking his athletes to complete. Discussion led to the generation of a whole range of different ideas under the common theme that variety (variability) is the spice of life (and key to learning) (McDonald, Oliver & Newell, 1995; Schmidt, 1975). A sample of the initiatives introduced included:

- Increased task switching through frequent alterations between stroke types or the athlete's focus of attention. This process became an enjoyable one for both of us. The coach would bring me his session plan illustrating the volume for the session and the stroke to be used. My task was to reorder the session to promote task switching without impacting on the prescribed volume. It was not long before the coach was generating his own sessions that would be more than suitable. A simple example involved distributing the volume of practice starts throughout the session rather than the customary blocked practice approach (see Barreiros, Figueiredo & Godinho 2007; Handford, Davids, Bennett & Button, 1997; Magill & Hall, 1990).

• As empirical evidence on the benefits of self-regulated practice approaches evolved (e.g. Keetch & Lee, 2007) I took this information to the coach and discussed how we might be able to introduce this within his programme. One successful strategy involved providing templates for the athletes, who then planned their own session. This was done one session per week (swimmers averaged 11 pool sessions per week) for an 8-week preparation period.

The final element to be refined, based on the practice evaluation, concerned instruction and feedback. The typical approach of the coach was to present lap time and stroke rate for each swimmer after every key effort in the main training set of a session. I considered this to be a consequence of the training focus typically being on the physiological aspects of performance. Another contextual factor that needed to be managed was the easy access to feedback technology, in particular, plasma screens located at the end of each lane that could provide feedback of the swimmers' performance from any camera perspective required (side-on, overhead or underwater) immediately after they completed a lap (see Figure 21.1). I challenged the coach to consider two fundamental feedback issues; first the feedback content, in particular the balance between the swimmers' need for knowledge of results and knowledge of performance information; and second the delivery and timing of the feedback (see Wulf & Shea, 2004 for a review). A range of strategies were implemented as a consequence, for example:

Figure 21.1 An AIS swimmer watching video feedback of her technique on a specially mounted plasma screen.

- Swimmers rated their effort on both technique and result. Two columns were drawn on a whiteboard so that the swimmer estimated lap time or stroke rate and then quality of the technical element of interest. Equally, on occasions only one type of information was prioritized on the basis of individual swimmer need.
- The ease of access to video feedback posed its own series of issues in terms of harnessing how often the swimmers could see themselves, usually accompanied by a coach commentary. The amount of laps a swimmer could view their video feedback was regulated to reduce the likelihood of dependency effects as well as requiring them to become more self-analytical about their own performance (i.e. feel it) rather than waiting to see it or hear the coach's evaluation.
- Related to the above point, the concept of bandwidth feedback (e.g. Chambers & Vickers, 2006) was introduced to reduce the swimmer's reliance on the coach and equally decrease his desire to provide more instruction or feedback. Consequently, feedback was provided only when a performance was outside a pre-agreed acceptable range of correctness, be it a lap time or a technical stroke component. In order to determine the pre-agreed range of correctness it was common to use video footage of the swimmer from a previous session or competition. Similarly, feedback was delayed and summarized to encourage the swimmers to attune and refine their own feedback/feel of their performance. Questioning was used to elicit these feelings.

I am into my second Olympic cycle with this programme because questions and challenges keep coming and equally because the combination of objective and subjective measures demonstrate continued improvement in the swimmers. Interestingly, the coach feels that the biggest change in the swimmers, since they adopted a more formalized skill acquisition approach, is their flexibility to adapt their technique or make subtle changes in a relatively efficient manner. Similarly, athlete feedback focuses on how they bring their brain to training more than ever before. Importantly, we have discussed leaving the brain at home when competing – but that is another story!

When reflecting on how my research and applied work experiences have influenced each other, having been immersed in a practical context for more than a decade has strongly influenced my perspective. In simple terms, practical significance is more relevant to me than theoretical significance. Hence, although I adopt a specific theoretical framework when examining a particular issue, I prioritize the need for an evidence-based practical outcome as compared with a theoretical contribution to the field. This is evidenced in the premium I have placed on high ecological validity, primarily through experimentation in naturalistic settings using complex sport skills rather than more simplified tasks in a well-controlled laboratory setting (see also Wulf & Shea, 2002). As time has evolved I have also felt more comfortable being not locked to a specific theoretical framework but rather open to the application of alternative approaches dependent upon my interpretation of which framework better addresses the issue to be examined.

Challenges and solutions

We hope that these case studies will bring some awareness of the typical challenges that are faced by skill acquisition specialists working in high-performance sport. Below we list a number of common issues that we have faced and discuss potential solutions.

What can you do for me?

Coaches (and athletes) may have little awareness of skill acquisition and what it has to offer. It is of value to form a trusting relationship by explaining some key principles of skill acquisition and discussing examples within the sport in question. Analysing practice together is a useful way to begin sharing information and to prioritize learning and performance in different training activities.

Remember you are not the coach

One of the reasons for the relative infancy of skill acquisition as a stand-alone sports science discipline is that historically it has been considered the domain of the coach. This is not surprising as many of the concepts and issues we consider are very much what the coach is responsible for delivering on a daily basis. However, it is important not to confuse an athlete by blurring the distinction between scientific provider and coach. Focus on developing the coaches' skills rather than your coaching skills.

How can I ensure the athlete plays an active role in learning?

A skill acquisition specialist and the coach need to create an effective learning environment for the athlete(s). Practice should be mentally and physically demanding, mimicking as many of the factors found in competition as possible. Whereas simplification of a practice activity (e.g. batting against a bowling machine in cricket) may be an *efficient* way to adapt an established movement pattern, the aim should always be to develop perception–action relationships that will be *effective* in competition (Wilson et al., 2009). In order to achieve consistently high performance levels, many skilled athletes have already developed effective error correction and self-regulation strategies (Aglioti, Cesari, Romani & Urgesi, 2008). However, large volumes of repetitive training activities with relatively low perceived challenge may lead to a more passive role in the learning process, which is to be avoided if at all possible.

How can you monitor and evaluate the effectiveness of skill acquisition interventions?

Any scientist should be looking for empirical evidence to better understand the situation in question. For skill acquisition support there are a range of sources of evidence that can be gathered (some listed below), in the absence of any direct measures of learning it is advisable to look for evidence of adaptation, skill retention, and maintenance of performance under pressure.

- Performance outcomes
- Qualitative video analysis
- Quantitative measures of behaviour (e.g. times, distances, speeds)
- Biomechanical analysis
- Coach and player feedback

What if the answer is 'I don't know'?

There is not always a firm empirical base in skill acquisition research upon which to build answers to applied problems. Furthermore, the research literature predominantly focuses on novice or early learners and there is much less information regarding advanced performers. Skill acquisition is still a relatively young discipline and there is often a considerable gap between theory and practical suggestions. Coaches may not like to hear it, but rarely are solutions black and white. Obviously in such situations honesty (i.e. 'I don't know') is usually a better strategy than complete guesswork. However, in our experience, an open-minded coach will often be prepared to give an informed and justified suggestion a try.

Who has the final say?

Nowadays, high-performance sports are serviced by a team of different specialists, each of whom is keen to have his or her say. Inevitably competing or conflicting advice can arise from the complexity of the high-performance environment (e.g. periodization, practice versus performance, injury avoidance). Clearly, in relation to skill acquisition, coaches should have the final word in terms of the content of a training programme, as the buck stops with them. Regular team meetings and effective communication can help the situation, but the reality is that the coach must filter and manage the information he or she receives to the best of his or her ability.

Can I juggle academic demands with support work?

Support work does take considerable time, which means that many academics choose to avoid it rather than risk compromising their research or teaching. However, in our view, the different roles do not necessarily compete with each other. For example, there are plenty of nice examples for teaching settings to be gained from support work and good opportunities to be exploited for applied research if you can convince practitioners of its potential value (see recent special issues of the *International Journal of Sport Psychology* in 2009 and *International Journal of Sport Science and Coaching* in 2011). Good time management is vital and it helps to consider strategies to work on the go and segregate certain important jobs (e.g. find your best space/time for writing). Ultimately, one can learn a lot about motor learning by observing and analysing it up close and, by integrating aspects of your teaching, research and applied work, you will soon discover the potential benefits. Admittedly, in our specific cases the nature of our current, and previous, academic positions have been flexible enough to allow us the luxury of fostering productive relationships with sports administrators and coaches. Although juggling academia with support work has certainly kept us busy, neither of us would wish to have it any other way!

Summary and conclusions

We hope that our applied work has been, and continues to be, an interesting insight into skill acquisition in the real world. In our careers to date both authors feel fortunate to have worked alongside many excellent practitioners and athletes, the large majority of whom have been eager to challenge and develop their own behaviours by embracing skill acquisition support. With the advances in skill acquisition knowledge and practice described in detail throughout this book comes considerable responsibility in communicating the current state of the discipline effectively. As evidenced by this chapter, there are a multitude of issues that require greater understanding. There are times when we have felt we had a solid empirically supported answer for the coach. Equally, there are occasions when we felt the literature could not provide the level of confidence we required to recommend a strategy to the coach, highlighting the need for more applied research. Spending time in the field has been essential for us to fully explain what skill acquisition is and how it can benefit practitioners as well as to develop an effective balance between research and performance driven outcomes. Furthermore, with each sport there has been a considerable amount for us to learn about the high-performance environments we have encountered. We feel that our experiences in the field have been invaluable in terms of providing real-world, credible examples within our teaching and supervision of students. Although there is a constant ebb and flow in academia between different demands on our time, we are privileged to have some choice over what we do and when we do it, and for both of us that means getting out into the field as often as possible.

We doubt if there are too many tangible differences between the issues we have encountered and those raised by our Northern Hemisphere neighbours. Admittedly in Australasia academics have only recently begun to experience the same level of scrutiny that comes with regular research and teaching assessments common for some time at most Northern Hemisphere institutions. How these academic pressures and expectations will affect our ability to continue engaging in applied support work remains to be seen. One particularly pleasing aspect of the relatively small and isolated population of skill acquisition researchers in Australasia is the multitude of support opportunities that seem to exist and our willingness to collaborate and share ideas. At the time of writing, skill acquisition seems to be riding the crest of a wave in terms of profile in high-performance sport in Australasia. We hope it can keep riding that wave for many years to come!

References

Aglioti, S. M., Cesari, P., Romani, M., & Urgesi, C. (2008). Action anticipation and motor resonance in elite basketball players. *Nature Neuroscience, 11*(9), 1109–1116.

Barreiros, J., Figueiredo, T., & Godinho, M. (2007). The contextual interference effect in applied settings. *European Physical Education Review, 13*, 195–208.

Bransford, J. D., Franks, J. J., Morris, C. D., & Stein, B. S. (1979). Some general constraints on learning and memory research. In Cermak, L. S., and Craik, F. I. M. (Eds.), *Levels of processing in human memory* (pp. 351–354). Hillsdale, NJ: Erlbaum.

Button, C., Chow, J.-Y., & Rein, R. (2008). Exploring the perceptual–motor workspace: New approaches to skill acquisition and training. In Hong, Y., & Bartlett, R. (Eds.) *Handbook of biomechanics and human movement science* (pp. 538–553). London: Routledge.

Chambers, K. L., & Vickers, J. N. (2006). Effects of bandwidth feedback and questioning on the performance of competitive swimmers. *Sport Psychologist, 20*, 184–197.

Davids, K., Button, C., & Bennett, S. J. (2008). *Dynamics of skill acquisition: A constraints-led approach.* Champaign, IL: Human Kinetics.

Davids, K., Glazier, P., Araújo, D., & Bartlett, R. M. (2003). Movement systems as dynamical systems: The role of functional variability and its implications for sports medicine. *Sports Medicine, 33*, 245–260.

Farrow, D., Abernethy, B., & Jackson, R. C. (2005). Probing expert anticipation with the temporal occlusion paradigm: Experimental investigations of some methodological issues. *Motor Control, 9*, 330–349.

Handford, C., Davids, K., Bennett, S., & Button, C. (1997). Skill acquisition in sport: Some applications of an evolving practice ecology. *Journal of Sports Sciences, 15*, 621–640.

Keetch, K. M., & Lee, T. D. (2007). The effect of self-regulated and experimenter-imposed practice schedules on motor learning for tasks of varying difficulty. *Research Quarterly for Exercise and Sport, 78*, 476–486.

Kwan, M., Andersen, M., Cheng, C.-L., Tang, W.-T., & Rasmussen, J. (2011). Investigation of high-speed badminton racket kinematics by motion capture. *Sports Engineering, 13*(2), 57–63.

Lavery, J. J. (1962). The retention of simple motor skills as a function of type of knowledge of results. *Canadian Journal of Psychology, 16*, 300–311.

Lee, B. K. (1993). The effects of the kinematic link principle on performance. In Hamill, J., Derrick, T. R., & Elliott, E. H. (Eds.), *Proceedings of the XI International Symposium on Biomechanics in Sport* (pp. 239–242). Amherst, MA: ISBS.

Lee, T. D. (1988). Transfer appropriate processing: A framework for conceptualising practice effects in motor learning. In Meijer, O. G., & Roth, K. (Eds.), *Complex movement behaviour: The motor-action controversy* (pp. 201–215). Amsterdam: Elsevier Science.

Magill, R. A., & Hall, K. G. (1990). A review of the contextual interference effect in motor skill acquisition. *Human Movement Science, 9*, 241–289.

McDonald, P. V., Oliver, S. K. and Newell, K. M. (1995). Perceptual–motor exploration as a function of biomechanical and task constraints. *Acta Psychologica, 88*, 127–166.

Ollis, S., Button, C., & Fairweather, M. (2005). The influence of professional expertise and task complexity upon the potency of the CI effect. *Acta Psychologica, 118*(3), 229–244.

Salmoni, A. W., Schmidt, R. A., & Walter, C. B. (1984). Knowledge of results and motor learning: A review and critical reappraisal. *Psychological Bulletin, 95*, 355–386.

Schmidt, R. A. (1975). A schema theory of discrete motor skill learning. *Psychological Review, 82*, 225–260.

Schmidt, R. A., & Lee, T. D. (1999). *Motor control and learning: A behavioral emphasis* (5th edn.). Champaign, IL: Human Kinetics.

Sherwood, D. E. (1988). Effect of bandwidth knowledge of results on movement consistency. *Perceptual and Motor Skills, 66,* 535–542.

Wilson, C., Simpson, S., & Hamill, J. (2009). Movement coordination patterns in triple jump training drills. *Journal of Sports Sciences, 27*(3), 277–282.

Wulf, G., & Shea, C. H. (2002). Principles derived from the study of simple skills do not generalize to complex skill learning. *Psychonomic Bulletin & Review, 9,* 185–211.

Wulf, G., & Shea, C. H. (2004). Understanding the role of augmented feedback: The good, the bad and the ugly. In Williams, A. M., & Hodges, N. J. (Eds.), *Skill acquisition in sport: Research, theory and practice.* London: Routledge.

Index